LECTURES ON

THE INDIAN EVIDENCE ACT

First Edition 2015
Reprint 2016
Reprint 2021
Reprint 2021
Reprint 2021
Reprint 2022
Reprint 2022
Reprint 2022
Reprint 2022
Reprint 2022

LECTURES ON

THE INDIAN EVIDENCE ACT

JUSTICE U.L. BHAT
Former Chief Justice of the High Court of Gauhati
& High Court of Madhya Pradesh

Foreword by

JUSTICE K.T. THOMAS
Former Judge, Supreme Court of India

Universal

LexisNexis

LexisNexis®

This book is a publication of LexisNexis
(A Division of RELX India Pvt Ltd)
14th floor, Building No 10, Tower-B, DLF Cyber City, Phase-II,
Gurgaon-122002, Haryana, India.
Tel : + 91 124 4774444 Fax: + 91 124 4774100
Website : www.lexisnexis.co.in / E-mail : help.in@lexisnexis.com

---

Justice U.L.Bhat Lectures on The Indian Evidence Act.

ISBN: 978-93-5035-523-7

Printer: Nice Printing Press, Sahibabad, U.P.

Printed and bound in India.

K.T. Thomas
Former Judge
Supreme Court of India

FOREWORD

Normally it is very difficult task for any author to write a commentary on Indian Evidence Act, mostly due to the toughness of the subject and partly due to its dreariness. But the author of this commentary, Justice U.L.Bhat (former Chief Justice) has done a commendable exercise in writing impressive annotations on every provision of the pristine statute. I had glanced through this book and found it tremendously useful to members of both the legal profession and the judiciary. He mastered the subject over the long period of association with the legal profession and also the judiciary.

Justice Bhat and I studied law in the same college (Madras Law College, as it then was) though at different periods and I learnt that the same professor taught both of us this subject – Evidence. To me, as a student, the lectures on the Evidence Act were dry and monotonous. But when I joined the chambers of my senior for apprenticeship (it was compulsory during those days) I realized that my senior was a wizard in this apparently wearisome subject. As days moved on, law of evidence became interesting to me. By the time I left the Bar and joined judiciary, I could acquire rich experience in utilising the provisions of the Indian Evidence Act. It helped me a lot in the discharge of my functions as judge at different levels. In the case of Justice U.L.Bhat, he was purely a civil lawyer while he was in the Bar and did not engage himself in any criminal litigation. After he became a judge (first at the level of District and Sessions and then as Judge of the High Court) the speed with which he mastered criminal law was amazing. He took special interest in imparting his knowledge and learning to the new entrants in the judicial arena. His lectures on criminal law were considered to be superb analysis on the applications of penal provisions, procedural law and particularly the law of evidence. No wonder, after his retirement he became the most sought after jurist in judicial academies both at High Court level and national level.

When I browsed through this book, I realized that Justice U.L.Bhat took particular care in adopting brevity in making his annotations. This book provides an advantage that any curious searcher could locate the point without much strain.

I remember how some academicians expressed that as the Evidence Act was enacted about one and a half century ago, that too during the Colonial period, its contents became outmoded and even anachronistic. But none of the critics could bring forth suggestions to substitutes for the provisions except a few marginal alterations. Even those alterations are intended to take care of the crimes identified by the advancement of civilization *e.g.*, when crimes against women involving demands for dowry became a social meance, the law makers brought new provisions in the penal statute and then sections 113(A) and 113(B) were inserted in the Evidence Act to aid the criminal courts as to the standards of the onus of proof in such cases. Similarly, to deal with the new crimes created by the advent of Information Technology the law makers have rightly incorporated necessary provisions in the Evidence Act to be of assistance in judicial exercise, Barring such additions, the primary provisions in the Evidence Act – such as different standards of proof, various facets of presumptions, admissions, confessions, corroborations etc., remain intact in spite of lapse of such long period of one and a half century. The case law developed on them during this long period had only strengthened the worth of such concepts.

In my assessment Justice U.L.Bhat holds a view that the provisions of the pristine enactment shall not be mutilated in the name of freshening up the statute.

I have no doubt that this commentary would receive wide welcome from all quarters concerned.

K.T. THOMAS

PREFACE

I have been delivering lectures on law of evidence and various branches of civil and criminal law in various centers of training for judges and National and State judicial academies. I have collected scripts of my lectures on law of evidence and updated and revised them. This book is the result of such efforts. The book which deals with all important aspects of law of evidence in India refers to over two thousand decisions of courts in India and abroad.

Judicial officers of the Kerala and Karnataka Judicial Academies of Kerala and Karnataka have been helpful to me in making this compilation. In particular, I am grateful to Sri. B.G. Harindranath, a District & Sessions Judge of Kerala and Sri. M.A. Rashid, author and advocate of Kerala who have been very helpful to me in getting this book published.

All comments and suggestions for improvement of the book are welcome.

Thanks are due also to M/s. Universal Law Publishing Company Pvt. Ltd., New Delhi for the neat printing and publication of the book.

Bangalore
December 2014

Justice U.L. Bhat (Retd)
Former Chief Justice, Gauhati High Court and
High Court of Madhya Pradesh

CONTENTS

TABLE OF CASES

A

B

C

D

E

F

G

I

J

K

L

M

N

Q

R

S

T

W

Y

Z

INDIAN EVIDENCE ACT

CHAPTER I

PRELIMINARY

(1) In 1868, the Indian Law Commission prepared a draft bill which was circulated to local governments for opinion. This bill was rejected ultimately as being unsuitable for Indian conditions. Two years later, Sir James Stephen prepared a new bill which was finally passed and enacted as Act I of 1872. The draft report of the select committee together with their draft bill was presented to the council of the Governor General of India on 31-3-1871, the first signatory being J.F. Stephen. The 1872 Act was inspired by the philosophy of (1) Insistence on the best evidence, (2) Necessity of relevancy and admissibility, and (3) discretion in appreciation of evidence.

The second report of the select committee was presented on 30.1.1872 by the same members. This was a little more than an attempt to reduce the English law of evidence to express formulations, with some modifications to suit peculiar conditions in India.

(2) The Indian Evidence Act, 1872, for short, the Act, extends to the whole of India; by the definition of *'India'* in section 3 of the Act, India means, the territory of India, excluding the State of Jammu and Kashmir.

(3) The object in adducing evidence is to find out the truth or otherwise of the disputed facts. The principle of fair trial manifests itself in virtually every aspect of our practice and procedure, including the law of evidence.[1] The Indian Evidence Act is a consolidating Act; it is expected that this Act is the whole law or complete code and hence principles of equity, justice and good conscience cannot be applied by a Court relying on principles of law in England. This Act is based, generally, on the English Law of Evidence, though arranged in their natural order with some modifications thought necessary by the peculiar or special circumstances of India. In case of doubt or ambiguity in the understanding the provisions of this Act, Courts in India can, with advantage, look to the English Common Law for ascertaining the true meaning of the provisions.[2] Yet importation of any principle of English Common Law relating to evidence is not permissible.[3] This Act deals with the subject of law of evidence in general; there are other rules of evidence contained in other enactments.

(4) The Act applies to all judicial proceedings in or before any Court, including Courts-martial, other than Courts-martial convened under the following Acts, *i.e.,*

---

1. *Zahira Habibulla H. Sheikh* v. *State of Gujarat,* (2004) 4 SCC 158: 2004 SCC (Cri) 999: AIR 2004 SC 3114: 2004 AIR SCW 2325: 2004 Cr LJ 2050.
2. *State of Punjab* v. *Sodhi Sukhdev Singh,* AIR 1961 SC 493: (1961) 1 SCJ 691: (1961) 2 SCR 371: (1961) 2 MLJ 203.
3. *Hira H. Advani* v. *State of Maharashtra,* (1969) 2 SCC 662: (1970) 1 SCR 821: AIR 1971 SC 44: 1971 Cr LJ 5 (SC): 1983 ELT 1413.

(1) The Army Act,

(2) The Naval Discipline Act,

(3) Indian Navy (Discipline) Act, and

(4) Air Force Act –

but not to affidavits presented to any Court or Officer nor to proceedings before an arbitrator. The provisions of the Act are applicable in proceedings under Foreign Exchange Regulation Act, 1947.[1] The Act does not apply to enquiry by Tribunals, even though they may be judicial in character, though such Tribunals are required to follow rules of natural justice. Income Tax authorities are not strictly bound by rules of evidence.[2] Strict rules of the Act and standard of proof envisaged therein do not apply to domestic proceedings or domestic tribunals. It is open to such authorities to receive all necessary, relevant and material evidence though not strictly in conformity with the Act.[3]

(5) The words *"Judicial Proceedings"* are not defined in section 3; they include any proceedings in the course of which evidence is or may be legally taken on oath. An enquiry is judicial if the object is to determine jural relation between two persons or a group of persons or between two persons or a group of persons or between him and the public generally.

(6) General rules of natural justice are that the authority prescribed to act in a matter must act in good faith and fairly listen to both sides and act without bias. The result of the process should be just.[4] In India domestic tribunals and departmental authorities are expected by the judiciary to follow principles of natural justice and avoid hearsay evidence. All materials which are logically probative for a prudent mind are admissible. Fair play is the basis. Sufficiency of evidence in proof of the finding by a domestic tribunal is beyond judicial scrutiny, while absence of evidence in support of the finding is an error of law apparent on the record.[5] Rules of evidence do not generally apply to domestic enquiries.[6]

(7) The Evidence Act is not a complete code containing the whole law of evidence. Certain rules of evidence are also contained in other statutes, *e.g.* Bankers Book Evidence Act (17 of 1891) Order XXVI of C.P.C. Commercial Documents Evidence Act (30 of 1930), Code of Criminal Procedure (sections 291, 292, 293 etc.).

---

1. *Shanti Prasad Jain* v. *Director of Enforcement, Foreign Exchange Regulation Act*, AIR 1962 SC 1764: (1963) 2 SCR 297: (1963) 33 Com Cas 231 (Coram 5).
2. *Commissioner of Income-tax, West Bengal* v. *East Coast Commercial Co. Ltd.*, AIR 1967 SC 768: 1967 (1) SCJ 433: (1967) 1 SCR 821 (Coram 3).
3. *Maharashtra State Board of Secondary and Higher Secondary Education* v. *K.S. Gandhi*, 1991 AIR SCW 879: (1991) 2 SCC 716; *Cholan Roadways Ltd.* v. *G. Thirugnanasambandam*, 2005 AIR SCW 84: AIR 2005 SC 570: (2005) 3 SCC 241.
4. *Board of Education* v. *Rice*, 1911 AC 179: 104 LT 689: 80 LJKB 796; Dunfermline in *Local Government Board* v. *Arlidge*, (1915) AC 120: 84 LJKB 72: 111 LT 905 (HL).
5. *Kesoram Cotton Mills Ltd.* v. *Gangadhar*, AIR 1964 SC 708: (1964) 2 SCR 809: 1965 (1) SCJ 71; *Employers of Firestone Tyre and Rubber Co. (Private) Ltd.* v. *Workmen*, AIR 1968 SC 236: 1968 (2) SCJ 83: (1968) 1 SCR 307; *Central Bank of India Ltd.* v. *Karunamoy Banerjee*, AIR 1968 SC 266: (1968) 1 SCR 251: 1968 (1) SCJ 850.
6. *State of Haryana* v. *Rattan Singh*, AIR 1977 SC 1512: (1977) 2 SCC 491: 1977 (2) SCJ 140.

CHAPTER 2
SECTION 2 (REPEALED)

1. Section 2, as it stood originally, read as follows—

"On and from that day the following laws shall be repealed:—

(1) all rules of evidence not contained in any Statute, Act or Regulation in force in any part of British India;

(2) all such rules, laws and regulations as have acquired the force of law under the 25th section of the Indian Council's Act, 1861, in so far as they relate to any matter herein provided for; and

(3) The enactments mentioned in the Schedule thereto, to the extent specified in the third column of the said Schedule."

"But nothing herein contained shall be deemed to affect any provision of any Statute, Act or Regulation in force in any part of British India and not hereby expressly repealed."

2. Since the above provisions worked themselves out or otherwise became unnecessary, the repealing section was repealed by the Repealing Act I of 1938.

3. Section 2 (as it stood before the Repealing Act) repealed all rules of evidence which were not contained in any Statute, Act or Regulation then in force. Such rules included the English Common Law[1] and rules of the Hindu[2] and Mohammedan laws,[3] which were then in force, as also rules which had their origin in principles of equity, justice and good conscience. Section 2 left undisturbed all rules of evidence contained in any Statute, Act and Regulation not expressly repealed by section 2.

---

1. *Srish Chandra Nandy* v. *Rakhalananda Thakur*, AIR 1941 PC 16: ILR (1941) Kar PC 54: 68 IA 34: 193 IC 220: 1941 ILR 1 Cal 468.
2. *Dhondo Bhikaji* v. *Ganesh Bhikaji*, ILR Bom 433.
3. *Miraj Fatima* v. *Abdul Waheed*, AIR 1921 All 175.

CHAPTER 3
INTERPRETATION CLAUSE (SECTION 3)

COURT

1. "Court" includes all Judges, Magistrates, and all persons legally authorised to take evidence, except arbitrators. This is an inclusive definition and hence is not meant to be exhaustive. This definition is framed only for the purpose of this Act and hence cannot be extended where such extension is not warranted.[1]

FACT

2. "Fact", as defined in section 3, means and includes anything, state of things, or relation of things, capable of being perceived by the senses and any mental condition of which any person is conscious. The Legislature has furnished certain illustrations of "fact", that is, that there are certain objects arranged in a certain order in a certain place, that a person heard or saw something, that a person said certain words, that a person holds a certain opinion or has a certain intention, acts in good faith or fraudulently or uses a particular word in a particular sense or is or was at a specified time conscious of a particular sensation. That a certain person has a certain reputation is a fact. The definition together with illustrations refers to two kinds of facts, that is, physical fact and psychological fact. They can be proved by direct or indirect evidence. The draft report of the select committee[2] stated that each of the two classes of facts has one common feature which entitles them to the description of "facts", and that can be directly perceived either with or without the intervention of five external human senses. Clause (1) of definition of "fact" refers to external facts covered by illustrations (a) to (c), facts which can be perceived by the five human senses while clause (2) refers to internal facts which are the subjects of consciousness as seen in illustrations (d) and (e). According to Best, there are two other divisions of fact, namely, (1) events or states of things, and (2) positive or affirmative, and negative. *e.g.*, the fall of a tree is an event, while the existence of a tree is a state of thing. Yet, both are "facts". Existence of certain state of things is a positive fact, while the non-existence of it is a negative fact.[3] Non-availability of an alternative accommodation to a tenant refers to a state of things and hence is a positive fact within the definition of "fact". It is not absence of a fact. Question of prejudice is a fact.[4] Question of intention is a fact[5]. The term "fact" is used in different senses, namely, information provided by witnesses and other evidence, conclusions drawn by the court from the information presented before it as to what actually happened, and the legal concepts, being the facts in issue that must be established if a particular party in a case is to succeed. "Matter of Law" is the general law of the land of which courts will take judicial cognizance.

---

1. *Brajnandan Sinha* v. *Jyoti Narain*, AIR 1956 SC 66: 1956 SCJ 155: (1955) 2 SCR 955.
2. Published in Gazette of India dated 1-7-1871, Part 5 at page 273.
3. Best on evidence 10th Edn., – Section 13.
4. *Willie (William) Slaney* v. *State of M.P.*, AIR 1956 SC 116: 1956 Cr LJ 291: (1955) 2 SCR 1140.
5. *Talab Haji Hussain* v. *Madhukar Purshottam Mondkar*, AIR 1958 SC 376: 1958 SCJ 672: 1958 SCR 1226.

FACTS IN ISSUE

3. The expression "Facts in issue" means and includes – any fact from which either by itself or in connection with other facts, the existence, non-existence, nature of extent of any right, liability, or disability, asserted or denied in any suit or proceeding, necessarily follows. The words "liability", "disability" or "proceeding" have reference to civil and criminal cases, while the words "right", "liability", "disability" and "suit" have reference to civil cases. The illustration to the definition is confined to a criminal case involving a charge of committing murder and defence raised is one of denial or under exception I to section 300 I.P.C. or/and section 84 I.P.C. The illustration states as follows:

- *A* is accused of the murder of *B*.

  At his trial the following facts may be in issue:—
- That *A* caused *B*'s death. (*i.e., Actus Reus*)
- That *A* intended to cause *B*'s death (*i.e., Mens Rea*)
- That *A* received grave and sudden provocation from *B* (Explanation I to section 300 I.P.C.)
- That *A*, at the time of doing the act which caused *B*'s death, was, by reason of unsoundness of mind, incapable of knowing it's nature (section 84 I.P.C.).

One may furnish the following facts in issue in a suit for recovery of money due under a demand promissory note where the defendant denies due execution of the D.P. Note and denies receipt of consideration:

- That *B* duly executed the D.P. Note in favour of defendant (*i.e.*, that the DP Note is true and genuine).
- That the D.P. Note is fully supported by consideration.

Facts in issue, which are the "principal" or "ultimate" facts are those necessary by law to establish the claim, liability or defence, constituting the subject-matter of the suit or other proceeding and which are in dispute. Principal matters which are affirmed by one party and denied by the other may be regarded as facts in issue. Identification of or locating facts in issue is made on the basis of the substantive law relating to the subject-matter of the case (for example, I.P.C., or T.P. Act or Contract Act, etc.,) and provisions of Chapter VII of the Act (Indian Evidence Act, 1872) or, in some cases, by the laws of procedure which regulate the law of pleadings, civil or criminal. Facts in issue are those disputed facts which a party to a civil or criminal litigation must prove in order to succeed in his claim or defence and show his entitlement to a relief (in a civil case) or to obtain conviction (in a criminal case) or to have defence raised by the defendant or accused, as the case may be, upheld by court. The words "Fact in issue" are employed in sections 5 to 9, 11, illustration (d) of section 21, sections 36 and 43 of the Evidence Act.

RELEVANT FACTS

4. In defining "Relevant", the definition in section 3 states that one fact is relevant to another, when the one is so connected with the other in any of the ways referred to in the provisions of the Evidence Act relating to relevancy of facts. Such provisions are contained in Chapter 2 of the Evidence Act. Facts relevant to the issue which are also called "evidentiary" facts, are facts which tend, either directly or indirectly, to prove or disprove a fact in issue.

Sections 6 to 55 in Chapter II of the Evidence Act furnish the methods one should adopt to know whether a particular fact is relevant for the determination of the issues in a case. According to Sir James Stephens' *"Digest of Law of Evidence"* (1893 Edition, Page 2), the word "relevant" as used in the Evidence Act means that any two facts to which it is applied are so related to each other that, according to the common course of events, one either by itself or in connection with other facts, proves or renders probable the past, present or future, existence or non-existence of the other. "Relevant", in a manner of speaking, means admissible in evidence, that is, when a fact is relevant, evidence can be adduced in proof of that fact. Relevant fact must have some connection (relationship) with the fact in issue and such fact must be provable in the trial. Relevancy of facts or admissibility of evidence to prove a relevant fact are based on certain statutory principles.

Often the expressions "Relevancy" and "Admissibility" are used as synonyms, but their legal implications are distinct and different. Some facts which are relevant may not be admissible. *e.g.*, communication between spouses during subsistence of their marriage are relevant but not admissible. Similarly some facts which are admissible may not be relevant *e.g.*, Questions permitted in cross-examination to test the veracity of a witness or to impeach his credit, though not relevant are admissible.[1] Relevant facts are facts other than facts in issue which are, in the eye of the law, so connected with or related to the facts in issue that they render the latter probable. Phipson on Evidence at page 49, stated;

> "The legal admissibility of facts is for the most part determined by their logical relevancy to the issue, or that connection between the two which, in the ordinary course of events, renders the latter probable from the existence of the former."

Every fact which is the basis of an inference is evidence, and is thus called often as "evidentiary fact" while the fact which is inferred from it is called "ultimate fact" or "principal fact".

DOCUMENT

5. Document means any matter expressed or described upon any substance by means of letters, figures or marks, or by more than one of these means, intended to be used, or which may be used, for the purpose of recording that matter. A writing, words printed, lithographed or photographed, map, plan, inscription on a metal plate or stone, caricature, tape recording or television film are documents. But a photograph of a writing can be used to prove the writing and can be received in evidence only if the original cannot be obtained and the photograph is faithful and genuine.[2] In case of tape recording of a speech which is also a document, the accuracy of the recording has to be proved and sound or voice recorded has to be identified.[3] *See* also section 3(18) of the General

1. *Ram Bihari Yadav* v. *State of Bihar*, AIR 1998 SC 1850: (1998) 4 SCC 517: 1998 Cr LJ 2515: 1998 AIR SCW 1647: 1998 SCC (Cri) 1085.
2. *Laxmipat Choraria* v. *State of Maharashtra*, AIR 1968 SC 938: (1968) 2 SCR 624: 1968 Cr LJ 1134: (1968) 2 SCJ 589; *Ziyauddin Burhanuddin Bukhari* v. *Brijmohan Ramdass Mehra*, AIR 1975 SC 1788: 1975 SCR 281: (1976) 2 SCC 17 "when it was disputed or in issue whether a person's speech, on a particular occasion, contained a particular statement there could be no more direct or better evidence of it than its tape record, assuming its authenticity is duly established."
3. *Yusufalli Esmail Nagree* v. *State of Maharashtra*, AIR 1968 SC 147: 1968 Cr LJ 103: 1967 SCR 720: (1968) 1 SCJ 511: 70 Bom LR 76.

Clauses Act, 1897, section 29 I.P.C., section 138C of the Sea Customs Act and section 36B Central Excise Act.

EVIDENCE

6. "Evidence" in the popular sense means that by which facts are established to the satisfaction of persons enquiring into them. It is any matter of fact, the effect, tendency or design of which, when presented to the mind, is to produce in the mind a persuasion concerning the existence of some other matter of fact – a persuasion either affirmative or dis-affirmative of its existence.[1] Under section 3 of the Evidence Act, "evidence" is defined as meaning and including – (1) all statements which the Court permits or requires to be made before it by witnesses in relation to matters of fact under inquiry (which statements are called oral evidence, and (2) all documents including electronic records produced for the inspection of the Court – (which are called documentary evidence). Going by this definition, materials such as confession or statement made by an accused in his trial, his statement under section 313 Criminal Procedure Code, note about demeanour of witness under examination in Court, result of local inspection and material objects are not "Evidence", though these fall within the scope of "matters" referred to in the definition of "Proved".

Thus, statement of a witness recorded under section 164 of Criminal Procedure Code is not substantive evidence, though it can be used for corraboration or contradiction.[2] Result of investigation also is not legal evidence.[3] First Information Statement, generally speaking, is not substantive evidence (except when it attracts sections 8, 21, 32 of the Evidence Act) and can be used only for corroboration or contradiction of the evidence given in court by the maker of the FIS.[4] The factual statements in FIS but not deposed to in Court by the informant cannot be treated as evidence in a case.[5]

First Information Statement (FIS) is, generally speaking, not substantive evidence.[6]

Statement in *Panchanama* is not substantive evidence; it can be used for corroboration or contradiction of the witness whose statement is contained in the *panchanama*.[7] Police diaries can be used only to contradict the investigating

1. Bentham's Judicial Evidence at page 17.
2. *Bhuboni Sahu* v. *King*, AIR 1949 PC 257: 50 Cr LJ 872: 51 BLR 955: 53 CWN 609: 1949 ALJ 283: 51 PLR 311: 76 Ind App 147; *Brij Bhushan Singh* v. *E.*, (1946) 47 Cr LJ 336: AIR 1946 PC 38: 223 IC 1: 73 IA 18: 50 Cal WN 348.
3. *Dalip Singh* v. *State of Punjab*, AIR 1997 SC 2985: 1997 Cr LJ 3647: 1997 AIR SCW 3015; *Vijender* v. *State of Delhi*, (1997) 6 SCC 171: JT 1997 (3) SC 131.
4. *Bhuboni Sahu* v. *King*, AIR 1949 PC 257: 50 Cr LJ 872: 51 BLR 955: 53 CWN 609: 1949 ALJ 283: 51 PLR 311: 76 Ind App 147; *State of Bombay* v. *Rusy Mistry*, AIR 1960 SC 391: 1960 Cr LJ 532; *State of Delhi* v. *Ram Lohia*, AIR 1960 SC 490: 1960 Cr LJ 679.
5. *Ramdas* v. *State of Maharashtra*, (2007) 2 SCC 170: AIR 2007 SC 155: 2006 AIR SCW 5675.
6. *Nanhku Singh* v. *State of Bihar*, AIR 1973 SC 491: 1972 Cr LJ 1204: (1972) 3 SCC 590; *Shankar* v. *State of Uttar Pradesh*, AIR 1975 SC 757: 1975 Cr LJ 634: (1975) 3 SCC 851; *Sheikh Hasib* v. *State of Bihar*, AIR 1972 SC 283: (1972) 4 SCC 773: 1972 Cr LJ 233; *Bijoy Singh* v. *State of Bihar*, AIR 2002 SC 1949: 2002 AIR SCW 1873: 2002 Cr LJ 2623; *Andrews* v. *State of Kerala*, (2002) 10 SCC 126; *Asharam* v. *State of M.P.*, AIR 2007 SC 2594: 2007 AIR SCW 4619: (2007) 6 SCALE 140, *Dharma Ram Bhagare* v. *State of Maharashtra*, AIR 1973 SC 476: (1973) 1 SCC 537: 1973 Cr LJ 680; *Ravi Kumar* v. *State of Punjab*, 2005 Cr LJ 1742: AIR 2005 SC 1929: 2005 AIR SCW 1359, *Harkirat Singh* v. *State of Punjab*, AIR 1997 SC 3231: 1997 Cr LJ 3954: 1997 AIR SCW 3288.
7. *Kanu Ambu Vish* v. *State of Maharashtra*, AIR 1971 SC 2256: 1971 Civ Ap R (SC) 181: 1971 Cr LJ 1547.

officer.[1] Court is empowered to call for case diary not to use it as evidence but to use it as an aid to find out anything that happened during the investigation of the case.[2] A statement made by a witness to a police officer in the course of investigation can be used only to contradict the witness in the manner provided by section 145 of Evidence Act and for no other purpose.[3] Statement made by a witness during investigation is not substantive evidence. It can be used only to contradict the witness when examined in Court and can be considered only to weigh the credibility of the evidence actually adduced in Court.[4] When a witness is so contradicted, then only that part of the statement put to the witness will be considered to determine his veracity. The whole of the previous statement cannot be treated as substantive evidence.[5] The case diary statement of the injured in a case, if he succumbed to his injuries later and if it contains statement as to the cause of his (subsequent) death, or as to any of the circumstances of the transaction which resulted in his death, can be proved as substantive evidence in a criminal trial in which the cause of death comes into question as contemplated in section 32(1) of the Evidence Act.[6] However, the practice of the police officer recording dying declaration is unwholesome and cannot be encouraged.[7] It is always the duty of the police officer to secure the services of the Magistrate to record the dying declaration. In every case of a dying declaration recorded by a Police Officer, the explanation offered by the prosecution for his inability to secure the presence of a magistrate or even secure the services of a doctor has to be considered by the Court in deciding whether the particular dying declaration could be acted upon. In some cases, Supreme Court declined to act on such dying declarations.[8] A part of case diary statement of an accused can also be proved for the purpose of section 27 of Evidence Act. Statement made to police during investigation can be used in civil cases since the bar or restriction of user stipulated in section 162 of the Criminal Procedure Code is only regarding the trial of the criminal case involving the particular crime during the investigation of which the statement was recorded.[9]

Broadly speaking, evidence can be classified into (1) Direct and Indirect or circumstantial evidence, (2) Primary and Secondary evidence, (3) Oral and

1. *Queen* v. *Mannu*, ILR 19 All 390 FB; *Dal Singh* v. *E.*, AIR 1917 PC 25: 44 IA 137: 44 C 876: 39 IC 311: 18 Cr LJ 471: 12 WR (PC) 32.
2. *Sidharth* v. *State of Bihar*, (2005) 12 SCC 545: AIR 2005 SC 4352: 2005 Cr LJ 4499: 2005 AIR SCW 5010.
3. *Prakash Chand* v. *State (Delhi Administration)*, AIR 1979 SC 400: (1979) 3 SCC 90: 1979 Cr LJ 329: 1979 MLJ (Cri) 419.
4. *Baladin* v. *State of Uttar Pradesh*, AIR 1956 SC 181: 1956 Cr LJ 345.
5. *Som Nath* v. *Union of India*, AIR 1971 SC 1910: 1971 Cr LJ 1429: 1971 (Supp) SCR 848.
6. *Charipalli Shankararao* v. *Public Prosecutor, High Court of Andhra Pradesh, Hyderabad*, AIR 1995 SC 777; *Ramawati Devi* v. *State of Bihar*, AIR 1983 SC 164: (1983) 1 SCC 211: 1983 Cr LJ 221; *State of Punjab* v. *Amarjit Singh*, AIR 1988 SC 2013: 1988 Supp SCC 704; *State of Uttar Pradesh* v. *Ram Sagar Yadav*, (1985) 1 SCC 552: 1985 SCC (Cri) 127: AIR 1985 SC 416: 1986 Cr LJ 836; *Tapinder Singh* v. *State of Punjab*, AIR 1970 SC 1566: (1971) 1 SCJ 871: 1970 Cr LJ 1415; *P.V. Radhakrishna* v. *State of Karnataka*, AIR 2003 SC 2859: 2003 AIR SCW 3587: 2003 Cr LJ 3717.
7. *Munnu Raja* v. *State of Madhya Pradesh*, AIR 1976 SC 2199: (1976) 2 SCR 764: (1976) 3 SCC 104: 1976 Cr LJ 1718; *State of Punjab* v. *Amarjit Singh*, AIR 1988 SC 2013: 1988 Supp SCC 704.
8. *Meera* v. *State of Rajasthan*, AIR 2004 SC 1879: 2004 Cr LJ 5038: 2004 AIR SCW 1721; *Keshav Gangaram Navge* v. *State of Maharashtra*, 1971 Cr LJ 798: (1971) 1 SCC 513: AIR 1971 SC 953; *Shaikh Rafiq* v. *State of Maharashtra*, (2008) 2 Supreme 66: AIR 2008 SC 1362: 2008 Cr LJ 1592.
9. *Ranjit Satardekar* v. *Joe Mathias*, 2006 Cr LJ 2237: 2007 (3) Civ LJ 75: 2006 (3) CCC 344.

Documentary evidence, (4) Real evidence, (5) Original and Hearsay evidence and (6) Presumptive evidence. Direct evidence is evidence which, if believed, establishes a fact in issue. Direct evidence consists either of the testimony of the witness who perceived the fact or the production of the documents which constitute the fact which is in question. Indirect or circumstantial evidence is evidence which gives rise to logical inference that a fact in issue exists. It may be conclusive or presumptive; it is the former when there is a connection between the fact in issue and the evidentiary or circumstantial or basic or primary fact and it is presumptive where the fact in issue rests on a greater or a less degree of probability. By presumptive or indirect evidence is meant that other facts are thus proved, from which the existence of the given fact may be logically inferred.[1] It consists of evidence of circumstances, none of which speak directly to the facts in issue, but from which those facts may be inferred.[2] Circumstantial evidence means a combination of facts creating a chain or network through which there is no escape for the accused because the facts taken as a whole do not admit of any inference but of his guilt.[3] Relevant facts are also required to be proved by direct evidence.

Hearsay evidence is given when a witness recounts a statement made (orally, in a document or otherwise) by another person and where the proponent of the evidence asserts that what the person who made the statement said was true. The contents of a document without examination of the author are hearsay evidence.

Statement recorded under section 161 Criminal procedure Code is, generally speaking, not evidence, though it may be used for the purpose of impeaching the credibility of a witness[4]. Evidence illegally obtained (illegal search) is admissible evidence.[5]

PROVED

7. The above definition reads as follows:—

"Proved" – A fact is said to be proved when, after considering the matters before it, the court either believes it to exist, or considers its' existence so probable that a prudent man ought, under the circumstances of the particular case, to act upon the supposition that it exists".

The expression, "Disproved" is defined in a similar way, except that the court's belief or probability is that the disputed fact does not exist. A fact is said not to be proved when it is neither proved nor disproved.

---

1. *Cement Corporation of India Ltd.* v. *Purya,* (2004) 8 SCC 270: AIR 2004 SC 4830: 2004 AIR SCW 5534; Phipson on evidence, 15th edn. (2000) page 3.
2. *Hanumant Govind Nargundkar* v. *State of Madhya Pradesh,* AIR 1952 SC 343: 1952 SCR 1091: 1952 SCA 623; *Sudama Pandey* v. *State of Bihar,* 2002 (1) SCC 679: AIR 2002 SC 293: 2001 AIR SCW 5012; *Ashish Batham* v. *State of Madhya Pradesh,* (2002) 7 SCC 317: AIR 2002 SC 3206: 2002 Cr LJ 4676.
3. *Udaipal Singh* v. *State of Uttar Pradesh,* AIR 1972 SC 54: 1972 Cr LJ 7: (1972) 4 SCC 142.
4. *Ramswaroop* v. *State of Rajasthan,* 2004 AIR SCW 1729: AIR 2004 SC 2943: 2004 Cr LJ 5043.
5. *Radha Kishan* v. *State of Uttar Pradesh,* AIR 1963 SC 822: 1963 All LJ 397: 1963 BLJR 353; *R.M. Malkani* v. *State of Maharashtra,* (1973) 1 SCC 471: 1973 Cr LJ 228: AIR 1973 SC 157: (1972) 2 SCWR 776; *State of Madhya Pradesh (through C.B.I.)* v. *Paltan Mallah,* (2005) 3 SCC 169: 2005 Cr LJ 918: 2005 AIR SCW 455: AIR 2005 SC 733; *Pooran Mall* v. *Director of Inspection,* (1974) 1 SCC 345: AIR 1974 SC 348: (1974) 2 SCR 704; *Prathap Singh* v. *Director of Enforcement, Foreign Exchange Regulation Act,* AIR 1985 SC 989: (1985) 3 SCC 72: (1985) 155 ITR 166.

On a proper analysis, the requirements of the definition of "proved" appear to be the following:

1. The task of the Court is to decide whether a 'fact' is proved, disproved or not proved. For this purpose, the court "considers" the "matters" before it, and
2. After such consideration, the court believes the fact to exist, OR
3. After such consideration, the court considers the existence of the fact so probable that a prudent person ought, under the circumstances of the particular case, to act upon the supposition that the fact exists.

"Matters" is wider in import than "Evidence" and would include, *inter alia*, presumptions and facts of which judicial notice can be taken, observation of demeanour, result of local investigation, inspection of material objects, pleading, charge and section 313 answers.

8. Section 3 of the Act defines "fact" as follows:

Fact means and includes—

(1) anything, state of things or relation of things, capable of being perceived by the senses,

(2) any mental condition of which any person is conscious.

The senses are the five human senses, *i.e.*, sight, hearing, smell, touch and taste. Thus, anything, state of things, relation of things perceived by the five senses, that is, physical fact as also mental condition known to any person constitute "fact". Thus, a fact can be a perceivable physical fact or an intangible mental fact.

Examples of Physical facts:—That a witness saw or heard something is a fact. So also what a witness smells (that an assailant smelled of a particular scent or that an officer smelled putrid smell in a food article or smelled alcohol in a liquid), or that a witness's hands touched soft or hard skin of an assailant.

That there are certain objects arranged in a certain order in a certain way is a fact. That an accused or victim of a crime or a party to a document said certain words is a fact. That an expert holds a certain opinion, that the accused or a testator has a certain intention, acts in good faith or fraudulently or uses a certain word in a particular sense or is or was at a specified time conscious of a particular sensation is a fact. That a doctor attending on a sick testator or that a person living or working with a testator was conscious of the mental state of the testator is a fact.

9. That parties to a civil or criminal case are enabled to prove only two kinds of facts is the mandate of section 5 of the Evidence Act; as a matter of law they are not allowed to prove any fact which is not a fact in issue or a relevant fact (section 5). For example, hearsay is a matter which cannot be attempted to be proved except for certain purposes in specific situations.

'Fact in issue' means and includes, according to its' definition, any fact from which, either by itself or in connection with other fact or facts, the existence, non-existence, nature or extent of any right, liability, disability asserted or denied in any suit or proceeding, necessarily follows. In a civil case, under the provisions of Code of Civil Procedure, whenever any court records an issue of fact, the fact to be asserted or denied in answer to such issue, is also a fact in issue. For example, in a suit to recover principal amount and interest due under a promissory note allegedly executed by the defendant in favour of plaintiff, if defendant denies due execution of the D.P. Note and receipt of consideration, the two facts actually in issue are, genuineness of the D.P. Note and alleged passing of consideration. Consequently the civil court is, under the C.P.C., required to frame the following issues:

(1) Whether the suit D.P. Note is true and genuine, that is, duly executed by the defendant in favour of the plaintiff?

(2) If so, whether the D.P. Note is not supported by consideration (Because, if due execution is proved, burden is on defendant to show that the D.P. Note is not supported by consideration. If the D.P. Note was not duly executed, the question of passing of consideration does not arise for decision unless plaintiff alternately sues on the original loan, if any)

10. In a trial of an accused for an offence punishable under section 326 I.P.C. by using a deadly weapon and defence is one of denial, the following are facts in issue:

(1) That accused caused grievous hurt to the victim.

(2) That the hurt was caused using a deadly weapon.

(3) That the hurt was caused "voluntarily",

If there is an express or implied plea of private defence, the following additional fact in issue would arise:

(4) That the grievous hurt was caused in exercise of the right of private defence.

In framing points for consideration, it would be necessary to frame the following points also:

(5) What, if any, is the offence proved against accused?

(6) What, if any, is the sentence to be imposed on accused?

11. Section 3 of Evidence Act, defines "Relevant fact" by stating that one fact is relevant to another fact, when the one is connected with the other in any of the ways referred to in the provisions of the Evidence Act relating to "relevancy of facts", Chapter II of the Evidence Act relates to "relevancy of facts". Sections 6 to 23, 27 to 29, 32 to 38 and 40 to 55 indicate that certain facts referred to therein are relevant facts; Sections 24 to 26 indicate what facts are not relevant. If a particular fact is a relevant fact, parties have a right to adduce evidence in proof or disproof of it. "Evidence" as defined means all oral statements permitted or required to be made before court in relation to matters of fact under enquiry, as also all documents for inspection of Court.

12. It is crystal clear that the definitions and provisions referred to above apply to civil as well as criminal cases. In ***C.H. Razik Ram*** v. ***C.H. Jaswant Singh***,[1] it was held as follows:

> "It is true that there is no difference between the general rules of evidence in **civil and criminal cases** and the definition of "proved" in section 3 of the Evidence Act does not draw a distinction between **civil and criminal cases.**"
>
> (Emphasis supplied)

1. *Razik Ram* v. *J.S. Chouhan*, AIR 1975 SC 667: (1975) 4 SCC 769.

This is also indicated in ***Vijayee Singh*** v. ***State of Uttar Pradesh***[1], (para 26).

13. Let us go back to the definition of "proved". It is in two parts. Under the first part, court "believes" a disputed fact to exist. The second part refers to a situation where the court considers the existence of the disputed fact "so probable that a prudent person ought, under the circumstances of the particular case, to act upon the supposition that the fact exists". In other words, the judge sitting in a prudent person's chair (thinking as he ought), considers the existence of disputed fact "so probable ...." that he arrives at a conclusion which a prudent ought to arrive at in the particular circumstances. This is what is otherwise termed "**preponderance of probability**". What is "so probable" is certainly preponderant probability. The judge, not being an eye-witness, is required to consider the matters before the court and arrive at a conclusion about existence of a disputed fact, based upon his own "belief" or "preponderance of probability" as a prudent person ought to find.

14. Does the definition postulate two different standards of proof and of the two standards, does the former (belief) postulate a standard higher or lower or different in degree than the degree postulated by the latter (preponderance of probability)? If so, why did the legislature provide two such standards? Would it not have been sufficient to stipulate the lower standard as the only standard since evidence in proof of a disputed fact, taken along with other matters before the court which makes the court believe (assuming it is a higher standard) in the existence of such a fact will necessarily satisfy the assumed lower standard of preponderance of probability? And if it is sufficient for a party in any judicial proceeding to satisfy the assumed lower standard, what impelled the legislature to provide a higher standard too? Is "belief" really a higher or lower or different standard than "preponderance of probability"?

15. It would be more reasonable to construe the second part, that is, "preponderance of probability" on which a prudent person ought to act as being explanatory of the first part, namely "belief"; this is particularly so since the first part does not lay down any criteria for "believing" in the existence of a fact. Yet, it is clear that 'belief' cannot be wholly subjective and ought to be objective. Such a belief can be entertained only if the probability of the existence is preponderant and such a probability ought to be acted upon by a prudent person. The two parts do not therefore, lay down two different standards. It is not possible to think that a Court can believe in the existence of a fact even though such existence is not supported by preponderance of probability or appears to be wholly improbable. Thus, the second part is linked to the first part of the definition.

16. In ***M.G. Agarwal*** v. ***State of Maharashtra***,[2] a Constitution Bench of the Supreme Court (five judges) dealt with a case in which three officials of the Income-tax department were charged with commission of offences punishable under sections 120-B, 467 and 471 of the I.P.C. and section 5(2) of the P.C. Act. The trial judge acquitted accused nos. (1) and (2) of all the charges, but convicted the 3rd accused under sections 467 and 471 I.P.C. and section 5(2) of P.C. Act, but acquitted him of the charge under section 120B, I.P.C. The Bombay

1. *Vijayee Singh* v. *State of Uttar Pradesh*, AIR 1990 SC 1459: (1990) 3 SCC 190: 1990 Cr LJ 1510.
2. *M.G. Agarwal* v. *State of Maharashtra*, AIR 1963 SC 200: 1963 (1) Cr LJ 235: 64 Bom LR 773: (1963) 2 SCR 405

High Court which heard the state appeal against acquittal, held that the charge under section 120B, I.P.C. was proved beyond reasonable doubt against all the accused and convicted and sentenced them accordingly. The High Court also convicted accused No. (2) under sections 467 and 471 I.P.C. as also section 5(2) of P.C. Act. Accused 1 and 2 approached the Supreme Court. Prosecution case was governed entirely by circumstantial evidence. Circumstances relied were, the established office procedure, office duties assigned to the three accused respectively, the verification of various matters which had to be conducted by the accused and which were not conducted, statements of the accused during departmental enquiry, the role played by each of the accused in relation to the incriminating documents, the falsity of the case setup by 1st accused that 3rd accused destroyed documents which would allegedly show that the refund orders were true and genuine, the *modus operandi* adopted by the three accused as seen from the proved office records, the non-existence of the alleged assessees in whose favour refund orders had been issued, that though all the alleged assessees being new assessees, absence of any enquiry being conducted by the 1st accused before passing the refund orders, the nature of income purported to be disclosed in the alleged returns, the fact that in respect of returns for such income no refund could be legally allowable under the particular statutory provision, absence of assessment orders in most of the cases, absence of entries showing advance payment of tax in some instances and absence of cancellation of certain papers required to be made under law etc. This narration will clearly show that entire evidence relied on consisted only of "circumstances".

17. Naturally, the Constitution Bench had to consider the principles of criminal jurisprudence regarding the manner of proof of "circumstances" or "primary facts" or "basic facts" or "circumstantial facts" and the basis on which such proved facts could lead to finding of guilt of the accused. The Bench held as follows in paragraph 18:

> "But in applying this principle, it is necessary to **distinguish between facts which may be called primary or basic** on the one hand **and inference of facts to be drawn** from them on the other. **In regard to the proof of basic or primary facts, the court has to judge the evidence in the ordinary way,** ***and in the appreciation of evidence in respect of basic or of primary facts there is no scope for the application of the doctrine of benefit of doubt.*** **The court considers the evidence and decides whether that evidence proves a particular fact or not.** When it is held that a certain fact is proved, **the question arises whether that fact leads to an inference of guilt of the accused person** or not and **in dealing with this aspect of the problem,** the **doctrine of benefit of doubt would apply** and an inference of guilt can be drawn only if the proved fact is wholly inconsistent with the innocence of the accused and is consistent only with his guilt. It is in the **light of this legal position** that the evidence in the present case has to be appreciated".

(Emphasis supplied)

The judgment of the Constitution Bench did not specifically advert to the definition of "proved" in section 3 of the Act; but the language in the above quotation makes it clear that the Bench had in mind this definition when it referred to "proof of basic or primary facts" and "judging the evidence in the ordinary way". The ordinary way is the way prescribed by the law of evidence, that is, the Act and definition contained in the Act. This was how the editor of the law journal also understood the decision as is clear from the explicit reference to section 3 in head note (b).

18. The conclusion of the Constitution Bench in ***M.G. Agarwal's*** case and the passage extracted above have been quoted in later decisions with approval as the law laid down by the Supreme Court. For example ***Balu Sonba Shinde*** v. ***State of Maharashtra,***[1] (Para 4), ***Abdul Ghani*** v. ***State of Uttar Pradesh,***[2] ***Alamgir*** v. ***State NCT of Delhi,***[3] ***Sharad Biridhichand Sarda*** v. ***State of Maharashtra,***[4] ***Kanhai Misra*** v. ***State of Bihar.***[5] In ***Kishore Chand*** v. ***State of Himachal Pradesh,***[6] and ***G. Parshwanath*** v. ***State of Karnataka,***[7] the Court used almost the same language as employed by the Constitution Bench quoted earlier, though without making reference to the earlier decision. The conclusion quoted above of the Constitution Bench deserves serious consideration and appreciation. The case dealt with prosecution based entirely on circumstantial evidence. In such cases, the circumstantial facts are only facts which have been declared to be relevant under chapter II of the Act. Such facts are referred to in ***M.G. Agarwal's*** case as "basic facts" or "primary facts". They are governed by the definition of "proved" in section 3 of the Act. The court believes in the existence of such facts or accepts such facts as proved by preponderance of probabilities. This was what was referred to in ***M.G. Agarwal's*** case as judging "the evidence in the ordinary way", that is, the way mandated by the definition of "proved" in section 3 of the Act.

19. In ***C.H. Razik Ram*** v. ***C.H. Jaswant Singh*** (supra), the Supreme Court observed as follows:

> "Nor does this definition insist on **perfect proof** because **absolute certainty** amounting to demonstration is rarely to be had in the affairs of life. Nevertheless the standard of measuring proof prescribed by the definition, is that of a person of **prudence and practical good sense** .... Judged by the standard of a prudent man, in the light of the nature of the *onus* cast by the law, the probative effect of evidence in civil and criminal proceedings is markedly different ....".
>
> (Emphasis supplied)

In ***Maharashtra Ed. Bd.*** v. ***K.S. Gandhi,*** (1991) 2 SCC 716,[8] the Supreme Court stated as follows:

> "There must be evidence, direct or circumstantial, to deduce necessary inferences in proof of the facts in issue. In some cases, the other facts,

1. *Balu Sonba Shinde* v. *State of Maharashtra*, AIR 2002 SC 3137: (2002) 7 SCC 543: 2002 Cr LJ 4650.
2. *Abdul Ghani* v. *State of Uttar Pradesh*, AIR 1973 SC 264: 1973 Cri LJ 280: (1973) 4 SCC 17.
3. *Alamgir* v. *State (NCT Delhi)*, AIR 2003 SC 282: 2003 Cr LJ 456: 2002 AIR SCW 4749: (2003) 1 SCC 21.
4. *Sharad Biridhichand Sarda* v. *State of Maharashtra*, AIR 1984 SC 1622: 1984 4 SCC 116: 1984 Cr LJ 1738.
5. *Kanhai Mishra* v. *State of Bihar*, AIR 2001 SC 1113: 2001 Cr LJ 1259: 2001 AIR SCW 857.
6. *Kishore Chand* v. *State of Himachal Pradesh*, AIR 1990 SC 2140: (1991) 1 SCC 286: 1990 Cr LJ 2289: 1991 SCC (Cri) 172.
7. *G. Parashwanath* v. *State of Karnataka*, AIR 2010 SC 2914: 2010 AIR SCW 5052: (2010) 8 SCC 593.
8. *Maharashtra State Board of Secondary and Higher Secondary Education* v. *K.S. Gandhi*, 1991 AIR SCW 879: (1991) 2 SCC 716.

can be inferred, as much as is practicable, as if they had been actually observed. **In other cases, the inferences do not go beyond reasonable probability**............".

(Emphasis supplied)

20. What is the precise meaning of the expression "fact" used in the definition of "proved" furnished in the Act? The "fact" referred to therein embraces any fact in issue or relevant fact, since any fact which is neither a fact in issue nor a relevant fact cannot be and will not allowed to be proved by evidence, by virtue of section 5 of the Act. The standard prescribed in the definition of "proved" in the Act is belief on preponderance of probability. But the definition does not expressly or impliedly embrace the idea of "proof beyond reasonable doubt". The requirement of "proof of beyond reasonable doubt" does not and cannot apply to basic or primary facts as made clear in ***M.G. Agarwal's*** case and other cases. Such basic or primary facts are to be proved in the ordinary way as explained in ***M.G. Agarwal's*** case and other cases, that is, merely satisfying the requirements of the definition of "proof". The requirement of "proof of the charge or guilt of accused beyond reasonable doubt" has never been a statutory requirement in India. This requirement was introduced originally by the judges in England as part of the common law and adopted by judges in India ever since the British rulers established courts in India. In the United States of America, the judges introduced this requirement borrowing from the common law of England and later by judicially holding that the requirement is inherent in and flows from the due process clause in the XIV amendment.

21. In what context exactly does the requirement of proof beyond reasonable doubt arise? There can be no dispute that such a burden rests on the prosecution in establishing the **charge** against the accused or proving his **guilt** for the offence alleged against him. It is worthwhile quoting again the following conclusion of the Constitution Bench in the case of ***M.G. Agarwal***:

> "When it is held that a certain fact is proved, the question arises whether that fact leads to the inference of **guilt of the accused person or not, and in dealing with this aspect of the problem, the doctrine of benefit of doubt would apply** and an inference of guilt can be drawn only if the proved fact is wholly inconsistent with the innocence of the accused and is consistent only with his guilt".

(Emphasis supplied)

In ***Garib Singh*** v. ***State of Punjab***,[1] (Para 7) the Supreme Court observed as follows:

> "Section 3 of the Evidence Act **enables a court to employ only the standards of a prudent man** in judging what is to be deemed to be proved according to law. Section 114 of the Evidence Act enables courts to presume only that which accords with the ordinary course of events and human nature and not what would be an aberration from such a course........................ **the degree which must reach before a court trying a criminal case will convict is no doubt that which a prudent man will employ in reaching a conclusion beyond reasonable doubt** whereas an accused need not prove his case to the same extent in order to succeed. **But the standards employed in judging each version are those of a reasonable and prudent man**. Such

1. *Garib Singh* v. *State of Punjab*, AIR 1973 SC 460: 1972 Cr LJ 1286: 1972 3 SCR 978.

a man can only adopt what is natural to expect and what accords with common sense and ordinary experience but not what is extra-ordinary and unexpected as a reliable test of credibility of witnesses."

(Emphasis supplied)

22. In ***Rana Pratap*** v. ***State of Haryana,***[1] (Para 11), the Supreme Court dealt with a case in which the prosecution alleged that "R" and "S" held the victim and "M" gave him stab injuries which caused his death. Though the trial court acquitted all the three accused of the charge, the High Court convicted them under section 302 I.P.C. read with section 34 I.P.C. In an appeal by the three accused, the Supreme Court held as follows on the question of "common intention":

"The evidence is not very clear whether Rama Pratap and Satpal continued to hold the deceased even after Manmohan Singh started stabbing him. (After referring to the words uttered by each of the three accused which indicated merely a desire to teach the victim a lesson). In the circumstances, we are unable to hold that **the only inference** possible is that Rama Pratap and Satpal **shared the common intention** with Manmohan to kill the deceased. No doubt they held the deceased and this facilitated the stabbing by Manmohan. But there is nothing whatever to indicate that they knew that Manmohan would cause fatal injuries. It is one of those **borderline cases** where one may with equal justification infer that the common intention was to commit murder or to cause grievous injury. But the **benefit of any such doubt** must go to the accused. In the circumstances, we conclude but not without hesitation, **that the common intention of the accused has not been established beyond reasonable doubt**, to be to cause the death of deceased. But it certainly was to cause grievous injuries to the deceased".

(Emphasis supplied)

The Supreme Court altered the conviction of "R" and "S" into one under section 326 I.P.C. read with section 34 I.P.C., while maintaining the conviction of "M" under section 302 I.P.C. I may comment that the court did not consider the aspect whether "R" and "S" were aware, immediately preceding and at the time of the commencement of the incident, that "M" had a knife with him and wonder whether the finding on this aspect would have persuaded the Supreme Court to a arrive at a different conclusion.

This decision made no reference to the earlier Constitution Bench decision in *M.G. Agarwal's* case.

23. In ***Vijayee Singh*** v. ***State of Uttar Pradesh,***[2] a three-judge bench of the Supreme Court observed as follows:

Para 28: "……………….. Section 3 while explaining the meaning of the words "proved", "disproved" and "not proved" **lays down the standard of proof**, namely about the existence or non-existence of the circumstances **from the point of view of a prudent man.** The section is so worded as to provide **for two conditions of mind**, first, that in which a man feels **absolutely certain of a fact**, in other words, "believe it to exist" and secondly, in which though he may not feel

1. *Rana Pratap* v. *State of Haryana*, AIR 1983 SC 680: (1983) 3 SCC 327: 1983 Cr LJ 1272.
2. *Vijayee Singh* v. *State of Uttar Pradesh*, AIR 1990 SC 1459: (1990) 3 SCC 190: 1990 Cr LJ 1510.

absolutely certain of a fact, he thinks it so extremely probable that a prudent man would under the circumstances act on the assumption of its' existence. **The Act while adopting the requirement of the prudent man as an appropriate concrete standard** by which to measure proof at the same time contemplates of giving full effect to be given to circumstances or **condition of probability or improbability. It is this degree of certainly to be** arrived at where the circumstances before a fact can be said to be proved".

This decision made no reference to the earlier Constitution Bench decision in *M.G. Agarwal's* case.

24. The idea expressed in Para 28 of the above decision that a fact is believed to exist when a person feels "absolutely certain" of the existence of the fact can lead to confusion. "Absolute certainty" is a standard not known to law of evidence. "Absolute certainty" presupposes "perfect evidence". How can any court or law-person expect "perfect evidence" to be adduced in this imperfect world? Particularly in the case of direct testimony of eye witnesses, one always expects to find some error, exaggeration, weakness or deficiency on account of substantial interval of time between the date of commission of offence and date on which the evidence of eye witness is recorded by court, which may lead to lapse of memory. Such perfect evidence is sometimes seen by courts as indicative of strenuous tutoring of the witness. Perfect evidence and absolute certainty are words relatable to mathematics or even science, and not to the realm of evidence and proof. In ***Inder Singh*** v. ***Delhi Administration,***[1] the Supreme Court observed as follows:

"While it is necessary that proof beyond reasonable doubt should be adduced in all criminal cases, it is **not necessary that it should be perfect evidence."**

(Emphasis supplied)

Recall also the observations in ***C.H. Rajik Ram's*** case quoted in para 12 above.

25. Further, in ***Vijayee Singh*** v. ***State of Uttar Pradesh***[2] case, the Court did not advert to the meaning and content of the words "belief" or "believes". *Blacks' Law Dictionary* (Abridged sixth edition) at page 106, explains the meaning of the word "belief" this:

"A conviction of truth of a proposition, existing **subjectively in the mind** and induced by argument, persuasion or proof addressed to the judgment. A conclusion arrived at from external sources **after weighing probability**. Conviction arising not from actual perception, but by way of inference or evidence received from other persons. ....**belief is an assurance** gained by evidence, and from other persons. **Suspicion is weaker than "belief"** since suspicion requires no real foundation for its' existence, while belief is necessarily based on atleast assumed facts".

(Emphasis supplied)

Advanced Law Lexicon (3rd Edition) by P. Ramanatha Aiyar at pages 498 and 499 of volume I explains "belief" thus:

---

1. *Inder Singh* v. *State,* AIR 1978 SC 1091: 1978 Cr LJ 766: (1978) 4 SCC 161.
2. *Vijayee Singh* v. *State of Uttar Pradesh,* AIR 1990 SC 1459: (1990) 3 SCC 190: 1990 Cr LJ 1510.

> "A persuasion of the truth .... of .... alleged fact.................... formed in the way of inference from some other fact..................... **Belief admits of all degrees from the slightest suspicion to the fullest assurance**..................... a **state of mind** that regards the existence of something **as likely or relatively certain**..................... To put **credit** or **confidence** in the veracity of testimony, to have **belief, to satisfy, to suppose, to think**....................."
>
> (Emphasis supplied)

The *Compact Oxford English Dictionary* explains the meaning of "believe" thus:—

> "To accept that (something) is or (someone) is telling the truth, **have faith in** the truth or existence of, have religious faith or **to think or suppose**".
>
> (Emphasis supplied)

Look at the range of meanings attached to the words "belief" or "believe". The range is very wide. Therefore, it is difficult to say these words convey the idea only of the highest degree of persuasion.

26. *Vijaya Singh's* case juxtaposed "belief" with "absolute certainty"; this was done without specific advertence to the possible meaning and content of the expression "belief". 'Belief" is not different in quality from "believes". One who has belief, believes; one who believes has belief. Belief does not indicate only a single degree of proof, that too at the highest level. When one uses words "absolute certainty", one has in mind highest degree or level of conviction. Actually "belief" or "belives", as we see from P.R. Aiyar, indicates a range or degrees or levels ranging from "suspicion" to "fullest assurance". Black indicates that belief is state of mind reached after weighing probability and satisfied by assurance. P.R. Aiyar also explains "Belief" is a state of mind that regards the existence of something as likely or relatively (not absolutely) certain. "Likelihood" and "relative certainty" are conclusions which can be arrived at after "weighing probability"; that is precisely what the second part of the definition of "proved" (that is, existence of a fact is it so probable that a prudent, ought, under the circumstances of the case ought to act upon the supposition that it exists) indicates. Both belief and preponderance of probability are based on probability arrived at on consideration of evidence and other matters before the Court. The two different parts of the definition have logical basis only if they involve different standards or degrees of proof. If 'belief' arises only in case of "absolute certainty", it is certainly a higher standard than "preponderance of probability" (second part). If, on the other hand, 'belief' means only likely, it reflects a standard lower in degree or level than "preponderance of probability". If "belief" connotes merely "relative certainly" it is nothing different from "preponderance of probability".

27. In ***In re: Winship***, 397 US 358, Justice Brennan, speaking for the majority of judges in the Supreme Court of USA observed (P. 364) as follows:

> ".....................the fact finder cannot acquire unassailably accurate knowledge of what happened. Instead, all the fact finder **can acquire is a belief of what probably happened. The intensity of this belief – the degree to which a fact finder is convinced** that a given fact actually occurred **can of course, vary**".
>
> (Emphasis supplied)

28. Reference may again be made to ***Garib Singh*** v. ***State of Punjab,***[1] where Supreme Court observed as follows:

> "Section 3 of the Indian Evidence Act enables a court to employ **only the standards of a prudent man** in judging what is deemed to be proved according to law............... The degree which proof must reach before a court trying a criminal case will convict is no **doubt that which a prudent man will employ** in reaching a conclusion beyond reasonable doubt whereas an accused need not prove his case to the same extent in order to succeed. But the standards employed in judging each version are those of **a reasonable and prudent man."**
>
> (Emphasis supplied)

Does this decision mean that the Supreme Court was not aware that the definition was in two parts and the first part dealt with "belief" or "believes"? It is apparent that the Supreme Court found no practical difference between the burden of proof prescribed in the two parts and both parts inhered only preponderant probability – which a prudent man ought to accept. Segregation of the two parts may mean that legislature was not concerned that "belief" should be entertained on the basis of what a prudent ought to do, certainly an absurd idea!

29. In another case dependent entirely on circumstantial evidence, *i.e.,* ***Rama Nand*** v. ***State of H.P.,***[2] the Supreme Court held as follows: (Para 16)

> "It is well-settled that where the inference of guilt of an accused person is to be drawn from circumstantial evidence only, those circumstances must, in the first place, be cogently established. Further, those circumstances should be of a definite tendency pointing towards the guilt of the accused, and in their totality, must unerringly lead to the conclusion that **within all human probabilities**, the offence was committed by the accused and none else."
>
> (Emphasis supplied)

30. In ***Maharashtra Ed. Board*** v. ***K.S. Gandhi,***[3] which dealt with proof of a corrupt practice which is treated akin to a criminal charge, the Supreme Court held as follows (Para 38):

> "......................There must be evidence, direct or circumstantial, to deduce necessary inferences in proof of facts in issue. There can be no inferences unless there are objective facts, direct or circumstantial from which to infer the other fact which it is sought to be establish. **In some cases, the other facts, can be inferred, as much as is practical, as if they had been actually observed. In other cases, the inferences do not go beyond reasonable probability**. If there are no positive proved facts, oral or documentary or circumstantial from which inferences can be made the method of inference fails and what is left if mere speculation or speculation."
>
> (Emphasis supplied)

---

1. *Garib Singh* v. *State of Punjab,* AIR 1973 SC 460: 1972 Cr LJ 1286: 1972 3 SCR 978.
2. *Rama Nand* v. *State of Himachal Pradesh,* 1981 CAR 75: 1981 Cr LR 340: 1981 SCR 444: 1981 UJ 424: (1981) 1 SCC 511: (1981) 1 SCALE 24: AIR 1981 SC 738: (1981) 87 Cr LJ 298.
3. *Maharashtra State Board of Secondary and Higher Secondary Education* v. *K.S. Gandhi,* 1991 AIR SCW 879: (1991) 2 SCC 716.

Quoting the above passage with approval, the Supreme Court in *R. Puthinayanar* v. *P.H. Pandian,*[1] said (Para 7):

> "Therefore, we hold that to draw an inference that a fact in dispute has been established, there must exist, on record, some direct material facts or circumstances from which such an inference should be drawn. **The standard of proof required cannot be put in a straight jacket formula.** .... **The probative force** could be gauged from the facts and circumstances of the case."
>
> (Emphasis supplied)

In this case the court also observed in para 9 as follows:

> "The burden of proof of the charge in a criminal case is always on the prosecution. **The guilt of the accused beyond reasonable doubt** should be established by the prosecution."
>
> (Emphasis supplied)

31. In ***M. Narsing Rao*** v. ***State of Andhra Pradesh,***[2] the Court had to consider whether an offence under the Prevention of Corruption Act, 1988 was brought home to the accused. The three-judge bench speaking through K.T. Thomas. J. observed as follows in Para 15:

> "The word "proof" need be understood in the sense in which it is defined in the Evidence Act because proof depends upon the admissibility of evidence. (After reproducing the definition in section 3 of the Act)—This is the definition given for the word "proof" in the Evidence Act. What is required is the production of such materials on which the court can reasonably act to reach the supposition that a fact exists. Proof of the fact **depends on the degree of probability of it having existed. The standard required for reaching the supposition is that of a prudent man** acting in any important matter concerning him."
>
> (Emphasis supplied)

The Court proceeded to quote the following observations of Fletcher Moulton. L.J. in ***Hawkins* v. *Powells Tillery Steam Coal Co. Ltd.***[3]

> **"Proof does not mean proof to rigid mathematical demonstration because that is impossible**; it must mean such evidence as would **induce a reasonable man to come to a particular conclusion."**
>
> (Emphasis supplied)

The Supreme Court continued as follows (Para 16):

> "The said observation **has stood the test of time** and can now be followed as the standard of proof. In reaching the conclusion, **the court can use the process of inferences to be drawn from facts produced or proved.** Such inferences **are akin to presumptions in law**. Law gives absolute discretion to the court to presume the existence of any fact which it thinks likely to have happened. In that process the court may have regard to common course of natural events, human conduct, public or private business

---

1. *R. Puthunainar Alhithan* v. *P.H. Pandian*, (1996) 3 SCC 624: (1996) 3 SCALE 317: AIR 1996 SC 1599.
2. *M. Narsinga Rao* v. *State of Andhra Pradesh*, (2001) 1 SCC 691: AIR 2001 SC 318: 2000 AIR SCW 4427: 2001 Cr LJ 515.
3. *Hawkins* v. *Powells Tillery Steam Coal Co. Ltd.*, (1911) 1 KB 988: 104 LT 365: 80 LJKB 769.

vis-à-vis the facts of the particular case. This discretion is clearly envisaged in section 114 of the Evidence Act."

(Emphasis supplied)

32. ***M. Narasing Rao's*** case, quoted above in para 25, recited the definition of "proved" occurring in section 3 of the Act (*i.e.*, either believes it to exist or considers..................... so probable.................... a prudent man.....................), but followed it by stating emphatically regarding the **standard prescribed by the definition** as follows (already quoted):—

"**Proof of the fact depends upon the degree of probability of it having existed**. The standard required for reaching the supposition **is that of a prudent man**....................."

(Emphasis supplied)

It is obvious that the Bench did not think that the first part of the definition (believes it exist) prescribes a standard higher or lower or different from the standard prescribed in the second part, suggesting thereby that the two parts, worded differently, mean the same thing and convey the same idea.

33. The Evidence Act contains provisions to control the uninhabited discretion of judges in the matter of conduct of trial, receiving evidence, method of proof, burden of proof and various other matters. The object sought to be achieved is to enable a fair trial, protecting the rights of all parties to litigation. The basic objective is fairness, speedy trial, without cluttering court record with all kinds of evidence of little credibility or proof of facts which will really not assist the judges in coming to as correct a conclusion as humanly possible. Framers of the bill preceding the Act had the benefit of experience of the common law of England and did try to avoid some pitfalls. When a fact can be said to have been proved, would have been one of the matters which received their serious attention.

34. In ***State NCT of Delhi*** v. ***Navjot Sandu* alias *Afsan Guru***[1] (Parliament attack case), the Supreme Court had to, among other questions, consider the charge of conspiracy and charges under sections 120A, 120B, 121, 121A and 122 of IPC. During the course of the discussion on the aspect of conspiracy, the court made the following observations:

"One more principle which deserves notice is that cumulative effect of the proved circumstances should be taken into account in determining the guilt of the accused rather than adopting an isolated approach to each of the circumstances. Of course, **each one of the circumstances should be proved beyond reasonable doubt**."

(Emphasis supplied)

If the last sentence is taken to mean that each of the primary or basic facts whose cumulative effect could lead to a conclusion that the charge of conspiracy (which includes the object and other relevant aspects) is required to be "proved beyond reasonable doubt" in the sense of "charge against the accused" or "guilt of the accused" being required to be proved beyond reasonable doubt, that would go against the decision of the Constitution Bench in ***M.G. Agarwal***.[2] The

1. *State (NCT of Delhi)* v. *Navjot Sandhu @ Afasan Guru*, AIR 2005 SC 3820: 2005 AIR SCW 4148: (2005) 11 SCC 600: 2005 Cr LJ 3950 (SC): 122 (2005) DLT 194 (SC).
2. *M.G. Agarwal* v. *State of Maharashtra*, AIR 1963 SC 200: 1963 (1) Cr LJ 235: 64 Bom LR 773: (1963) 2 SCR 405.

above observation was made without noticing the conclusion of the Constitution Bench in para 18 of that judgment, which was as follows:

> "In regard to the proof of basic or primary facts, the court has to judge the evidence **in the ordinary way**, and in the appreciation of evidence in respect of proof of **basic or primary facts, there is no scope for the application of the doctrine of benefit of doubt."**
>
> (Emphasis supplied)

The doctrine of "benefit of doubt" and requirement of "proof beyond reasonable doubt" are two faces of the same coin. It must follow that doctrine of benefit of doubt has no role to play in the area of appreciation of evidence for the purpose of deciding whether prosecution has proved "basic or primary facts" or the various basic or primary circumstances whose cumulative effect requires to be taken into consideration. If in regard to any matter, "proof beyond reasonable doubt" is not required, in reference to proof of that matter, the doctrine of benefit of doubt cannot apply and *vice versa.*

35. Referance is already made to the decision of the Supreme Court of U.S.A. in ***In re: Winship***[1]. The question which arose for consideration was whether the juvenile before the New York family court was "a person .... who did any act which, if done by an adult, would constitute a crime?" Section 744(b) of the New York Family Court Act provided that any determination at the conclusion of an adjudicatory hearing that the juvenile did commit such a act or acts must be based on a **"preponderance of the evidence"** (not preponderance of probability, which may be a different matter). The Supreme Court held that even in the proceeding against a juvenile in respect of an offence allegedly committed, the standard of proof **"of essential elements of crime" is one of proof beyond reasonable doubt** and this standard must necessarily apply to proceeding before the family court in respect of an act, which, if committed by an adult, would be a criminal offence; this is so by virtue of the **due process clause** introduced by the XIV amendment to the Constitution and the different and lower standard prescribed by the New York statute would be unconstitutional as violative of the due process clause. There are observations to the following effect in the majority judgment:

(a) Page 359: "It is now accepted in **common law jurisdiction** as the **measure of persuasion** by which the prosecution must convince the trier of **all the essential elements of guilt.**"

"Expressions in many opinions of this court indicate that it has long **been assumed that proof of a criminal charge beyond a reasonable doubt is constitutionally required.**"

(b) Page 360: "Mr. Justice Frankfurter stated that (it is) the duty of the government to **establish guilt beyond a reasonable doubt**. This notion basic in our law and rightly one of the boasts of a free society – is a requirement and a safeguard of **due process** of law in the historic and procedural content of "due process of law".........

In a similar vein, the court said in ***Brinegar*** v. ***U.S.***, supra, 338 U.S. at 174[2] .... that **"guilt in a criminal case must be proved beyond reasonable doubt............"**

(Emphasis supplied)

1. 397 US 358.
2. *Brinegar* v. *U.S.*, 338 US 174.

(c) In ***Davis* v. *U.S.*,**[1] the court considered the question of degree of burden of proof regarding sanity of the accused. The court said:

"On the contrary, he (accused) is entitled to an acquittal of the specific crime charged, if upon all evidence, there is **reasonable doubt whether he was capable in law of committing crime**..................... No man should be deprived of his life under the norms of law unless the jurors who try him are able, upon their conscience, to say that the evidence before them ....is sufficient to **show beyond a reasonable doubt the existence of every fact necessary to constitute the crime charges."**

(Emphasis supplied)

(d) Page 361: (Quoted from ***Speiser* v. *Randall*,**[2] "Where one party has at stake an interest of transcending value as a criminal defendant his liberty – this margin of error (in factfinding) is reduced as to him by the factfinder **at the conclusion of the trial of his guilt beyond reasonable doubt**. Due process commands that no man shall lose his liberty unless the government has borne the burden of ....convincing the fact finder of **his guilt**.

To this end, the reasonable doubt standard is indispensable for it "impresses on the trier of fact the necessity of reaching a **subjective state of certitude of the facts in issue"**.

(e) Lest there remain any doubt about the constitutional stature of the reasonable doubt standard, we explicitly hold that the due process clause protects the accused against conviction except **upon proof beyond a reasonable doubt of every fact necessary to constitute the crime with which he is charged.** (Emphasis supplied)

36. Here are a few observations in the concurring judgement delivered by Mr. Justice Harlan:

(f) Page 364: "I begin by stating two propositions .... First, in a judicial proceeding in which there is a dispute about the facts of some earlier event, the fact finder cannot acquire unassailably accurate knowledge of what happened. Instead, all the fact finder can acquire is **a belief of what probably happened. The intensity of this belief can, of course, vary.** In this regard, a standard of proof represents an attempt to instruct the fact finder concerning the degree of confidence our society thinks he should have in the correctness of the factual conclusions for a particular type of adjudication. ...."

(Emphasis supplied)

(g) Page 365: Mr. Justice Harlan also observed—

"(A preponderance of evidence standard) ....simply requires the trier of fact to "believe that the existence of a fact is **more probable than it's non-existence before** he may find in favour of the party who has the burden to persuade the (judge) of the fact's existence. .... Where one party has at stake an interest of transcending value as a criminal defendant his liberty this margin of error is reduced as to him by the process of placing on the other party the burden of persuading the

1. *Davis* v. *U.S.*, 160 US 488.

2. *Speiser* v. *Randall*, (1958) 357 US 513: 2 Law Ed 2d 1460.

factfinder at the conclusion of the trial of **his guilt beyond a reasonable doubt."**

(Emphasis supplied)

37. ***In re: Winship*** (Majority and concurring judgments) does not contain any other observations relating to degree of proof of "fact in issue" or "relevant fact" or "basic or primary facts" except those quoted in paragraphs 28 and 29 supra and serialized as (a) to (g). Do they support any proposition that proof of all "facts" in a criminal case must be proved beyond reasonable doubt? In the said judgments, it is repeatedly stated that burden which lies on the prosecution is to **prove the charge or guilt of the accused or the "essential elements of crime" beyond reasonable doubt.** *See* quotations in clauses (a), (b), (d) and (g). This, of course, is unexceptionable. By "essential elements of the crime" are meant '*Actus reus*' and '*Mens rea*'

Quotations (c) and (e) refer to need to prove beyond reasonable doubt, "the existence of every fact necessary to **constitute the crime charged**". This does not comprehend every "relevant fact" as defined in Indian Evidence Act, but only the facts necessary to constitute the crime, that is, "facts in issue" which means '*actus reus*' and '*mens rea*'. "Every fact necessary to constitute the crime" means the facts in issue and not relevant or circumstantial facts.

Quotation (f) refers to "factual conclusions". There is an accepted way for a judge to proceed to arrive at a final conclusion regarding the charge or the guilt of the accused. Prosecution may rely on direct testimony (of eye witnesses) or indirect testimony (*i.e.*, relating to circumstances) spoken to by witnesses, such as motive, previous quarrel, previous threat or behaviour, acts of preparation such as procuring a weapon or poison, opportunity, subsequent conduct of accused such as hiding his own blood-stained clothes or knife, absconding, judicial confession, extra-judicial confession not hit by sections 24 to 26 of the Act and other circumstances. These are the obviously the facts or circumstances referred to as "basic or primary facts" by the Constitution Bench in ***M.G. Agarwal's*** case. There can be no doubt that the observations in ***In re: Winship*** are to the effect that proof beyond reasonable doubt is required in respect "of every fact **necessary to constitute the crime**". What are the facts necessary to constitute the crime? There may several basic or primary facts whose cumulative effect leads to an inference of guilt beyond reasonable doubt. These facts which enable such an inference are not "facts which constitute crime" which are really "facts in issue" as defined in section 3 of the Act in the light of the illustrations. In other words, those facts which constitute the crime are the ingredients found in the definition of the offence in the penal law (*actus reus, mens rea*, common intention, common object, conspiracy, constructive liability, etc.) Ingredients of crime constitute, "facts in issue" and these are "facts necessary to constitute the crime". These facts in issue or facts necessary to "constitute" the crime are, according to ***In re: Winship***, required to be proved beyond reasonable doubt. Other facts, which may be just introductory facts (in the general sense) and relevant facts (under the Act) are not facts in issue and fall within the description of "basic or primary facts" mentioned in ***M.G. Agarwal's*** case and such facts are required to be proved in the ordinary way, that is, as prescribed in the definition of "proved" in section 3 of the Act which means belief, that is to say, preponderance of probability.

38. In this connection, referance may be made to certain passages in Wigmore "on evidence in trials at common law" (Tillers edition) Vol. IX.

Page 405: "The tribunal must be persuaded to believe the affirmation of the burden bearer before it can be asked to act as desired, but that persuasion or conviction in the mind of the tribunal **may have more than one degree of quality or persuasion."**

(Emphasis supplied)

Pages 412 to 414: "It is generally and properly said that **this measure of reasonable doubt need not be applied to the specific detailed facts, but only to the whole of the issue and herein is given** an opportunity for much vain argument whether the strands of a cable or the links of a chain furnish the better similar for listing the measure of persuasion."

The truth is that no one has yet invented or discovered a mode of measurement for the **intensity of human belief**.

(Emphasis supplied)

Page 416: (Footnote 2 bottom). "A later case, ***Jackson*** v. ***Virgenia,***[1] expounds the doctrine; "WINSHIP presupposes as an essential of the due process guaranteed by the Fourteenth Amendment that no person shall be made to suffer the *onus* of a criminal conviction except upon sufficient proof – defined as evidence necessary to convince a trier **of fact beyond reasonable doubt, of the existence of every element of the offence**."

(Emphasis supplied)

Pages 416 and 417: "In ***In re: Winship***, the Supreme Court held, for reasons set forth below that the due process clause protects the accused against conviction, except upon proof beyond a reasonable doubt **of every fact necessary to constitute the crime with he is charged**."

(Emphasis supplied)

Page 418: "In ***Patterson*** v. ***New York,***[2] under the New York Law, White J. reasoned for the majority as follows:—

"........we therefore will not disturb the balance struck in previous cases holding that the due process clause requires the prosecution to prove beyond a reasonable doubt all of the **elements included in the definition of the offence of which the defendant is charges**."

(Emphasis supplied)

Page 413: (Footnote 2) ***"California People*** v. ***Kelinbinberg,*** 90 Cal App 2d 608 (632, 634, 638),[3]– **"It is not the law ....that each fact in a chain of circumstances that will establish a defendants' guilt must be proved beyond reasonable doubt...................... Doctrine of reasonable doubt applies to proof of guilt and not to establishment of each incident or event inculpating the defendant**.""

"The strict standard is not applicable to evidence of criminal acts offered evidentially to show motive, intent etc. Cases cited in para 216 note 4 supra."

(Emphasis supplied)

---

1. *Jackson* v. *Virgenia*, 443 US 307 (1979).
2. *Patterson* v. *New York*, 432 US 197 (1977).
3. *California People* v. *Kelinbinberg*, 90 Cal App 2d 608 (632, 634, 638).

39. The following statements in *Criminal Evidence* (4th Edn.) by Richard May are also significant:

Page 65 – Para 4-37: "Proof of guilt beyond a reasonable doubt .... many attempts have been made to define a reasonable doubt .... the standard of proof is a high one, but it is important that it **should not be confused with absolute certainty (*Bracewell,*** (1979) 68 Cr Appeal R 44 CA). Thus in ***R.H. (minors),*** (1996) 2 WLR 8 (24) Lord Nicholls said **"The law looks for probability, not certainty, certainty is seldom attainable.** But probability is an unsatisfactorily vague criterion because there are degrees of probability.

(Emphasis supplied)

In ***Miller*** v. ***Minister of Pensions,*** 372, 373[1], Lord Denning said "That degree is well-settled. **It need not reach certainty, but it must carry a high degree of probability.** Proof beyond doubt does not mean proof beyond **a shadow** of reasonable doubt.

(Emphasis supplied)

Page 67 – Para 4-39: In ***Miller*** v. ***Minister of Pensions*** supra, Lord Denning observed, dealing with the burden resting on the defence, that if the evidence is such that the Tribunal says "we think it more probable than not, the burden is discharged, but if the probabilities are equal, it is not". That, according to **Miles. J.** in ***Cooper*** v. ***Slade,***[2] is exactly the burden in a civil case, that is, preponderance of probability."

(Emphasis supplied)

40. Here are some of the observations in *Halsburys' Laws of England,* Vol. 17, 4th Edition:

"To succeed on any issue the legal burden of proof must (1) satisfy a judge or jury of the **likelihood of truth of his case** by adducing a greater weight of evidence than his opponents and (2) adduce evidence sufficient to satisfy them to the required standard of proof. The standard differs in criminal and civil cases ....

In civil cases, the standard of proof is satisfied on a **balance of probabilities** (***Miller*** v. ***Minister of Pensions***)[1] the more serious the allegation, for example, fraud, crime or professional misconduct, the higher will be the required degree of proof, although it will not reach the criminal law standard............

In Criminal case, the standard required of the prosecution is proof beyond reasonable doubt.

Page 23 – Para 29: **Proper evaluation of the weight of evidence given by different witnesses is a matter for the common sense and impression of the judge or jury.**

Page 74: **"Sure" does not mean certainty. To require certainty of legal proof would produce absurdity.**"

(Emphasis supplied)

1. *Miller* v. *Minister of Pensions,* 1947 (2) All ER 372 (373): 177 LT 536: 63 TLR 474.
2. *Cooper* v. *Slade,* (1857-58) 6 HL Case 746.

41. Following are of the statements found in Criminal Pleadings, Evidence and Practice by Archibald:

> Page 447 – Para 4-384: **"While the prosecution do not have to make the jury feel certain of the accuseds' guilt** (*Miller*, 1947 (2) All ER 372)[1] per Denning at Pages 373, 374, ***R.*** v. ***Bracewell,*** 68 Cr Appeal R 44 (A) they must satisfy the jury, upon the whole evidence called by all the parties, of the accuseds' guilt beyond all reasonable doubt...................... it is well established that the **standard of proof is less than certainty**. Expressions (in instructions to juries) such as **"pretty certain, reasonably sure and pretty sure" were disapproved by** the court of criminal appeal. ***R.*** v. ***Law,*** (1961) Crl R 52, ***R.*** v. ***Head and Warren,*** 45 Cr Appeal R 225 and ***R.*** v. ***Woods,*** (1961) Crl R 324. It is therefore better to give "reasonable doubt" direction. In ***R.*** v. ***Bentley,*** (1999) Cr LR 330, the court of appeal said, as to standard of proof, that a jury should be instructed that if on reviewing all evidence, **they are unsure or left in any reasonable doubt as to the accuseds' guilt**, that doubt must be resolved in accuseds' favour.

(Emphasis supplied)

42. Here are some of the statements in Jeremy Bentham's *Rationale of Judicial Evidence*, Prevention of Deception:

> Page 60: **"Quantity of probative force incident to the body of evidence, is manifestly, as above explained, susceptible of degrees and conformable to the tendency of the evidence. It is not necessary that the probative force of it should in every instance be at the highest degree**.

(Emphasis supplied)

43. The following principles emerge from the above discussion:

Definition of "proved" in section 3 of the Act applies equally in civil and criminal cases. "Fact" referred to in the definition includes—

"facts in issue" and "relevant facts" . The definition apparently has two parts. The first part refers to "believes" and the second part uses language which means "preponderance of probability". The two parts do not indicate two different alternative standards. The first part "believes" is not self explanatory and has no guidelines; the guidelines are actually provided in the second part, which is explanatory or expository or interpretative. A judge believes the existence of a fact when there is a preponderance of probability in favour of it. The true question is not whether the testimony in a given case may be false, but whether there is sufficient probability of its' truth, that is, whether the facts are shown by competent and satisfactory evidence. The element of "proof beyond reasonable doubt" is not comprised in the definition. This element regarding proof of "facts in issue" in criminal cases, that is to say, guilt of accused of the crime or offence charged was introduced by judges in England and India. The requirement of "proof beyond reasonable doubt" does not apply to proof in civil cases or proof of "basic or primary facts" (that is, facts which are merely relevant facts) in criminal cases. Proof of any fact under section 3 of the Act depends on preponderance of probability in civil and criminal cases (except that, in criminal cases, the facts in issue, that is, the offence or the ingredients of the offence charged must be proved beyond reasonable

1. *Miller* v. *Minister of Pensions*, 1947 (2) All ER 372 (373): 177 LT 536: 63 TLR 474.

doubt). The words "belief" and "believes", by themselves do not point to any particular degree or standard of proof. These words, by their natural meaning inhere different degrees of intensity. These words do not give rise to the idea of "absolute certainty" for such certainty can be achieved only by "perfect evidence", both of which are unattainable or unavailable through the medium of human witness. See ***Inder Singh*** v. ***(State) Delhi Administration***.[1] The expression "relatively certain" would be a more appropriate one.

The decision of the Constitution Bench of the Supreme Court in ***M.G. Agarwal*** v. ***State of Maharashtra***,[2] Para 18 has stood the test of time. It has not been "explained" or "read down" in any later decision. On the other hand, it has been followed in later decisions.

---

1. *Inder Singh* v. *State*, AIR 1978 SC 1091: 1978 Cr LJ 766: (1978) 4 SCC 161.
2. *M.G. Agarwal* v. *State of Maharashtra*, AIR 1963 SC 200: 1963 (1) Cr LJ 235: 64 Bom LR 773: (1963) 2 SCR 405.

CHAPTER 4
RELEVANCY OF FACTS
(SECTIONS 5 TO 16)

Relevancy of facts is different from admissibility of evidence. Looked at this way, all that is relevant is not admissible and *vice versa*[1]. Primary duty of courts is to ascertain facts about which parties are at issue. "Facts in issue" means and includes any fact from which, either by itself or in conjunction with other facts, the existence, non-existence, nature or extent of any, right, liability, or disability asserted or denied in any suit or proceeding, necessarily follows, as per the definition in section 3, Indian Evidence Act. One fact is said to be relevant to another when the one is connected with the other in any of the ways referred to in the provisions of the Act relating to relevancy of facts. Relevant means what is logically probative. Stephen, in his introduction to one of the editions of Woodroffe and Amir Ali on 'Law of Evidence' stated that "The word 'relevant' means that any two facts to which it is applied are so related to each other that according to the common course of events, one either taken by itself or in connection with other facts proves or renders probable the past, present or future existence or non-existence of the other". But this is 'relevancy' in a logical sense. Legal relevancy requires a higher standard of evidentiary force and the interconnection should not be misleading or remote. Fact as defined means and includes (a) anything, state of things, or relation of things capable of being perceived by the senses, and (b) any mental condition of which any person is conscious, that is, physical facts and psychological facts. Inferences are not facts. Substantive law defines rights and liabilities of persons which are vindicated or enforced by means of litigation, civil or criminal. Object of litigation is to ascertain whether the right claimed or liability sought to be enforced does or does not exist. A party to a litigation has to establish all such facts as go to constitute such right or liability. The necessary constituents of "right" or "liability" are called "facts in issue". Every fact which one party must prove in order to secure a favourable verdict in a litigation is a fact in issue, if the parties are not agreed about the existence or non-existence of such fact. What are the 'facts in issue' in a given case depends on the substantive law governing the case and the procedural law which deals with framing of issues or points of fact. Rules (1) and (2) of Order XIV C.P.C. may be seen. In criminal cases, all the ingredients of the offence charged are 'facts in issue'.

The means by which courts inform themselves of existence of facts is called "evidence". Evidence means and includes all statements which the court permits or requires to be made before it by witnesses in relation to matters of fact under enquiry as also all documents produced for inspection of the court. (*See*

1. *Ram Bihari Yadav* v. *State of Bihar*, AIR 1998 SC 1850: (1998) 4 SCC 517: 1998 Cr LJ 2515: 1998 AIR SCW 1647: 1998 SCC (Cri) 1085.

definition in section 3). Evidence is the instrument by means of which disputed facts are brought before the court and by which Court is convinced of these facts. It is the medium of proof.[1]

When trying a case, court must know:

(a) what facts are in issue; (Order XIV C.P.C. in civil cases)

(b) what facts, other than facts in issue, may or may not be proved; (Relevancy – Chapter II, Evidence Act)

(c) what kind of evidence can be adduced in proof of disputed facts; (Admissibility – Chapters III to VI, IX and X of Evidence Act)

(d) by whom and in what manner evidence must be produced and by which party any fact is to be proved (Burden of proof – Chapter VII of Evidence Act).

The broad principles to be borne in mind are:

(a) Evidence must be confined to facts in issue and relevant facts.

(b) Hearsay evidence is barred, except in certain specified cases.

(c) Best evidence must be given in all cases.

2. SECTION 5: Evidence can be given only in respect of facts in issue and relevant facts. Relevancy and admissibility are not the same thing. Relevancy is what is logically probative; admissibility is the fitness for being received in evidence. All that is relevant is not necessarily admissible (for example, as being against public policy) and all that is admissible is not necessarily relevant. (Statements under section 155 or 157). A fact is logically relevant to another, when it bears such casual relation with the other as to render probable the existence or otherwise of the latter. The Act exhaustively enumerates the kinds of causal connection which makes a fact legally relevant to another. The two facts must be so related to each other that, according to the common course of events, one, either taken by itself or in connection with other facts, proves or renders probable the existence of the other. No fact which is not a fact in issue or a relevant fact under Chapter II of the Indian Evidence Act can be allowed to be proved in the court of law.

Question of relevancy is a question of law and can be raised at any time. It is the duty of the court to exclude all irrelevant evidence, even if no objection is taken to it by the opposite party. Provisions of C.P.C. also have a bearing as seen from illustration (b) to section 5.

The Evidence Act is a special law dealing with the subject of evidence, including the admissibility of evidence. Hence no rule about relevancy of evidence in this Act is affected by any provision of Criminal Procedure Code, 1973. Statement of a witness recorded during investigation of a crime, being traceable to sections 161 and 162 of the Criminal Procedure Code, is governed by these provisions which restrict the use of contradictions in such a statement for a specific purpose (Section 162 Criminal Procedure Code).

Sections dealing with relevancy enumerate specifically the different instances of the connection between the cause and effect which arise commonly in judicial proceedings. They are worded widely and in such a way as to overlap each

1. *Himachal Pradesh Administration* v. *Om Prakash*, AIR 1972 SC 975: (1972) 1 SCC 249: 1972 SCC (Cri) 88: (1972) 1 SCJ 691; *Hira H. Advani* v. *State of Maharashtra*, (1969) 2 SCC 662: (1970) 1 SCR 821: AIR 1971 SC 44: 1971 Cr LJ 5 (SC): 1983 ELT 1413.

other in some instances. Motive for a fact in issue (section 8) is part of its cause (section 7). Subsequent conduct influenced by a fact in issue (section 8) is part of its effect (section 7). Facts relevant under section 11 may be relevant under some other sections.

Sections 6 to 16, 21, 22, 22A, 23, 27, 28, 29, 32 to 38, 41 to 55 set out what are relevant facts. Sections 24 to 26 deal with facts which are not relevant. Section 30 is in a different category.

3. SECTION 6: Section 6 incorporates the principle of *res gestae*[1]. Bar of hearsay is implicit in the illustrations to the definition of "Fact" in section 2. Hearsay is generally regarded as not relevant and not admissible. Principle of *res gestae* is one of the exceptions to the bar against hearsay. (*See* the illustrations to section 6). The bar against heresay evidence is the reflection of judicial awareness that admission of such evidence involves two dangers. The first is that repetition of any statement involves the risk of error or distortion, which increases as the number of repetitions and complexity of the statement. The second is that it is practically impossible to effectively cross-examine a witness testifying to a heresay statement, because the witness did not perceive the events in question. Heresay is not the best evidence and is not delivered on oath. But the rule against heresay has certain exceptions one of which is that the words may be proved when they form part of *res gestae*. The reasons for this exception are two-fold. One is that human speech is both a fact and a means of communication; the other is that action of men may be so interwoven with words that the significance of the action cannot be understood without the correlative words and the dissociation of the words from the action would obstruct the discovery of truth[2]. If the whole of a transaction is a fact in issue or relevant, a part thereof is also relevant. A transaction may be a single occurrence lasting only a few moments or a variety of acts, declarations and circumstances, occupying a length of time and occurring on distinct occasions. When only a part of a transaction is the fact in issue, every other part of the transaction is relevant, according to section 6. Circumstances to be borne in mind are proximity of time, unity or proximity of place, continuity of action and community of purpose or design. Unity of time and of place, though material, are not essential. It is essential that the words sought to be proved should be, if not absolutely contemporaneous with the actual event, at least so clearly associated with it in time, place and circumstance, that they are part of the thing being done. Criteria of necessity and reliability are to be borne in mind[3]. Facts which form part of *res gestae*, and are consequently provable as acts relevant to the issue, include acts, declarations and incidents which themselves constitute, or accompany and explain the facts or

---

1. *Sardul Singh Caveeshar* v. *State of Bombay*, AIR 1957 SC 747: 1957 SCJ 780: 1958 SCR 161; *Gentela Vijayavardhan Rao* v. *State of Andhra Pradesh*, AIR 1996 SC 2791: (1996) 3 Crimes 197: (1996) 3 SCJ 247: (1996) 6 SCC 241: (1996) 6 SCALE 231: (1996) 102 Cr LJ 4151; *Rattan Singh* v. *State of Himachal Pradesh*, AIR 1997 SC 768: (1997) 4 SCC 161: (1996) 9 SCALE 258: 1997 AIR SCW 587: 1997 Cr LJ 833: *Chandra Kala* v. *Ram Krishna*, AIR 1985 SC 1268: (1985) 4 SCC 212: 1985 Cr LJ 1490; *Sukhar* v. *State of Uttar Pradesh*, (1999) 9 SCC 509: 2000 SCC (Cri) 419: AIR 1999 SC 3883: 2000 Cr LJ 29.
2. *Union of India* v. *S.L. Dutta*, AIR 1991 SC 363: (1991) 1 SCC 505: 1991 Lab IC 290; *Pawan Kumar* v. *State of Haryana*, (2003) 11 SCC 241: 2003 AIR SCW 3671: 2003 Cr LJ 3552: AIR 2003 SC 2987.
3. *Sukhar* v. *State of Uttar Pradesh*, (1999) 9 SCC 509: 2000 SCC (Cri) 419: AIR 1999 SC 3883: 2000 Cr LJ 29; *Gentela Vijayavardhan Rao* v. *State of Andhra Pradesh*, AIR 1996 SC 2791: (1996) 3 Crimes 197: (1996) 3 SCJ 247: (1996) 6 SCC 241: (1996) 6 SCALE 231: (1996) 102 Cr LJ 4151.

transactions in issue[1]. Many jurists have criticized the word *"res gestae"* as being vague and ambiguous. In its original meaning, the word imported only a 'fact', 'transaction' or 'event'. In the context of section 6 the word *"res gestae"* means only "accompanying facts",[2] or "utterances constituting a verbal part of an act" and what may be called declaration accompanying acts"[3]. The declaratory words must explain the act and must be uttered during or immediately before or after the occurrence, but not at such an interval from it as to allow of fabrication or reduce them to a mere narrative of a past event[4]. On hearing gunshots from the house of the victim, his neighbours rushed to the spot within minutes and he told them the names of the assailants who shot him. His statement would be relevant under section 6.[5]

Even hearsay statement is admissible if it forms part of the same transaction as the fact in issue[6]. *E.g.*, Utterances while killing, immediate statements of victim[7], spontaneous outbursts of by-standers, immediate confession of accused, contemporaneous dialogue between the accused and the injured.[8] A statement which may not be relevant under section 6 may be covered under sections 32 or 155 or 157. A statement by the victim made the next day to her husband and co-workers, though not relevant under section 6, is covered by section 157, provided it is corroborated.[9] Statement of an eyewitness that the accused killed the victim, made to another witness who reached the scene of occurrence immediately after the occurrence, is relevant under section 6. Utterances, during or immediately after the occurrence, by bystanders are relevant under section 6. Illustration (a) to the section may be seen with advantage.

Statement of a rape victim soon after the rape is relevant[10]. Absconding is a relevant circumstance.[11]

FIS which is ordinarily not substantive evidence, and can be used ordinarily only to corroborate or contradict the testimony of the informant, may be relevant as evidence of his conduct or as one of *res gestae*.

Earlier statement of accused at about the time and place of occurrence is relevant. Attempt of accused to put people on a false track by telling lies about the whereabouts of the victim is clearly part of *res gestae* under section 8.[12] Where

1. Halsbury's Laws of England, Vol. 13 (1934) at page 522.
2. Phipson on Evidence, 8th edition, P. 65.
3. John Henry Wigmore, on Anglo American system of evidence in trials at Common Law, III Edn., P. 1772.
4. Phipson, Evidence, XI Edn., P. 82.
5. *Nathuni Yadav* v. *State of Bihar*, AIR 1993 SC 1808: 1997 AIR SCW 1158: (1998) 9 SCC 238.
6. *Yusufalli Esmail Nagree* v. *State of Maharashtra*, AIR 1968 SC 147: 1968 Cr LJ 103: 1967 SCR 720: (1968) 1 SCJ 511: 70 Bom LR 76.
7. *Sukhar* v. *State of Uttar Pradesh*, (1999) 9 SCC 509: 2000 SCC (Cri) 419: AIR 1999 SC 3883: 2000 Cr LJ 29.
8. *Pershadi Lal* v. *State of Uttar Pradesh*, 1957 Cr LJ 328: AIR 1957 SC 211; *Yusufalli Esmail Nagree* v. *State of Maharashtra*, AIR 1968 SC 147: 1968 Cr LJ 103: 1967 SCR 720: (1968) 1 SCJ 511: 70 Bom LR 76; *Sawal Das* v. *State of Bihar*, AIR 1974 SC 778: (1974) 4 SCC 193: (1974) 3 SCR 74; *Rattan Singh* v. *State of Himachal Pradesh*, AIR 1997 SC 768: (1997) 4 SCC 161: (1996) 9 SCALE 258: 1997 AIR SCW 587: 1997 Cr LJ 833; *Brij Bhushan* v. *Emperor*, AIR 1946 PC 38.
9. *Chandra Kala* v. *Ram Krishna*, AIR 1985 SC 1268: (1985) 4 SCC 212: 1985 Cr LJ 1490.
10. *Sheikh Zakir* v. *State of Bihar*, AIR 1983 SC 911: (1983) 4 SCC 10: 1983 Cr LJ 1285.
11. *Raghav Prapanna Tripathi* v. *State of Uttar Pradesh*, AIR 1963 SC 74: (1963) 1 Cr LJ 70: 1963 3 SCR 239.
12. *Basanti* v. *State of Himachal Pradesh*, AIR 1987 SC 1572: 1987 Cr LJ 1869: 1987 3 SCC 227.

the injured witness narrated the incident to a witness who came to the scene immediately and saw a dead body with injuries, such a narration is relevant under Section 6.[1]

It is sometimes said that the statement and act must be by the same person[2]. But this rule is not so strictly observed. There could the statements of victim as also of accused. Exclamations of bystanders could be relevant[3]. Statements are no proof of any fact they accompany and the latter must be proved independently.

Stephen described 'transaction' as a group of facts so connected together as to be referred to by a single name, as a crime, contract a wrong or any other subject of enquiry which may be in issue. The question is whether the fact in issue and the fact claimed to be a relevant fact under section 6 are so connected together as to be referred to by a single legal name, as the alleged crime. Every fact which is part of the same transaction as the fact in issue is deemed to be relevant to the fact in issue, although it may not actually be in issue and although, if it were not part of the same transaction, it might be excluded as hearsay. In a transaction consisting of both physical acts and the words accompanying such physical acts, whether spoken by the person doing such acts (accused), the person to whom they were done (victim) or any other person or persons (bystanders, eyewitnesses, witness who rushed to the spot immediately after the occurrence), such words are relevant and admissible as part of the same transaction. Illustration (a) to section 6 may be seen. The other illustrations indicate that acts done at different places and times may form part of the same transaction. In illustrations (b) to (d), the word "transaction" is used in a wider sense while in illustration (a) it is used in a limited sense.

In a case where children of the victim were heard crying out that their mother was being killed, it was held that such statements of the children would be relevant under section 6.[4] So also statement by a witness that he was told by other witnesses at about the time of the occurrence that the accused was beating the victim[5]. Statement made by accused to his father soon after the murder of a person held responsible for the murder of the son of the accused is relevant under this section[6]. A tape recorded conversation between the accused and the complainant where the voices were identified was held to be relevant as it was a contemporaneous conversation[7]. The section is concerned with the question whether one of the tests of relevancy is whether a fact sought to be proved, though not a fact in issue, is so connected with the fact in issue as to form part of the same transaction. The real test is whether the fact sought to be proved and the fact in issue are part of the same transaction. That the statement made and said to form part of the same transaction was made due to extraneous factors

1. *Bisna* v. *State of West Bengal*, (2005) 12 SCC 657: AIR 2006 SC 302: 2005 AIR SCW 5798.
2. *Delhi Transport Corporation* v. *Shyam Lal*, AIR 2004 SC 4271: 2004 AIR SCW 4711: (2004) 8 SCC 88: 2004 SCC (L&S) 1053.
3. Woodroffe and Amir Ali's, Law of Evidence Vol. I Page 922.
4. *Sawal Das* v. *State of Bihar*, AIR 1974 SC 778: (1974) 4 SCC 193: (1974) 3 SCR 74.
5. *Badruddin Rukonddim Karpude* v. *State of Maharashtra*, 1981 Cr LJ 729: AIR 1981 SC 1223: 1981 Scc (Cri) 610 (SC).
6. *Pershadi Lal* v. *State of Uttar Pradesh*, 1957 Cr LJ 328: AIR 1957 SC 211.
7. *Yusufalli Esmail Nagree* v. *State of Maharashtra*, AIR 1968 SC 147: 1968 Cr LJ 103: 1967 SCR 720: (1968) 1 SCJ 511: 70 Bom LR 76.

may affect the credibility of the evidence adduced in proof of the fact alleged to be relevant, but can have no impact on the question whether the fact sought to be proved, that is, the statement is relevant.

Where a lady who was shot at, stated to others just before she died on account of the shots, that she saw the accused standing in her courtyard with a gun and firing shots at her, such statement is part of the same transaction as the murder[1]. Of course, her statement would be relevant also under section 32(1) of the Evidence Act. In a case where the deceased was sleeping in a room with his child and the child, awakened by the sound of axeblow inflicted on her father by the accused, shouted to her mother for help saying that the accused (naming him) as her father's assailant and hearing her shouts, other family members gathered at the spot, the words uttered by the child are relevant under this section[2]. The shouts by children of the deceased on hearing the cries of her mother on being pushed into a room by the accused, are covered by this section[3].

4. SECTION 7: Facts, which are the occasion, cause or effect, immediate or otherwise, of relevant facts or facts in issue, or which constitute the state of things under which they happened, or which afforded an opportunity for their occurrence or transaction are relevant. (*See* illustrations.) The section deals with five instances of causal connection or *res gestae* when it goes to the root of the matter concerning the commission of a crime.

Physical presence of accused within a specific time and place is relevant. Proof of "occasion" excludes or negatives a number of hypotheses and reduces the number of persons who might have possibly committed the crime to a limited number. This is important in cases of poisoning. That the victim had money and exhibited or mentioned it provides "occasion" for the subsequent robbery. Marks on the ground caused due to a struggle have relevance. "Last seen alive in the company of accused" theory is an indication of "occasion" and "opportunity". A contemporaneous tape record of a relevant conversation is relevant under section 7.[4] Tape record is relevant provided the voice of the person is identified by the maker of the record, accuracy of the record is established and possibility of tampering is ruled out and the subject-matter recorded is also relevant. Supreme Court in a later decision said that the record must have been sealed and kept in safe custody and voice of the speaker must be audible[5].

Evidence of similar facts or crimes committed by the accused is not relevant, except as indicative of motive, *modus operandi* in peculiar crimes or for enhanced sentence.

5. CAUSATION: Section 7 provides for admission of several kinds of facts, which, though not forming part of the disputed transaction, are yet connected with it in particular modes as provided in the section *i.e.*, (1) Occasion, (2)

---

1. *Rattan Singh* v. *State of Himachal Pradesh*, AIR 1997 SC 768: (1997) 4 SCC 161: (1996) 9 SCALE 258: 1997 AIR SCW 587: 1997 Cr LJ 833.
2. *Uttam Singh* v. *State of Madhya Pradesh*, 2003 Cr LJ 560: 2002 Cr LR (SC and MP) MPJ 434.
3. *Sawal Das* v. *State of Bihar*, AIR 1974 SC 778: (1974) 4 SCC 193: (1974) 3 SCR 74.
4. *Yusufalli Esmail Nagree* v. *State of Maharashtra*, AIR 1968 SC 147: 1968 Cr LJ 103: 1967 SCR 720: (1968) 1 SCJ 511: 70 Bom LR 76; *R.M. Malkani* v. *State of Maharashtra*, (1973) 1 SCC 471: 1973 Cr LJ 228: AIR 1973 SC 157: (1972) 2 SCWR 776; *Ziyauddin Burhanuddin Bukhari* v. *Brijmohan Ramdass Mehra*, AIR 1975 SC 1788: 1975 SCR 281: (1976) 2 SCC 17.
5. *R.M. Malkani* v. *State of Maharashtra*, (1973) 1 SCC 471: 1973 Cr LJ 228: AIR 1973 SC 157: (1972) 2 SCWR 776.

Cause, (3) Effect, (4) Giving Opportunity, (5) Constituting the state of things under which they happened and they are relevant when the transaction itself is sought to be proved. These modes are really different modes of the process of causation. Each of the five facts dealt with in this section is one step in the process of concluding that the accused committed the act. For example, the physical presence near the place of occurrence at or about the time of the occurrence is one such step. The proof of the opportunity available to the accused, by itself, rules out several hypotheses as he would perhaps be the only person, among others, who had the opportunity. Opportunity and not exclusive opportunity, is a sufficient reason for its' relevancy.[1] Contrarily, that a person had no opportunity of committing the crime is of great advantage to the decision making process. (*e.g.*, successful plea of *alibi*). It is said by several jurists that there cannot be a crime without opportunity though there is a long distance to be traversed between opportunity and actual commission of the crime. That the accused owed money to the deceased and the latter had gone to meet the former on the fateful day of murder to demand the money are relevant facts showing the occasion, cause or effect of the fact in issue[2]. Such collateral facts as are referred to in the section can be proved.

This section renders relevant a large category of facts which may not form part of the transaction. Certain types of collateral facts are rendered relevant when such facts, if proved, will lead to a reasonable inference regarding a fact in issue. Such collateral facts must be connected with the main fact in any one or more of the following ways:

(i) A fact being the occasion of a relevant fact or fact in issue; illustration (a) to the section deals with this aspect

(ii) A fact being the cause of a relevant fact or fact in issue

(iii) A fact being the effect of a relevant fact or fact in issue. Illustration (b) deals with this aspect.

(iv) A fact which constitutes the state of things under which a relevant fact or fact in issue happened. Illustration (c) deals with this aspect.

(v) A fact which afforded an opportunity for the occurrence or transaction of a relevant fact or fact in issue.

6. SECTION 8: Any fact which shows motive or preparation for any fact in issue or relevant fact is relevant. So also conduct of a party to a proceeding or of his agent in reference to any proceeding or in reference to any fact in issue therein or relevant thereto and the conduct of accused are relevant. This is so, provided the conduct influences or is influenced by any fact in issue or relevant fact. It does not matter if the conduct was previous or subsequent thereto. "Conduct" will not include statements unless the statements accompany and explain acts other than statements. Where conduct is relevant, any statement made to him or in his presence and hearing, which affects such conduct are also relevant. (*See* illustrations to section 8). Sometimes, existence of motive may be seen to increase the probability that the offence was committed by the accused[3].

1. Wigmore on Evidence, III Ed. Section 131.
2. Norton on Evidence Page 104; Best on Evidence Section 453.
3. Woodroffe and Amir Ali on Law of Evidence, 18th Ed., Vol. I page 856.

Motive is that which induces a person to act in a certain way. Motive is sometimes difficult to prove, since one cannot always look into mind of a human being. It cannot therefore be said that no act can be seen to be criminal unless motive is proved. Motive is distinct from "intention". Evidence of motive is relevant[1]. Though motive is not an element of crime (unlike *Mens Rea*), it is made relevant under section 8.[2] Motive could lead to preparation and both could be succeeded by the actual commission of the crime. This could be regarded as part of *res gestae*. Preparation is an instance of previous conduct influencing the fact in issue or a relevant fact. Where section 27 may not strictly be applicable, this section may apply.

Knowledge of a situation leads to a motive which produces intention and deliberation of choice of means to achieve an end; in other words, preparation. This is followed by an attempt, which, if successful, amounts to commission of an offence.[3] Absence of motive has to be treated in the background of the factual scenario[4] Presence of motive lends additional support to the prosecution case and absence of motive does not automatically warrant an acquittal[5]. Where eyewitnesses allege motive, it could be considered to test their credibility[6]. Where motive is alleged, it is relevant to enquire if the pattern of crime fits in with the alleged motive. Often it is only the perpetrator of the crime who knows his motive for committing the crime[7]. Where motive fails, the court should be careful in examining the remaining prosecution evidence[8].

Adequacy of motive alleged is not in all cases necessary. Atrocious crimes have been committed from very slight motive[9]. Motive is rarely a fact in issue, the exception being a case of transfer alleged to be in fraud of creditors in which case and such other cases good faith or bad faith may be in issue. Presence or absence of motive acquires some significance regarding the probability of the prosecution version[10]. When the other evidence is sufficient to hold accused guilty, motive receeds to the background.[11] Motive lacks significance even in a case of circumstantial evidence, if all other proved circumstances undoubtedly

1. *Udaipal Singh* v. *State of Uttar Pradesh*, AIR 1972 SC 54: 1972 Cr LJ 7: (1972) 4 SCC 142; *Suresh Chandra Bahri* v. *State of Bihar*, AIR 1994 SC 2420: 1995 (Supp) 1 SCC 80: 1994 AIR SCW 3420: 1994 Cr LJ 3271; *Gurmej Singh* v. *State of Punjab*, AIR 1992 SC 214: 1991 Supp (2) SCC 75: 1991 AIR SCW 2935.
2. *Babu Lodhi* v. *State of Uttar Pradesh*, AIR 1987 SC 1268: 1987 Cr LJ 1119: (1987) 2 SCC 352.
3. Woodrofe and Amir Ali, Law of Evidence, 18th Edn. Vol. I, pages 845, 846.
4. *Ranganayaki* v. *State by Inspector of Police*, AIR 2005 SC 418: (2004) 12 SCC 521: 2004 AIR SCW 6613: 2004 (8) SCALE 734: 2004 (7) Supreme 350.
5. *Sardul Singh* v. *State of Haryana*, AIR 2002 SC 3462: 2002 AIR SCW 4048: (2002) 8 SCC 372.
6. *Hem Raj* v. *State of Punjab*, AIR 2003 SC 4259: 2003 Cr LJ 4987: 2003 AIR SCW 4899.
7. *Suresh Chandra Bahri* v. *State of Bihar*, AIR 1994 SC 2420: 1995 (Supp) 1 SCC 80: 1994 AIR SCW 3420: 1994 Cr LJ 3271.
8. *Mani Kumar Thapa* v. *State of Sikkim*, AIR 2002 SC 2920: 2002 Cr LJ 4069: 2002 AIR SCW 3409.
9. *Jagdish* v. *State of Madhya Pradesh*, AIR 1981 SC 1167: 1981 Cr LJ 630: 1981 SCC (Cri) 676; *Krishna Pillai Sree Kumar* v. *State of Kerala*, AIR 1981 SC 1237: 1981 Cr LJ 743: 1981 SCC (Cri) 669.
10. *Badam Singh* v. *State of Madhya Pradesh*, (2003) 12 SCC 792: AIR 2004 SC 26: 2004 Cr LJ 22.
11. *Narayan Nathu Naik* v. *State of Maharashtra*, AIR 1971 SC 1656: 1971 (1) SCJ 72: (1971) 1 SCR 133; *Krishna Pillai Sree Kumar* v. *State of Kerala*, AIR 1981 SC 1237: 1981 Cr LJ 743: 1981 SCC (Cri) 669; *State of Andhra Pradesh* v. *Bogam Chandraiah*, AIR 1986 SC 1899: 1986 Cr LJ 1903: (1986) 3 SCC 637.

point to the guilt of accused.[1] When the foundation of prosecution case collapses, motive becomes inconsequential.[2]

7. PREPARATION/ATTEMPT

Motive as also preparation, by themselves, do not prove the crime alleged; but they are steps in proof of the commission of crime. Preparation may be in devising or arranging means necessary for commission of an offence, *e.g.*, purchase of a knife. An attempt, on the otherhand, is the direct movement towards the commission after preparation is made.[3] The test for determining whether an act constitutes an attempt or merely preparation is whether the overt act already done is such that if the offender changes his mind and does not proceed further in its progress, the act already done would be completely harmless.[4] An attempt is an intentional preparatory action which fails its object – which so fails through circumstances independent of the accused.[5] Preparation consists in arranging means necessary for the commission of the offence. Mere preparation is not an attempt.

Conduct made relevant by section 8 is conduct which is directly and immediately influenced by a fact in issue or relevant fact and does not include actions resulting from some intermediate cause. Preparation and previous attempts to commit the offence are instances of previous conduct, influencing the fact in issue or relevant fact. Some of the illustrations throw light on such previous or subsequent conduct. It is the conduct of parties to the litigation which is relevant. Party includes the victim also. Relevant conduct can be past or future and is not required to be contemporaneous.

"Conduct" does not include statements, unless those statements accompany and explain acts other than statements, subject to other sections of the Act. When the conduct of any person is relevant, any statement made to him or in his presence and hearing, which affects such conduct, is relevant.

What is relevant is that the statement and act must be so blended together as to form part of a thing observed by the witnesses and sought to be proved.[6] A statement is not relevant if there is no conduct to be explained.[7] The statement must really explain the act and must relate to and explain the act it accompanies and not previous or subsequent act, unless the transaction is of a continuous nature.[8]

Section 8 has a wider object than section 7. Illustrations (a), (b) relate to motive, (c), (d) relate to preparation, (e), (f) relate to conduct of accused,

1. *Mani Kumar Thapa* v. *State of Sikkim*, AIR 2002 SC 2920: 2002 Cr LJ 4069: 2002 AIR SCW 3409; *Uday Kumar* v. *State of Karnataka*, 1998 Cr LJ 4622: AIR 1998 SC 3317: 1998 AIR SCW 3254; *Rajinder Kumar* v. *State of Punjab*, AIR 1966 SC 1322: 1963 (2) SCJ 418: (1966) 1 SCWR 891; *Bahal Singh* v. *State of Haryana*, AIR 1976 SC 2032: 1976 Cr LJ 1568: (1976) 3 SCC 564.
2. *State of Punjab* v. *Sucha Singh*, AIR 2003 SC 1471: (2003) 3 SCC 153: 2003 AIR SCW 813.
3. *Abhayanand Mishra* v. *State of Bihar*, (1962) 2 SCR 241: AIR 1961 SC 1698: (1961) 2 Cr LJ 822; *His Holiness Kesavananda Bharati Sripadgalvaru* v. *State of Kerala*, AIR 1973 SC 1461: (1973) 4 SCC 225.
4. *Malkiat Singh* v. *State of Punjab*, 1970 Cr LJ 750 (SC): AIR 1970 SC 713: (1969) 2 SCR 663 (SC).
5. *King* v. *Tustipada Mandal*, AIR 1951 Ori 284: 1952 Cr LJ 837: 15 Cut LT 12.
6. *Zwinglee Ariel* v. *State of Madhya Pradesh*, AIR 1954 SC 15: 1954 Cr LJ 230.
7. *Nika Ram* v. *State of Himachal Pradesh*, 1971 Sim LJ (HP) 190: 1972 Cr LJ 204 (SC).
8. *Alek Mohammad* v. *State of West Bengal*, AIR 1974 SC 889: 1974 Cr LJ 747: (1974) 4 SCC 599.

(f) to (h) relate to statement affecting the conduct of the accused and (f), (g) relate to statements explaining and accompanying acts, which would form part of *res gestae*.

Evidence of motive as also other factors dealt with in section 8 loose importance, when the prosecution is able to prove by clear, cogent and convincing evidence the commission of the crime by the accused.[1] When the evidence of eyewitnesses is found to be truthful, motive assumes a secondary role.[2] But where the occular evidence appears to the suspect, the motive assumes importance. Mere existence of motive cannot give rise to an inference of guilt.[3]

When the other evidence is sufficient to hold the accused guilty, motive receds to the background.[4] Motive lacks significance even in a case of circumstantive evidence, if all other proved circumstances undoubtedly point to the guilt of the accused.[5] When the foundation of prosecution collapses, motive becomes inconsequential.[6]

8. The following are instances of relevant conduct:

Conduct of accused regarding property of deceased before and after her death.[7] preparation and previous attempts (illustrations (c) and (d)), fabricating false evidence to support plea of *alibi*, altering a deed to fit in with the defence case, pretending insanity, agitated demeanour, destroying or concealing evidence (illustrations (e) and (f)) concealing one's identity or disguising one's person, stifling evidence, being in possession of subject-matter of crime (illustration (i)), delay in filing a suit or filing complaint, absconding after the crime, pointing out stolen articles or scene of occurrence (subject to section 162 of Code)[8] or scene

1. *Narayan Nathu Naik* v. *State of Maharashtra*, AIR 1971 SC 1656: 1971 (1) SCJ 72: (1971) 1 SCR 133; *Gurucharan Singh* v. *State of Punjab*, AIR 1956 SC 460: 1956 Cr LJ 827 (SC); *Shivaji Genu Mohite* v. *State of Maharashtra*, AIR 1973 SC 55: 1973 Cr LJ 159: (1973) 3 SCC 219; *Podda Narayana* v. *State of Andhra Pradesh*, AIR 1975 SC 1252: 1975 Cr 1062: (1975) 4 SCC 153; *Yeshwant* v. *State of Maharashtra*, AIR 1973 SC 337: 1972 Cr LJ 1254: (1972) 3 SCC 639; *Bahal Singh* v. *State of Haryana*, AIR 1976 SC 2032: 1976 Cr LJ 1568: (1976) 3 SCC 564; *Sardar Hussain* v. *State of Uttar Pradesh*, AIR 1988 SC 1766; *Baitullah* v. *State of Uttar Pradesh*, (1998) 1 SCC 509: AIR 1997 SC 3946: 1997 Cr LJ 4644.
2. *Murarilal Jivaram Sharma* v. *State of Maharashtra*, AIR 1997 SC 1593: 1997 Cr LJ 782: 1997 AIR SCW 360; *Bikan Pandey* v. *State of Bihar*, AIR 2004 SC 997: 2003 AIR SCW 6624: 2004 AIR Jhar HCR 313; *Sarup Singh* v. *State of Punjab*, AIR 2005 SC 4345: 2005 Cr LJ 4518: 2005 AIR SCW 5057; *State of Uttar Pradesh* v. *Nahar Singh*, AIR 1998 SC 1328: 1998 Cr LJ 2006: (1998) 3 SCC 561; *Bhagirath* v. *State of Haryana*, AIR 1996 SC 3431: 1996 Cr LJ 3499: 1996 AIR SCW 3016.
3. *Jaipal* v. *State of Haryana*, AIR 2002 SC 3447: 2002 Cr LJ 4703: 2002 AIR SCW 4028.
4. *Narayan Nathu Naik* v. *State of Maharashtra*, AIR 1971 SC 1656: 1971 (1) SCJ 72: (1971) 1 SCR 133; *State of Andhra Pradesh* v. *Bogam Chandraiah*, AIR 1986 SC 1899: 1986 Cr LJ 1903: (1986) 3 SCC 637; *Krishna Pillai Sree Kumar* v. *State of Kerala*, AIR 1981 SC 1237: 1981 Cr LJ 743: 1981 SCC (Cri) 669.
5. *Atley* v. *State of Uttar Pradesh*, AIR 1955 SC 807: 1955 Cr LJ 1653: 1956 SCC 159; *Balbir Singh Nehra* v. *State of Haryana*, 1998 Cr LJ 4722: 1999 (1) All Cri LR 331: 1998 (4) Rec Civ R 157; *Rajinder Kumar* v. *State of Punjab*, AIR 1966 SC 1322: 1963 (2) SCJ 418: (1966) 1 SCWR 891; *Bahal Singh* v. *State of Haryana*, AIR 1976 SC 2032: 1976 Cr LJ 1568: (1976) 3 SCC 564.
6. *State of Punjab* v. *Sucha Singh*, AIR 2003 SC 1471: (2003) 3 SCC 153: 2003 AIR SCW 813.
7. *Anant Chintaman Lagu* v. *State of Bombay*, AIR 1960 SC 500: (1960) 2 SCR 460: 1960 Cr LJ 682.
8. *Prakash Chand* v. *State (Delhi Administration)*, AIR 1979 SC 400: (1979) 3 SCC 90: 1979 Cr LJ 329: 1979 MLJ (Cri) 419; *Malkhan Singh* v. *State of Uttar Pradesh*, AIR 1975 SC 12: 1975 Cr LJ 32: (1975) 3 SCC 311; *State (NCT of Delhi)* v. *Navjot Sandhu @ Afasan Guru*, AIR 2005 SC 3820: 2005 AIR SCW 4148: (2005) 11 SCC 600: 2005 Cr LJ 3950 (SC): 122 (2005) DLT 194 (SC).

of hiding weapon or stolen articles or evidence of crime etc.[1] Flight, silence, evasive or false response, possession of documents or property connected with the offence are examples of conduct. If the statement of accused is not relevant under section 27 of Evidence Act, it can be relevant under section 8 as conduct of accused (such as pointing out).[2] A man's conduct is not only what he does but also what he refrains from doing.

Only conduct which supports, destroys or dents the presumption of innocence is relevant.[3] Conduct of accused by way of immediate reaction to an illegal overture of bribe is relevant.[4] Creating false records is conduct which is relevant.[5] False explanation or false plea by an accused is relevant.[6] Evidence of absconding is relevant.[7] Conduct of accused before and after poisoning is relevant.[8] Conduct of one accused is relevant only against him and not against his co-accused. Conduct if an accused must have nexus with the crime charged.[9]

If shortly after the crime, the accused files a complaint, relevant conduct was the act of making the complaint, the circumstances under which the complaint was made and contents of the complaint because they accompany and explain the act of making the complaint. A mere statement is not a complaint. 'Complaint need not be to a court or to some one in authority like the police; it can be to parents, elders, neighbours etc. (Statement immediately after rape or robbery or violence – *See* illustration (k)). Terms of a complaint can be used under section 155 or 157, if the conditions of these sections are satisfied.

Filing First Information Statement (FIS) is relevant conduct. Contents of FIS by the accused, which do not amount to confession, may be relevant

1. *Himachal Pradesh Administration* v. *Om Prakash,* AIR 1972 SC 975: (1972) 1 SCC 249: 1972 SCC (Cri) 88: (1972) 1 SCJ 691; *Prakash Chand* v. *State (Delhi Administration),* AIR 1979 SC 400: (1979) 3 SCC 90: 1979 Cr LJ 329: 1979 MLJ (Cri) 419.
2. *Ram Kishan* v. *State of Bombay,* 1955 Cr LJ 196 (208): AIR 1955 SC 104: 1955 SCR 903; *Prakash Chand* v. *State (Delhi Administration),* AIR 1979 SC 400: (1979) 3 SCC 90: 1979 Cr LJ 329: 1979 MLJ (Cri) 419; *Bahadul* v. *State of Orissa,* AIR 1979 SC 1262: (1979) 4 SCC 346: 1979 Cr LJ 1075.
3. *Anant Chintaman Lagu* v. *State of Bombay,* AIR 1960 SC 500: (1960) 2 SCR 460: 1960 Cr LJ 682; *Prakash Chand* v. *State (Delhi Administration),* AIR 1979 SC 400: (1979) 3 SCC 90: 1979 Cr LJ 329: 1979 MLJ (Cri) 419; *State of Madras* v. *A. Vaidyanatha Iyer,* AIR 1958 SC 61: 1958 SCR 580: 1958 Cr LJ 232: (1958) 2 LLJ 653; *State of Madras* v. *A. Vaidyanatha Iyer,* AIR 1958 SC 61: 1958 SCR 580: 1958 Cr LJ 232: (1958) 2 LLJ 653; *Rao Shiv Bahadur Singh* v. *State of Vindhya Pradesh,* AIR 1954 SC 322: 1954 SCR 1098: 1954 Cr LJ 910; *Zwinglee Ariel* v. *State of Madhya Pradesh,* AIR 1954 SC 15: 1954 Cr LJ 230; *Himachal Pradesh Administration* v. *Om Prakash,* AIR 1972 SC 975: (1972) 1 SCC 249: 1972 SCC (Cri) 88: (1972) 1 SCJ 691; *A.N. Venkatesh* v. *State of Karnataka,* (2005) 7 SCC 714: AIR 2005 SC 3809: 2005 Cr LJ 3732; *State (NCT of Delhi)* v. *Navjot Sandhu @ Afasan Guru,* AIR 2005 SC 3820: 2005 AIR SCW 4148: (2005) 11 SCC 600: 2005 Cr LJ 3950 (SC): 122 (2005) DLT 194 (SC).
4. *Maha Singh* v. *State (Delhi Administration),* AIR 1976 SC 449: 1976 CAR 94: 1976 Cr LR 86: (1976) 1 SCC 644: (1976) 3 SCR 119: 1976 Cr LJ 346; *State of Madras* v. *A. Vaidyanatha Iyer,* AIR 1958 SC 61: 1958 SCR 580: 1958 Cr LJ 232: (1958) 2 LLJ 653.
5. *State of Uttar Pradesh* v. *Ram Sagar Yadav,* (1985) 1 SCC 552: 1985 SCC (Cri) 127: AIR 1985 SC 416: 1986 Cr LJ 836.
6. *Sharad Biridhichand Sarda* v. *State of Maharashtra,* AIR 1984 SC 1622: 1984 4 SCC 116: 1984 Cr LJ 1738.
7. *Atley* v. *State of Uttar Pradesh,* AIR 1955 SC 807: 1955 Cr LJ 1653: 1956 SCC 159; *Matru* v. *State of Uttar Pradesh,* (1971) 2 SCC 75: AIR 1971 SC 1050: (1971) 3 SCR 914: 1971 Cr LJ 913.
8. *Anant Chintaman Lagu* v. *State of Bombay,* AIR 1960 SC 500: (1960) 2 SCR 460: 1960 Cr LJ 682.
9. *Vikramjit Singh* v. *State of Punjab,* (2006) 12 SCC 306: 2006 AIR SCW 6197: 2007 Cr LJ 1000.

as an admission under section 21.[1] Accused giving FIS is a relevant conduct under section 8. Silence may, in certain circumstances, amount to conduct. Silence, when the occasion was such that a contradiction or explanation may reasonably be expected and there was opportunity to speak, may be seen as an admission. If an injured, while talking to a third person in the presence of the accused, named the accused as the assailant and the accused did not deny it, the statement and conduct are relevant under section 8. Illustration (g) may be seen in this connection. Failure to send reply to notice of demand is also conduct relevant under this section. Evidence regarding incidents pertaining to previous acceptance of bribes is not relevant in a trial under section 161 I.P.C. Confession to a Patel is relevant under section 8. Statement of rape victim to witnesses shortly after the rape shows consistency of her conduct with her evidence in court and is relevant.[2]

A criminal trial is not an enquiry into the conduct of the accused for any purpose other than to determine whether he is guilty of the offences charged. In appropriate cases, his conduct can be held to be incriminatory, if it has no reasonable explanation except on the hypothesis that he is guilty. Only conduct, which destroys the presumption of innocence, can be considered as relevant material.[3] Evidence of false explanation given by accused apparently designed to give the facts an appearance favorable to him is not only relevant conduct but also important.[4] Similarly, conduct of the victim, the complainant and even a witness would be relevant. For example, failure of an eye witness well-acquainted with the accused, to name him to the neighbours who come to the scene soon after the occurrence is relevant, though it may not render the charge untrue unless the prosecution case rested entirely on the evidence of this eye witness.[5] To discard the evidence of a witness on the ground that he did not react in any particular manner is unrealistic.[6] Human behaviour depends upon the facts and circumstances of each given case. There is no set rule of natural reaction.[7]

Where accused refuses to appear for Test Identification Parade (T.I.P.) an adverse inference can be drawn. In such a case, evidence of the witness identifying the accused in court can be relied on.[8] Where, in the face of the prosecution case that accused was known to eyewitnesses even earlier which was under denial by him and he filed a petition for holding T.I.P., the Court while dealing with the prayer should consider if his denial is *bona fide* or a mere pretense without holding a mini enquiry. If the Court concludes that the denial

1. *Aghnoo Nagesia* v. *State of Bihar*, AIR 1966 SC 119: 1966 Cr LJ 100: (1966) 1 SCJ 193: (1966) 1 SCR 134.
2. *Rameshwar* v. *State of Rajasthan*, AIR 1952 SC 54: 1952 SCJ 46: 1952 Cr LJ 547: (1952) 3 SCR 377.
3. *Anant Chintaman Lagu* v. *State of Bombay*, AIR 1960 SC 500: (1960) 2 SCR 460: 1960 Cr LJ 682 (Woodroffe and Amir Ali at Vol. I page 918.
4. *Golam Majibuddin* v. *State of West Bengal*, 1972 Cr LJ 1342: (1972) 4 SCC (N) 39 (SC).
5. *Harbajan Singh* v. *State of Jammu and Kashmir*, AIR 1975 SC 1814: (1975) 4 SCC 480: 1975 Cr LJ 1553.
6. *State of Uttar Pradesh* v. *Kishori Lal Minocha*, AIR 1980 SC 680: (1980) 3 SCC 8: (1980) 2 SCJ 74.
7. *State of Uttar Pradesh* v. *Devendra Singh*, 2004 AIR SCW 3656: AIR 2004 SC 3690: 2004 Cr LJ 3118.
8. *Munna* v. *State (NCT of Delhi)*, AIR 2003 SC 3805: 2003 Cr LJ 4440: 2003 AIR SCW 4355; *State of Haryana* v. *Surender*, AIR 2007 SC 2312: 2007 AIR SCW 4009: 2007 (4) Supreme 492.

is *bona fide*, it may direct TIP to be held, and if not, question of ordering TIP would not arise.[1]

9. SECTION 9: This section renders relevant the following:

(a) Facts necessary to explain or introduce fact in issue or relevant fact,

(b) Facts which support or rebut an inference suggested by a fact in issue or relevant fact,

(c) Facts which establish the identity of anything or person whose identity is relevant,

(d) Facts which fix the time or place at which any fact in issue or relevant fact happened, and

(e) Facts which show the relation of parties by whom any such fact was transacted – insofar as they are necessary for that purpose.

(*See* illustrations – *See* also illustration (c) to section 6 and (d) to section 8)

Illustrations (d) to (f) to section 9 relate to statements made by someone other than the party or his agent. Statements under illustration (d) are relevant only as explanation of C's conduct which is a fact in issue. Statement under illustration (e) is relevant regarding delivery of stolen property to *A*'s wife which is relevant under section 6 as part of the transaction. In both these instances, statement is made in the absence of the accused and these are exceptions to the hearsay rule. The statements are not relevant to show the truth of matters mentioned in the statement, but merely as explanatory of some other fact. Illustration (a) is also an example of an explanatory or introductory fact. Illustration (f) relates to a statement explanatory of the common object.

Identification or failure to identify are relevant.[2] Evidence of identification in a T.I.P. is not substantive evidence but is only corroborative evidence.[3] Substantive evidence is the identification made in Court.[4] T.I.P. need be resorted to only in cases where the witnesses had no previous acquaintance with the accused. Result of T.I.P., though not substantive evidence, has relevancy.[5] Identification by gait and voice by a person who knew accused is relevant.[6] It is safe to

1. *Dana Yadav* v. *State of Bihar*, AIR 2002 SC 3325: 2002 AIR SCW 3867: (2002) 7 SCC 295: 2002 SCC (Cri) 1698.
2. *Budhsen* v. *State of Uttar Pradesh*, AIR 1970 SC 1321: 1970 CAR 337: 1970 UJ 689: (1970) 2 SCC 128: 1970 Cr LJ 1149: (1971) 1 SCR 564.
3. *Matru* v. *State of Uttar Pradesh*, (1971) 2 SCC 75: AIR 1971 SC 1050: (1971) 3 SCR 914: 1971 Cr LJ 913; *Hari Nath* v. *State of Uttar Pradesh*, AIR 1988 SC 345: (1987) 2 SCALE 980: (1987) 3 Crimes 667: 1988 Cr LR 55: (1988) 1 SCC 14: (1988) 1 SCR 848: 1988 Cr LJ 422; *Santokh Singh* v. *Izhar Hussain*, (1973) 2 SCC 406: AIR 1973 SC 2190: 1973 Cr LJ 1176; *State of Andhra Pradesh* v. *Dr. M.V. Ramana Reddy*, 1991 AIR SCW 2154: AIR 1991 SC 1938: 1991 Cr LJ 2703; *Sir Shadilal Distillery and Chemicals Works* v. *State of Uttar Pradesh*, (1998) 8 SCC 428; *Shaikh Umar Ahmed Shaikh* v. *State of Maharashtra*, AIR 1998 SC 1922: (1998) 5 SCC 103: 1998 SCC (Cri) 1276; *Umesh Kamat* v. *State of Bihar*, AIR 2005 SC 726: 2005 Cr LJ 908: 2005 AIR SCW 435; *Md. Kalam* v. *State of Rajasthan*, AIR 2008 SC 1813: 2008 Cr LJ 2602: 2008 AIR SCW 2501; *Mahabir* v. *State of Delhi*, 2008 AIR SCW 3869: AIR 2008 SC 2343: 2008 Cr LJ 3036: (2008) 16 SCC 481.
4. *Raj Kishore Singh* v. *State of Bihar*, 1971 SCD 62: 1971 Cr LJ 921: AIR 1971 SC 1058; *Matru* v. *State of Uttar Pradesh*, (1971) 2 SCC 75: AIR 1971 SC 1050: (1971) 3 SCR 914: 1971 Cr LJ 913; *Munshi Singh Gautam* v. *State of Madhya Pradesh*, (2005) 9 SCC 631: AIR 2005 SC 402: 2004 AIR SCW 6537: 2005 Cr LJ 320 (SC); *Sheikh Hasib* v. *State of Bihar*, AIR 1972 SC 283: (1972) 4 SCC 773: 1972 Cr LJ 233.
5. *Ram Nath Mahto* v. *State of Bihar*, (1996) 8 SCC 630: AIR 1996 SC 2511: 1996 AIR SCW 3119.
6. *Kirpal Singh* v. *State of Uttar Pradesh*, AIR 1965 SC 712: (1964) 1 SCJ 411: (1964) 3 SCR 992.

have T.I.P. in case of stranger witness.[1] T.I.P. is not necessary where witness implicated accused by name in FIS.[2] Exposing parts of the body for purpose of identification does not offend article 20(3) of the Constitution.[3] Accused has no right to disguise or cover up marks on his face or body in such a way as to deny prosecution witness an opportunity of seeing as much of him as is necessary for identification.

Identification of a skull may be made by the superimposition procedure.[4] Memorandum prepared by a Magistrate containing description of the present condition of the house where the victim of abduction was kept and the evidence given by him on the basis of the memorandum are relevant.[5]

Evidence of expert tracker as to the identity of foot prints of accused with those found at the crime scene is relevant.[6] Evidence relating to footprints, if found satisfactory, may be used only to reinforce the conclusions as to identity of culprit based on other evidence (*ibid*). DNA test result is relevant. Photographic evidence is relevant. Report of enquiry into a railway accident under Railway Act is relevant in a suit for compensation.[7]

Identification of property can also be done.

Where accused refuses to appear for T.I.P., an adverse influence can be drawn. In such a case, evidence of the witness identifying the accused in court can be relied on.[8] Where, in the face of the prosecution case that accused was known to eyewitnesses even earlier which was under denial by him and he filed a petition for holding T.I.P., the Court while dealing with the prayer should consider if his denial is bonafide or a mere pretense without holding a mini enquiry. If the Court concludes that the denial is bonafide, it may direct TIP to be held, and if not, the question of ordering T.I.P. would not arise.[9]

In a case where a superimposed photo showed the shape and contours of the bones of the face of the victim as they looked when he was alive and the prosecution sought, by this method, to establish the identity of the victim, it was held that the photo was relevant under section 9.[4]

It is common knowledge that women have an uncanny sense of identifying their belongings, particularly articles of common use in the house. Identification

---

1. *C. Chellappan* v. *State of Kerala*, (1979) 4 SCC 312: AIR 1979 SC 1761: 1979 Cr LJ 1335; *State of Andhra Pradesh* v. *Dr. M.V. Ramana Reddy*, 1991 AIR SCW 2154: AIR 1991 SC 1938: 1991 Cr LJ 2703; *Mahabir* v. *State of Delhi*, 2008 AIR SCW 3869: AIR 2008 SC 2343: 2008 Cr LJ 3036: (2008) 16 SCC 481.
2. *Asha* v. *State of Rajasthan*, AIR 1997 SC 2828: 1997 Cr LJ 3508: 1997 AIR SCW 2831.
3. *State of Bombay* v. *Kathi Kalu Oghad*, AIR 1961 SC 1808: (1962) 3 SCR 10: (1961) 2 Cr LJ 856: 64 Bom LR 240.
4. *Ram Lochan Ahir* v. *State of West Bengal*, AIR 1963 SC 1074: 1963 Cr LJ 170: (1963) 2 SCR 852: (1964) 1 SCJ 82: (1981) 3 SCC 689; *Golakonda Venkateswara* v. *State of Andhra Pradesh*, AIR 2003 SC 2846: 2003 Cr LJ 3731: 2003 AIR SCW 3612: (2003) 9 SCC 277.
5. *Deepchand* v. *State of Rajasthan*, AIR 1961 SC 1527: 1961 Cr LJ 705: (1962) 1 SCR 662: (1962) 2 SCJ 658.
6. *Pritam Singh* v. *State of Punjab*, 1956 Cr LJ 805: AIR 1956 SC 415 (SC).
7. *Union of India* v. *Sugauli Sugar Works (P) Ltd.*, (1976) 3 SCC 32: AIR 1976 SC 1414: (1976) 3 SCR 614.
8. *Munna* v. *State (NCT of Delhi)*, AIR 2003 SC 3805: 2003 Cr LJ 4440: 2003 AIR SCW 4355; *State of Haryana* v. *Surender*, AIR 2007 SC 2312: 2007 AIR SCW 4009: 2007 (4) Supreme 492.
9. *Dana Yadav* v. *State of Bihar*, AIR 2002 SC 3325: 2002 AIR SCW 3867: (2002) 7 SCC 295: 2002 SCC (Cri) 1698.

of their ornaments and clothes by a woman in court is relevant and cannot be rejected merely on the ground that such articles are common articles available in the market.[1]

10. SECTION 10: In the case of conspiracy by two or more persons to commit an offence, anything said, done or written by any of such persons in reference to their common intention, after the time when such intention was entertained by any of them, is relevant against each of those persons as also for the purpose of proving the existence of such conspiracy and proving that any such person was a party to it.

To render this section applicable, existence of reasonable ground to believe the existence of conspiracy is sufficient. This provision is based on the theory of agency. A conspirator is an agent of his associates in carrying out the object of the conspiracy. Therefore his acts and declarations are relevant and admissible against the others. An act of one is an act of all. Each is an agent of the others.[2] Before section 10 can be invoked, some *prima facie* evidence should be before the court to enable it to form an opinion that there is reasonable ground to believe that two or three persons have conspired together.[3]

This section is an exception to the general rule that the acts, statements or writings of a person are admissible only against him and not against others. Anything said, done or written can be used only for the purpose of proving the existence of the conspiracy, or for showing that the other person was a party to it. It cannot be used in favour of the other party.[4]

The words "in reference to their common intention" are very wide and comprehensive and give wider scope than the words "in furtherance of".[5]

---

1. *Earabhadrappa* v. *State of Karnataka,* AIR 1983 SC 446: 1983 Cr LJ 846: (1983) 1 SCC 330: 1983 SCC (Cri) 447: (1983) 2 SCR 552; *Nagappa Dondiba Kalal* v. *State of Karnataka,* AIR 1980 SC 1753: 1980 Cr LJ 1270; *Abdul Sattar* v. *Union Territory, Chandigarh,* 1985 SCC (Cri) 505: AIR 1986 SC 1438: 1986 Cr LJ 1072.
2. *Badri Rai* v. *State of Bihar,* AIR 1958 SC 953: 1958 Cr LJ 1434: 1959 SCJ 1141: 1959 SCR 1171; *Madhya Pradesh Special Police Establishment* v. *State of Madhya Pradesh,* (2004) 8 SCC 788: AIR 2005 SC 325: 2004 AIR SCW 6843; *In R/o Smt. Sayalee Sanjeev Joshi, Member, Maharashtra Public Service Commission,* AIR 2007 SC 2809: 2007 AIR SCW 5103: (2007) 7 SCALE 631; *Sardul Singh Caveeshar* v. *State of Bombay,* AIR 1957 SC 747: 1957 SCJ 780: 1958 SCR 161; *Bhagwan Swarup Lal Bishan Lal* v. *State of Maharashtra,* AIR 1965 SC 682: 1965 Cr LJ 608: (1964) 2 SCR 178: (1964) 2 SCJ 771; *Mirza Akbar* v. *E.,* AIR 1940 PC 176: 43 Bom LR 20: 41 Cr LJ 871: 190 IC 233: 67 IA 336.
3. *Shivnarayan* v. *State of Maharashtra,* AIR 1980 SC 439: (1980) 2 SCC 465: 1980 SCC (Cri) 493: 1980 Cr LJ 388; *Kehar Singh* v. *State (Delhi Administration),* (1988) 3 SCC 609: AIR 1988 SC 1883: JT 1988 (3) SC 191; *Bhagwan Swarup Lal Bishan Lal* v. *State of Maharashtra,* AIR 1965 SC 682: 1965 Cr LJ 608: (1964) 2 SCR 178: (1964) 2 SCJ 771; *Bhagwandas Keshwani* v. *State of Rajasthan,* AIR 1974 SC 898: 1974 Cr LJ 751: (1974) 4 SCC 611; *Topandas* v. *State of Bombay,* AIR 1956 SC 33: (1956) 2 SCR 881: 1956 Cr LJ 138: 58 Bom LR 492.
4. *Bhagwan Swarup Lal Bishan Lal* v. *State of Maharashtra,* AIR 1965 SC 682: 1965 Cr LJ 608: (1964) 2 SCR 178: (1964) 2 SCJ 771; *Badri Rai* v. *State of Bihar,* AIR 1958 SC 953: 1958 Cr LJ 1434: 1959 SCJ 1141: 1959 SCR 1171; *Bhagwandas Keshwani* v. *State of Rajasthan,* AIR 1974 SC 898: 1974 Cr LJ 751: (1974) 4 SCC 611; *Tribhuvan Nath* v. *State of Maharashtra,* AIR 1973 SC 450: 1972 Cr LJ 1277: (1972) 3 SCC 511.
5. *State of Maharashtra* v. *Damu,* AIR 2000 SC 1691: (2000) 6 SCC 269: 2000 Cr LJ 2301: 2000 SCC (Cri) 1088: JT 2000 (5) SC 575; *Bhagwan Swarup Lal Bishan Lal* v. *State of Maharashtra,* AIR 1965 SC 682: 1965 Cr LJ 608: (1964) 2 SCR 178: (1964) 2 SCJ 771; *Ram Narain Poply* v. *Central Bureau of Investigation,* 2003 SCC (Cri) 869: AIR 2003 SC 2748: 2003 Cr LJ 4801.

Common intention must exist at the time when the "thing" was said, done or written by one of them.[1]

Strict proof of conspiracy is not necessary before section 10 is invoked; *prima facie* evidence is sufficient.[2] It is sufficient to place before court materials for establishing reasonable ground to believe the existence of such conspiracy. (*See* also second paragraph of section 136). Conspiracy is invariably hatched in secrecy and direct evidence is seldom available. In most cases only circumstantial evidence will be available.[3] If no such reasonable ground is made out, section 10 cannot be invoked.[4] Section 10 comes in to play only when there is reasonable ground to believe the existence of a conspiracy. If so, anything said or done or written by one of them in reference to the common intention is relevant against the others. Reasonable ground for belief depends upon the proof of facts. Once such a conspiracy is proved, act of one conspirators becomes the act of the others.[5] "Anything said, done or written" refer to such things which took place when the intention was first entertained by any one of them and before such intention ceased to exist.[6] Such a statement made by an accused after his arrest will not attract section 10.[7]

Once the common intention ceased to exist, any statement made by a former co-conspirator is inadmissible.[1] *E.g.*, a post-arrest statement.[8] Evidence of conduct of a deceased conspirator is not relevant.[6] If a specific instance of the particular offence is proved against any accused, that would furnish the best corroboration of the offence of conspiracy because conspiracy is the root and the specific instances are the fruits.[9] The section will not apply to a period after the conspiracy ended. The act shall be in reference to their common intention and in respect of a period after such intention was first entertained by any of them.[2]

In order that section 10 is invoked, it is not necessary that there be a charge under section 120(B) I.P.C.[9]

The offence of criminal conspiracy consists in a meeting of minds of two or more persons for agreeing to do or causing to be done, an illegal act or an act by illegal means and the performance of an act in terms thereof. If those persons commit several offences, all of them will be liable for all those offences even if

---

1. *Mirza Akbar* v. *E.*, AIR 1940 PC 176: 43 Bom LR 20: 41 Cr LJ 871: 190 IC 233: 67 IA 336.
2. *Bhagwan Swarup Lal Bishan Lal* v. *State of Maharashtra*, AIR 1965 SC 682: 1965 Cr LJ 608: (1964) 2 SCR 178: (1964) 2 SCJ 771.
3. *Suresh Chandra Bahri* v. *State of Bihar*, AIR 1994 SC 2420: 1995 (Supp) 1 SCC 80: 1994 AIR SCW 3420: 1994 Cr LJ 3271.
4. *Abdul Sattar* v. *Union Territory, Chandigarh*, 1985 SCC (Cri) 505: AIR 1986 SC 1438: 1986 Cr LJ 1072.
5. *Shivnarayan* v. *State of Maharashtra*, AIR 1980 SC 439: (1980) 2 SCC 465: 1980 SCC (Cri) 493: 1980 Cr LJ 388.
6. *Sardul Singh Caveeshar* v. *State of Bombay*, AIR 1957 SC 747: 1957 SCJ 780: 1958 SCR 161.
7. *Mirza Akbar* v. *E.*, AIR 1940 PC 176: 43 Bom LR 20: 41 Cr LJ 871: 190 IC 233: 67 IA 336; *State of Tamil Nadu through Superintendent of Police CBI/SIT* v. *Nalini*, AIR 1999 SCW 1889: (1999) 5 SCC 253: 1999 Cr LJ 3124: AIR 1999 SC 2640: 1999 SCC (Cri) 691; *State (NCT of Delhi)* v. *Navjot Sandhu @ Afasan Guru*, AIR 2005 SC 3820: 2005 AIR SCW 4148: (2005) 11 SCC 600: 2005 Cr LJ 3950 (SC): 122 (2005) DLT 194 (SC).
8. *State of Gujarat* v. *Mohammed Atik*, AIR 1998 SC 1686: (1998) 4 SCC 351: 1998 Cr LJ 2251: 1998 SCC (Cri) 936.
9. *Badri Rai* v. *State of Bihar*, AIR 1958 SC 953: 1958 Cr LJ 1434: 1959 SCJ 1141: 1959 SCR 1171.

some of them had not actively participated in the commission of the offences.[1] It is not necessary that a person should be a participant in a conspiracy from start to finish; some conspirators may appear and disappear from stage to stage in the course of the conspiracy.[2] The acts done by any of them in reference to the common intention are considered to be the acts of all. These acts are relevant for the purpose of proving the conspiracy as well as the part of each of them.[3] The evidence of a co-conspirator (approver) is that of an accomplice and hence the rule of caution regarding corroboration is required to be borne in mind.[4]

Once section 10 is applied, whatever is said or done by the parties to the conspiracy becomes relevant evidence as against the co-conspirators, even for the purpose of proving conspiracy itself.[5]

11. The elements of the offence of "conspiracy" under section 120A of I.P.C. are – (i) An agreement between two or more persons, (ii) to do an illegal act, (iii) or to do a legal act by illegal means, and (iv) an overt act done in pursuance of the conspiracy. In the case of conspiracy to commit an offence, there is no requirement of some act independent of the agreement and the above ingredients (i) to (iii) are sufficient to constitute the offence of criminal conspiracy. In the case of conspiracy to commit only an illegal act or a lawful act by illegal means and the act does not amount to an offence, there must be proof of some act done by one or more parties in pursuance of their agreement. An act may be illegal, without being criminal. The requirement of an agreement between two or more persons makes it clear that one person alone cannot conspire.[6] An agreement and not mere intention has to be proved. Joint evil intent is necessary.[7]

A conspiracy is hatched in secrecy and executed in secrecy. Therefore, it is not feasible for prosecution to connect each isolated act or statement of one accused with acts or statements of others unless there is a common bond linking all of them together. In a criminal case, ordinarily, one person cannot be held responsible for the acts or statements of another. It is only when there is evidence of a concerted action in furtherance of a common responsibility that the principle that everyone concerned in a conspiracy is acting as the agent of the rest of them applies. Once there are sufficient materials to reasonably believe that there was concert and connection between persons charged with a common design, it is immaterial as to whether they were strangers to each other or ignorant of the actual role of each of them or that they did not perform any one or more of such acts by joint efforts in unison.[8] Where the charge is against three persons and two of them were found having no concern with the conspiracy, the third person also cannot be convicted even on his own confession.[6] There need not be proof of direct physical meeting. An agreement can be inferred from circumstances raising presumption of a common concerted plan to carry out the unlawful design. It is not necessary that more than one person should be convicted of

---

1. *State of Himachal Pradesh* v. *Krishan Lal Pardhan*, AIR 1987 SC 773: 1987 Cr LJ 709: (1987) 2 SCC 17.
2. *Raghubir Singh* v. *State of Bihar*, AIR 1987 SC 149: 1987 Cr LJ 157: (1986) 4 SCC 481.
3. Stephen's: Digest of Evidence 3rd Ed. – Vol. I, page 160.
4. *Sardul Singh Caveeshar* v. *State of Bombay*, AIR 1957 SC 747: 1957 SCJ 780: 1958 SCR 161.
5. *Baburao Bajirao Patil* v. *State of Maharashtra*, 1971 SCC (Cri) 680: (1971) 3 SCC 432.
6. *Topandas* v. *State of Bombay*, AIR 1956 SC 33: (1956) 2 SCR 881: 1956 Cr LJ 138: 58 Bom LR 492.
7. Woodroffe and Amir Ali on Law of Evidence, 18th Ed., Vol. I pages 1079 to 1086.
8. *Government of NCT of Delhi* v. *Jaspal Singh*, (2003) 10 SCC 586: JT 2003 (7) SC 302.

the offence of criminal conspiracy; it is enough if the Court can find that two or more persons were actually concerned in the criminal conspiracy.[1] Conspiracy can be proved by direct or circumstantial evidence or by both.[2]

Section 10 is not intended to make the confession of a co-accused substantive evidence, though it may be considered under section 30.[3] The principle of this provision applies to civil cases also. If the charge specifies the period, evidence of acts of co-conspirators outside the period is not relevant. But evidence may necessitate reference to and narration of acts of co-conspirators beyond such period, but within reasonable limits.[4] Every conspirator need not have been present at every stage of the conspiracy.[5]

12. "Common Intention": Section 10 refers to "in furtherance to their common intention". These words are deliberately used to give a wide scope, with the result that anything said, done or written by a co-conspirator, after the conspiracy is formed will be evidence against the other before he entered the field of conspiracy or after he left it.[6] The section does not comprehend a statement made by one conspirator, in the absence of the other, with reference to past acts done in the actual course of carrying out the conspiracy, after the conspiracy has been completed. There is a distinction between communication between conspirators while the conspiracy was going on with reference to the carrying out the transaction and the statements made after the arrest or after the conspiracy was over, by way of description of past events. A document not enacted in the course of carrying out the transaction, but made by one of the conspirators after the object (say fraud) was completed would not be relevant or admissible. A mere statement made by one conspirator to a third party or any act of such conspirator not done in pursuance of the conspiracy is not evidence for or against another conspirator.[7]

A confession by a conspirator to a Magistrate after arrest, disclosing the existence of a conspiracy, its objects and the names of its members is not relevant under section 10 against the co-conspirators jointly tried with him, though it can be considered under Section 30. When one of the accused in a case voluntarily enters the witness box and gives evidence and is therefore, subject to cross-examination by the co-accused, his evidence can be used against them.[8]

1. *Dalip Singh* v. *State of Punjab*, (1954) 1 SCR 145: AIR 1953 SC 364: 1953 SCJ 532: 1953 Cr LJ 1465; *Bimadhar Pradhan* v. *State of Bombay*, AIR 1956 SC 469: 1956 SCR 206: 1956 Cr LJ 831: (1956) 2 MLJ (SC) 13.
2. *Nazir Khan* v. *State of Delhi*, AIR 2003 SC 4427: (2003) 8 SCC 461: 2003 AIR SCW 5068; *Baburao Bajirao Patil* v. *State of Maharashtra*, 1971 SCC (Cri) 680: (1971) 3 SCC 432.
3. *Mirza Akbar* v. *E.*, AIR 1940 PC 176: 43 Bom LR 20: 41 Cr LJ 871: 190 IC 233: 67 IA 336; *Haricharan Kurmi* v. *State of Bihar*, AIR 1964 SC 1184: (1964) 2 Cr LJ 344: (1964) 6 SCR 623: (1964) 1 SCWR 399: 1964 (2) SCJ 454; *Baburao Bajirao Patil* v. *State of Maharashtra*, 1971 SCC (Cri) 680: (1971) 3 SCC 432; *Kehar Singh* v. *State (Delhi Administration)*, (1988) 3 SCC 609: AIR 1988 SC 1883: JT 1988 (3) SC 191.
4. *Sardul Singh Caveeshar* v. *State of Bombay*, AIR 1957 SC 747: 1957 SCJ 780: 1958 SCR 161.
5. *V. Govindarajulu* v. *State of Mysore*, 1962 Mys LJ 494.
6. *Bhagwan Swarup Lal Bishan Lal* v. *State of Maharashtra*, AIR 1965 SC 682: 1965 Cr LJ 608: (1964) 2 SCR 178: (1964) 2 SCJ 771; *State of Maharashtra* v. *Damu*, AIR 2000 SC 1691: (2000) 6 SCC 269: 2000 Cr LJ 2301: 2000 SCC (Cri) 1088: JT 2000 (5) SC 575.
7. *Emperor* v. *Abani Bhusan*, ILR 38 CAL 169 (PC); "*Ranganatham* v. *Ethirajulu*" AIR 1940 PC 176; *Sardul Singh Caveeshar* v. *State of Bombay*, AIR 1957 SC 747: 1957 SCJ 780: 1958 SCR 161.
8. *King* v. *James Paul*, (1920) 2 KB 183: 89 LJ KB 801; *Rex* v. *Hadwen*, (1902) 1 KB 882: 71 LJ KB 581; *Tribhuvan Nath* v. *State of Maharashtra*, AIR 1973 SC 450: 1972 Cr LJ 1277: (1972) 3 SCC 511.

"Against each of the persons": This expression is intended to prove the existence of a conspiracy *i.e.,* to show that a person was a party to it, and cannot be used in favour of the other party to it.[1] This section applies to acts and declarations of one of the conspirators in respect of the common design of all. Everything said or done by any one of them in furtherance of the common object is evidence against each and all the parties concerned, whether they were present or not.

Confession of a co-accused is not substantive evidence against other accused and can be used only when the court is inclined to accept other evidence and feels the need for an assurance in support of the conclusion deductible from the said evidence.[2] Where only circumstantial evidence is available and the broad features of the case are proved by trustworthy evidence connecting all the links forming a complete chain, then, on isolated events, confession of a co-accused can be considered for lending assurance to the conclusions of court.[3] In the absence of reliable evidence, such a confession cannot be used in a conspiracy case.[4] Confessions recorded after the termination of the conspiracy are of no use.[5] A retracted confession of a co-accused is not substantive evidence and can only be taken into consideration under section 30 (*ibid*). Section 10 would apply to statement of an approver with reference to anything said, done or written by him.

13. SECTION 11: Facts not otherwise relevant will be treated as relevant if:

(a) They are inconsistent with any fact in issue or relevant fact;

(b) By themselves or in conjunction with other facts they make the existence or non-existence of any fact in issue or relevant fact highly probable or improbable.

The language of this section is very wide. Yet collateral facts which have practically no connection with the main fact are not attracted. The connection between the two facts must be so immediate as to render the co-existence of the two highly probable.

14. *Alibi* is relevant under this provision.[6] It has to be proved.[7] Alibi is only a rule of evidence, not an exception. It need be considered only when the burden on the prosecution is discharged.[8] Evidence of claimant that she learnt the place of her birth from her mother is relevant.[9]

1. *M.D. Dhanwatey* v. *Commissioner of Income-tax, Madhya Pradesh, Nagpur and Bhandara,* AIR 1968SC 682: (1968) 1 SCWR 463.
2. *Haricharan Kurmi* v. *State of Bihar,* AIR 1964 SC 1184: (1964) 2 Cr LJ 344: (1964) 6 SCR 623: (1964) 1 SCWR 399: 1964 (2) SCJ 454.
3. *Baburao Bajirao Patil* v. *State of Maharashtra,* 1971 SCC (Cri) 680: (1971) 3 SCC 432.
4. *Kehar Singh* v. *State (Delhi Administration),* (1988) 3 SCC 609: AIR 1988 SC 1883: JT 1988 (3) SC 191.
5. *Jayendra Saraswathi Swamigal* v. *State of Tamil Nadu,* 2005 AIR SCW 323: AIR 2005 SC 716: 2005 Cr LJ 883: (2005) 2 SCC 13.
6. *Dudh Nath Pandey* v. *State of Uttar Pradesh,* AIR 1981 SC 911: (1981) 2 SCC 166: 1981 SCC (Cri) 379: 1981 Cr LJ 618.
7. *Brijala Pd. Sinha* v. *State of Bihar,* 1998 AIR SCW 2440: AIR 1998 SC 2443: 1998 Cr LJ 3611; *Union of India* v. *Onkar S. Kanwar* 2002 SCC (Cri) 1873: AIR 2002 SC 3563: 2002 AIR SCW 4179.
8. *Union of India* v. *Onkar S. Kanwar* 2002 SCC (Cri) 1873: AIR 2002 SC 3563: 2002 AIR SCW 4179.
9. *Alicia* alias *Alice* v. *Percival Felix Pinto,* 1967 (2) Mys LJ 210.

When the question is whether a particular claim or charge is established or not, any fact which either proves or tends to prove, or disproves or tends to disprove it, is also relevant. The language employed in this section has a wide import; yet it cannot be taken in its widest possible sense as it would complicate every trial and would defeat one of the objects of the law of evidence, namely to restrict the investigation by the court within the limits prescribed by general convenience; and this object would be totally defeated by the reception on all occasions, of every circumstance on either side having some remote and conjectural probative force. The court has to exercise reasonable discretion to ensure that the connection between the fact to be proved and the fact sought to be proved under this section must be so immediate as to render their co-existence highly probable.

According to this section, facts not otherwise relevant under sections 6 to 10, 12 and later sections are relevant if they fall within clause (1) or clause (2).

Regarding inconsistency referred to in clause (1) of the section, John Henry Wigmore in his treatise on evidence (III Edition, section 135), provides five common examples *i.e.*, (i) presence of accused in another place (*alibi*), (ii) absence of the husband (non-access) in a dispute about paternity, (iii) that the person allegedly killed is really alive, (iv) the commission of the crime by a third person, and (v) the self-infliction of the harm by the injured. Evidence of inconsistency between medical evidence and ocular evidence is relevant under section 11.

If the plea of *alibi* fails, there is a presumption that the accused was present where the prosecution alleges to him to be at the time of the crime. If the defence evidence does not show that it was physically impossible for the accused to be present at the place and time of occurrence, the plea of *alibi* fails.[1] However, the adverse inference cannot be that the accused committed the crime. Burden of proof on the accused arises out of section 103 of the Evidence Act.[2] Where prosecution case has not been proved beyond reasonable doubt, failure of accused to prove *alibi* cannot be used to convict him.[3] It is also possible for the accused to raise a reasonable doubt about his presence at the scene at the time of occurrence.[4] A plea of *alibi* can, in appropriate cases, be spelt out from the prosecution evidence. For a plea of *alibi* to be accepted adequate proof is required.[5]

Where the disputed fact is whether payment of a sum of money was made to a person, the absence of entries in the account books of the payee would be inconsistent with the receipt of the amount and hence is a relevant fact under

---

1. *State of Maharashtra* v. *Narsingrao Gangaram Pimple*, AIR 1984 SC 63: (1984) 1 SCC 446: 1984 Cr LJ 4; *Dhanjay Chatterjee* v. *State of West Bengal*, JT 1994 (1) SC 33: 1994 SCC (Cri) 358: (1994) 2 SCC 220.
2. *State of Uttar Pradesh* v. *Sughar Singh*, AIR 1978 SC 191: (1978) 1 SCC 178: 1978 Cr LJ 141; *State of Haryana* v. *Sher Singh*, AIR 1981 SC 1021: (1981) 2 SCC 300: 1981 Cr LJ 714; *Gurucharan Singh* v. *State of Punjab*, AIR 1956 SC 460: 1956 Cr LJ 827 (SC).
3. *State of Haryana* v. *Prabhu*, AIR 1979 SC 1019: (1979) 4 SCC 189: 1979 Cr LJ 892; *Gayadin* v. *State of Madhya Pradesh*, (2005) 12 SCC 267.
4. *Jayantibhai Bhenkaarbhai* v. *State of Gujarat*, AIR 2002 SC 3569: (2002) 8 SCC 165: 2002 SCC (Cri) 1873: 2002 Cr LJ 4734: 2002 AIR SCW 4187.
5. *Binay Kumar Singh* v. *State of Bihar*, AIR 1997 SC 322: (1997) 1 SCC 283: 1997 Cr LJ 362: 1997 SCC (Cri) 333; *Rajesh Kumar* v. *Dharamvir*, (1997) 4 SCC 496: AIR 1997 SC 3769: 1997 AIR SCW 1847; *Vijayee Singh* v. *State of Uttar Pradesh*, AIR 1990 SC 1459: (1990) 3 SCC 190: 1990 Cr LJ 1510.

Section 11.[1] Absence of mutation entry in the revenue record would be relevant, though there could be an acceptable explanation for such absence.

15. CLAUSE (2) OF SECTION 11

Facts which tend to render the existence or non-existence of the fact in issue highly probable or improbable are relevant under this clause. "Probability" means likelihood of anything to be true, inferred from our knowledge, observation and experience.[2] Mere probability or improbability is not sufficient; it must be highly probable or improbable. The language of this clause shows that the connection between the fact in issue and the fact sought to be proved under section 11 must be so immediate as to render their co-existence highly probable or improbable.[3] Where the evidence adduced by the opposing parties is conflicting, the court has to consider which case fits best with the admitted circumstances and the resulting probabilities.

Serious contradictions and significant omissions in F.I. Statement affecting the probabilities of the case are relevant under this section.[4] Recitals in documents not *inter-partes* are not facts within the meaning of this section unless the existence of the recitals itself is a matter in issue. This section makes the existence of facts relevant, and not the statements as to such existence, unless the fact of making that statement itself is a matter in issue. What is stated above applies to recitals in documents. Documents between a party to a suit and a stranger which lend strength to the party to the suit is not relevant. Admissions stand on a different basis. A judgment not-*interpartes* in a land acquisition case (regarding market value) or any other case is not relevant under this section as such a judgment is not a 'fact'. Some such judgment may become relevant under Section 43 read with this section and section 13. But previous judgment not-*interpartes* in respect of other nearby land is relevant in deciding quantum of compensation for acquisition. Recitals of boundaries in documents not-interpartes may have relevance under sections 11, 13 and 32(3) and may be capable of being used under section 157 if conditions of those provisions are satisfied. For a full discussion on clause (2) of this section, reference may be made usefully to *Ram Chander* v. *State of Haryana*.[5]

16. SECTION 12: In suits for damages, any fact which will enable the Court to quantify the damages which ought to be awarded, is relevant. That is because amount of damages is a fact in issue, unless the defendant admits quantification made by plaintiff. "Bad character" of plaintiff assumes relevance in suits for damages for defamation, for breach of promise to marry and in suits for damages against alleged adulterer. Plaintiff's good character and reputation may also be relevant under this section, even without recourse to section 55.

Damages can be claimed either in an action on contract or tort. To understand under what circumstances damages can be recovered, one has to look at the substantive law in accordance with which the action is brought. If in such an action, it is found that damages are awardable, the question arises regarding

1. *State of Andhra Pradesh* v. *Cheemalapati Ganeswara Rao*, 1963 (2) Cr LJ 671: (1964) 3 SCR 297: AIR 1963 SC 1850: (1964) 2 SCA 38.
2. (Woodroffe and Amir Ali on Evidence, 18th Edition, Vol. I, Page 981).
3. *S.H. Jhabawala* v. *Emperor*, 145 IC 481: AIR 1933 All 690: 34 Cr LJ 967.
4. *Ram Kumar Pandey* v. *State of Madhya Pradesh*, AIR 1975 SC 1026: 1975 CAR 101: 1975 Cr LR 215: 1975 UJ 423: (1975) 3 SCC 815: (1975) 3 SCR 519: 1975 Cr LJ 870.
5. AIR 1981 SC 1036: 1981 Cr LJ 609: (1981) 3 SCC 191.

quantification of damages. Section 12 deals with question as to what are the facts relevant to such quantification. In every suit for recovery of damages, amount of damages is a fact in issue when the amount of the claim in the plaint is disputed by defendant. Factors affecting mitigation or aggravation of damages are relevant and hence provable.

Injury to feelings has no relevance in an action on contract, while it is a relevant factor in an action on tort. Examples of the former are actions for breach of contract to marry and examples of the latter are actions for libel. Extent of damages for libel may depend on the kind of imputation made, occasion and time of such libel. Damages cannot be too remote. Equally, good faith, honesty of purpose, absence of malice can be relevant in mitigation of damages in torts. *See* also section 55. *See* also section 73 of the Contract Act. In the case of contracts, the parties may expressly vary their rights and obligations which may arise under the law (say, Contract Act) and if they do so, the express agreement will govern them.[1]

17. SECTION 13: This section relates to cases in which existence of any right or custom is in issue. In such cases, any transaction by which the right or custom was created, claimed, modified, recognized, asserted, or denied or was inconsistent with its existence is relevant. So also, particular instance in which the right or custom was claimed, recognised or exercised or in which its existence was disputed, asserted or departed from, is relevant.

Clause (a): The term "right" includes right to ownership, possession and every right to know to law, including incorporeal rights. An assertion that a property is joint family property falls within the ambit of this section.[2] The section covers all kinds of rights and customs, public or private as could be seen in the illustration to the Section. Description in a mortgage deed regarding title is relevant.[3]

The English rule that a custom need not have been observed beyond living memory[4] does not apply to conditions in India. Custom could be a family custom a local custom, a general custom or of public custom, a special custom, a trade custom or usage.[5] Custom must be pleaded in precise terms and proved by evidence.[6]

This clause refers to "transaction". A transaction is a group of acts so connected together as to be referred to by a single name as a crime, a wrong or a contract or any other subject of enquiry which may be in issue. Every fact which is part of the same transaction as the fact in issue[7] is deemed to be relevant to the facts in issue (*Stephens' Digest of Criminal Law*). Sale deeds are transactions

---

1. *Thawardas Pherumal* v. *Union of India*, AIR 1955 SC 468: 1955 SCJ 445: (1955) 2 SCR 48.
2. *Shrinivas Krishnarao Kango* v. *Narayan Devji Kango*, AIR 1954 SC 379: 1954 SCJ 408: 1955 SCR 1.
3. *Harihar Prasad Singh* v. *Deo Narain Prasad*, AIR 1956 SC 305: 1956 SCJ 279: 1956 SCR 1.
4. *Subhani* v. *Nawab*, AIR 1941 PC 21: 193 IC 436: ILR 1941 Lah 154; *Gokul Chand* v. *Pravin Kumari*, AIR 1952 SC 231: 1952 SCJ 331: 1952 SCR 825; *Harihar Prasad Singh* v. *Balmiki Prasad Singh*, AIR 1975 SC 733: (1975) 1 SCC 212: 1975 2 SCR 932.
5. *Mirza Raja Pushpavathi Vijayaram Gajapathi Raj Manne Sultan Bahadur* v. *Sri Pushapathi Visweswar Gajapathiraj Rajkumar of Vizianagram*, AIR 1964 SC 118: (1964) 2 SCR 403; *Dattajirao Bahirojirao Ghorpade* v. *Vijayasinhrao*, AIR 1960 SC 1272: 1961 (1) SCJ 434: (1960) 3 SCR 789.
6. *Ram Kishore* v. *State of Uttar Pradesh*, AIR 1966 SC 1820: 2 SCJ 137: 1966 SCR (Supp) 68.
7. Stephens' Digest on Criminal Law referred to in Ratanlal and Dhirajlal on Law of Evidence 23rd Edn. Page 321.

and instances in which rights are asserted and recognised and hence relevant under this clause. A Will also could be such a transaction. So also a litigation between two persons, though the plaint or written statement is not a transaction. It has been held that the description in a mortgage deed by the mortgagor of the mortgaged land as belonging to him or in his possession is not an admission by the mortgagee, but is relevant under this section as containing an assertion of title.[1] Assertion of relationship of the executee of a document to the original owner is an assertion within the meaning of clause (1). So also recital as to the character of the land in question. If the executant of a document not *inter-partes* is examined as a witness, the recitals contained in the document may be used to corroborate his evidence under section 157.

The words "by which" used in clause (a) carry a different connotation from the words "in which", used in clause (b). The creation, claim, modification, recognisation, assertion or denial must be "by" the document and "in" the document.

Clause (b) deals not with "transactions" by which, but with "instances" in which the right or custom was claimed, recognised etc.

The importance of the Section is that it renders relevant transactions which are not *inter-partes*. They are relevant, though they may not be binding on the opposite party. The section relates to "transactions" and "instances" not mere previous statements. The words "by which" in clause (a) and "in which" in clause (b) are significant. Therefore, a recital in a sale deed that the vendor has certain rights in the property is not relevant in a suit which is not *inter-partes.* A recital is not a transaction by which a right is asserted, but is a mere instance of the assertion of an existence of a right. It will not be relevant unless section 21 or section 32 is attracted. A bare statement may or may not be a "claim" under clause (b). There is a distinction between a claim and a statement of a claim, though in certain circumstances, a statement may amount to a claim. A claim is made with reference to a right in a thing which was at the time being dealt with or directly in contemplation. A statement of claim may be casual or made with reference to some other right or thing. "Claim" means assertion to the knowledge and in the presence of the person whose right will be derogated by the establishment of the claim. Mere assertion of a right in a document not inter-partes is not to "claim" the right. A mere recital of a right is not relevant under clause (b). Such a recital is barred under section 21 as a gratuitous, self-serving statement. A right is not asserted merely because it is recited in a certain document. It is asserted only when the transaction concerned is itself entered into in exercise of that right *e.g.*, transfer of interest in the property such as mortgage or lease. Recitals regarding character of land are relevant.

Documents, to attract section 13, need not be *inter-partes*.[2] Pleadings, judgments are also relevant to show assertion of a right.[3] Previous judicial determination of market value of similarly situated land is relevant in the assessment of market value.[4]

1. *Harihar Prasad Singh* v. *Deo Narain Prasad*, AIR 1956 SC 305: 1956 SCJ 279: 1956 SCR 1.
2. *Ashfaque Ali* v. *Ashafi Mahaseth*, AIR 1951 Pat 641.
3. *Shrinivas Krishnarao Kango* v. *Narayan Devji Kango*, AIR 1954 SC 379: 1954 SCJ 408: 1955 SCR 1.
4. *Land Acquisition Officer, City Improvement Trust Board* v. *H. Narayanaiah*, AIR 1976 SC 2403: (1976) 4 SCC 9: (1977) 1 SCR 178.

Supreme Court has held that a judgment not inter-partes which is not relevant under sections 40 and 42 and does not fulfill the conditions of section 43 cannot be relevant under section 13. But it has to be noticed that section 43 itself states that "unless .... is relevant under some other provisions of this Act."[1]

18. JUDGMENT: A Judgment is admissible in support of a plea of *res judicata* in a civil case (section 11 C.P.C., section 40 Evidence Act) or that of *autre fois* acquit in a criminal case (Section 40) or when it is a judgment *in rem* (section 41) or when it relates to a matter of public nature (section 42).

Privy Council justified the reception of previous proceedings not inter-partes in evidence for certain purposes.[2] To similar effect are the decisions of Supreme Court.[3] However a finding of fact in such a judgment is not relevant as proof of that fact in subsequent proceedings.[4] Relevancy is to a limited extent contemplated in section 13. The reasoning in the previous judgment cannot be taken into consideration.[5]

However, Supreme Court has held that 'other provisions of the Act' referred to in section 43 cannot cover section 13 because this section does not deal with judgments at all.[6] Privy Council held that a judgment not *inter-partes* may be relevant under section 13 and though so relevant, the findings of fact arrived at on the evidence in one case are not evidence of that fact in another case.[7] The Supreme Court has upheld relevancy of such judgments relating to similar lands in the matter of quantification of compensation for land acquisition.[8]

19. RECITALS OF BOUNDARIES IN DOCUMENTS

(a) If the document is inter-partes, the recital is a joint statement made by both parties and hence relevant as an admission of both.

(b) If the document is between a party and a stranger, the recital is relevant against that party as an admission, but is not admissible in his favour, unless the fact recited is deposed to in court by the executant of the document, in which case, the recital will be admissible under section 157 or section 155 for corroboration or contradiction.

1. *State of Bihar* v. *Radha Krishna Singh*, AIR 1983 SC 684: (1983) 1 SCALE 789: (1983) 2 SCR 808: (1983) 3 SCC 118: 1983 Cur Civ LJ (SC) 273.
2. *Dinomoni Chowdhrani* v. *Brojo Mohini Chowdhrani*, (1901) 29 Ind App 24: ILR 29 Cal 187 (PC): 6 CWN 386 (PC); *Ram Ranjan Chakerbati* v. *Ram Narain Singh*, ILR (1895) 22 Cal 533: 22 IA 60 (PC); *Collector of Gorakhpur* v. *Ram Sunder Mal*, AIR 1934 PC 157 (PC): 56 A 468: 150 IC 545; *Kumar Gopika Raman Roy* v. *Atal Singh*, ILR 56 Cal 1003: 56 IA 119: 114 IC 561: AIR 1929 PC 99; *Kesho Prasad Singh* v. *Bhagjogna Kuer*, AIR 1937 PC 69: 41 Cal WN 577: ILR 16 Pat 258.
3. *Shrinivas Krishnarao Kango* v. *Narayan Devji Kango*, AIR 1954 SC 379: 1954 SCJ 408: 1955 SCR 1; *See* also *Tirumala Tirupati Devasthanams* v. *K.M. Krishnaiah*, AIR 1998 SC 1132: (1998) 3 SCC 331: 1998 AIR SCW 945.
4. *Coca Cola Company* v. *Pepsi Cola Company*, AIR 1942 PC 40: 202 IC 203; *Gobinda Narain Singh* v. *Sham Lal Singh*, AIR 1931 PC 89: ILR 58 Cal 1187: 58 IA 125: 1931 IC 753; *Kumar Gopika Raman Roy* v. *Atal Singh*, ILR 56 Cal 1003: 56 IA 119: 114 IC 561: AIR 1929 PC 99.
5. *Gobinda Narain Singh* v. *Sham Lal Singh*, AIR 1931 PC 89: ILR 58 Cal 1187: 58 IA 125: 1931 IC 753; *Shankarrao Dagadujirao* v. *Shambhu Nath*, AIR 1940 PC 192: 43 Bom LR 1: ILR (1941) Bom 107 (PC).
6. *State of Bihar* v. *Radha Krishna Singh*, AIR 1983 SC 684: (1983) 1 SCALE 789: (1983) 2 SCR 808: (1983) 3 SCC 118: 1983 Cur Civ LJ (SC) 273.
7. *Govinda Narayana* v. *Shyamlal*, AIR 1939 PC 89.
8. *Land Acquisition Officer, City Improvement Trust Board* v. *H. Narayanaiah*, AIR 1976 SC 2403: (1976) 4 SCC 9: (1977) 1 SCR 178.

(c) If the document is between strangers, the recital is neither a particular instance in which the right is exercised nor a transaction by which a right is claimed or asserted and is not relevant, unless the executant appears as a witness attracting operation of section 155 or 157. A mere statement of boundary cannot be classed with any of the verbs used in clause (a).

What applies to "right" applies to "custom" also. Evidence afforded by judicial decisions in enforcement of a custom is most satisfactory.[1]

20. SECTION 14

(1) When the existence of any state of mind such as intention, knowledge, good faith, negligence, rashness, ill-will or goodwill towards any particular person, and

(2) When the existence of any state of body or bodily feeling is in issue or relevant—

Facts showing the existence of such state of mind or of body or of bodily feeling are relevant.

The section has two clarificatory explanations. The eleven illustrations to the section make clear the intendment of the section.

Facts from which mental or bodily state or feeling may be inferred are relevant. The second explanation represents a particular application of the general rule contained in the section. The rejection of the "general" fact in the first explanation is on the basis that the collateral matter has too remote a connection, if at all, with the fact in issue.

A witness must be swear to facts within his knowledge and recollection and cannot swear to his belief. State of a person's mind can be ascertained either by his own confession or by presumptive inference from physical facts. A witness has to speak to facts within his own knowledge and let the inference from those facts be drawn by the Court. Can the facts presented show the existence of the state of mind or body under enquiry? If a collateral fact is relevant, its remoteness can effect only the weight to be attached to it. When the charge against accused was that he acted out of hatred towards a particular community, he was entitled to adduce evidence to show that his behaviour towards members of that community throughout his career was good and he could not have attacked them physically.[2]

Evidence of facts similar to but not part of the same transaction as the main fact cannot be received to prove the occurrence of the main fact in dispute. But if the main fact has been established, evidence of similar acts committed by the accused can be looked into to decide the state of mind of the person who did the acts, that is, whether it was done accidentally or with a particular knowledge or intention. This section applies only where the criminality of the act depends on the state of mind or feeling of the person who did the act. Evidence of a collateral offence cannot be received as substantive evidence of the offence for which the offender is being tried.

Both previous and subsequent events may be relevant as showing a state of mind.

1. *Kehar Singh* v. *Dewan*, AIR 1966 SC 1555: (1966) 3 SCR 393: 1966 (2) SCJ 363.
2. *Habeeb Mohammad* v. *State of Hyderabad*, AIR 1954 SC 51: 1953 SCJ 678: 35 Cr LJ 338: 1954 SCR 475.

Illustrations (e), (i), (j) relate to "intention", (a), (b), (c) and (d) to "knowledge"; (f), (g) (h) to "good faith", (n) to "negligence" and "knowledge", (k), (l), (m) to "mental and bodily feeling". (n), (o), and (p) illustrate the explanation.

To prove guilty knowledge of an accused, that he committed similar offences is relevant. This principle may not apply to all offences. It may be applicable in the prosecution of an accused for forging a bank note with the requisite knowledge where it could be shown that he had earlier committed similar acts. Where the question is whether *A* voluntarily shot at *B* with intention to kill, evidence that *A* previously or subsequently shot at *B* is relevant to show *mens rea*. But evidence that *A* killed other persons is not relevant. Death by poisoning of other inmates of the house is relevant to show that poisoning in the instant case was not accidental, but intentional.[1]

Knowledge may be inferred from the fact that a person had reasonable means of knowledge or information. This principle cannot be followed beyond reasonable limits. For example, notification in a newspaper cannot amount to actual knowledge unless his attention was drawn to it. "Notice" of a fact has been dealt with in the Transfer of Property Act, 1882 and Indian Trusts Act, 1882. Notice may be either actual or constructive. Notice to an agent could sometimes be regarded as notice to his principal. Willful abstention from making enquires or inspection of documents can impute "knowledge". In appropriate cases, court can raise a presumption of notice. Whatever is sufficient to put a person of ordinary prudence on enquiry is constructive notice of all that enquiry would lead to.[2] Where a party deliberately abstains from enquiry for the purpose of avoiding notice, court may draw an inference of constructive notice. There could be presumption of knowledge where a party is guilty of gross negligence. Such negligence must be something which raises a positive equity against the negligent person. Where a doctor was charged with negligence on account of administering a particular injection given by him, in order to show that the particular injection was too strong and to rebut the defence case that death of a particular patient to whom it was given was due to an exceptional reaction to the drug, evidence was held to be admissible to show the symptoms and illness and death of other patients to whom same injection was given.[3]

Fraud is rarely capable of being proved directly, as it is by its' nature a matter of secrecy. In the generality of cases only circumstantial evidence will be available in proof of fraud and in overcoming the natural presumption of honesty and raising a contra-presumption. A party's good faith in doing an act may generally be inferred from facts which would justify its' doing.[4] To show the *bona fides* of a party's' belief as to any matter, it is allowable to show the state of his knowledge and that he had reasonable grounds for such belief. A false statement made though carelessness, and without reasonable belief that it is true, may be evidence of fraud. Fraud is proved, where it is shown that a false representation was made knowingly or without belief in its truth, or recklessly, careless whether it is true or false. If fraud is proved, the defendants' motive is immaterial.

1. *Juggan Khan Jamshankan* v. *State*, AIR 1963 SC 102; *John Oni Akerale* v. *King*, AIR 1943 PC 72: (1943) 44 Cr LJ 569.
2. Phipson on Evidence, 13th Edn., P. 171.
3. *John Oni Akerale* v. *King*, AIR 1943 PC 72: (1943) 44 Cr LJ 569.
4. Phipson on Evidence, 13th Edn., P. 178.

Negligence is a tort resulting from the failure to exercise the care, which the circumstances demand. Where there is no duty to exercise care, negligence in the general sense has no legal consequence. Where there is a duty to exercise reasonable care, care must be taken to avoid acts and omissions which can be reasonably foreseen to be likely to cause injury to person or property. The degree of care required in a given case depends upon the accompanying circumstances and may vary according to the amount of risk to be encountered and the magnitude of the prospective injury. Absence of care owed by one party to the other in the given circumstances and the damage suffered by the plaintiff on account of the cause and effect between the two, are to be examined.

A party guilty of a rash act neither intends evil nor does he know that evil is likely nor has he reason to believe that it is likely. He does not think that evil will ensue. He thinks of the probable consequences of his act or omission, but from insufficient thought, assumes that the consequences will not ensue. Rashness is different from heedlessness (where a person acts because he does not think of the probable consequences of his conduct at all). In the Indian Penal Code, there is no distinction drawn between rashness and heedlessness. Culpable rashness is acting with the consciousness that the mischievous and illegal consequences may follow, but with the hope that they will not. Culpable negligence is acting without the consciousness that an illegal and mischievous result will follow, but in circumstances which indicate that the culprit has not exercised the caution expected from him, and that, if he had, he would have had the consciousness.

Malice in the doing of an act is generally proved by the previous or subsequent conduct and relationship of the parties, such as prior enmity, threats etc., in which case, previous conduct showing goodwill may be shown.

Illustrations (l) and (m) relate to state of body or bodily feeling.

22. A state of mind relevant as showing the existence of a state of mind must show that state of mind in reference to the particular matter in question and not generally. That a person is generally dishonest or malicious or negligent or criminal in his conduct does not have sufficient directness to his conduct on any particular occasion. Dishonesty, if that is the charge, must be dishonesty in the particular case. In such a case, the probability of his having been dishonest in the particular case is perhaps increased, but only in a vague and indefinite way. However, if at the time, he was found in possession of a number of other stolen articles, this would throw a particular light on his knowledge and intention regarding those articles. The general tendency of an accused cannot be attempted to be proved, as that would amount to proving his bad character which is barred by section 54.

Any person must be taken to intend the natural consequences of his act. The word "intent" cannot be read as if it were identical with "wish" or "desire". A person may not wish to annoy the owner of a land as a result of trespass, but, if the annoyance is the natural consequence of his act and if it is known to him that such is the natural consequence, it can be inferred that there is an intent to annoy. When a person voluntarily does an act, knowing at the time that in the natural course of events a certain result will follow, he intends to bring about that result. Section 114 has considerable bearing in such situations.

Explanation (2) does not extend the scope of the section. If, in a given case, previous commission of an offence is relevant, conviction in that case is also relevant. The mode of proof is indicated in section 298, Cr.P.C. Code. Under explanation (2), previous conviction is relevant as evidence to prove habit and association. Previous offences must be of a cognate character so as to reasonably permit an inference as to the state of mind of the person charged.

23. SECTION 15: When there is a question whether an act was accident or intentional, or an act was done with a particular knowledge or intention, the fact that such act formed part of a series of similar occurrences in each of which the person doing the act was concerned, is relevant.

This section is an application of the principle underlying section 14. Section 15 enables facts to be allowed to be proved to show a system. If there is no common link between the fact to be proved (fact in issue) and the evidentiary fact, they cannot form a series. The purpose of the provision is to enable establishment of the *animus* of the act for which the accused is charged. In an anticipatory rebuttal of a defence of accident, mistake or other innocent condition of mind, evidence may be given to prove that the accused has been concerned in a systematic course of conduct of the same specific kind as that in question. It is not necessary that all the acts should form part of one transaction but such acts should form part of a series of similar occurrences. This section must be read as subject to section 14 so far as evidence of knowledge and intention are concerned. When there is an issue whether the act of the accused was deliberate or accidental or done with guilty knowledge, evidence can be let of a series of similar acts by him on other occasions because a series of acts with similar characteristics is unlikely to be produced by accident or in advertence.[1] In a case where the accused was tried for murder of the victim by poisoning, prosecution sought to rely on an earlier incident in which the wife of accused was administered poison under similar circumstances. The Privy Council held that there was no relevancy since in neither case was there direct evidence that the accused had administered the poison, observing further that if the accused was proved to have administered poison in the case under trial in circumstances consistent with accident, then proof that he had previously administered poison to another person in similar circumstances might well have been relevant.[2] When a boy aged 12 years was drowned in a tank, it was possible that it was by accidental, but the fact of previous attempt to kill the boy would be relevant.[3] *Woodroffe and Amir Ali on Law of Evidence*, 18th Edition at pages 1271 to 1274 refer to English cases having a bearing on this question. It has been held by the Privy Counsel that evidence that the accused were connected with similar cases of user of forged challans was admissible to prove their knowledge and intention in regard to the cases under trial against them.[4]

24. SECTION 16: When the question is whether something was done, the existence of any course of business, according to which it naturally would have been done, is a relevant fact. Illustration (a) relates to the question whether a particular letter was dispatched. In such a case, the fact that it was done in the ordinary course of business for all letters put in a certain place in the office to be carried to the post box and that the particular letter was put in that place

1. *C.N. Krishna Murthy* v. *Abdul Subban*, AIR 1965 Mys 128: (1965) 1 Cr LJ 565: ILR 1964 Mys 1011.
2. *Davis and Co.* v. *H.M. Procurator General.*
3. *R.* v. *Shnakaraya*, AIR 1940 Bom 365.
4. *Srinivas Mall* v. *Emperor*, AIR 1947 PC 135: 49 Bom LR 688.

are relevant. Illustration (b) relates to the question whether a particular letter reached the addressee. The facts that it was posted in due course and was not returned through the Dead Letter office are relevant. Illustration (f) to section 114 may also be referred to. All these presumptions are permissive and not mandatory. The Court, on consideration of the evidence before it, may conclude that the presumption stood rebutted.[1]

This section relates private and public offices. Where registration of a document was performed by a competent person appointed to act as registrar and all necessary endorsements and signatures are found to have been made by or before him, all these acts can be presumed to have been duly done and in order, subject only to strong evidence of fraud. Suspicion may prevent a court from drawing such a presumption. Where there is evidence that certain land was attached, in the absence of any evidence to the contrary, it may be presumed that all necessary formalities had been complied with.[2]

The fixed methods and systematic operation of the postal and telegraphic service is evidence of due delivery of the matter placed for that purpose in the custody of the proper authority. Where it is shown that a letter correctly addressed is delivered to the post office, it may be presumed, from the known course of business in that department of public service, that it reached its destination at the regular time and was received by the addressee.[3]

A notice under section 106, Transfer of Property Act, sent by registered post which returned with endorsement of refusal, may be deemed to have been served. As to under what circumstances the presumption will stand rebutted would vary from case to case and a mere denial may not be sufficient.[4] The endorsement of refusal can also be taken to mean that the registered letter was refused by the addressee or his agent.[5] It is not necessary to examine the postman as a witness.[6]

It is important to bear in mind that this section deals not with presumption, but with relevance.[7] Drawing a presumption depends on the facts and circumstances of each case. Postal seals on postal articles also have relevance.

---

1. *L.M.S. Ummu Saleema* v. *B.B. Gujral*, AIR 1981 SC 1191: (1981) 3 SCC 317: (1981) 3 SCR 647.
2. *Mohammad Akbar Khan* v. *Mian Musharraf Shah*, AIR 1934 PC 217: 151 IC 221.
3. *Harihar Banerji* v. *Ramshashi Roy*, AIR 1918 PC 102: 45 Ind App 222: 16 All LJ 969.
4. *Om Prakash* v. *Divisional Superintendent, Northern Rly.*, AIR 1970 All 440: 1970 All WR (HC) 107: 1970 All LJ 223 FB.
5. *Har Charan Singh* v. *Shiv Rani*, AIR 1981 SC 1284: (1981) 2 SCC 535: (1981) 2 SCR 962; *Thakur Chandra Nandi* v. *Arun Kumar Roy Chowdhury*, AIR 1986 Cal 249: (1986) 1 Ren CJ 387: (1986) 2 Ren CR 87.
6. *Radha Kishan* v. *State of Uttar Pradesh*, AIR 1963 SC 822: 1963 All LJ 397: 1963 BLJR 353; *Puwada Venkateswara Rao* v. *C.V. Ramana*, AIR 1976 SC 869: (1976) 2 SCC 409: (1976) 3 SCR 551.
7. *Mobarik Ali Ahmed* v. *State of Bombay*, AIR 1957 SC 857: 1957 Cr LJ 1346: 1958 SCR 328: (1957) 61 Bom LR 58: 1958 SCJ 111.

CHAPTER 5

ADMISSIONS
(SECTIONS 17 TO 23 AND 31)

Statement is genus, admission is the species and confession is the sub-species.[1] Admissions are exception to hearsay rule. They are treated as relevant since they are statements against the interests of the maker and so are probably true. Probative value does not depend on communication.[2] What is admitted by a party to be true may be presumed to be true unless the contrary is shown.

2. "The statements made out of Court by a party – opponent are universally deemed admissible when offered against him .... when offered against the party the statements have the same logical status as a witness'es self-contradiction .... the party opponent is discredited when it appears that on some other occasion he has made a statement inconsistent with his present claim against him .... Thus, in effect and broadly, anything said by a party opponent may be used against him as an admission, provided it exhibits the quality of inconsistency with the fact now asserted by him in pleadings or in testimony ....".[3] Wigmore does not agree that admissions are important since they are statements made against one's own interest, a view not favoured by judges in India. By definition (section 17), an admission is a statement which suggests any inference as to any fact in issue or relevant fact. If *A* in his present case against *B* seeking declaration of title to a property and ancillary reliefs, which title is denied by *B* who sets up title in himself, *B* may prove a previous statement made by *A* to the effect that he had no title to the property. That statement contradicts the present claim of *A* and constitutes a statement made against his own interest, which is the main reason why *B* seeks to prove as relevant the previous statement. If the earlier statement of *A* is not against the present claim of *A, B* would not seek to rely on it.

3. **SECTION 17:** Admission is an oral or documentary statement which suggests any inference as to any fact in issue or relevant fact, and which is made by any of the persons, and under the circumstances hereafter mentioned (in sections 18 to 20). This definition is incomplete and must be read alongwith sections 18 to 20. Admissions by conduct are not covered by section 17, but by section 8. While every confession is an admission, every admission may not be confession. 'Statement' only means "what is stated".[2]

An admission may be direct or indirect.[4] Form of an admission is immaterial so far as its relevancy (admissibility) is concerned.[5] Admissions

1. *Aghnoo Nagesia* v. *State of Bihar*, AIR 1966 SC 119: 1966 Cr LJ 100: (1966) 1 SCJ 193: (1966) 1 SCR 134; *Sahoo* v. *State of Uttar Pradesh*, AIR 1966 SC 40: 1966 Cr LJ 68: (1965) 3 SCR 86: (1965) 2 SCWR 464: (1965) 2 SCA 292: 1965 SCD 809: (1965) 2 Andh LT 215.
2. *Bhogilal Chunilal Pandya* v. *State of Bombay*, AIR 1959 SC 356: 1959 Supp (1) SCR 310: 1959 Cr LJ 389.
3. Wigmore on Eivdence in trials at common law 1972 Ed., Vol. IV Pages 2 to 4.
4. Taylor Evidence, Section 800.
5. Best, Evidence Section 521.

are relevant, whether they are oral or contained in books of account or letters, maps, pleadings, depositions, answers to interrogatories, affidavits, recitals in documents, horoscopes, receipts, negotiable securities, bank pass books, income tax related.[1] Admission of a signature of a person on a document does not amount to admission of due execution of the document by that person. Execution implies conscious execution and knowledge of its contents. Statement that a person signed on a blank paper does not amount to admission of execution of document. In matrimonial cases, admissions of parties can be acted upon if there was no collusion between them.[2]

A judgment is generally irrelevant between strangers. Yet it may be relevant as between strangers if it is an admission. Where *A* sued *B*, a carrier of goods delivered by *A* to *B*, a judgment obtained by *B* against a person to whom he had delivered the goods, is relevant as an admission by *B* that he had the goods with him at some time. *A* plea of guilty by an accused in a case of trespass may be considered as an admission.

4. An admission serves the following purposes depending on their value:

(a) It shifts the burden of proof regarding the fact so admitted, on the party making the admission.

(b) It casts on the person who made the admission, the burden of showing it to be wrong or mistaken or to explain it.

(c) It serves as substantive evidence and not merely as a contradiction.[3]

(d) When an admission of a party is satisfactorily proved, it can reasonably be presumed to be true, unless rebutted by other evidence.[4]

(e) An admission is never conclusive unless it creates estoppel.[5]

(f) By reason of an admission of a party, title to the property does not pass, since transfer of title can take place only by a registered instrument.[6]

Where a third person makes an admission in a document, that is not relevant against a party to a case, who did not make the admission, unless he can be said to be bound by the admission.[7]

An admission made by an accused to the doctor examining him as to the cause of injuries sustained by him is an admission.[8] If an accused not in custody makes a confession to a doctor, that is relevant. A purported admission in a

1. Taylor, Evidence, 91-100, 858, 860, 804.
2. *Mahendra Manilal Nanavati* v. *Sushila Mahendra Nanavati*, AIR 1965 SC 364: 66 Bom LR 681: 1965 Mah LJ 365.
3. *Union of India* v. *Moksh Builders and Financiers*, AIR 1977 SC 409: 1978 UPTC 75: (1977) 1 SCC 60: (1977) 1 SCR 967; *Thiru John* v. *Returning Officer*, AIR 1977 SC 1724: (1977) 3 SCC 540: (1977) 3 SCR 538; *Sushil Kumar* v. *Rakesh Kumar*, AIR 2004 SC 230: 2003 AIR SCW 6005: (2003) 8 SCC 673.
4. *Nagubai Ammal* v. *B. Shama Rao*, AIR 1956 SC 593: 1956 SCC 321: 1956 SCR 451: 1956 SCA 959: 1956 SCJ 655.
5. *K.S. Srinivasan* v. *Union of India*, AIR 1958 SC 419: 1958 SCA 544: 1958 SCR 1295: 1958 SCJ 777.
6. *Ambika Prasad Thakur* v. *Ram Ekbal Rai*, AIR 1966 SC 612: 1966 (1) SCA 35: (1966) 1 SCR 758.
7. *Sitaram Motilal Kalal* v. *Santanuprasad Jaishanker Bhatt*, AIR 1966 SC 1697: (1966) 1 SCWR 974: (1966) 3 SCR 527.
8. *Ammini* v. *State of Kerala*, (1998) 2 SCC 301: AIR 1998 SC 260: 1997 AIR SCW 4231: 1998 Cr LJ 481: 1998 SCC (Cri) 618.

deposition must be examined for error in recording the deposition.[1] A stray sentence may not have much value as an admission.

5. An admission cannot be split up and part of it used against the maker. It must be used as a whole or not at all.[2] All parts of the admission must be taken together even if they operate in favour of the maker. If the admission is subject to a condition or qualification, the condition and the qualifying part must also be considered.[3] In the case of a suit on a lost document, the defendant admits execution of the document and pleads discharge endorsed on the document, admission of execution cannot be relied on eschewing the latter part of the statement. However, in the light of the other evidence in the case, the court may disbelieve a part of a statement. The court must start with the other evidence and form an opinion on it, thereafter consider the admission to receive assurance to support its conclusion.[4]

Admission on a question of law is not binding.[5]

Admission is best evidence, though not conclusive and is decisive unless successfully withdrawn or proved to be erroneous.[6]

6. Admission may be judicial admission (by a party during the proceedings of a case) or extra-judicial admission (informal, in documents accounts, letters, etc., not in Court proceedings). Admission in a pleading is a judicial admission.[7] Such an admission may result in a certain right accruing to the opposite party. If such a right has accrued, the maker of the admission cannot be allowed to retract the same. Thus pleadings cannot be allowed to be amended so as to delete an admission contained therein.[8] Admission incorrectly made in ignorance of facts can be allowed to be withdrawn.[9]

7. An admission must be clear and unambiguous.[10] If an admission is capable of two interpretations, the interpretation unfavourable to the maker cannot be accepted.

---

1. *S. Venugopal* v. *A. Karruppusami*, AIR 2006 SC 1930: 2006 AIR SCW 2295: (2006) 4 SCC 507.
2. *Jwala Das* v. *Pir Sant Das*, AIR 1930 PC 245; *Hanumant Govind Nargundkar* v. *State of Madhya Pradesh*, AIR 1952 SC 343: 1952 SCR 1091: 1952 SCA 623; *Palvinder Kaur* v. *State of Punjab*, AIR 1952 SC 354: 1952 SCJ 545: 1953 Cr LJ 154: 1953 SCR 94: ILR 1953 Punj 107; *Dadarao* v. *State of Maharashtra*, AIR 1974 SC 388: 1974 Cr LJ 447: (1974) 3 SCC 630; *Haji C.H. Mohammad Koya* v. *T.K.S.M.A. Muthukoya*, (1979) 2 SCC 8: AIR 1979 SC 154: (1979) 1 SCR 664.
3. *Matabhoy Mulla Essabhoy* v. *Mulji Harielas*, AIR 1915 PC 2: 29 IC 223: 42 IA 103: 29 B 399 (PC).
4. *Kashmira Singh* v. *State of Madhya Pradesh*, AIR 1952 SC 159: 1952 SCR 526: 1952 SCJ 201: 1952 Cr LJ 839.
5. *Banarsi Das* v. *Kanshi Ram*, AIR 1963 SC 1165: (1964) 1 SCR 316: ILR (1963) 2 All 678.
6. *Narayan Bhagwantrao Gosavi Balajiwale* v. *Gopal Vinayak Gosavi*, AIR 1960 SC 100: (1960) 1 SCR 773: (1960) 2 SCA 153: 1960 SCJ 263; *Kishorilal* v. *Chaltibai*, AIR 1959 SC 504: 1959 SCJ 560: 1959 Supp (1) SCR 698; *Nagubai Ammal* v. *B. Shama Rao*, AIR 1956 SC 593: 1956 SCC 321: 1956 SCR 451: 1956 SCA 959: 1956 SCJ 655; *Ramji Dayawala and Sons (P) Ltd.* v. *Invest Import*, AIR 1981 SC 2085: (1981) 1 SCC 80: (1981) 1 SCR 899.
7. *Nagindas Ramdas* v. *Dalpatram Ichharam*, AIR 1974 SC 471: (1974) 1 SCC 242: (1974) 3 SCR 544.
8. *Modi Spinning and Weaving Mills Co. Ltd.* v. *Ladha Ram and Co.*, AIR 1977 SC 680: (1976) 4 SCC 320: (1977) 1 SCR 728; *Jagan Nath* v. *Chander Bhan*, AIR 1988 SC 1362: JT 1988 (2) SC 441.
9. *Panchdeo Narain Srivastava* v. *Jyoti Sahay*, AIR 1983 SC 462: 1983 UJ (SC) 406: 1983 BLJ 394.
10. *Daulat Singhji* v. *Khachar Mansur*, AIR 1936 PC 150: 162 IC 17: 60 B 634: 63 IA 248; *Sita Ram Bhau Patil* v. *Ramchandra Nago Patil*, AIR 1977 SC 1712: (1977) 2 SCC 49: (1977) 2 SCR 671; *Nagubai Ammal* v. *B. Shama Rao*, AIR 1956 SC 593: 1956 SCC 321: 1956 SCR 451: 1956 SCA 959: 1956 SCJ 655; *C. Koteshwara Rao* v. *C. Subbarao*, AIR 1971 SC 1542: (1970) 1 SCC 558: 1970 (2) SCJ 679.

Admissions made in previous cases, petitions, letters, deeds, account books, horoscopes, returns, FIR, Razi deeds, invalid instruments, unstamped documents are relevant.

8. An admission must be properly proved in any of the ways in which a statement is allowed to be proved. An admission (by a party) is relevant as substantive evidence and not merely to contradict the party if examined as a witness. Hence, the party need not be confronted with the admission as required by section 145.[1] An admission by a witness (other than a party) must be put to the witness.[2] It is for the party making the admission to explain the admission or prove that it is not true. Admission is relevant, but not conclusive.

Admission shifts burden of proof. What a party himself admitted to be true may reasonably be presumed to be so, though the party making it may rebut the presumption.[3]

Admission of signature in a document does not amount to admission of execution. Admission in a letter not communicated to the addressee attracts section 17. Oral admission cannot be received in evidence of contents of documents except when secondary evidence is allowed (section 65). Execution of a document which is not required to be attested by law, may be proved by admission (section 78). Even where attestation is compulsory admission of a party of its execution by himself is sufficient proof of it, (section 70).

What weight is to be attached to an admission is a matter different from its relevancy.[4]

9. An admission which is wrong in point of fact and evidently made in ignorance of legal rights has no binding effect.[5] An admission in relation to a matter which is not a fact in issue or relevant fact in the case is not an admission attracting section 17.[6] An admission is a voluntary acknowledgement made by a party, of the existence of certain facts which are inconsistent with his claim in the case.[7]

10. An admission cannot be proved by a recital in a judgment.[8] Recitals in judgment are no evidence to prove the exact admission made by a party or a witness unless the whole of the statement is recited therein.[9] A judgment is no more than secondary evidence of pleadings and it is doubtful whether it would be admissible as evidence of contents of pleadings where original pleadings are available. So also recital in a judgment regarding a statement in a deposition.

---

1. *Bharat Singh* v. *Mst. Bhagirthi*, AIR 1966 SC 405: (1966) 1 SCR 606: 1966 (2) SCJ 53; *Union of India* v. *Moksh Builders and Financiers*, AIR 1977 SC 409: 1978 UPTC 75: (1977) 1 SCC 60: (1977) 1 SCR 967.
2. *Ambika Prasad Thakur* v. *Ram Ekbal Rai*, (1966) 1 SCA 35: AIR 1966 SC 605: (1966) 1 SCR 758.
3. *Nathoo Lal* v. *Durga Prasad*, AIR 1954 SC 355: 1955 SCR 51: 1954 SCJ 557: 1954 SCA 921; *Thiru John* v. *Returning Officer*, AIR 1977 SC 1724: (1977) 3 SCC 540: (1977) 3 SCR 538; *Sushil Kumar* v. *Rakesh Kumar*, AIR 2004 SC 230: 2003 AIR SCW 6005: (2003) 8 SCC 673.
4. *Bharat Singh* v. *Mst. Bhagirthi*, AIR 1966 SC 405: (1966) 1 SCR 606: 1966 (2) SCJ 53.
5. *Delhi Transport Corporation* v. *Shyam Lal*, AIR 2004 SC 4271: 2004 AIR SCW 4711: (2004) 8 SCC 88: 2004 SCC (L&S) 1053.
6. *Sita Ram Bhau Patil* v. *Ramchandra Nago Patil*, AIR 1977 SC 1712: (1977) 2 SCC 49: (1977) 2 SCR 671.
7. Black's Law Dictionary.
8. *Dundbahadur Singh* v. *Durga Prasad Singh*, AIR 1953 Pat 346: 1953 BLJR 234.
9. *Collector of Gorakhpur* v. *Ram Sunder Mal*, AIR 1934 PC 157 (PC): 56 A 468: 150 IC 545.

An admission must be based on personal knowledge. A person's admission of his age, though based on hearsay, is evidence of the fact.

When an admission has been acted upon by the other party it operates as an estoppel and is conclusive. If not, he can prove that the admission was not correct or was made under mistake.[1]

Admissions by non-traverse are relevant for the purpose of the particular litigation in which they are made, but are not covered by section 17.

11. An admission is a very strong piece of evidence and is almost conclusive if not explained or not shown to be wrong.[2] It is for the maker to show that admission was made under circumstances which do not making it binding on him. He may show that he was mistaken or was not telling the truth.[3] But an admission is decisive of the matter unless successfully withdrawn or proved to be erroneous by adducing necessary evidence for the purpose.[4] Until then, an admission has evidentiary value. An admission can be shown to be wrong, so long as the person to whom it is made has not acted upon it to his detriment when it might become conclusive by way of estoppel.[5] As the value of an admission depends on the circumstances in which it was made, evidence of such circumstances can be given to affect the weight of the admission. He may show it was made in ignorance of law or facts. A clear admission of a party is relevant irrespective of whether he is examined as a witness and whether, if appears, he was confronted with it under section 145 or not. Purpose of Section 145 is only to contradict him under section 145. Purpose of section 155(3) is to impeach his credibility. A previous admission of a party is relevant and is substantive evidence of fact admitted.[6] But a previous statement used to contradict a witness does not become substantive evidence and merely serves to throw doubt on the veracity of the witness.[7] Where the admission is unclear and ambiguous, the party who made the admission has to be confronted with it, when examined as a witness, failing which, the admission does not become substantive evidence.[8] The Court has to consider the evidentiary value of an admission along with the other evidence.

An admission of a party, as substantive evidence, need not be brought to the attention of the maker.[9]

A self-serving statement cannot be used.[10]

---

1. *Kishorilal* v. *Chaltibai*, AIR 1959 SC 504: 1959 SCJ 560: 1959 Supp (1) SCR 698.
2. *Ramji Dayawala and Sons (P) Ltd.* v. *Invest Import*, AIR 1981 SC 2085: (1981) 1 SCC 80: (1981) 1 SCR 899.
3. *Basant Singh* v. *Janki Singh*, AIR 1967 SC 341: 1967 All LJ 1: (1967) 1 SLJ 476.
4. *Narayan Bhagwantrao Gosavi Balajiwale* v. *Gopal Vinayak Gosavi*, AIR 1960 SC 100: (1960) 1 SCR 773: (1960) 2 SCA 153: 1960 SCJ 263.
5. *Nagubai Ammal* v. *B. Shama Rao*, AIR 1956 SC 593: 1956 SCC 321: 1956 SCR 451: 1956 SCA 959: 1956 SCJ 655; *K.S. Srinivasan* v. *Union of India*, AIR 1958 SC 419: 1958 SCA 544: 1958 SCR 1295: 1958 SCJ 777.
6. *Nathoo Lal* v. *Durga Prasad*, AIR 1954 SC 355: 1955 SCR 51: 1954 SCJ 557: 1954 SCA 921; *Bharat Singh* v. *Mst. Bhagirthi*, AIR 1966 SC 405: (1966) 1 SCR 606: 1966 (2) SCJ 53.
7. *Biswanath Prasad* v. *Dwarka Prasad*, AIR 1974 SC 117: (1974) 1 SCC 78: (1974) 2 SCR 124.
8. *Sita Ram Bhau Patil* v. *Ramchandra Nago Patil*, AIR 1977 SC 1712: (1977) 2 SCC 49: (1977) 2 SCR 671; *Biswanath Prasad* v. *Dwarka Prasad*, AIR 1974 SC 117: (1974) 1 SCC 78: (1974) 2 SCR 124; *Bharat Singh* v. *Mst. Bhagirthi*, AIR 1966 SC 405: (1966) 1 SCR 606: 1966 (2) SCJ 53.
9. *Biswanath Prasad* v. *Dwarka Prasad*, AIR 1974 SC 117: (1974) 1 SCC 78: (1974) 2 SCR 124.
10. *Krishnawati* v. *Hans Raj*, AIR 1974 SC 280: 1975 (1) SCJ 87: (1974) 2 SCR 524.

In a prosecution for Adultery or Bigamy, mere admission of second marriage is not sufficient.[1]

Weight of an admission increases with the knowledge and deliberation of the maker or the solemnity of the occasion when it was made. Evidence of oral admission must always be received with great caution.

12. **SECTION 18:** Following statements are admissions:

(a) Made by a party to the proceedings;

(b) Made by his agent – if was expressly or impliedly authorised to make the statement;[2]

(c) Made by parties to representative suits only if made while the party making the statement held that character;

(d) Made by persons having any proprietary or pecuniary interest in the subject-matter of the case and who make them in such character;

(e) Made by persons who were predecessors-in-interest of the parties *vis-à-vis* the subject-matter.[3]

Provided, the statements were made during the continuance of such interest.[4]

Definition of "admission" must now include statements contained in an electronic form in view of the amendment of section 17 by the Information Technology Act, 2000.

An admission by an agent is never relevant in criminal cases, except in cases covered by section 30 where both the principal and the agent are accused. In a criminal case, accused is a party but a victim of a crime is not regarded as party, except in the case of a non-cognizable case where the victim filed a private complaint. Admission made by a wife as such does not affect the husband unless she had express or implied authority from him to make the admission.[5]

Directors of company, Manager of joint Hindu Family, partners, trustees are such agents. So also lawyers regarding question of fact.

Statements by persons outside the framework of section 18 are not relevant as admissions.[4]

A self-serving statement is not an admission.[6]

An admission in a previous suit by a witness who was not a party to the subsequent suit is not relevant against a party to the later suit. The deposition of a person in a suit to which he is not a party is, in a subsequent suit in which he was the defendant, relevant against him though he was not called as a witness in the later suit.

---

1. *Kanwal Ram* v. *Himachal Pradesh Administration,* AIR 1966 SC 614: 1966 (1) SCJ 210: (1966) 1 SCR 532; *Priya Bala Ghosh* v. *Suresh Chandra Ghosh,* AIR 1971 SC 1153: 1971 Cr LJ 939: (1971) 1 SCC 864.
2. *Kedar Nath Bajoria* v. *State,* AIR 1954 SC 660: 1954 Cr LJ 1679.
3. *Bhim Singh* v. *Kan Singh,* (1980) 3 SCC 72: AIR 1980 SC 727.
4. *Shrichand Gupta* v. *Gulzar Singh,* AIR 1992 SC 123: 1991 AIR SCW 2813: (1992) 1 SCC 143.
5. Taylor's Evidence, Section 765 to 771.
6. *Idandas* v. *Anant Ramchandra,* AIR 1982 SC 127: (1982) 1 SCC 27: 1982 MHLJ 328; *Mahendra Manilal Nanavati* v. *Sushila Mahendra Nanavati,* AIR 1965 SC 364: 66 Bom LR 681: 1965 Mah LJ 365.

The recital of boundary in a document between a party and a stranger, is relevant against the party as an admission, but is not relevant in his favour, unless the fact recited is deposed to in court by the executant of the document, in which case, the recital will be admissible under section 157 or 155 to corroborate or contradict as the case may be. Where a mortgage deed describes the mortgaged land as belonging to mortgagor in a particular right and as being in his actual possession, it is not an admission by the mortgagees, but such recitals are relevant under section 13 as assertions of fact in documents under which the mortgagee claims.[1]

Where an admission was deliberately made and precisely identified, its evidentiary value is highly satisfactory.[2] Value of an admission depends very much on the circumstances under it was made. Possible motives for incorrect statements by interested parties cannot be ignored. If the fact admitted was within the personal knowledge of the party admitting and there is no evidence of any convincing explanation, its value is considerable. If the fact admitted is an inference from evidence and circumstances, it is like an opinion and its value is very little.

13. **ADMISSION BY AGENT IN CRIMINAL CASES:** To make a client criminally liable for a letter written by his lawyer, it is necessary to show that such letter was written on instructions of the client. When personal knowledge and instructions are shown, the admission will be relevant.[3] Admission by the father of the accused would be of no avail. (*ibid* page 1369). In civil cases, a lawyer has implied authority to make an admission of fact against his client during the actual progress of the litigation. Such an opinion of the lawyer which is not in accordance with the law applicable in the case is not binding on the party. (*ibid* pages 1370, 1371). The admission must have been necessary for the purpose of the matter in dispute. An erroneous concession made by a lawyer does not bind his client.[4] Admission by a lawyer on a question of law has no binding force and court can always give free effect to it's view of law.[5] An admission of a fact by the lawyer cannot bind the party where it was made under misapprehension or mistake; nor can such an admission be binding if it related to a matter outside the scope of the case.[6] Such a concession or admission made in one case cannot bind the party in another case.[7] A concession made on a question of fact cannot be disregarded.[8]

Except by a plea of guilty, admissions dispensing with proof, as distinguished from admissions which are evidential, are not allowed in a criminal trial. No consent by the counsel of accused to dispense with the medical witness can relieve the prosecution of the duty of proving by evidence, the nature of injuries received by the deceased and that the injuries were the cause of death.[9] Under

1. *Harihar Prasad Singh* v. *Deo Narain Prasad*, AIR 1956 SC 305: 1956 SCJ 279: 1956 SCR 1.
2. Taylor, Evidence Section 861.
3. Woodroffe and Amir Ali on Law of Evidence, 18th Edn., Vol. I page 1368.
4. *Sha Mulchand and Co. Ltd.* v. *Jawahar Mills Ltd., Salem*, AIR 1953 SC 98: 1953 SCJ 68: 1953 SCR 351.
5. *Societe Beige De Bauque* v. *Girdhari Lal*, AIR 1940 PC 90: ILR (1940) Kar PC 208.
6. Woodroffe and Amir Ali on Law of Evidence, Vol. I Page 1371, 1372.
7. *Union of India* v. *S.R. Dhareshwar*, AIR 1971 SC 1753: (1971) 2 Lab LJ 117: (1972) 4 SCC 703.
8. *Special Land Acquistion Officer* v. *Pari Kashavlal Jamnadas*, (1987) 3 SCC 306.
9. Woodroffe and Amir Ali on Law of Evidence (Vol-I) – Page 1376.

section 206 of Cr.P.C., 1973, in case of petty offences, the counsel, if so authorized by the accused, can plead guilty on his behalf. Under section 294 of the Code, the accused or his counsel may admit the genuineness of a document whereupon it can become part of evidence. Letters written by accused are relevant against him.

14. When several persons are jointly interested in the subject-matter of a suit, the general rule is that admissions of any one of those persons are receivable against himself and the others, if they be all jointly suing or sued, provided the admission relates to the subject-matter in dispute and be made by him in his character as a person jointly interested with the party against whom the evidence is tendered.[1] (*Ibid* P. 1380). The representation of a fact made by one partner binds the firm if made in the ordinary course of business. So also an admission made by one co-sharer will bind the other co-sharers.

An admission made at one stage of a legal proceeding cannot be permitted to be withdrawn at a subsequent stage of the proceedings.[2] What is admitted by a party must be presumed to be true unless the contrary is shown, provided the admission is clear and unambiguous.[3] A court can base it's finding on the admission of parties.[4] An admission of a fact in written statement in a previous case, though not conclusive, in the absence of any reasonable and acceptable explanation, is good evidence.[5] But the tenor of the entire statement must be seen, and not merely a word here or there taken out of context.[6] A clear and categorical admission is the best piece of evidence against the person making the admission though it is open to him to show why it cannot be acted upon.[7] An admission by a co-owner regarding the right of the other co-owner can be relied upon.[8] An admission made by one defendant is not binding on a co-defendant unless interests of both in the suit are joint.[9] Where there was no privity of contract between two persons, an admission of one will not bind the other.[10]

15. **SECTION 19:** Purpose of this section is to add to the category of persons whose statements may amount to admissions. This Section is an exception to the rule that admissions of persons who are strangers to the suit are not relevant as against the parties.

Statement by a servant is relevant against the master, both for deciding whether he is a servant and also as regards his liability as such servant.

1. Woodroffe and Amir Ali on Law of Evidence (Vol-I) – Page 1380.
2. *State of Haryana* v. *M.P. Mohla*, (2007) 1 SCC 457.
3. *Nathoo Lal* v. *Durga Prasad*, AIR 1954 SC 355: 1955 SCR 51: 1954 SCJ 557: 1954 SCA 921.
4. *Mahendra Manilal Nanavati* v. *Sushila Mahendra Nanavati*, AIR 1965 SC 364: 66 Bom LR 681: 1965 Mah LJ 365.
5. *Sitaramacharya* v. *Gururajacharya*, AIR 1997 SC 806: 1997 AIR SCW 630: (1997) 2 SCC 548.
6. *Rachakonda Venkat Rao* v. *R. Satya Bai*, AIR 2003 SC 3322: 2003 AIR SCW 4717: (2003) 7 SCC 452.
7. *Delhi Transport Corporation* v. *Shyam Lal*, AIR 2004 SC 4271: 2004 AIR SCW 4711: (2004) 8 SCC 88: 2004 SCC (L&S) 1053.
8. *Raj Kumar* v. *Chiranji Lal Ram Chand, Ludhiana*, AIR 1996 SC 941: 1996 AIR SCW 349: (1996) 2 SCC 288.
9. *Ambika Prasad Thakur* v. *Ram Ekbal Rai*, (1966) 1 SCA 35: AIR 1966 SC 605: (1966) 1 SCR 758.
10. *K.S. Venkataraman and Co. (P) Ltd.* v. *State of Madras*, AIR 1966 SC 1089: 1966 (1) SCJ 515: (1966) 2 SCR 229.

Ordinarily statements by strangers to a case are not relevant as against any party to the suit.[1] This section enables reception of evidence of admissions of strangers in circumstances described in section 19. The admission of a stranger against his own interest, when it affects his position or liability and when that position or liability has to be proved as against a party to a case, is relevant against that party. This is explained by the illustration. *A* undertakes to collect rent for *B*. *B* sues *A* for not collecting rent due from *C* to *B*. *A* denies that rent was due from *C* to *B*. Any statement by C that he owed rent to *B* is an admission and is a fact relevant to be proved against *A*.

The word "statement" used in sections 17 to 21 is used in its ordinary sense, that is, "something said". Communication of the statement is not necessary.[2]

16. **SECTION 20:** Statement made by a "Referee" is relevant.[3]

Where there was an undertaking to be bound by special oath, if the oath is taken and statement is made, the statement would be deemed to be an admission.[4] This principle applies to criminal cases also.

According to the illustration, where the question is about the condition of a house sold by *A* to *B*, *A* told *B* – "Go and ask *C*, *C* knows all about it". *C*'s statement to *B* about the condition of the house is an admission of the referee from *A* and treated as an admission by *A* and thus relevant. The referring party is deemed to have approved of the view to be expressed by the person to whom reference is made.[3] It is sometimes said that such a reference is akin to arbitration.[5]

17. **SECTION 21:** According to this section, admission is relevant and may be proved against the maker or his representative in interest. Admission, however, cannot be proved in favour of the maker or his representative except in the following cases:

(a) Where the admission would attract section 32 if the maker was dead [Illustrations (b) and (c)];

(b) Where the admission relates to existence of any state of mind or body relevant or in issue, made at or about the time when such state of mind or body existed, and is accompanied by conduct rendering its falsehood improbable. [Illustrations (d) and (e)]. (*See* sections 14 and 15 also)

(c) If it is relevant otherwise as an admission.

The principle is that while an admission is always relevant against the maker, it is relevant in favour of the maker only in the specified exceptional cases.

The most acceptable ground of reception of admission is that a party's earlier statement, whether for or against his interest when made, may always be taken to be true as against himself. The weight of such statement is, of course, a different matter; this may vary with the circumstances, and will, no doubt, be

1. Stephen on Evidence, 3rd Edn. Vol. I Sec. 18
2. *Bhogilal Chunilal Pandya* v. *State of Bombay*, AIR 1959 SC 356: 1959 Supp (1) SCR 310: 1959 Cr LJ 389.
3. *Hirachand Kothari* v. *State of Rajasthan*, AIR 1985 SC 998: (1986) 1 Supreme 37: (1985) 2 Cur CC 632.
4. *K.M. Singh* v. *Secretary, Association of Indian Universities*, AIR 1992 SC 1356: (1992) 3 SCC 129: (1992) 2 SCR 630.
5. Stephen's Digest 7th Edn. Note to Article 19 at page 1789.

greater if against interest at the time, than the contrary.[1] Illustration (a) illustrates the true meaning of the section. Admission, for the purpose of section, means a previous admission or an admission outside the proceedings. Statement made several years subsequent to a transaction that it was benami would be relevant under this provision since it was a statement against the maker's interest.[2]

An admission by a party in a plaint signed and verified by him can be used against him in his other cases, though it is not conclusive and is capable of being shown as not true.[3] Court will not be able to determine the value of an admission without examining the circumstances in which it was made.[4] The admission must be free from any ambiguity.[5] Failure of defendants in the prior suit to deny an averment in the plaint may be taken as an admission of the claim therein for the purpose of that suit, but not for the purpose of a subsequent case. An admission can be relevant without confronting the maker with his earlier statement.[6]

18. Where a judicial confession was recorded without following the requirements of section 164 Cr.P.C., the test is to see whether the non-compliance was so vital as to cut at the root of the jurisdiction or so abhorrent to natural justice and cause serious prejudice to accused. When such is not the case, even a departure from the strict terms of section 164 may not necessarily render such a confession irrelevant.[7] Sections 24 to 26 apply only to confessions and not admissions. An admission of a gravely incriminating fact is not, of itself, a confession.[8] Letter written by accused to third parties concerning the offence is relevant against him.[9] FIS given by a person, who later became an accused, which does not contain confession and contains only certain admissions is relevant in the trial of the accused.[10] A statement given by the accused to the police about his version of the occurrence stating that he had acted in self-defence, is an exculpatory statement and not a confession.[8] An admission regarding existence of a motive is relevant.[11] Letter written by an accused to a third party concerning the offence under investigation is admissible against him.[12]

1. Phipson on Evidence, 15th Edn., p. 708-709.
2. *Bhim Singh* v. *Kan Singh*, (1980) 3 SCC 72: AIR 1980 SC 727.
3. *Basant Singh* v. *Janki Singh*, AIR 1967 SC 341: 1967 All LJ 1: (1967) 1 SLJ 476.
4. *Prem Ex-Serviceman Co-op. Tenant Farming Society Ltd.* v. *State of Haryana*, AIR 1974 SC 1121: (1974) 2 SCC 319: 1974 Pun LJ 272.
5. *Nagubai Ammal* v. *B. Shama Rao*, AIR 1956 SC 593: 1956 SCC 321: 1956 SCR 451: 1956 SCA 959: 1956 SCJ 655; *C. Koteshwara Rao* v. *C. Subbarao*, AIR 1971 SC 1542: (1970) 1 SCC 558: 1970 (2) SCJ 679.
6. *Biswanath Prasad* v. *Dwarka Prasad*, AIR 1974 SC 117: (1974) 1 SCC 78: (1974) 2 SCR 124.
7. *Willie (William) Slaney* v. *State of Madhya Pradesh*, AIR 1956 SC 116: 1956 Cr LJ 291: (1955) 2 SCR 1140 departing.
8. *Narayana Swami* v. *E.*, AIR 1939 PC 47: (1939) 40 Cr LJ 364: 180 IC 1: 1939 ALJ 298: 69 CLJ 273: 41 Bom LR 428: 1939 MWN 185: 43 CWN 473.
9. *Soni Vallabhadas Liladhar* v. *Assistant Collector of Customs, Jamnagar*, AIR 1965 SC 481: 1965 Cr LJ 490: (1965) 1 SCJ 208: 66 BLR 282.
10. *Faddi* v. *State of Madhya Pradesh*, AIR 1964 SC 1850: (1964) 6 SCR 312: (1964) 2 SCWR 140: 1964 MLJ 519: 1964 SCD 779: (1964) 2 Cr LJ 744.
11. *Belashwar Rai* alias *Nepali Master* v. *State of Bihar*, 1964 Cr LJ 564: (1963) 2 SCJ 128: (1963) 3 SCR 433 (SC).
12. *Sardul Singh Caveeshar* v. *State of Bombay*, AIR 1957 SC 747: 1957 SCJ 780: 1958 SCR 161.

Procedure in section 145 does not apply to admissions falling within the purview of sections 17 and 21. Previous statement which is in favour of a party seeking to use it does not attract these sections.[1] An admission is not conclusive unless it operates as estoppel.[2] Where the FIS was given by the accused, it cannot be used to contradict any witness and can be used only against the accused.[3] Where the admission is not clear, unequivocal and unambiguous, it cannot be used as an admission.[2] A self-serving statement cannot be used as an admission.[4]

Admissions cannot be proved by or on behalf of person who made it or by his representatives in interest, except when (a) it is of such a nature that, if the person making it were dead, it would be relevant as between third persons under section 32, (b) it consists of a statement of the existence of any state of mind or body made at or about the time when such state of mind or body existed and is accompanied by conduct rendering its falsehood improbable, and (c) it is relevant otherwise as an admission. Section 21(b) has to be read with section 14. A person's state of mind or feeling can be manifested to others only by countenance, attitude, gesture, by sounds or words, spoken or written. Evidence that he expressed that intention at that time, is direct evidence of the fact. Hence, his letters to his family or friends are the natural evidence of his intention. A fact which may not constitute an admission may be relevant under other sections such as sections 6, 8, 11(1), 11(2), 13(b), 14, and other sections.

When an accused in police custody found to have injuries on his person is produced before a doctor for treatment and he tells the doctor that he was injured by the victim in the case, such a statement is only an admission and not a confession and is relevant under section 21 read with section 17.[5] An admission made in a FIS given by an accused would be relevant under section 21 as long as the statement does not amount to a confession; it may be relevant as conduct under section 8.[6] If the FIS contains incriminating materials and it is difficult to sift the exculpatory materials therefrom, the whole of it must be excluded from evidence.[7]

Statement made in counterfoil of receipt to the tenant, being an admission in favour of the landlord, cannot be proved against the tenant (on the question whether tenancy was annual or monthly).

19. **SECTION 22:** Oral admission of contents of documents are not relevant except in the following cases:

---

1. *Mahendra Manilal Nanavati* v. *Sushila Mahendra Nanavati*, AIR 1965 SC 364: 66 Bom LR 681: 1965 Mah LJ 365; *Hukumdev Narian Yadav* v. *Lalit Narian Mishra*, AIR 1974 SC 480: (1974) 2 SCC 133: (1974) 3 SCR 31.
2. *Nagubai Ammal* v. *B. Shama Rao*, AIR 1956 SC 593: 1956 SCC 321: 1956 SCR 451: 1956 SCA 959: 1956 SCJ 655.
3. *Nagubai Ammal* v. *B. Shama Rao*, AIR 1956 SC 593: 1956 SCC 321: 1956 SCR 451: 1956 SCA 959: 1956 SCJ 655; *Krishnawati* v. *Hans Raj*, AIR 1974 SC 280: 1975 (1) SCJ 87: (1974) 2 SCR 524.
4. *Krishnawati* v. *Hans Raj*, AIR 1974 SC 280: 1975 (1) SCJ 87: (1974) 2 SCR 524.
5. *Kanda Padayachi* alias *Kandaswamy* v. *State of Tamil Nadu*, AIR 1972 SC 66: 1972 Cr LJ 11: 1971 CAR 453: (1971) 2 SCC 641: 1972 SCR 450: (1972) 1 SCJ 395.
6. *Nisar Ali* v. *State of Uttar Pradesh*, AIR 1957 SC 366: 1957 SCR 657: 1957 Cr LJ 550: 1957 All LJ 447.
7. *Aghnoo Nagesia* v. *State of Bihar*, AIR 1966 SC 119: 1966 Cr LJ 100: (1966) 1 SCJ 193: (1966) 1 SCR 134.

(a) Where the party relying on the admission shows that he is entitled to give secondary evidence of the contents of the document under the certain sections. (Sections 65, 66).

(b) Where the genuineness of the document is in question.

Contents of document, must normally be proved by production of the document (section 62, 64), unless secondary evidence of contents becomes admissible under section 65. Oral admissions of contents are merely secondary evidence (section 63(5)). Written admissions of such contents are relevant whether or not the document is produced (section 65(b)).

20. **SECTION 22A:** Oral admission as to contents of electronic records are not relevant, unless the genuineness of the electronic record produced is in question. This section was added by the Information Technology Act, 2000.

21. **SECTION 23:** No admission is relevant in civil cases, if it is made in two circumstances, namely (a) upon an express condition that evidence of it is not to be given, or (b) under circumstances from which the court can infer that parties agreed together that evidence of it should not be given (*i.e.*, implied condition). But no lawyer is exempt from giving evidence of any matter of which he may be compelled to give evidence under section 126.

This section is based on public policy and as a privilege of confidentiality. Public policy is served if parties in dispute can settle their differences without recourse to or continuation of litigation. But for the principle underlying this section parties may not talk frankly and with open mind which is necessary to promote a settlement. This section provides communication made "without prejudice". If parties were to be prejudiced later on by their efforts to compromise a dispute, settlement of dispute will become impossible. Negotiations conducted with a view to settlement should be deemed to be conducted without prejudice so that it can be inferred that parties agreed together that no evidence of it should be given. Parties often make admissions for the purpose of effecting a compromise to which it would be unfair to hold them if compromise falls through. An offer to accept a smaller amount as a result of compromise, cannot be treated as an admission.[1] It is open to a party to waive this privilege. The rule underlying section 23 does not apply to admissions made before an arbitrator.

SECTION 31: Admissions are not conclusive proof of the matters admitted but they may operate as estoppels under the provisions hereinafter contained (*i.e.*, sections 115 to 118 in Chapter VIII of the Evidence Act).

Ordinarily an admission is open to rebuttal, unless the principle of estoppel is attracted. Principle of estoppel applies if three conditions are satisfied, *i.e.*, (a) There was a representation, oral or in writing, by a person to another, (b) the other person must have acted upon the said representation taking the admission as true, and (c) he should suffer some prejudice by believing the representation or must have acted in detriment to his interest by reason of the representation.[2]

Admission is not conclusive proof of the facts admitted and may be explained or shown to be wrong; it may shift the burden of proof. Unless explained or

---

1. *Chandrika Prasada* v. *Bombay Baroda and Central India Ry. C.*, AIR 1935 PC 59: 39 Cal WN 552: 154 Ind Cas 945 (PC).
2. *Nagubai Ammal* v. *B. Shama Rao*, AIR 1956 SC 593: 1956 SCC 321: 1956 SCR 451: 1956 SCA 959: 1956 SCJ 655.

shown to be wrong, it is an efficacious proof of the fact admitted.[1] It is the best available evidence unless explained or shown to be wrong.[2] The circumstances under which an admission was made are sometimes important and may be such that the admission losses weight.[3]

When a fact is declared to be conclusively proved court cannot allow evidence to be given for disproving it. (Section 4). An admission of a fact, if it operates as an estoppel, is conclusive proof of the fact.

---

1 *Avadh Kishore Das* v. *Ram Gopal*, AIR 1979 SC 861: 1979 UJ (SC) 251: (1979) 4 SCC 790; *United India Insurance Co. Ltd.* v. *Samir Chandra Chaudhary*, (2005) 5 SCC 784.

2. *Narayan Bhagwantrao Gosavi Balajiwale* v. *Gopal Vinayak Gosavi*, AIR 1960 SC 100: (1960) 1 SCR 773: (1960) 2 SCA 153: 1960 SCJ 263.

3. *Kishorilal* v. *Chaltibai*, AIR 1959 SC 504: 1959 SCJ 560: 1959 Supp (1) SCR 698; *Daulat Singhji* v. *Khachar Mansur*, AIR 1936 PC 150: 162 IC 17: 60 B 634: 63 IA 248; *Nagubai Ammal* v. *B. Shama Rao*, AIR 1956 SC 593: 1956 SCC 321: 1956 SCR 451: 1956 SCA 959: 1956 SCJ 655.

CHAPTER 6

CONFESSION

(SECTIONS 24 TO 26 AND SECTIONS 28 TO 30)

1. No statement which contains self-exculpatory matter can amount to a confession. A confession must, in terms, admit the offence or at any rate, substantially all the ingredients which constitute the offence. An admission even of a gravely incriminating fact is not, of itself, a confession.[1] Confession may be oral or in writing. Communication of statement is unnecessary.[2] Each and every admission of an incriminating fact is a confession.[3] Every confession is an admission, but every admission is not a confession. A deliberate confession, found to be true and voluntary, is conclusive regarding guilt.

2. A confession also must be considered as a whole. But it is open to the court to believe a part and disbelieve another part in the light of the other evidence.[4] Inculpatory part can be accepted if the exculpatory part is found to be inherently improbable or where it is contradicted by other evidence or by the accused himself under Section 342 of old Code.[5] If confession covers two distinct and separate matters, rule against splitting does not apply.[6]

---

1. *Narayana Swami* v. *E.*, AIR 1939 PC 47: (1939) 40 Cr LJ 364: 180 IC 1: 1939 ALJ 298: 69 CLJ 273: 41 Bom LR 428: 1939 MWN 185: 43 CWN 473; *Palvinder Kaur* v. *State of Punjab*, AIR 1952 SC 354: 1952 SCJ 545: 1953 Cr LJ 154: 1953 SCR 94: ILR 1953 Punj 107; *Om Prakash* v. *State of Uttar Pradesh*, AIR 1960 SC 409; *Faddi* v. *State of Madhya Pradesh*, AIR 1964 SC 1850: (1964) 6 SCR 312: (1964) 2 SCWR 140: 1964 MLJ 519: 1964 SCD 779: (1964) 2 Cr LJ 744; *Aghnoo Nagesia* v. *State of Bihar*, AIR 1966 SC 119: 1966 Cr LJ 100: (1966) 1 SCJ 193: (1966) 1 SCR 134; *Kanda Padayachi* alias *Kandaswamy* v. *State of Tamil Nadu*, AIR 1972 SC 66: 1972 Cr LJ 11: 1971 CAR 453: (1971) 2 SCC 641: 1972 SCR 450: (1972) 1 SCJ 395; *Veera Ibrahim* v. *State of Maharashtra*, AIR 1976 SC 1167: (1976) 2 SCC 302: 1976 Cr LJ 860: 1976 SCC (Cri) 278; *Ayyub* v. *State of Uttar Pradesh*, AIR 2002 SC 1192: (2002) 3 SCC 510: 2002 AIR SCW 968; Stephen's Digest, 12th Edn., Article 22.
2. *Shiva Karam Payaswami Tewar* v. *State of Maharashtra*, AIR 2009 SC 1692: 2009 AIR SCW 1226: 2009 (1) Rec Cri R 877.
3. *Aghnoo Nagesia* v. *State of Bihar*, AIR 1966 SC 119: 1966 Cr LJ 100: (1966) 1 SCJ 193: (1966) 1 SCR 134.
4. *Hanumant Govind Nargundkar* v. *State of Madhya Pradesh*, AIR 1952 SC 343: 1952 SCR 1091: 1952 SCA 623; *Palvinder Kaur* v. *State of Punjab*, AIR 1952 SC 354: 1952 SCJ 545: 1953 Cr LJ 154: 1953 SCR 94: ILR 1953 Punj 107; *Aghnoo Nagesia* v. *State of Bihar*, AIR 1966 SC 119: 1966 Cr LJ 100: (1966) 1 SCJ 193: (1966) 1 SCR 134; *Bhagwan Singh* v. *State of Haryana*, AIR 1976 SC 1797: (1976) 3 SCC 101: 1976 SCC (Cri) 373: 1976 Cr LJ 1379; *Nishi Kant Jha* v. *State of Bihar*, AIR 1969 SC 422: (1969) 1 SCC 347: 1969 Cr LJ 671: (1969) 1 SCJ 844: 1969 ALJ 638.
5. (313 New Code); *Nishi Kant Jha* v. *State of Bihar*, AIR 1969 SC 422: (1969) 1 SCC 347: 1969 Cr LJ 671: (1969) 1 SCJ 844: 1969 ALJ 638; *Hira H. Advani* v. *State of Maharashtra*, AIR 1976 SC 44: (1970) 2 SCA 10; *Keshoram Bora* v. *State of Assam*, AIR 1978 SC 1096: 1978 (2) SCJ 502: (1978) 2 SCR 788.
6. *Karnail Singh* v. *State of Punjab*, AIR 1954 SC 204: 1954 SCJ 269: 1954 Cr LJ 580; *Keshoram Bora* v. *State of Assam*, AIR 1978 SC 1096: 1978 (2) SCJ 502: (1978) 2 SCR 788.

3. "Of course, confessions are also one species of admissions, namely, that species which consists of a direct acknowledgement of guilt in a criminal charge".[1] Confessions may be judicial or non-judicial; the latter are made either to investigating police officers or other persons. So far as criminal cases are concerned, confession is different from admission. Confession is an admission by an accused of his guilt for the offence charged against him, that is, all the essential ingredients of the offence; admission of an accused is admission of any incriminating fact falling short of a confession of guilt. Sections 24 to 27 deal with confessions while section 14 to 23 deal with admissions in relation to civil and criminal cases provided, in criminal cases, they fall short of confession.

4. Confessions which are excluded under sections 24 to 26 are not irrelevant under section 8. The reference in section 8 to "Conduct" must be read along with section 24 to 26; therefore a statement cannot be admitted under section 8 as evidence excluded by sections 24 to 26. Rationale underlying reception of admission or confession rests on the presumption that a rational human being will not make such statements prejudicial to his interest, except when urged by his inclination to speak the truth and prompting of his conscience.[2] A confession which is otherwise relevant, must have been made voluntarily and freely.

5. Confessions may be judicial or extra judicial. Judicial confessions are those made before a Magistrate or Court in the course of the legal proceedings after observing all statutory safeguards. Extrajudicial confessions are those made before anyone other than a magistrate or court; it may be made before a police officer or anyone else while the accused was in police custody or before a friend, relation or any official other than police. Such confessions are subject to provisions of sections 24 to 26. Courts have generally approached extrajudicial confessions with some degree of caution and described them as weak type of evidence. But there is no rule of law that extra-judicial confession cannot be relied upon without corroboration.[3] Where an accused pleads guilty before the trial court, it is open to the court to accept the plea and convict him or go on with the trial if the circumstances of the case so justify. A confession recorded by a Magistrate, after observing all requisite formalities and precautions can be acted upon by a court trying the accused.

6. Extra-judicial confessions (E.J.C.) may be oral or in writing; they are more often oral and made to a close relation, friend or colleague, neighbor, etc. The exact words of such a confession (E.J.C.) may not be available in every case because, in most cases, laymen to whom confession is made, do not note down the words as they are uttered by the accused. Therefore, generally speaking, only the substance of the confession will be available to the court. Thus, there is always the risk of a mistake arising from misapprehension or interestedness of the witness who speaks to the E.J.C., as also misuse of words, infirmity of memory of and misunderstanding by the witness. These are generally the reasons why E.J.C. is sometimes considered to be weak type of evidence, particularly if the witness had a strong motive for implicating the accused.[4] Yet E.J.C. may be

1. Wigmore on Eivdnec, Page 290.
2. Taylor's Treatise on Law of Evidence Vol I.
3. *Ram Singh* v. *State of Uttar Pradesh*, AIR 1967 SC 152: 1962 (2) SCJ 136: 1967 Cr LJ 9; *Pyara Singh* v. *State of Punjab*, AIR 1977 SC 2274: (1978) 1 SCR 597: (1977) 4 SCC 452; *Palanisamy* v. *State of Tamil Nadu*, AIR 1986 SC 593: 1986 Cr LJ 551: (1986) 1 SCC 693; *Shrishail Nageshi Pare* v. *State of Maharashtra*, AIR 1985 SC 866: (1985) 2 SCC 341: 1985 Cr LJ 1173.
4. *Mohd. Azad @ Samin* v. *State of West Bengal*, AIR 2009 SC 1307: 2009 AIR SCW 752: 2009 (1) Cal LT 57; *Keshav* v. *State of Maharashtra*, (2007) 13 SCC 284: AIR 2007 SC (Supp) 1150.

made in such circumstances so as to leave no legitimate suspicion as to its truth. It has to be accepted when the evidence is clear, consistent and convincing and requires no corroboration; this is particularly so where the witness to whom E.J.C., was said to have been made is a trustworthy witness. The value of evidence as to confession, as in other matters, depends on the veracity of the witness. Evidence can be acted upon if it proves E.J.C. satisfactorily.[1] There can be no initial presumption that E.J.C. is a weak type of evidence. It would depend on the nature of circumstances, the time when the confession was made and kind of person to whom the confession was made and his credibility.[2] Courts have sometimes found evidence of E.J.C. a weak piece of evidence, but there is no rule of law nor of prudence that it is in general not to be acted upon. If an E.J.C., is found reliable and trustworthy, the same can be relied upon and conviction founded thereon.[3] The value of evidence regarding E.J.C. would be just like that of any other evidence, depending on the veracity of the witness who speaks to it. It is for the court to judge all relevant factors.[4] The court has to consider the capacity of the witness to reproduce the exact words or the substance thereof, motive for the confession, whether the person to whom the confession was allegedly made is one in whom the accused was likely to have reposed confidence. Prudence may require the court to seek some corroboration of the E.J.C.[5] Words attributed to accused must be clear and unambiguous.[2] The court may consider if the witness had motive to implicate the accused falsely. Credibility depends on the nature of the circumstances, the time when the confession was made and the credibility of the witness (*Ibid*). Court may consider for what reason the accused confessed to the particular witness, what kind of relationship he had with the witness, whether the confession was consistent with other facts and circumstances and the motivation of the witness.[6] Court has to consider if it was natural conduct for the accused to confide in the particular witness or witnesses. Prosecution story which otherwise appears to be a false story affects the credibility of E.J.C.[7] So also where the E.J.C. is wholly inconsistent with the medical evidence. Some decisions have taken the view that the exact words of the confession must be reproduced in evidence.[8] Another

1. *Mulk Raj* v. *State of Uttar Pradesh*, 1959 Cr LJ 1219: AIR 1959 SC 902: 1960 All Cr R 37.
2. *Narayan Singh* v. *State of Madhya Pradesh*, (1985) 4 SCC 26: AIR 1985 SC 1678: 1985 Cr LJ 1862.
3. *State of Uttar Pradesh* v. *M.K. Anthony*, AIR 1985 SC 48: (1985) 1 SCC 505: 1985 Cr LJ 493: 1985 Cr LR (SC) 41; *Pyara Singh* v. *State of Punjab*, AIR 1977 SC 2274: (1978) 1 SCR 597: (1977) 4 SCC 452; *Jagta* v. *State of Haryana*, AIR 1974 SC 1545: (1975) 1 SCR 165: 1974 Cr LJ 1010; *State of Punjab* v. *Bhajan Singh*, AIR 1975 SC 258: (1975) 4 SCC 472: 1975 SCC (Cri) 584: 1975 Cr LJ 282: (1975) 1 SCR 747; *Madan Gopal Kakkad* v. *Naval Dubey*, (1992) 3 SCC 204: 1992 AIR SCW 1480: JT (1992) 3 SC 270: 1992 SCC (Cri) 598; *Gura Singh* v. *State of Rajasthan*, AIR 2001 SC 330: (2001) 2 SCC 205: 2001 SCC (Cri) 323: 2001 Cr LJ 487: 2000 AIR SCW 4439; *Ram Singh* v. *Sonia*, (2007) 3 SCC 1: AIR 2007 SC 1218: 2007 AIR SCW 1278.
4. *Mulk Raj* v. *State of Uttar Pradesh*, 1959 Cr LJ 1219: AIR 1959 SC 902: 1960 All Cr R 37; *Kulwinder Singh* v. *State of Punjab*, (2006) 12 SCC 538: AIR 2007 SC 2868: 2007 Cr LJ 4290.
5. *Gagan Kanojia* v. *State of Punjab*, (2006)13 SCC 516: (2006) 12 SCALE 479; *Sukhwant Singh* v. *State*, AIR 2003 SC 3362: 2003 AIR SCW 4776: 2003 Cr LJ 4974.
6. *Ram Chandra* v. *State of Uttar Pradesh*, AIR 1957 SC 381: 1957 Cr LJ 559; *Ratan Gond* v. *State of Bihar*, AIR 1959 SC 18: 1959 SCR 1336: 1959 Cr LJ 180: 1959 SCJ 222; *Thimma and Thimma Raju* v. *State of Mysore*, AIR 1971 SC 1871: 1970 SCC (Cr) 320: (1970) 2 SCC 105: 1971 Cr LJ 1314; *Rahim Beg* v. *State of Uttar Pradesh*, AIR 1973 SC 343: 1972 Cr LJ 1260: (1972) 3 SCC 75; *Keshav* v. *State of Maharashtra*, (2007) 13 SCC 284.
7. *Jagta* v. *State of Haryana*, AIR 1974 SC 1545: (1975) 1 SCR 165: 1974 Cr LJ 1010.
8. *Rahim Beg* v. *State of Uttar Pradesh*, AIR 1973 SC 343: 1972 Cr LJ 1260: (1972) 3 SCC 75.

view taken is that E.J.C. cannot be rejected if the witness gives only the substance of the words and not the exact words, since it is the substance which really matters.[1] Some decisions of the Supreme Court contain an observation to the effect that E.J.C. is a weak type of evidence.[2] There are a number of other cases where the Supreme Court acted on such confessions. Any decision can depend only on the facts and circumstances of each case and other factors referred to earlier. The ultimate test, based on the evidence, is whether the relevant evidence inspires confidence.[3] E.J.C. can be retracted at the time of the trial.

7. **Retracted Confession**: When a confession is made voluntarily and is also true, but is subsequently retracted by the accused, there is no legal bar in basing conviction on such retracted confession. However, rule of prudence requires that, to form the basis of conviction, the retracted confession should be corroborated by independent evidence as it is not safe to act upon such a confession which, though made before a magistrate, was retracted during the sessions trial. When at any stage after confession was recorded by a magistrate, accused denies having made it, it is treated as a retracted confession. An extra-judicial confession also can be retracted by denying the same during the trial.[4] Yet a retracted judicial confession can form the legal basis of conviction if the court is satisfied that it was true and voluntarily made.[5] Court, if so satisfied, can use a retracted confession in convicting the accused. Wherever corroboration is deemed necessary, it need not be in respect of each material particular; general corroboration of the important incidents mentioned in the confession is sufficient.[6] The court has to evaluate the evidence concerning the confession by looking at all aspects to satisfy itself that the confession was voluntary and true. If these two tests are satisfied and if there is no other reason not to act on the retracted confession, it can be believed.[7] General corroboration can serve to reassure the court.[8] The reason for making the confession and its' retraction must be weighed.

8. **SECTION 24**: Under this section, confession of the nature referred to therein is irrelevant, that is, such a confession cannot be allowed to be proved in the course of the trial. The section covers a confession which appears to the court to have been caused by an **inducement, threat** or **promise** having **reference to the charge** against the accused person and **proceeding** from a person in **authority** and having, in the **opinion** of the court, to give the accused **sufficient grounds**, which would **appear** to him to be **reasonable**, for **supposing** that by

1. *Heramba Brahma* v. *State of Assam*, AIR 1982 SC 1595: (1982) 3 SCC 351: 1983 SCC (Cri) 40.
2. *Madhab Roy* v. *State of West Bengal*, AIR 1975 SC 255: 1974 Cr LJ 1335: (1974) 4 SCC 548.
3. *Gura Singh* v. *State of Rajasthan*, AIR 2001 SC 330: (2001) 2 SCC 205: 2001 SCC (Cri) 323: 2001 Cr LJ 487: 2000 AIR SCW 4439; *Madan Gopal Kakkad* v. *Naval Dubey*, (1992) 3 SCC 204: 1992 AIR SCW 1480: JT (1992) 3 SC 270: 1992 SCC (Cri) 598; *Ram Singh* v. *Sonia*, (2007) 3 SCC 1: AIR 2007 SC 1218: 2007 AIR SCW 1278.
4. *Palanisamy* v. *State of Tamil Nadu*, AIR 1986 SC 593: 1986 Cr LJ 551: (1986) 1 SCC 693.
5. *Balbir Singh* v. *State of Punjab*, AIR 1957 SC 216: 1957 Cr LJ 481; *Kehar Singh* v. *State (Delhi Administration)*, (1988) 3 SCC 609: AIR 1988 SC 1883: JT 1988 (3) SC 191; *State of Uttar Pradesh* v. *M.K. Anthony*, AIR 1985 SC 48: (1985) 1 SCC 505: 1985 Cr LJ 493: 1985 Cr LR (SC) 41.
6. *Shrishail Nageshi Pare* v. *State of Maharashtra*, AIR 1985 SC 866: (1985) 2 SCC 341: 1985 Cr LJ 1173.
7. *Paramananda Pegu* v. *State of Assam*, AIR 1958 SC 66.
8. *Sabramania Goundan* v. *State of Madras*, AIR 1958 SC 66: 1958 SCR 428: 1958 Cr LJ 238: 1958 SCJ 321.

making it he would **gain** any **advantage** or avoid any **evil** of a **temporal nature** in reference to the proceedings against him.[1] This section is intended to protect the interest of the accused on ground of public policy and for administration of justice. It is abhorrent to notions of justice and fair play, and is also dangerous, to allow a person to be convicted on the strength of a confession unless it is made voluntarily and unless he knows that anything he says may be used against him; any attempt by a person in authority to make a person into making a confession, by any threat or coercion would at once invalid it, if the fear was still operating on his mind at the time he made the confession and if it would appear to him reasonable for supposing that by making it he would gain any advantage or avoid any evil of a temporal nature in reference to the proceedings against him.[2] Moral or religious exhortation is not covered by section 24. The section is based on public policy.[3]

9. **"Appears to the Court":** Use of the words "appears to the court" indicates that Section 24 does not require positive proof within the meaning of the definition of "proved" in section 3 of the Evidence Act, of improper inducement etc., to justify the rejection of the confession; a lesser degree of probability than contemplated by the definition of "proved" would be sufficient. It may "appear" to be so, even if the court might hesitate say it was proved. "Appears" means "Seems", which conveys a lesser degree of assurance than "preponderance of probability". Yet court's view cannot be based on mere surmise. A *prima-facie* opinion based on appreciation of evidence and circumstances could be adopted as the standard required to be satisfied. It is not possible to lay down a inflexible standard for guidance of courts; it is the court which has to decide whether if "appears" to be so.[4] A mere bald assertion by accused that he was so threatened or induced etc., cannot be accepted as probable without anything more, so as to so "appear" to the court.[5]

When the prosecution wants to rely on a purported confession as a relevant fact and substantive evidence, at the outset, it has to prove the voluntariness of the confession.[6] Accused is entitled to give evidence in support of his stand. The decision of the court at that stage is only as to it's relevancy or admissibility and not its weight. A judicial confession duly recorded by the Magistrate after following all requirements of law and caution and with the prescribed certificate appended to it may be presumed to be voluntary, subject to challenge based on section 24.[7] Of course such a presumption as stated earlier in favour of the prosecution is not available in the case of extra-judicial confession. If the accused does not challenge the voluntariness of the confession at the stage of evidence,

---

1. *Percy Rustomji Basta* v. *State of Maharashtra*, 1971 Cr LJ 933: AIR 1971 SC 1087: 1971 Cri Ap R 305 (SC): (1971) 1 SCC 847: 1971 SCC (Cri) 345; *Veera Ibrahim* v. *State of Maharashtra*, AIR 1976 SC 1167: (1976) 2 SCC 302: 1976 Cr LJ 860: 1976 SCC (Cri) 278.
2. *Aher Raja Khima* v. *State of Saurashtra*, AIR 1956 SC 217: (1955) 2 SCR 1285: 1956 Cr LJ 421: 1956 SCJ 24.
3. *Aghnoo Nagesia* v. *State of Bihar*, AIR 1966 SC 119: 1966 Cr LJ 100: (1966) 1 SCJ 193: (1966) 1 SCR 134.
4. *Pyare Lal Bhargava* v. *State of Rajasthan*, (1963) 2 Cr LJ 178: 1963 Supp (1) SCR 689: AIR 1963 SC 1094: 1963 All LJ 459.
5. *Hemraj Devilal* v. *State of Ajmer*, AIR 1954 SC 462: 1954 Cr LJ 1313: 1954 SCR 1133: 1954 SCJ 449.
6. *Ibrahim* v. *E.*, 23 IC 678: AIR 1914 PC 155: 15 Cr LJ 326: 18 CWN 705.
7. Law of Evidence by Woodroffe and Amir Ali, 18th Edn., Vol. 1, Page 1537.

the court can presume that it is voluntary, unless there are highly suspicious circumstances surrounding the confession or evidence in support of it.

10. **Inducement Threat or Promise:**—Confession becomes irrelevant or not provable if it appears to the Court that making of the confession was caused by inducement, threat or promise of the kind described in the section.[1] A mere assertion by the accused when questioned under section 313 of Cr.P.C. is not sufficient to attract the operation of section 24.[2] In a case where the BSF commandant, having failed to obtain confession from the accused (his subordinate) through another agency, himself succeeded in obtaining confessional statement, it was held that it could be inferred that there was some hope generated in the mind of the accused of receiving support of a person in authority.[3] Mere denial of the confession does not give rise to an inference that any coercion or inducement was practiced.[4] The burden of showing the applicability of the section is on the accused.[5] Prolonged custody of the accused immediately preceeding the making of a confession is sufficient to hold it to be involuntary unless such delay is properly explained.[6] If an accused had been administered oath by his departmental superior not empowered to administer oath before recording his confession, that would amount to concealed threat.[7] It is not necessary that the confession is made to the person in authority holding out the threat. Inducement may be express or implied.

11. **"Person in Authority"**: This expression is not defined in the Act. It must be understood in a wide sense. Generally speaking, he is one who is engaged in the investigation of the particular offence and his superiors or officers authorised by him. Any officer, for example, a Tahasildar, Panchayat President or Member, who has no interest in the investigation or prosecution is not a person in authority. In each case, whether the person in question is a person in authority is a question of fact.[8] The threat, inducement etc., must emanate from a person in authority over the accused. Where the law required a person summoned under section 108, Customs Act, 1962 to speak the truth, it was held that the threat did not emanate from a "person in authority" but from the statute itself.[9] Mere warning of prosecution for perjury if truth was not stated is not a threat falling under the scope of the section.[10] So also a warning to the

1. *Sevantilal* v. *State of Maharashtra,* AIR 1979 SC 705: (1979) 2 SCC 58: 1979 Cr LJ 645; *Pyare Lal Bhargava* v. *State of Rajasthan,* (1963) 2 Cr LJ 178: 1963 Supp (1) SCR 689: AIR 1963 SC 1094: 1963 All LJ 459.
2. *Ammini* v. *State of Kerala,* (1998) 2 SCC 301: AIR 1998 SC 260: 1997 AIR SCW 4231: 1998 Cr LJ 481: 1998 SCC (Cri) 618.
3. *Satbir Singh* v. *State of Punjab,* AIR 1977 SC 1294: (1977) 3 SCR 195: 1977 Cr LJ 985.
4. *Abdul Rajak Murtaja Dafedar* v. *State of Maharashtra,* (1969) 2 SCC 234: AIR 1970 SC 283: 1969 (2) SCJ 870: 1970 Cr LJ 373.
5. *Sevantilal* v. *State of Maharashtra,* AIR 1979 SC 705: (1979) 2 SCC 58: 1979 Cr LJ 645.
6. *Natha* v. *State of Uttar Pradesh,* 1956 Cr LJ 152: AIR 1956 SC 56; *Shivappa* v. *State of Karnataka,* AIR 1995 SC 980: AIR 1995 SCW 956.
7. *Brijbasi Lal Shrivastava* v. *State of Madhya Pradesh,* AIR 1979 SC 1080: (1979) 4 SCC 521: 1980 SCC (Cri) 116: 1979 Cr LJ 913.
8. *Pyare Lal Bhargava* v. *State of Rajasthan,* (1963) 2 Cr LJ 178: 1963 Supp (1) SCR 689: AIR 1963 SC 1094: 1963 All LJ 459.
9. *Percy Rustomji Basta* v. *State of Maharashtra,* 1971 Cr LJ 933: AIR 1971 SC 1087: 1971 Cri Ap R 305 (SC): (1971) 1 SCC 847: 1971 SCC (Cri) 345
10. *Veera Ibrahim* v. *State of Maharashtra,* AIR 1976 SC 1167: (1976) 2 SCC 302: 1976 Cr LJ 860: 1976 SCC (Cri) 278.

accused in departmental proceedings that if he did not disclose the truth the matter will be placed in the hands of police, is not a threat within the mischief of the section.[1] If a confession is made to a person in authority without any inducement etc., it does not fall within the mischief of section 24.[2]

12. **"Have reference to the charge":** The inducement, threat or promise must have reference to the charge against the accused person, which means, the charge of an offence in the court and made for the purpose of securing a confession from him in respect of the specific offence in the charge. An inducement etc. relating to some collateral matter unconnected with the specific charge will not attract section 24[3] though a different view has been taken in England.[4] The inducement need not be express; it can be implied from the conduct of the person in authority, declarations of the accused or circumstances of the case.[5] It need not be made directly to the prisoner; it is sufficient if it may be reasonably presumed to have come to his knowledge.[6]

13. **"An Accused Person":** Use of these words in the section does not mean than an accusation of an offence must necessarily have been in existence at the time of the making of the confession.[7] The section will apply even if the maker of the confession was charged subsequently. It is sufficient that criminal proceedings was, at the time, in prospect. The section would apply even if the confession was made before a report was made to the police. "Accused person" only signifies the person against whom evidence is sought to be lead in a criminal proceeding.[7] A customs officer conducting an enquiry under section 107 or 108 of Customs Act is not a police officer and person against whom the enquiry is conducted is not an "accused person" and a statement made by such a person in that enquiry is not a statement by "a person accused of any offence" and the statement is not hit by section 24 or 25.[8]

14. **Inducement etc. must have reference to the charge**: Inducement must have reference to the charge against the accused person in a criminal court. This condition implies that the prisoner's position with reference to the charge will be made better or worse, according as he does or does not confess. If the inducement does not relate to the charge in question but to some other charge, the section will not apply. The inducement should not relate to a collateral matter unconnected with the charge.[9] The advantage to be gained, in the mind of the accused, must be of a temporal nature and relatable to the charge.

15. **"Sufficient to give the accused grounds":** It must appear to the court that the inducement etc. must have been sufficient to give the accused person

---

1. *Kedar Nath* v. *State*, 1962 II Cr LJ 178 (SC).
2. *Soni Vallabhadas Liladhar* v. *Assistant Collector of Customs, Jamnagar*, AIR 1965 SC 481: 1965 Cr LJ 490: (1965) 1 SCJ 208: 66 BLR 282.
3. Taylor Evidence section 880.
4. Phipson Evidence, 13th Edition, Page 432, 433.
5. Phipson Evidence, P. 433.
6. Taylor Evidence, section 885.
7. *State of Uttar Pradesh* v. *Deoman Upadhyaya*, AIR 1960 SC 1125: (1961) 1 SCR 14: 1960 Cr LJ 1504: (1960) 2 SCA 371.
8. *Ramesh Chander Mehta* v. *State of West Bengal*, AIR 1970 SC 940: 1970 Cr LJ 863: (1969) 2 SCR 461; *Illias* v. *Collector of Customs, Madras*, AIR 1970 SC 1065: (1969) 2 SCR 613: 1970 Cr LJ 998 (SC); *Percy Rustomji Basta* v. *State of Maharashtra*, 1971 Cr LJ 933: AIR 1971 SC 1087: 1971 Cri Ap R 305 (SC): (1971) 1 SCC 847: 1971 SCC (Cri) 345.
9. Taylor Evidence, section 880.

grounds which would appear to him reasonable for "supposing ....". Thus it is seen, application of the section depends on the court's opinion about what could have been in the mind of the accused at the time he made the confession. Therefore, the actual words uttered accompanying the conduct of the person in authority may be judged to find what their effect might have been on the mind of the accused. Of course nothing much turns merely on the actual words used; in each case, whatever the words used may be, the court has to consider whether the words used and the attitude adopted by the person in authority were such as to convey to the mind of the accused the idea that it will be better for him to confess that he committed the crime or worse for him if he does not. A confession induced by a promise of pardon or of being made an approver is not relevant.

16. **SECTION 25:** No confession made to a Police Officer is relevant against the maker in a criminal trial.[1] Such a confession cannot proved in the trial of a criminal case. Statement made by an accused to the police in the course of investigation cannot be used for any purpose under section 162 of Cr.P.C. If the statement is a confession, it is rendered irrelevant under section 25 of the Evidence Act. This is because of the realization that powers of police are often misused for the purpose of extorting confession.[2] Section 25 does not bar proving a confession made by a prosecution witness in his capacity as an accused in another case, if it is relevant otherwise. The policy underlying this section is that any confession made to police unless in the presence of a Magistrate, is presumed to have been obtained under circumstances mentioned in section 24.[3] A confession made while accused was in custody but in the presence of a Magistrate who did not record it under section 164 Cr.P.C.[4] is not relevant.

The word "Police Officer' has not been defined in the Evidence Act. It is not restricted to S.H.O. But he must have some of the powers exercised by police, such as power of investigation and prosecution.[5] The term "Police Officer" should not be used in a strict technical sense, but in it's more comprehensive and popular meaning. It applies to every police officer and not merely to officers in a regular police force.[1] Where an officer was invested with powers of office-in-charge of a police station but did not have the power to submit a report under section 157 Criminal Procedure Code, it was held that he was not a police officer for the purpose of this section.[5]

17. **The following officers have been held to be not police officers:**

(1) IPS Officer working in a purely administrative post.[6]

(2) Officer of Railway Protection Force or Railway Property (Unlawful Possession) Act, 1966.[7]

---

1. *Narayana Rao* v. *State of Andhra Pradesh*, AIR 1957 SC 737: 1958 SCR 283: 1957 Cr LJ 1320.
2. I-Report of the Law Commission of India.
3. *Commissioner of Police* v. *Narender Singh*, (2006) 4 SCC 265: AIR 2006 SC 1800.
4. *Zwinglee Ariel* v. *State of Madhya Pradesh*, AIR 1954 SC 15: 1954 Cr LJ 230.
5. *Raj Kumar Karwal* v. *Union of India*, AIR 1991 SC 45: 1990 CAR 113: 1990 Cr LR 358: (1990) 1 SCALE 509: (1990) 2 Crimes 435: (1990) 2 SCC 409: (1990) 2 UJ 373: (1990) 48 ELT 496: 1991 Cr LJ 97.
6. *Seethamanian* v. *State of Kerala*, 1996 Cr LJ 308.
7. *Balakishan A. Devi Dayal* v. *State of Maharashtra*, AIR 1981 SC 379: 1980 Cr LJ 1424: (1980) 4 SCC 600.

(3) Central Reserve Officer of Central Reserve Police Force.[1]

(4) Constable of Rajasthan Armed Constabulary.[2]

(5) Sub-Divisional Officer.[3]

(6) Officer of the Security Force.[4]

(7) Prohibition Officer.[5]

(8) Food Inspector.[6]

(9) Forest Officer.[7]

(10) Officers under the Narcotic Drugs Act or FERA.[8]

18. **The following Officer have been held to be Police Officers:—**

(a) Officer under NDPS Act.[9]

(b) Customs Officer.[10]

(c) Reserve Police Officer under S.R.P.F. Act.[11]

(d) R.P.F. Police Officer.[12]

(e) Food Grains Inspector, Central Excise Officer under Central Excise and Salt Act.[13]

Excise officer having power of investigation and Police Patil are police officer.[14]

---

1. *Jagjitsingh Tannasingh* v. *State of Kutch*, 1956 Cr LJ 217: AIR 1956 Kutch 1.
2. *Ramesh Kumar* v. *State of Rajasthan*, 1999 (1) Raj Cri C 397: 1999 (1) Raj LR 554: 1999 Cr LJ 871 Raj.
3. *Haru* v. *State of Madhya Pradesh*, 1980 Cr LJ 762: 1979 MPLJ 616: 1979 Jab LJ 643.
4. *Darshan Lal* v. *State*, AIR 1975 SC 898: 1975 Cr LJ 774: (1975) 4 SCC 33.
5. *P.T. Vadivel Gounder (in re:)*, AIR 1952 Mad 299: 1952 WN Cr 5: 1952 Cr LJ 640: (1952) 1 MLJ 69.
6. *Badku Jyoti Savant* v. *State of Mysore*, AIR 1966 SC 1746: 1966 Cr LJ 1353: (1966) 3 SCR 698.
7. *Ramesh Chander Mehta* v. *State of West Bengal*, AIR 1970 SC 940: 1970 Cr LJ 863: (1969) 2 SCR 461.
8. *Kanhaiyalal* v. *Union of India*, AIR 2008 SC 1044: 2008 AIR SCW 627: (2008) 4 SCC 668 and Ibid 438.
9. *Raj Kumar Karwal* v. *Union of India*, AIR 1991 SC 45: 1990 CAR 113: 1990 Cr LR 358: (1990) 1 SCALE 509: (1990) 2 Crimes 435: (1990) 2 SCC 409: (1990) 2 UJ 373: (1990) 48 ELT 496: 1991 Cr LJ 97.
10. *Illias* v. *Collector of Customs, Madras*, AIR 1970 SC 1065: (1969) 2 SCR 613: 1970 Cr LJ 998 (SC); *Ramesh Chander Mehta* v. *State of West Bengal*, AIR 1970 SC 940: 1970 Cr LJ 863: (1969) 2 SCR 461; *Percy Rustomji Basta* v. *State of Maharashtra*, 1971 Cr LJ 933: AIR 1971 SC 1087: 1971 Cri Ap R 305 (SC): (1971) 1 SCC 847: 1971 SCC (Cri) 345; *Hira H. Advani* v. *State of Maharashtra*, (1969) 2 SCC 662: (1970) 1 SCR 821: AIR 1971 SC 44: 1971 Cr LJ 5 (SC): 1983 ELT 1413; *State of Punjab* v. *Barkat Ram*, AIR 1962 SC 276: 1962 Cr LJ 217: (1962) 3 SCR 338; *Soni Vallabhadas Liladhar* v. *Assistant Collector of Customs, Jamnagar*, AIR 1965 SC 481: 1965 Cr LJ 490: (1965) 1 SCJ 208: 66 BLR 282.
11. *State of Gujarat* v. *Anirudh Sing*, AIR 1997 SC 2780: (1997) 6 SCC 514: (1997) 3 Crimes 82: 1997 Cr LJ 3397 (SC).
12. *Balakishan A. Devi Dayal* v. *State of Maharashtra*, AIR 1981 SC 379: 1980 Cr LJ 1424: (1980) 4 SCC 600; *State of Uttar Pradesh* v. *Durga Prasad*, AIR 1974 SC 2136: (1975) 1 SCR 881: 1974 Cr LJ 1465.
13. *Badku Jyoti Savant* v. *State of Mysore*, AIR 1966 SC 1746: 1966 Cr LJ 1353: (1966) 3 SCR 698; *Raja Ram Jaiswal* v. *State of Bihar*, (1964) 2 SCR 752: 1964 Cr LJ 705: AIR 1964 SC 828.
14. *Ramaji Ramappa Malagi* v. *State of Mysore*, 1972 (II) Mys LJ 6

This section refers to a person accused of an offence which means the same thing as "accused" occurring in section 24. The accused means the person prosecuted in a criminal case, though at the time he made the confession there was no formal accusation against him. A letter containing a confession and addressed to a police officer is not covered by section 25.[1]

Confession made to a private person in the presence of a police officer is also not relevant.[2]

The confession is barred for all purposes. It may be used in favour of the accused or co-accused in connection with conviction or sentence.[3] It can be used to impeach the credit of the maker who is examined in another criminal case. It can be used to discredit a subsequent confession made to a Magistrate.

Section 25 is not qualified by section 26.

For the ban to be effective, the maker need not have been accused of the offence at the time of the confession.[4] He need not have been in custody.

A confessional First Information Statement (FIS) by accused is also barred.[5] FIS which does not contain any confession, but contains admission of facts having a bearing on the question involved in the case is relevant.[6] The fact of his giving first information is relevant under section 8. Severability test has been discarded in *Aghnoo Nagesia* v. *State of Bihar*.[7] In a later decision[8] it was stated that inculpatory part has to be excluded.

19. **SECTION 26:** Confession made by any person while in the custody of a police officer is not relevant, unless it is made in the immediate presence of a Magistrate exercising powers of Magistrate under the Code. This bar applies even if the confession is not made to a police officer but to a private individual.[9] Section 26 does not control section 25.[10] Object of this section is to prevent the abuse of their powers by the police. Section 26 interdicts confession made to anyone when the person making the confession is in police custody. The policy underlying sections 25 and 26 is to make it a substantive rule of law that confession wherever and whenever made to the police or while in the custody of police shall be presumed to have been obtained under circumstances mentioned in section 24 and hence irrelevant except to the extent provided in

1. *Sitaram* v. *Uttar Pradesh*, AIR 1966 SC 1906: (1967) 1 SCJ 809: 1966 Cr LJ 1519.
2. *Bhulakiram Koiri* v. *State*, 1970 Cr LJ 403: 73 Cal WN 467: ILR (1969) 1 Cal 39.
3. *Lal Khan* v. R., AIR 1948 Lah 43: 48 Cr LJ 977; *Walli Mohammad* v. *King*, AIR 1949 PC 103: 1949 All LJ 154:1949 Cr LJ 340.
4. *State of Uttar Pradesh* v. *Deoman Upadhyaya*, AIR 1960 SC 1125: (1961) 1 SCR 14: 1960 Cr LJ 1504: (1960) 2 SCA 371.
5. AIR 1966 SC 119: 1966 Cr LJ 100: (1966) 1 SCJ 193: (1966) 1 SCR 134; *Khatri Hemraj Amulakh* v. *State of Gujarat*, AIR 1972 SC 922: 1972 Cr LJ 626: 1972 2 SCJ 299.
6. *Faddi* v. *State of Madhya Pradesh*, AIR 1964 SC 1850: (1964) 6 SCR 312: (1964) 2 SCWR 140: 1964 MLJ 519: 1964 SCD 779: (1964) 2 Cr LJ 744; *Dal Singh* v. *E.*, AIR 1917 PC 25: 44 IA 137: 44 C 876: 39 IC 311: 18 Cr LJ 471: 12 WR (PC) 32.
7. *Aghnoo Nagesia* v. *State of Bihar*, AIR 1966 SC 119: 1966 Cr LJ 100: (1966) 1 SCJ 193: (1966) 1 SCR 134.
8. *State of Karnataka* v. *Yarappa Reddy*, AIR 2000 SC 185: (1999) 8 SCC 715: 2000 Cr LJ 400.
9. *Dhanjay Chatterjee* v. *State of West Bengal*, JT 1994 (1) SC 33: 1994 SCC (Cri) 358: (1994) 2 SCC 220.
10. *Udai Bhan* v. *State of Uttar Pradesh*, AIR 1962 SC 1116: 1962 Cr LJ 251: ILR (1962) 2 All 522: 1962 Supp (2) SCR 830.

section 27.[1] Section 26 bars confessions made by persons in police custody unless it is made to a magistrate.[2] Confession made to a doctor (before whom the accused was produced by police), fellow-prisoner etc., is covered by section 26.[3] An admission made by accused to a doctor or other persons is not barred by this section.[4] A statement by an accused in police custody to a doctor that his injuries were caused by the victim is only an admission.[4]

"Custody" does not mean formal custody and includes, some sort of surveillance or restriction.[5] Such custody need not be legal.[6] Bar will apply even if he was in custody for some other offence.[7] Formal arrest need not have been made.[8] There may be custody without arrest.[9] This section applies to a confession made by a person who is in surveillance of the police during which his movements are restricted.[10] Custody does not mean a person being in actual custody. It means control of a person's movements. A formal arrest is not necessary.

When a person not in custody approaches a police officer and offers information leading to discovery, he may be regarded as being in custody for the purpose of section 27.[11] Custody and arrest are not synonymous terms. In every arrest, there is custody but not *vice versa*. Custody may amount to an arrest in certain cases, but not in all cases.[12] Presence of the Magistrate secures the free and voluntary nature of the confession and uncontrolled by any fear of police.[13] This section is based on the principle that custodial interrogation is inherently coercive.[14]

The underlying principle is that the custody renders the confession involuntary. The reason is not because the law presumes the confession to be

1. *Commissioner of Police* v. *Narender Singh*, (2006) 4 SCC 265: AIR 2006 SC 1800.
2. *Udai Bhan* v. *State of Uttar Pradesh*, AIR 1962 SC 1116: 1962 Cr LJ 251: ILR (1962) 2 All 522: 1962 Supp (2) SCR 830.
3. *Narayana Swami* v. *E.*, AIR 1939 PC 47: (1939) 40 Cr LJ 364: 180 IC 1: 1939 ALJ 298: 69 CLJ 273: 41 Bom LR 428: 1939 MWN 185: 43 CWN 473; *Emperor* v. *Mallangowda Bin Parwatgowda*, AIR 1917 Bom 130: 19 Bom LR 683: 18 Cr LJ 981.
4. *Kanda Padayachi* alias *Kandaswamy* v. *State of Tamil Nadu*, AIR 1972 SC 66: 1972 Cr LJ 11: 1971 CAR 453: (1971) 2 SCC 641: 1972 SCR 450: (1972) 1 SCJ 395.
5. *Maharani* v. *E.*, AIR 1948 All 7: 1947 All WR HC 273: 1947 ALJ 265: 48 Cr LJ 939, *Ram Singh* v. *State*, AIR 1959 All 518: 1958 All LJ 660: 1959 Cr LJ 940; *Paramhansa Jadab* v. *State*, AIR 1964 Ori 144: (1964) 1 Cr LJ 680: 31 Cut LT 17, *Mihir Adhikary* v. *State*, 1983 Cal WN 723: 1983 (2) Crimes 499: 1983 Cr LJ 1559 Cal.
6. *Emperor* v. *Mt. Jagia*, AIR 1938 Pat 308: 39 Cr LJ 428.
7. *Kamakshi Naidu (in re:)*, AIR 1943 Mad 89: 1942 Mad WN 750: 44 Cr LJ 304; *Public Prosecutor* v. *Kandikatla Nagabhushanam* alias *Bhushanam*, AIR 1943 Mad 661.
8. *Maharani* v. *E.*, AIR 1948 All 7: 1947 All WR HC 273: 1947 ALJ 265: 48 Cr LJ 939.
9. *Gurdial Singh* v. *Emperor*, AIR 1932 Lah 609: 33 Cr LJ 756; *Mannem Edukondalu (in re:)*, AIR 1957 AP 729: 1957 Cr LJ 1086.
10. *Jacob George (Dr)* v. *State of Kerala*, 1994 Cr LJ 3851: JT 1994 (3) SC 225: 1994 AIR SCW 2282 (SC).
11. *State of Uttar Pradesh* v. *Deoman Upadhyaya*, AIR 1960 SC 1125: (1961) 1 SCR 14: 1960 Cr LJ 1504: (1960) 2 SCA 371; *See* also *State of Karnataka* v. *David Razario*, (2002) 7 SCC 728: AIR 2002 SC 3272: 2002 Cr LJ 4127 and *Bodhraj* v. *State of Jammu and Kashmir*, (2002) 8 SCC 45: AIR 2002 SC 3164: 2002 AIR SCW 3655: 2002 Cr LJ 4664.
12. *Vinod Kumar Arora* v. *Administrator, Union Territory of Delhi*, 1984 Cr LJ 1344: 1984 (26) DLT 275: 1984 (2) Rec Cri R 309.
13. *Ram Singh* v. *Sonia*, (2007) 3 SCC 1: AIR 2007 SC 1218: 2007 AIR SCW 1278.
14. *Nandini Satpathy* v. *P.L. Dani*, AIR 1978 SC 1025: 1978 Cr LJ 968: (1978) 2 SCC 424.

untrue, but having regard to the tainted nature of the source of this confession, law prohibits it from being received in evidence.[1] Once the accused is arrested by a police officer and in his custody, the mere fact that, for some purpose the officer is temporarily absent and leaves the accused in charge of a private individual, does not terminate police custody and accused is deemed to continue in police custody.[2] Jail custody is still police custody.[3] Prosecution has always the duty of showing that any confession is voluntary.[4] Mere presence of a Magistrate is not sufficient. This section saves confessions recorded by Magistrate under section 164 Criminal Procedure Code.[5] Section 26 saves confession made in the immediate presence of a Magistrate; it is not required to be made to a Magistrate.

20. **SECTION 28**: If a confession as is referred to in section 24 is made after the impression caused by any such inducement, threat or promise has, in the opinion of the court, been fully removed, it is relevant. In other words, the section over comes section 24. The question is,[6] was the inducement (contemplated in section 24) brought to an end? If originally there was a statement (confession) made under threat or inducement, and if the threat, inducement still persists when the second confession is made, the latter will be inadmissible; only where during the time which elapses between the making of the two statements, the circumstances and the giving of any caution are such that, it can be said that the original threat or inducement has been dissipated will the second statement (confession) be admitted is being voluntary.[7]

The effect of threat, inducement or promise must have fully or thoroughly or completely obliterated. Since there is a presumption of continuance of a state [on the analogy of illustration (d) to section 114] prosecution has to prove that the impression caused by inducement, threat was fully removed when the accused made the second confession.[8]

21. **SECTION 29**: A confession otherwise relevant will not be irrelevant on account of promise of secrecy or inconsequence of deception practiced on the accused or when he was drunk or because it was made in response to questions he need not have answered or because he was not warned that he was not bound to make such confession and that it might be used against him. The confession attracting this section must be a confession not attracting sections 24 to 26. "Such a confession" means confession not referred to in the preceding Sections and is admissible.[9]

The non-invalidating origins of a confession under this section are (a) promise of secrecy, (b) deception, (c) drunkenness (d) absence of warning and

1. *State of Uttar Pradesh* v. *Deoman Upadhyaya*, AIR 1960 SC 1125: (1961) 1 SCR 14: 1960 Cr LJ 1504: (1960) 2 SCA 371.
2. *Emperor* v. *Mt. Jagia*, AIR 1938 Pat 308: 39 Cr LJ 428.
3. *Rambharose* v. *E.*, AIR 1944 Nag 105: ILR 1944 Nag 274 (FB).
4. *Natha* v. *State of Uttar Pradesh*, 1956 Cr LJ 152: AIR 1956 SC 56.
5. *Zwinglee Ariel* v. *State of Madhya Pradesh*, AIR 1954 SC 15: 1954 Cr LJ 230; *Surjan* v. *State of Rajasthan*, AIR 1956 SC 425.
6. Wigmore on Evidence (13th Edition, Section 853 to 855).
7. Halsbury's Laws of England (4th Edition, Vol. 71, Page 234)
8. *Shobha Param Kachhi* v. *State of Madhya Pradesh*, AIR 1959 MP 125: 1958 MPLJ 752: 1959 Cr LJ 476.
9. *Rangappa Hanamappa* v. *State*, AIR 1954 Bom 285: 1954 Cr LJ 887: ILR 1954 Bom 484.

(e) responses be to questions he need not have answered (f) absence of warning that he was not bound to make such confession. A confession which is otherwise relevant does not become irrelevant on account of any one of the situations referred to above.

Section 164(2) of the Code does not override section 29. Failure to comply with section 164 of the Code will not render a confession inadmissible. Relevancy and admissibility have to be decided as per the provisions of Evidence Act. However, strict compliance with section 164 of Code affords, in a large measure, the guarantee that the confession was voluntary.[1]

22. **SECTION 30**: It is said that self-implication by one accused affords some measure of guarantee of truth for the truth of his accusation against the other.[2] The guarantee is a weak one. Such a confession is weaker than the evidence of an approver. It is not tested by cross-examination. Under section 30, confession of a co-accused can only be "taken into consideration". Clearly there must be other evidence.[3] Confession of co-accused can only reassure the court in support of its conclusion deducible from other evidence.[4] Where the other evidence is unsatisfactory, the confession of a co-accused can be of no use. It cannot be used as substantive evidence.[5] This is so, though the confession may amount to evidence in a general way. Where the other evidence against the co-accused is sufficient, if believed, to support his conviction, confession of the other accused may be thrown into the scale as an additional reason for believing such evidence. There may be cases where the other evidence may be sufficient but the court may not be prepared to act on it as it stands. In such an event, court may call in aid the confession of co-accused and use it to lend assurance to the other evidence.[6] It is strictly not "evidence" within the scope of section 3.[7] It can be used only for corroboration.[8] Acquittal of one accused would not render his confession inadmissible if it corroborated circumstantial evidence against other accused.

---

1. *Dagdu* v. *State of Maharashtra*, AIR 1977 SC 1579: 1977 Cr LJ 1206: 1977 SCC (Cri) 421: (1977) 3 SCC 68.
2. *Khuban* v. *Emperor*, AIR 1930 All 29: 31 Cr LJ 26; *Hefajuddin Talukdar* v. *Nabi Nasya*, AIR 1928 Cal 416 (2).
3. *Sidharth* v. *State of Bihar*, (2005) 12 SCC 545: AIR 2005 SC 4352: 2005 Cr LJ 4499: 2005 AIR SCW 5010.
4. *Kashmira Singh* v. *State of Madhya Pradesh*, AIR 1952 SC 159: 1952 SCR 526: 1952 SCJ 201: 1952 Cr LJ 839; *Govt. of NCT of Delhi* v. *Jaspal Singh*, (2003) 10 SCC 586: JT 2003 (7) SC 302; *Mohd. Khalid* v. *State of West Bengal*, (2002) 7 SCC 334: JT 2002 (6) SC 486; *Haroon Haji Abdulla* v. *State of Maharashtra*, 70 Bom LR 540: 1968 Cr LJ 1017: AIR 1968 SC 832: (1968) 2 SCR 641: (1968) 1 SCWR 243: (1968) 2 SCJ 534; *Haricharan Kurmi* v. *State of Bihar*, AIR 1964 SC 1184: (1964) 2 Cr LJ 344: (1964) 6 SCR 623: (1964) 1 SCWR 399: 1964 (2) SCJ 454.
5. *Haricharan Kurmi* v. *State of Bihar*, AIR 1964 SC 1184: (1964) 2 Cr LJ 344: (1964) 6 SCR 623: (1964) 1 SCWR 399: 1964 (2) SCJ 454; *Param Hans Yadav and Sadanand Tripathi* v. *State of Bihar*, AIR 1987 SC 955: 1987 Cr LJ 789: (1987) 2 SCC 197; *Ram Chandra* v. *State of Uttar Pradesh*, AIR 1957 SC 381: 1957 Cr LJ 559; *Kalpnath Rai* v. *State (through CBI)*, 1997 AIR SCW 4166: (1997) 8 SCC 732: 1998 Cr LJ 369: AIR 1998 SC 201; *State of Tamil Nadu through Superintendent of Police CBI/SIT* v. *Nalini*, 1999 AIR SCW 1889: (1999) 5 SCC 253: 1999 Cr LJ 3124: AIR 1999 SC 2640: 1999 SCC (Cri) 691.
6. *Kashmira Singh* v. *State of Madhya Pradesh*, AIR 1952 SC 159: 1952 SCR 526: 1952 SCJ 201: 1952 Cr LJ 839; *Haricharan Kurmi* v. *State of Bihar*, AIR 1964 SC 1184: (1964) 2 Cr LJ 344: (1964) 6 SCR 623: (1964) 1 SCWR 399: 1964 (2) SCJ 454; *Shantilal Rameshwar* v. *State of Rajasthan*, AIR 1976 SC 739.
7. *Mohan Singh Balwant Singh* v. *State*, AIR 1965 Punjab 291: (1965) 2 Cr LJ 127: 66 Pun LR 1230.
8. *Sasi* v. *State of Kerala*, (2000) 10 SCC 360.

One pre-condition of this section is that in order that confession of one accused implicating another accused is treated as relevant, the confessing accused must implicate himself substantially, at-least to the same extent as he implicates the other accused. The section should be construed strictly.[1]

The other precondition is that confessing accused and the other accused must be tried jointly. If the confessing accused had been discharged initially, there is no joint trial and this section is not attracted.[2] So also where the confessing accused pleads guilty and is convicted and trial proceeds only against the other accused or where he died before trial. Both accused must be tried for the same offence. According to the explanation to the section, "offence" includes the abetment of or attempt to commit the offence. An accomplice is examined and cross-examined in court; his evidence is substantive evidence unlike the confession (a previous statement) of a co-accused which is not "evidence" but a material which court can be "take into consideration". The confession has to be "proved" in court. A retracted confession of one accused can be taken into consideration against his co-accused though it has lesser value.[3]

---

1. *Balbir Singh* v. *State of Punjab*, AIR 1957 SC 216: 1957 Cr LJ 481.
2. *Suresh Budharmal Kalani* alias *Pappu Kalani* v. *State of Maharashtra*, AIR 1998 SC 3258: 1998 SCC (Cri) 1625: (1998) 7 SCC 337: 1998 Cr LJ 4592.
3. *Haroon Haji Abdulla* v. *State of Maharashtra*, 70 Bom LR 540: 1968 Cr LJ 1017: AIR 1968 SC 832: (1968) 2 SCR 641: (1968) 1 SCWR 243: (1968) 2 SCJ 534; *Ram Parkash* v. *State of Punjab*, AIR 1959 SC 1: 1959 SCJ 181: 1959 SCR 1219.

CHAPTER 7

DISCOVERY (SECTION 27)

1. **SECTION 27:** Where any fact is disposed to as discovered in consequence of information received from a person accused of any offence in the custody of a police officer, so much of such information, whether it amounts to a confession or not, as relates distinctly to the fact thereby discovered may be proved. It is the connection of the fact discovered with the crime and the accused which renders its discovery relevant and this renders relevant the information leading to the discovery of the relevant fact.[1] Discovery of a relevant fact must be the consequence and information must be cause of the discovery.

2. Reason for not admitting confession under sections 24 to 26 is the danger of admitting false confession. But this danger disappears when the truth of the confession is guaranteed by the discovery of any relevant fact in consequence of information contained in the confession. It is this guarantee which is the reason for enacting section 27. The fact discovered shows that part of the confession is true and perhaps voluntary.[2] Extent of the information admissible depends on the exact nature of the fact discovered. The "fact discovered" includes the place from which object is produced and the knowledge of the accused as to this and the information given must relate distinctly to this fact. The part of the statement leading to discovery is admissible, whether are not it amounts to confession.[3] Interrogation need not be in the presence of any witness. Hence witnesses need not hear the statement being made.[4] The court has to be cautious that no effort is made by the prosecution to make out a statement of accused with a simple case of recovery as a case of discovery of fact in order to attract the section.[5]

3. Validity of the section as not violating articles 14 and 20(3) of the Constitution has been upheld several cases.[6] If the information was extorted by

1. *Basanti* v. *State of Himachal Pradesh*, AIR 1987 SC 1572: 1987 Cr LJ 1869: (1987) 3 SCC 227; *Anter Singh* v. *State of Rajasthan*, (2004) 10 SCC 657: AIR 2004 SC 2865: 2004 AIR SCW 743.
2. *Puliguri Kotayya* v. *Emperor*, AIR 1947 PC 67: (1947) 1 MLJ 219: 51 CWN 474: 60 MLW 258: 230 IC 135: 1947 ALJ 355: 49 BLR 508: (1946-47) 74 1A 65: 48 Cr LJ 533; *Ram Kishan* v. *State of Bombay*, 1955 Cr LJ 196 (208): AIR 1955 SC 104: 1955 SCR 903; *State of Rajasthan* v. *Bhup Singh*, (1997) 10 SCC 675: 1997 SCC (Cri) 1032: JT 1997 (1) SC 479; *State of Karnataka* v. *David Razario*, (2002) 7 SCC 728: AIR 2002 SC 3272: 2002 Cr LJ 4127; *Bodhraj* v. *State of Jammu and Kashmir*, (2002) 8 SCC 45: AIR 2002 SC 3164: 2002 AIR SCW 3655: 2002 Cr LJ 4664.
3. *K. Chinnaswamy Reddy* v. *State of Andhra Pradesh*, (1963) 1 Cr LJ 8: AIR 1962 SC 1788: (1963) 3 SCR 412.
4. *State of Himachal Pradesh* v. *Jeet Singh*, AIR 1999 SC 1293: 1999 AIR SCW 982: 1999 Cr LJ 2025: (1999) 4 SCC 370.
5. *Geejaganda Somaiah* v. *State of Karnataka*, AIR 2007 SC 1355: 2007 Cr LJ 1792: 2007 AIR SCW 1681.
6. *M.P. Sharma* v. *Satish Chandra*, AIR 1954 SC 300: 1954 SCR 1077: 1954 Cr LJ 865; *State of Uttar Pradesh* v. *Deoman Upadhyaya*, AIR 1960 SC 1125: (1961) 1 SCR 14: 1960 Cr LJ 1504: (1960) 2 SCA 371; *R.K. Dalmia* v. *Delhi Administration*, AIR 1962 SC 1821: (1962) 2 Cr LJ 805: (1963) 1 SCR 253; *State of Bombay* v. *Kathi Kalu Oghad*, AIR 1961 SC 1808: (1962) 3 SCR 10: (1961) 2 Cr LJ 856: 64 Bom LR 240; *Mohammed Dastagir* v. *State of Madras*, AIR 1960 SC 756: 1960 Cr LJ 1159: (1960) 3 SCR 116; *State of Uttar Pradesh* v. *Deoman Upadhyaya*, AIR 1960 SC 1125: (1961) 1 SCR 14: 1960 Cr LJ 1504: (1960) 2 SCA 371.

duress, the evidence of discovery would be hit by article 20(3).[1] Mere handcuffing does not amount to compulsion.[2]

4. That the place of recovery is open or accessible to all is not a criterion. Test is whether the place was ordinarily visible to others. There can be concealment in open place accessible to all.[3]

5. Sections 161 and 162 of the Code do not affect section 27. What is excluded under section 162 of the Code is the statement made to a police officer in the course of investigation and not the evidence relating to the conduct of an accused person (not amounting to a statement) when confronted by a police officer. Evidence of the circumstance that an accused person led a police officer and pointed out the place where stolen articles or weapons were hidden, would be admissible as conduct under section 8, irrespective of any statement by the accused contemporariously with or antecedent to such conduct which falls within the purview of section 27.[4] The officer who received the information and the officer who recovered the article need not be the same.

6. It has been held that Section 27 is a proviso to section 26.[5] It has been held in other cases that section 27 is an exception to sections 25 and 26.[6] In order that section 27 should apply, five conditions must be satisfied, *viz.*, (a) the person must be accused of an offence; (b) he must be in the custody or deemed to be in the custody of a police officer; (c) a relevant fact must have been discovered; (d) the discovery must have been in consequence of information received from the accused, and (e) information must be deposed to in Court.[7] If these conditions are satisfied, so much of such information as distinctly relates to the fact thereby discovered is relevant. It does not matter whether information amounts to confession or not.[8] Discovery furnishes guarantee to the truth of the information and hence can be safely allowed to be given in evidence. Extent of the information must depend on the exact nature of the fact discovered. It is

1. *In Re: Madugula Jermiah*, AIR 1957 AP 611: 1957 Cr LJ 1071: ILR 1956 Andh 173; *State of Bombay* v. *Premdas Sukritdas Gadhewal Koshti*, AIR 1960 Bom 483: 1960 Cr LJ 1426: ILR 1961 Bom 529; *Ahmedmiyan Bhaimiya* v. *State*, AIR 1963 Guj 159: (1963) 2 Cr LJ 16: (1963) 4 Guj LR 543; *Dasan* v. *State of Kerala*, 1987 Cr LJ 180: 1986 Ker LJ 603: 1986 Ker LT 598.
2. *Dasan* v. *State of Kerala*, 1987 Cr LJ 180: 1986 Ker LJ 603: 1986 Ker LT 598.
3. *State of Himachal Pradesh* v. *Jeet Singh*, AIR 1999 SC 1293: 1999 AIR SCW 982: 1999 Cr LJ 2025: (1999) 4 SCC 370.
4. *Prakash Chand* v. *State (Delhi Administration)*, AIR 1979 SC 400: (1979) 3 SCC 90: 1979 Cr LJ 329: 1979 MLJ (Cri) 419; *Bahadul* v. *State of Orissa*, AIR 1979 SC 1262: (1979) 4 SCC 346: 1979 Cr LJ 1075; *Himachal Pradesh Administration* v. *Om Prakash*, AIR 1972 SC 975: (1972) 1 SCC 249: 1972 SCC (Cri) 88: (1972) 1 SCJ 691
5. *Puliguri Kotayya* v. *Emperor*, AIR 1947 PC 67: (1947) 1 MLJ 219: 51 CWN 474: 60 MLW 258: 230 IC 135: 1947 ALJ 355: 49 BLR 508: (1946-47) 74 1A 65: 48 Cr LJ 533
6. *Pershadi Lal* v. *State of Uttar Pradesh*, 1957 Cr LJ 328: AIR 1957 SC 211; *Ram Kishan* v. *State of Bombay*, 1955 Cr LJ 196 (208): AIR 1955 SC 104: 1955 SCR 903; *K. Chinnaswamy Reddy* v. *State of Andhra Pradesh*, (1963) 1 Cr LJ 8: AIR 1962 SC 1788: (1963) 3 SCR 412; *Anter Singh* v. *State of Rajasthan*, (2004) 10 SCC 657: AIR 2004 SC 2865: 2004 AIR SCW 743; *Bodhraj* v. *State of Jammu and Kashmir*, (2002) 8 SCC 45: AIR 2002 SC 3164: 2002 AIR SCW 3655: 2002 Cr LJ 4664; *Delhi Administration* v. *Balkrishnan*, (1972) 1 SCJ 347: AIR 1972 SC 3: 1972 Cr LJ 1; *Mohd. Inayatullah* v. *State of Maharashtra*, AIR 1976 SC 483: (1976) 1 SCC 828: 1976 Cr LJ 481.
7. *Prathap Singh* v. *Director of Enforcement, Foreign Exchange Regulation Act*, AIR 1985 SC 989: (1985) 3 SCC 72: (1985) 155 ITR 166.
8. *Puliguri Kotayya* v. *Emperor*, AIR 1947 PC 67: (1947) 1 MLJ 219: 51 CWN 474: 60 MLW 258: 230 IC 135: 1947 ALJ 355: 49 BLR 508: (1946-47) 74 1A 65: 48 Cr LJ 533; *K. Chinnaswamy Reddy* v. *State of Andhra Pradesh*, (1963) 1 Cr LJ 8: AIR 1962 SC 1788: (1963) 3 SCR 412.

fallacious to equate the "fact" discovered with the object produced. The recovery of an object is not discovery of fact.[1] The "fact" discovered embraces the place from which the object is produced and the knowledge of the accused as to this.[2] Information as to past user or past history of the object produced is not related to its discovery.[3] Section 27 is based on the doctrine of confirmation by subsequent events.[4] The words of accused that he had hidden ornaments and will show the place to the police are relevant if the ornaments were actually found hidden at the place stated or shown by him.[5] Statement that the weapon used and blood stained clothes of accused were in his house do not lead to discovery of any relevant fact.[6]

The weapon recovered must be shown to have been used in committing the crime.[7] Mere recovery of the dead body of deceased has no significance if there is no substantive evidence to connect the accused with the crime alleged against him or if the body does not show indications of homicidal death.[8]

Section 27 will not apply when accused is not in custody or is in custody but not an accused or neither an accused nor in custody, even if there is discovery.[9]

It is necessary to bring on record the exact words used by the accused.[10]

---

1. *Puliguri Kotayya* v. *Emperor,* AIR 1947 PC 67: (1947) 1 MLJ 219: 51 CWN 474: 60 MLW 258: 230 IC 135: 1947 ALJ 355: 49 BLR 508: (1946-47) 74 1A 65: 48 Cr LJ 533; *Prabhoo* v. *State of Uttar Pradesh*, AIR 1963 SC 1113: (1963) 2 Cr LJ 182: 1962 All LJ 1097: 1963 (2) SCJ 165: (1963) 2 SCR 881; *State of Maharashtra* v. *Damu*, AIR 2000 SC 1691: (2000) 6 SCC 269: 2000 Cr LJ 2301: 2000 SCC (Cri) 1088: JT 2000 (5) SC 575; *Anter Singh* v. *State of Rajasthan,* (2004) 10 SCC 657: AIR 2004 SC 2865: 2004 AIR SCW 743; *Amit Singh Bhikamsingh Thakur* v. *State of Maharashtra,* (2007) 2 SCC 310: 2007 AIR SCW 286: AIR 2007 SC 676; *Udai Bhan* v. *State of Uttar Pradesh,* AIR 1962 SC 1116: 1962 Cr LJ 251: ILR (1962) 2 All 522: 1962 Supp (2) SCR 830; *Pandurang Kalu Patil* v. *State of Maharashtra*, AIR 2002 SC 733: 2002 Cr LJ 1007: (2002) 2 SCC 490; *State of Karnataka* v. *David Razario*, (2002) 7 SCC 728: AIR 2002 SC 3272: 2002 Cr LJ 4127.
2. *State of Uttar Pradesh* v. *Jogeshwar*, AIR 1983 SC 349: (1983) 2 SCC 305: 1983 Cr LJ 686; *State of Maharashtra* v. *Damu*, AIR 2000 SC 1691: (2000) 6 SCC 269: 2000 Cr LJ 2301: 2000 SCC (Cri) 1088: JT 2000 (5) SC 575.
3. *Puliguri Kotayya* v. *Emperor,* AIR 1947 PC 67: (1947) 1 MLJ 219: 51 CWN 474: 60 MLW 258: 230 IC 135: 1947 ALJ 355: 49 BLR 508: (1946-47) 74 1A 65: 48 Cr LJ 533; *Ram Kishan* v. *State of Bombay*, 1955 Cr LJ 196 (208): AIR 1955 SC 104: 1955 SCR 903; *Pershadi Lal* v. *State of Uttar Pradesh,* 1957 Cr LJ 328: AIR 1957 SC 211; *Udai Bhan* v. *State of Uttar Pradesh,* AIR 1962 SC 1116: 1962 Cr LJ 251: ILR (1962) 2 All 522: 1962 Supp (2) SCR 830; *K. Chinnaswamy Reddy* v. *State of Andhra Pradesh,* (1963) 1 Cr LJ 8: AIR 1962 SC 1788: (1963) 3 SCR 412; *Prabhoo* v. *State of Uttar Pradesh,* AIR 1963 SC 1113: (1963) 2 Cr LJ 182: 1962 All LJ 1097: 1963 (2) SCJ 165: (1963) 2 SCR 881; *Mohd. Inayatullah* v. *State of Maharashtra,* (1976) 1 SCC 828: 1976 Cr LJ 481: AIR 1976 SC 483; *Earabhadrappa* v. *State of Karnataka,* AIR 1983 SC 446: 1983 Cr LJ 846: (1983) 1 SCC 330: 1983 SCC (Cri) 447: (1983) 2 SCR 552.
4. *State of Karnataka* v. *David Razario,* 2002 SCC (Crl) 1852: AIR 2002 SC 3272: 2002 Cr LJ 4127.
5. *K. Chinnaswamy Reddy* v. *State of Andhra Pradesh,* (1963) 1 Cr LJ 8: AIR 1962 SC 1788: (1963) 3 SCR 412.
6. *Prabhoo* v. *State of Uttar Pradesh,* AIR 1963 SC 1113: (1963) 2 Cr LJ 182: 1962 All LJ 1097: 1963 (2) SCJ 165: (1963) 2 SCR 881.
7. *Baboo* v. *State of Madhya Pradesh,* AIR 1979 SC 1042: (1979) 4 SCC 74: 1979 Cr LJ 908.
8. *Mohammed Dastagir* v. *State of Madras,* AIR 1960 SC 756: 1960 Cr LJ 1159: (1960) 3 SCR 116; *State of Uttar Pradesh* v. *Deoman Upadhyaya,* AIR 1960 SC 1125: (1961) 1 SCR 14: 1960 Cr LJ 1504: (1960) 2 SCA 371.
9. *State of Uttar Pradesh* v. *Deoman Upadhyaya,* AIR 1960 SC 1125: (1961) 1 SCR 14: 1960 Cr LJ 1504: (1960) 2 SCA 371.
10. *State of Karnataka* v. *David Razario,* (2002) 7 SCC 728: AIR 2002 SC 3272: 2002 Cr LJ 4127; *Bodhraj* v. *State of Jammu and Kashmir,* (2002) 8 SCC 45: AIR 2002 SC 3164: 2002 AIR SCW 3655: 2002 Cr LJ 4664.

This section will not apply if the fact was discovered otherwise than on the information given by the accused or if already known to police.[1]

7. "Any Fact": "Fact" as defined in section 3 includes anything, state of things or relation of things capable of being perceived by the senses and any mental condition of any person in conscious.[2] It refers to physical fact (place of concealment) suggesting a mental fact (knowledge of concealment). The thing discovered may be the stolen article, the crime weapon, the dead body or any material thing or place.[3] "Fact" means some concrete material fact to which information relates.[4] Obviously police would not have the particular information without the same being given by the accused. If what was stolen was gold ornament and recovery was of gold ingot, there would be no discovery in consequence of information given by accused unless it is shown that the ingot was made out of the particular ornament.[5] If knife was not used in the occurrence according to the prosecution case, alleged recovery of a knife at the instance of accused has no relevance.[6]

8. Subject-matter of discovery cannot be a person, such as a witness.[7] Pointing out the person from whom accused purchased the weapon is conduct relevant under section 8. Where accused led police to the house of another and knocked at the door and when the door was opened by another, as instructed by accused, the other gave the incriminating article to the police, section 27 was held to be applicable.[8]

Failure to detect human blood in the weapon so recovered will not render the recovery useless.[9] Dead body was found at the place pointed by accused. In Court, accused did not explain that he saw another person concealing the body or he came know of it from another person. Court can presume that it

---

1. *State of Haryana* v. *Jagbir Singh*, AIR 2003 SC 4377: (2003) 1 SCC 261: 2001 SCC (Cri) 126: (2003) 1 SCW 5180; *Krishan Mohan Singh Dugal* v. *State of Goa*, AIR 1999 SC 3842: (1999) 8 SCC 552: 2000 Cr LJ 18; *State of Karnataka* v. *M.V. Mahesh*, 2003 SCC (Cri) 795; *Jaffer Hussein Dastigir* v. *State of Maharashtra*, AIR 1970 SC 1934: (1969) 2 SCWR 550: (1969) 2 SCC 872: 1970 Cr LJ 1659; *Aher Raja Khima* v. *State of Saurashtra*, AIR 1956 SC 217: (1955) 2 SCR 1285: 1956 Cr LJ 421: 1956 SCJ 24; *State of Bombay* v. *Kathi Kalu Oghad*, AIR 1961 SC 1808: (1962) 3 SCR 10: (1961) 2 Cr LJ 856: 64 Bom LR 240; *Karan Singh* v. *State of Uttar Pradesh*, AIR 1973 SC 1385: 1973 3 SCC 662: 1973 Cr LJ 1136; *Thimma and Thimma Raju* v. *State of Mysore*, AIR 1971 SC 1871: 1970 SCC (Cr) 320: (1970) 2 SCC 105: 1971 Cr LJ 1314; *Hemraj Devilal* v. *State of Ajmer*, AIR 1954 SC 462: 1954 Cr LJ 1313: 1954 SCR 1133: 1954 SCJ 449.
2. *Puliguri Kotayya* v. *Emperor*, AIR 1947 PC 67: (1947) 1 MLJ 219: 51 CWN 474: 60 MLW 258: 230 IC 135: 1947 ALJ 355: 49 BLR 508: (1946-47) 74 1A 65: 48 Cr LJ 533 followed in *Mohd. Inayatullah* v. *State of Maharashtra*, AIR 1976 SC 483: (1976) 1 SCC 828: 1976 Cr LJ 481; *Himachal Pradesh Administration* v. *Om Prakash*, AIR 1972 SC 975: (1972) 1 SCC 249: 1972 SCC (Cri) 88: (1972) 1 SCJ 691; *Earabhadrappa* v. *State of Karnataka*, AIR 1983 SC 446: 1983 Cr LJ 846: (1983) 1 SCC 330: 1983 SCC (Cri) 447: (1983) 2 SCR 552.
3. *Aloke Nath Dutta* v. *State of West Bengal*, (2007) 12 SCC 230: (2006) 13 SCALE 467.
4. *State of Karnataka* v. *David Razario*, (2002) 7 SCC 728: AIR 2002 SC 3272: 2002 Cr LJ 4127.
5. *C.V. Puttanna Setty* v. *A.V. Balasubramanyam*, 1969 (1) Mys LJ 417.
6. *Deva* v. *State of Rajasthan*, AIR 1999 SC 214: JT 1998 (8) SC 8: 1999 SCC (Cri) 41: 1999 Cr LJ 265.
7. *Himachal Pradesh Administration* v. *Om Prakash*, AIR 1972 SC 975: (1972) 1 SCC 249: 1972 SCC (Cri) 88: (1972) 1 SCJ 691.
8. *Prasad Ramakant Khade* v. *State of Maharashtra*, (1999) 8 SCC 493: AIR 2000 SC 138: 2000 Cr LJ 55.
9. *State of Rajasthan* v. *Teja Ram*, AIR 1999 SC 1776: (1999) 3 SCC 507: 1999 Cr LJ 2588: (1999) 3 SCC 507.

was accused who concealed body. He is the only person who knows the source of his knowledge.[1]

Part of the confession or statement which directly and distinctly does not lead to discovery is not relevant.[2] The words "where I had hidden them" are relevant and the words 'which I had stolen from' relate to past history and are inadmissible.[3] The words "with which I stabbed" are not relevant since they do not lead to discovery. If the information leading to discovery is contained in the F.I. Statement given by the accused, section 27 would apply to such information. Where the information is capable of two interpretations, the one which is favourable to the accused has to be adopted.[4]

Where the accused merely takes out a weapon, section 27 will not apply, but section 8 may apply.[5] Discovery without information has no relevance.

9. **Discovery:** If the fact was already known to the police from other sources, Section 27 will not apply as there is no "discovery" on the information purportedly given by accused.[6] Recovery from a place accessible to all is of no moment.[7] Discovery leading only to "knowledge" is not by itself incriminating.[8] Recovery from tall grass in field or buried in field (open space) indicates they were hidden. Hence reliance could be placed on such recovery.[9] A person sharing knowledge with others about the fact that certain article is lying in tank will not give rise to the inference of participation in the crime. Knowledge may be exclusive as where the article is well hidden though in a place open to others also.[10] If the discovery is as a result of search by police and not information given by the accused, section 27 will not apply.[11] If the disclosure statement was subsequent to the discovery, section 27 is not attracted.[12]

1. *State of Uttar Pradesh* v. *Babu Ram,* AIR 2000 SC 1735: JT 2000 (4) SC 456: (2000) 4 SCC 515: 2000 Cr LJ 2457: 2000 All LJ 1439.
2. *Puliguri Kotayya* v. *Emperor,* AIR 1947 PC 67: (1947) 1 MLJ 219: 51 CWN 474: 60 MLW 258: 230 IC 135: 1947 ALJ 355: 49 BLR 508: (1946-47) 74 1A 65: 48 Cr LJ 533.
3. *Mohd. Inayatullah* v. *State of Maharashtra,* AIR 1976 SC 483: (1976) 1 SCC 828: 1976 Cr LJ 481.
4. *Puliguri Kotayya* v. *Emperor,* AIR 1947 PC 67: (1947) 1 MLJ 219: 51 CWN 474: 60 MLW 258: 230 IC 135: 1947 ALJ 355: 49 BLR 508: (1946-47) 74 1A 65: 48 Cr LJ 533; *Pohalya* v. *State of Maharashtra,* AIR 1979 SC 1949: 1979 Cr LJ 1310: (1980) 1 SCC 530.
5. *Bahadul* v. *State of Orissa,* AIR 1979 SC 1262: (1979) 4 SCC 346: 1979 Cr LJ 1075.
6. *Makhan Singh* v. *State of Punjab,* AIR 1988 SC 1705: 1988 Supp SCC 526: 1988 Cr LR 501; *Jaffer Hussein Dastigir* v. *State of Maharashtra,* AIR 1970 SC 1934: (1969) 2 SCWR 550: (1969) 2 SCC 872: 1970 Cr LJ 1659; *Aher Raja Khima* v. *State of Saurashtra,* AIR 1956 SC 217: (1955) 2 SCR 1285: 1956 Cr LJ 421: 1956 SCJ 24.
7. *Abdul Sattar* v. *Union Territory, Chandigarh,* 1985 SCC (Cri) 505: AIR 1986 SC 1438: 1986 Cr LJ 1072; *State of Maharashtra* v. *Bharat Fakira Dhiwar,* AIR 2002 SC 16: (2002) 1 SCC 622: JT 2001 (9) SC 407: 2002 Cr LJ 218: 2001 AIR SCW 4609 (SC); *Anter Singh* v. *State of Rajasthan,* (2004) 10 SCC 657: AIR 2004 SC 2865: 2004 AIR SCW 743; *Mani* v. *State of Tamil Nadu,* AIR 2008 SC 1021: 2008 AIR SCW 576: 2008 Cr LJ 1046.
8. *Pohalya* v. *State of Maharashtra,* AIR 1979 SC 1949: 1979 Cr LJ 1310: (1980) 1 SCC 530.
9. *State of Maharashtra* v. *Bharat Fakira Dhiwar,* AIR 2002 SC 16: (2002) 1 SCC 622: JT 2001 (9) SC 407: 2002 Cr LJ 218: 2001 AIR SCW 4609 (SC); *State of Himachal Pradesh* v. *Jeet Singh,* AIR 1999 SC 1293: 1999 AIR SCW 982: 1999 Cr LJ 2025: (1999) 4 SCC 370; *Narpal Singh* v. *State of Haryana,* AIR 1977 SC 1066: (1977) 2 SCC 131: 1977 Cr LJ 642: 1977 Cr LJ 642.
10. *In Re: Murugan* alias *Thannasi,* AIR 1958 Mad 451: (1957) 1 Mad LJ (Cri) 829: 1958 Cr LJ 1196.
11. *Barkat Ram Kishan Lal* v. *State,* AIR 1959 Punj 287: 1959 Cr LJ 764: ILR 1959 Punj 458; *Abdul Sattar* v. *Union Territory, Chandigarh,* 1985 SCC (Cri) 505: AIR 1986 SC 1438: 1986 Cr LJ 1072.
12. *Kalu Khan* v. *State,* AIR 1957 Ori 102: 1957 Cr LJ 530: ILR 1951 Cut 468.

Where, in the case of dacoity and murder, a huge quantity of gold ornaments were recovered at the instance of the accused and were duly identified by the witnesses, and there was no occasion to plant the ornaments to falsely implicate the accused, recovery of the ornaments could not be doubted merely because of some delay in the recovery.[1] That the police displayed the seized weapons in a press conference would be no ground to disbelieve the factum of recovery (*ibid*). That the recovery was made some time after the disclosure statement was made is no reason to render the statement irrelevant.[2] Where the weapon used by accused had been recovered on the information given by accused, proof of ownership is not necessary.[3] Recovery after lapse of a long period does not dilute its evidentiary value.[4]

Ordinarily there must be evidence of exclusive possession of the accused of the place of recovery. If the accused was the author of the concealment in the compound of another, and accused made such a statement and the weapon was found in the place stated by accused, section 27 is attracted though obviously the accused had no possession over the place.[5] If the recovery was not from such a place and was on the initiative of police, section 27 will not apply.[6] When there was delay in securing information from accused or in effecting recovery, the circumstances of each case must be examined with great care to see if relevant evidence can be acted upon.[7] Mere production of weapon by taking it from under his cot without any statement is not incriminating in the absence of evidence to show he had concealed it in a place known to him only and none else had knowledge of it.[8] When the statement is vague as to the authorship of concealment, mere pointing out the weapon may at best prove knowledge of place of concealment.[9]

10. **Information**: "Information" is not synonymous with "statement". "Information" connotes means employed for imparting knowledge possessed by one person to another and the knowledge so derived by the other person. It is necessary to depose to the exact words uttered by the accused, absence of which may affect its reliability. The information must be proved like any other circumstance.[10] But no witness need hear the statement.[11] Recording of the

1. *Narayan Prasad* v. *State of Madhya Pradesh*, AIR 2006 SC 204: 2006 Cr LJ 123: 2005 AIR SCW 5696.
2. *Praveen Kumar* v. *State of Karnataka*, (2003) 12 SCC 199: 2004 SCC (Cri) Supp 357; *Nisar Khan* v. *State of Uttaranchal*, (2006) 9 SCC 386.
3. *Sivakumar* v. *State by Inspector of Police*, AIR 2006 SC 653: 2006 Cr LJ 536: 2005 AIR SCW 6360.
4. *Mano* v. *State of Tamil Nadu*, (2007) 13 SCC 795: 2007 Cr LJ 2736 (SC): 2007 AIR SCW 2736: 2007 (3) Supreme 708.
5. *State of Maharashtra* v. *Bharat Fakira Dhiwar*, AIR 2002 SC 16: (2002) 1 SCC 622: JT 2001 (9) SC 407: 2002 Cr LJ 218: 2001 AIR SCW 4609 (SC).
6. *Abdul Sattar* v. *Union Territory, Chandigarh*, 1985 SCC (Cri) 505: AIR 1986 SC 1438: 1986 Cr LJ 1072; *Kora Ghasi* v. *State of Orissa*, AIR 1983 SC 360: 1983 Cr LJ 692 (2): (1983) 2 SCC 251; *Chandran* v. *State of Madras*, AIR 1978 SC 1574: 1978 Cr LJ 1693: (1978) 4 SCC 90.
7. *State of Himachal Pradesh* v. *Wazir Chand*, AIR 1978 SC 315: (1978) 1 SCC 130: 1978 Cr LJ 347; *Chandran* v. *State of Madras*, AIR 1978 SC 1574: 1978 Cr LJ 1693: (1978) 4 SCC 90; *Ashish Batham* v. *State of Madhya Pradesh*, (2002) 7 SCC 317: AIR 2002 SC 3206: 2002 Cr LJ 4676; *State of Andhra Pradesh* v. *Patnam Anandam*, 2005 Cr LJ 894: AIR 2005 SC 764: 2005 AIR SCW 362 (SC); *Mano* v. *State of Tamil Nadu*, 2007 Cr LJ 2736 (SC): 2007 AIR SCW 2736: 2007 (3) Supreme 708.
8. *Bahadul* v. *State of Orissa*, AIR 1979 SC 1262: (1979) 4 SCC 346: 1979 Cr LJ 1075.
9. *Dudh Nath Pandey* v. *State of Uttar Pradesh*, AIR 1981 SC 911: (1981) 2 SCC 166: 1981 SCC (Cri) 379: 1981 Cr LJ 618.
10. *Chandran* v. *State of Madras*, AIR 1978 SC 1574: 1978 Cr LJ 1693: (1978) 4 SCC 90.
11. *State of Himachal Pradesh* v. *Jeet Singh*, AIR 1999 SC 1293: 1999 AIR SCW 982: 1999 Cr LJ 2025: (1999) 4 SCC 370.

information is for the benefit of both sides and hence the information should be recorded and proved; if it is not so recorded, the exact information must be proved through evidence.[1] Statement need not be in the presence of independent witnesses.[2]

11. **Accused Of Any Offence:** These words are merely descriptive of the person. They do not indicate that a formal accusation should have been made against him at the time.[3] It is not necessary that when he gave the information, he should be an accused; it is enough if he is an accused person when it is sought to be proved in Court.[4]

12. **Custody**: This section will not apply if the person giving information was not in custody at that time.[5] "Custody" does not mean physical custody by arrest.[6] When a person goes to police station and gives a statement implicating himself, he may deemed to have surrendered himself to the police and may be deemed to be in custody of police.[7] "Custody" means some kind of restraint on movements.[8] Police surveillance means custody.[9]

13. **"Distinctly"**: The entire information is not relevant; only that part which distinctly leads to discovery is relevant. The extent of information which is relevant depends on the exact nature of the fact discovered. The fact embraces the place and knowledge. Information must relate distinctly to this fact.[10] "Distinctly" means directly clearly, positively. If the statement is a compound one, court should divide it into it's component parts and admit only that part which distinctly led to the discovery.[11] Statement that he had buried the article

---

1. *Bodhraj* v. *State of Jammu and Kashmir*, (2002) 8 SCC 45: AIR 2002 SC 3164: 2002 AIR SCW 3655: 2002 Cr LJ 4664.
2. *Sanjay @ Kaka* v. *State (N.C.T. of Delhi)*, AIR 2001 SC 979: (2001) 3 SCC 190: 2001 SCC (Cri) 449: 2001 Cr LJ 1231: 2001 AIR SCW 767; *State Govt. of NCT of Delhi* v. *Sunil*, 2001 Cr LJ 504: 2000 AIR SCW 4398: (2001) 1 SCC 652.
3. *State of Uttar Pradesh* v. *Deoman Upadhyaya*, AIR 1960 SC 1125: (1961) 1 SCR 14: 1960 Cr LJ 1504: (1960) 2 SCA 371.
4. *Mohammed Dastagir* v. *State of Madras*, AIR 1960 SC 756: 1960 Cr LJ 1159: (1960) 3 SCR 116.
5. *Manoranjan Singh* v. *State of Delhi*, (1998) 3 SCC 523: AIR 1998 SC 2811: 1998 Cr LJ 2062.
6. *State of Bihar* v. *Madanlal Agarwalla*, AIR 1967 Pat 63: 1967 Cr LJ 237: 1966 BLJR 133.
7. *State of Uttar Pradesh* v. *Deoman Upadhyaya*, AIR 1960 SC 1125: (1961) 1 SCR 14: 1960 Cr LJ 1504: (1960) 2 SCA 371; contra observation in *State of Karnataka* v. *David Razario*, (2002) 7 SCC 728: AIR 2002 SC 3272: 2002 Cr LJ 4127; see also *Bodhraj* v. *State of Jammu and Kashmir*, (2002) 8 SCC 45: AIR 2002 SC 3164: 2002 AIR SCW 3655: 2002 Cr LJ 4664.
8. *Paramhansa Jadab* v. *State*, AIR 1964 Ori 144: (1964) 1 Cr LJ 680: 31 Cut LT 17.
9. *Chhotey Lal* v. *State of Uttar Pradesh*, AIR 1954 All 687: 1954 All LJ 93: 1954 Cr LJ 1445.
10. *Ram Kishan* v. *State of Bombay*, 1955 Cr LJ 196 (208): AIR 1955 SC 104: 1955 SCR 903; *Puliguri Kotayya* v. *Emperor*, AIR 1947 PC 67: (1947) 1 MLJ 219: 51 CWN 474: 60 MLW 258: 230 IC 135: 1947 ALJ 355: 49 BLR 508: (1946-47) 74 1A 65: 48 Cr LJ 533; *Mohd. Inayatullah* v. *State of Maharashtra*, AIR 1976 SC 483: (1976) 1 SCC 828: 1976 Cr LJ 481.
11. *State of Himachal Pradesh* v. *Jeet Singh*, AIR 1999 SC 1293: 1999 AIR SCW 982: 1999 Cr LJ 2025: (1999) 4 SCC 370; *Limbaji* v. *State of Maharashtra*, (2001) 10 SCC 340: AIR 2002 SC 491: 2002 AIR SCW 22; *Deepak Chandrakant Patil* v. *State of Maharashtra*, (2006) 10 SCC 151: AIR 2006 SC 1708: 2006 AIR SCW 1637; *Bodhraj* v. *State of Jammu and Kashmir*, (2002) 8 SCC 45: AIR 2002 SC 3164: 2002 AIR SCW 3655: 2002 Cr LJ 4664; *K. Chinnaswamy Reddy* v. *State of Andhra Pradesh*, (1963) 1 Cr LJ 8: AIR 1962 SC 1788: (1963) 3 SCR 412; *Mohd. Inayatullah* v. *State of Maharashtra*, AIR 1976 SC 483: (1976) 1 SCC 828: 1976 Cr LJ 481; *Anter Singh* v. *State of Rajasthan*, (2004) 10 SCC 657: AIR 2004 SC 2865: 2004 AIR SCW 743; *Aloke Nath Dutta* v. *State of West Bengal*, (2007) 12 SCC 230: (2006) 13 SCALE 467; *State of Uttar Pradesh* v. *Deoman Upadhyaya*, AIR 1960 SC 1125: (1961) 1 SCR 14: 1960 Cr LJ 1504: (1960) 2 SCA 371.

at a particular place is relevant.[1] If the accused merely pointed out the place where the weapon was hidden, that may prove only his knowledge as to where the weapon was hidden. That by itself, will not show he hid the weapon there.[2] Such an inference can be drawn from the other proved facts in the case.

Statement made while producing the article is not relevant.[3] If the accused described the weapon as the one used by him in the occurrence, that part of the "information" is not relevant.[4]

The statement made by an accused that he will show the place where he hid the ornaments would be relevant under section 27.[5] The words "whether it amounts to confession or not" qualify information and not the words "so much".[6] Information must be recorded in first person in the exact words of the accused.[7]

14. **Two or more accused:** Discovery on joint information given by two accused would not attract Section 27.[8] It is only information received first which is relevant.[9] Two accused cannot speak at once and there cannot be a joint statement. Evidence must be given of words uttered by each separately. A composite statement has no significance since recovery has to be connected to information given by a specific accused. This way of recording statements is most unsatisfactory. It is obligatory on the investing officer to state and record who gave the information when he is dealing with more than one accused, what words were used by him so that a recovery pursuant to the information received may be connected to the person giving information so as to provide incriminaling evidence against him.[10] Evidence that all the accused pointed out the property has no value.[11] If several accused give vague information and only

1. *Karan Singh* v. *State of Uttar Pradesh,* AIR 1973 SC 1385: 1973 3 SCC 662: 1973 Cr LJ 1136; *Pohalya* v. *State of Maharashtra,* AIR 1979 SC 1949: 1979 Cr LJ 1310: (1980) 1 SCC 530; *Dudh Nath Pandey* v. *State of Uttar Pradesh,* AIR 1981 SC 911: (1981) 2 SCC 166: 1981 SCC (Cri) 379: 1981 Cr LJ 618.
2. *Dudh Nath Pandey* v. *State of Uttar Pradesh,* AIR 1981 SC 911: (1981) 2 SCC 166: 1981 SCC (Cri) 379: 1981 Cr LJ 618.
3. *Annika Lakshmudu (in re:),* 1941 MWN 956: AIR 1942 Mad 237: 199 IC 87: (1942) 43 Cr LJ 463.
4. *Puliguri Kotayya* v. *Emperor,* AIR 1947 PC 67: (1947) 1 MLJ 219: 51 CWN 474: 60 MLW 258: 230 IC 135: 1947 ALJ 355: 49 BLR 508: (1946-47) 74 1A 65: 48 Cr LJ 533; *Ram Lochan Ahir* v. *State of West Bengal,* AIR 1963 SC 1074: 1963 Cr LJ 170: (1963) 2 SCR 852: (1964) 1 SCJ 82: (1981) 3 SCC 689; *Baboo* v. *State of Madhya Pradesh,* AIR 1979 SC 1042: (1979) 4 SCC 74: 1979 Cr LJ 908.
5. *K. Chinnaswamy Reddy* v. *State of Andhra Pradesh,* (1963) 1 Cr LJ 8: AIR 1962 SC 1788: (1963) 3 SCR 412.
6. *K. Chinnaswamy Reddy* v. *State of Andhra Pradesh,* (1963) 1 Cr LJ 8: AIR 1962 SC 1788: (1963) 3 SCR 412.
7. *Bodhraj* v. *State of Jammu and Kashmir,* (2002) 8 SCC 45: AIR 2002 SC 3164: 2002 AIR SCW 3655: 2002 Cr LJ 4664; *In Re: Kattameedi Chenna Reddi,* AIR 1940 Mad 710: ILR (1940) Mad 254: 42 Cr LJ 582; *Chandran* v. *State of Madras,* AIR 1978 SC 1574: 1978 Cr LJ 1693: (1978) 4 SCC 90.
8. *Mohd. Abdul Hafeez* v. *State of Andhra Pradesh,* AIR 1983 SC 367: 1983 Cr LJ 689: (1983) 1 SCC 143.
9. *Lachman Singh* v. *State,* AIR 1952 SC 167: 1952 ALJ 437: 1952 Cr LJ 863: 1952 SCJ 230: 1952 SCR 839.
10. *Mohd. Abdul Hafeez* v. *State of Andhra Pradesh,* AIR 1983 SC 367: 1983 Cr LJ 689: (1983) 1 SCC 143.
11. *Lachman Singh* v. *State,* AIR 1952 SC 167: 1952 ALJ 437: 1952 Cr LJ 863: 1952 SCJ 230: 1952 SCR 839.; *Mohd. Abdul Hafeez* v. *State of Andhra Pradesh,* AIR 1983 SC 367: 1983 Cr LJ 689: (1983) 1 SCC 143.

one of them gives sufficient information so as to lead to discovery, section 27 can apply to his statement.[1]

Supreme Court has observed that the question of joint disclosures assumes relevance in the context of joint disclosures by more than one accused (in that case, two accused) leading to discovery of hideouts of deceased terrorists and recovery of laptop computer, a mobile phone and Rs. 10 lakhs from the truck in which they were found in Srinagar. The Supreme Court observed that some High Courts took the view that the mention in section 27 of "a person" excludes the applicability of the section to more than one person. The Supreme Court held that this was too narrow a view to be taken and joint disclosures – to be more accurate, simultaneous disclosures, were not irrelevant under Section 27. "A person" need not necessarily be a single person, but it could be plurality of accused. The court felt that the real reason for not acting upon joint information supposed to have been given by two accused at a time is that such joint information is a myth, because two or more persons would not have uttered informatory words in a chorus. At best, one person would have made the statement orally and the other person would have stated substantially in similar terms a few seconds or minutes later, or the second person would have given a clear nod to what had been said by the first person. Or, two persons in custody might be interrogated separately and simultaneously and both of them might furnish similar information leading to the discovery of fact. Or, in rare cases, both accused might reduce the information to writing and handover the written notes to the police officer at the same time. Supreme Court observed that such disclosures did not go out of the purview of section 27 altogether. If information was given one after the other without any break, almost simultaneously, and if such information was followed up by pointing out the material thing by both of them, there was no good reason to eschew such evidence from the scope of section 27. However, there might be practical difficulties in placing reliance on such evidence. It might be difficult for the witness (generally, a police officer) to depose which accused spoke what words and in what order; in other words, the deposition regarding information given by the two accused might be exposed to criticism from the stand point of credibility and it's nexus with the discovery. Admissibility and credibility are two different aspects.[2]

It is not proper to associate eye witness as witness to the recovery mahazar or memo.[3] "Information" relevant under section 27 is not relevant against co-accused.

15. **Evidentiary Value:** Conduct of concealment is an incriminating circumstance.[4] Recovery of weapon at the instance of the accused, by itself, cannot prove that he wielded it. Where the information given by the accused does not indicate authorship of the concealment, the pointing out may prove only knowledge of the accused regarding the place of concealment and factum of concealment. Such discovery, in the light of surrounding facts, may lead to inference that accused was the author of concealment.[5] Mere knowledge, without

1. *Tippa Reddy* v. *Gondamma*, 1952 Cr LJ 567: ILR 1952 Hyd 60: AIR 1952 Hyd 53 (SC).
2. Woodroeffe and Amir Ali's Law of Evidence, 18th Edn. Vol. II Page 522.
3. *Narpal Singh* v. *State of Haryana*, AIR 1977 SC 1066: (1977) 2 SCC 131: 1977 Cr LJ 642: 1977 Cr LJ 642.
4. *State of Uttar Pradesh* v. *Jogeshwar*, AIR 1983 SC 349: (1983) 2 SCC 305: 1983 Cr LJ 686.
5. *Dudh Nath Pandey* v. *State of Uttar Pradesh*, AIR 1981 SC 911: (1981) 2 SCC 166: 1981 SCC (Cri) 379: 1981 Cr LJ 618; *Pohalya* v. *State of Maharashtra*, AIR 1979 SC 1949: 1979 Cr LJ 1310: (1980) 1 SCC 530.

exclusive possession of the place may not ordinarily connect accused with the crime. Knowledge and possession are different aspects. Except in cases in which possession or concealment of an object constitutes the gist of the offence alleged (*e.g.*, being in conscious possession of stolen goods), it can seldom happen that information relating to discovery of a fact forms the foundation of the prosecution case. It is only a link in the chain of proof, and the other links must be forged in the manner required by law.[1]

Recovery under section 27 provides significant support to evidence of eye-witnesses.[2] Evidence of the investigating officer regarding such recovery of relevant material objects, if convincing, need not be rejected on the ground that seizure panch witnesses do not support the prosecution version.[3] Recovery of dead body on the information given by accused raises strong suspicion against him.[4] Evidence relevant under section 27 is corroborative piece of evidence.[5] That the panch witnesses were not examined to support the prosecution case of recovery at the instance of accused, would not introduce any serious infirmity in the evidence regarding recovery (*ibid*). In appreciating evidence in this regard, court has to consider the broad probabilities as in the case of other evidence.

---

1. *Udai Bhan* v. *State of Uttar Pradesh*, AIR 1962 SC 1116: 1962 Cr LJ 251: ILR (1962) 2 All 522: 1962 Supp (2) SCR 830; *Prabhoo* v. *State of Uttar Pradesh*, AIR 1963 SC 1113: (1963) 2 Cr LJ 182: 1962 All LJ 1097: 1963 (2) SCJ 165: (1963) 2 SCR 881.
2. *Bhagwan Dass* v. *State of Rajasthan*, 1974 Cr LJ 1168: AIR 1974 SC 1699: (1974) 4 SCC 781.
3. *Modan Singh* v. *State of Rajasthan*, (1978) 4 SCC 435: AIR 1978 SC 1511: 1978 WLN 357; *Mohd. Aslam* v. *State of Maharashtra*, (2001) 9 SCC 362: JT 2000 (8) SC 104; *Anter Singh* v. *State of Rajasthan*, (2004) 10 SCC 657: AIR 2004 SC 2865: 2004 AIR SCW 743.
4. *Bakshish Singh* v. *State of Punjab*, AIR 1971 SC 2016: 1971 UJ (SC) 281: 1971 Cr LJ 1452.
5. *Delhi Administration* v. *Mohammad Iqbal*, AIR 1971 SC 472: 1971 UJ (SC) 91: 1971 Cr LJ 509.

CHAPTER 8
SECTIONS 32 AND 33

SECTION 32:

1. Section 32 constitutes a further exception to the hearsay rule.[1] As a general rule, oral evidence must be direct (section 60). Section 32 is an exception to this rule, based on the principle of necessity and practicality and circumstantial guarantee of their trustworthiness. Hearsay is rejected because of its inherent untrustworthiness on account of absence of oath and cross-examination. One reason for the relevancy under section 32 is that no better evidence can be had in regard to the matters in question. Practical convenience or inability to obtain evidence of the same value are some of the other reasons.

Section 32 is not controlled by section 33. Section 32 exhaustively deals with law relating to relevancy of statements made by persons falling in four categories mentioned therein. Evidence relevant under section 32 is substantive evidence. Burden of showing the applicability of the section lies on the party who wishes to avail the benefit of the section.

2. Section 32 relates to previous statements written or verbal, of relevant facts, made by persons falling under four different categories, namely,

(a) a deceased person;

(b) a person who cannot be found;

(c) a person who has become incapable of giving evidence;

(d) a person whose attendance cannot be procured without reasonable delay or expense.

Such statements are relevant in the cases falling under the eight categories mentioned in clauses (1) to (8).

These circumstances have to be proved and reasons for invoking one or the other of the above must be proved to the satisfaction of the court. The above must be proved by relevant materials. Written or verbal statements of relevant facts made by such persons are themselves relevant facts in the eight cases mentioned in the section. If such statements of relevant facts are relevant, there is no reason why such statements of facts in issue are not relevant.[2] Some of the illustrations relate to facts in issue.

3. When a person though alive at the time the plaintiff closed his case was not called as a witness, his earlier statement in support of plaintiff's claim is not relevant under section 32.[3] When a witness has been fully examined and

---

1. *Tapinder Singh* v. *State of Punjab,* AIR 1970 SC 1566: (1971) 1 SCJ 871: 1970 Cr LJ 1415; *State of Rajasthan* v. *Kishore,* 1996 AIR SCW 1392: AIR 1996 SC 3035: 1996 Cr LJ 2003.
2. *Jadavkumar Liladhar Mainthia* v. *Pushpabai Mainthia Nee,* AIR 1944 Bom 29; *Biro* v. *Atma Ram,* AIR 1937 PC 101: 64 IA 92: 167 IC 346.
3. *Rai Jagatpal Singh* v. *Raja Jogeshwar Baksh Singh,* ILR 25 All 143: 30 Ind App 27 (PC).

cross-examined and died subsequently, his previous statement cannot thereafter be admitted under this section.[1]

Some solemnity attaches to the statement of a dying man.[2]

4. **Clause (1):** Statements referred to in the main part of section are relevant, when the statement is made by a person as to the cause of his death, or to any of the circumstances of the transaction which resulted in his death, in cases in which the cause of that person's death comes into question. Such statements are relevant whether the person who made them was or was not, at the time when they were made, under expectation of death, and whatever may be the nature of the proceeding in which the cause of his death comes into question. The words "dying declaration" are not used in clause (1), though these words are used commonly while discussing the clause. The statement has hearsay character. This clause applies to death by homicide or suicide.[3] There is no reason why the clause should not apply to a case of death by negligence. The statement must be as to the cause of death or to any of the circumstances of the transaction leading to death and not to any previous or subsequent transaction. If death was not the result of injuries received in the particular incident, his statement cannot be said to be the statement as to the cause of his death etc.[4] It is not necessary to investigate whether when he made the statement he was under expectation of death or not, though presence or absence of such expectation may have an effect on the evidentiary value of the statement.[5] That he lingered for a few days after receiving fatal injuries does not matter.

5. The words "circumstances of the transaction which resulted in his death" are wider in scope than the expression "cause of his death". It is immaterial whether the circumstances of the transaction are distant or near.[6] Circumstances must have some proximate relation to the actual occurrence. Words "which resulted in his death" are not to be understood as synonymous with "cause of his death". The two are distinct; one is wider than the other. Statement about anything which has nexus with the death is relevant.[7]

6. Clause (1) comprehends Dying Declaration. The statement may be made before the cause of death has arisen or before the deceased has any reason to anticipate being killed. Statement that deceased was proceeding to the spot where he was later killed, or as to the reasons for so proceeding, or that he was going to meet a particular person or that he had invited a particular person or was invited by a particular person would, each of them, be a circumstance of the transaction.

1. *Sahdeo* v. *State of Bihar*, AIR 1920 Pat 291.
2. *K. Ramachandra Reddy* v. *Public Prosecutor*, AIR 1976 SC 1994: 1976 Cr LJ 1548: (1976) 3 SCC 618.
3. *Sharad Biridhichand Sarda* v. *State of Maharashtra*, AIR 1984 SC 1622: (1984) 4 SCC 116: 1984 Cr LJ 1738; *Vajrala Paripurnachry* v. *State of Andhra Pradesh*, AIR 1998 SC 2680: 1998 Cr LJ 4031: 1998 AIR SCW 2723.
4. *Mod Singh* v. *State of Uttar Pradesh*, AIR 1964 SC 900: (1964) 1 SCR 688: 1963 Cur LJ 87: (1963) 2 SCJ 714.
5. *Narayana Swami* v. *E.*, AIR 1939 PC 47: (1939) 40 Cr LJ 364: 180 IC 1: 1939 ALJ 298: 69 CLJ 273: 41 Bom LR 428: 1939 MWN 185: 43 CWN 473; *Tehal Singh* v. *State of Punjab*, AIR 1979 SC 1347: 1979 Cr LJ 1031: 1980 Supp SCC 400: 1979 SCC (Cri) 722; *Sharad Biridhichand Sarda* v. *State of Maharashtra*, AIR 1984 SC 1622: 1984 4 SCC 116: 1984 Cr LJ 1738
6. *Narayanan* v. *State of Orissa*, 1992 (II) Crimes 363.
7. *Patel Hiralal Joitaram* v. *State of Gujarat*, AIR 2001 SC 2944: 2001 AIR SCW 4411: (2002) 1 SCC 22.

Circumstances must have some **proximate relation** to the actual occurrence. Transaction must be the one which resulted in death of declarant. In homicidal death or suicidal death, the cause of death comes into question.[1] In that case, the statement made two days prior to murder was that the declarant was setting out to the place of the accused to meet his wife (*See* also[2]). However the test of proximity cannot be too literally construed and reduced to a formula of universal application. Distance or time would depend or vary with the circumstances of each case.[3] If death was the logical culmination of a long continuous drama, the statements regarding each step directly connected with the culmination have to be read as an organic whole. Sometimes statement relevant to or furnishing immediate motive would be relevant as being part of the transaction of death. In the case of slow poisoning or continuous cruelty, the proximity may extend even to a period of a few years.[4] What is relevant under Clause (1) is not merely statement regarding cause of death, but also regarding all the circumstances of the transaction.[5] The matters which are the subject matter of the statement must be closely connected with the events leading to death.[1] Where infection set in because of surgery or post-surgery complications (Surgery for injury caused in the occurrence), statement of the patient recorded in hospital would be dying declaration.[6] Statement regarding event which was the motive for the murder is relevant.[7] Statement regarding death of another person is not relevant.[8] The statement may have been made before the occurrence.[1] Statements and letters written by deceased which are directly connected with or related to the death and which reveal a tell-tale story would be relevant.[3]

7. Relevancy of the statement is only in proceedings in which the cause of declarant's death comes into question, though the charge may be murder or even rape or dacoity etc. It may be even a civil case.[9] It may be that on a final consideration of the evidence, cause of death is found to be not connected with the injuries caused; but the test is not what the final finding in the case is, but whether the cause of death of the maker **comes into question** in the case.[10]

---

1. *Narayana Swami* v. *E.*, AIR 1939 PC 47: (1939) 40 Cr LJ 364: 180 IC 1: 1939 ALJ 298: 69 CLJ 273: 41 Bom LR 428: 1939 MWN 185: 43 CWN 473.
2. *Shivkumar* v. *State of Uttar Pradesh*, 1966 Cr AppR. (SC) 281.
3. *Sharad Biridhichand Sarda* v. *State of Maharashtra*, AIR 1984 SC 1622: 1984 4 SCC 116: 1984 Cr LJ 1738.
4. *Sharad Biridhichand Sarda* v. *State of Maharashtra*, AIR 1984 SC 1622: (1984) 4 SCC 116: 1984 Cr LJ 1738; *Manohar Lal* v. *State of Punjab*, 1981 Cr LJ 1373.
5. *Parag* v. *State of Rajasthan*, 1981 Cr LJ 1244: 1981 Raj LW 370: 1981 WLN (SC) 274.
6. *Vijay Singh* v. *State of Madhya Pradesh*, 2000 Cr LJ 650; *Jageshwar Singh* v. *State of Bihar*, 1968 Crl App R 73 (SC).
7. *Lachhmilal* v. *Firm Sriniwash Ram Kumar*, AIR 1939 Pat 354: 179 Ind Cas 538; *Bhaiyalal* v. *Rai Beharilal*, AIR 1924 Nag 115; *Findal* v. *State*, AIR 1954 HP 11: 1953 Cr LJ 1900; *T. Retnakaran* v. *State*, AIR 1955 TravCo 87: 1954 Ker LT 801: 1955 Cr LJ 847; *Baggam Appalanarasayya (in re:)*, AIR 1941 Mad 101; *Public Prosecutor* v. *Munigan*, AIR 1941 Mad 359: 1941 (42) Cr LJ 664; *Fr. Benedict* v. *State of Kerala*, 1967 Ker LT 466.
8. *Dannu Singh* v. *Emperor*, AIR 1925 All 227; *Kanwarpal Singh* v. *E.*, AIR 1948 All 170: 1947 ALJ 627: 49 Cr LJ 140: ILR 1948 All 122; *Lukka Ulahannan* v. *Travancore-Cochin State*, AIR 1955 TC 104: 1954 Ker LT 920: 1955 Cr LJ 852; *Loorthia Odayar* v. *Gopalasami Aiyar*, AIR 1924 Mad 450: 19 Mad LW 135; *Ratan Gond* v. *State of Bihar*, AIR 1959 SC 18: 1959 SCR 1336: 1959 Cr LJ 180: 1959 SCJ 222.
9. *Parmanand Ganga Prasad* v. *E.*, (1941) 42 Cr LJ 17: AIR 1940 Nag 340: ILR 194 Nag 110; *Mohammad Hayat Khan* v. *Emperor*, AIR 1928 Pat 162.
10. *State* v. *Ramprasad Singh*, AIR 1953 Pat 354: 1953 Cr LJ 1751: 1953 BLJR 333.

8. Where the declaration was in Punjabi which was written down in Urdu, it was held that this would not be a ground for saying that recorded statement did not correctly reproduce what was stated by the declarant. In all cases it is the substance and not the form which matters.[1] It is the substance of the information which matters and not the language in which it is recorded. The statement or declaration must be complete.[2] But even if it is incomplete by reason of his not being able to answer further questions, but is complete so far as the accused having killed the deceased was concerned, it is relevant.[3] Where the injured became unconscious after several questions put by doctor and before the question "what more you want to say" could be put, the statement would not be regarded as incomplete.[2] The statement (dying declaration) need not be exhaustive. It cannot be disregarded on account of omission to refer to a particular circumstance.[4] Elaborate dying declaration may excite suspicion of tutoring.[5] Mere brevity is not fatal. He may have been in dreadful agony on account of injuries.[3] Sometimes, brevity may be guarantee of truth.[6] Details depend upon his capacity for observation, his anxiety to mention details and the manner of putting questions.[7] Exact words of deceased are important.[8] Words must be free from ambiguity.[9] Mere absence of name of accused did not matter since FIR was lodged within one hour of the occurrence.[10] That the dying declaration did not explain how the injuries were sustained did not matter.[11] Absence of names of eyewitnesses in the dying declaration, by itself, was not an infirmity.[12] Medical evidence has importance, sometimes, in deciding whether to act on the dying declaration or not.[13]

9. One important aspect is whether the injured was in a fit condition to make the statement. His fitness has to be considered.[14] Wherever possible, doctor's evidence must be made available. This aspect is important because courts attach

1. *Bakhshish Singh* v. *State of Punjab*, AIR 1957 SC 904: 1958 SCR 409: 1957 Cr LJ 1459: 1958 SCJ 106.
2. *Kusa* v. *State of Orissa*, (1980) 2 SCC 207: 1980 Cr LJ 408: AIR 1980 SC 559.
3. *Abdul Sattar* v. *State of Mysore*, 1956 Cr LJ 334: AIR 1956 SC 168; *Muniappan* v. *State of Madras*, AIR 1962 SC 1252: 1962 SCR 869: 1962 Cr LJ 404.
4. *Sitaram Bhola Ram* v. *State*, 1953 Cr LJ 600: AIR 1953 MB 79.
5. *Munnu Raja* v. *State of Madhya Pradesh*, AIR 1976 SC 2199: (1976) 2 SCR 764: (1976) 3 SCC 104: 1976 Cr LJ 1718.
6. *Surajdeo Oza* v. *State of Bihar*, (1980) Supp SCC 769: 1979 SCC (Cri) 519: AIR 1979 SC 1505; *Satto* v. *State of Uttar Pradesh*, AIR 1979 SC 1519: 1979 Cr LJ 943: 1979 2 SCC 628.
7. *Tehal Singh* v. *State of Punjab*, AIR 1979 SC 1347: 1979 Cr LJ 1031: 1980 Supp SCC 400: 1979 SCC (Cri) 722.
8. *Ramnath Madhoprasad* v. *State of Madhya Pradesh*, AIR 1953 SC 420: 1953 Cr LJ 1772.
9. *State of Himachal Pradesh* v. *Wazir Chand*, AIR 1978 SC 315: (1978) 1 SCC 130: 1978 Cr LJ 347; *Mohar Singh* v. *State of Punjab*, AIR 1981 SC 1578: 1981 Cr LJ 998: 1981 SCC (Cri) 638; *Gopal (Ram Gopal)* v. *State of Uttar Pradesh*, 1994 SCC (Cri) 169.
10. *Tirath Ram* v. *State of Uttar Pradesh*, AIR 1979 SC 1440: 1979 SCC (Cri) 501: 1979 All LJ 983.
11. *State of Maharashtra* v. *Krishnamurthy Laxmipati Naidu*, AIR 1981 SC 617: 1981 Cr LJ 9: 1981 SCC (Cri) 364 (SC): (1980) Supp SCC 455.
12. *Rabi Chandra* v. *State of Orissa*, AIR 1980 SC 1738: (1980) 1 SCC 240: 1980 Cr LJ 1257.
13. *State of Haryana* v. *Harpal Singh*, AIR 1978 SC 1530: 1978 Cr LJ 1603; *Somappa Vamanappa Madar Shankarappa Ravanappa Kaddi* v. *State of Mysore*, AIR 1979 SC 1831: 1979 Cr LJ 1358: (1980) 1 SCC 479.
14. *State (Delhi Administration)* v. *Laxman Kumar*, AIR 1986 SC 250: 1985 CAR 304: 1985 Cr LR 501: (1985) 2 Crimes 758: (1985) 2 SCALE 701: (1985) 4 SCC 476: (1985) 2 SCR 898: 1986 Cr LJ 155; *K. Ramachandra Reddy* v. *Public Prosecutor*, AIR 1976 SC 1994: 1976 Cr LJ 1548: (1976) 3 SCC 618.

some sanctity to what are regarded as words of a dying person. Court has to take into account the questions put and answers elicited, the nature, extent and seriousness of the injuries, his mental and physical condition, the site of injury and surrounding circumstances. Medial evidence may not always be decisive.[1] But it is important.[2] Absence of a medical certificate to the effect that declarant was in a fit condition to make the statement is not always fatal.[3] Opinion of the doctor cannot be conclusive on the ability of the declarant to talk. Medical opinion cannot wipeout direct testimony of eyewitness who deposed that the injured was in a fit condition to speak.[1] Where the executive magistrate who recorded the declaration deposed that the declarant was in a fit state of mind, it was held to be sufficient.[4] Medical evidence cannot override reliable evidence in proof of declaration.[1]

10. Dying declaration should also be voluntary and not tutored one. Mere presence of friends and relatives does not make it tutored.[5]

11. Oral dying declaration made to witnesses can be believed if it inspires confidence.[6] Statement recorded in an injury report by a doctor could be treated as dying declaration.[7] An FIS can contain dying declaration.[8] So also a complaint.[9] But the practice of police recording it ought not to be encouraged.[10] Yet such a dying declaration is relevant.[11] In the case of recorded dying declaration, if a doctor is available, he should be asked to record it.[12] Dying declaration recorded by a police officer before investigation has more value than the one by the investigator.[13] Declaration may be oral or written.[14]

1. *Nanahau Ram* v. *State of Madhya Pradesh*, 1988 Sup SCC 152: 1988 SCC (Cri) 342: AIR 1988 SC 912.
2. *Kanwar Pal Singh* v. *State of Haryana*, 1994 SCC (Cri) 150: AIR 1994 SC 1045: 1994 Cr LJ 1392; *State of Haryana* v. *Harpal Singh*, AIR 1978 SC 1530: 1978 Cr LJ 1603; *Somappa Vamanappa Madar Shankarappa Ravanappa Kaddi* v. *State of Mysore*, AIR 1979 SC 1831: 1979 Cr LJ 1358: (1980) 1 SCC 479; *Paniben* v. *State of Gujarat*, (1992) 2 SCC 474: 1992 Cr LJ 2919: AIR 1992 SC 1817: 1992 AIR SCW 2050; *K. Ramachandra Reddy* v. *Public Prosecutor*, AIR 1976 SC 1994: 1976 Cr LJ 1548: (1976) 3 SCC 618.
3. *Laxman* v. *State of Maharashtra*, (2002) 6 SCC 710: AIR 2002 SC 2973: 2002 AIR SCW 3479: 2002 SCC (Cri) 1491: 2002 Cr LJ 4095.
4. *Sohan Lal* v. *State of Punjab*, (2003) 11 SCC 534: AIR 2003 SC 4466: 2003 Cr LJ 4569.
5. *Habib Usman* v. *State of Maharashtra*, AIR 1979 SC 1181: (1979) 3 SCC 358: 1979 Cr LJ 708; contra *Balak Ram* v. *State of Uttar Pradesh*, AIR 1974 SC 2165: 1974 Cr LJ 1486: (1975) 1 SCR 753.
6. *Ananta Mahanto* v. *State of Orissa*, AIR 1979 SC 1433: (1979) 3 SCC 423: 1979 All Cri R 362.
7. *Ashok Kumar* v. *State of Rajasthan*, AIR 1990 SC 2134: (1991) 1 SCC 166: 1990 Cr LJ 2276.
8. *Munnu Raja* v. *State of Madhya Pradesh*, AIR 1976 SC 2199: (1976) 2 SCR 764: (1976) 3 SCC 104: 1976 Cr LJ 1718; *Lalaram* v. *State of Madhya Bharat*, AIR 1953 MB 249.
9. *Gowri Das Namasuder* v. *Emperor*, ILR 36 Cal 659.
10. *Munnu Raja* v. *State of Madhya Pradesh*, AIR 1976 SC 2199: (1976) 2 SCR 764: (1976) 3 SCC 104: 1976 Cr LJ 1718; *Balak Ram* v. *State of Uttar Pradesh*, AIR 1974 SC 2165: 1974 Cr LJ 1486: (1975) 1 SCR 753.
11. *Dalip Singh* v. *State of Punjab*, AIR 1979 SC 1173: 1979 Cr LR 81: 1979 UJ 334: (1979) 4 SCC 332: 1979 Cr LJ 700; *Ramawati Devi* v. *State of Bihar*, AIR 1983 SC 164: (1983) 1 SCC 211: 1983 Cr LJ 221; *State of Punjab* v. *Amarjit Singh*, AIR 1988 SC 2013: 1988 Supp SCC 704.
12. *Abdul Majid Abdul Rehman* v. *State of Gujarat*, AIR 1976 SC 1782: 1976 Cr LJ 1382: (1976) 4 SCC 351; *Suresh* v. *State of Madhya Pradesh* AIR 1987 SC 860: 1987 Cr LJ 775: (1987) 2 SCC 32.
13. *Munnu Raja* v. *State of Madhya Pradesh*, AIR 1976 SC 2199: (1976) 2 SCR 764: (1976) 3 SCC 104: 1976 Cr LJ 1718.
14. *Surinder Kumar* v. *State (Delhi Administration)*, AIR 1987 SC 692: (1987) 1 SCC 467: 1987 Cr LJ 537; *Ananta Mahanto* v. *State of Orissa*, AIR 1979 SC 1433: (1979) 3 SCC 423: 1979 All Cri R 362.

12. Evidentiary value depends upon the facts and circumstances of the case.[1] No hard and fast rule can be laid down regarding value of dying declaration recorded by police.[2] Such a dying declaration can be suspicious.[3] It requires close scrutiny. If it passes scrutiny, it can be relied on.[4] Great sanctity attaches to words of a dying person, provided the person was in a fit state of mind to make the statement. Court has to keep in mind circumstances like the opportunity to the dying person for observation, whether there was sufficient light if the crime was committed at night, whether the person's capacity to remember the facts stated had not been impaired and whether it was the result of tutoring. A declaration having suspicious features is unreliable.[5] If the court concludes that a declaration is a truthful version regarding the occurrence and identity of the assailant, there is no question of further corroboration.[6] Oral dying declaration made to relations who rushed there on hearing cries could be believed.[7] The fact that a dying declaration was not mentioned in the FIS is of no consequence.[8] Where prosecution deliberately withheld production of a dying declaration, adverse influence can be drawn against prosecution; however this will not justify rejection of other evidence of the occurrence, though such evidence requires to be subjected to careful scrutiny. Witnesses must be certain of the exact words.[9]

13. When a magistrate records a dying declaration, it should preferably be in question and answer form.[10] Such a dying declaration stands on a much higher footing than an oral dying declaration which depends on oral testimony. Statement by signs and nods in answer to questions amounts to oral statement.[11] But the opinion of witnesses as to the meaning of gestures is not admissible. It is for the Court to determine what the gestures meant.[12] It has to be noted that dying declaration is not made on oath. Feeble condition of the injured does not necessarily mean that injured was not in a fit condition, if the doctor had

---

1. *Ramawati Devi* v. *State of Bihar*, AIR 1983 SC 164: (1983) 1 SCC 211: 1983 Cr LJ 221.
2. *Dalip Singh* v. *State of Punjab*, AIR 1979 SC 1173: 1979 Cr LR 81: 1979 UJ 334: (1979) 4 SCC 332: 1979 Cr LJ 700; *State of Punjab* v. *Amarjit Singh*, AIR 1988 SC 2013: 1988 Supp SCC 704.
3. *State (Delhi Administration)* v. *Laxman Kumar*, AIR 1986 SC 250: 1985 CAR 304: 1985 Cr LR 501: (1985) 2 Crimes 758: (1985) 2 SCALE 701: (1985) 4 SCC 476: (1985) 2 SCR 898: 1986 Cr LJ 155.
4. *Jaswant Singh* v. *State (Delhi Administration)*, AIR 1979 SC 190: 1978 Cr LJ 1869: (1978) 4 SCC 85.
5. *Rasheed Beg* v. *State of Madhya Pradesh*, AIR 1974 SC 332: 1974 Cr LJ 361: (1974) 4 SCC 264; *Ram Manorath* v. *State of Uttar Pradesh*, 1981 SCC (Cri) 581: (1981) 2 SCC 654: 1981 Cur LJ 107: *Anil Prakash Shukla* v. *Aravind Shukla*, (2007) 9 SCC 513.
6. *Khushal Rao* v. *State of Bombay*, AIR 1958 SC 22: 1958 SCR 522: 1958 Cr LJ 106: 1958 SCJ 198.
7. *Anantha Mohantha* v. *State of Madhya Pradesh*, (1979) 48 Cuttack LT 515 (SC).
8. *Nanahau Ram* v. *State of Madhya Pradesh*, 1988 Sup SCC 152: 1988 SCC (Cri) 342: AIR 1988 SC 912.
9. *Ramnath Madhoprasad* v. *State of Madhya Pradesh*, AIR 1953 SC 420: 1953 Cr LJ 1772.
10. *Rabi Chandra* v. *State of Orissa*, AIR 1980 SC 1738: (1980) 1 SCC 240: 1980 Cr LJ 1257.
11. *Alexander Perera Chandrasekhara* v. *King*, AIR 1937 PC 24: 166 IC 330: 38 Cr LJ 281 (PC): (1937) 1 MLJ 600; *Meesala Ramakrishna* v. *State of Andhra Pradesh*, (1994) 2 SCJ 409; *Emperor* v. *Sadhu Charan Das*, AIR 1922 Cal 409; *Khushal Rao* v. *State of Bombay*, AIR 1958 SC 22: 1958 SCR 522: 1958 Cr LJ 106: 1958 SCJ 198.
12. *Chandrika Ram Kahar* v. *Emperor*, AIR 1922 Pat 535; *Darpan Potdarin* v. *E.*, AIR 1938 Pat 153: 39 Cr LJ 384; *Alexander Perera Chandrasekhara* v. *King*, AIR 1937 PC 24: 166 IC 330: 38 Cr LJ 281 (PC): (1937) 1 MLJ 600.

given a certificate that he was fit and deposed so.[1] If due to incapacity, injured could not affix signature, thumb impression would be sufficient.[2] Where dying declaration was given in one language and recorded in another, that could not be a ground to say that the recording was not correct.[3]

14. The test is whether the version is shown to be false in respect of the integral part of the case. There should be consistency in material particulars.[4] In one case, the Supreme Court preferred the earlier dying declaration.[5] Plurality of declarations do not add weight to the prosecution case; what matters is their qualitative worth.[6] Each declaration has to be considered independently on its' own merit as to its evidentiary value. One cannot be rejected because of the contents of the other. Court has to examine the circumstances under which each was recorded.[7] Serious inconsistency affects both declarations and can create serious doubt.[8] Naturalness and probability of each has to be considered.[9] Declaration recorded by respectable persons ought to carry weight.[10] Where one declaration is found reliable, conviction can be based on it.[11] Where there is more than one dying declaration, they must be compared and subjected to closer scrutiny and the surrounding circumstances must be examined critically. One which inspires confidence can be accepted.[12]

Evidence regarding dying declaration must be carefully and critically scrutinized as the accused cannot cross-examine the maker.[13] A person on the verge of death is most unlikely to make a false statement unless prompted or tutored by friends or relations.[14] Reliability must be judged in the light of

1. *State of Haryana* v. *Harpal Singh*, AIR 1978 SC 1530: 1978 Cr LJ 1603.
2. *Babu* v. *State of Uttar Pradesh*, AIR 1980 SC 443: (1980) 4 SCC 483: 1980 Cr LJ 392.
3. *Bakhshish Singh* v. *State of Punjab*, AIR 1957 SC 904: 1958 SCR 409: 1957 Cr LJ 1459: 1958 SCJ 106.
4. *Kamla* v. *State of Punjab*, AIR 1993 SC 374: 1992 AIR SCW 3420: 1993 Cr LJ 68.
5. *Mohanlal Gangaram Gehani* v. *State of Maharashtra*, AIR 1982 SC 839: (1982) 1 SCC 700: 1982 (1) SCJ 380.
6. *State of Maharashtra* v. *Sanjay D. Rajhans*, 2005 SCC (Guj) 231: 2004 AIR SCW 6320: AIR 2005 SC 97: 2005 Cr LJ 120.
7. *Nallam Veera Stayanandam* v. *Public Prosecutor, High Court of Andhra Pradesh*, AIR 2004 SC 1708: 2004 AIR SCW 1160: (2004) 10 SCC 769; *Lella Srinivasa Rao* v. *State of Andhra Pradesh*, AIR 2004 SC 1720: 2004 AIR SCW 1254: (2004) 9 SCC 713; *Chinnamma* v. *State of Kerala*, 2004 AIR SCW 1105: AIR 2004 SC 2816: 2004 Cr LJ 1447.
8. *Sanjay* v. *State of Maharashtra*, 2007 AIR SCW 1710: AIR 2007 SC 1368: 2007 Cr LJ 1801.
9. *Jorubha Juzer Singh* v. *State of Gujarat*, AIR 1980 SC 358: 1980 Cr LJ 314: (1980) 1 SCC 672.
10. *Ganpat Mahadeo Mane* v. *State of Maharashtra*, AIR 1993 SC 1180: 1993 Supp (2) SCC 242: 1993 Cr LJ 298.
11. *Harbans Lal* v. *State of Haryana*, AIR 1993 SC 819: 1993 (Supp) 4 SCC 641: 1992 Cr LR 802: 1993 Cr LJ 75.
12. *Kamla* v. *State of Punjab*, AIR 1993 SC 374: 1992 AIR SCW 3420: 1993 Cr LJ 68; *Mohanlal Gangaram Gehani* v. *State of Maharashtra*, AIR 1982 SC 839: (1982) 1 SCC 700: 1982 (1) SCJ 380; *Jorubha Juzer Singh* v. *State of Gujarat*, AIR 1980 SC 358: 1980 Cr LJ 314: (1980) 1 SCC 672; *Ganpat Mahadeo Mane* v. *State of Maharashtra*, AIR 1993 SC 1180: 1993 Supp (2) SCC 242: 1993 Cr LJ 298; *Harbans Lal* v. *State of Haryana*, AIR 1993 SC 819: 1993 Supp 4 SCC 641: 1992 Cr LR 802: 1993 Cr LJ 75; *Aher Rama Gova* v. *State of Gujarat*, AIR 1979 SC 1567: 1979 Cr LJ 1081: (1979) 4 SCC 500; *State of Maharashtra* v. *Sanjay D. Rajhans*, 2005 SCC (Guj) 231: 2004 AIR SCW 6320: AIR 2005 SC 97: 2005 Cr LJ 120; *Amol Singh* v. *State of Madhya Pradesh*, 2008 (3) RCR (Cri) 602 (SC): 2008 (4) Raj 343: (2008) 5 SCC 468.
13. *K. Ramachandra Reddy* v. *Public Prosecutor*, AIR 1976 SC 1994: 1976 Cr LJ 1548: (1976) 3 SCC 618.
14. *Union of India* v. *M.E. Reddy*, AIR 1980 SC 563: (1980) 2 SCC 15: (1980) 1 SCR 736.

attendant facts and circumstances. Opportunity to see and identify assailant, memory, condition of injured, consistency with other evidence and probabilities, time interval, brevity or otherwise, opportunity for prompting or tutoring, suspicious circumstances, clarity and coherence, circumstances in which it was made and intellectual power are some of the factors.[1] Merely because some friends and relatives were with the declarant before he made the dying declaration, it cannot be held to be tutored.[2]

It is possible to reject a part of dying declaration if found untrue and rely on another part, if the two parts are severable.[3] As far as possible, it must be considered as a whole.

Dying declaration cannot be rejected on the sole ground that it was not mentioned in the FIS. FIS given by the injured, who died later on account of his injuries, could be treated as dying declaration.

15. The earlier view was that conviction cannot be rested on an uncorroborated dying declaration.[4] Present view is that if it is found to be true and voluntary and the declarant had opportunity to see, and the declaration is not suspicious and is free from infirmity, conviction can rest on it.[5] Need for corroboration arises not from any inherent weakness of a dying declaration, but if in a given case the court has found some infirmities in it or other evidence disclosed some infirmities.[6] There is no rule of law that a dying declaration cannot be acted upon

1. *Kusa* v. *State of Orissa*, (1980) 2 SCC 207: 1980 Cr LJ 408: AIR 1980 SC 559; *Harbans Singh* v. *State of Punjab*, AIR 1962 SC 439: (1962) 1 Cr LJ 479: 1962 (2) SCJ 662: 1962 All Cri R 115; *Khushal Rao* v. *State of Bombay*, AIR 1958 SC 22: 1958 SCR 522: 1958 Cr LJ 106: 1958 SCJ 198; *V.S. More* v. *State of Maharashtra*, AIR 1978 SC 519: (1978) 1 SCC 622: 1978 Cr LJ 644; *State of Himachal Pradesh* v. *Wazir Chand*, AIR 1978 SC 315: (1978) 1 SCC 130: 1978 Cr LJ 347; *Nanahau Ram* v. *State of Madhya Pradesh*, 1988 Sup SCC 152: 1988 SCC (Cri) 342: AIR 1988 SC 912; *Vajrala Paripurnachry* v. *State of Andhra Pradesh*, AIR 1998 SC 2680: 1998 Cr LJ 4031: 1998 AIR SCW 2723; *Sharad Biridhichand Sarda* v. *State of Maharashtra*, AIR 1984 SC 1622: 1984 4 SCC 116: 1984 Cr LJ 1738.
2. *Habib Usman* v. *State of Maharashtra*, AIR 1979 SC 1181: (1979) 3 SCC 358: 1979 Cr LJ 708.
3. *Godhu* v. *State of Rajasthan*, AIR 1974 SC 2188: 1974 Cr LJ 1500: 1974 SCC (Cri) 859.
4. *Ramnath Madhoprasad* v. *State of Madhya Pradesh*, AIR 1953 SC 420: 1953 Cr LJ 1772.
5. *State of Uttar Pradesh* v. *Ram Sagar Yadav*, (1985) 1 SCC 552: 1985 SCC (Cri) 127: AIR 1985 SC 416: 1986 Cr LJ 836; *State of Assam* v. *Mafzuddin Ahmed*, AIR 1983 SC 274: 1983 Cr LJ 426: (1983) 2 SCC 14; *Ramawati Devi* v. *State of Bihar*, AIR 1983 SC 164: (1983) 1 SCC 211: 1983 Cr LJ 221; *Kusa* v. *State of Orissa*, (1980) 2 SCC 207: 1980 Cr LJ 408: AIR 1980 SC 559; *Tara Chand Damu Sular* v. *State of Maharashtra*, AIR 1962 SC 130: (1962) 2 SCR 775: 1962 Cr LJ 196; *Tara Chand Damu Sular* v. *State of Maharashtra*, AIR 1962 SC 130: (1962) 2 SCR 775: 1962 Cr LJ 196; *Harbans Singh* v. *State of Punjab*, AIR 1962 SC 439: (1962) 1 Cr LJ 479: 1962 (2) SCJ 662: 1962 All Cri R 115; *Khushal Rao* v. *State of Bombay*, AIR 1958 SC 22: 1958 SCR 522: 1958 Cr LJ 106: 1958 SCJ 198; *Munnu Raja* v. *State of Madhya Pradesh*, AIR 1976 SC 2199: (1976) 2 SCR 764: (1976) 3 SCC 104: 1976 Cr LJ 1718; *Gopal Singh* v. *State of Madhya Pradesh*, AIR 1972 SC 1557: (1972) 3 SCC 268: 1972 Cr LJ 1045; *Surendra Nath Mahton* v. *State of Bihar*, AIR 1979 SC 1497: 1979 Cr LJ 1129: (1979) 3 SCC 457; *Muniappan* v. *State of Madras*, AIR 1962 SC 1252: 1962 SCR 869: 1962 Cr LJ 404; *Lallubhai Devechand Shah* v. *State of Gujarat*, AIR 1972 SC 1776: (1971) 3 SCC 767: 1972 Cr LJ 828; *Tapinder Singh* v. *State of Punjab*, AIR 1970 SC 1566: (1971) 1 SCJ 871: 1970 Cr LJ 1415; *V.S. More* v. *State of Maharashtra*, AIR 1978 SC 519: (1978) 1 SCC 622: 1978 Cr LJ 644; *K. Ramachandra Reddy* v. *Public Prosecutor*, AIR 1976 SC 1994: 1976 Cr LJ 1548: (1976) 3 SCC 618; *Kusa* v. *State of Orissa*, (1980) 2 SCC 207: 1980 Cr LJ 408: AIR 1980 SC 559; *Muthu Kutty* v. *State by Inspector of Police*, (2005) 9 SCC 113: AIR 2005 SC 1473: 2004 AIR SCW 7396; *Bhayani Luhana Radhabai* v. *State of Gujarat*, (1977) 1 SCC 762; *Ramnath Madhoprasad* v. *State of Madhya Pradesh*, AIR 1953 SC 420: 1953 Cr LJ 1772.
6. *Khushal Rao* v. *State of Bombay*, AIR 1958 SC 22: 1958 SCR 522: 1958 Cr LJ 106: 1958 SCJ 198.

without corroboration but corroboration strengthens the evidentiary value of the declaration.[1] Dying declaration cannot be rejected on the ground of absence of precise description of manner of causing injuries or description of weapons.[2] If dying declaration differs from the prosecution version, it cannot be acted upon.[3]

16. If the maker survives, the statement is not relevant under section 32. It is not substantive evidence. It is admissible under section 157 as a former statement if the maker is examined as a witness under section 157 or 158.[4]

17. In several cases Supreme Court has found dying declarations in those cases unreliable.[5] Secondary evidence of declaration is admissible.[6]

Section 161 statement of injured will be relevant as dying declaration if he succumbs to the injuries later.[7] If a statement was made by several persons and one of them is dead, the statement of that person is relevant under this section.

18. **Clause(2):** This clause refers to a statement made by a person referred to in the main provision, in the ordinary course of business, and in particular, when it consists of any entry or memorandum made by him in books kept in the ordinary course of business, or in the discharge of professional duty, or of an acknowledgement written or signed by him of the receipt of money, goods, securities or property of any kind, or of a document used in commerce written or signed by him or of the date of letter or other document usually dated, written or signed by him. Reason for this rule is the difficulty in finding proof and circumstantial guarantee of truth. Though relevant, weight to be attached depends on facts and circumstances of each case.

Entries in accounts which are relevant only under section 34 are not by themselves sufficient to charge any person with liability and they require

---

1. *Girdhar Shankar Tawade* v. *State of Maharashtra*, AIR 2002 SC 2078: (2002) 5 SCC 177: 2002 Cr LJ 2814.
2. *Dalbir Singh* v. *State of Punjab*, AIR 1987 SC 1328: 1987 Cr LJ 1065: (1987) 3 SCC 360; *State of Maharashtra* v. *Krishnamurthy Laxmipati Naidu*, AIR 1981 SC 617: 1981 Cr LJ 9: 1981 SCC (Cri) 364 (SC): (1980) Supp SCC 455; *Surajdeo Oza* v. *State of Bihar*, (1980) Supp SCC 769: 1979 SCC (Cri) 519: AIR 1979 SC 1505; *Som Nath* v. *State of Haryana*, AIR 1980 SC 1226: 1980 3 SCC 301: 1980 Cr LJ 925; *Jayaraj* v. *State of Tamil Nadu*, 1976 Cr LJ 1186: AIR 1976 SC 1519: 1976 SCC (Cri) 293.
3. *State of Uttar Pradesh* v. *Madan Mohan*, (1989) 3 SCC 390: 1989 SCC (Cri) 585: AIR 1989 SC 1519.
4. *Ramnath Madhoprasad* v. *State of Madhya Pradesh*, AIR 1953 SC 420: 1953 Cr LJ 1772; *Maqsoodan* v. *State of Uttar Pradesh*, AIR 1983 SC 126: (1983) 1 SCC 218: 1983 Cr LJ 218: 1982 ALJ 1524.
5. *State (Delhi Administration)* v. *Laxman Kumar*, AIR 1986 SC 250: 1985 CAR 304: 1985 Cr LR 501: (1985) 2 Crimes 758: (1985) 2 SCALE 701: (1985) 4 SCC 476: (1985) 2 SCR 898: 1986 Cr LJ 155; *Mohd. Ekramul* v. *State of Bihar*, AIR 1973 SC 1395; *Godhu* v. *State of Rajasthan*, AIR 1974 SC 2188: 1974 Cr LJ 1500: 1974 SCC (Cri) 859; *Gopal Singh* v. *State of Madhya Pradesh*, AIR 1972 SC 1557: (1972) 3 SCC 268: 1972 Cr LJ 1045; *Ghurphekan* v. *State of Uttar Pradesh*, AIR 1972 SC1172: 1972 Cr LJ 746; *Nirmal Singh* v. *State of Rajasthan*, AIR 1972 SC 945: 1972 Cr LJ 580: (1972) 3 SCC 781; *Banka Naiko* v. *State of Orissa*, AIR 1976 SC 2013: (1976) 3 SCC 401: 1976 Cr LJ 1556; *Kake Singh* v. *State of Madhya Pradesh*, AIR 1982 SC 1021: 1981 Supp SCC 25: 1982 Cr LJ 986: (1981) Supp SCC 25: 1981 SCC (Cr) 645; *S. Guin* v. *Grindlays Bank Ltd.*, AIR 1986 SC 289: 1986 Cr LJ 255: (1986) 1 SCC 654; *Jagga Singh* v. *State of Punjab*, AIR 1995 SC 135: 1994 SCC (Cri) 1798: 1994 Supp (3) SCC 463: 1995 Cal Cr LR (SC) 18: JT 1994 (6) SC 99.
6. *Aher Rama Gova* v. *State of Gujarat*, AIR 1979 SC 1567: 1979 Cr LJ 1081: (1979) 4 SCC 500.
7. *Hazari Lal* v. *State*, AIR 1980 SC 873: (1980) 2 SCC 390: 1980 SCC (Cri) 458: 1980 Cr LJ 564; *Patel Hiral Joitram* v. *State of Gujarat*, 2002 SCC (Cri) 1.

corroboration.[1] But if the entries are such as to attract section 32(2), they constitute substantive evidence and there is no legal requirement of corroboration, unless circumstances of a given case warrant it.[2] This clause is also an exception to hearsay rule. *See* also section 16, illustration (a) and section 114, illustration (f).

19. **"Ordinary course of business"** means not only business as would be conducted by a man of business, but means, in the way that business (public, private) is conducted. It has no connection with a course of business which suggests a series of acts of business.[3] The occupation need not be a mercantile or an industrial one or even a secular one. Business includes trade, profession, occupation and calling of every kind.[4] Autopsy report is a statement made by a doctor in the ordinary course of business and in the discharge of professional duty.[5] The words in the clause have to be construed broadly and liberally.[6]

20. **"Book"** is a collective unity of sheets even at the time of making entries and intended as serving a permanent record. It need not be bound in any particular way.[7] In case of loose sheets with blanks left at different places so that the sheets and entries could be substituted or interpolated at different places, it cannot be said entries were made in the ordinary course of business.[8] A logbook in loose sheets and not in book bound form would not be reliable.[9] A notebook, not written from day to day but in an *adhoc* way from slips at a number of consecutive sittings is not admissible. Account book containing entry regarding birth of a baby and to expenses incurred on the occasion would be relevant.[10] Counterfoil entries in receipt books made in the ordinary course of business are relevant.[11] Entries in a diary maintained in a solicitor's office are relevant, even if they are unsigned, if they have come from proper custody and appear to have been kept regularly.[12]

21. **"Professional duty"** – Exercise of such a duty in a given case depends largely upon the nature and terms of the engagement. Examples are injury report, autopsy report, carbon copy of medical certificate, Commissioner's report, entries in palm leaf manuscripts or books of genealogy maintained by professional genealogists, register of marriages, policy diary.[13] Entries in Palm

1. *V.K. Abraham* v. *N.K. Abraham*, AIR 1978 Mad 56: (1978) 1 Mad LJ 331: ILR (1978) 2 Mad 95.
2. *Rampyari Bai* v. *Balaji*, ILR 28 Bom 284 (PC); *Maulvi A.R.M. Abdul Wahed* v. *Nagendra Chandra Lahiri*, AIR 1940 Cal 524; *Chaturbhuj Singh* v. *Sarada Charan Guha*, AIR 1933 Pat 6: ILR 11 Pat 701; *Babhnaji* v. *Ratanlal*, AIR 1934 Nag 106; *R.V.E. Venkatachala Gounder* v. *Arulmigu Vishweswara Swami & V.P. Temple*, AIR 2003 SC 4548: 2003 AIR SCW 5316: (2003) 8 SCC 752.
3. *Ramamurthi* v. *Subba Rao*, AIR 1937 Mad 19: 167 IC 30.
4. *Keolapati* v. *Raja Amar Krishna Narain Singh*, AIR 1939 PC 249.
5. *Mohan Singh* v. *E.*, 85 IC 647: AIR 1925 All 413: 26 Cr LJ 551; *Kochu* v. *State*, 1979 Ker LT 550.
6. *Devi Singh* v. *Phulma*, AIR 1961 HP 10; *M.V. Mfg. Co.* v. *K.J. Mills*, AIR 1969 Cal 496.
7. *Ambalavana Pillai* v. *Gouri Ammal*, AIR 1936 Mad 871: 44 Mad LW 467.
8. *Ganesh Prasad Ray* v. *Narendra Nath Sen*, AIR 1953 SC 431: 17 Cut LT 73: 1951 Ker LT (SC) 28.
9. *State of Kerala* v. *Thomas*, (1986) 2 SCC 411: 1983 Cri App R (SC) 114.
10. *Mirabai* v. *Kaushalayabai*, AIR 1949 Nag 235: ILR 1948 Nag 794: 1949 NLJ 154.
11. *P.K. Rukmini Bai* v. *Venkateswara Silk House, Bangalore*, IR 1972 Mysore 143: (1971) 2 Mys LJ 635: 1972 Ren CR 272.
12. *Mohd. Yusuf* v. *D.*, AIR 1968 Bom 112: 68 Bom LR 228: ILR 1966 Bom 420.
13. *Prithi Chand* v. *State of Himachal Pradesh*, AIR 1989 SC 702: 1989 CAR 56: 1989 Cr LR 235: (1989) 1 Crimes 384: (1989) 1 SCC 432: (1989) 1 SCR 123: (1989) 1 SCALE 74: JT 1989 (1) SC 106: 1989 Cr LJ 841; *Zakeri Begum* v. *Sakina Begum*, ILR 19 Cal 689: 19 Ind App 157 (PC).

leaf manuscripts of geneology maintained by professional genelalogists and systematically maintained are relevant.[1]

Personal knowledge of the person who made entries is not necessary.[2] Contemporaneousness is not also necessary, through lack of it may affect the weight.

22. **Acknowledgement written or signed**: Illustrations (e), (g) indicate that word "business" is to be understood not in a restricted or narrow sense. Account book not kept in the ordinary course of business would be relevant if it contains an admissions of liability.[3]

Section 32 relates only to relevancy and to the manner of its proof. Authorship of entries has to be proved. In appropriate cases section 60 can be invoked.[4]

23. **Clause (3):** This clause deals with a statement made by a person described in the main part of the section, when the statement is against the pecuniary or proprietary interest of the person making it or when, if true, it would expose him to or would have exposed him to a criminal prosecution or a suit for damages. The principle is that what a man states against his interest is probably true.[5] The place of test of oath and cross-examination is in some measure supplied by the circumstances of the making of the statement and the character of statement.

"Against interest": To decide whether a statement is against the interest of the maker one should look at the statement itself and not to the nature of the transaction in the course of which the statement was made. He might have given away something valuable in the transaction, but that does not matter. Question is, is the statement made in the transaction against his interest.[6] Entry against interest means an entry standing alone is *prima facie* against his interest. It is not a kind of interest which he may feel about a friend or relation.[7] The fact stated in the statement must be against his interest.[8] Admission of interest must have some value.

This principle will not apply unless the maker knew the statement was against his interest.[9] This would be a question of fact in each case, depending on the surrounding circumstances.[10] Knowledge or consciousness must be at the time of making the statement. It is not sufficient that it turns out to be against his interest subsequently.

---

1. *Sitaji* v. *Bijendra Narain Choudhary*, AIR 1954 SC 601: 1951 Pat 356: 28 Pat 447.
2. *Maroti Raghoba* v. *Mahadeo Chindhu*, AIR 1947 Nag 106.
3. *Ambalavana Pillai* v. *Gouri Ammal*, AIR 1936 Mad 871: 44 Mad LW 467.
4. *Venkatammal* v. *K.V. Ramaswami Aiyar*, AIR 1941 Mad 602.
5. *Savitri Devi* v. *Ram Ran Bijoy Prosad Singh*, AIR 1950 PC 1: 63 MLW 45: 54 CWN 233: 76 IA 255 1950 ALJ 134: 1950: 1 MLJ 163; *Dal Bahadur Singh* v. *Bijai Bahadur Singh*, AIR 1930 PC 79: 52 A 1: 57 IA 14: 122 IC 8.
6. *Bhim Singh* v. *Kan Singh*, (1980) 3 SCC 72: AIR 1980 SC 727; *Markhu Mahto* v. *Saharai Mahto*, AIR 1940 Pat 16: 184 IC 246.
7. *Arjun Sukla* v. *Jujesthi Sukla*, AIR 1954 Ori 52: 19 Cut LT 354; *Re Adams Benton*, AIR 1992 Pat 240A.
8. Wigmore on Evidence, III Edn. section 1462).
9. *Savitri Devi* v. *Ram Ran Bijoy Prosad Singh*, AIR 1950 PC 1: 63 MLW 45: 54 CWN 233: 76 IA 255 1950 ALJ 134: 1950: 1 MLJ 163.
10. *Ramrati Kuer* v. *Dwarika Prasad Singh*, AIR 1967 SC 1134: (1967) 2 SCJ 789: (1967) 1 SCR 153.

Pecuniary interest is affected where the entry has the effect of charging the maker with pecuniary liability.[1] Attestation of a deed of adoption by the natural sons of the adopter amounts to a statement against pecuniary interest.[2]

Proprietary interest:

Declaration by deceased persons (or others within the meaning of section 32) would be relevant as admissions, being statements against the maker's proprietary interest, both under section 21 and Section 32(3). Examples are, statement that a transaction was benami, statement by a coparcener that he has no further interest in family property or property left by the father, allegation of separation or, that a person has only life interest under a Will etc.[3]

So also recitals of boundaries in documents not interpartes.[4] Regarding such recitals in documents between parties, the judicial view is not uniform.

"If true would expose him to criminal….. or suit for damages. Susceptibility to such exposure should be at the time statement was made. (*See* Illustration (f)). Such a statement made after the expiry of period of limitation for suit or for criminal prosecution would cause no risk and is not relevant.

The statement must have been, to the maker's knowledge, contrary to his interest. Such knowledge is essential.[5]

24. **Clause (4):** Clause (4) section 32 deals with a statement made by a person described in the main part of the section, when the statement gives the opinion of any such person as to the existence of any public right or custom or matter of public or general interest, of the existence of which, if it existed, he would have been likely to be aware, and when such statement was made before any controversy as to such right, custom or matter had arisen.

Matter should relate to public right or custom or any matter of public or general interest. What is relevant is that the statement contains the opinion of the maker and not facts. The statement should have been made at a undisputed time.[6] The logic of this provision is founded upon the nature of such rights as are covered by the clause and reliability of the opinion with regard to them. Such statement may cover opinion relating to facts in issue or relevant facts.[7]

---

1. *Babhnaji* v. *Ratanlal*, AIR 1934 Nag 106; *Kalyan Rai* v. *Jagannath*, AIR 1925 All 130 (1); *Gulam Ali Saha* v. *Sultan Khan*, AIR 1967 Ori 55: 32 Cut LT 510: ILR 1966 Cut 571.
2. *Minor Nagammal* v. *Sankarappa Naidu* alias *Muthalagiri Naidu*, AIR 1931 Mad 264; *Gnanamuthu Nadan* v. *Veilukanda Nadathi, Wife of Guruswami Nadan*, AIR 1927 Bom 433; *Savitri Dei* v. *Bhaskar*, AIR 1972 Ori 148: (1971) 2 Cut WR 814.
3. *Bhim Singh* v. *Kan Singh*, (1980) 3 SCC 72: AIR 1980 SC 727; *Bhagwati Prasad Sah* v. *Dulhin Rameshwari Kuer*, AIR 1952 SC 72: 1951 SCR 603: 1952 SCJ 115; *Repaka Appalanarasimham* v. *Repaka Udalama*, AIR 1959 AP 407: ILR 1959 AP 208; *Manik Biswas* v. *Maharaja Jagadindra Nath Roy Bahadur*, AIR 1914 Cal 704; *Champat* v. *Balakdas*, AIR 1924 Nag 131.
4. *Thyagarajan Chitty* v. *Narayana Thevan*, AIR 1940 Mad 450: 51 Mad LW 509: 1940 MWN 80; *Tika Ram* v. *Moti Lal*, AIR 1930 All 299: 1930 All LJ 564; *Abdul Rahim Kazi* v. *Jonabali Sardar*, AIR 1923 Cal 299; *Ram Nandan Prasad* v. *Tilakdhari Lal*, AIR 1933 Pat 636: 145 Ind Cas 944; Contra decisions- *Kandasami Goundan* v. *Marudachala Goundan*, AIR 1928 Mad 105: 107 Ind Cas 293; *Abdul Karim* v. *Chhale Ahmed*, AIR 1926 Cal 479; *Brojo Mohan Das Adhikari* v. *Gaya Prosad Karan*, AIR 1926 Cal 948: 30 Cal WN 761: 45 Cal LJ 55; *Deokinandan Prasad* v. *Deoki Kumar*, AIR 1934 Pat 617:152 Ind Cas 829.
5. *Savitri Devi* v. *Ram Ran Bijoy Prosad Singh*, AIR 1950 PC 1: 63 MLW 45: 54 CWN 233: 76 IA 255 1950 ALJ 134: 1950: 1 MLJ 163.
6. *Ekradeshwar Singh* v. *Javeshwari Bahuasin*, AIR 1914 PC 76: 42 C 582: 41 IA 275: 25 IC 417.
7. *Raghu Bhushan Tirtha Swamy* v. *Vidya Varidhi Tirtha Swamy*, AIR 1917 Mad 809: 34 Ind Cas 875.

The statement of a person covered by this clause is a statement not covering facts within his own knowledge, but merely has opinion, of the general right, and not of particular facts which support or negate it.[1] The test of relevancy is whether the persons whose opinion is placed on record was likely to have had knowledge. Such opinion can be positive or negative, direct or indirect.

Sections 48 and 49 refer to opinion of living witness.[2] Reference may be made to the 4th para and the first proviso of section 60.

Public right or custom: Village administrative paper (Wajib-ul-arag) is prepared with due care and after due enquiry by a public servant in the discharge of his official duties and is part of the settlement record.[3] Entries in certain records (wajib-ul-arag) being opinion of lambardars etc., are relevant as evidence to prove custom.[4]

Matters of public or general interest: (Illustration (i))

The words "public" or "general" are used synonymously. The right must have been one the existence of which (if it existed) the declarant would have been likely to be aware. The word "interest" in "matters of public or general interest" means those which are connected with legal rights and liabilities of the community.[5] Examples are, boundaries of town, parish, existence of highway, pathway, liability to repair bridges. But private boundary, private right of way are matters of private nature.[6]

Statement may be oral or written and in any form. It may be in the form of recitals in deeds, maps, orders, judgments.

Statement must have been before the particular controversy commenced.[7]

25. **Clauses (5) and (6)** – Clause (5) deals with a statement made by a person described in the main part of the section, relating to the existence of any relationship by blood, marriage or adoption between persons as to whose relationship by blood, marriage or adoption the person making the statement had special means of knowledge, and when the statement was made before the question in dispute was raised.

Clause (6) deals with a statement made by a person described in the main part of the section, relating to the existence of any relationship by blood, marriage or adoption between persons deceased, and is made in any will or deed relating to the affairs of the family to which any such deceased person belonged, or in any family pedigree or upon any tombstone, family portrait or other things on which such statement is usually made, and when such statement was made before the question in dispute was raised.[8]

1. Stephen's Digest on Law of Evidence, 3rd Edn., Vol. 1 Article 30.
2. *Garuradhwaja Prasad* v. *Superundhwaja Prasad*, ILR 23 All 37: (1900) 10 Mad LJ 267: 27 Ind App 238 (PC).
3. *Avadh Kishore Das* v. *Ram Gopal*, AIR 1979 SC 861: 1979 UJ (SC) 251: (1979) 4 SCC 790.
4. *Digambar Singh* v. *Ahmad Sayeed Khan*, AIR 1914 PC 11: ILR 37 All 129; *Sheobaran Singh* v. *Kulsum-un-nissa*, AIR 1927 PC 113: ILR 49 All 367: 54 Ind App 204.
5. *Busoid* v. *Newaj Ahmed Khan*, AIR 1929 Cal 533: 33 Cal WN 439.
6. *Kesho Prasad Singh* v. *Bhagjogna Kuer*, AIR 1937 PC 69: 41 Cal WN 577: ILR 16 Pat 258.
7. *Ekradeshwar Singh* v. *Javeshwari Bahuasin*, AIR 1914 PC 76: 42 C 582: 41 IA 275: 25 IC 417; *Protap Chandra Deo Dhanbal Deb* v. *Sri Raja Jagadish Chandra Deo Dhabal Deb*, AIR 1925 Cal 116: 82 Ind Cas 886.
8. *Biro* v. *Atma Ram*, AIR 1937 PC 101: 64 IA 92: 167 IC 346; *Kalidindi Venkata Subbaraju* v. *Chintalapati Subbaraju*, AIR 1968 SC 947: (1968) 2 SCJ 513: (1968) 2 SCR 292.

Section 32(5) is not controlled by section 50 which operates in its own field. Under Clauses (5) and (6), the statement should have been made before the question in dispute was raised as required in the case of clause (4).[1] Clause (5) is wider in scope than clause (6). Under clause (6) relationship must be between deceased persons and the statement must have been made in the documents etc., referred to therein; Clause (5) relates to relationships between any persons but the statement must be by a person having special means of knowledge. Clause (5) does not limit the scope of the word "statement". These clauses should not be construed literally.[2]

A statement relating to existence of a particular relationship is admissible to prove the facts contained in the statement on any issue. Plaint in a prior suit was admissible to prove the order in which sons of a particular person were born and their ages.[3] Statement of age is admissible.[4] Statement regarding death is also admissible.[5] Statement in a will regarding adoption is relevant, though not conclusive.[6] "Existence" includes "non-existence".

In regard to relationship, special means of knowledge required should be presumed in the case of members of the family.[7] So also a family priest.[8] Evidence is not admissible to show general reputation regarding relationship.[9] Servants, friends and neighbours may be regarded is having special means of knowledge as to relationship. Special knowledge is not the same as personal knowledge. Special knowledge may have come through one's elders.[10] "Deed" referred in clause (6) takes in a horoscope.[11] However, it's evidentiary value regarding age is not very substantial.[12] School records have more probative value than horoscope.[13]

In the case of statement made by persons, some of whom are still living, it would be relevant since it was made also by deceased persons.[14]

1. *State of Bihar* v. *Radha Krishna Singh*, AIR 1983 SC 684: (1983) 1 SCALE 789: (1983) 2 SCR 808: (1983) 3 SCC 118: 1983 Cur Civ LJ (SC) 273; *Kalidindi Venkata Subbaraju* v. *Chintalapati Subbaraju*, AIR 1968 SC 947: (1968) 2 SCJ 513: (1968) 2 SCR 292.
2. *Kalidindi Venkata Subbaraju* v. *Chintalapati Subbaraju*, AIR 1968 SC 947: (1968) 2 SCJ 513: (1968) 2 SCR 292.
3. *Dhanmull* v. *Ramchander*, ILR 24 Cal 265: 1 CWN 270; *Chuah Hooi Gnoh Neoh* v. *Khaw Sim Bee*, AIR 1915 PC 45: 31 IC 637: 19 CWN 787; *Ram* v. *Jogeshwar*, ILR 20 Cal 758.
4. *Kalidindi Venkata Subbaraju* v. *Chintalapati Subbaraju*, AIR 1968 SC 947: (1968) 2 SCJ 513: (1968) 2 SCR 292; *Shivashanker Singh* v. *Raghubansh Singh*, AIR 1967 Pat 172: 1966 BLJR 406.
5. *Sayeruddin Akonda* v. *Samiruddin Akonda*, AIR 1923 Cal 378: 72 Ind Cas 985.
6. *Banwari Lal* v. *Trilok Chand*, AIR 1980 SC 419: (1980) 1 SCC 349: (1980) 1 SCR 998.
7. *Provincial Automobile Co.* v. *Narayan Krishnarao*, AIR 1943 Nag 252: ILR 1943 Nag 577; *Mohammad Asad Ali Khan* v. *Sadiq Ali Khan*, AIR 1943 Oudh 91.
8. *Balak Ram High School* v. *Nanu Mal*, AIR 1930 Lah 579: ILR 11 Lah 503.
9. *Lakshmi Reddi* v. *Venkata Reddi*, AIR 1937 PC 201: 31 Sind LR 575: 168 IC 881.
10. *State of Bihar* v. *Radha Krishna Singh*, AIR 1983 SC 684: (1983) 1 SCALE 789: (1983) 2 SCR 808: (1983) 3 SCC 118: 1983 Cur Civ LJ (SC) 273; *Sitaji* v. *Bijendra Narain Choudhary*, AIR 1954 SC 601: 1951 Pat 356: 28 Pat 447; *Devi Prasad* v. *Radha Choudhrani*, 31 Ind App 160: 32 Cal 84 (PC).
11. *Ramanathan* v. *Murugan*, AIR 1917 Mad 930: 33 Ind Cas 969.
12. *The Secretary to Government Home Department* v. *T.V. Hari Rao*, AIR 1978 Mad 42.
13. *State of Punjab* v. *Mohinder Singh*, (2005) 3 SCC 702: AIR 2005 SC 1868: 2005 AIR SCW 1476.
14. *Dolgobinda Paricha* v. *Nimai Charan Misra*, AIR 1959 SC 914: 1960 SCJ 879: (1959) 2 SCR 814: 1959 26 Cut LT 130: 1959 SCR Supp (2) 814.

The statement should have been made before the question in dispute was raised.[1]

26. **Clause (7):** deals with a statement made by a person described in the main part of the section, contained in any deed, will or other document which relates to any such transaction as is mentioned is section 13(a). This clause relates to both public and private rights and customs as in the case of section 13.

The opposite party need not have been a party to the transaction. Clause (4) deals with verbal and written statements relating to public or general rights and customs in general. Clause (7) does not take in oral statements. Ancient documents by which right of property purports to have been exercised are relevant, even in favour of grantor or his successor on, in proof of ancient possession. While clause (4) admits parol evidence of reputation in proof of public or private rights, clause (7) does not admit parol evidence of such a nature. The statement must have been made in relation to a transaction where it was necessary to make that statement. It should not have been a gratuitous statement.[2] Will also is a transaction.[3]

27. **Clause (8):** Statement by a number of persons *i.e.*, group of individuals and expressing feelings or impressions on the matter in question is relevant and may be proved by testimony of others. It is a common statement giving vent to feelings and impressions. Relevancy of individual statements and feelings is dealt with by sections 14 and 45 to 51. Illustration (n) brings out the meaning of the clause.

SECTION 33:

This section deals with depositions of witnesses in judicial proceedings or before any person authorised by law to take such evidence. Such depositions are relevant in a subsequent judicial proceeding or in a later stage of the same judicial proceeding for proving the truth of the facts which such depositions state. This can be done in the following five situations:

(1) When the witness is dead,[4]

(2) When the witness cannot be found,[5]

(3) When the witness is incapable of giving evidence,[6]

(4) When the witness is kept out of the way by the adverse party,[7] or

1. *Kalidindi Venkata Subbaraju* v. *Chintalapati Subbaraju*, AIR 1968 SC 947: (1968) 2 SCJ 513: (1968) 2 SCR 292; *State of Bihar* v. *Radha Krishna Singh*, AIR 1983 SC 684: (1983) 1 SCALE 789: (1983) 2 SCR 808: (1983) 3 SCC 118: 1983 Cur Civ LJ (SC) 273.
2. *Khudiram Ojha* v. *Amodebala Debi*, AIR 1948 Pat 426; *Governor-General of India in Council representing the Great Indian Peninsula Railway Administration* v. *Bhanwari Devi*, AIR 1961 All 14: 1960 All LJ 770: ILR (1960) 2 All 586.
3. *Hitnarain Singh* v. *Rambarai Rai*, AIR 1928 Pat 459: ILR 7 Pat 733.
4. *Sitaji* v. *Bijendra Narain Choudhary*, AIR 1954 SC 601: 1951 Pat 356: 28 Pat 447; *Tarlok Singh* v. *State of Punjab*, AIR 1974 SC 1797: (1973) 2 SCC 458: 1974 Cr LJ 1265.
5. *Gurdayal* v. *Emperor*, AIR 1949 Pun 228; *Jose* v. *State of Kerala*, (1973) 3 SCC 472: 1973 SCC (Cri) 372: AIR 1973 SC 944: 1973 Cr LJ 687.
6. *Ibid., Jose* v. *State of Kerala*, (1973) 3 SCC 472: 1973 SCC (Cri) 372: AIR 1973 SC 944: 1973 Cr LJ 687; *Chainchal Singh* v. *K.E.*, AIR 1946 PC 1: ILR (1944) Lah 451: ILR (1944) Lah 451.
7. *Abbas Mandal* v. *Emperor*, AIR 1931 Cal 473; *Mokshed* v. *Emperor*, AIR 1944 Mad 319.

(5) If his presence cannot be obtained without an amount of delay or expense which, under the circumstances of the case, the court considers unreasonable.[1]

Provided (a) that the proceeding was between the same parties or their representatives in interest, and

(b) the adverse party in the first proceedings had the right and opportunity to cross-examine, and

(c) that the questions in issue were substantially the same in the first and in the second proceeding.

The section further states by way of explanation, that a criminal trial or enquiry shall be deemed to be a proceeding between the prosecutor and the accused within the meaning of the section.

Primary evidence is evidence to be given by a witness in the subsequent proceedings; it is only when production of primary evidence is beyond the power of the party on the grounds mentioned in the section that secondary evidence in the form of prior deposition of the witness is allowed to be given. This Section provides yet another exception to the hearsay rule. The existence of one or the other of the five situations in which only this exception to the hearsay rule is available, must be proved as a precondition.[2] In a civil case, a party can waive such proof;[3] but in a criminal case, strict proof ought to be given of one or the other prerequisites.[4] An affidavit is not "evidence given by a witness" within the meaning of this section. Statement of approval under section 306(4) of Cr.P.C. is not attracted by this section.[5]

Evidence should have been given by a witness in a judicial proceeding or before any person authorised by law to take evidence; this means that the person taking evidence administers oath or solemn affirmation. Reference may be made in this connection to the presumption in section 80. Omission to take oath shall not invalidate the proceedings.

This section cannot apply to a case diary statement.[6] This section does not apply to a statement recorded under section 164, Cr.P.C. because the accused had no opportunity of cross examination.[7]

Where the records showed that the summons were received back with the report that the witnesses were dead, the earlier depositions of the witnesses would be relevant.[8] Where a witness was examined in a previous case to prove

---

1. *Prithi Chand* v. *State of Himachal Pradesh*, AIR 1989 SC 702: 1989 CAR 56: 1989 Cr LR 235: (1989) 1 Crimes 384: (1989) 1 SCC 432: (1989) 1 SCR 123: (1989) 1 SCALE 74: JT 1989 (1) SC 106: 1989 Cr LJ 841; *Bakhshish Singh* v. *State of Punjab*, AIR 1957 SC 904: 1958 SCR 409: 1957 Cr LJ 1459: 1958 SCJ 106.
2. *Bakhshish Singh* v. *State of Punjab*, AIR 1957 SC 904: 1958 SCR 409: 1957 Cr LJ 1459: 1958 SCJ 106; *Bal Gangadhar Tilak* v. *Shriniwas Pandit*, AIR 1915 PC 7: 39 B 441: 42 IA 135: 29 IC 639; *Chainchal Singh* v. *K.E.*, AIR 1946 PC 1: ILR (1944) Lah 451: ILR (1944) Lah 451.
3. *Kalyan Peoples' Co-operative Bank Ltd. (In both the Appeals)* v. *Dulhanbibi Aqual Aminsaheb Patil*, AIR 1966 SC 1072: 1963 (2) SCJ 176: (1963) 2 SCR 348.
4. *Chainchal Singh* v. *K.E.*, AIR 1946 PC 1: ILR (1944) Lah 451: ILR (1944) Lah 451.
5. *L.S. Ashokan* v. *State of Kerala*, 2005 Cr LJ 384.
6. *Sukhar* v. *State of Uttar Pradesh*, (1999) 9 SCC 509: 2000 SCC (Cri) 419: AIR 1999 SC 3883: 2000 Cr LJ 29.
7. *Arjun Biswas* v. *State of Assam*, 2005 Cr LJ 554.
8. *Nirmal Singh* v. *State of Haryana*, AIR 2000 SC 1416: (2000) 4 SCC 41: 2000 Cr LJ 1803.

the entries in a pedigree table maintained by Panjikars, such deposition would be relevant if the witness died in the meanwhile.[1] Mere statement of the police or the prosecutor that a witness summoned was unable to attend court is not sufficient compliance with requirement of the section. In the case of a doctor examined before the committal magistrate a police constable deposed in the Sessions Court that his enquiries showed that the whereabouts of the doctor were not known and the hospital superintendent reported that the doctor was no longer in government service and his whereabouts were not known and the Sessions Court treated the earlier deposition as relevant evidence, Supreme Court held that there was no infirmity in the action of the Court.[2] The action was justified on the ground that the doctor's presence could not be obtained without an amount of delay or expense which, under the circumstances of the case, the court considers unreasonable. In such a case, the carbon copy, made by a uniform process, of the doctors' certificate would be admissible.[3]

Relevancy of the previous evidence of a witness who is kept out of the way by the adverse party is justified on the principle of justice which will not permit a party to take advantage of his own wrong.

The explanation to the section indicates that the section applies to criminal cases also. Consequently, depositions in criminal cases may be used in civil cases and *vice versa*, if the other conditions are satisfied.[4] A private person at whose instance and report, the prosecution is launched by the police is a prosecutor within the meaning of this context.[5] A mere informant is not a prosecutor. He must be a person making a complaint upon which prosecution is launched.

Relevant evidence can be brought on the record without following the regular mode, if parties agree.[6] But in a criminal case, consent of counsel for accused cannot do away with the necessity of the court being satisfied about relevancy under the section.[7]

Even depositions of parties, though relevant as admissions against persons making them, are not relevant against persons who were not parties to previous litigation in which the depositions were recorded.[8] An admission of marriage by the accused is not evidence of it for the purpose of proving marriage in an adultery or bigamy case.[9]

According to section 158, whenever any statement relevant under section 32 or 33 is proved, all matters may be proved, either in order to contradict or to corroborate it or in order to impeach or confirm the credit of the person by

---

1. *Sitaji* v. *Bijendra Narain Choudhary*, AIR 1954 SC 601: 1951 Pat 356: 28 Pat 447.
2. *Bakhshish Singh* v. *State of Punjab*, AIR 1957 SC 904: 1958 SCR 409: 1957 Cr LJ 1459: 1958 SCJ 106.
3. *Prithi Chand* v. *State of Himachal Pradesh*, AIR 1989 SC 702: 1989 CAR 56: 1989 Cr LR 235: (1989) 1 Crimes 384: (1989) 1 SCC 432: (1989) 1 SCR 123: (1989) 1 SCALE 74.
4. Field on Evidence, 11th Edition, Vol. III, Page 2072.
5. *Gaya Prasad* v. *Bhagath Singh*, ILR 30 All 525: 35 Ind App 189 (PC); *S.T. Saheb* v. *Hassan Gani*, AIR 1957 Mad 646.
6. *Kalyan Peoples' Co-operative Bank Ltd. (In both the Appeals)* v. *Dulhanbibi Aqual Aminsaheb Patil*, AIR 1966 SC 1072: 1963 (2) SCJ 176: (1963) 2 SCR 348.
7. *Chainchal Singh* v. *K.E.*, AIR 1946 PC 1: ILR (1944) Lah 451: ILR (1944) Lah 451.
8. *Ambika Prasad Thakur* v. *Ram Ekbal Rai*, (1966) 1 SCA 35: AIR 1966 SC 605: (1966) 1 SCR 758.
9. *Kanwal Ram* v. *Himachal Pradesh Administration*, AIR 1966 SC 614: 1966 (1) SCJ 210: (1966) 1 SCR 532.

whom it was made, which might have been proved if that person had been called as a witness and had denied upon cross-examination of the truth of the matter suggested.

Identity of the deponent requires to be proved.[1] Privy Council has held that the mere description of the witness in the heading of the deposition is not part of the deposition.

Part of deposition abstracted in a judgment cannot be made use of.[2]

The party in the first proceeding must have represented the interest of the party in the second proceeding.[3] It is not necessary that all the questions in issue in the two cases should be substantially the same.[4]

Where the approver was examined before the committal court (under the old Code) and prosecution was unable to produce him before the Sessions Court, it was held that the approver's deposition is relevant evidence in the Sessions Court.[5] Where a witness who was examined and cross-examined in committal Court later suffered from paralysis at the time of session's trial, it was held that his prior deposition would be relevant under the section during the Sessions trial.[6]

Right and opportunity to cross-examine are important.[7] In a given case, there might have been right, but no opportunity and *vice-versa* (where accused could not go to the place where the witness was which was at a great distance and he was too poor to engage counsel.[8] In a civil case where defendant was *ex parte*, if witness was examined, his deposition would not be relevant in the subsequent case.[9] Right to cross-examine must be statutory and not merely permissive.[10] A question may arise whether in a warrant case accused has the right to cross-examine prosecution witnesses.

Opportunity does not mean that the party should have actually exercised his right, using the opportunity available to him. It is sufficient if he had the opportunity. Accused, if unrepresented, must know that witness would be produced and examined on the particular day in Court; witness should not have been sprung as a surprise. If not, in such circumstances, he is denied a

---

1. *Brajaballav Ghose* v. *Akhoy Bagdi*, AIR 1926 Cal 705: 93 Ind Cas 115.
2. *Nanduri Saradamba* v. *Parakala Pattabhiramayya* AIR 1931 Mad 207; *Narsayya* v. *Veerayya*, AIR 1935 Mad 268: 40 Mad LW 810.
3. *Krishnayya Rao* v. *Raja of Pittapur*, AIR 1933 PC 202: 57 M 1: 60 IA 336: 145 IC 216.
4. *State* v. *A.M. Kothandaraman*, (1984) 1 MLJ 590 (Mad); Contra *L.S. Ashokan* v. *State of Kerala*, 2005 Cr LJ 3848: 2006 (1) ALJ 265: 2005 (2) Ker LJ 700.
5. *Jose* v. *State of Kerala*, (1973) 3 SCC 472: 1973 SCC (Cri) 372: AIR 1973 SC 944: 1973 Cr LJ 687.
6. *Dal Bahadur Singh* v. *Bijai Bahadur Singh*, AIR 1930 PC 79: 52 A 1: 57 IA 14: 122 IC 8; *Mulkh Raj Sikka* v. *Delhi Administration*, AIR 1974 SC 1723: 1975 (3) SCC 2: 1974 Cr LJ 1171.
7. *V.M. Mathew* v. *V.S. Sharma*, 1995 AIR SCW 3788: AIR 1996 SC 109: JT 1995 (6) SC 318; *Dal Bahadur Singh* v. *Bijai Bahadur Singh*, AIR 1930 PC 79: 52 A 1: 57 IA 14: 122 IC 8; *Abdul Rahman S/o Ghola* v. *Emperor*, AIR 1946 Lah 275; *Sundara Rajali* v. *Gopala Thevan*, AIR 1934 Mad 100: 150 Ind Cas 132; *Bayava Shiddappa Desai* v. *Parvateva Basavaneppa Bellad*, AIR 1933 Bom 126; *Banwari Lal* v. *State*, AIR 1956 All 385: 1956 Cr LJ 841.
8. *Phool Chand* v. *Amrit Lal*, AIR 1980 P & H 122: 1980 Rev LR 80.
9. *Mool Chandra* v. *Jagdish Chandra*, AIR 1955 All 385.
10. *Mulkh Raj Sikka* v. *Delhi Administration*, AIR 1974 SC 1723: 1975 (3) SCC 2: 1974 Cr LJ 1171; *Gauri Dutt Marwari* v. *D.K. Dowring*, AIR 1934 Pat 413; *Tafiz Pramanik* v. *Emperor*, AIR 1930 Cal 228.

chance to prepare for cross-examination, the clause will not apply.[1] Ordinarily if deposition was recorded in the presence of accused and his counsel, it can be presumed that he had the opportunity.[2]

If the witness fell ill or died after chief-examination or before completion of cross-examination, the deposition would not be relevant under this clause.[2]

"Prosecutor" in the explanation is the real prosecutor.[3] The person actively instrumental in putting the criminal law in motion is regarded as the prosecutor. But a mere informant who merely stated his suspicion and did not do anything more cannot be regarded as the prosecutor. Hence, examination of his conduct is necessary.[4]

Section 299, Criminal procedure Code partially superceeds section 33. 3rd proviso to the section requires that the questions in issue should be substantially the same in the two proceedings. This is to ensure that in the former proceeding the parties were not without the opportunity of examining and cross-examining on the very same point upon which the evidence is adduced in the subsequent proceeding.[5] Recitals of boundaries in deeds not inter-parties cannot be looked into unless the executants are examined.[6] It is sufficient if principal question in issue in both proceedings is identical.[7]

---

1. *Abdul Rahman S/o Ghola* v. *Emperor*, AIR 1946 Lah 275.
2. *Tafiz Pramanik* v. *Emperor*, AIR 1930 Cal 228; *R.* v. *Ramachandra*, ILR 19 Bom 749; *Banwari Lal* v. *State*, AIR 1956 All 385: 1956 Cr LJ 841; *State* v. *Ramani Mohan Chanda*, AIR 1953 Assam 176: 1953 Cr LJ 1593.
3. *Gaya Prasad* v. *Bhagath Singh*, ILR 30 All 525: 18 Mad LJ 394: 35 Ind App 189 (PC); *State of Himachal Pradesh* v. *Charan Dass Dogra*, 1976 Cr LJ 1466: (1976) 2 DLT 23: ILR 1975 HP 647 (HP); *Fool Kissory Dasee* v. *Nobin Chander Bhujno*, ILR 23 Cal 441; *S.T. Sahib* v. *N. Hasan Ghani Sahib*, AIR 1957 Mad 646.
4. *Periya Goundan* v. *Kuppa Goundan*, AIR 1919 Mad 229 (2): ILR 42 Mad 880: 37 Mad LJ 234; *Rajagopala* v. *Spencer and Co. Ltd.*, AIR 1920 Mad 712: 12 Mad LW 87.
5. Taylor on Evidence, 12th Edition, Page 321.
6. *Sadhurajan* v. *Sriramulu Naidu*, AIR 1999 Mad 377
7. *Krishnayya Rao* v. *Raja of Pittapur*, AIR 1933 PC 202: 57 M 1: 60 IA 336: 145 IC 216.

CHAPTER 9
SECTIONS 34 TO 39

1. SECTION 34:

Entries in the books of accounts including those maintained in an electronic form, regularly kept in the ordinary course of business, are relevant whenever they refer to a matter into which court is to enquire, but such statements shall not alone be sufficient evidence to charge any person with liability. The Information Technology Act, 2000 incorporated the words "entries an electronic form" in the section.

This is also an exception to the hearsay rule and the principle underlying section 21. Habit and system of keeping a book with regularity ensures its accuracy. Influence of habit prevents casual inaccuracies. If regularly kept, mistake is liable to be detected and rectified. Regularity provides circumstantial guarantee of truth.[1] The book must be account book; it must be one regularly kept in the ordinary course of business.[2] "Book" ordinarily, is a collection of sheets of paper bound together with the intention that such binding shall be permanent and the papers used collectively as one volume.[3] Collective unity must exist even at the time of making entries. Unbound sheet of paper do not constitute a "book".[4] Spiral note book is a book.[2] A register kept at the hotel counter need not contain statement of accounts and the same cannot be treated as a book of accounts.[5] A logbook of a vehicle in loose sheets and not in a bound book form would not be free from doubt.[6]

Entries should have been made some time or the other. Book merely containing entries, without accounting, is not a book for the purpose of this clause.[7] Book containing only odd entries, interpolates and not kept continuously is not regularly kept.[8]

No particular form is necessary. Word "business" is of wide import and means an activity carried on continuously and systematically by the application of labour and skill with a view to earn income.[3]

---

1. Wigmore on Evidence, III Edition, Vol. 2 Section 1536.
2. *State of Andhra Pradesh* v. *Cheemalapati Ganeswara Rao*, 1963 (2) Cr LJ 671: (1964) 3 SCR 297: AIR 1963 SC 1850: (1964) 2 SCA 38; *Bankey Behari Lal* v. *Brij Behari Lal*, AIR 1929 All 170.
3. *Central Bureau of Investigation* v. *V.C. Shukla*, AIR 1998 SC 1406: (1998) 3 SCC 410: 1998 SCC (Cri) 761.
4. *Ganesh Prasad Ray* v. *Narendra Nath Sen*, AIR 1953 SC 431: 17 Cut LT 73: 1951 Ker LT (SC) 28; *State of Kerala* v. *Thomas*, (1986) 2 SCC 411: 1983 Cri App R (SC) 114.
5. *Manish Dixit* v. *State of Rajasthan*, (2001) 1 SCC 596: 2001 SCR 235: AIR 2001 SC 93: 2001 Cr LJ 133.
6. *State of Kerala* v. *Thomas*, (1986) 2 SCC 411: 1983 Cri App R (SC) 114.
7. *Mukundram* v. *Dayaram*, 23 IC 893: AIR 1914 Nag 44.
8. *Umed* v. *Raj Singh*, AIR 1975 SC 43: (1975) 1 SCC 76: (1975) 1 SCR 918.

2. "Regularly" means keeping according to a certain fixed method or form or a system, *i.e.*, systematically. The system need not be an elaborate one. Excellence of the system and the closeness with which it was followed affects the weight to be attached to the book. Even if a system is not closely followed, it is admissible, though it's weight may not be much.[1] Even roughest accounts kept by petty shopkeepers are relevant, if they are genuine. It is a matter of intrinsic evidence that books in question were books of account and regularly kept in the course of business.[2] Entries need not have been made day to day or hour to hour as and when the transactions take place.[3] Accounts prepared from loose sheets or rough books should be treated as original account book.[4] The time of making entries may affect the value of the entries. (ibid). From the fact that the practice was of noting down transactions once in eight days, it cannot be said that the books were not maintained in the regular course of business.[5] Where an entry regarding a transaction was written closely in a cramped style at the end of a page though it could have been written in the next page, and the total amount debited was written in a different ink, the entry cannot be said to have been made in the regular course of business.[6]

3. The entries in the books, by themselves, are not sufficient to charge any person with liability.[7] They should be considered along with other evidence in the case. Some independent evidence regarding the transactions covered by the entries would be necessary.[8] Absence of entries would be relevant under section 11.[9] Value to be attached to the entries is to be decided by the court. Section deals only with relevancy and not weight.[10]

Entries require proof by examination of the person who made them or the person under whose direction and supervision they were made or the person who had knowledge of the transactions.[11] Supreme Court has held that books of

---

1. *Kesheo Rao* v. *Ganesh*, AIR 1926 Nag 407, (29.03.1926).
2. *Chandradhar Goswami* v. *Gauhati Bank Ltd.*, AIR 1967 SC 1058: (1967) 1 SCR 898: 37 Comp Cas 108.
3. *Deputy Commissioner Barabanki* v. *Ram Parsad*, ILR 27 Cal 118: 26 Ind App 254 PC.
4. *Ibid.*, and *Pannalal* v. *Labh Chand*, AIR 1955 MB 49.
5. *Firm Ramlochan Ram Lakshmi Prasad* v. *Maikha Sethani*, AIR 1960 Pat 271: 1959 BLJR 769.
6. *Venkata Mallayya* v. *Ramaswami & Co.*, AIR 1964 SC 818: 1963 (2) SCJ 483: 1963 SCD 785.
7. *State of Andhra Pradesh* v. *Cheemalapati Ganeswara Rao*, 1963 (2) Cr LJ 671: (1964) 3 SCR 297: AIR 1963 SC 1850: (1964) 2 SCA 38.
8. *Chandradhar Goswami* v. *Gauhati Bank Ltd.*, AIR 1967 SC 1058: (1967) 1 SCR 898: 37 Comp Cas 108; *Central Bureau of Investigation* v. *V.C. Shukla*, AIR 1998 SC 1406: (1998) 3 SCC 410: 1998 SCC (Cri) 761; *Dadarao* v. *State of Maharashtra*, AIR 1974 SC 388: 1974 Cr LJ 447: (1974) 3 SCC 630.
9. *State of Andhra Pradesh* v. *Cheemalapati Ganeswara Rao*, 1963 (2) Cr LJ 671: (1964) 3 SCR 297: AIR 1963 SC 1850: (1964) 2 SCA 38; *Imam Bandi* v. *Haji Mutsaddi*, AIR 1918 PC 11: 45 Ind App 73: 16 All LJ 800.
10. *State of Andhra Pradesh* v. *Cheemalapati Ganeswara Rao*, 1963 (2) Cr LJ 671: (1964) 3 SCR 297: AIR 1963 SC 1850: (1964) 2 SCA 38; *Chandradhar Goswami* v. *Gauhati Bank Ltd.*, AIR 1967 SC 1058: (1967) 1 SCR 898: 37 Comp Cas 108.
11. *Balmukund* v. *Jagan Nath*, AIR 1963 Raj 212: 1963 Raj LW 195: ILR (1963) 13 Raj 579; *Arakkan Narayanan* v. *Indian Handloom Traders*, AIR 1999 Ker 279: 1999 (3) Civ LJ 26: 1999 (2) CCC 44; *Kaka Ram Sohanlal* v. *Firm Thakar Das Mathra Das*, AIR 1961 Pun 27; *Ramgobind Prasad* v. *Gulab Chand Sahu*, AIR 1941 Pat 430: ILR 20 Pat 273; *Ram Janki Devi* v. *Juggilal Kamlapat*, AIR 1971 SC 2551: 1972 (1) SCJ 638: (1971) 3 SCR 573; *State Bank of India* v. *Yumnam Gouramani Singh*, AIR 1994 SC 1644: 1994 AIR SCW 1375: (1993) 3 SCC 631.

account must be held to have been proved even in the absence of examining the writer as a witness, provided, there is proof of proper maintenance of the books in the regular course of business and of the impossibility of securing the presence of the writer.[1] Someone competent to speak about it should be examined.[2] Proper custody also must be proved. There need not be independent evidence to prove each and every transaction entered in the book. What is necessary is to see is whether besides the entries, there is any evidence to prove that the transaction actually took place and in whose presence it took place.[3] Entries carry weight unless there are elements throwing sufficient doubt on their correctness.[4] They have corroborative value.[5]

Entries require corroboration.[6] They may be used to refresh memory under section 159. Books have to be tested for their probative value.[7] Absence of an entry in defendant's account book is relevant when there is an entry in plaintiffs' book.[8] Veracity of entries in ledger maintained properly and regularly cannot be doubted on the ground that day books supporting the ledger entries were not produced and the person who made the ledger entries was not examined.[9] Ledger book is relevant only in conjunction with the cash book or day book.[10] However entries in ledger require to the corroborated before they are accepted as true.[11] Each relevant entry must be proved.[12]

4. SECTION 35:

According to this section an entry in any public or other official book, register or record or an electronic record, stating a fact in issue or relevant fact, and made by a public servant in the discharge of his official duty or by any other person in performance of a duty specially enjoined by the law of the country in which such book, register or record or an electronic record is kept, is itself a relevant fact. The words "or an electronic record" were incorporated by Central Act 21 of 2000.

---

1. *Ram Janki Devi* v. *Juggilal Kamlapat*, AIR 1971 SC 2551: 1972 (1) SCJ 638: (1971) 3 SCR 573.
2. *Sankaran Ezuthachan* v. *Velayudhan Ezuthachan*, ILR (1978) 1 Ker 619.
3. *State Bank of India* v. *Yumnam Gouramani Singh*, AIR 1994 SC 1644: 1994 AIR SCW 1375: (1993) 3 SCC 631.
4. *Maidhandas* v. *Sricharan*, AIR 1956 Ass 170: 1956 Cr LJ 1283; *Shamaraya* v. *Beloor Sri Mariamma Temple*, AIR 1974 Kant 10: (1973) 2 Mys LJ 131.
5. *Hagami Lal Ram Prasad, a firm* v. *Bhuralal Ram Narain*, AIR 1961 Raj 52: ILR (1960) 10 Raj 1304; *Emperor* v. *Narbada Prasad*, AIR 1930 All 38: 31 Cr LJ 356; *Haribux Gouri Sankar Firm* v. *Subhakaran Tulsiram*, AIR 1965 Ori 211; *Shubhkaran Rameshwarlal Agarwal* v. *Durgaprasad Private Ltd.*, AIR 1972 Guj 208: (1972) 13 Guj LR 179.
6. *State Bank of India* v. *Yumnam Gouramani Singh*, AIR 1994 SC 1644: 1994 AIR SCW 1375: (1993) 3 SCC 631.
7. *B. Siddalingappa* v. *M.C. Moben*, AIR 1978 Kant 10: (1977) 1 Kant 385: ILR (1977) 1 Kant 756; *R.R. Chari* v. *State*, AIR 1959 All 149: 1959 Cr LJ 268.
8. *State of Andhra Pradesh* v. *Cheemalapati Ganeswara Rao*, 1963 (2) Cr LJ 671: (1964) 3 SCR 297: AIR 1963 SC 1850: (1964) 2 SCA 38; *Imam Bandi* v. *Haji Mutsaddi*, AIR 1918 PC 11: 45 Ind App 73: 16 All LJ 800.
9. *R.V.E. Venkatachala Gounder* v. *Arulmigu Vishweswara Swami & V.P. Temple*, AIR 2003 SC 4548: 2003 AIR SCW 5316: (2003) 8 SCC 752.
10. *Zenna Sorabji* v. *Mirabelle Hotel Co. (P.) Ltd.*, AIR 1981 Bom 446.
11. *Mohan Lal Bodj Raj* v. *Dwarka Nath Kuldeep Kumar*, AIR 1985 J&K 85: 1985 Kash LJ 341.
12. *D.K. Aswathanarayanaiah* v. *Nallapula Sanjeeviah*, AIR 1965 AP 33: (1964) 1 Andh WR 69: (1964) 1 Andh LT 82.

The principle underlying, rests upon the public duty of the person who keeps the record to make the entries after satisfying himself of their truth. It is assumed he performs his duty with accuracy and fidelity.[1] His personal knowledge is irrelevant. Unavailability of the person, on account of death or otherwise is not necessary to be shown. But his inconvenience in attending court is taken into consideration.

Three conditions must be satisfied: (a) entry must be in any public or other official book; (b) it must be an entry stating a fact in issue or relevant fact; and (c) it must be made by a public servant in the discharge of his official duty or by any other person in performance of duty specially enjoined by the law.[2] The clause covers public documents and also record of official acts.[3]

5. The clause deals with relevancy and not probative value. Probative value of documents which do not disclose the source of their information or have not achieved publicity is not much.[4] In the case of entries made by public servants in the discharge of their official duty, no express statute or statutory rule is needed.[5] A document which is prepared under a statute which requires certain conditions to be fulfilled carries greater weight. Entries in public registers are evidence of the facts recorded therein, provided the registers were required by law to be kept for public reference and entries were made promptly by the proper officer.

6. "Public Official": Reference may be made to sections 74, 78 of this Act and section 21 of I.P.C. Certain other Acts also declare who are public servants (Registrar of Births, Census Officers etc.). Government school teacher is a public officer. Official correspondence by a Forest Officer to his superior in the due performance of his duty is relevant.[6] Where a register is not maintained by a person who is a public servant, the person who maintained it should have done so in performance of duty specially enjoined by statutes or statutory rule. This duty may be expressly provided by a statute or it may be implied from the nature and functions of the office held by the official.[4]

7. "Duty specially enjoined by law": Duty may be enjoined by statute or statutory rules.[7] Finger print slips cum descriptive rolls of criminals maintained under Police Manual are relevant.[8] So also Register of Births and Deaths.[9] Duty may be implied from the nature and functions of the office.[4] The words "..........

1. *Ram Prasad Sharma* v. *State of Bihar*, AIR 1970 SC 326: (1971) 1 SCJ 184: (1969) 2 SCC 359: 1970 Cr LJ 496.
2. *Birad Mal Singhvi* v. *Anand Purohit*, 1988 (Supp) SCC 604: AIR 1988 SC 1796; *State of Bihar* v. *Radha Krishna Singh*, AIR 1983 SC 684: (1983) 1 SCALE 789: (1983) 2 SCR 808: (1983) 3 SCC 118: 1983 Cur Civ LJ (SC) 273.
3. *Bakhshish Singh Dhaliwal* v. *State of Punjab*, AIR 1967 SC 752: 1967 Cr LJ 656: (1967) 1 SCR 211.
4. *State of Bihar* v. *Radha Krishna Singh*, AIR 1983 SC 684: (1983) 1 SCALE 789: (1983) 2 SCR 808: (1983) 3 SCC 118: 1983 Cur Civ LJ (SC) 273.
5. *Chandran Nair* v. *Kunhambu Nair*, AIR 1982 Ker 232.
6. *Maharaj Bhanudas Narayanboa Gosavi* v. *Krishnabai Chintaman Deshpande*, AIR 1927 Bom 11.
7. *Shyam Pratap Singh* v. *Collector of Etawah*, AIR 1946 PC 103: ILR (1946) Kar PC 111: (1946) 2 Mad LJ 235: 59 Mad LW 483 (PC).
8. *Bandra Nayak* v. *State*, 1974 Cuttack LR (Cr) 19.
9. *Mohammad Zafar* v. *Kaniz Saiyada*, AIR 1925 All 79: ILR 46 All 637.

specially enjoined by law" do not apply to registers maintained by public servants in discharge of their official duties.

8. Entries should have been made contemporaneously or without such long delay as to affect their credibility.[1] Erasures, alterations and minor irregularities affect the weight and not relevancy. In appropriate cases, court may presume that the official or official body did their duty to the best of their ability and based on materials the accuracy of which they were satisfied.[2] Where a document is prepared with due care and after due enquiry by a public official and is part of settlement record, a statutory presumption of correctness attaches to it.[3] The entries in such record are subject to rebuttal.[4] The entry in public register can be initially presumed to be correct subject to its being reliable and trustworthy. An entry relating to date of birth made in a school register is relevant under this Section; but, the age so recorded is not of much significance to prove the age in the absence of material on which the age was recorded.[5] If the informant is examined as a witness and supports the entry, it has probative value.[5] An entry of age made before dispute arose is entitled to weight. If the entry was made on the basis of information given by parents or someone having special means of knowledge, it has probative force.[6]

Entries must have been made by or under the direction of the public servant or officer concerned.[7]

9. The following documents have been held to be relevant: Inam Register, Quinquennial Register, Revenue Register, Record of Rights, Settlement Records, Survey and Settlement Record, Guardianship Certificate, Official Reports, Mutation Orders, Reports of Judicial (but not Revenue) enquiry, Order Sheets, Register of Official Communications, FIR, Registrars Endorsement, Postal Endorsement, School Register of Government Schools, SSLC certificate, Secondary Board marks list, Marriage Register, Municipal Register, Jail Register, Vaccination Report, Govt. Hospital Register, Voters List, Police General Diary Cultivation Registers, Ship Log Books, Report of Public Meeting by CID, etc.[8]

1. *Bishnath Prasad* v. *Emperor*, AIR 1948 Oudh 1: 48 Cr LJ 542.
2. *Shyam Pratap Singh* v. *Collector of Etawah*, AIR 1946 PC 103: ILR (1946) Kar PC 111: (1946) 2 Mad LJ 235: 59 Mad LW 483 (PC).
3. *Avadh Kishore Das* v. *Ram Gopal*, AIR 1979 SC 861: 1979 UJ (SC) 251: (1979) 4 SCC 790.
4. *Beg* v. *Allah Ditta*, AIR 1916 PC 129: 45 PR 1917: 44 C 749: 44 IA 89: 38 IA 354; *Saleh Mohammad* v. *Zawar Hussain*, AIR 1944 PC 18: ILR (1944) Lah 195 (PC); *Ram Kumar Das* v. *Jagdish Chandra Deo, Dhabal Deb*, AIR 1952 SC 23: 1951 SCJ 813: 1952 SCR 269; *Salig Ram* v. *Maya Devi*, AIR 1955 SC 266: (1955) 1 SCR 1911: ILR 1955 Punj 167: 1955 FCJ 248 (SC).
5. *Birad Mal Singhvi* v. *Anand Purohit*, 1988 (Supp) SCC 604: AIR 1988 SC 1796.
6. *Birad Mal Singhvi* v. *Anand Purohit*, 1988 (Supp) SCC 604: AIR 1988 SC 1796; *State of Chhattisgarh* v. *Lekhram*, AIR 2006 SC 1746: 2006 AIR SCW 1982: 2006 Cr LJ 2139 (SC).
7. *Shaikh Abdur Rashid* v. *Musammat Qudrat-Un-Nissa*, AIR 1922 All 510 (1); *Madho Saran Singh* v. *Manna Lal*, AIR 1933 Pat 473: 14 Pat LT 441: 149 IC 129.
8. *Arunachalam Chetty* v. *Venkatachalapathi Guruswamigal*, AIR 1919 PC 62: LR (1919) 46 IA 204: 53 IC 288; *Kondavitti Brahmayya* v. *Rajeswaraswami Temple*, AIR 1953 Mad 580: 1953 MWN 45: (1953) 1 MLJ 164; *Ramanandhan Sahay* v. *Jaigovind Pandey*, AIR 1924 Pat 213; *Sheojee* v. *Prema Kuer*, AIR 1964 Pat 187: 1964 BLJR 152; *Karicherry Charadan Nair* v. *Edayillam Kunhambu Nair*, AIR 1982 Ker 232; *Gangabai* v. *Fakirgowda*, AIR 1930 PC 93: 57 Ind App 61; AIR 1932 PC 217; *Charu Chandra* v. *Kamakhya Narain (Sir John Wallis)*, AIR 1931 PC 5; *Shikharchand Jain* v. *Digamber Jain Praband Karini Sabha*, AIR 1974 SC 1178: (1974) 1 SCC 675: 1974 SCR 101; *Vimla Bai* v. *Hiralal Gupta*, 1990 II SCC 22.

11. Probative value depends on the facts and circumstances of each case. It must be taken along with the other evidence. Basis on which entry was made would be relevant in considering probative value.[1]

12. Relevancy does not depend on the personal knowledge of the maker of the entry.[2] The Court presumes that the public officer did his duty to the best of his ability and based the entries on material the accuracy of which he was satisfied.[3] That the entries were made not by the officer but by his subordinates under his supervision did not matter.[4]

13. Special Marriage Act, Hindu Marriage Act, Births, Deaths and Marriages Registration Act, Bankers Books Act, Indian Partnership Act, L.A. Act, Trade Marks Act, Trade Unions Act, TADA Act, Panchayath Act are special laws within the meaning of this clause.

14. An entry in Birth Register is admissible without examining the maker of the entry.[5] But it is not conclusive evidence.[6] It is not necessary to prove the manner in which the entry was made.[7] Probative value of entry in Registers of Births in the matter of disputed paternity depends upon the identity of the informant.[8] The entry must also be connected with the person in regard to whom the dispute exists.[9]

Certified copies are admissible under section 77 read with section 78.[10]

15. SECTION 36:

The section deals with two classes of maps, (a) published maps or charts generally offered for sale; (b) maps or plans made under the authority of Government. The first class of maps are admissible on the ground that they are published and hence accessible to the entire community and open to criticism and challenges. The second class of maps are made relevant because they must have been made as the result of thorough study or enquiry. According to section 83, court shall presume that maps or plans purporting to be made by the authority of government were so made and are accurate. The presumption regarding accuracy is rebuttable.[11]

16. A map so made for a private purpose or for a cause is not covered by this clause.[12] Such maps must be proved to be accurate by other evidence. A survey

1. *Kamalnarayan Ramsaranlal* v. *Ram Kishorelal*, AIR 1958 MP 246: 1958 MPLJ 198: 1958 Jab LJ 289; *National Investment Co. Ltd.* v. *Mohendra Nath Kundu*, AIR 1960 Cal 724: ILR (1961) 1 Cal 295; *Ramanna* v. *Sambamoorthy*, AIR 1961 AP 361; *Wali Mohammed* v. *Mohammad Baksh*, AIR 1930 PC 91: 57 Ind App 86.
2. *Graham* v. *Panindra*, AIR 1916 Cal 617: 19 Cal WN 1038.
3. *Shyam Pratap Singh* v. *Collector of Etawah*, AIR 1946 PC 103: ILR (1946) Kar PC 111: (1946) 2 Mad LJ 235: 59 Mad LW 483 (PC).
4. *Rani Lekraj Kuar* v. *Babu Mahpal Singh*, (1879) 7 Ind App 63: ILR 5 Cal 744: 6 CLR 593 (PC).
5. *Harpal Singh* v. *State of Himachal Pradesh*, AIR 1981 SC 361: 1981 Cr LJ 1: (1981) 1 SCC 560.
6. *H. Subba Rao* v. *Life Insurance Corporation of India*, AIR 1976 Kant 231: (1976) 1 Kant LJ 283: ILR 1976 Kant 800.
7. *Ghuia Devi* v. *Shyamlal Mandal*, AIR 1974 Pat 68.
8. *B. Mahadeva Rao* v. *Yesoda Bai*, AIR 1962 Mad 141: (1962) 1 Cr LJ 437 (2): (1962) 2 Mad LJ 107.
9. Phipson on Evidence, 14 Edition, Page 781.
10. *Manikrao* v. *Deorao*, AIR 1955 Nagpur 290.
11. *Kumar Kamakhya Narain Singh* v. *Abhiman Singh*, AIR 1934 PC 182: 13 P 589: 150 IC 807; *Shib Chandra Roy Choudhary* v. *Harendra Lal Roy Choudhary*, AIR 1919 Cal 752.
12. *Kantu Prasad Hazari* v. *Jagath Chandra Dutta*, ILR 23 Cal 335.

map is cogent evidence of possession at the particular time when it was made.[1] Maps prepared after due enquiry are presumed to be correct, unless they are shown to be wrong.[2] They are not conclusive.[3] Presumptions can be rebutted.[4] A site plan relating to the offence prepared by a police officer is not relevant as it was prepared relying on the statement of witnesses during investigation and would be affected by section 162 Criminal Procedure Code.[5] But a site plan prepared by a police officer basing on his own observation is relevant.[6] Where a witness showed the same to a draughtsman who thereupon prepared a plan to scale and the witness corroborated in Court the statement of the draughtsman, the map is not hit by section 162 Criminal Procedure Code.[7]

17. If a document is evidence of possession, it is evidence of title also; but it is not direct evidence of title. Value depends upon the facts of the particular case.[8]

18. SECTION 37:

Recitals in Statutes and Gazette Notifications referred to in section 37 are relevant regarding existence of any fact of public nature in respect of which court has to form an opinion. Under section 81, the Court shall presume the genuineness of these documents.

The documents are documents of public character made by public servants in the course of official duty and published under public authority.

Notice of dissolution of partnership, sale proclamation or notice, assent of President to any statute, commencement of a statute, resolution winding up a company are instances of matters which require to be gazetted.

19. SECTION 38:

Statement of law contained in a government publication of the particular country and any report of court ruling of the country are relevant when the court has to form an opinion as to the law of that country.[9] *See* also sections 57 and 84. Statement in books of law and law reports are relevant on grounds similar to those stated in sections 35 to 37. Under section 3 of Indian Law Reports Act, 1875 only those reports of cases decided by any of the High Courts as reported in a report published under the Act require the authority of the Governor General in council.

20. SECTION 39:

According to this section, what is admissible is that portion of a statement in a document or electronic record or a connected series of letters or papers

---

1. *Ram Kishore Sen* v. *Union of India*, AIR 1966 SC 644: (1966) 1 SCR 430.
2. *Tarakdas Acharjee Choudhury* v. *Secretary of State*, AIR 1935 PC 125: 156 IC 548.
3. *Secretary of State* v. *Birendra Kishore*, AIR 1916 PC 182.
4. *Secretary of State* v. *Birendra Kishore*, AIR 1916 PC 182; *Kumar Kamakhya Narain Singh* v. *Abhiman Singh*, AIR 1934 PC 182: 13 P 589: 150 IC 807.
5. *Dharam Singh* v. *State of Uttar Pradesh*, (1964) 1 Cr LJ 78: 1962 B L LJ R 749: 1962 All Cri R 331 (SC).
6. *Tori Singh* v. *State of Uttar Pradesh*, AIR 1962 SC 399: (1962) 1 Cr LJ 469: (1962) 3 SCR 580.
7. *Santa Singh* v. *State of Punjab*, AIR 1956 SC 526: 1955 Cr LJ 930.
8. *Debendra* v. *Surendra*, AIR 1927 Cal 345; *Nasarul Nazi Haq* v. *Abdul Wahab Khan*, AIR 1923 Pat 58: ILR 1 Pat 674.
9. *Hindustan Chloride* v. *Karbi*, ILR (1972) 1 Cal 506, *See* also sections 57 and 84.

which the court finds necessary in order that the statement may be intelligible. Court is entitled to look into the contents of the document and make use of it as it deems fit. It cannot be said all recitals and statements in the document are to be used. The inadmissible part can be rejected. This principle applies where the statement is contained in part of connected series of letters or papers also.

If it is necessary to read the document as a whole to find the intent and meaning thereof, that must be done. It is not correct to say that a statement does not attract the provisions in this Act relating to "statements" unless they are communicated.[1]

This section refers to statements rendered relevant under the preceding sections and also for the purpose of cross-examination, and documents referred to for refreshing memory. It is for the court to consider what is necessary to make the a statement intelligible. Where a police officer has a police diary to refresh his memory, the accused is entitled to see so much of the diary as in the opinion of the court may be necessary to the proper understanding of the entry.

---

1. *P.C. Purushothama Reddiar* v. *S. Perumal*, AIR 1972 SC 608: (1972) 1 SCC 9: 1972 SCJ 469; *Food Corporation of India* v. *Assam State Coop. Marketing and Consumer Federation Ltd.*, (2004) 12 SCC 360.

CHAPTER 10

RELEVANCY OF JUDGMENTS (SECTIONS 40 TO 44)

1. SECTION 40:

The existence of any judgment, order or decree which by law prevents any court from taking cognizance of a suit or holding trial, is a relevant fact when the question is whether such court ought to take cognizance of such suit or to hold such trial. Ancient Indian Jurisprudence calls *Res judicata* as the plea of former judgment or *Poorva Nyaya*. "If a person, though defeated at law, sues again, he should be answered – you were defeated formerly". *Woodroffe and Ameer Ali on Law of Evidence*, 18th Edition, Vol. II at page 2354 refers to ancient text writers in this connection.

2. Section 40 effectuates the prinicples of *Res judicata* and *autre fois* acquit and *autre fois convict.*[1] If judgment or order prevents the court from taking cognizance of a case or trying a case, the existence of such judgment or order is a relevant fact. It is the existence of the previous judgment that is relevant. This principle does not apply when a court has no jurisdiction to decide the matter[2] or where the person against whom the previous judgment is sought to be used was not a party.[3] But land acquisition judgments not interpartes have relevance regarding valuation.[4] The principle of *autre fois* acquit which is recognized in section 300, Criminal Procedure Code arises when a person is tried again for the same offence or on the same facts for some other offence for which a different charge might have been made.[5] "The same offence" means the same act or one punishable under the same provision of law. When the act is punishable under different provisions of law, the accused cannot be said to have committed the same offence.[5] If the offences are different, section 300(1) Criminal Procedure Code will not apply. The bar will not also apply to continuing offences. Even if plea of *autre fois* acquit is not technically available, the principle of it is available for the accused when the interest of justice requires its' extension in his favour.[6]

---

1. *Chhadek Karikar* v. *Sayad Ali Kaviraj*, 85 IC 979: AIR 1925 Cal 1046; (*Padmanabhini*) *Ramanamma* v. *Appala Narasaiah*, AIR 1932 Mad 254: 62 Mad LJ 230: 33 Cr LJ 307; *Ramparokha Pande* v. *Mst. Ramjhari Kuer*, AIR 1933 Pat 690: 149 IC 1158; *Mahabir Mahton* v. *Sonmati Kuer*, AIR 1964 Pat 66.
2. *Lakshan Chandra* v. *Ramdas*, AIR 1964 Pat 66.
3. *Hira Lal* v. *Hari Narain*, AIR 1964 All 302.
4. *Land Acquisition Officer, City Improvement Trust Board* v. *H. Narayanaiah*, AIR 1976 SC 2403: (1976) 4 SCC 9: (1977) 1 SCR 178.
5. *Kharkan* v. *State of Uttar Pradesh*, ILR (1964) 1 All 519: AIR 1965 SC 83: (1965) 1 Cr LJ 116.
6. *Yusofalli Mulla Noorbhoy* v. *The King*, AIR 1949 PC 264: 1949 Cr LJ 889: 76 Ind App 158.

If a judgment does not fall within sections 40 to 43, it is not relevant.[1] These sections only exclude judgments as pieces of conclusive evidence. They do not bar admission of judgment as proof of the fact of litigation, or its result and effect upon the parties which make a certain course of conduct probable or improbable on the part of one of the parties. If as a result of previous litigation, one of the parties was in possession, that fact can be used in the subsequent litigation.[2]

3. Bar of a suit may arise on the following grounds:

(a) The matter in issue is the subject of a previously instituted pending suit. (Section 10 C.P.C.).

(b) The relief sought forms part of a claim which plaintiff omitted to sue in a former suit or was one of the remedies in respect of the same cause of action, which plaintiff in a former suit omitted to claim without the leave of court. (Order II, rule 2 C.P.C.).

(c) There is estoppel by judgment, matter in issue being *res judicata* (Section 11 C.P.C.).

4. In a civil case, decision of criminal court is not *res judicata.*[3] When a question in probate proceedings whether the son of the testator murdered him or in a suit for damages for malicious prosecution or defamation, the judgment of criminal court can be looked into for the purpose of seeing how it ended, but not for the grounds for acquittal.[4] It has not relevance in a suit for damages for accident, except to show the result of the criminal case.[5] Conviction in a criminal case is not evidence of the facts on which the conviction was based, in a civil case in which these facts are in issue. But if the conviction was based on a plea of guilty by, accused plea is relevant and to prove it, the judgment of conviction is relevant.[6] Judgment of a civil court is admissible in a criminal court as the best evidence of the civil rights of the parties but not as conclusive evidence.[7] Decision of a civil court is binding on a criminal court. The converse is not true.[8] It has been held that finding of criminal court stands superceded by the finding recorded by a civil court.[9] It has to be seen that this view has been over ruled.[10] An order of civil court rejecting a previous claim on land is relevant in a subsequent criminal case for alleged theft of crops in that land. It is the existence of the judgment that is relevant; the reasons for acquittal or

1. *Purnima Debya* v. *Nand Lal Ojha*, ILR 11 Pat 50: 136 IC 577: AIR 1932 Pat 105; *Shankar Ganesh Kesheo* v. *Kesheo*, AIR 1930 Nag 1; *Kesho Prasad Singh* v. *Bhagjogna Kuer*, AIR 1937 PC 69: 41 Cal WN 577: ILR 16 Pat 258.
2. *Shiv Charan* v. *State*, AIR 1965 All 511: (1965) 2 Cr LJ 578; *Ram Sarup* v. *Puran*, AIR 1971 P&H 106: 1970 Cur LJ 870: ILR (1972) 2 P&H 141.
3. *Adi Pherozshah Gandhi* v. *H.M. Seervai, Advocate General of Maharashtra, Bombay*, AIR 1971 SC 385: 1971 (2) SCJ 71: (1971) 1 SCR 863; *Ramekbal Tiwary* v. *Madan Mohan Tiwary*, AIR 1967 SC 1156: 1967 (2) SCJ 191: (1967) 2 SCR 368.
4. *Ramanamma* v. *Appala Narasaiah*, AIR 1932 Mad 254: 62 Mad LJ 230: 33 Cr LJ 307.
5. *Seethamma* v. *Benedict D'Sa*, (1966) 1 Mys LJ 576: 1967 Cr LJ 216: AIR 1967 Mys 11.
6. *Vasappan* v. *Sarada*, AIR 1958 Ker 39: 1957 Ker LJ 842: 1957 Ker LT 977.
7. *Emperor* v. *Ma. Pwa Chone; Hosnaki* v. *State*, AIR 1956 All 81: 1955 All WR (HC) 654: 1956 Cr LJ 168.
8. *Karam Chand Ganga Prasad* v. *Union of India*, (1970) 3 SCC 694: 1971 Cr LJ 1072: AIR 1971 SC 1244.
9. *V.M. Shah* v. *State of Maharashtra*, AIR 1996 SC 339: 1995 AIR SCW 4140: JT 1995 (6) SC 433; Contra *M.S. Sheriff* v. *State of Madras*, AIR 1954 SC 397: 1954 SCJ 458: 1954 SCR 1144.
10. *K.G. Premshankar* v. *Inspector of Police*, AIR 2002 SC 3372: 2002 Cr LJ 4343: (2002) 8 SCC 87.

the evidence recorded in the earlier trial are not relevant.[1] The decision which was not necessary for the disposal of the previous suit is not relevant.[2] Where a judgment is not *in rem*, nor relating to matters of public nature nor interpartes, it is not relevant for decision of the same point in a later suit.[3]

General principle of *res judicata* is applicable to criminal cases. *See* section 300 of Cr.P.C.[4] Issue estoppel bars reception of evidence to disturb a finding in an earlier prosecution even for a distinct offence.[5] Though the effect of *res judicata* results in estoppel, it is different from the latter. Estoppel covered by section 115 is based on doctrine of equity, while *res judicata* is based on the principle that no person should be vexed twice for the same cause.

General principles of *res judicata* may be applicable even where section 11, C.P.C. is not applicable.[6]

5. SECTION 41:

A final judgment, order or decree of a competent court, in the exercise probate, matrimonial, admiralty or insolvency jurisdiction, which confers upon or takes away from any person any legal character, or which declares any person to be entitled to any such character, or to be entitled to any specific thing, not as against any specified person but absolutely, is relevant when the existence of any such legal character, or the title of any such person to any such thing, is relevant. The second part of this section declares that such judgment order or decree is conclusive proof in the following four different purposes[7]:

(1) that any legal character, to which it confers accrued at the time when such judgment, order or decree came into operation,

(2) that any legal character, to which it declares any such person to be entitled, accrued to that person at the time when such judgment, order or decree declares it to have accrued to that person,

---

1. *Ali Hasan* v. *State*, 1975 Cr LJ 345.
2. *A. Venkateshwarlu* v. *M.M. Mosque*, AIR 1972 AP 132.
3. *Kesho Prasad Singh* v. *Bhagjogna Kuer*, AIR 1937 PC 69: 41 Cal WN 577: ILR 16 Pat 258.
4. *Manipur Administration, Manipur* v. *Thokchom Bira Singh*, AIR 1965 SC 87: 1965 Cr LJ 120: 1964 7 SCR 123; *S.A. Venkataraman* v. *State*, AIR 1958 SC 107: 1958 Cr LJ 254: 1958 SCR 1037; *State of Madhya Pradesh* v. *Veereshwar Rao Agnihotri*, AIR 1957 SC 592: 1957 Cr LJ 892: 1957 SCC 317; *Mohar Rai* v. *State of Bihar*, AIR 1968 SC 1281: (1968) 3 SCR 525: 1968 Cr LJ 1479; *Piara Singh* v. *State of Punjab*, (1969) 3 SCR 236: AIR 1969 SC 961: 1969 Cr LJ 1435; *Ravinder Singh* v. *State of Haryana*, AIR 1975 SC 856: (1975) 3 SCC 742: (1975) 3 SCR 453.
5. *Masud Khan* v. *State of Uttar Pradesh*, AIR 1974 SC 28: 1975 (1) SCJ 129: (1974) 1 SCR 793.
6. *Satyadhyan Ghosal* v. *Deorjin Debi*, AIR 1960 SC 941: (1961) 1 SCA 10: (1960) 3 SCR 590; *Gulabchand Chhotalal Parikh* v. *State of Gujarat*, AIR 1965 SC 1153: 1965 (2) SCJ 58: (1965) 2 SCR 547; *Raj Lakshmi Dasi* v. *Banamali Sen*, AIR 1953 SC 33: 1952 SCJ 618: 1953 SCR 154; *Gokul Mundar* v. *Pudammud Singh*, ILR 29 Cal 707 (PC); *Workmen of Balmer Lawrie and Co. Ltd.* v. *Balmer Lawrie and Co. Ltd.*, AIR 1964 SC 728: (1964) 5 SCR 344: 1965 (1) SCJ 190; *Associated Cement Staff Union* v. *Associated Cement Co. Ltd. Bombay*, AIR 1964 SC 914: (1964) 1 Lab LJ 12: (1964) 1 SCWR 265; *Workmen of the Straw Board Manufacturing Co., Ltd.* v. *Straw Board Manufacturing Co., Ltd.*, AIR 1974 SC 1132: (1974) 4 SCC 881: (1974) 3 SCR 703; *Punjab Co-operative Bank Ltd.* v. *R.S. Bhatia*, AIR 1975 SC 1898: (1975) 4 SCC 696: 1975 Lab IC 1439; *Gulam Abbas* v. *State of Uttar Pradesh*, AIR 1981 SC 2198: 1981 Cr LJ 1835; *Workmen of Cochin Port Trust* v. *Board of Trustees of the Cochin Port Trust*, AIR 1978 SC 1283: (1978) 3 SCC 119: 1978 (2) SCJ 518; *G.K. Dudani* v. *S.D. Sharma*, AIR 1986 SC 1455: 1986 (2) SCJ 183: 1986 Lab IC 1454.
7. *Satrucharla Vijaya Rama Raju* v. *Nimmaka Jaya Raju*, AIR 2006 SC 543: 2005 AIR SCW 6197: (2006) 1 SCC 212.

(3) that any legal character which it takes away from any such person ceased at the time from which such judgment, order or decree declared it had ceased or should cease,

(4) and that anything to which it declares any person to be so entitled was the property of that person at the time from which such judgment, order or decree declares that it had been or should be his property.

6. This section deals generally with judgments *in rem.*[1] Judgments *in rem* generally declare status of a person or a thing.[2] Such judgments are binding on the whole world and not merely against the parties thereto. Therefore, anyone who can possibly be affected by the decision is entitled to appear and assert his own rights by becoming a party to the case.[3]

7. The first part of the section makes certain judgments relevant *i.e.,* final judgments in the exercise of probate, matrimonial, admiralty or insolvency jurisdiction which confer upon or take away from any person any legal character, or which declares any person to be entitled to such character or to be entitled to any specific thing, not as against any specified person but absolutely, provided the judgment is of a competent court. A judgment *in rem* is an adjudication made upon the status of some particular subject-matter by a competent Tribunal.[1] This section applies also to judgments of courts in foreign countries provided the foreign court had jurisdiction and the judgment was not obtained by fraud or collusion.[4]

The judgment of a probate court granting probate of a will in favour of petitioner must be presumed to have been obtained as per proper procedure and is a judgment *in rem* binding on the whole world and failure to implead other legal heirs would be of no consequence.[5] Matrimonial jurisdiction is conferred on courts by special statutes, such as Indian Divorce Act Indian Christian Marriage Act, Special Marriage Act, Hindu Marriage Act etc. A judgment of a matrimonial Court is binding as to the status of the parties concerned and is a judgment *in rem.*[6] Similar is the position regarding judgments rendered in Admiralty and Insolvency jurisdictions. Section 41 lays down a conclusive presumption.[7]

8. The second part of the section makes such judgments conclusive evidence in certain specified matters. Conclusiveness attaches only to the extent (a) that any legal character which it confers accrued at the time when the judgment came into operation; (b) that any legal character to which it declares any such person to be entitled, accrued to him at the time when such judgment declares it to have accrued to him; (c) that any legal character which it takes away from

1. *Satrucharla Vijaya Rama Raju* v. *Nimmaka Jaya Raju,* AIR 2006 SC 543: 2005 AIR SCW 6197: (2006) 1 SCC 212.
2. *R. Viswanathan* v. *Rukn-ul-Mulk Syed Abdul Wajid,* AIR 1963 SC 1: (1963) 1 Cr LJ 1: (1963) 2 SCWR 117; Halsbury's Laws of England
3. Taylor on Evidence, 12th Edition P 1054.
4. *R. Viswanathan* v. *Rukn-ul-Mulk Syed Abdul Wajid,* AIR 1963 SC 1: (1963) 1 Cr LJ 1: (1963) 2 SCWR 117; *Satya* v. *Teja Singh,* AIR 1975 SC 105: 1975 Cr LJ 52: 1975 (2) SCJ 294.
5. *Surinder Kumar* v. *Gian Chand,* AIR 1957 SC 875: 1958 SCR 584: 1957 SCJ 159: 1958 SCA 412.
6. *S.M. Pandey* v. *Manohar Shamarao,* AIR 1971 Bom 83; *Siddaiah* v. *Penchalamma,* (1962) 2 Andh WR 259: AIR 1963 AP 158: ILR (1964) AP 387.
7. *Ashok Layland Ltd.* v. *State of Tamil Nadu,* AIR 2004 SC 2836: 2004 AIR SCW 1001: (2004) 3 SCC 1.

him ceased at the time from which the judgment declared it had ceased or should cease; (d) that anything to which it declares him to be so entitled was his property at the time from which the judgment declared that it had been or should be his property.

9. Judgment *in rem* is an adjudication made upon the status of a person or thing by a competent court and pronounced to the world generally.[1] But it is not conclusive evidence except to the extent provided in the section. It is admissible in all cases whether inter-partes or not.[2] The section is not exhaustive of judgments *in rem*. Judgments under section 92 CPC have the same effect though not covered by this section.[3] Judgment under section 92 C.P.C. is not a judgment *in rem*.[4] Where there are more than one judgment *in rem* the whole matter is at large again.[5]

Regarding foreign judgments, section 13 C.P.C. may be seen. A foreign judgment is accepted as analogous to a judgment *in rem*.

10. Judgment in rem is valid "inter omnes" or against the whole world.

"Final judgment, order or decree". "Final" does not mean "not subject to appeal"; "final" is used as distinct from 'interlocutory' or "reversed".

Competent Court means the court having jurisdiction over the parties and subject-matter and to pass the judgment.[6]

11. Legal character: Declaration of a legal right is different from a declaration of a legal character. "Character" means status.[7] It is something more than a legal right. Right is in relation to a person or group of persons; status is something which defines a person's position, not in relation to a particular person or group, but in relation to the rest of the world. The word "legal character" must be construed narrowly.[8]

Conclusiveness of the judgments is only in regard to matters enumerated in the second part of the section.

12. Foreign Matrimonial Judgments can be recognised given if the jurisdiction assumed by that court, grounds on which relief was granted are in accordance with the law under which parties were married. The exceptions are where the action is filed in the forum where respondent is domiciled and the relief is granted on a ground available under the law under which parties were married, where respondent voluntarily submits to the jurisdiction of the forum and

---

1. *Anjuman Islamia* v. *Latafat Ali*, AIR 1950 All 109: 1950 ALJ 776; *Sriram* v. *Prabhu Dayal*, AIR 1972 Raj 180: 1972 WLN 49: 1972 Raj LW 169.
2. *State of Bihar* v. *Radha Krishna Singh*, AIR 1983 SC 684: (1983) 1 SCALE 789: (1983) 2 SCR 808: (1983) 3 SCC 118: 1983 Cur Civ LJ (SC) 273.
3. *Hassanulla Khan* v. *Royal Mosque Trust Board*, AIR 1948 Mad 134: ILR (1948) Mad 257; *Sunni Central Board* v. *Sirajul Haq Khan*, AIR 1954 All 88: 1953 All WR (HC) 527: 1953 All LJ 587.
4. 1959 MYs LJ 234.
5. Phipson on Evidence, 14th Edition P 856 and 857.
6. *Menahem Messa* v. *Moses Menahem Messa*, AIR 1938 Bom 394: ILR 1938 Bom 529; *Satya* v. *Teja Singh*, AIR 1975 SC 105: 1975 Cr LJ 52: 1975 (2) SCJ 294.
7. *Lakshmayee* v. *Ponna Goundan*, 88 Madras LW 445
8. *Amar Kaur* v. *Shiv Karan*, ILR (1965) 1 Punj 160: AIR 1965 Punj 206; In the matter of *P.C. Venkataramanayya Fantulu*, AIR 1931 Mad 441: ILR 54 Mad 601 (SB); *Sriram* v. *Prabhu Dayal*, AIR 1972 Raj 180: 1972 WLN 49: 1972 Raj LW 169.

contests the claim which is based on a ground available under the law under which parties were married and where respondent consented to grant relief.[1]

Modern theory of conflict of laws recognizes the jurisdiction of the State which has the most intimate contact with the issues arising in the case. Jurisdiction is not attracted in child custody case by the operation or creation of fortuitous circumstances such as to where the child is brought or for the time being lodged.[2]

13. SECTION 42:

Judgments, orders and decrees other than those mentioned in section 41, are relevant if they relate to matters of a public nature relevant to the enquiry; but such judgments, orders or decrees are not conclusive proof of that which they state. *A* sues *B* for trespass on his land; *B* alleges the existence of a public right of way over the land, which *A* denies. The existence of a decree in favour of the defendant in a suit by *A* against *C* for trespass on the same land, in which *C* alleged existence of the same right of way is relevant, but it is not conclusive proof that the right of way exists.[3] On account of the public nature of the earlier proceedings, an exception is made in regard to judgments relating to matters of a public nature; but they are not conclusive.[4] "Public Nature" means such of those matters in which public are interested and not matters in which only individuals may be interested.[5] Such matters are those in which a large section of the public is interested.[6]

Custom is a matter of public nature.[7] A judgment is evidence of a custom dealt with therein.

The judgment need not have been given before the present dispute started.[8] A Judgment by compromise is also relevant, though it may not have much value.[9] An *ex-parte* judgment is relevant and not less useful.[9] Probative value depends upon the nature of the finding and of the issues involved in the two cases. Such a judgment is not conclusive.[10]

---

1. *Y. Narasimha Rao* v. *Y. Venkata Lakshmi*, 1991 CAR 290: 1991 Cr LR 555: (1991) 2 Crimes 855: (1991) 2 SCR 821: (1991) 2 SCALE 1: (1991) 3 SCC 451: JT (1991) 3 SC 33.
2. *Surinder Kaur Sandhu* v. *Harbax Singh Sandhu*, AIR 1984 SC 1224: (1984) 3 SCC 698: 1984 SCC (Cri) 464; *Elizabeth Dinshaw* v. *Arvand M. Dinshaw*, AIR 1987 SC 3: 1987 (1) SCJ 134: (1987) 1 SCC 42.
3. *Salekh Chand* v. *Satya Guptha*, (2008) 13 SCC 119: AIR 2009 SC (Supp) 418: 2008 AIR SCW 4211; *K.G. Premshankar* v. *Inspector of Police*, AIR 2002 SC 3372: 2002 Cr LJ 4343: (2002) 8 SCC 87; *Syed Askari Hadi Ali Augustine Imam* v. *State*, (2009) 5 SCC 528: AIR 2009 SC 3232: 2009 AIR SCW 3251.
4. *Gopi Sundari Dasi* v. *Kherod Gobinda Chowdhury*, AIR 1925 Cal 194: 82 Ind Cas 99; *Secretary of State* v. *Syed Ahmed Badshah Sahib*, AIR 1921 Mad 248: ILR 44 Mad 778:14 Mad LW 128 (FB).
5. *Ram Ranjan Chakerbati* v. *Ram Narain Singh*, ILR (1895) 22 Cal 533: 22 IA 60 (PC); *Dinomoni Chowdhrani* v. *Brojo Mohini Chowdhrani*, (1901) 29 Ind App 24: ILR 29 Cal 187 (PC).
6. *Tula* v. *Sadh*, AIR 1962 HP 28.
7. *Ram Kishore Jaiswal* v. *B. Kavindra Narain*, AIR 1955 All 59: 1954 All LJ 726: ILR (1955) 1 All 557 (FB); *Raja Rama Rao* v. *Raja of Pittapur*, AIR 1918 PC 81: 1918 LR 45 IA 148; *Subhani* v. *Nawab*, AIR 1941 PC 21: 193 IC 436: ILR 1941 Lah 154.
8. *Amar Chand* v. *Shankari*, AIR 1956 Raj 51: ILR (1955) 5 Raj 32.
9. *Abdul Karim* v. *Shiv Narain*, AIR 1952 Punjab 356: (1952) 54 Punj LR 255.
10. Phipson, Evidence, 14th Edition Pages 911, 912.

14. A judgment under section 92 C.P.C. is relevant under this section.[1] It binds the entire world.[2] It has been held that a stranger may assert a title which is paramount to the trust and may have the scheme displaced.

15. This section also forms an exception to the general rule that no one shall be affected by judgments to which he is not a party or privy; such judgments are relevant not as *res judicata,* but as evidence and such judgment are not conclusive.

16. SECTION 43:

Judgments, other than those covered by sections 40 to 42 are irrelevant unless the existence of such judgment is a fact in issue or is relevant under some other provision of this Act. Sections 11 is another provision which renders judgments relevant.

See discussion in *Gujjulal* v. *Fatehlal*[3] Example – *B* slanders *A* by saying *A* had been convicted for forgery. *B*'s defence was of justification by truth. He has to prove *A*'s conviction like any other fact. The criminal court judgment, though not relevant under sections 40 to 42, would be relevant under section 43 to show there was conviction or acquittal.[4] It has been held that the words" "other provisions of the Act" do not comprehend section 13.[5] But land acquisition judgments quantifying compensation are relevant.[6] Finding of a civil court regarding possession of land can be used in a later criminal case.[7] Findings in a judgment relevant under this section are not binding in a suit not inter-partes.[8]

16. Judgment, to show motive for a subsequent crime, is relevant.[9] Judgment against surety is relevant in the suit filed by the surety against the principal debotor. Judgment of acquittal is relevant in a suit for damages.[10] A judgment relevant under this section is not admissible as evidence of the truth of the facts found or observations made.[11] Such a judgment cannot be used to prove the

1. *Sri Ram* v. *Prabhu Dayal,* AIR 1972 Raj 180: 1972 WLN 49: 1972 Raj LW 169.
2. *Ramdoss* v. *Hanumantha Rao,* ILR 36 Mad 364: 21 Mad LJ 952: 12 Ind Cas 449; *Sakharam Daji* v. *Ganu Raghu Gurao,* AIR 1921 Bom 297: 23 Bom LR 125: 45 Bom 683; *Suraj Gir* v. *Bramh Narain,* AIR 1946 All 148: 1945 All LJ 486: ILR 1946 All 107; *Hassanulla Khan* v. *Royal Mosque Trust Board,* AIR 1948 Mad 134: ILR (1948) Mad 257; *Anjuman Islamia* v. *Latafat Ali,* AIR 1950 All 109: 1950 ALJ 776; *Sunni Central Board* v. *Sirajul Haq Khan,* AIR 1954 All 88: 1953 All WR (HC) 527: 1953 All LJ 587.
3. *Gujjulal* v. *Fateh Lal,* 6 Cal LR 439: ILR 6 Cal 171 (FB).
4. *Anil Behari Ghose* v. *Laika Bala Dassi,* AIR 1955 SC 566: 1955 SCJ 578: (1955) 2 SCR 270; *See* also *Chandra Bai* v. *State of Uttar Pradesh,* (1971) 3 SCC 983.
5. *State of Bihar* v. *Radha Krishna Singh,* AIR 1983 SC 684: (1983) 1 SCALE 789: (1983) 2 SCR 808: (1983) 3 SCC 118: 1983 Cur Civ LJ (SC) 273.
6. *State of Uttar Pradesh* v. *Nathhoo,* AIR 1986 All 172: 1985 All WC 733; *Mariam* v. *State,* AIR 1980 Ker 176; *Mohd. S. Labbai* v. *Mohd Hanifa,* AIR 1976 SC 1569: 1976 4 SCC 780: (1976) 3 SCR 721; *State of Bihar* v. *Mosafir Thakur,* AIR 1984 Pat 40: 1984 BLJR 18: (1984) 1 Civ LJ 156; *H. Narayaniah* v. *Land Acquisition Officer, Bangalore,* AIR 1981 Kant 26: (1980) 2 Kant LJ 441: 1981 Land LR 7.
7. *Hari Panda* v. *State,* AIR 1956 Ori 212: ILR 1956 Cut 241: 1956 Cr LJ 1421.
8. *Dinomoni Chowdhrani* v. *Brojo Mohini Chowdhrani,* (1901) 29 Ind App 24: ILR 29 Cal 187 (PC): 6 CWN 386 (PC) (PC); *S.M. Jakati* v. *S.M. Borkar,* AIR 1959 SC 282: 1959 SCJ 719: 1959 SCR 1384.
9. *Hitendra Singh* v. *Rameshwar Singh Bahadur,* ILR 4 Pat 510: 87 IC 849: AIR 1925 Pat 625.
10. *Shubrati* v. *Shamshuddin,* AIR 1928 All 337: ILR 50 All 713; *Pedda Venkatapathi* v. *Ganagunta Balappa,* AIR 1933 Mad 429: 65 Mad LJ 146: ILR 56 Mad 641; *Gobind Chandra Sambarsingh Mohapatra* v. *Upendra Padhi,* AIR 1960 Ori 29: 25 Cut LT 366.
11. *Muneswari* v. *Jugal Mohini,* AIR 1952 Cal 368.

conclusion arrived at on the particular evidence in the previous suit. A decision by the civil court binds the criminal court.[1]

17. SECTION 44:

Judgment relevant under any of the sections 40 to 42 may be shown to be the result of fraud or collusion or by an incompetent court. These circumstances go to the root of the matter and vitiate the sanctity, finality and binding nature of a judgment. A decree or order of court is normally binding on those who are parties to it, subject to section 44.[2] Section 44 applies to judgments *in rem* or *in personem* as also to civil and criminal proceedings.[3] It is not necessary for the party against whom such a judgment is sought to be used, to bring a separate suit to have it set aside; it is open to such party to the suit in which such judgment is sought to be used against him, to show that the judgment relied upon by the other side was delivered by a Court not competent to deliver it, or was obtained by fraud or collusion. The principle underlying this section is that a party who had secured a judgment by fraud or collusion should not be allowed to enjoy the fruits thereof.[4] A party or a stranger can invoke this section.[5]

Judgment by an incompetent court is a nullity.[6] Jurisdiction must be at the date of the former suit.[7] Competency and Jurisdiction are synonymous terms.[8]

Section 44 does not apply to judgments relevant under section 43.[9]

An executing Court can consider if the decree was passed without jurisdiction.[10]

The words "by a Court not competent" refer to a court acting without jurisdiction. "Jurisdiction" may have to be considered with reference to place, value, nature of the subject-matter.[11] Defect of jurisdiction strikes at the very authority of the court to pass any order. This rule is subject to exceptions. Section 11 of Suits Valuation Act and section 21 C.P.C. provide for two exceptions. It

---

1. *Shanti Kumar Panda* v. *Shakuntala Devi*, (2004) 1 SCC 438: AIR 2004 SC 115: 2004 Cr LJ 1249; See also *K.G. Premshankar* v. *Inspector of Police*, AIR 2002 SC 3372: 2002 Cr LJ 4343: (2002) 8 SCC 87.
2. *Som Dev* v. *Rati Ram*, (2006) 10 SCC 788: AIR 2006 SC 3297: 2006 AIR SCW 4806.
3. *Satya* v. *Teja Singh*, AIR 1975 SC 105: 1975 Cr LJ 52: 1975 (2) SCJ 294; *R. Viswanathan* v. *Rukn-ul-Mulk Syed Abdul Wajid*, AIR 1963 SC 1: (1963) 1 Cr LJ 1: (1963) 2 SCWR 117.
4. *Hamza Haji* v. *State of Kerala*, (2006) 7 SCC 416: AIR 2006 SC 3028: 2006 AIR SCW 4168.
5. *Satya* v. *Teja Singh*, AIR 1975 SC 105: 1975 Cr LJ 52: 1975 (2) SCJ 294.
6. *Kiran Singh* v. *Chaman Paswan*, AIR 1954 SC 340: 1954 SCJ 514: (1955) 1 SCR 117 (SC); *Chief Justice of Andhra Pradesh* v. *L.V.A. Dixitulu*, (1979) 2 SCC 34: AIR 1979 SC 193: 1978 Lab IC 1672; *Nai Bahu* v. *Lala Ramnarayan*, AIR 1978 SC 22: (1978) 1 SCC 58: (1978) 1 SCR 723.
7. *Jeevantha* v. *Hanumantha*, AIR 1954 SC 9: ILR 1953 Hyd 400.
8. Stephen quoted in Field on Evidence, 9th Edition, Vol. 3, Page 2336.
9. *Venkata Rangacharyalu* v. *Akkappa Rao*, AIR 1941 Mad 569; *Bishunath Tewari* v. *Mirchi*, AIR 1955 Pat 66.
10. *Haji Sk. Subhan* v. *Madhorao*, AIR 1962 SC 1230: 1962 2 SCJ 575: 1962 Supp (1) SCR 123; *Hiralal* v. *Kalinath*, AIR 1962 SC 199: 1961 (2) SCJ 592: (1962) 2 SCR 747; *Gora Chand Haldar* v. *P.K. Roy*, AIR 1925 Cal 907: ILR 53 Cal 166 (FB); *Vasudev Dhanjibhai Modi* v. *Rajabhai Abdul Rehman*, AIR 1970 SC 1475: 1970 Ren CR 427: 1970 Ren CJ 716; *Kiran Singh* v. *Chaman Paswan*, AIR 1954 SC 340: 1954 SCJ 514: (1955) 1 SCR 117 (SC).
11. *Hirday Nath Roy* v. *Ramchandra Barna Sarma*, AIR 1921 Cal 34: ILR 48 Cal 138; *Hiralal Patni* v. *Sri Kali Nath*, AIR 1955 All 569; *Kiran Singh* v. *Chaman Paswan*, AIR 1954 SC 340: 1954 SCJ 514: (1955) 1 SCR 117 (SC).

must be inherent lack of jurisdiction, not lack of territorial jurisdiction.[1] Lack of territorial jurisdiction can be waived.[2]

Section 44 refers to fraud and not negligence.[3] A judgment obtained by practicing fraud on a court is nullity.[4] It can be challenged before a higher court or in collateral proceedings.[5] Fraud and collusion are not defined in this Act; Indian Contract Act defines these words.

Fraud must be in procuring the judgment, such as collusion or the like between the parties; fraud on the court must be actual fraud. Mere perjury is not fraud.[6]

Fraud is act of deliberate deception and design of securing some unfair benefit by taking undue advantage of another. Fraud is an extrinsic collateral act which vitiates all judicial acts.[7] Even a stranger who is confronted by a judgment, may avoid it's affects by proving that it was obtained by fraud.[8] Finding of fraud cannot be founded on mere suspicion.[9]

Such a judgment can be challenged in a collateral proceeding.[10] Fraud can be pleaded as a defence to an action. Section 44 is an exception to section 11, Civil Procedure Code. Where an inference of fraud or collusion can be drawn from negligence of the next friend of a minor, the minor can avoid the judgment in the earlier case by invoking section 44, without filing a suit to set aside the judgment.

Fraud has to be established by cogent evidence.[11]

"Collusion" is uniting for the purpose of fraud or deception. It is deceitful agreement or compact to do some act in order to prejudice another or for some improper purpose.

Parties or strangers can allege fraud, provided they were not party to the fraud.[12] But where the act in which parties concur is against the principles of

1. 1972 II Mys LJ 123.
2. *Mohanlal Goenka* v. *Benoy Kishna Mukherjee*, AIR 1953 SC 65: 1953 SCJ 130: 1953 SCR 377; *Hiralal* v. *Kalinath*, AIR 1962 SC 199: 1961 (2) SCJ 592: (1962) 2 SCR 747; *Bahrein Petroleum Co. Ltd.* v. *P.J. Pappu*, AIR 1966 SC 634: (1966) 1 SCR 461: 1967 (1) SCJ 49.
3. *W.M.S. Muttu Mohammado* v. *S.K.R.A.A.R. Ramasami Chetty*, AIR 1934 PC 1; *Chand Khan* v. *State of Uttar Pradesh*, AIR 1995 SC 2140
4. *Jai Narain Parasrampuria* v. *Pushpa Devi Saraf*, (2006) 7 SCC 756.
5. *A.V. Papayya Sastry* v. *Government of Andhra Pradesh*, (2007) 4 SCC 221: AIR 2007 SC 1546: 2007 AIR SCW 2212; *K.D. Sharma* v. *Steel Authority of India Limited*, (2008) 12 SCC 481: AIR 2009 SC (Supp) 1309: 2008 AIR SCW 6654; *S.P. Chengalvaraya Naidu* v. *Jagannath*, JT 1993 (6) SC 331: (1994) 1 SCC 1: AIR 1994 SC 853.
6. 1972 I Mys LJ 473.
7. *A.V. Papayya Sastry* v. *Government of Andhra Pradesh*, (2007) 4 SCC 221: AIR 2007 SC 1546: 2007 AIR SCW 2212; *K.D. Sharma* v. *Steel Authority of India Limited*, (2008) 12 SCC 481: AIR 2009 SC (Supp) 1309: 2008 AIR SCW 6654.
8. *Gurdit Singh* v. *State of Punjab*, AIR 1974 SC 1791: (1974) 2 SCC 260: (1974) 3 SCR 896.
9. *Narayanan* v. *Official Assignee, Rangoon*, AIR 1941 PC 93: (1941) 31 NY Supp 2(d) 631; *Union of India* v. *Chaturbhai M. Patel and Co.*, AIR 1976 SC 712: (1976) 1 SCC 747: (1976) 2 SCR 902.
10. *Jai Narain Parasrampuria* v. *Pushpa Devi Saraf*, (2006) 7 SCC 756; *North Eastern Railway Admn.* v. *Bhagwan Das*, (2008) 8 SCC 511: AIR 2008 SC 2139: 2008 AIR SCW 3159.
11. *Hansraj Gupta* v. *Dehra Dun Mussoorie Electric Tramway Co. Ltd.*, AIR 1940 PC 98: ILR (1940) Kar PC 216; *Narayanan* v. *Official Assignee, Rangoon*, AIR 1941 PC 93: (1941) 31 NY Supp 2(d) 631; *Union of India* v. *Chaturbhai M. Patel and Co.*, AIR 1976 SC 712: (1976) 1 SCC 747: (1976) 2 SCR 902.
12. *Kondi Ravjiu* v. *Chunnilal Rupechandra*, AIR 1929 Bom 1: 53 Bom 75.

morality or public policy, court may interfere even at the instance of a party to the fraud. These principles apply to "collusion" also.

The principle of this section cannot be extended to other grounds like misrepresentation or undue influence or natural mistake as to a material fact. Courts cannot treat gross negligence as fraud or collusion unless fraud or collusion is the proper inference from facts.[1] But section 44 does not affect the right of an erstwhile minor, on attaining majority, to get the decree obtained against him earlier (when he was minor) set aside on the ground of gross negligence or fraud by a guardian, by filing an independent suit.[2] Section 44 is only permissive; it allows a party to avoid a judgment, but does not destroy his substantive right which exists independently of the Evidence Act.[3]

---

1. *T. Venkata Seshayya* v. *T. Kotiswara Rao*, AIR 1937 PC 1: ILR (1937) Mad 263: 64 Ind App 17.
2. *Venkatappa Naik* v. *Subba Naik*, (1906) ILR 29 Mad 179: 16 Mad LJ 59.
3. *Kothandarama Gramani* v. *Sellammal*, AIR 1959 Mad 524: (1959) 2 Mad LJ 218.

CHAPTER 11

OPINIONS OF EXPERTS AND CERTAIN OTHERS (SECTIONS 45 TO 51)

SECTIONS 45 AND 46:

Section 45 of Evidence Act states, *inter alia*, that when the court has to form an opinion upon a point of foreign law, or of science, or art, or as to identity of handwriting or finger-impressions, the opinions upon that point of persons specially skilled in such subjects are relevant facts. Such persons are called experts. According to section 46, facts not otherwise relevant, are relevant, if they support or are inconsistent with opinions of experts, when such opinions are relevant. Section 51 states that whenever the opinion of any living person is relevant, the grounds on which such opinion is based are also relevant. Section 57 states, *inter alia*, that on all matters of public history, literature, science or art the Court may resort for its aid to appropriate books or documents of reference. Section 60 states, *inter alia*, that oral evidence must be direct, that is to say, if it refers to an opinion or to the grounds on which that opinion is held, it must be the evidence of the person who holds that opinion on those grounds; but opinion of expert in any book commonly offered for sale, and the grounds on which such opinion is held, may be proved by the production of the book if the author is dead or cannot be found or is otherwise unavailable to give evidence. Section 159 enables an expert to refresh his memory by reference to his notes and treatises written by others.

2. The general rule regarding oral evidence is the one contained in section 60 *i.e.*, a witness has only to state facts, which he has seen, heard or perceived i.e., facts immediately within his knowledge. The general rule excludes opinion of a witness. Formation of opinion or conclusion is the function of the judge. Section 45 dealing with expert evidence is an exception to the general rule. Opinion of an expert is the statement of an inference by him as to the existence or otherwise of a fact in issue or a relevant fact, based upon other facts presented directly to his senses. The reason behind the rule is that judges do not have expertise in technical or scientific matters and have to be assisted by skilled persons. Expert is a person who has special knowledge and skill in the particular subject to which the enquiry relates.

3. The competency of an expert is a matter of proof. He must be shown to be an expert. In America *'voire diare' i.e.*, preliminary examination is allowed for ascertaining the qualifications of the expert. In India, this is not allowed. As observed by Lord Russel[1] the question is, is he peritus, is he skilled? Has he adequate knowledge? But he need not have acquired his knowledge professionally. It is sufficient if he has made a special study of the subject or acquired special experience therein.[2] If there is no evidence of the nature of training received

1. *United States Shipping Board* v. *Ship St. Albans*, AIR 1931 PC 189: 1931 AC 632: 131 IC 771.
2. *R.* v. *Silver lock*, (1894) 2 KB 766 (768).

by him and qualifications, he is no expert.[1] Doctor who performs autopsy is a witness of fact also. His evidence is a check on eye-witnesses.[2] The following persons have been held to be experts:—Surveyor or broker regarding value of property,[3] Excise Officer who is able to distinguish liquors,[4] Excise Officer who is able to distinguish liquor and illicit liquor.[5] Excise Officer regarding wash,[6] Goldsmith who bases his opinion on test by touchstone.[7] His opinion about purity must be supported by data. Expert must indicate his qualification and experience. A Police Officer having certificate of technical competency and long experience of fire arms is an expert on Arms.[8]

4. Opinion of witnesses possessing special skills is admissible, whenever the subject-matter of enquiry is such that inexperienced persons are unlikely to prove capable of forming a correct judgment upon it without such assistance. This is so when it so far partakes of the character of a science or art as to require a course of previous habit or study to obtain a competent knowledge of its' nature.[9] In applying section 45 or 47, the evidence is of opinion and the court must satisfy itself by such means as are open that the opinion may be acted upon.[10] Expertise may be derived from experience and not merely from formal training.[11]

5. An expert is one who has devoted time to study a special branch of learning. All persons who practice a business or profession which requires them to possess a certain knowledge of the matter are experts. Opinion of an experienced obstetrician cannot be rejected merely because she has not specialized in gynecology.[12] An excise inspector who had twenty years' experience in testing a large number of samples of liquor and whose competence to test the contents and strength of seized liquor was not questioned, has to be regarded as an expert.[13] The decision of Supreme Court may be usefully read to understand the manner of appreciaton of opinion evidence of an expert.[14]

1. *Lakshmi Chand Khajuria* v. *Ishroo Devi*, AIR 1977 SC 1694: 1977 J and K LR 127; *Mahmood* v. *State of Uttar Pradesh*, AIR 1976 SC 69: 1976 Cr LJ 10: (1976) 1 SCC 542; *Chatt Ram* v. *State of Haryana*, AIR 1979 SC 1890: (1980) 1 SCC 460: 1979 Cr LJ 1411; *Chatt Ram* v. *State of Haryana*, AIR 1979 SC 1890: (1980) 1 SCC 460: 1979 Cr LJ 1411.
2. *Badri Prasad* v. *State of Madhya Pradesh*, AIR 1970 SC 706: (1969) 2 SCR 380: 1970 1 SCJ 757; *Mohd. Zahid* v. *State of Tamil Nadu*, AIR 1999 SC 2416: 1999 Cr LJ 3699: 1999 AIR SCW 2556; *Prithi Chand* v. *State of Himachal Pradesh*, AIR 1989 SC 702: 1989 CAR 56: 1989 Cr LR 235: (1989) 1 Crimes 384: (1989) 1 SCC 432: (1989) 1 SCR 123: (1989) 1 SCALE 74: JT 1989 (1) SC 106: 1989 Cr LJ 841.
3. *Nelson Fernandes* v. *Special L.A. Officer, South Goa*, (2007) 9 SCC 447: AIR 2007 SC 1414: 2007 AIR SCW 1782.
4. *Oli (in re:)*, 1976 Cr LJ 1339: 1976 Mad LW (Cri) 38 Mad.
5. *Sri Chand Batra* v. *State of Uttar Pradesh*, AIR 1974 SC 639: 1974 CAR 105: 1974 Cr LR 97: 1974 UJ 149: (1974) 2 SCR 821: (1974) 4 SCC 247: 1974 Cr LJ 590.
6. *Rajabather*, AIR 1959 Mad 450: 1959 Cr LJ 1189.
7. *Assistant Collector of Central Excise, Calicut* v. *V.P. Sayed Mohammed*, AIR 1983 SC 168: 1983 Cr LJ 225: (1983) 1 SCC 370.
8. *Brij Patel* v. *State (Delhi Administration)*, 1996 SCC (Cri) 392.
9. Taylor on Evidence 12th Edition, Page 902.
10. *Fakhruddin* v. *State of Madhya Pradesh*, AIR 1967 SC 1326: (1967) 2 SCJ 885: 1967 Cr LJ 1197: 1967 MPLJ 473: (1967) 1 SCWR 449: 1967 All LJ 303.
11. Phipson on Evidence, 15th Edition, Page 962; and *State of Himachal Pradesh* v. *Jai Lal*, AIR 1999 SC 3318: (1999) 7 SCC 280: 1999 SCC (Cri) 1184.
12. *Baldev Raj Miglani* v. *Urmila Kumari*, AIR 1979 SC 879: (1979) 3 SCC 782: 1979 SCC (Cri) 875.
13. *Srichand Batra* v. *State of Uttar Pradesh*, AIR 1974 SC 639: 1974 CAR 105: 1974 Cr LR 97: 1974 UJ 149: (1974) 2 SCR 821: (1974) 4 SCC 247: 1974 Cr LJ 590.
14. *Murari Lal* v. *State of Madhya Pradesh*, AIR 1980 SC 531: (1980) 1 SCC 704: (1980) 2 SCR 249: 1980 Cr LJ 396.

The words "science" and "art" have to be construed broadly. "Science" or "art" would include all branches of human knowledge requiring a course of special study, skill or experience.

The study of footprints has been accepted as a science, though not an exact science.[1] Evidence relating to footprints, if satisfactory, may be used only to reinforce the conclusions as to identity of a culprit which, alongwith other circumstances, would point to the identity of the culprit.[2]

6. Expert has to state his opinion and the facts or data which he noticed and on which his opinion is based. His testimony regarding the facts noticed is direct testimony. (Doctor describing injuries), while statement of his opinion is as an expert. (opinion as to cause of death, nature of weapon used, time of death, whether injuries are ante mortem etc.). Nevertheless, it has to be recognised that in certain cases, even the perception of facts may require expertise (comparison of injuries described in inquest report and autopsy certificate). When the expert himself collects the special facts, that part of his testimony could also be treated as expert testimony. Expert can also give opinion on the basis of data collected by other experts or proved by ordinary witnesses. The facts perceived by him, his opinion, the grounds for the opinion are relevant. "Fact", under Section 3, includes any mental condition of which any person is conscious. Illustration (d) to the definition says, that a person holds a certain opinion is a fact. That Modi in his treatise on *Medical Jurisprudence* expresses a certain opinion can be relied on by the expert by citing passages from Modi. Expert may rely on facts relating to other similar cases in support of his opinion. *See* illustration (a) to section 46. Evidence of expert as to the existence of facts on which his opinion is based is not relevant unless perceived by himself. Expert should not be asked his opinion on other evidence in this case. No hypothetical questions can be asked without foundation in evidence. Expert cannot determine the very question which is to be decided by court. If an expert is to be contradicted by an opinion in a treatise, his attention must be drawn to the relevant passages.[3] Expert evidence is a weak type of evidence and is not conclusive. Court must look for some reliable corroboration.[4] This is a rule of caution. The weight of expert evidence depends on the correctness of the report, reasons given and his expertise in the field. It is important that the expert gives reasons in support of his opinion so that court may verify the correctness of the reasons. In a case where majority of finger prints found are partially smudged, expert has to state which of the marks are usable as finger print evidence and give his opinion whether opinion can be formed on eight or less identical characteristics in a given case.[5]

7. Expert opinion is a relevant fact and is brought into evidence. Evidence given by an expert which remains positive inspite of cross-examination can be acted upon even in the presence of minor deficiencies like non-production of

1. *Basudeo Gir* v. *State of Bihar*, AIR 1959 Pat 534: 1959 Cr LJ 1355: ILR 38 Pat 69.
2. *Pritam Singh* v. *State of Punjab*, 1956 Cr LJ 805: AIR 1956 SC 415 (SC); *Mohd. Aman* v. *State of Rajasthan*, AIR 1997 SC 2960: 1997 Cr LJ 3567: 1997 AIR SCW 2980; *Surajpal Singh* v. *State of Madhya Pradesh*, 1972 Cr LJ 1668: 1972 MPWR 394: 1972 MPLJ 1029.
3. *Sunderlal* v. *State of Madhya Pradesh*, AIR 1954 SC 28: 1954 Cr LJ 257; *Bhagwan Das* v. *State of Rajasthan*, AIR 1957 SC 589: 1957 Cr LJ 889: 1957 SCC 308; *State of Madhya Pradesh* v. *Sanjay Rai*, AIR 2004 SC 2174: 2004 Cr LJ 2006: 2004 AIR SCW 1919.
4. *Magan Behari Lal* v. *State of Punjab*, AIR 1977 SC 1091: 1977 Cr LJ 711: (1977) 2 SCC 210.
5. *Mohan Lal* v. *Ajit Singh*, AIR 1978 SC 1183: (1978) 3 SCC 279: 1978 Cr LJ 1107.

original workbook.[1] Expert opinion is not binding on the court. The reasons given by an expert require probe and verification by the court. Opinions of authors of expert treatises may be of help to the expert and the court. Views expressed by such authors may be of persuasive value, though not binding. Opinion of an author cannot be given higher value than expert evidence given in court.[2]

8. Need for expert evidence: Science is becoming increasingly important in criminal investigation. Experts are even attached to police organisations and more and more policemen are being trained as experts. It has been found that individual copper wire has distinctive marks, that nicks on the blade of a knife can match the window forced upon by a knife, that blood stains can be seen through infrared rays, that grass stains, powder grains, hair etc., can be removed from clothes and identified and that, identification of skull can be made by superimposition process, blood can be matched etc. Expert evidence can play an important role in identification, particularly where the body is uncognizably decomposed or only bones remain. It can be found if the remains are of a male or female, of a young, middle aged or old person. It can disclose an old but recognizable injury, missing tooth or deformity. Expert evidence can be useful in identification of living persons. Science relating to blood, handwriting, fingerprints, foot prints, horoscopy can be helpful. Identification of weapon can be assisted by experts, particularly in the case of fire arms. It may be necessary to show that injuries on a body are likely to have been caused by the weapon with which and the manner in which they are alleged to have been caused. Medical jurist can throw a flood of light on intoxication and its degree, the age and nature of injuries, manner of infliction of injuries, nature of weapon used, ante-mortem nature of injuries, degree of force used, time of death, cause of death, whether injuries are self-inflicted, suicidal, homicidal or accidental, whether a child was born alive or dead, age of a raped girl, whether there was rape etc. Chemical examiner can tell us if viscera contains poison and the particular kind of poison, presence and percentage of alcohol etc. Hence the importance of expert assistance cannot be overemphasized.

9. Case of suspected homicide: In case of death by physical violence, medical cause of death could be syncope, shock, asphyxia or coma. Syncope is caused by sudden and excessive hemorrhage from wounds of large blood vessels or internal organs. Shock inhibits action of heart from sudden freight, blows on the head or on the epigastrium or from extensive injuries to the spine or other parts of the body. Asphyxia on account of physical violence is due to mechanical obstruction of air passages by blocking their lumen from within as in suffocation and drowning or by their compression from without as in strangulation or hanging or stoppage of movements of the chest resulting from mechanical pressure on the chest or abdomen or collapse of the lungs from punctured wounds of the thorax. Coma due to physical violence is due to compression of the brain from injuries to the brain or its membranes or effusion of blood on or in the brain consequent on fracture of the skull.

10. Death by some pathological condition must be ruled out. A simple injury could have fatal consequence in case of diseased spleen or other organ. In case of several injuries (perhaps inflicted by several persons) it is necessary to know

1. *Baso Prasad* v. *State of Bihar,* (2006) 13 SCC 65: AIR 2007 SC 1019: 2007 AIR SCW 807.
2. *State of Madhya Pradesh* v. *Sanjay Rai,* AIR 2004 SC 2174: 2004 Cr LJ 2006: 2004 AIR SCW 1919.

which particular injury was fatal. Where an injured dies after a longer or shorter period, the expert must all the more be careful. In such a case it is important to distinguish between the purely medical aspect of the immediate cause of death from the medico-legal question as to whether death could be strictly and clearly traceable to the injury. Where disease intervenes, it is necessary to know if the supervening disease was itself the direct and natural result of the wound. Expert evidence assumes greater importance where the immediate cause of death is an operation necessitated by the injury. In such a case necessity for the operation and skill employed are relevant.

11. Death by asphyxia could be due to drowning, hanging, strangulation or suffocation. In the case of drowning it is necessary to know if the person was dead before being thrown into water. In the case of hanging, care must be taken to see if dead body or living person was hanged. In cases of poisoning, death could be caused by syncope, asphyxia or coma, according to the nature and action of poison (poisoning by strychnine – asphyxia, by opium or alcohol – coma). Expert is expected to have a good general knowledge of various poisons and their effect and symptoms. The ultimate opinion is the result of medical as well as chemical examination.

12. In appreciating expert evidence, the first question to be answered is whether he is an expert. It must be verified whether any part of his evidence is inadmissible in view of the provisions of Evidence Act. His opinion and grounds for his opinion must be tested, as he is liable to err. Bias cannot be assumed; it has to be proved. Other evidence in the case could be tested with the aid of expert evidence. Nevertheless, expert evidence is only a piece of evidence. It will have to be considered along with other evidence. Which is the main evidence and which is the corroborative evidence depends upon facts and circumstances of each case.[1] Generally speaking, expert evidence has corroborative value only. Ocular or other evidence, if cogent and acceptable, could be preferred to expert evidence.[2] It is also independent evidence since it establishes certain facts.[3]

13. Medical and Chemical examination: Supreme Court has held that "to furnish evidence" is not equivalent to "to be compelled to be a witness against himself" within the meaning of article 20(3) of the Constitution.[4] It is thus indicated that there is no legal bar to subjecting an accused to medical examination for purpose of criminal investigation. It stands on the same footing as taking specimen handwriting, thumb impressions, foot prints etc. An accused in custody, suspected to be of unsound mind could be directed by the court to be kept under observation in a hospital. During investigation, an accused can be medically examined for detection of intoxicated condition. Injured in an occurrence, including accused, can be sent for medical treatment. In medico-legal cases, great care must be taken to ensure thorough clinical and specialised examination (*e.g.*, suspected fracture – X-ray examination). In the case of victims of indecent assault and rape or attempted rape, medical (and chemical re: objects)

1. *Guntaka Hussenaiah* v. *Busetti Yerraiah*, AIR 1954 Andhra 39: (1954) 2 Mad LJ 39: 67 Mad LW 1052.
2. *Anant Chintaman Lagu* v. *State of Bombay*, AIR 1960 SC 500: (1960) 2 SCR 460: 1960 Cr LJ 682.
3. *Nagindra Bala Mitra* v. *Sunil Chandra Roy*, AIR 1960 SC 706: (1960) 3 SCR 1: 1960 Cr LJ 1020.
4. *Gorkha Ram* v. *Custodian General of India, Delhi*, AIR 1961 SC 1805: (1962) 2 SCR 151: 1962 (1) SCJ 564.

examination of the victim and the offender is of the highest importance. In the case of some contraband goods, chemical examination will yield good results *i.e.*, liquor, opium, drugs, etc. Medical examination can be made and tests can be performed to determine age *e.g.*, X-ray examination or Radiological test,[1] growth of hair on the pubes, development of organs. Ossification is perhaps the most reliable test. Blood grouping gives negative indication of paternity.

14. Importance of a thorough post-mortem examination in the case of suspected unnatural death cannot be overstressed. If autopsy is held in location, Doctor should also note the condition and position of body, position of any weapon found at the scene, the condition of the clothing etc. Careful examination of wounds to find out nature (incised, incised looking, lacerated etc.,) and direction of the wound (to detect manner of stab or cut) must be conducted. It is relevant to note if the body is warm or cold, rigid or pliant, contents of digestive organs and condition of all internal organs. Other particulars like sex, colour, indications of age, deformities and abnormalities, colour of hair may be relevant, particularly in the case of unidentified bodies. All necessary data to determine time of death have to be collected. In case of death of infant, all relevant data having a bearing on the question whether the infant was born alive or not have to be collected. In case of suspected poisoning and in cases without injuries, viscera must be preserved and sent for chemical examination. Post-mortem findings must be reduced to writing and correctly interpreted. Injuries must be categorised as simple or grievous, likely to cause death, sufficient in the ordinary course of nature to cause death or necessarily fatal. Internal injuries must be carefully described. Condition of chambers of heart and other internal organs must be thoroughly examined. Exudation from orifices must be recorded.

15. Ordinarily the medical expert has to be examined in court subject to section 291 of Code of Criminal Procedure. Autopsy report or wound certificate is relevant under section 32(2) of Evidence Act. Post-mortem notes and case sheets can be secured in appropriate cases; so also X-ray photographs and other relevant records.

16. Importance of medical evidence in homicidal cases cannot be overstated. In cases of conflict of evidence, attempt has to be made to reconcile them.[2] Limitation of medical evidence has to be borne in mind.[3]

17. Regarding cause of death and also *mens rea*, medical evidence is of crucial significance. Prosecutor has the duty to place relevant medical evidence before court. When the doctor who performed post-mortem is before court, it is the duty of the prosecutor to bring out all necessary particulars regarding the injuries, their size, nature and effect. Prosecutor should show the alleged weapon to the doctor and elicit from him whether it would or would not be possible for such an injury to be caused by such a weapon and the reason for the opinion.[4] It is also his duty to elicit from the expert all materials which would help the Court to arrive at a conclusion regarding the degree of culpability of the act involved

---

1. *Jaya Mala* v. *Government of Jammu and Kashmir*, (1982) 2 SCC 538: AIR 1982 SC 1297: 1982 Cr LJ 1777.
2. *Punjab Singh* v. *State of Haryana*, AIR 1984 SC 1233: (1984) 1 Crimes 859: 1984 Cr LJ 921; *Solanki Chimanbhai Ukabhai* v. *State of Gujarat*, AIR 1983 SC 484: (1983) 2 SCC 174: 1983 Cr LJ 822.
3. *Nagindra Bala Mitra* v. *Sunil Chandra Roy*, AIR 1960 SC 706: (1960) 3 SCR 1: 1960 Cr LJ 1020.
4. *Ishwar Singh* v. *State of Uttar Pradesh*, AIR 1976 SC 2423: 1976 Cr LJ 1883: 1976 SCC (Cr) 629.

in the case. The injury may be necessarily fatal or it may be only of such a nature as likely to cause death. Attention of the expert must be drawn to these differences. Opinion given by the expert must be supported by reasons which can be tested by the court. Medical jurisprudence is not an exact science.

Court has to consider not merely medical evidence, but also other evidence and circumstances appearing on the point.[1] Medical evidence can never be absolutely certain so far as age of injuries is concerned.[2] Medical opinion pointing out alternative possibilities cannot be treated as conclusive.[3] Court should not normally substitutes its' opinion as to the murder weapon for that of the expert.[4] Court should not substitute its' opinion for that of the expert regarding nature of injuries and cause of death unless there is something inherently defective in the opinion.[5] Evidence of a doctor has to be appreciated like evidence of any other witness.[6] The weapon alleged to have been used must be shown to the doctor so as to enable him to comment whether all or any of the injuries could have been caused with it.[7] A medical certificate cannot be admitted in evidence unless the doctor who issued it is examined. But if the doctor had left his job and was not traceable, another doctor who is conversant with the formers' handwriting can be examined to prove the certificate. If the medical evidence is deficient, the court can come to its' own conclusions on a consideration of the nature of injuries and other relevant evidence.[8] A doctor is not a ballistic expert and his opinion, in the case of death by a projectile, that a bullet caused death is of no consequence.[9]

Where the doctor who examined the injured first in Primary Health Centre noticed only a single injury on the head and the doctor who conducted postmortem examination noticed injuries on head, back and left shoulder, it was held that the inconsistency was not material because while giving emergency treatment at the P.H.C., the doctor must have devoted his entire attention only to the serious head injury.[10] If evidence of two doctors in conflicting, they must be scrutinized carefully and the more reliable opinion may be accepted, after carefully examining the discrepancies.

Even though the doctor does not suspect death due to poisoning, he cannot destroy the viscera until he finally hears from the investigating officer that the viscera could be destroyed.[11]

1. *Mani Ram* v. *State of Rajasthan*, AIR 1993 SC 2453: 1993 Cr LJ 2530: 1993 AIR SCW 1885.
2. *Ram Swaroop* v. *State of Uttar Pradesh*, AIR 2000 SC 715: 2000 Cr LJ 808: 2000 All LJ 391: (2000) 2 SCC 461.
3. *State of Uttar Pradesh* v. *Krishna Gopal*, AIR 1988 SC 2154: 1989 Cr LJ 288: (1988) 4 SCC 302: JT 1988 (3) SC 544; *Ravi Kumar* v. *State of Punjab*, 2005 Cr LJ 1742: AIR 2005 SC 1929: 2005 AIR SCW 1359; *State of Madhya Pradesh* v. *Kasiram*, (2009) 4 SCC 26.
4. *State of Uttar Pradesh* v. *Shanker*, AIR 1981 SC 897: 1980 Supp SCC 489: 1981 Cr LJ 23.
5. *Mafabhai Nagarbhai Raval* v. *State of Gujarat*, AIR 1992 SC 2186: JT 1992 (4) SC 555: 1992 AIR SCW 2592; *State of Punjab* v. *Jugraj Singh*, AIR 2002 SC 1083: (2002) 3 SCC 234: 2002 Cr LJ 1503: 2002 AIR SCW 823.
6. *Mayur Panabhai Shah* v. *State of Gujarat*, AIR 1983 SC 66: 1982 Cr LJ 1972: (1982) 2 SCC 396.
7. *Ishwar Singh* v. *State of Uttar Pradesh*, AIR 1976 SC 2423: 1976 Cr LJ 1883: 1976 SCC (Cr) 629.
8. *Brij Bhukhan* v. *State of Uttar Pradesh*, AIR 1957 SC 474: 1957 Cr LJ 591; *Union Territory of Mizoram* v. *Venkatachallamma @ lallawmma*, 1977 Cr LJ 1831.
9. *Mahmood* v. *State of Uttar Pradesh*, 2007 AIR SCW 7385: 2008 Cr LJ 696: AIR 2008 SC 515.
10. *Prakash* v. *State of Madhya Pradesh*, 2007 Cr LJ 798: 2006 AIR SCW 6216: 2007 (2) Crimes 74.
11. *State of Maharashtra* v. *Manglya Dhavu Kongil*, AIR 1972 SC 1797: 1972 Cr LJ 570.

18. The medical report, by itself is not substantive evidence; it is the doctor's evidence in court which is substantive evidence. The value of the report is as a contemporaneous document which can be used to refresh one's memory or for corroboration or contradiction.[1] Post-mortem report is more valuable than the inquest report.[2] Non-examination of the doctor who conducted autopsy is a serious flaw, except where the accused admits that the death of the victim in the case was a homicidal one.[3] In a case of death by gun shot injuries, the autopsy report need not specifically state the cause of injuries in the report.[4] Non-ascertainment of the blood group of the blood found on the clothes of accused and the weapon of offence cannot be the basis for discarding the evidence of eyewitnesses who, otherwise, inspire confidence of the court.[5]

19. In cases of homicidal death, time of death, if death was instantaneous, may assume importance. Process of digestion is not uniform in all human beings. The degree of digestion of the contents cannot always be relied on in determining the time of death. This is particularly so since, as stated in *Modi's Medical Jurisprudence*, power of digestion may remain in abeyance for a long time in conditions of privation, shock and coma.[6] It would be risky to guess the probable time of death on the basis of the appearance or disappearance of rigor mortis in a dead body. The doctor who conducts autopsy generally takes into consideration the result of autopsy, rigor mortis, lividity, coolness and nature and extent of injuries found on the body.[7] In fixing the time of death, court has to consider the materials provided by the expert.[8] Condition of stomach contents has to be considered along with the time when the victim had his last meal and when he relieved himself.[9] The time taken normally for digestion would also depend on the quality and quantity of food consumed also.[10] The time of death furnished by the doctor is only an approximate one.[11]

Opinion as to time of death depends upon condition of body at the time of its receipt for autopsy, degree of digestion of the stomach contents, rigor mortis, climatic factors, age and vigour at the time of death, presence or absence of

1. *Munshi Prasad* v. *State of Bihar*, (2002) 1 SCC 351: 2001 Cr LJ 4708: AIR 2001 SC 3031: 2001 AIR SCW 4174; *State of Haryana* v. *Ram Singh*, 2002 (1) SCC 426: AIR 2002 SC 620: AIR 2002 SCW 219: 2002 (1) Supreme (Criminal) 11.
2. *Maula Bux* v. *State of Rajasthan*, (1983) 1 SCC 379.
3. *State of Uttar Pradesh* v. *Lakhami*, AIR 1998 SC 1007: 1998 Cr LJ 1411: (1998) 4 SCC 336.
4. *State of Punjab* v. *Jugraj Singh*, AIR 2002 SC 1083: (2002) 3 SCC 234: 2002 Cr LJ 1503: 2002 AIR SCW 823.
5. *Keshavlal* v. *State of Madhya Pradesh*, AIR 2002 SC 1221: 2002 Cr LJ 1776: 2002 AIR SCW 1007.
6. *Aziz Khan* v. *State of Bihar*, AIR 1964 Pat 158: (1964) 1 Cr LJ 426; *State of Uttar Pradesh* v. *Sheo Sanehi*, AIR 2004 SC 4974: 2004 Cr LJ 4650: 2004 AIR SCW 5602.
7. *Tanviben Pankajkumar Divetia* v. *State of Gujarat*, AIR 1997 SC 2193: 1997 AIR SCW 2055: 1997 Cr LJ 2535.
8. *Gambhir* v. *State of Maharashtra*, (1982) 2 SCC 351: AIR 1982 SC 1157: 1982 Cr LJ 1243.
9. *Bhim Singh* v. *State of Haryana*, AIR 2003 SC 693: (2002) 10 SCC 461: 2003 Cr LJ 857: 2002 AIR SCW 5373; *Ram Kishan* v. *State of Uttar Pradesh*, AIR 2004 SC 4678: 2004 Cr LJ 4236: 2004 AIR SCW 5169.
10. *Ram Bali* v. *State of Uttar Pradesh*, AIR 2004 SC 2329: AIR 2004 SCW 2748: (2004) 10 SCC 2598: 2004 Cr LJ 2490; *Pattipati Venkaiah* v. *State of Andhra Pradesh*, AIR 1985 SC 1715: 1985 Cr LJ 2012: (1985) 4 SCC 80; *Nihal Singh* v. *State of Punjab*, AIR 1965 SC 26: 1965 (1) SCJ 160: (1964) 4 SCR 5.
11. *A.N. Venkatesh* v. *State of Karnataka*, (2005) 7 SCC 714: AIR 2005 SC 3809: 2005 Cr LJ 3732; *Thangavelu* v. *State of Tamil Nadu*, AIR 2002 SC 2759: 2002 AIR SCW 3118: 2002 Cr LJ 3558.

clothing, temperature of the surrounding media etc. These aspects require careful consideration.[1] Reliance on degree of digestion of stomach contents is not safe.[2] In case of conflict between medical opinion and evidence of reliable eyewitnesses, Courts have not hesitated to reject the former.[3] Opinion unsupported by sound reasons is not reliable.[4]

Where the prosecution case is that the weapon seized during investigation had been used to cause injury on the victim, this aspect should be brought to the notice of the doctor who examined the victim or conducted autopsy.

20. Age:—Evidence furnished by birth register and family members with regard to age has to be preferred over a doctor's opinion, but if the former evidence is unsatisfactory and the ossification test is successful and complete, the test result can be accepted. If the entry in the school register is not genuine, medical evidence can be preferred.[5] Ossification test is not conclusive.[6] Ossification test result cannot be accepted if it is contrary to the hospital register entry relating to the child's birth.[7] In the result of radiological test, margin of error could be two years on either side.[8] Doctor's opinion based merely on physical examination has no merit.[9]

21. Where the prosecution case was that the dead bodies were dragged by the accused but autopsy did not show any injuries on the back though such injuries were noted down in the inquest report, it was held that the theory of dragging could not be discarded merely because of non-mention of corresponding injuries on the back in the autopsy report.[10] Minor variations between medical evidence and ocular evidence do not take away the primacy of ocular evidence.[11] This is so unless the medical evidence goes so far that it completely rules out all possibility of injuries being inflicted in the manner alleged by eye-witnesses.[12]

1. *Sucha Singh Nigahia Singh* v. *State*, AIR 1951 Simla 283
2. *Gopal Singh* v. *State of Uttar Pradesh*, (1978) 3 SCC 327: 1980 Cr LJ 832: AIR 1979 SC 1822; *Shivaji Sahabrao Babade* v. *State of Maharashtra*, (1974) 1 SCR 489: (1973) 2 SCC 793: AIR 1973 SC 2622: 1973 Cr LJ 1783; *Sheo Darshan* v. *State of Uttar Pradesh*, 1971 Cr LJ 1306: (1972) 3 SCC 74: AIR 1971 SC 1794; *Charan Singh* v. *State of Punjab*, AIR 1975 SC 246: (1975) 3 SCC 39: (1975) 1 SCR 561; *Pattipati Venkaiah* v. *State of Andhra Pradesh*, AIR 1985 SC 1715: 1985 Cr LJ 2012: (1985) 4 SCC 80.
3. *Lachman Singh* v. *State*, AIR 1952 SC 167: 1952 ALJ 437: 1952 Cr LJ 863: 1952 SCJ 230: 1952 SCR 839; *Doddamani* v. *State*, 1961 Cr LJ 120: AIR 1961 Mys 21: 1960 Mad LJ (Cri) 808.
4. *Haji Mohammad Ekramul Haq* v. *State of West Bengal*, AIR 1959 SC 488: 1959 SCJ 443: 1959 Supp (1) SCR 922: 1959 SCA 47.
5. *Brij Mohan Singh* v. *Priya Brat Narain Sinha*, AIR 1965 SC 282: 1964 BLJR 538: (1964) 1 SCWR 588: (1965) 3 SCR 86: 26 ELR 781: (1964) 2 SCJ 644.
6. *Ram Deo Chauhan* v. *State of Assam*, AIR 2001 SC 2231: 2001 AIR SCW 2159: 2001 Cr LJ 2902.
7. *Vishnu* v. *State of Maharashtra*, (2006) 1 SCC 283: AIR 2006 SC 508: 2005 AIR SCW 6149; *Babloo Pasi* v. *State of Jharkhand*, (2008) 13 SCC 133: AIR 2009 SC 314: 2008 AIR SCW 7332.
8. *Jaya Mala* v. *Government of Jammu and Kashmir*, (1982) 2 SCC 538: AIR 1982 SC 1297: 1982 Cr LJ 1777.
9. *Kamal Kishore* v. *State of Himachal Pradesh*, AIR 2000 SC 1920: (2000) 4 SCC 502: 2000 Cr LJ 2292; *Babloo Pasi* v. *State of Jharkhand*, (2008) 13 SCC 133: AIR 2009 SC 314: 2008 AIR SCW 7332.
10. *Ganesh K. Gulve* v. *State of Maharashtra*, AIR 2002 SC 3068: 2002 AIR SCW 3528: (2002) 7 SCC 71.
11. *Kamaljit Singh* v. *State of Punjab*, 2003 AIR SCW 5613: AIR 2004 SC 69: 2004 Cr LJ 28.
12. *Solanki Chimanbhai Ukabhai* v. *State of Gujarat*, AIR 1983 SC 484: (1983) 2 SCC 174: 1983 Cr LJ 822; *Jai Karan* v. *State of Uttar Pradesh*, AIR 2004 SC 1148: 2004 Cr LJ 403: 2003 AIR SCW 5948; *State of Uttar Pradesh* v. *Krishna Gopal*, AIR 1988 SC 2154: 1989 Cr LJ 288: (1988) 4 SCC 302: JT 1988 (3) SC 544.

Medical evidence can be used to repel testimony of eye-witnesses only if it is so conclusive as to rule out even the possibility of the version of the latter to be true.[1] Where the opinion of the doctor was that the injury in question could not be caused by a particular kind of weapon as spoken to by the eye-witnesses, but the unimpeachable eye-witness testimony was that the injury was caused by the particular kind of weapon, it has been held that the eye-witness testimony could not be nullified by the medical evidence.[2] An eye-witness could be confused between an entry gunshot and an exit wound and inconsistency on that account with medical evidence would not matter.[3] In a case of gunshot, eye witness'es version was that firing took place from a long range while medical evidence showed firing was from a close range based on the tattooing marks of the injury, it was held that tattooing or charring of injuries would depend also upon the constituents of the propellant charge and the nature of the gun and the conflict was of no consequence and it was for the court to arrive at an opinion as to which version should be accepted and whether in a given situation, ocular evidence should be believed in preference to medical evidence or *vice-versa*.[4] If appropriate, benefit of doubt could be given to the accused.[5] Such a conclusion would depend upon the facts and circumstances of each case and no hard and fast rule can be laid down.[6]

22. Credibility of medical expert depends on the reasons stated by him in support of his conclusion and data and material furnished by him which form the basis of his conclusions.[7] At the same time, expert evidence is a check upon the evidence of eye-witnesses.[8]

23. The court has a duty to put questions to witnesses when it is necessary to do so. This is much more so in the case of expert witnesses. The court has to be vigilant and see that all relevant or necessary materials are elicited from expert witnesses, to enable the court to arrive at a just and correct decision. Where the prosecutor fails to discharge his duties by putting necessary questions to expert witnesses, it is the duty of the court to put such questions and bring the relevant material on record. This must be done without any hint of partisanship and in a just and fair manner.[9] There is no irrebuttable presumption that a medical witness is always a witness of truth.[10]

24. Chemical Examination, Explosive Expert, Public Analyst: Section 293 of Cr.P.C. states that report of Chemical Examiner or Asst. Chemical Examiner to Government, Chief Inspector of Explosives or Director of F.B. Bureau and

1. *State of Uttar Pradesh* v. *Harban Sahai*, (1998) 6 SCC 50: JT 1998 (3) SC 443.
2. *Prem* v. *Daula*, AIR 1997 SC 715: 1997 Cr LJ 838: 1997 AIR SCW 530.
3. *Surendra Narain* alias *Munna Pandey* v. *State of Uttar Pradesh*, AIR 1998 SC 192: (1998) 1 SCC 76: 1998 Cr LJ 359; *Adhya Singh* v. *State of Bihar*, AIR 1998 SC 3011: 1998 Cr LJ 4052: 1998 AIR SCW 2866; *State of Bihar* v. *Ram Padarath Singh*, AIR 1998 SC 2606: 1998 Cr LJ 4007: 1998 AIR SCW 2640.
4. *Baso Prasad* v. *State of Bihar*, (2006) 13 SCC 65: AIR 2007 SC 1019: 2007 AIR SCW 807.
5. *Mohar Singh* v. *State of Punjab*, AIR 1981 SC 1578: 1981 Cr LJ 998: 1981 SCC (Cri) 638.
6. *Kailash* v. *State of Madhya Pradesh*, (2006) 11 SCC 420.
7. *State of Himachal Pradesh* v. *Jai Lal*, AIR 1999 SC 3318: (1999) 7 SCC 280: 1999 SCC (Cri) 1184.
8. *Nagindra Bala Mitra* v. *Sunil Chandra Roy*, AIR 1960 SC 706: (1960) 3 SCR 1: 1960 Cr LJ 1020.
9. *Ram Chander* v. *State of Haryana*, AIR 1981 SC 1036: 1981 Cr LJ 609: (1981) 3 SCC 191.
10. *Mayur Panabhai Shah* v. *State of Gujarat*, AIR 1983 SC 66: 1982 Cr LJ 1972: (1982) 2 SCC 396.

Haffkeine Institute, Bombay, Director (Deputy and Assistant) of Central or State Forensic Science Laboratory, Serologist upon any matter or thing submitted to him for examination or analysis and report in the course of any proceedings under the Code may be used as evidence. Court may, if it thinks fit, and shall, on application of either party, summon and examine him as to the subject-matter of the report. According to section 292 of the Code, report of any notified gazetted officer of the Mint or of India Security Press (including office of controller of Stamps and Stationery) may be used as evidence. Expert can be summoned. (*See* restrictions in sub-section 3). Section 13 of PFA Act requires Public Analyst to deliver a report of analysis. It contemplates sending a sample to Director of Central Food Laboratory. Their reports may be used as evidence. But there must be proof of identity of articles sent to their experts.

OTHER EXPERTS:

25. Fingerprints: (*See* sections 45, 73 of Evidence Act and sections 2 and 6 of Identification of Prisoners Act). Supreme Court has held that taking finger impressions is not barred by article 20(3) of the Constitution.[1] This applies to specimen handwriting also.[2] Finger prints of deceased may also be relevant *i.e.*, in the case of unidentified bodies. Finger prints on the weapon, in various articles at the scene, in the table or box broken open, provide valuable clues and can become good evidence if the formalities are properly observed and chain of various links properly established. Infallibility and certainty are the positive aspects of fingerprints system. Similarly of marks and features is the basis of this branch of science. Naturally the court should apply its own mind to the features in finger prints, similarities and dissimilarities, opinion of the expert and the grounds for the opinion and arrive at a conclusion. Science of identifying finger impressions is an exact science.[3] The basis consists of ridges forming many varieties of pattern and by creases. This science has developed to a stage of exactitude.[4] The prints must be clear and there must be a minimum number of similar features.[5] Ten points of similarities are sufficient. Court may direct any person present to give his fingerprints.[6]

26. Foot prints: Science of identification of footprints is no doubt a rudimentary science and must be viewed as such. Track evidence may be relied upon as a circumstance and taken along with other circumstances.[7] Foot print evidence has not been recognized as conclusive.[8]

---

1. *State of Bombay* v. *Kathi Kalu Oghad*, AIR 1961 SC 1808: (1962) 3 SCR 10: (1961) 2 Cr LJ 856: 64 Bom LR 240.
2. *State of Kerala* v. *K.K. Sankaran Nair*, AIR 1960 Ker 392: 1960 Ker LJ 805: 1960 Ker LT 684.
3. *Jaspal Singh* v. *State of Punjab*, AIR 1979 SC 1708: (1980) 1 SCC 487: 1979 Cr LJ 1386; *Arjan Singh* v. *Hazara Singh*, AIR 1979 SC 1236: 1979 Cr LJ 1029.
4. *Govinda Reddy (in re:)*, 1958 Cr LJ 1489: AIR 1958 Mys 150: 1958 Mad LJ (Cri) 341.
5. *Mohan Lal* v. *Ajit Singh*, AIR 1978 SC 1183: (1978) 3 SCC 279: 1978 Cr LJ 1107.
6. *State (Delhi Administration)* v. *Pali Ram*, 1979 Cr LJ 17: 1978 Cri App R (SC) 374: AIR 1979 SC 14: (1979) 2 SCC 158; *State of Uttar Pradesh* v. *Ram Babu Misra*, AIR 1980 SC 791: (1980) 2 SCC 343: (1980) 2 SCWR 25.
7. *Pritam Singh* v. *State of Punjab*, 1956 Cr LJ 805: AIR 1956 SC 415 (SC); *Shankaria* v. *State of Rajasthan*, AIR 1978 SC 1248: 1978 Cr LJ 1251: (1978) 3 SCC 435; *Mohd. Aman* v. *State of Rajasthan*, AIR 1997 SC 2960: 1997 Cr LJ 3567: 1997 AIR SCW 2980.
8. *In re Paramban Mammadu*, AIR 1951 Mad 737: 1949 MWN 634: (1949) 2 MLJ 544; *In Re: Mylaswami Goundan*, AIR 1937 Mad 951; *In re: Balija Pullayya*, AIR 1941 Mad 88: 42 Cr LJ 316; *Basudeo Gir* v. *State of Bihar*, AIR 1959 Pat 534: 1959 Cr LJ 1355: ILR 38 Pat 69.

27. Hand writing: Rogers, Osborne and Wigmore are strong protagonists of efficacy of comparison of handwriting. Efficacy depends on availability of undisputed or clearly proved standard writing. Opinion must be based on similarities and dissimilarities. Court has power to direct any person present in court to provide specimen handwriting, (*See* section 73(2)) though the possibility of disguise is present. Conclusion based on mere comparison must yield to the positive evidence in the case.[1] It is not safe to rest conviction solely on expert evidence without corroboration.[2] Adverting to most of these decisions, it is explained in *Vareed Kunju Kunju* v. *Chellappan*:[3]

"Undoubtedly expert evidence in proof or disproof of genuineness of hand writing or signature is rendered relevant under section 45; at the same time, other evidence which supports or detracts from expert opinion is also relevant under section 46. This is the rule of relevancy. In arriving at a decision whether to act upon expert evidence or not, an important feature of such evidence must be kept in mind. Expert opinion, like other opinion evidence, is only evidence based on opinion. It should be realised that science of identification of hand writing is a science which is imperfect and not exact.......(it) may not be conclusive; normally it may not be safe to base the Court's finding only on opinion evidence. This is only a rule of caution. Such expert evidence could be acted upon if supported by internal or external evidence, direct or circumstantial. Court may of its own observation of the admitted or proved writing and comparison with disputed writing, verify the premises of and the reasons given by the expert in support of his opinion. If the reasons given by the expert are unchallenged or are found acceptable, there is no reason to say that the finding of the Court cannot rest on such evidence. The only rule is rule of caution. How the court is to apply the rule of caution in a given case depends on the facts and circumstances of each case. Expert evidence is as fallible as any other opinion evidence. Prudence requires that it must be approached with caution; caution is to be exercised by looking for internal and external evidence – call it corroboration, if you must – supporting the opinion. Corroboration may be forthcoming as a result of court's own observations and comparison and testing of reasons given by the expert; or it may be forthcoming in the form of external evidence, direct or circumstantial.......If the reasons given by the expert are convincing and if there is no other acceptable evidence inconsistent with the expert evidence, Court may act upon it".

---

1. *Kishore Chandra Singh Deo* v. *Ganesh Prasad Bhagat*, AIR 1954 SC 316: (1954) 1 Mad LJ 622: 1954 SCR 919: 1954 SCJ 395; *Bhagwan Kaur* v. *Shri Maharaj Krishan Sharma*, AIR 1973 SC 1346: 1973 Cr LJ 1143: (1973) 4 SCC 46.
2. *Ram Chandra* v. *State of Uttar Pradesh*, AIR 1957 SC 381: 1957 Cr LJ 559; *Ishwari Prasad Mishra* v. *Mohammad Isa*, (1963) 3 SCR 722: AIR 1963 SC 1728: 1963 BLJR 226; *Shashi Kumar Banerjee* v. *Subodh Kumar Banerjee*, AIR 1964 SC 529; *Fakhruddin* v. *State of Madhya Pradesh*, AIR 1967 SC 1326: (1967) 2 SCJ 885: 1967 Cr LJ 1197: 1967 MPLJ 473: (1967) 1 SCWR 449: 1967 All LJ 303; *State of Gujarat* v. *Vinaya Chandra Chhota Lal*, (1967) 1 SCJ 821: 1967 Cr LJ 668: AIR 1967 SC 778; *Ram Narain* v. *State of Uttar Pradesh*, AIR 1973 SC 2200: (1973) 2 SCC 86: 1973 Cr LJ 1187; *Bhagwan Kaur* v. *Shri Maharaj Krishan Sharma*, AIR 1973 SC 1346: 1973 Cr LJ 1143: (1973) 4 SCC 46; *Magan Behari Lal* v. *State of Punjab*, AIR 1977 SC 1091: 1977 Cr LJ 711: (1977) 2 SCC 210; *Chatt Ram* v. *State of Haryana*, AIR 1979 SC 1890: (1980) 1 SCC 460: 1979 Cr LJ 1411; *Murari Lal* v. *State of Madhya Pradesh*, AIR 1980 SC 531: (1980) 1 SCC 704: (1980) 2 SCR 249: 1980 Cr LJ 396.
3. 1983 Ker LT 281.

28. Expert evidence must yield to the positive evidence in the case.[1] Conviction cannot rest entirely on opinion evidence.[2] Court should not act as an expert.[3] Court must critically examine expert evidence by its own observation.[4] It is only where the Court is satisfied that the circumstances lead to the inference that the person must have signed the disputed document that it arrives at a conclusion.[5] Science of identification of handwriting is an imperfect one and Court must be careful in placing implicit reliance on expert opinion of a handwriting expert.[6] Mere variation in the appearance of handwriting or signatures need not disprove their authenticity because nature of the pen and the nib, pen pressure, haste or deliberation in writing, health and posture can radically change the appearance or quality of writing. Dissimilarity due to difference in ink or angle of impression cannot have any impact.[7] In appropriate cases, Court can act on the opinion of the expert without corroboration.[8] Handwriting can be proved by other means also.[9] The Court must see for itself and with assistance of the expert come to its' own conclusion which is not to say that the Court must play the role of an expert, but to say that the Court may accept the fact proved only when it has satisfied itself on its' observation that it is safe to accept the opinion of the expert.[4] Proof of handwriting is no proof of contents.[10] Where signature is in dispute, it would be proper for Court to take assistance from an expert instead of itself making a comparison.[11] It is necessary to examine the expert as a witness.[12] Opinion of expert can be sought for determining the age of the disputed writing.[13]

29. Ballistics: No two types of fire arms and no two projectiles from the same type of fire arm, nor even from the same firearm discharged at different times, have exactly the same marks in all details (Bullet marks). This science helps to establish whether a particular bullet or cartridge was used in a particular weapon and also the distance from which it was fired, the direction of firing, approximate time since when the weapon was last fired and whether the wound was accidental, suicidal or homicidal. This science can bring home the guilt of

1. *Kishore Chandra Singh Deo* v. *Ganesh Prasad Bhagat*, AIR 1954 SC 316: (1954) 1 Mad LJ 622: 1954 SCR 919: 1954 SCJ 395.
2. *Magan Behari Lal* v. *State of Punjab*, AIR 1977 SC 1091: 1977 Cr LJ 711: (1977) 2 SCC 210.
3. *State (Delhi Administration)* v. *Pali Ram*, 1979 Cr LJ 17: 1978 Cri App R (SC) 374: AIR 1979 SC 14: (1979) 2 SCC 158; *Nagappa Chendappa Kolli* v. *Nannibu*, AIR 1960 Mys 220: ILR 1959 Mys 523.
4. *Fakhruddin* v. *State of Madhya Pradesh*, AIR 1967 SC 1326: (1967) 2 SCJ 885: 1967 Cr LJ 1197: 1967 MPLJ 473: (1967) 1 SCWR 449: 1967 All LJ 303.
5. *Baru Ram* v. *Prasanna*, AIR 1959 SC 93: 1959 SCR 1403: 1959 SCJ 42.
6. *State of Maharashtra* v. *Sukhdev Singh*, AIR 1992 SC 2100: 1992 Cr LR 678: (1992) 2 SCALE 9: (1992) 3 Crimes 5: (1992) 3 SCC 700: (1992) 3 SCR 480: 1992 Cr LJ 3454; *Murari Lal* v. *State of Madhya Pradesh*, AIR 1980 SC 531: (1980) 1 SCC 704: (1980) 2 SCR 249: 1980 Cr LJ 396.
7. *Arjan Singh* v. *Hazara Singh*, AIR 1979 SC 1236: 1979 Cr LJ 1029.
8. *Murari Lal* v. *State of Madhya Pradesh*, AIR 1980 SC 531: (1980) 1 SCC 704: (1980) 2 SCR 249: 1980 Cr LJ 396.
9. *State of Gujarat* v. *Vinaya Chandra Chhota Lal*, (1967) 1 SCJ 821: 1967 Cr LJ 668: AIR 1967 SC 778.
10. *Ramji Dayawala and Sons (P) Ltd.* v. *Invest Import*, AIR 1981 SC 2085: (1981) 1 SCC 80: (1981) 1 SCR 899.
11. *O. Bharathan* v. *K. Sudhakaran*, (1996) 2 SCC 704: AIR 1996 SC 1140: 1996 AIR SCW 685.
12. *State of Maharashtra* v. *Damu*, AIR 2000 SC 1691: (2000) 6 SCC 269: 2000 Cr LJ 2301: 2000 SCC (Cri) 1088: JT 2000 (5) SC 575.
13. *Pawan Kumar* v. *State of Haryana*, (2003) 11 SCC 241: 2003 AIR SCW 3671: 2003 Cr LJ 3552: AIR 2003 SC 2987.

the weapon and not the individual. When a firearm is discharged, the gases generated by the combustion eject the bullet with considerable velocity and drive back the cartridge against the breech face of the weapon. The pressure with which the latter occurs causes the cap and base of the cartridge to take an imprint of the breech face (like wax pressed on a seal takes impression of the design). It is this imprint which enables cartridges to be identified as fired from a particular gun. Several trial shots are fired from the gun. The markings on the cartridges are compared with those on the suspected cartridge. Marks in the case of bullets are caused by rifling and other characteristics of the barrel which carries individual peculiarities due to the same causes as those on the breach face. Bullet identification is practicable only with bullets from a rifled arm, since shotgun bullets cannot carry marks. Evidence of Ballistics Expert is very useful.[1] Of course, it must be tested in the same way as evidence of other experts. Expert evidence cannot be rejected on the ground that photographs had not been taken.[2] If the opinion of Ballistic expert is reliable, that can be preferred to that of medical expert.[3]

30. Distance from which the shot was fired has great effect on the markings around the wound. Test firing from various distances can lead to determination of distance from which fatal shot was fired. Generally speaking, missile has a tendency to continue in a straight line from the point of entry to the point of resting or to the exit wound. This would indicate direction of firing. Often the wound may be curved, the missile being deflected by bones etc. Study of state of residue left behind in the gun barrel and experiments with similar powder until a comparable condition is obtained helps determination of the time when the weapon was last fired. This evidence may not be conclusive; nevertheless it may be useful. Whether the shot was accidental, suicidal or homicidal may be determined from the situation of the wound, the design, the distance from which the weapon was fired, position of the weapon when found after death, direction of the wound, nature of the projectile, powder, etc.

There can be no general rule that in every case where a firearm was allegedly used, prosecutor must lead the evidence of a Ballistic expert irrespective of the quality of direct evidence available on record. Where the direct evidence is of an unimpeachable character and nature of injuries is consistent with direct evidence, examination of the expert may not be regarded as essential.[4] If the opinion of the expert is given after conducting all necessary tests and there is no reason to distrust his opinion, it can be accepted.[5] This is particularly so, when expert evidence is corroborated the eye-witnesses testimony.[6]

31. Where the expert compared the markings on the bullet under a microscope but had not taken photographs, it has been held that his evidence could not be

1. *Kalua* v. *State of Uttar Pradesh*, AIR 1958 SC 180: 1958 Cr LJ 300: ILR (1957) 1 All 15 (SC); *Kartar Singh* v. *State of Punjab*, AIR 1977 SC 349: (1976) 3 SCC 478: 1977 Cr LJ 214.
2. *Ramnathan* v. *State of Tamil Nadu*, AIR 1978 SC 1204: (1978) 3 SCC 86: 1978 Cr LJ 1137.
3. *Raza Pasha* v. *State of Madhya Pradesh*, AIR 1983 SC 575: 1983 Cr LJ 977: (1983) 1 Crimes 969.
4. *Vineet Kumar Chauhan* v. *State of Uttar Pradesh*, AIR 2008 SC 780: 2008 Cr LJ 1367: 2008 AIR SCW 1.
5. *Kalua* v. *State of Uttar Pradesh*, AIR 1958 SC 180: 1958 Cr LJ 300: ILR (1957) 1 All 15 (SC); *Bhola Singh* v. *State of Punjab*, AIR 1994 SC 137: 1993 Cr LJ 3904: 1993 AIR SCW 3771.
6. *Kartar Singh* v. *State of Punjab*, AIR 1977 SC 349: (1976) 3 SCC 478: 1977 Cr LJ 214; *Bhola Singh* v. *State of Punjab*, AIR 1994 SC 137: 1993 Cr LJ 3904: 1993 AIR SCW 3771.

rejectled because of absence of photographs.[1] This is also so where the expert has given convincing reasons to support his opinion about identifiable marks on the pellets.[2] But where failure to take photographs of empty cartridges and test cartridges was compounded by his failure to state the points of similarity between empty and test cartridges, his opinion cannot be conclusive. If there is sufficient direct evidence to prove the charge, failure to secure a proper expert report is inconsequential.[3] It is impossible to state the precise distance from which it is possible to produce marks of burning since it depends on the quantity and nature of the powder, the method of charging and the nature of the weapon. But it is unusual to get burn marks beyond a yard or a yard and a half with a shot by a gun or at more than half a yard with a revolver.[4] The skin around the entry wound being blackened is an indication that it was a close range firing (ibid). The opinion of a doctor who has no knowledge of ballistics and firearm is not helpful distinguishing and interpreting fire arm injuries.[5] Report of Ballistic expert submitted under signature of junior scientific officer (Ballistic) of the Central Forensic Laboratory can be read in evidence.[6] Evidence of Ballistic expert or police officer who is trained in handling of guns is sufficient to prove that its' mechanism was in order.[7] Firing capability need not necessarily be verified by test firing, so far as an expert is concerned.[8] A police officer can test workability of a weapon.[9]

32. Anthracone is used in the Technique for trapping in corruption cases. Anthracone powder is not visible to the naked eye. It can only be seen when ultra-violet light is focused on it which results in emission of light of a particular colour. The technique is also conducted using phenophthelene solution. Scrupulous care must be taken in operating the technique and giving evidence in court. Procedure is explained in AIR 1960 Guj 7 and AIR 1961 Guj 1.[10]

33. Radiologists and Photographers can be treated as experts. So also Anthropologists, polygraph experts. Evidence of dog tracking, even if admissible, is not ordinarily of much weight.[11] A dog is not a person within the meaning of section 3(42) of General Clauses Act; Section 45 refers to opinion of "persons", regarding photography.[12]

---

1. *Ramnathan* v. *State of Tamil Nadu*, AIR 1978 SC 1204: (1978) 3 SCC 86: 1978 Cr LJ 1137.
2. *State of Madhya Pradesh (through C.B.I.)* v. *Paltan Mallah*, (2005) 3 SCC 169: 2005 Cr LJ 918: 2005 AIR SCW 455: AIR 2005 SC 733.
3. *Chatar Singh* v. *State of Haryana*, AIR 1976 SC 2474: (1976) 2 SCC 263: 1976 Cr LJ 1891; *Gurucharan Singh* v. *State of Punjab*, AIR 1963 SC 340: (1963) 1 Cr LJ 823: 1963 SCD 211.
4. *Bhupendra Singh A. Chudasama* v. *State of Gujarat*, AIR 1997 SC 3790: 1997 AIR SCW 3938: (1998) 2 SCC 603.
5. *Mohan Singh* v. *State of Punjab*, AIR 1975 SC 2161: (1975) Cr LJ 1865: (1975) 4 SCC 254.
6. *State of Himachal Pradesh* v. *Mast Ram*, 2004 AIR SCW 5754: AIR 2004 SC 5056: 2004 Cr LJ 4973.
7. *Jarnail Singh* v. *State of Punjab*, AIR 1999 SC 321: (1998) 8 SCC 126: 1999 Cr LJ 453.
8. *Sukhpal* v. *State of Haryana*, (1995) 1 SCC 10: AIR 1995 SC 578: 1994 AIR SCW 4856.
9. *Manoj Kumar Achhelal Brahimram* v. *State of Gujarat*, (1980) 2 SCC 354.
10. *Ramsing Badharsing* v. *State*, 1960 Cr LJ 1207: AIR 1960 Guj 7; *Oswal Damji Tejsi* v. *State*, AIR 1960 Guj 1.
11. *Abdul Rajak Murtaja Dafedar* v. *State of Maharashtra*, (1969) 2 SCC 234: AIR 1970 SC 283: 1969 (2) SCJ 870: 1970 Cr LJ 373.
12. *Govind Reddy* v. *State*, 1958 Mys LJ 278.

34. The basis of relevance of expert opinion is the supposed superior knowledge or experience, skill or training of experts. But the opinion is not determinative of the question. Section 293 of the Code prevails over section 45 of the Evidence Act. Expert has to give his opinion, the reasons therefore and the data. Court has to evaluate the same like any other evidence. Court has to judge whether the opinion is correct on the available data and for the reasons stated.[1] Weight to be attached to the opinion depends on it's reasonableness and scientific quality. Expert opinion alone cannot form the basis for conviction. Value of expert opinion is that it assists the court in reaching a particular conclusion where technical assistance is necessary. If the opinion is obscure and oscillating, it is not proper to reject the direct testimony of eye-witnesses.[2] There is no requirement of law that expert evidence must be corroborated. But courts do not ordinarily base the decision on expert evidence alone, unless it is supported by other evidence, external and internal. In AIR 1980 SC 531[3] Supreme Court has held that while in appropriate cases corroboration can be sought, if reasons for the opinion are carefully probed and are convincing and there is no reliable evidence to throw any doubt, there can be conviction on the uncorroborated testimony of hand writing expert. In many cases courts have preferred direct testimony to expert opinion.[4] Slight inconsistency does not matter.[5]

35. "Science and Art" include all subjects on which a course of study or experience is necessary to the formation of an opinion.[6] These words comprehend study of customs of tribes and castes, their residential areas and other matters. A particular subject or matter can be regarded as a science if inexperienced persons cannot form correct judgment on it without the assistance of experts *i.e.*, persons with previous study and experience.

'Science and Art" must not be understood narrowly. Authoritative books on Tribes and Castes have been held to be admissible as books written by persons who made a special systematic study of the subject.[7] Opinion of brokers and surveyors on land valuation is relevant. But it must be supported by data.[8]A contractor who owns several lorries and fits a large number of tyres every month was held to be an expert on the quality, wear and usage of tyres. Assistant Mint Master of Mint is an expert. Firearms expert is an expert.[9] Telephony is a science on which expert evidence is relevant.[10] Artists are experts. That science of identification of hair has not attained the certainty of a scientific study.[11] But progress and development of the aspect has to be studied whenever the question arises for consideration. Opinion of experts on foot prints, typewriting are also

1. *State* v. *Kanhu Charan Barik*, 1983 Cr LJ 133.
2. *Anvaruddin* v. *Shakoor*, AIR 1990 SC 1242: (1990) 3 SCC 266: 1990 Cr LJ 1269.
3. *Murari Lal* v. *State of Madhya Pradesh*, AIR 1980 SC 531: (1980) 1 SCC 704: (1980) 2 SCR 249: 1980 Cr LJ 396.
4. *State of Uttar Pradesh* v. *Krishna Gopal*, AIR 1988 SC 2154: 1989 Cr LJ 288: (1988) 4 SCC 302: JT 1988 (3) SC 544.
5. *State of Uttar Pradesh* v. *Sughar Singh*, AIR 1978 SC 191: (1978) 1 SCC 178: 1978 Cr LJ 141.
6. Stephen's Digest. 12th Edn. Article 49.
7. *Mahadeo Dewanna* v. *Viankamma Bai*, AIR 1948 Nag 287.
8. *Secretary of State* v. *Sarakdevi Chouwdhary*, AIR 1924 Lah 548.
9. *Kalua* v. *State of Uttar Pradesh*, AIR 1958 SC 180: 1958 Cr LJ 300: ILR (1957) 1 All 15 (SC).
10. *Bachraj Factories Ltd.* v. *Bombay Telephone Company Ltd.*, AIR 1939 Sind 245.
11. *Himangshu Pahari* v. *State*, 1986 Cr LJ 622.

relevant as the expertise relates to "Science" or "Art". Type writing comes within the ambit of "hand writing" also.[1]

36. In case of conflict of opinion between two medical experts, court will normally accept the evidence of expert which is supported by direct evidence,[2] or which accords with prosecution version.[3] But the entire evidence must be scrutinized with care and caution. Court may rely on the opinion of the doctor who has superior qualifications and experience in the particular branch of medical science.[4] Where the doctor who examined the victim before her death found only four injuries while the doctor who conducted autopsy noted six injuries, it was held that it was likely that the first doctor did not examine her thoroughly keeping her modesty in mind.[5]

37. Exceptional cases referred to in books on medical jurisprudence cannot be relied on against positive and clear evidence before the court.[6] It is the duty of the prosecution and no less of the court to see that the weapon is shown to the expert and his opinion invited as to whether all or any of the injuries could be caused with that weapon.[7] Where the weapon has not been recovered, its nature can be assessed from the injuries.[8]

38. Direct evidence must be preferred to expert evidence, unless the latter goes so far that it completely rules out all possibility whatsoever of injuries taking place as alleged by eye-witnesses.[9] Attempt should, however be made to reconcile the two, if possible. Sometimes conflicting medical evidence may discredit prosecution case.[10]

39. Typewriting: Each machine has its own idiosyncracies by which it may be recognized. Machines change their characteristics with age.[11] It has been held that expert opinion that a particular letter was typed on a particular machine does not attract section 45 and is not relevant. The matter was referred to a larger

1. *State (Through CBI/New Delhi)* v. *S.J. Choudhary*, AIR 1996 SC 1491: (1996) 1 Crimes 96: (1996) 2 SCC 428: (1996) 2 SCJ 327: (1996) 2 SCALE 37: (1996) 64 ECR 185: 1996 Cr LJ 1713.
2. *Pyara Singh* v. *State of Punjab*, AIR 1977 SC 2274: (1978) 1 SCR 597: (1977) 4 SCC 452.
3. *Makan Jivan* v. *State of Gujarat*, AIR 1971 SC 1797: 1971 Cr LJ 1310: 1971 UJ (SC) 634.
4. *Mahendra Manilal Nanavati* v. *Sushila Mahendra Nanavati*, AIR 1965 SC 364: 66 Bom LR 681: 1965 Mah LJ 365.
5. *Sukpal* v. *State of Madhya Pradesh*, AIR 1997 SC 468: 1997 AIR SCW 381: (1997) 9 SCC 773; *State Govt. of NCT of Delhi* v. *Sunil*, 2001 Cr LJ 504: 2000 AIR SCW 4398: (2001) 1 SCC 652; *Prakash* v. *State of Madhya Pradesh*, 2007 Cr LJ 798: 2006 AIR SCW 6216: 2007 (2) Crimes 74.
6. *Baldev Raj Miglani* v. *Urmila Kumari*, AIR 1979 SC 879: 1979 3 SCC 782: 1979 SCC (Cri) 875.
7. *Ishwar Singh* v. *State of Uttar Pradesh*, AIR 1976 SC 2423: 1976 Cr LJ 1883: 1976 SCC (Cr) 629; *Mohinder Singh* v. *State*, 1950 SCR 821: AIR 1953 SC 415: 1953 Cr LJ 1761.
8. *Sakharam* v. *State of Maharashtra*, (1969) 3 SCC 730: AIR 1969 NSC 85: 1969 UJ (SC) 423.
9. *Solanki Chimanbhai Ukabhai* v. *State of Gujarat*, AIR 1983 SC 484: (1983) 2 SCC 174: 1983 Cr LJ 822; *State of Uttar Pradesh* v. *Krishna Gopal*, AIR 1988 SC 2154: 1989 Cr LJ 288: (1988) 4 SCC 302: JT 1988 (3) SC 544; *Punjab Singh* v. *State of Haryana*, AIR 1984 SC 1233: (1984) 1 Crimes 859: 1984 Cr LJ 921.
10. *Ram Narain* v. *State of Punjab*, AIR 1975 SC 1727: 1975 Cr LJ 1500: (1975) 4 SCC 497; *Amar Singh* v. *State of Punjab*, AIR 1987 SC 826: 1987 Cr LJ 706: (1987) 1 SCC 679; *Mayappa Dhondanna Padeade* v. *State of Maharashtra*, AIR 1981 SC 173: 1981 UJ (SC) 119: (1981) 3 SCC 669; *Purshottam* v. *State of Madhya Pradesh*, AIR 1980 SC 1873: 1980 Cr LJ 1298; *Hallu* v. *State of Madhya Pradesh*, AIR 1974 SC 1936: (1974) 4 SCC 300: (1974) 3 SCR 652.
11. *Hanumant Govind Nargundkar* v. *State of Madhya Pradesh*, AIR 1952 SC 343: 1952 SCR 1091: 1952 SCA 623.

Bench by *State (Through CBI / New Delhi)* v. *S.J. Choudhary*.[1] In*State (Through CBI/ New Delhi)* v. *S.J. Choudhary* (5 Judges),[2] the Court held that opinion of typewriter expert is relevant, overruling AIR 1952 SC 343.

40. Tracker dog: In the present state of scientific knowledge, evidence of dog-tracking, even if admissible, is not ordinarily of much weight.[3] Tracker evidence can be admitted. Where the dogs of the police dog squad pointed towards the husband of the victim, it is not a circumstance which could exclude the possibility of guilt of anyone other than that of the accused or be compatible only with the guilt of the accused.[4]

41. Forensic Science deals, *inter alia*, with the following:

Dirt, dust and debris collected at the scene, inorganic matter like soil, glass and paint collected at the scene, biological material like grass, vegetable, wood fragments, human hair, cloth fibres, paper found at the scene, marks on an object made by a weapon, tyre impressions, erased identification marks, blood stains, seminal fluid, drugs, burnt or partially burnt objects, burnt gun powder, particles of explosives, fire arms, cartridges, questioned documents, ink marks, samples of blood, of urine, poison, chemicals, food items, cosmetics etc.

42. Foreign Law: Opinion of an expert on foreign law is relevant. For a judgment to be accepted as a foreign judgment, there must be an adjudicatory process or a judicial decision of a foreign court.[5]

43. SECTION 47:

This section does not deal with expert evidence. Opinion of any person acquainted with the handwriting or signature of the writer of any document is relevant.[6] To be regarded as so acquainted, the person must have seen the writer write or must have received documents written by the writer in answer to documents written by himself or under his authority or when in the ordinary course of business, such documents have been habitually submitted to him.[7] This section deals with the opinion of a non-expert.

The opinion evidence of a non-expert becomes good evidence to go by if his familiarity with the hand writing or signature of the writer is proved.[8] The value of the opinion depends on the degree of such familiarity. If the familiarity is insufficient, the opinion is to be discarded.[9] Proof may be also by internal

1. *State (Through CBI / New Delhi)* v. *S.J. Choudhary*, AIR 1990 SC 1050: 1990 Cr LJ 1112: JT 1990 (2) SC 15.
2. *State (Through CBI/New Delhi)* v. *S.J. Choudhary*, AIR 1996 SC 1491: (1996) 1 Crimes 96: (1996) 2 SCC 428: (1996) 2 SCJ 327: (1996) 2 SCALE 37: (1996) 64 ECR 185: 1996 Cr LJ 1713.
3. *Abdul Rajak Murtaja Dafedar* v. *State of Maharashtra*, (1969) 2 SCC 234: AIR 1970 SC 283: 1969 (2) SCJ 870: 1970 Cr LJ 373.
4. *Surinder Pal Jain* v. *Delhi Administration*, 1993 Cr LJ 1871: AIR 1993 SC 1723: 1993 AIR SCW 1561 SC.
5. *Technip S.A.* v. *SMS Holding (Pvt) Ltd.*, (2005) 5 SCC 465.
6. *Rahim Khan* v. *Khurshid Ahmed*, AIR 1975 SC 290: (1974) 2 SCC 660: (1975) 1 SCR 643; *H. Venkatachala Iyengar* v. *B.N. Thimmajamma*, AIR 1959 SC 443: 1959 SCJ 507: (1959) 2 SCA 1: 1959 SCR Supp (1) 426.
7. *Fakhruddin* v. *State of Madhya Pradesh*, AIR 1967 SC 1326: (1967) 2 SCJ 885: 1967 Cr LJ 1197: 1967 MPLJ 473: (1967) 1 SCWR 449: 1967 All LJ 303.
8. *Dalim Kumar* v. *Nandarni Dassi*, AIR 1970 Cal 292: 73 Cal WN 877: ILR (1970) 2 Cal 31; *Bhupendra Narain Mandal* v. *Ek Narain Lal Das*, AIR 1965 Pat 332; *In re: Basawarajaswami*, AIR 1967 Mys 210: (1967) 1 Mys LJ 548: (1967) Cr LJ 1536.
9. *Devi Prasad* v. *State*, AIR 1967 All 64: 1967 Cr LJ 134; *Dhani Bai* v. *Neem Kanwar*, AIR 1972 Raj 9: 1971 Raj LW 103.

evidence of contents of the document, such as a document which is a link in the chain of correspondence, some links of which have already been proved.[1] This section is often used in proving medical reports.[2]

If original letters are suppressed by the accused, evidence of photographs as to contents and as to the handwriting is admissible.[3]

44. Handwriting may be proved by the writer or by a person who saw the document being written[4] or by the opinion of expert under section 45, by the opinion of a non-expert under section 47 or by comparison under section 73.

45. "Habitually" means "usually" or "generally", not the frequency of the occasions, but the invariability of practice.[5] A servant who habitually carried his master's letters to the post is a person covered by this section.[6]

It is enough if the witness states in chief-examination that he is acquainted with handwriting. It is for the opposite side to probe into the matter in cross-examination.[7] But it is safer to elicit the details even in chief-examination. The conditions laid down in the section must be proved.[8]

The opinion is not conclusive. Court can refuse to act upon it.[9] But it may be more valuable than that of an expert.[10] Before relying on such evidence, the court is to apply its own observation to the writings, not to become an expert but only to apprise the evidence of the non-expert.[11]

46. SECTION 47A: When the court has to form an opinion as to the electronic signature of any person, the opinion of the Certifying Authority which has issued the electronic signature certificate is relevant fact. Section 47 must be read with Section 67.

47. SECTION 48:

Opinion as to the existence of any general custom or right, of persons who would be likely to know of its existence if it existed, is relevant. Such persons are depositories of customary law.[12] According to the explanation, "general right or custom" includes customs or rights common to any considerable class of persons.

Section 13 refers to all rights and customs, public, general or private and to specific facts which may be given in evidence. Section 32(4) refers to reception

1. *Mobarik Ali Ahmed* v. *State of Bombay*, AIR 1957 SC 857: 1957 Cr LJ 1346: 1958 SCR 328: (1957) 61 Bom LR 58: 1958 SCJ 111.
2. *Rameshwar Prasad Srivasthava* v. *State of Uttar Pradesh*, 1984 Cr LJ 996
3. *Laxmipat Choraria* v. *State of Maharashtra*, AIR 1968 SC 938: (1968) 2 SCR 624: 1968 Cr LJ 1134: (1968) 2 SCJ 589.
4. *Hafiz Abdul Basit* v. *Hafiz Ahmad Mian*, AIR 1973 Del 280.
5. *P.B. Ponde* v. *Emperor*, AIR 1925 Bom 429.
6. *Surendra Krishna Mandal* v. *Rani Dassi*, AIR 1921 Cal 677: 24 Cal WN 860: ILR 47 Cal 1043.
7. *Shankerappa* v. *Sushilabai*, AIR 1984 Kant 112: (1984) 1 Kant LC 265.
8. *Rahim Khan* v. *Khurshid Ahmed*, AIR 1975 SC 290: (1974) 2 SCC 660: (1975) 1 SCR 643.
9. *Chandreshwar Singh* v. *Ramchandra Singh*, AIR 1973 Pat 215: 1973 Pat LJR 393.
10. *Ramanlal Rathi* v. *State of West Bengal*, AIR 1951 Cal 305: 52 Cr LJ 301.
11. *Fakhruddin* v. *State of Madhya Pradesh*, AIR 1967 SC 1326: (1967) 2 SCJ 885: 1967 Cr LJ 1197: 1967 MPLJ 473: (1967) 1 SCWR 449: 1967 All LJ 303; *State (Delhi Administration)* v. *Pali Ram*, 1979 Cr LJ 17: 1978 Cri App R (SC) 374: AIR 1979 SC 14: (1979) 2 SCC 158.
12. *Jugmohan* v. *Mangal Das*, ILR 10 Bom 528.

of second hand opinion evidence in cases in which the declarant cannot be brought to court, upon the question of existence of any public right or custom or matter of public or general interest made at undisputed time. Section 32(7) refers to statements contained in document. Section 48 refers to opinion evidence of living person produced before court who would be likely to know of the existence of right or custom.[1] Section 48 read with section 60 requires him to give evidence in court. Necessarily his opinion is based on hearsay, not mere repetition of hearsay.[2] Section 48 refers to general rights or customs, not public rights or customs. Every public right is a general right; but every general right is not a public right. By 'general' is meant what is common to any considerable class of persons. Evidently "private" rights are not included in the operation of this section; so also a customary right of easement is outside the scope of this section.

Evidence regarding "usage" is also relevant as the section is not limited to ancient customs.[3] "Usage" would mean that people are now or recently were in the habit of doing something in a particular place.

The person's personal knowledge is not necessary, but he should have sufficient experience as may suggest likelihood of his knowledge of the custom. Section 31 has to be read with section 48. Hence, grounds for his opinion are relevant.

Tribal or family custom can be proved by general evidence by members thereof who would naturally be cognizant of its existence and exercise without controversy.[2]

Authoritative treatises on customary law by public servants are relevant under section 35.[4] Settlement report is relevant under this section.

48. SECTION 49:

Opinion of persons having special means of knowledge are relevant in regard to usages and tenets of any body of men or family, the constitution and governance of any religious or charitable foundation, or the meaning of words or terms used in particular districts or by particular class of people. Section 49 must be read with sections 51, 60.

The person should be examined as a witness.[5] "Usage" includes usages of trade, agriculture, mercantile, or any other usage common to a body of persons. Special means of knowledge may be derived from witness'es business or activities, family affairs etc. Weight of evidence would depend upon the character and position of the witness and his experience or knowledge.[6] Conversation with elders could lead to knowledge.[7] He should have acquired the necessary knowledge. A police officer who had long experience among people who

1. *Garuradhwaja Prasad* v. *Superundhwaja Prasad*, ILR 23 All 37: (1900) 10 Mad LJ 267: 27 Ind App 238 (PC).
2. *Daniraiji Vrajlalji* v. *Vahuji Maharaj Chandraprabha*, AIR 1971 Guj 188.
3. *Sariatullan* v. *Prannath*, ILR 26 Cal 184; *Bajrangi Singh* v. *Manokernika Baksh Singh*, ILR 30 All 1: 35 Ind App 1 (PC).
4. *Subhani* v. *Nawab*, AIR 1941 PC 21: 193 IC 436: ILR 1941 Lah 154.
5. *Kandan Soren* v. *Jitan Hembrom*, ILR (1974) 53 Pat 21: AIR 1973 Pat 206: 1973 Pat LJR 153.
6. *Ahmad Khan* v. *Mt. Channi Bibi*, AIR 1925 PC 267: ILR 6 Lah 502: 52 Ind App 379.
7. *Kameshwar Prasad Singh* v. *Mithilesh Kishori Devi*, AIR 1964 Pat 150.

indulged in *satta* gambling in a particular district may give evidence regarding the "code" followed by them.[1]

49. SECTION 50:

Opinion expressed by conduct of any person, who as a member of the family or otherwise, has special means of knowledge on the subject of relationship of one person to another, is relevant. But such opinion is not sufficient to prove marriage in proceedings under Indian Divorce Act or in prosecution under sections 494, 495, 497 or 498 I.P.C.[2] It is for the Court to weigh such evidence and arrive at its' own opinion as to the alleged relationship. This section does not make evidence of general reputation (without conduct) relevant. That the opinion is expressed by conduct is an additional guarantee of its "trustworthiness".

There is no express provision making evidence of general reputation admissible as proof of relationship. Reputation is the cumulation of ordinary 'perception testimonies" heard and gathered and reduced to a single implied assertion which is deposed to in court by the witness who perceived the cumulative assertions. Evidence under section 50 is akin to reputation evidence. Evidence of mere general reputation is not relevant.[3] What is relevant is opinion expressed by conduct and opinion means something more than mere repetition of gossip or hearsay. It means judgment or belief or conviction resulting from what one thinks on a particular question. It is the conduct or outward behaviour which must be proved in the manner laid down in section 60.[4] His sources of information and the time at which he acquired knowledge (*e.g.* whether before the dispute arose or not) would affect its' weight but not its' relevancy.[5] If sections 50 and 114 are read together, an act of marriage can be presumed from the common course of natural events and the conduct of the parties as they are seen from the facts of the case.[6]

Section 50 refers to opinion expressed by conduct, *i.e.*, overt act.[7] Conduct must be of such a tenor as to be the result of an inner existence of an opinion.[8] The item of evidence offered is "conduct" but what is admissible is "opinion", that is, the opinion expressed by such conduct. It is for the court to weigh such evidence and come to its own opinion. When a person has been treated as an adopted son for a long period, oral evidence of neighbours or relatives that they heard the son addressing adopted parents as father/mother is relevant.[9] The person whose conduct expresses his opinion need not be called as a witness.

1. *Harilal Gordhan* v. *Emperor*, 39 Bom LR 613: AIR 1937 Bom 385: 38 Cr LJ 1047.
2. *Dolgobinda Paricha* v. *Nimai Charan Misra*, AIR 1959 SC 914: 1960 SCJ 879: (1959) 2 SCR 814: 1959 26 Cut LT 130: 1959 SCR Supp (2) 814; *Bant Singh* v. *Niranjan Singh*, AIR 2008 SC 1512: 2008 AIR SCW 1611: (2008) 4 SCC 75; (1996) 11 SCC 88; *Munshi Dass* v. *R. Mal Singh (Dead) by LRS*, (1977) 4 SCC 65: AIR 1977 SC 2002: 1977 U J (SC) 555.
3. *Lakshmi Reddi* v. *Venkata Reddi*, AIR 1937 PC 201: 31 Sind LR 575: 168 IC 881.
4. *Dolgobinda Paricha* v. *Nimai Charan Misra*, AIR 1959 SC 914: 1960 SCJ 879: (1959) 2 SCR 814: 1959 26 Cut LT 130: 1959 SCR Supp (2) 814.
5. *Sitaji* v. *Bijendra Narain Choudhary*, AIR 1954 SC 601: 1951 Pat 356: 28 Pat 447.
6. *Tulsa* v. *Durghatiya*, AIR 2008 SC 1193: 2008 AIR SCW 1148: (2008) 4 SCC 520.
7. *Baruni* v. *Padan*, AIR 1987 Ori 187; *Dolgobinda Paricha* v. *Nimai Charan Misra*, AIR 1959 SC 914: 1960 SCJ 879: (1959) 2 SCR 814: 1959 26 Cut LT 130: 1959 SCR Supp (2) 814; *Krishnappa* v. *N. Jayamma*, 1966 1 Mys LJ 235.
8. *Bhagavathy Ummini* v. *Ramankutty*, AIR 1976 Ker 34.
9. *Jagabandhu Senapati* v. *Bhagu Senapati*, AIR 1974 Ori 120: (1973) 1 Cut WR 809: ILR (1973) Cut 553.

Such opinion can be proved by another who has seen the conduct.[1] "Special means of knowledge" must be of the person whose opinion is sought to be proved and not of the person who comes to prove the opinion.[2] Conduct means a conduct which is expression in outward behaviour of the opinion entertained as to relationship.[3] What is relevant is the opinion. To enable to infer the opinion, the conduct must be of a tenor which suggests opinion held by the person.

See also section 32(5) which is different from section 50. There can be a combination of the two provisions.[4] The two illustrations to section 50 bring out the true scope and effect of the section. Opinion means something more than repetition of gossip. It means judgment or belief which may manifest itself in conduct or behaviour which indicates the existence of the belief or opinion.[5] Evidence that parents or close relatives acknowledged and recognised a person as legitimate son of another is relevant.[6] Evidence of treatment accorded to the marriage by relations is relevant to prove its validity.[7] Distribution and devolution of family property is often evidence of conduct.[8] Mention or non-mention of names from list of ancestors in Shradda Ceremony, observance of pollution are conduct.[9] Conduct expressed in documents (dissolution and treatment of family property) is relevant as conduct expressing relationship.[10] Long cohabitation is conduct.[11] Non-challenge in a suit, of legitimacy, is conduct.[12] The section comprehends also non-existence of relationship.[13] Special means of knowledge as a member of family or otherwise is necessary. Personal knowledge is not necessary.[14] His source of information would affect the weight of evidence, and not its admissibility.

50. The word 'Otherwise" shows the conduct need not be of a member of the family. It can be a neighbor also.[15] Traditional barber of a family is a competent

1. *Amar Singh* v. *Chhaju Singh*, AIR 1973 P&H 213: ILR (1972) 2 P&H 424: 1972 Cur LJ 591; *Balaram Das* v. *Jayakrishna Das*, (1972) 38 CLT 44: AIR 1972 Ori 141.
2. *Hazara Singh* v. *Attar Kaur*, AIR 1976 P&H 24: 1975 Rev LR 567.
3. *Ramadhar Chaudhary* v. *Janki Chaudhary*, AIR 1956 Pat 49: 1955 BLJR 705.
4. *S.M. Dawood Bibi* v. *Abu Bakker Pulavar*, AIR 1972 Mad 228: 85 Mad LW 225: (1972) 1 Mad LJ 491.
5. *Dolgobinda Paricha* v. *Nimai Charan Misra*, AIR 1959 SC 914: 1960 SCJ 879: (1959) 2 SCR 814: 1959 26 Cut LT 130: 1959 SCR Supp (2) 814.
6. *Sivalingiah* v. *Chowdamma*, AIR 1956 Mys 17: ILR (1955) Mys 578; *Dolgobinda Paricha* v. *Nimai Charan Misra*, AIR 1959 SC 914: 1960 SCJ 879: (1959) 2 SCR 814: 1959 26 Cut LT 130: 1959 SCR Supp (2) 814.
7. *Sivalingiah* v. *Chowdamma*, AIR 1956 Mys 17: ILR (1955) Mys 578;.
8. *Seshammal* v. *Kuppanaiyyangar*, AIR 1926 Mad 475: 91 Ind Cas 462.
9. *Ramakrishna Aiyar* v. *Chinnavengammal*, AIR 1915 Mad 953.
10. *Amar Singh* v. *Chhaju Singh*, AIR 1973 P&H 213: ILR (1972) 2 P&H 424: 1972 Cur LJ 591; *Balaram Das* v. *Jayakrishna Das*, (1972) 38 CLT 44: AIR 1972 Ori 141; *Hazara Singh* v. *Attar Kaur*, AIR 1976 P&H 24: 1975 Rev LR 567.
11. *Ranganath Parmeshwar Panditroo Mali* v. *Eknath Gajanan Kulkarni*, AIR 1996 SC 1290: 1996 AIR SCW 1389: (1996) 7 SCC 681; *Gokul Chand* v. *Pravin Kumari*, AIR 1952 SC 231: 1952 SCJ 331: 1952 SCR 825; *Dolgobinda Paricha* v. *Nimai Charan Misra*, AIR 1959 SC 914: 1960 SCJ 879: (1959) 2 SCR 814: 1959 26 Cut LT 130: 1959 SCR Supp (2) 814.
12. *Sheodhar Prasad Singh* v. *Jagdhar Prasad Singh*, AIR 1964 Pat 316.
13. *Subaravt* v. *Dindayal Choudhury*, AIR 1941 Pat 205.
14. *Sitaji* v. *Bijendra Narain Choudhary*, AIR 1954 SC 601: 1951 Pat 356: 28 Pat 447.
15. *Dukhiram Dey* v. *Mrityunjoy Prosad Daw*, AIR 1982 Cal 294: (1982) 1 Cal LJ 256: 1982 (1) Cal HN 206.

person.[1] Doctor who was frequently visiting the house is a competent person. In the face of evidence that a man and a woman were treated as husband and wife for a number of years, a presumption can be drawn that they were lawfully married, though the presumption is rebuttable.[2] Where a child bride never lived with her husband, but cohabited for a long time with another person and had a number of children from him and divorce was permissible in the community, it was held that it could be presumed that her first marriage had been terminated.[3]

A statement made by persons not having special means of knowledge, though not relevant under section 50, may be relevant under section 32(5) provided the witness states that he had the information from a deceased person (or person described in the first para of section 32) long before the dispute.[4] A member of a family had been told about his ancestors based on which he forms an independent opinion, as the opinion is expressed by conduct by making offerings, such opinion is relevant.[5]

51. Proviso: Such opinion evidence is not sufficient to prove marriage in cases covered by the proviso. Proof of marriage ceremony would be necessary.[6] The proviso does not include Section 125 of the Code and hence in a case under Section 125 of the code the standard of proof therein is not as high as in the cases covered by the proviso.[7]

52. SECTION 51:

Where opinion of a living person is relevant, grounds or reasoning upon which such opinion was based are also relevant. Value of opinion will depend on the tenability of the grounds.[8] This section applies to opinions relevant under sections 45 to 50.

---

1. *Bishnu Charan Mohanty* v. *State of Orissa*, AIR 1973 Ori 199: (1973) 1 Cut WR 469: ILR (1972) Cut 339.
2. *Gokul Chand* v. *Pravin Kumari*, AIR 1952 SC 231: 1952 SCJ 331: 1952 SCR 825; *Sobha Hymavathi Devi* v. *Setti Gangadhara Swamy*, AIR 2005 SC 800: 2005 AIR SCW 718: (2005) 2 SCC 244; *Savitaben Somabhai Bhatiya* v. *State of Gujarat*, (2005) 3 SCC 636: 2005 AIR SCW 1601: AIR 2005 SC 1809; *Tulsa* v. *Durghatiya*, AIR 2008 SC 1193: 2008 AIR SCW 1148: (2008) 4 SCC 520.
3. *Sobha Hymavathi Devi* v. *Setti Gangadhara Swamy*, AIR 2005 SC 800: 2005 AIR SCW 718: (2005) 2 SCC 244.
4. *Bujhawan Singh* v. *Shyama Devi*, AIR 1964 Pat 301.
5. *S.M. Dawood Bibi* v. *Abu Bakker Pulavar*, AIR 1972 Mad 228: 85 Mad LW 225: 85 Mad LW 225: (1972) 1 Mad LJ 491; *Sheojee* v. *Prema Kuer*, AIR 1964 Pat 187: 1964 BLJR 152.
6. *Vanjakshamma* v. *P. Gopalakrishna*, AIR 1970 Mys 305: (1970) 2 Mys LJ 15: 1970 Cr LJ 1584; *Kanwal Ram* v. *Himachal Pradesh Administration*, AIR 1966 SC 614: 1966 (1) SCJ 210: (1966) 1 SCR 532; *Bhaurao Shankar Lokhande* v. *State of Maharashtra*, AIR 1965 SC 1564: (1965) 2 Cr LJ 544: (1965) 1 SCWR 579.
7. *Vanjakshamma* v. *P. Gopalakrishna*, AIR 1970 Mys 305: (1970) 2 Mys LJ 15: 1970 Cr LJ 1584; *K.J.B. David* v. *Nilamoni Devi*, AIR 1953 Ori 10: ILR 1952 Cuttack 511.
8. *Nekram* v. *Emperor*, AIR 1931 All 273; *K.N. Katju and Binod Beharilal* v. *P.L. Banerji*, AIR 1931 All 399; *Gobardhan* v. *State*, AIR 1959 All 53: 1956 All WR (HC) 216: 1959 Cr LJ 13.

CHAPTER 12
CHARACTER EVIDENCE
(SECTIONS 52 TO 55 AND RELATED SECTIONS)

Character may be of witnesses or of parties. Character of a witness, whether a party or not, is always material, as affecting his credit, to see if he is creditworthy. In the case of parties, there may be cases where character is in issue or not. Where a party's character is in issue, whether in a civil or a criminal case, evidence of character is relevant. Where general character of a party is not in issue, evidence of character is generally excluded. The exception in a civil case is evidence of character as affecting damages and in a criminal case, good character is relevant and except in specified cases, bad character is not relevant.

2. SECTION 52:

In civil cases, the fact that character of any person concerned is such as to render probable or improbable any conduct imputed to him is irrelevant, except insofar as such character appears from facts otherwise relevant. Evidence of character of a party in civil cases is excluded as too remote, and such evidence of character of a party to prove the probability or improbability of any conduct imparted to him is irrelevant. If character is not in issue, evidence would only cause prejudice and hence offend public policy and fairness. Evidence of a person cannot be rejected on the sole ground of his being an ex-convict.[1] The business of the court is to try the case, and not try the parties and a very bad person might have a righteous cause.[2] To admit or reject character evidence in every case would be equally fatal to justice.[3] Explanation to section 55 defines the word "Character" in section 52 to 55 as including both reputation and disposition and except as provided in section 54, evidence may be given only of general reputation and general disposition and not of particular acts by which reputation or Character were shown. "character of any person concerned" in section 52 refers to character of parties and not to character of witnesses whose credibility is always in issue.[4] *See* sections 146(3), 148, 149, 155(1) of the Evidence Act.

Under sections 52 and 54, distinction must be drawn between cases where character of a party is in issue (action for defamation or seduction, for example) and where it is not issue, but is tendered in support of some other issue. In the latter case, it is not relevant. Evidence of character of defendant is relevant to mitigate damages.[5]

---

1. *Safi Devi* v. *Mahadeo Prasad*, AIR 1978 All 215: (1978) 4 All LR 181.
2. Wigmore on Evidence, sec. 135.
3. Best on Evidence 8th Edn. P. 245.
4. Best on Evidence, sec. 263.
5. *Bhagwan Swarup Lal Bishan Lal* v. *State of Maharashtra*, AIR 1965 SC 682: 1965 Cr LJ 608: (1964) 2 SCR 178: (1964) 2 SCJ 771; 1962 II SCR 771.

3. SECTION 53:

In criminal cases, the fact that the accused is of good character is relevant. The evidence has importance in weighing probabilities in doubtful cases and this principle affords a presumption against the commission of the crime.[1] The influence of this presumption from character will necessarily vary according to the circumstances of different cases.[2] Character evidence is very weak evidence; it cannot outweigh positive evidence in regard to guilt of accused.[3] In *Bhagwan Swarup Lal Bishan Lal* v. *State of Maharashtra*[4] the Supreme Court declined to interfere with conviction of accused under section 409 read with 120B I.P.C., despite the evidence of good character of the accused given by Jawaharlal Nehru (Later Prime Minister) and Sriprakasa (Later Governor), observing that the two witnesses believed the accused was a person of integrity but this is of no avail in the face of positive evidence in the case establishing the guilt of the accused. A person's character may be useful in doubtful cases to tilt the balance in favour of accused or in explaining his conduct and in judging his alleged criminality. Many acts of accused would be suspicious or innocent depending on his character.[5]

4. SECTION 53A:

This section introduced by section 25 of the Criminal Law (Amendment) Act, No. 13 of 2013, reads as follows:

> "53A. In a prosecution for an offence under section 354, section 354A, section 354B, section 354C, section 354D, section 376, section 376A, section 376B, section 376C, section 376D or section 376E of the Indian Penal Code or for attempt to commit such offence, where the question of consent is in issue, evidence of the character of the victim or of such person's previous sexual experience with any person shall not be relevant on the issue of such consent or the quality of the consent".

This new section has to be appreciated in the light of the provisio to section 146 introduced by the Indian Evidence (Amendment) Act, 4 of 2003 and the deletion of clause (4) of section 155 by the same Amending Act 4 of 2003. Section 146 refers to questions allowed in cross-examination to test the witness'es veracity, to discover who he is and what his position in life is, or to shake his credit by injuring his character...........Amending Act 4 of 2003 introduced the following proviso to section 146:

> "Provided that in a prosecution for rape or attempt to commit rape, it shall not be permissible to put questions in the cross-examination of the prosecutrix as to her general immoral character".

Section 155 allowed impeaching the credit of witness in four different ways as laid down therein; the fourth way was as follows:

---

1. *M.L. Sethi* v. *R.P. Kapur*, AIR 1967 SC 528: 1967 Cr LJ 528: (1967) 1 SCR 520 (FB).
2. *Kasam Abdullah Haji* v. *State of Maharashtra*, AIR 1998 SC 1451: 1998 AIR SCW 831: 1998 Cr LJ 1422.
3. *Bhagwan Swarup Lal Bishan Lal* v. *State of Maharashtra*, AIR 1965 SC 682: 1965 Cr LJ 608: (1964) 2 SCR 178: (1964) 2 SCJ 771; *Uday Kumar* v. *State of Karnataka*, 1998 Cr LJ 4622 (SC): AIR 1998 SC 3317: 1998 AIR SCW 3254.
4. *Bhagwan Swarup Lal Bishan Lal* v. *State of Maharashtra*, AIR 1965 SC 682: 1965 Cr LJ 608: (1964) 2 SCR 178: (1964) 2 SCJ 771.
5. *Habeeb Mohammad* v. *State of Hyderabad*, AIR 1954 SC 51: 1953 SCJ 678: 35 Cr LJ 338: 1954 SCR 475; *Satya Dev Bushahri* v. *Padam Dev*, AIR 1954 SC 587: (1955) 1 SCR 549: 1954 SCJ 764.

"(4) When a man is prosecuted for rape or an attempt to ravish, it may be shown that the prosecutrix was of generally immoral character.

Amending Act 4 of 2003 deleted this clause (4) to bring section 155 in harmony with the provisio newly introduced in section 146. The purpose of the two amendments introduced by Act 4 of 2003 was to make it clear that the testimony of a prosecutrix cannot be impeached by trying to show that she was a female of general immoral character. Such women, if they exist, are also entitled to protection against rape or attempted rape.

5. The Amending Act 13 of 2013 brought about important changes in Indian Penal Code etc. This Act, *inter alia*, created several new offences by introducing section 354A to 354D, by substituting sections 375 to 376D by modified sections 375 to 376D. Consequently chapter IV of Amending Act 13 of 2017 introduced in the Indian Evidence Act, new section 53A and substituted certain other sections (Sections 114A, 119) and introduced a provisio to section 146 to the following effect:

> "Provided that in a prosecution for an offence under section 376, section 376A, section 376B, section 376C, section 376D or section 376E of the Indian Penal Code or for attempt to commit any such offence, where the consent of victim is an issue, it shall not be permissible to adduce evidence or put questions in the cross-examination of the victim as to the general immoral character, or of previous sexual experience of such victim with any person, for proving such consent or the quality of consent."

6. Thus, in the context of extensive revision of law relating to sexual offences against members of the female sex, the legislature has made it clear that the victim's general immoral character or that she had previous sexual experience shall not be attempted to be proved by direct evidence or by cross-examination of the victim, since such past, cannot probablise to any extent consent for the sexual offence under trial. Thus, section 53A is only one among the package of provisions introduced in the Indian Evidence Act.

7. SECTION 54:

In criminal cases, the fact that the accused has a bad character is irrelevant, unless evidence has been given of his good character in which case it becomes relevant.[1] This rule will not apply where bad character is itself a fact in issue. (Expln. I). Previous conviction is relevant as evidence of bad character. (Expln. II).

Character evidence may be useful, in doubtful cases, to tilt the balance in favour of the accused or it may afford background for appreciating his reaction in a given situation.[2] It must yield to acceptable positive evidence.[3] Evidence of good character is given as tending to explain his conduct. When such evidence is given, rebuttal evidence of bad character may be adduced.[1] In the case of an accused found in possession of a watch belonging to another, a friend of his, and who pleaded that he found it and was holding it for his friend, evidence of

---

1. *Ram Lakhan Singh* v. *State of Uttar Pradesh*, AIR 1977 SC 1936: (1978) 1 SCR 125: 1977 Cr LJ 1566.
2. *Habeeb Mohammad* v. *State of Hyderabad*, AIR 1954 SC 51: 1953 SCJ 678: 35 Cr LJ 338: 1954 SCR 475.
3. *Bhagwan Swarup Lal Bishan Lal* v. *State of Maharashtra*, AIR 1965 SC 682: 1965 Cr LJ 608: (1964) 2 SCR 178: (1964) 2 SCJ 771.

good character as an honest person has importance in probabilishing his case. Good character has importance in a bribery case. Where an act amounts to an offence only by reason of being done with a vicious intention, good character has importance.[1] Where the intention is not the essence of the offence, such evidence may be of use only if it be doubtful whether the accused was the person who committed the act. Evidence of character is admissible in mitigation of sentence.[2] Evidence which is otherwise relevant does not became irrelevant merely because it shows bad character of the accused.[3] Section 54 as it originally stood allowed evidence of previous conviction as admissible in all cases. Section 54 was amended by Act III of 1891 to alter it to its present form. Such evidence is irrelevant except where evidence of bad character is relevant.[4] Section 236 of Cr.P.C. renders evidence of previous conviction relevant in the matter of sentence. Previous conviction may be relevant under section 8 as showing motive.[5] If the evidence is otherwise relevant, it is not rendered irrelevant under this section merely because it shows bad character of accused.[6] An accused, who is examined as his own witness may be cross-examined as to his character.

According to explanation I, if the charge implies bad character, evidence of such character is relevant.[7] Evidence of bad character must be confined to such traits which the charge is concerned about.[8] Reputation for honesty would be relevant on a charge of theft. Such a reputation has no relevance on a charge of cruelty. Evidence of a habit may be allowed, though it may speak to character also.[9]

There are two stages at which previous conviction can be proved. One is before conviction, for a subsequent offence, the other is after conviction as in section 211 of the Code. A previous conviction of accused is not relevant except where he would be liable for enhanced punishment under section 75 I.P.C. or unless in rebuttal when accused adduced evidence of good character. A previous conviction may be relevant under section 8 to prove motive or under section 14, explanation (2).

In a charge of murder, it has been held that evidence which disclosed certain unsavoury things about the accused could be let in to furnish the motive for killing.[5] Even where the accused is said to possess good qualities, unimpeachable prosecution evidence against him cannot thereby become unbelievable.[10]

1. *Re: Loganathaiyar*, 1911 Cr LJ 30.
2. *Habeeb Mohammad* v. *State of Hyderabad*, AIR 1954 SC 51: 1953 SCJ 678: 35 Cr LJ 338: 1954 SCR 475.
3. *Saroj Kumar Chakravrty* v. *Emperor*, AIR 1932 Cal 474; *Raikhan Boro* v. *Emperor*, AIR 1936 Cal 469; *Teka Ahir* v. *Emperor*, AIR 1920 Pat 351.
4. *Ram Lakhan Singh* v. *State of Uttar Pradesh*, AIR 1977 SC 1936: (1978) 1 SCR 125: 1977 Cr LJ 1566.
5. *Mangal Singh* v. *State of Madhya Bharat*, AIR 1957 SC 199: 1957 Cr LJ 325.
6. *Mangal Singh* v. *State of Madhya Bharat*, AIR 1957 SC 199: 1957 Cr LJ 325; *Lakshmandas* v. *State*, AIR 1968 Bom 400: 69 Bom LR 808: 1968 Cr LJ 1584.
7. *Rash Behari Sanyal* v. *Gosto Behari Goswami*, AIR 1935 Cal 243: 39 Cal WN 110: ILR 62 Cal 331: 60 Cal LJ 216.
8. *Noor Mohamed* v. *King*, AIR 1949 PC 161: 50 Cr LJ 770.
9. *Motiram Hari* v. *Emperor*, AIR 1925 Bom 195: 26 Bom LR 1223: 26 Cr LJ 1391; *Bai Chaturi* v. *State*, AIR 1960 Guj 5: 1960 Cr LJ 1204.
10. *Uday Kumar* v. *State of Karnataka*, 1998 Cr LJ 4622 (SC): AIR 1998 SC 3317: 1998 AIR SCW 3254.

8. SECTION 55:

In civil cases, the fact that the character of any person is such as to affect the amount of damages which he ought to receive, is relevant. This principle has significance in mitigation of damages for defamation, breach of promise, etc. This section has to be read with section 12 of the Act in cases where damages are claimed. Evidence of good character, however, is not admissible in aggravation of damages as there is always a presumption in favour of good character. But it is to rebut this, that evidence of bad character is made relevant.

Character is what a person really is, while reputation is what he is supposed to be by general repute. Both are distinct. According to the explanation to this section, character includes both reputation and disposition. Reputation is what the neighbours say he is, what is thought by others and is constituted by public opinion. It is the general credit which a person has obtained in that opinion.[1] Rumour is not reputation. Reputation is the collective opinion of several persons. Rumour can ripen into reputation. Reputation is different from hearsay.[2] If one hears of reputation from others, it is hearsay.[3]

Disposition is not based on opinion of others, but is to be inferred from acts which he has done or certain demonstrable facts directly connected with them. It means "natural tendency". The best character, it is stated in Wharton on Evidence (Vol. 1 page 468), is that which is least talked of!. The word 'habit' used in section 110 of the Criminal Procedure Code is not different from 'disposition'.

Evidence of existence of bad or good character, wherever they are relevant, is not by itself proof of or defence to a crime, but when proved it should be taken into consideration in connection with all the other evidence in the case and be given weight under all facts and circumstances of the case as it merits.[4] Evidence of good character, may sometimes, raise such a doubt as to justify acquittal.[5] If his guilt is proved beyond reasonable doubt, conviction must follow, inspite of his otherwise good character.

Character evidence is weak evidence and cannot outweigh the positive evidence in the case regarding guilt of the accused. It may be useful in some cases to tilt the balance in favour of the accused or it may also afford a background for appreciating his reactions in a given situation.[6]

9. SECTION 140:

Witnesses to character may be cross-examined and reexamined. In England, it is not usual to cross-examine witness called merely to speak to character, except in exceptional circumstances, but there is no rule which forbids it. Sections 146(3) and 155(1) of the Act may be seen in this connection.

1. *Isri Pershad* v. *Queen – Empress*, ILR 23 Cal 628.
2. *Firangi Rai* v. *Emperor*, AIR 1933 Pat 189: 34 Cr LJ 643.
3. *Firangi Rai* v. *Emperor*, AIR 1933 Pat 189: 34 Cr LJ 643; *Baso Rai* v. *Emperor*, AIR 1948 Pat 84.
4. *Mangal Singh* v. *State of Madhya Bharat*, AIR 1957 SC 199: 1957 Cr LJ 325.
5. *Habeeb Mohammad* v. *State of Hyderabad*, AIR 1954 SC 51: 1953 SCJ 678: 35 Cr LJ 338: 1954 SCR 475.
6. *Bhagwan Swarup Lal Bishan Lal* v. *State of Maharashtra*, AIR 1965 SC 682: 1965 Cr LJ 608: (1964) 2 SCR 178: (1964) 2 SCJ 771.

10. SECTION 146:

Cross-examination is regulated by sections 137 to 140, 142 to 145. Cross-examination must relate to relevant facts, though it is not confined to facts spoken in chief-examination. It may relate to previous statements in writing. In addition, under section 146, questions may be asked which tend to test his veracity, to discover who he is and his position in life and to shake his credit, by injuring his character though the answer might tend to criminate him or might expose him to penalty or forfeiture. But the lawyer must have some reasonable ground for thinking that the imputation conveyed by the question is well-founded.[1] Questions can be put to show his *mala fides*, immorality, dishonesty or falsehood. Even indecent and scandalous questions can be put if they have a bearing upon the fact in issue.[2] Irrelevant questions which tend to harass or embarrass are not permissible.[3]

11. SECTION 147:

If any such question relates to a matter relevant to the proceeding, section 132 will apply and witness will not be excused from answering it.

12. SECTION 148:

If a question is put under section 146(3), Court shall decide whether or not the witness shall be compelled to answer it and may, if it thinks fit, warn the witness that he is not obliged to answer it. In exercising the discretion, court shall have regard to the four circumstances referred to the section 149. This is to protect the witness from improper cross-examination.

Trustworthiness of a witness is very important.[4]

13. SECTION 149:

No such question as is referred to in section 148 ought to be asked, unless the person asking it has reasonable grounds for thinking that the imputation which it conveys is well-founded. Proper instructions from a client or other person is sufficient to enable the lawyer to think the imputation is well-founded.[5] Statement must be put in good faith or for public good or for the protection of the person making it. There is a presumption of good faith on the part of the lawyer.[6]

14. SECTION 150:

If any such question is asked without reasonable grounds, court may report it to the High Court or other authority to which the Advocate is subject to in the exercise of his profession.

15. SECTION 151:

Court may forbid questions which it regards as scandalous or indecent, through such questions may have some bearing on the grounds before the Court,

---

1. *Deepchand* v. *Sampathraj*, AIR 1970 Mys 34: (1969) 1 Mys LJ 606: 1970 Cr LJ 260.
2. *Prakash Rajaram* v. *State of Maharashtra*, 1975 Cr LJ 1297: 1974 Mah LJ 416.
3. *Dr. Baburao Patel* v. *Bal Thackeray*, 1977 Cr LJ 1637: (1977) 3 UCR (Bom) 371.
4. *Rameshwar Prasad Sahu* v. *Parameshwar Prasad Sahu*, AIR 1951 PC 1.
5. *Narayana Chandra* v. *Harish Chandra*, AIR 1933 Cal 185: 34 Cr LJ 865; *Deepchand* v. *Sampathraj*, AIR 1970 Mys 34: (1969) 1 Mys LJ 606: 1970 Cr LJ 260; *Rev. Father P. Mesaric* v. *Rai Ramani Mohan Banerjee Bahadur*, AIR 1938 Cal 766.
6. *Piter* v. *Mahomed Idoo Miah*, AIR 1914 Cal 255.

unless they relate to facts in issue or the matters necessary to be known to determine whether or not the facts in issue existed. What is relevant cannot be scandalous.[1]

16. SECTION 152:

Question intended to insult or annoy or which though proper in itself, appears to be needlessly offensive in form, may be forbidden.[2] Personal inconvenience to a witness may be justified only by a real necessity. It is not so justified when the imputation, if true, would not affect his credibility or when the injury to his character is very serious while the importance of the evidence is very small.[3] Court cannot forbid scandalous or indecent questions if they relate to facts in issue.[4] If they have only some bearing on the question before the Court, it has a discretion and may forbid them. Duty of court is to see that questions forbidden by law are not asked. Half the mischief is done by mere asking the questions.[3]

17. SECTION 153:

When a witness has answered a question intended to shake his credit by injuring his character, no evidence shall be given to contradict him. But if he answers falsely, he may later be charged with perjury. In the face of denial of previous conviction, evidence may be given of such conviction. If a question impeaching impartiality is asked and denied, he may be contradicted.

This section restricts the right to give evidence in contradiction so that the attention of Court may be confined to specific issues arising in the case and not diverted to collateral matters which may result in protraction of the case.[5] This section must be construed strictly. The reason for the restriction is that the witness cannot be expected to come prepared to defend by independent proof all the actions of his life and that to admit contradicting evidence on such points would lead to confusion by raising endless series of collateral issues.[6] The section provides for two expectations. Ordinarily the answer must conclude the matter (except in the two exceptional cases).

18. SECTION 155:

This section prescribes three methods of impeaching the credit of a witness, *i.e.*, oral evidence regarding credit, proof of bribery etc., proof of former statements contradicting his present evidence.

The section is to be strictly construed.[7] In view of section 6 of Commission of Enquiry Act, 1952, the statement of a witness recorded by the Commission

---

1. *In re G. Vasantha Pai*, AIR 1960 Mad 73: ILR 1959 Mad 958: (1960) 1 Mad LJ 21; *T. Vetriselvan* v. *Tamil Nadu Merchantile Bank Ltd.*, 1970 II MLJ 119.
2. *Prakash Rajaram* v. *State of Maharashtra*, 1975 Cr LJ 1297: 1974 Mah LJ 416; *Dr. Baburao Patel* v. *Bal Thackeray*, 1977 Cr LJ 1637: (1977) 3 UCR (Bom) 371.
3. *Ayeasha Bi* v. *Peerkhan Sahib*, AIR 1954 Mad 741: 1954 Cr LJ 1239.
4. *Mhomed Mion* v. *Emperor*, AIR 1919 Pat 515; *Hara Sundar* v. *Lahabara Singh*, AIR 1923 Cal 315: 67 Ind Cas 277.
5. *Bhogi Lal Bhika Chand* v. *Royal Insurance Co. Ltd.*, AIR 1928 PC 54: 6 R 142: 108 IC 1: 47 Cr LJ 550.
6. 1990 SC Cr R 339.
7. *Kamal Kanto* v. *State*, 1959 Cr LJ 694: AIR 1959 Cal 342: ILR (1960) 1 Cal 292; *Bhogi Lal Bhika Chand* v. *Royal Insurance Co. Ltd.*, AIR 1928 PC 54: 6 R 142: 108 IC 1: 47 Cr LJ 550.

cannot be used at the trial of a case for the purpose of cross-examination for impeaching his credit.[1]

Sections 52 and 155 deal with different matters. Section 52 deals with character evidence in regard to subject-matter of a suit while section 155 deals with manner of impeaching credit.[2] Sections 146 and 155 are not contradictory. Section 146 permits questions injuring character to be put to him in cross-examination. Section 155 deals with independent evidence to be adduced to discredit a witness. Section 145 does not control section 155.[3] Section 155 applies to civil and criminal cases.

19. Clause (1): Independent evidence is allowed regarding a general reputation for untruthfulness or moral turpitude generally. But evidence of general bad character is not allowed. In chief-examination, particular instances cannot be given. Witness's credit cannot be decided on the basis of what another Court thought of the witness in another case.[4]

20. Clause (2): Mere offer of a bribe to a person does not disparage him. His acceptance of the offer is disparaging.

21. Clause (3): Illustrations (a) and (b) may be seen. 'Statement' may be verbal or written. If it is written, section 145 must be followed. Witness must be given an opportunity even if it is a verbal statement. Recitals in deeds are statements.[5] Evidence of previous statement cannot be given without the previous cross-examination of the witness as to such statement.[6] The former statement need not be signed.[7] Tape-recorded statement can be used for this purpose.[8]

---

1. *Kehar Singh* v. *State (Delhi Administration)*, (1988) 3 SCC 609: AIR 1988 SC 1883: JT 1988 (3) SC 191.
2. *Maitri* v. *Hemraj*, AIR 1954 Andhra 30.
3. *Ramratan* v. *State*, AIR 1956 Raj 196: 1956 Cr LJ 1432: ILR (1956) 6 Raj 762; Contra 1958 Cr LJ (Cr) 942.
4. *Chandreshwar Prasad Narain Singh* v. *Bisheshwar Pratab Narain Singh*, AIR 1927 Pat 61: 101 Ind Cas 289: ILR 5 Pat 777.
5. *Rangayyan* v. *Innasimithu Mudali*, AIR 1956 Mad 226: (1955) 2 Mad LJ 687: 69 Mad LW 513.
6. *Stephen Seneviratne* v. *King*, AIR 1936 PC 289: 37 Cr LJ 963 (PC).
7. *Narayanan* v. *Krishnan*, 1981 Cr LJ 563.
8. *N. Sri Ram Reddy* v. *V.V. Giri*, AIR 1971 SC 1162: (1971) 1 SCR 399: (1970) 2 SCC 340; *Rup Chand* v. *Mahabir Parshad*, AIR 1956 Punj 173: 58 Punj LR 441: ILR (1956) Punj 1351; *Muncipal Corporation of City Hubli* v. *Subba Rao Hanumantharao*, 1976 I Kar LJ SC 45.

CHAPTER 13

FACTS WHICH NEED NOT BE PROVED (SECTIONS 56 TO 58)

SECTIONS 56, 57: According to section 56, no fact of which court will take judicial notice needs to be proved. Section 57 enumerates the facts of which court shall take judicial notice.

2. All disputed facts in issue and relevant facts arising in a case require to be proved by oral evidence, production of documents, material objects, admissions or confessions. The two exceptions to this rule are – (i) facts judiciably noticeable and, (ii) facts admitted. Facts covered by these two exceptions need not be proved.

The definition of "proved" in section 3 of the Act requires consideration of the "matters" before the Court, before conducting the exercise of finding if whether a disputed fact is proved or not. Such matters are brought before the court by the parties or otherwise appear in the particular proceeding. Judge's belief in the existence of facts dealt with in section 56 is induced by general knowledge acquired otherwise than in such proceedings and independently of the action of the parties to the cause.[1] Court can take judicial notice of certain facts. Section 57 directs that the courts shall take judicial notice of facts referred to in the several clauses therein. The clauses in section 57 are not exhaustive; other facts within public knowledge may be judicially noticed. For example, the date of birth and date of martyrdom of Mahatma Gandhi cannot be required to be proved. As a means of establishing widely known facts, taking judicial notice is superior to formal means of proof.[2] Certain matters are specifically referred to in section 57, because regarding those facts, the court is given no discretion; in other words, courts shall take judicial notice of those matters specified in section 57. As to other matters, court has wide discretion to take judicial notice. That is because the court assumes that the matter is so well-known that it will not be disputed; but the opposite party can dispute the matter by evidence.

"Taking judicial notice" means taking cognizance, without proof, of something as existing, or as being true. This principle is based on convenience and expediency. It is desirable that proof of matters within the common knowledge of all or many, is dispensed with.

3. Clauses (1) to (13) of section 57 refer to laws in force in India and United Kingdom, Articles of war, parliamentary proceeding in the two countries and proceedings of State Legislatures, National Flag of every country recognised

1. Woodroffe and Amir Ali on Law of Evidence, 18th Edn., Vol. 2, page 2863.
2. *Onkar Nath* v. *Delhi Administration*, AIR 1977 SC 1108: (1977) 2 SCC 611: 1977 Cr LJ 957: 1977 SC 1108.

by Government of India, and so forth. Notifications issued under statutory provisions have the force of law.[1]

4. Courts have taken judicial notice of facts outside the scope of section 57 *e.g.* that many of industrial workers are illiterate[2] that among hill tribes there is low expectation of life, that communal disturbances have taken place in the country[3] that war with Pakistan started in June 1965,[4] regarding prices of commodities, general level of wages[5] of the loss of purchasing power of rupee[6] that rents of buildings have increased enormously, particularly in urban areas[7] that sometimes prescribed registers and case diaries are not maintained in the prescribed form,[8] that a railway strike was on,[9] that prices of urban and rural land have increased[10] that construction cost of buildings has gone up[11] that where the Authority concerned had a low toll income from Taj Mahal visitors, it reflected on the lack of care in preservation of Taj and in maintaining the cleanliness of Agra city,[12] that municipal authorities are unwilling or unable or incapable of preventing illegal construction and/or demolishing the same,[13] that law and order situation is deteriorating,[14] that it is common knowledge that in central India rice is not the principal meal or eaten exclusively and rice in small quantity is cooked and served along with "Dal Roti".[15]

5. It is a matter of common practice that on a date a case is posted for hearing, the presence of counsel and not of the parties is recorded in the order

---

1. *State of Bombay* v. *F.N. Balsara*, AIR 1951 SC 318: 1951 SCR 682: (1951) 52 Cr LJ 1361; *Jayantilal Amratlal* v. *F.N. Rana*, AIR 1964 SC 648: (1964) 5 SCR 294: (1964) 2 SCA 284; *Kalyani Stores* v. *State of Orissa*, AIR 1966 SC 1686: (1966) 1 SCR 865: 1966 (2) SCJ 367, *Kailash Nath* v. *State of Uttar Pradesh*, AIR 1957 SC 790: (1957) 8 STC 358; *Saraswati Industrial Syndicate Ltd.* v. *Union of India*, AIR 1975 SC 460: (1974) 2 SCC 630: 1975 (2) SCJ 332; *Additional Commissioner of Income Tax, Gujarat, Ahmedabad* v. *Surat Art Silk Cloth Manufactures Association, Surat*, AIR 1980 SC 387: 1980 Tax LR 230: (1980) 2 SCC 31.
2. *Kesoram Cotton Mills Ltd.* v. *Gangadhar*, AIR 1964 SC 708: (1964) 2 SCR 809: 1965 (1) SCJ 71.
3. *Shiv Nath Rai Ram Dhari* v. *Union of India*, AIR 1965 SC 1666: 1965 Punj LR (Supp) 231.
4. *State of Assam* v. *Banshidhar Shewbhagavan and Co.*, AIR 1981 SC 1957: (1981) 4 SCC 283.
5. *Kamini Metals and Alloys Ltd.* v. *Workmen*, AIR 1967 SC 1175: (1967) 2 SCR 463: (1967) 1 SCWR 730.
6. *Bharat Petroleum MSP* v. *Bharat Petroleum Corporation Ltd.*, AIR 1988 SC 1407: (1988) 3 SCC 32: 1988 SCC (L&S) 706.
7. *Rattan Arya* v. *State of Tamil Nadu*, AIR 1986 SC 1444: (1986) 3 SCC 385: 1986 (2) SCJ 429; *D.C. Oswal* v. *V.K. Subbiah*, AIR 1992 SC 184: 1991 AIR SCW 2894: (1992) 1 SCC 370.
8. *State of Madhya Pradesh* v. *Dhirendra Kumar*, AIR 1997 SC 318: 1997 AIR SCW 74: (1997) 1 SCC 93.
9. *Onkar Nath* v. *Delhi Administration*, AIR 1977 SC 1108: (1977) 2 SCC 611: 1977 Cr LJ 957: 1977 SC 1108.
10. *Modi Spinning and Weaving Mills* v. *Virendra*, (1998) 5 SCC 718; *Land Acquisition Officer Revenue Divisional Officer, Chittor* v. *L. Kamalamma*, (1998) 2 SCC 385: AIR 1998 SC 781: 1998 AIR SCW 497.
11. *Haryana Urban Development Authority* v. *A.K. Rampal*, AIR 2004 SC 4138: 2004 AIR SCW 4569: (2005) 9 SCC 443.
12. *M.C. Mehta* v. *Union of India*, (1998) 8 SCC 711.
13. *Supreme Court Monitoring Committee* v. *Mussoorie Dehradun Development Authority*, AIR 2002 SC 2876: 2002 AIR SCW 3275: (2003) 10 SCC 445.
14. *Shashi Nayar* v. *Union of India*, AIR 1992 SC 395: (1992) 1 SCC 96: 1992 SCC (Cri) 24: 1992 Cr LJ 514.
15. *Babu Ram* v. *State of Uttar Pradesh*, AIR 2002 SC 2815: 2002 Cr LJ 3745: 2002 AIR SCW 3192: (2002) 6 SCC 518.

sheet.[1] In assessing the value of oral evidence, judge is bound to call upon his experience of life.[2] There is a difference between the personal knowledge of a Judge as a private person and his knowledge as a Judge; he can make use of his experience as a judge by taking judicial notice of facts transpiring in the court. Court can take judicial notice of institutions of repute, such as National Institute of Mental Health and Neurosciences (NIMHANS).[3] Court can take judicial notice of the increasing practice of courts to direct parties to bear their own costs which encourages filing of frivolous litigation.[4] Court cannot take judicial of the fact that FIR was sent to the Magistrate concerned; it is a matter which requires to be proved.[5] Judicial notice cannot be taken of matters stated in newspapers; they require proof.[6] Court can take judicial notice of the fact that the Government in any particular year fixed a particular rate of interest under a statutory provision. Judicial notice can be taken of the fact that more and more of the younger generation in our country are getting addicted to liquor. Practices prevailing in transactions comprising purchase and sale of shares by investors may be taken judicial notice of.[7] Judicial notice can be taken of fact that specific political parties are in power in the Centre or the States.[8] Judicial notice can be taken of historical facts, geographical truths, scientific inventions, socio-economic conditions at a given time, natural phenomena, axiomatic truths, common affairs of life, general knowledge of people, religious history etc., prevailing prices of any commodity in different states, ages of retirement in various services in the country,[9] and of subsequent events having a material bearing in cases.[10]

For the purpose of section 57, court can refer to statements in books and journals.

6. SECTION 58: No fact need be proved in any proceeding which the parties thereto or their agents agree at the hearing, or which, before the hearing, they agree to admit by any writing under their hands, or which by any rule of pleading in force at the time they are deemed to have admitted by their pleadings: provided that the court may, in its' discretion, require the facts admitted to be proved otherwise by such admissions.

Admissions by prior to before suit are dealt with by sections 17 and 21. Section 58 deals with admissions made "before or at" the hearing. Admissions constitute the best evidence, even conceding that admissions do not create any title. The principle underlying section 58 is that what is admitted need not be

---

1. *State of Punjab* v. *Hardan Singh*, AIR 2003 SC 4343: 2003 Cr LJ 5048: 2003 AIR SCW 5131.
2. *Chaturbhuj Pande* v. *Collector, Raigarh*, AIR 1969 SC 255: (1969) 1 SCR 412.
3. *K. Shekar* v. *V. Indiramma*, AIR 2002 SC 1230: 2002 LabIC 971: 2002 AIR SCW 1018.
4. *Salem Advocate Bar Association, Tamil Nadu* v. *Union of India*, AIR 2005 SC 3353: 2005 AIR SCW 3827: (2005) 6 SCC 344.
5. *Bir Singh* v. *State of Uttar Pradesh*, AIR 1978 SC 59: (1977) 4 SCC 420: 1978 Cr LJ 177.
6. AIR 1988 SC 1290.
7. *M.S. Narayana Menon* v. *State of Kerala*, (2006) 6 SCC 39: AIR 2006 SC 3366: 2006 Cr LJ 4607.
8. *T.N. Cauvery Neerppasana Vilaiporulgal Vivasayigal Nala Urimai Padhugappu Sangam* v. *Union of India*, AIR 1990 SC 1316: (1990) 3 SCC 440: JT 1990 (2) SC 397.
9. *Life Insurance Corporation of India* v. *S.S. Srivastava*, AIR 1987 SC 1527: JT 1987 (3) 529: 1987 (3) SCJ 99.
10. *Atma S. Berar* v. *Muktiar Singh*, AIR 2003 SC 624: 2002 AIR SCW 5282: (2003) 2 SCC 3; *Shipping Corporation of India Ltd.* v. *Machado Brothers*, AIR 2004 SC 2093: (2004) 11 SCC 168: (2004) 110 DLT 649.

proved.[1] The object of this provision is to save time and expense at the trial. A court is required to try the question on which parties are at issue, and not those on which they are agreed. Admission in pleading, or judicial admission admissible under section 58 made by parties or their agents at or before the hearing of the case, stand on a higher footing than evidentiary admissions. The former class of admissions are fully binding on the parties who made them and constitute proof and can become the basis of the rights of the parties. Evidentiary admissions which are receivable at the trial as evidence are by themselves not conclusive as they can be shown to be wrong.[2] Where the defendant does not file a written statement, it does not amount to an admission of the facts stated in the plaint. But this legal position is altered by rule 5(2) of Order VIII, C.P.C., introduced by Central Act 104 of 1976. Rule 5(2) makes it lawful for a court, where the defendant has not filed written statement, to pronounce judgment on the basis of the facts contained in the plaint, except as against a person under disability, but the court may, in its' discretion, require any such fact to be proved. Every allegation of fact in the plaint, if not denied specifically or by necessary implication, or not stated to be not admitted in the written statement, shall be deemed to be admitted. Yet, under the proviso to sub-rule (1) of rule 5 of Order VIII C.P.C., it is open to the court, in its' discretion, to require any fact so admitted to be proved otherwise than by such admission.

7. Rules (1) and (2) of Order X, provisions of Order XI, XII provide further opportunities for parties to make admission of facts asserted by opposite party. Parties get such opportunity at the hearing. There are also admissions which can be implied from pleadings.[3] An admission in pleadings must be clear and specific.[4] Admission must be taken as a whole.[5] An admission of a document is admission of facts contained therein.[6] Where execution of a gift deed was admitted in the written statement and the document was marked with consent of the parties, the contents of the document need not be separately proved.[7]

Stephen in his Digest (Art. 60) stated that the section appears to allow an accused person to admit at the trial such facts as he pleases to admit. However, there is no case law in support of this view. Madras High Court has taken a

1. *Shreedhar Govind Kamerkar* v. *Yesahwant Govind Kamerkar*, (2006) 13 SCC 481: (2006) 14 SCALE 174; *Oriental Insurance Co. Ltd.* v. *Premlata Shukla*, (2007) 13 SCC 476: 2007 AIR SCW 3591; *Avtar Singh* v. *Gurdial Singh*, (2006) 12 SCC 552; *Commissioner Excise* v. *Manoj Ali*, (2006) 13 SCC 88; *Chairman & MD V.S.P.* v. *Goparaju Sri Prabhakara Hari Babu*, (2008) 5 SCC 569: AIR 2008 SC (Supp) 1694; *Harendra Nath Chakraborty* v. *State of West Bengal*, (2009) 2 SCC 758: AIR 2008 SC (Supp) 775; *Bhuwan Singh* v. *Oriental Insurance Company Ltd.*, (2009) 5 SCC 136: AIR 2009 SC 2177: 2009 AIR SCW 2865; *B.S.N.L.* v. *Abhishek Shukla*, (2009) 5 SCC 368.
2. *Nagindas Ramdas* v. *Dalpatram Ichharam*, AIR 1974 SC 471: (1974) 1 SCC 242: (1974) 3 SCR 544.
3. *Mahendra Manilal Nanavati* v. *Sushila Mahendra Nanavati*, AIR 1965 SC 364: 66 Bom LR 681: 1965 Mah LJ 365; *Uttam Singh Duggal and Co. Ltd.* v. *United Bank of India*, AIR 2000 SC 2740: (2000) 7 SCC 120: 2010 AIR SCW 2924; *Charanjit Lal Mehra* v. *Kamal Saroj Mahajan*, (2005) 11 SCC 279: AIR 2005 SC 2765: 2005 AIR SCW 1697.
4. *Thayyil Mammo* v. *Kottiath Ramunni*, AIR 1966 SC 337: 1966 (1) SCJ 138; *M.P. Wakf Board* v. *Subhan Shah*, (2006) 10 SCC 696: 2006 AIR SCW 5540.
5. *Mahendra Manilal Nanavati* v. *Sushila Mahendra Nanavati*, AIR 1965 SC 364: 66 Bom LR 681: 1965 Mah LJ 365.
6. *Sitaram Motilal Kalal* v. *Santanuprasad Jaishanker Bhatt*, AIR 1966 SC 1697: (1966) 1 SCWR 974: (1966) 3 SCR 527.
7. *P.C. Purushothama Reddiar* v. *S. Perumal*, AIR 1972 SC 608: (1972) 1 SCC 9: 1972 SCJ 469.

contrary view.[1] It has to be noticed that if on any fact required to be established by prosecution some evidence is advanced by the prosecution, the accused has to be questioned about it under section 313 Criminal Procedure Code and at that stage, it is open to the accused to admit the fact or evidence to be true. But then, such an admission cannot be used to fill up any gap in the prosecution evidence.[2] But in a criminal case, there is no preliminary stage at which court can question accused about facts or ingredients of the offence charged, except in recording his plea after reading out the charge. Such a stage is reached only at the stage of section 313 questioning, which, however, cannot be converted into a fishing expedition.

---

1. AIR 1926 Mad 426.
2. *Miss Hardevi Malkani* v. *State*, AIR 1969 All 423: 1968 All LJ 466: 1969 Cr LJ 1089; *Yalavarthi Ramakrishnayya* v. *Yalavarthi Rattayya*, ILR 1927 Mad 238.

CHAPTER 14
ORAL EVIDENCE (SECTIONS 59 AND 60)

SECTION 59:

1. All facts, except the contents of documents, may be proved by oral evidence. Any method of communicating thought which the circumstances and condition of the witness demand, may, with discretion of the court may be employed. A deaf-mute may testify by signs, by writing or through an interpreter; A dying person may answer by signaling by hand.[1]

Oral evidence is defined in section 3 of the Evidence Act as all statements which the court permits or requires to be made before it by witnesses, in relation to matters of fact under inquiry. All facts, except contents of documents, (subject to section 63(5) read with section 65), can be proved by oral evidence. Credibility of the witnesses has to be tested, intrimiscally and extrinsically.[2] Where the entire case is based upon a construction a document; oral evidence is not called for.[3] Where division of joint property was by an unregistered deed, parties are entitled to adduce oral evidence to prove the size of the building.[4] Oral evidence could be adduced for a collateral purpose, say of showing nature of possession.[5]

2. SECTION 60:

Oral evidence must be direct. In the case of facts which could be seen or heard or perceived by any other sense, evidence must be given by those who saw, heard or perceived respectively. In the case of opinion, evidence must be by the person who holds the opinion. In case of opinion, treatises are admissible. This Section incorporates rule against hearsay.[6]

What a witness heard from somebody else is not admissible ordinarily. But it can corroborate or contradict the evidence of the person who had spoken. News item is hearsay.[7]

---

1. *R.* v. *Abdullah*, ILR 7 All 385 (FB).
2. *Mahanth Bhagwan Bhagat* v. *Girija Nandan Bhagat*, AIR 1972 SC 814: 1972 (2) SCJ 730: (1972) 2 SCR 1005.
3. *Peacock Plywood (P) Ltd.* v. *Oriental Insurance Co. Ltd.*, (2006) 12 SCC 673: (2006) 14 SCALE 300.
4. *Hriday Narain Chaudhury* v. *Shyam Kishore Singh*, AIR 2002 SC 2526: 2002 AIR SCW 2734: 2002 AIR Jhar HCR 806.
5. *Virendra Nath Thr. P.A. Holder R.R. Gupta,* v. *Mohd. Jamil*, AIR 2004 SC 3856: 2004 AIR SCW 4121: (2004) 6 SCC 140.
6. *Bhugdomal Gangaram* v. *State of Gujarat*, AIR 1983 SC 906: (1984) 1 SCC 319: 1984 SCC (Cri) 67: 1983 Cr LJ 1276.
7. *Samant N. Balakrishna* v. *George Fernandez,* AIR 1969 SC 1201: (1969) 3 SCR 603: (1970) 1 SCA 376; *Laxmi Raj Shetty* v. *State of Tamil Nadu*, AIR 1988 SC 1274: (1988) 3 SCC 319: 1988 SCC (Cri) 633: (1988) 2 Crimes 107.

3. This section prescribes that oral evidence must be direct. "Fact" as defined in section 3 is anything, state of things or relation of things, capable of being "perceived" by the senses and any mental condition of which any person is conscious. Section 60 follows the principle underlying the definition and requires every disputed fact to be proved by the person or persons who "perceived" it. Section 60 is also based on bar of hearsay. This section excludes opinions given by a second person, subject to the first proviso. It is the duty of the court to exclude all oral evidence which is not direct; this obligation is that of the court irrespective of whether the opposite party objects or not. The word "direct" used here is in contradistinction to "hearsay".

Where documentary evidence available was not produced, plaintiff could not rest his case on oral evidence.[1] The section is based on the rule of "Best Evidence". It is cardinal rule of evidence that a party to a case should produce the best evidence. Sections 60, 64 and 91 are based on this principle.[2] Court cannot compel any party to examine any particular witness. But in weighing evidence, court can take note of the fact that the best available evidence was not produced by a particular party on whom the burden of proof lies and draw an adverse inference against that party.[3] No value could be attached to hearsay evidence.[4] The word hearsay is used in several senses. It may mean what a person is heard to say, or what a person declares on information given by someone else.[5]

4. The select committee in their report observed:

> "This provision, taken in connection with the provisions of relevancy contained in Chapter II, will, we hope, set the whole doctrine of hearsay in a perfectly plain light, for their joint effort is that:—(1) the sayings and doings of third persons are, as a rule, irrelevant, so that no proof of them can be admitted; (2) in some excepted cases they are relevant; (3) every act done or spoken which is relevant on any ground must (if proved by oral evidence) be proved by someone who saw it with his own eyes or heard it with his own ears."

5. A hearsay statement to *A* by *B*, who is not called as a witness may or may not be hearsay. It is hearsay and inadmissible when the object of the evidence is to establish what is contained in the statement. It is admissible if such evidence proposed merely to establish the factum of the statement made by *B* to *A* and not the truth of the statement as there is a distinction between proving the factum of a statement and proving the truth of the statement.[6] Where a draftsman prepared a map of the scene of occurrence, the different spots being pointed out to him by the eye-witnesses and the draftsman himself took measurement of various relevant distances and he deposed to the correctness of the distances, it was held

1. *Bharat Commerce and Industries Ltd.* v. *Commissioner of Income Tax, Central-II*, AIR 1998 SC 1795: 1998 AIR SCW 1584: (1998) 3 SCC 510.
2. *State of Maharashtra through Khar Police Station* v. *Alister Anthony Pareira*, (2006) 3 SCC 374.
3. *Rama Paswan* v. *State of Jharkhand*, 2007 Cr LJ 2750: (2007) 3 AIR Jhar R 203: 2007 AIR SCW 2779 (SC).
4. *Rajendra Prabhu Chikane* v. *State of Maharashtra*, (2007) 13 SCC 511: 2007 CR LJ 3410 (SC): 2007 AIR SCW 2936.
5. *J.D. Jain* v. *Manager of SBI*, AIR 1982 SC 673: (1982) 1 SCC 143: (1982) 1 SCWR 243.
6. *J.D. Jain* v. *Manager of SBI*, AIR 1982 SC 673: (1982) 1 SCC 143: (1982) 1 SCWR 243; *Balram Prasad Agrawal* v. *State of Bihar*, AIR 1997 SC 1830: (1997) 9 SCC 338: 1997 Cr LJ 1640.

that his evidence given in proof of the map was not hearsay.[1] Evidence of a Bank officer in proof of a transaction given on the basis of the material on record since he had no personal knowledge, was held to be hearsay.[2] What someone else told a witness is hearsay as long as that someone did not give evidence in court stating that he told the witness so and that he personally knew about it.[3] Newspaper report is hearsay unless proved by examining the reporter as a witness.[4] Hearsay statement which attracts section 157 is admissible.[5]

6. The statement in the inquest report which is based on the actual observation of the witness at the scene is direct evidence admissible under section 60, when spoken to by a signatory to the report.[6] Matters in the observation report of the police officer are not hit by section 162 Criminal Procedure Code and are admissible when spoken to by him in court. In the case of an officer working in the office of the Food Inspector, his oral evidence to that effect, would be direct evidence and production of the appointment order would become necessary only if his oral evidence is challenged.[7] Recitals in panchnama do not constitute substantive evidence of the facts recited, and have to be proved by the oral evidence of the investigating officer or the panchas.

7. Section 60 does not exclude circumstantial evidence of a fact which could be seen, heard or felt.[8] Concept of hearsay evidence has nothing to do with circumstantial evidence. Circumstantial facts such as motive, section 27 recovery etc. are required to be proved by direct evidence. It is the duty of court to insist on direct evidence and disallow hearsay evidence even if no objection is raised by the opposite party.[9] No particular evidence, by itself, can be termed as "hearsay". Under particular circumstances, a particular evidence may amount to hearsay and yet in some other circumstances, the same evidence may not amount to hearsay. If a witness says that he heard something and desires to speak about in his evidence, he is allowed to do so provided he heard that matter or words directly. If a person desires to depose about what he saw, it must be what he saw directly. Where a dying declaration was made to a doctor, the evidence of the doctor in that regard is relevant and also admissible under section 60; that is because he heard directly from the dying person. If the purpose of this evidence is merely to know what the doctor heard from the dying person, it is

1. *Santa Singh* v. *State of Punjab*, AIR 1956 SC 526: 1955 Cr LJ 930.
2. *S.R. Ramaraj* v. *Special Court, Bombay*, AIR 2003 SC 3039: 2003 AIR SCW 3962: 2003 Cr LJ 3863.
3. *Pawan Kumar* v. *State of Haryana*, (2003) 11 SCC 241: 2003 AIR SCW 3671: 2003 Cr LJ 3552: AIR 2003 SC 2987; *Sakatar Singh* v. *State of Haryana*, AIR 2004 SC 2570: 2004 AIR SCW 2388: 2004 Cr LJ 2076; *Ram Kishan* v. *State of Uttar Pradesh*, AIR 2004 SC 4678: 2004 Cr LJ 4236: 2004 AIR SCW 5169; *Ram Anup Singh* v. *State of Bihar*, 2002 AIR SCW 3347: AIR 2002 SC 3006: 2002 Cr LJ 3927; *S. Partap Singh* v. *State of Punjab*, AIR 1964 SC 72: 1966 1 Lab LJ 458: (1964) 4 SCR 733; *State of Andhra Pradesh* v. *Patnam Anandam*, 2005 Cr LJ 894: AIR 2005 SC 764: 2005 AIR SCW 362 (SC); *Subhash Haranaryanji Ladda* v. *State of Maharashtra*, (2006) 12 SCC 545.
4. *Quamarul Islam* v. *S.K. Kanta*, AIR 1994 SC 1733: 1994 AIR SCW 1598: (1994) 1 SCR 210; *Laxmi Raj Shetty* v. *State of Tamil Nadu*, AIR 1988 SC 1274: (1988) 3 SCC 319: 1988 SCC (Cri) 633: (1988) 2 Crimes 107.
5. *Mukhtear Singh* v. *State of Punjab*, AIR 2009 SC 1854: 2009 Cr LJ 1744: 2009 AIR SCW 1475.
6. *Rameshwar Dayal* v. *State of Uttar Pradesh*, AIR 1978 SC 1558: 1978 2 SCC 518: 1978 All LJ 1011.
7. *State of Kerala* v. *V.P. Enadeen*, AIR 1971 Ker 193: 1971 Ker LT 19: 1971 Ker LJ 177 FB.
8. *Makbul Ahmad Mallik* v. *Abdul Rahman Akhand*, AIR 1952 Cal 494: 1952 Cr LJ 944.
9. *Lim Yam Hong* v. *Lam Choon and Co.*, AIR 1928 PC 127: 107 IC 457.

not hearsay; but if the purpose is to show that the dying person was stabbed by a particular individual, then what the doctor heard from the dying person would be hearsay. It is the purpose, which makes a particular piece of evidence hearsay. There are, of course, exceptions to the hearsay rule which are statutorily recognized, such as resgestae and other matters covered by some of the Sections in chapter II of the Evidence Act.

8. Hearsay evidence has been defined to be all the evidence which does not derive its' value solely from the credit given to the witness himself, but which rests also in part on the veracity and competency of some other person.[1] Sometimes, "hearsay" means whatever a person declares on the basis of information given by somebody else.[2] The evidence of witness of what he was told by others is hearsay.[3] The test to distinguish between direct and hearsay evidence is that it is direct, if, to act upon it, the court has to rely only upon that witness, whereas if it is hearsay, if it has to rely upon not only the witness but on some other person also.[4] Where a father whose daughter was killed received some information from neighbours which roused suspicion against the accused, the father rushed to the police with that information, the information would be admissible as explaining the conduct of the father.[5] The fact that a person identified the accused in a test identification parade is hearsay and cannot be taken note of, if that person is not examined as a witness.[6] Observations made by investigating officer in the inquest report regarding injuries found on the dead body of the victim are not hit by section 162 of Criminal Procedure Code and are admissible if deposed to by the officer.[7] A map consists only of lines and pictorial representation instead of word of mouth as to the description of the scene of occurrence and the objects found there. To admit the map in evidence without calling the officer who prepared it as a witness to speak to the details will go against section 60. Even a doctors' evidence is hearsay if it is based entirely on hearsay.[8] Even a report of the commissioner appointed in a case is not *per se* evidence if he is not examined as a witness.[9] The report can be received in evidence by consent of both parties. Marks made by investigating officer on the basis of the statement made to him by eye-witness would be affected by

1. Taylor on Evidence, P. 570.
2. AIR 1982 SC 676; *Shiromani Gurudwara Prabhandhak Committee, Amritsar* v. *Mahant Kirpa Ram*, (1984) 2 SCC 614: 1984 UJ (SC) 613.
3. *Yasin Gulam Haider* v. *State of Maharashtra*, AIR 1980 SC 878: (1980) 4 SCC 600: 1980 Cr LJ 568; *Sharad Biridhichand Sarda* v. *State of Maharashtra*, AIR 1984 SC 1622: (1984) 4 SCC 116: 1984 Cr LJ 1738; *State of Uttar Pradesh* v. *Satish Chandra*, AIR 1986 SC 313: 1985 Cr LJ 1921: (1985) 2 Crimes 861.
4. *Jagroop* v. *Rex*, AIR 1952 All 276: 1952 Cr LJ 588.
5. *Balram Prasad Agrawal* v. *State of Bihar*, AIR 1997 SC 1830: 1997 Cr LJ 1640: 1997 SCC (Cri) 612; *Bhugdomal Gangaram* v. *State of Gujarat*, AIR 1983 SC 906: (1984) 1 SCC 319: 1984 SCC (Cri) 67: 1983 Cr LJ 1276; *J.D. Jain* v. *Manager of SBI*, AIR 1982 SC 673: (1982) 1 SCC 143: (1982) 1 SCWR 243.
6. *Caetano Piedade Fernandes* v. *Union Territory of Goa*, AIR 1977 SC 135: (1977) 1 SCC 707: 1977 Cr LJ 167: 1977 SCC (Cri) 154; *Chandan* v. *State of Rajasthan*, AIR 1988 SC 599: 1988 Cr LJ 842: (1988) 1 SCC 696.
7. *Rameshwar Dayal* v. *State of Uttar Pradesh*, AIR 1978 SC 1558: 1978 2 SCC 518: (1978) All LJ 1011.
8. *Judah* v. *Isolyne Shrojbashini Bose*, AIR 1945 PC 174: ILR (1945) Kar PC 351: 1945 OWN 287.
9. *Shib Singh* v. *Sridhar*, 1952 ALJ 19: 1953 Cr LJ 794: AIR 1953 All 371.

the bar in section 162 of Criminal procedure Code and the same would violate section 60.[1]

The first proviso deals with expert opinion found in treatises. The second proviso empowers court to order production of material objects.

---

1. *Tori Singh* v. *State of Uttar Pradesh*, AIR 1962 SC 399: (1962) 1 Cr LJ 469: (1962) 3 SCR 580.

CHAPTER 15
DOCUMENTARY EVIDENCE (SECTIONS 61 TO 73A)

Document, as defined in section 3, means any matter expressed or described upon any substance by means of letters, figures, marks or by more than one of those means, intended to be used, or which may be used, for the purpose of recording that matter. It includes a writing, words printed or lithographed or photographed, a map or plan and inscription on a metal plate or stone or a caricature. (*see* illustrations). Evidence means, oral evidence, electronic records and documents produced for inspection of the court. Such documents are called documentary evidence.

2. Superiority in performance and in many respects, trustworthiness of written over verbal proof has been noticed since ancient times. Oral evidence has many imperfections, namely, weak memory, imperfect recollection, and willful misrepresentation and certainty of extinction of primary source by death. The imperfections, either do not exist, or exist only in a smaller measure in documentary evidence. It is valuable where there is conflict of oral evidence, as a guide to truth. Hence, the rule of best evidence requires production of document itself or an explanation for its absence. Object for which writing is used is to perpetuate the memory of what is written down. In the face of documentary evidence, generally speaking, oral evidence has no weight.[1]

Yet Privy Council has commented on the "Propensity" of our people to forge documents.[2]

Mere marking of a document as an exhibit does not dispense with proof of its contents.[3] Execution of a document has to be proved unless such execution is admitted by the opposite party.[3]

3. The Evidence Act deals, *inter alia*, with three aspects – how the contents of documents are to be proved (Section 61-66, 59, 22), how document is to be proved as genuine (sections 67-73, 79-90) or how far and in what cases oral evidence is excluded by it (Chapter III of the Act).

4. SECTION 61:

Contents of documents may be proved either by primary or secondary evidence. Documents do not prove themselves. Witness must be examined to prove the documents and their contents, unless the same are admitted.[4]

1. AIR 1978 SC 360.
2. (1875) 3 IA 175, (1858) 7 Moo IA 148.
3. *Sait Tarajee Khimchand* v. *Yelamarti Satyam* Alias *Satteyya*, AIR 1971 SC 1865: 1971 UJ (SC) 644: (1972) 4 SCC 562; *Narbada Devi Gupta* v. *Birendra Kumar Jaiswal*, AIR 2004 SC 175: (2003) 8 SCC 745: 2003 AIR SCW 5861.
4. *Rajwati Devi* v. *Jt. Dir., Consolation*, AIR 1989 Pat 66: 1988 BLJR 698: 1988 BLJ 1069; *Oriental Insurance Co. Ltd.* v. *Premlata Shukla*, (2007) 13 SCC 476: 2007 AIR SCW 3591.

Mere proof of handwriting would not amount to proof of the contents or facts stated, if the truth thereof is in issue. Truth of contents has to be proved by examining persons who can vouchsafe the truth.[1] In the absence of such evidence, it may be hearsay evidence. Probative value is weak in the absence of such oral evidence.[2] Account books are not admissible without proof of entries by other evidence.[3] Primary evidence is the document itself. Even on proof of the contents, Court will accept it only on being satisfied about its truth. If a document has been exhibited in evidence without objection, admissibility cannot be challenged.[4] But the opposite party can impeach the contents.[5] Once the document is properly admitted, contents are also admitted in evidence, though they may not be conclusive evidence.[6]

Primary evidence is the document itself. For example, Doctor's report. The document itself must be produced.[7] Proving the document does not prove the contents.

A cyclostyle copy of a government order is not primary evidence. It may be secondary evidence under section 63(2).[8] Recitals of legal necessity in a document cannot be relied on as true, unless the truth is otherwise proved.[9]

Objection to mode of proof must be taken before the document is admitted.[10] But mere marking of the document as an exhibit does not dispense with proof.[11] When a document is marked by consent, formal proof is not required.[12]

5. SECTION 62:

Primary evidence means the document itself produced for inspection of Court. If the document is in several parts, each part is primary evidence of the document. If the document is executed in counterpart, each counterpart being executed by one or some of the parties only, each is primary evidence as against the party executing it. When a number of documents are made by one uniform process as in the case of printing, lithography, photography, each is primary

1. *Ramji Dayawala and Sons (P) Ltd.* v. *Invest Import*, AIR 1981 SC 2085: (1981) 1 SCC 80: (1981) 1 SCR 899.
2. *Bishwanath Rai* v. *Sachidanand*, AIR 1971 SC 1949: 1971 (2) Civ App J (SC) 245: (1972) 4 SCC 707.
3. *Chandrakantaben* v. *Vadilal Bapalal*, AIR 1989 SC 1269: 1989 1 APLJ (SC) 76: (1989) 2 SCC 630.
4. *Bhagat Ram* v. *Khetu Ram*, AIR 1929 PC 110; 116 Ind Cas 394; *P.C. Purushothama Reddiar* v. *S. Perumal*, AIR 1972 SC 608: (1972) 1 SCC 9: 1972 SCJ 469.
5. *Sailendra Kishore Patnaik* v. *Harekrushna Satpathy*, AIR 1978 Ori 125: 44 Cut LT 597: (1977) 2 Cut WR 779.
6. *P.C. Purushothama Reddiar* v. *S. Perumal*, AIR 1972 SC 608: (1972) 1 SCC 9: 1972 SCJ 469.
7. *Mohd. Ikram Hussain* v. *State of Uttar Pradesh*, AIR 1964 SC 1625: (1964) 1 SCWR 328: (1964) 2 Cr LJ 590: (1964) 5 SCR 86.
8. *Union of India* v. *Nirmal Singh*, AIR 1987 All 83: 1986 All WC 692: 1987 All CJ 35.
9. *Banga Chandra Dhur Biswas* v. *Jagat Kishor*, AIR 1916 PC 110: 43 IA 249: 44 IC 186 (199): 36 IC 420.
10. *P.C. Purushothama Reddiar* v. *S. Perumal*, AIR 1972 SC 608: (1972) 1 SCC 9: 1972 SCJ 469; *Gopal Das* v. *Thakurji*, AIR 1943 PC 83: ILR (1943) Kar PC 69: 1943 All LJ 292 (PC): 47 CWN 607.
11. *Sait Tarajee Khimchand* v. *Yelamarti Satyam* Alias *Satteyya*, AIR 1971 SC 1865: 1971 UJ (SC) 644: (1972) 4 SCC 562.
12. *A.V.S. Perumal* v. *Vadivelu Asari*, AIR 1986 Mad 341: (1986) 99 Mad LW 561: (1986) 1 Mad LJ 283; *Karuppanna Thevar* v. *Rajagopala Thevar*, AIR 1975 Mad 257: (1974) 2 Mad LJ 260: 87 Mad LW 777.

evidence of the contents of the rest; If they are all copies of the original they are not primary evidence of the contents of the original.

A written statement filed in court on behalf of accused is not a document produced for inspection of court.[1] An anonymous letter is not primary or secondary evidence of its contents.[2] Recitals in a decree of contents of a plaint are not secondary evidence of contents of plaint. Relevant document produced in original before court is primary evidence.[3] Documentary evidence must be formally proved.

6. Explanation (1): First part of explanation (1) refers to duplicates, triplicates etc. Each is an original and is primary evidence. (1976 I MLJ 89, AIR 1959 Orissa 113, AIR 1983 All 90). Cash memo prepared at the same time and in the same process, is not a copy, but is primary evidence. If each document is signed by both parties, each is original. If each is signed by one party only, they are counterparts and each is primary evidence against the party signing it.[4]

7. Explanation 2: Any copy of an issue of a newspaper is primary evidence. This is useful in defamation case. It is necessary to prove the original from which the article was put up, printed issue being only secondary evidence of the manuscript. Carbon copies duly made are primary evidence.[5] A tape record is primary evidence of the record.[6]

Each printed copy is primary evidence of contents of another copy. If they are all copies of the original, they are not primary evidence of contents of the original.[7] Photograph would be primary evidence, provided the person who took the photograph and developed it, speaks about it as a witness. An enlarged photograph cannot be admitted in evidence without its' negative being produced and proved by the photographer.[8]

Once a document is properly admitted, the contents are also admitted in evidence, though this may not be conclusive evidence.[9] Probative value has to be judged.[10]

8. SECTION 63:

Secondary evidence means and includes five types of evidence referred to in the section. The first few are documents, namely, certified copies, copies from the original made by mechanical process which ensures accuracy and copies compared with such copies, copies made from or compared with original and counterparts as against parties who do not execute them and the last is oral

1. *Emperor* v. *Tuti Babu*, AIR 1946 Pat 373: 25 Pat 33: 47 Cr LJ 937.
2. *Ayyamperumal Pillai* v. *Emperor*, AIR 1925 Mad 879.
3. *State of Andhra Pradesh* v. *T.G. Lakshmainah Setty and Sons*, AIR 1994 SC 237.
4. *Kruttivasa Padhy* v. *Malati Padhani*, AIR 1959 Ori 113; *Katihar Jute Mills Ltd.* v. *Calcutta Match Works (India) Ltd.*, AIR 1958 Pat 133.
5. *Prithi Chand* v. *State of Himachal Pradesh*, AIR 1989 SC 702: 1989 CAR 56: 1989 Cr LR 235: (1989) 1 Crimes 384: (1989) 1 SCC 432: (1989) 1 SCR 123: (1989) 1 SCALE 74: JT 1989 (1) SC 106: 1989 Cr LJ 841.
6. *N. Sri Ram Reddy* v. *V.V. Giri*, AIR 1971 SC 1162: (1971) 1 SCR 399: (1970) 2 SCC 340.
7. *Ramachandra* v. *Emperor*, AIR 1930 Lah 371; *T. Shivshankaram* v. *Agali Narayana Rao*, AIR 1937 Mad 807.
8. *Laxman Ganpati Khot* v. *Anusuyabai*, AIR 1976 Bom 264: 1977 Mah LJ 68.
9. *P.C. Purushothama Reddiar* v. *S. Perumal*, AIR 1972 SC 608: (1972) 1 SCC 9: 1972 SCJ 469.
10. *State of Bihar* v. *Radha Krishna Singh*, AIR 1983 SC 684: (1983) 1 SCALE 789: (1983) 2 SCR 808: (1983) 3 SCC 118: 1983 Cur Civ LJ (SC) 273.

evidence of contents given by a witness who has himself seen it. This Section is exhaustive of the kinds of admissible secondary evidence.[1] But in AIR 1986 All 302 held it was not exhaustive, because of the word "includes". A photo of an original is secondary evidence, though the two have not been compared, if it is proved that the thing photographed was the original. A copy, compared with a copy of a letter, made by a copying machine is secondary evidence of the contents of the letter, if it is shown that the copy was made from the original. A copy transcribed from a copy, but afterwards compared with the original is secondary evidence, but the copy not so compared is not secondary evidence of the original, although the copy from which it was transcribed was compared with the original. The five kinds of secondary evidence are exhaustive. A piece of written paper cannot be admitted as secondary evidence by calling it a draft, unless there is evidence that it was compared with the original.[2]

Newspaper reports are not themselves evidence of the contents thereof and are not admissible unless original manuscript is produced and proved by concerned person.[3] A news item without any further proof by any witness of what actually happened is of no value.[4] Newspaper report of a speech is hearsay.[5]

"Certificate" of birth based on entries in Register is not admissible".[6] Such a certificate is not a "certified copy". Correctness of a certified copy will be presumed under section 79. A purported certified copy not issued as per the requirements of law is not a certified copy.

If the original is found to be inadmissible for want of proof, secondary evidence is barred. An admission cannot be used as secondary evidence of a document inadmissible for want of stamp or registration or is found to be forgery.

Certified copy is a copy signed and certified as true by the officer to whose custody the original is entrusted. *See* sections 76 to 78. An ordinary copy of sale deed is not secondary evidence.[7] *See* sections 79, 86 and C.P.C. Order XI, rule 19. A copy of a copy is not a certified copy.[8] Mere registration is not proof of execution.

9. Mechanical Process (Clause 2) must ensure accuracy of the copy. *See* section 62, explanation (2). Illustration (a) must be read with first part of clause (2). Illustration (b) must be read with second part of clause (2). A copy of a copy is admissible as secondary evidence if it has been compared with the original

---

1. *Commissioner of Income-tax* v. *Taj Mahal Hotel, Secunderabad*, AIR 1972 SC 168: (1972) 1 SCR 168: 1972 (2) SCJ 673; *Girdhar Prasad* v. *Ambika Prasad Thakur*, AIR 1969 Pat 218: 1969 Pat LJR 82: 1969 BLJR 1096.
2. *Girdhar Prasad* v. *Ambika Prasad Thakur*, AIR 1969 Pat 218: 1969 Pat LJR 82: 1969 BLJR 1096.
3. *A. Devegowda* v. *Puttanna*, AIR 1994 SC 1733; *Borgaram Deuri* v. *Premodhar Bora*, AIR 2004 SC 1386: 2004 AIR SCW 292: (2004) 2 SCC 227.
4. *Samant N. Balakrishna* v. *George Fernandez*, AIR 1969 SC 1201: (1969) 3 SCR 603: (1970) 1 SCA 376.
5. *Laxmi Raj Shetty* v. *State of Tamil Nadu*, AIR 1988 SC 1274: (1988) 3 SCC 319: 1988 SCC (Cri) 633: (1988) 2 Crimes 107.
6. *Harendra Nath* v. *Suprova*, AIR 1989 Cal 120: (1988) 93 Cal WN 102: (1989) 1 Hindu LR 228.
7. *Kalyan Singh, London Trained Cutter, Johri Bazar, Jaipur* v. *Chhoti*, AIR 1990 SC 396: (1989) 2 SCALE 1238: (1989) 2 SCR 356: (1990) 1 SCC 266: 1990 RD 198.
8. *Adiraja Ariga* v. *K. Beeranna Rai*, AIR 1957 Mad 14: 69 Mad LW 700: 1956 2 Mad LJ 218.

or if this copy is taken from the original by a mechanical process.[1] Copy of a copy not compared with the original is not secondary evidence of the original. See illustration (d).

"Photographs properly verified on oath by a person able to speak to their accuracy are generally admissible to prove identity of persons etc. as it existed at a particular time. The person who look the photograph should be called unless his evidence is dispensed with by consent"[2] X-ray photograph is admissible in evidence to determine the extent of physical injury or disease provided it is proved that the photograph is a photograph of the person injured or diseased. The person who took the photograph should be called, unless his evidence is dispensed with by consent. (ibid). A Photostat copy is receivable in evidence if the other conditions of the section are satisfied.[3] But, it should have been compared with the original. But the copy should be shown to be genuine and signature must be admitted or proved. Where genuineness of a tape recording and identity of voices heard in the tape are not in dispute, the tape can be legal evidence for corroborating the evidence of the person who overheard the conversation.[4] If a statement is relevant, an accurate tape recording of the statement is also relevant and admissible, the place and accuracy of the recording being proved by competent witnesses and voices being identified.[5] But since the recording can be erased and reused, the evidence must be received with caution and court must be satisfied that the recording was not tampered with.[6] Tape itself is primary and direct evidence of the matter recorded; it can be used also for corroboration under section 156 and contradiction under section 145, impeaching credit under section 155 and to test his veracity under section 146.[7] The conditions for admissibility have been prescribed by the Supreme Court in AIR 1986 SC 3.[8]

Clause (3) must be read with illustration (c). Making of the copy or comparison with the original must be proved.[9] Clause (3) prescribes two alternatives, being made from the original or being compared with the original.[10] Making from the

---

1. *Prithi Chand* v. *State of Himachal Pradesh*, AIR 1989 SC 702: 1989 CAR 56: 1989 Cr LR 235: (1989) 1 Crimes 384: (1989) 1 SCC 432: (1989) 1 SCR 123: (1989) 1 SCALE 74: JT 1989 (1) SC 106: 1989 Cr LJ 841.
2. Halsburys Laws of England, 4th Edition Volume 17 – P 158.
3. *Government of Andhra Pradesh* v. *Karri Chinna Venkata Reddy*, AIR 1994 SC 591: 1995 Supp (1) SCC 462.
4. *Babu Lal* v. *State of Uttar Pradesh*, AIR 1964 SC 725: (1964) 1 SCWR 180: (1964) 1 Cr LJ 555; *Mahabir Prasad Verma* v. *Dr. Surinder Kaur*, AIR 1982 SC 1043: (1982) 2 SCC 258: 1982 (1) SCJ 362.
5. *Yusufalli Esmail Nagree* v. *State of Maharashtra*, AIR 1968 SC 147: 1968 Cr LJ 103: 1967 SCR 720: (1968) 1 SCJ 511: 70 Bom LR 76.
6. *Ziyauddin Burhanuddin Bukhari* v. *Brijmohan Ramdass Mehra*, AIR 1975 SC 1788: 1975 SCR 281: (1976) 2 SCC 17; *R.M. Malkani* v. *State of Maharashtra*, (1973) 1 SCC 471: 1973 Cr LJ 228: AIR 1973 SC 157: (1972) 2 SCWR 776; *C.K. Narayana Chary* v. *Pothepalli Ashanna*, AIR 1986 SC 317: (1986) 1 SCC 9: (1986) 1 Supreme 232.
7. *N. Sri Ram Reddy* v. *V.V. Giri*, AIR 1971 SC 1162: (1971) 1 SCR 399: (1970) 2 SCC 340.
8. *C.K. Narayana Chary* v. *Pothepalli Ashanna*, AIR 1986 SC 317: (1986) 1 SCC 9: (1986) 1 Supreme 232.
9. *Narendra Chandra De* v. *Rajendra Chandra Chanda*, AIR 1941 Cal 506: 197 IC 45: 73 Cr LJ 159; *Suganchand* v. *Balchand*, AIR 1957 Raj 89: 1957 Raj LW 31: ILR (1957) 7 Raj 204.
10. *Harijiwan Sahu* v. *Jairam Sahu*, AIR 1989 Pat 96.

original and comparison, cumulatively, are not necessary. When a document is an accurate or true reproduction of the original, it would be a copy.[1]

Reading of clauses (2) and (3) as well as illustrations (b) and (c) together, it appears that copy of a copy is admissible if it has been compared with the original or a copy of the original taken by means of a mechanical process.[2] Certified copy of a registered sale deed is admissible in evidence, but to prove the transaction, the person connected with the sale deed requires to be examined as witness.[3] A copy of a copy is not admissible when the original itself was not accounted for satisfactorily.[4] Copy of a copy which was kept in the registration office and signed and sealed by the officer concerned as required under section 57(5) of the Registration Act is admissible for proving the contents of the document.[5]

A copy of deposition in the printed record of High Court is a copy of a copy and without evidence of comparison with the original, it is inadmissible.[6] Abstracts of document or deposition in a judgment is not secondary evidence.[7] If the judgment sets out the document fully, it is a copy of a copy made from the original and admissible.[8]

10. As an example of counterpart referred in clause (4), consider Pattah and Qabuliat.[9] Counterfoils maintained by the landlord of rent receipts issued to the tenant containing self-serving recitals are not admissible against the tenant and they cannot be called counterparts.[10]

11. Under clause (5), the witness, who gives oral account of contents of a document, must have seen the original.[11] Witness cannot be a person unable to read.[12] It is not sufficient that the document had been read over to him.[9] A newspaper report of a speech is not admissible. The speaker or listener or a reporter must be examined as a witness.[13] Newspaper report is only hearsay.[14] The witness must have read the document.

1. *Hindustan Construction Company Ltd.* v. *Union of India*, AIR 1967 SC 526: (1967) 1 SCR 843: 1967 (2) SCJ 219.
2. *Hanuman Bax Agarwalla* v. *Bibhuti Prosad Singh*, AIR 1950 Assam 17; *Krishna Subala Bose* v. *Dhanapati Dutta*, AIR 1957 Cal 59; *Rajendra Narayana Singh* v. *Bihari Lal*, AIR 1932 Pat 157: ILR 11 Pat 569.
3. *A.P. State Road Transport Corporation, Hyderabad* v. *P. Venkaiah*, AIR 1997 SC 2600: (1997) 10 SCC 128: 1997 AIR SCW 2556.
4. *Raja Mahadeva Royal Y.B.* v. *Raja Virabasava Chikka Royal*, AIR 1948 PC 114: 1948 ALJ 216: 50 BLR 638: 61 MLW 454: ILR 1949 M 72.
5. *Suganchand* v. *Balchand*, AIR 1957 Raj 89: 1957 Raj LW 31: ILR (1957) 7 Raj 204.
6. *Alapati Narasimham* v. *Ailoori Babu Rao*, AIR 1939 Mad 40: ILR 1939 Mad 333; *K.S. Ganapathi Aiyar* v. *Jokharayappa Mudaliar*, AIR 1929 Mad 187.
7. *Hafiz Mohammad Suleman* v. *Hari Ram*, AIR 1937 Lah 370: 39 Pun LR 602; *(Nanduri) Saradamba* v. *(Parakala) Pattabhiramayya*, AIR 1931 Mad 207.
8. *Kundan Bibi* v. *Magan Lal*, AIR 1932 All 710.
9. AIR 1927 PC 16.
10. *Idandas* v. *Anant Ramchandra*, AIR 1982 SC 127: (1982) 1 SCC 27: 1982 MHLJ 328.
11. AIR 1927 PC 16; *Katihar Jute Mills Ltd.* v. *Calcutta Match Works (India) Ltd.*, AIR 1958 Pat 133.
12. *Ramkrishna Panda* v. *Arjuno Padhano*, AIR 1963 Ori 29.
13. *Khilumal* v. *Arjun Das*, AIR 1959 Raj 280: ILR (1959) 9 Raj 524: 22 Ele LR 404; AIR 1961 Mys 706.
14. *Laxmi Raj Shetty* v. *State of Tamil Nadu*, AIR 1988 SC 1274: (1988) 3 SCC 319: 1988 SCC (Cri) 633: (1988) 2 Crimes 107.

Tape recorded conversion can be used only as corroborative evidence. Conversion must be proved by a party thereto or a person who heard it.[1] In *N. Sri Ram Reddy* v. *V.V. Giri*,[2] it was held that the tape itself to be primary evidence. But the time, place and accuracy of the recording must be proved and voice must be identified.[3] Court must be satisfied that the tape was not tampered with.[4] In several countries, Videotapes have been held to be admissible.[5] Video recording of a confession is admissible if the accused look part voluntarily and it had been shown to him as soon as practicable after it was completed with the opportunity to make and have recorded any comments which he wish to make of the film.[6] Copy means a full reproduction.[7]

Certified copy of sale deed is admissible.[8] Section 64 does not strictly apply to M.V.A. Tribunals.[9]

12. SECTION 64:

Documents must be proved by primary evidence except in cases covered by the succeeding sections. This section reflects the rule of best evidence. What is in writing shall be proved by the writing itself. The principle is that it is risky to rely on dishonest or poor recollection of witnesses and the court must have occasion to see the entire contents of the document. It is open to the other party to impeach the contents.[10] Mere marking of a document does not dispense with proof.[11] This section applies to all writing. This section has to be read along with sections 61, 62 and 65 to 67.

This section is distinct from section 91. Section 91 deals with matters which the parties have put in writing or which the law requires to be in writing. Section 64 only states that if it is desired to prove the contents of document, the document itself must be produced. Where a document is marked on admission without any reservation, the contents are also to be taken as admitted.[12] Mere marking of a document, by itself, does not distance with the proof.[11]

---

1. *Mahabir Prasad Verma* v. *Dr. Surinder Kaur*, AIR 1982 SC 1043: (1982) 2 SCC 258: 1982 (1) SCJ 362.
2. AIR 1971 SC 1162: (1971) 1 SCR 399: (1970) 2 SCC 340
3. *Yusufalli Esmail Nagree* v. *State of Maharashtra*, AIR 1968 SC 147: 1968 Cr LJ 103: 1967 SCR 720: (1968) 1 SCJ 511: 70 Bom LR 76; *N. Sri Ram Reddy* v. *V.V. Giri*, AIR 1971 SC 1162: (1971) 1 SCR 399: (1970) 2 SCC 340; *D.R. Punjab Montogomery Transport Co.* v. *Raghuvanshi Pvt. Ltd.*, AIR 1983 Cal 343: (1982) 86 Cal WN 759: (1982) 2 Cal LJ 74.
4. *Yusufalli Esmail Nagree* v. *State of Maharashtra*, AIR 1968 SC 147: 1968 Cr LJ 103: 1967 SCR 720: (1968) 1 SCJ 511: 70 Bom LR 76; *K.S. Mohan* v. *Sandhya Mohan*, AIR 1993 Mad 59: 1993 Marri LJ 366.
5. 1988 III All ER 138, 1961 III All ER 88.
6. 1988 III All ER 138.
7. *Hindustan Construction Company Ltd.* v. *Union of India*, AIR 1967 SC 526: (1967) 1 SCR 843: 1967 (2) SCJ 219.
8. *Nani Bai* v. *Gita Bai Kom Rama Gunge*, AIR 1958 SC 706: 1958 SCJ 925: 1959 SCR 479; *Kalyan Singh, London Trained Cutter, Johri Bazar, Jaipur* v. *Chhoti*, AIR 1990 SC 396: (1989) 2 SCALE 1238: (1989) 2 SCR 356: (1990) 1 SCC 266: 1990 RD 198.
9. ILR 1973 KAR 339.
10. *Sailendra Kishore Patnaik* v. *Harekrushna Satpathy*, AIR 1978 Ori 125: 44 Cut LT 597: (1977) 2 Cut WR 779.
11. *Sait Tarajee Khimchand* v. *Yelamarti Satyam* Alias *Satteyya*, AIR 1971 SC 1865: 1971 UJ (SC) 644: (1972) 4 SCC 562.
12. *P.C. Purushothama Reddiar* v. *S. Perumal*, AIR 1972 SC 608: (1972) 1 SCC 9: 1972 SCJ 469.

Question of relevancy is a question of law which can be raised even in appeal. Question of proof of a document is a question of procedure and can be waived.[1] When the question is one of forgery, the document has to be produced.[2]

Where the whole or part of the document is missing, secondary evidence is allowable.[3]

Where a sale deed is required to be brought on record, the execution of the sale deed has to be proved and the original sale deed is required to be produced by way of primary evidence.[4] Where neither the sale deed nor it's certified copy is produced, mere oral evidence of the transaction is not admissible.[5] Where the correctness of a document is in issue, it should be proved by examining the executant or the attester or the scribe or anyone who has personal knowledge about the contents. Where a party desires to rely on an entry in an account book, the original account book must be produced as primary evidence in proof of the entry.[6] Where books of account are the sole evidence of payment of money, production of mere extracts of accounts would not be sufficient.[7] Any document must be able to stand the test of genuineness. Oral admissions of contents of documents are not relevant, unless the party proposing to prove them shows that he is entitled to adduce secondary evidence of the contents of the document.[8] The rule of exclusion of secondary evidence where primary evidence is available will not be insisted upon where no objection is taken by the opposite party.[9] Where a party has admitted the contents of a document in his pleadings or during the course of the proceedings, the opposite party can rest on such admission and need not produce and prove the original document.[10] Where a document is marked by consent, it means the party consenting is willing to waive his right to have the document proved.[11] But such consent does not have the effect of dispensing with the proof of the truth or otherwise of the contents. Where the original autopsy certificate was not available, the register containing the original entries regarding the autopsy could be taken not of.[12] An uncertified carbon copy of a autopsy certificate could not be marked; it would not come within the purview of any other clause of section 65 and any attempt to get it proved

---

1. *Ajjarapu Subbarao* v. *Pulla Venkata Rama Rao,* AIR 1964 AP 53.
2. *Sarala Sundari Dassya* v. *Dinabandhu Roy Brajaraf Saha (Firm),* AIR 1944 PC 11.
3. AIR 1963 HP 234; *Mohd. Ikram Hussain* v. *State of Uttar Pradesh,* AIR 1964 SC 1625: (1964) 1 SCWR 328: (1964) 2 Cr LJ 590: (1964) 5 SCR 86.
4. *Cement Corporation of India Ltd.* v. *Purya,* (2004) 8 SCC 270: AIR 2004 SC 4830: 2004 AIR SCW 5534; *Church of South India Trust Assn* v. *Land Acquistion Officer & Tehsildar,* (2006) 9 SCC 676.
5. *Chintaman* v. *State of Maharashtra,* AIR 1997 SC 448: 1996 AIR SCW 3832: (1996) 10 SCC 36.
6. *Paras Nath Hira Lal* v. *Kishan Lal Chuni Lal,* AIR 1965 All 189: 1964 All LJ 738.
7. *Trimbak Narayan Hardas* v. *Babulal Motaji,* AIR 1973 SC 1363: (1973) 2 SCC 154.
8. *Murarka Properties Private Limited* v. *Beharilal Murarka,* AIR 1978 SC 300: (1978) 1 SCC 159: (1978) 2 SCR 261.
9. *Alacs Finanz Ltd.* v. *Oksh Technologies,* AIR 2005 Del 376: 2006 (3) Bank Cas 283: 2005 (2) CurCC 483.
10. AIR 1926 All 741; *M.P. Rajya Beej Avam Farm Vikas Nigam* v. *Shri Durga Transport Service, Banapura, District, Hoshangabad, M.P,* AIR 1996 MP 208: 1996 (2) Civ LJ 829: 1996 MPLJ 497.
11. *A.V.S. Perumal* v. *Vadivelu Asari,* AIR 1986 Mad 341: (1986) 99 Mad LW 561: (1986) 1 Mad LJ 283.
12. *Shakila Abdul Gafar Khan* v. *Vasant Raghunath Dhoble,* AIR 2003 SC 4567: 2003 Cr LJ 4548: 2003 AIR SCW 5343.

through a clerk when the doctor who prepared the certificate is available to give evidence could not be allowed.[1]

Regarding proof of a document, objection has to be taken at the time when the document is tendered in evidence and cannot be raised at any subsequent stage.[2] Yet mere marking of a document cannot preclude the opposite party from raising appropriate objection later.

Section 64 deals with the mode of proof of the document and the contents thereof. Section 91 requires that in circumstances mentioned therein, no oral evidence at all can be given in proof of the terms of the contract etc. except by tendering the document itself.

13. SECTION 65:

Secondary evidence of the existence, condition and contents of documents may be given in the several contingencies referred to in clauses (a) to (g) of the section. Section 65 constitutes an exception to Section 64. Conditions in section 65 must be satisfied before secondary evidence can be given.[3] It must be shown that there is or was a document in existence capable of being proved by secondary evidence and proper foundation is laid for reception of the same.[4] This section applies to Civil, Revenue and Criminal cases.[5] Oral evidence of registration of firm is not admissible.[6] Objection has to be raised at the time of marking the document. Objection can also be raised in the appellate court.[7]

Clauses (a) to (g) of section 65 are:

(a) When the original is shown or appears to be in the possession or power—

- of the person against whom the document is sought to be proved; or
- of any person out of reach of, or not subject to the process of the court, or
- of any person legally bound to produce it,

And when, after the notice mentioned in section 66, such person does not produce it:

(b) When the existence, condition or contents of the original have been proved to be admitted in writing by the person against whom it is proved or by his representative in interest;

---

1. *Vijendar* v. *State of Delhi*, 1997 SCC (Cri) 857.
2. *Gopal Das* v. *Thakurji*, AIR 1943 PC 83: ILR (1943) Kar PC 69: 1943 All LJ 292 (PC): 47 CWN 607; *Alacs Finanz Ltd.* v. *Oksh Technologies*, AIR 2005 Del 376: 2006 (3) Bank Cas 283: 2005 (2) CurCC 483.
3. *Anand Bihari Lal* v. *Dinshaw & Co.*, AIR 1946 PC 24: 1945 FCR 90; AIR 1933 Pat 468; *Phiroze Temulji Anklesaria* v. *H.C. Vashistha*, AIR 1980 Bom 9; AIR 1925 Mad 345; *Jaldu Ananta Raghuram Arya* v. *Rajah Bommadevara Naga Chayadevamma*, AIR 1958 AP 418: 1958 Andh LT 440.
4. *Roman Catholic Mission* v. *State of Madras*, AIR 1966 SC 1457: 1967 (1) SCJ 605; *Rajeswari Amma* v. *Joseph*, (1995) 1 SCC 71; *Ashok Dulichand* v. *Madhavlal Dube*, AIR 1975 SC 1748: (1975) 4 SCC 664: (1976) 1 SCR 246: 1975 UJ (SC) 601; *Sital Das* v. *Sant Ram*, AIR 1954 SC 606.
5. *Chandranath* v. *Tusharika*, 1958 SCJ 874: AIR 1958 SC 521: 1959 SCR 226; AIR 1933 All 498; *S.H. Jhabawala* v. *Emperor*, 145 IC 481: AIR 1933 All 690: 34 Cr LJ 967.
6. 1975 I KAR LJ 461.
7. *Dayamathi Bai* v. *K.M. Shaffi*, (2004) 7 SCC 107: 2004 AIR SCW 4419: AIR 2004 SC 4082.

(c) When the original has been destroyed or lost or when the party offering evidence of its' contents cannot, for any other reason not arising from his own default or neglect, produce it in reasonable time;

(d) When the original is of such a nature as not to be easily movable;

(e) When the original is public document within the meaning of section 74;

(f) When the original is a document of which a certified copy is permitted by this Act, or by any other law in force in India to be given in evidence;

(g) When the originals consist of numerous accounts or other documents which cannot conveniently be examined in court and the fact to be proved is the general result of the whole collection.

The purpose of the section is to enable proof of existence, condition or contents of a document by secondary evidence, in the unavoidable absence of the best evidence.[1] A Photostat copy of a registered document cannot be received as secondary evidence.[2] When the original document filed by a party to prove title is insufficiently stamped and unregistered and hence inadmissible, no secondary evidence could be allowed to prove title.[3] Where a party could not produce the original option of a teacher regarding the P.F. scheme but was able to produce sufficient materials to show that the teacher had opted for a certain scheme, such materials could not be ignored.[4] Where both the lessor and lesser denied being in possession of the lease deed, photo copies of the original could be received.[5]

14. The basic premise on which section 65 rests is that the original document is not available for one of the reasons mentioned in the section. It is a general and well-known rule that no secondary evidence of a document can be received until an excuse such as the law deems sufficient, is given for non-production of the primary evidence.[6] Unless the conditions laid down in one of the seven clauses of section is satisfied, no secondary evidence in liew of primary evidence can be received.[7] The question of invoking the provision enabling secondary evidence is not one of fact, but of procedure.[8] Before invoking the provisions of this section, foundation must be laid for reception of secondary evidence by fulfilling the conditions in one or the other of the seven clauses.[9] Opportunity should be given to the party concerned to lay such a foundation.[10]

1. Halsbury, 4th Edition, Volume 17, Para 9.
2. *Jupudi Kesava Rao* v. *Pulavarthi Venkata Subbarao*, AIR 1971 SC 1070: (1971) 1 SCC 545: 1972 (1) SCJ 643: (1971) 3 SCR 590; *Hariom Agrawal* v. *Prakash Chand Malviya*, (2007) 8 SCC 514: AIR 2008 SC 166: 2007 AIR SCW 6368.
3. *Jupudi Kesava Rao* v. *Pulavarthi Venkata Subbarao*, AIR 1971 SC 1070: (1971) 1 SCC 545: 1972 (1) SCJ 643: (1971) 3 SCR 590; *Hariom Agrawal* v. *Prakash Chand Malviya*, (2007) 8 SCC 514: AIR 2008 SC 166: 2007 AIR SCW 6368; *Shankar Lal* v. *Civil Judge (Jr. Division), Shahpura*, AIR 2006 Raj 187: 2006 (2) Raj LR 274: 2006 (3) Raj LW 2049.
4. *D. Dwarakanatha Reddy* v. *Chaitanya Bharathi Educational Society*, (2007) 6 SCC 13: AIR 2007 SC 1794: 2007 AIR SCW 2997.
5. *Bharat Sewa Sansthan* v. *U.P. Electronic Corpn. Ltd.*, (2007) 7 SCC 737: AIR 2007 SC 2961: 2007 AIR SCW 5399.
6. Best on Evidence, 8th Edition P416.
7. *Ram Lal Dutt Sarkar* v. *Dhirendra Nath*, AIR 1943 PC 24: 70 Ind App 18; *Roman Catholic Mission* v. *State of Madras*, AIR 1966 SC 1457: 1967 (1) SCJ 605.
8. *Raja Jagadish Chandra Deo Dhabal Deb* v. *Gour Hari Mahato*, AIR 1936 PC 258: 164 Ind Cas 17: 1936 All WR 717.
9. *Sital Das* v. *Sant Ram*, AIR 1954 SC 606.
10. *Ramchandra Sakharam Mahajan* v. *Damodar Trimbak Tanksale*, AIR 2007 SC 2577: 2007 AIR SCW 4583: 2007 (5) AIR Bom R 183.

15. CLAUSE (A): This clause deals with three situations under which secondary evidence can be given. Requirement of "the original is shown or appears to be in the possession or power" must be shown by some evidence or circumstances arising from the record itself, as otherwise secondary evidence will not be allowed. Under this clause, there are three sub-clauses.

Possession of or power over the document must be of persons falling under two categories, namely:

(i) person against whom the document is sought to be proved, *i.e.*, the opposite party.[1] Any person out of reach of, or not subject to, process of the court, *i.e.*, witness to be summoned to produce the document,

(ii) Any person legally bound to produce the document. This category has created some controversy. The "person" referred to cannot obviously be a party to litigation as he is covered by category (i); he can only be a third person. On a plain reading, the clause relates to a situation where a witness summoned to produce the document unjustifiably withholds it. But if the witness objects to do so and the court uphold the objection, such a document is obviously not a document which the witness is legally bound to produce it. Ratanlal and Dhirajlal have suggested that it may be, however, that the court will admit secondary evidence in such a case upon general principles of the English Law and the decisions of English Courts.[2]

Applicability of clause (a) is subject to the condition that "such person" referred to in clause (a) does not produce the document even after notice mentioned in section 66. The purpose of the notice is to secure the production of the original document.[3] Where in-spite of the notice, the person concerned does not produce the document referred to in the notice, secondary evidence could be adduced.[4]

16. CLAUSE (B): This clause has to be read with section 22 of the Act, according to which, oral admissions of the contents of a document are not relevant unless and until the party proposing to prove them shows that he is entitled to give secondary evidence of the contents of such a document.[5] Where in a letter the opposite party admitted the existence and contents of a document, secondary evidence could be adduced.[6] Such secondary evidence could be received as genuine if the existence of the document is admitted.[7] For clause (b) "admission" is a precondition. This clause will not apply if the original document though required to be in stamp paper and registered, was in stamp paper but not registered.

1. *Brij Bhushan* v. *State of Delhi*, AIR 1950 SC 129: 1950 SCR 605: 1950 Cr LJ 1525; *Chandranath* v. *Tusharika*, 1958 SCJ 874: AIR 1958 SC 521: 1959 SCR 226; *T. Mohan* v. *Kannammal*, (2002) 10 SCC 82.
2. Ratanlal and Dhirajlal Law of Evidence, 23rd Edition, Page 930.
3. *Antonio Dias Caldeira* v. *Frederick Augustus Gray*, AIR 1936 PC 15.
4. *Brij Bhushan* v. *State of Delhi*, AIR 1950 SC 129: 1950 SCR 605: 1950 Cr LJ 1525.
5. Law of Evidence by Ratanlal and Dhirajlal, 23rd Edition, Page 932 and *Biswambar Singh* v. *State of Orissa*, AIR 1954 SC 139: 1954 SCJ 219: 1954 SCR 842: ILR 1954 Cut 398; AIR 1949 All 677.
6. *Biswambar Singh* v. *State of Orissa*, AIR 1954 SC 139: 1954 SCJ 219: 1954 SCR 842: ILR 1954 Cut 398.
7. *T. Mohan* v. *Kannammal*, (2002) 10 SCC 82.

17. CLAUSE (C): This clause is in two parts. The two parts are independent of each other. The first part relates to a case where the original document has been destroyed or lost. The second part applies when a party offering evidence of contents of a document cannot, for any other reason, (*i.e.*, other than the reason given in the first part) not arising from his default or neglect, produce the original within a reasonable time.

Where a party admitted that he did not preserve the original, the opposite party can give secondary evidence.[1] There must be evidence that the original existed and its' destruction or loss after search at appropriate places.[2] Where records of the registrar had been destroyed and a party produced a copy prepared from a certified copy which the defendant had produced in a former suit but which was not available as court records also had been destroyed, the copy produced by plaintiff was held admissible.[3] Where a person in whose custody a document was alleged to be, deposed to it's loss or that he was not in possession of the document, unless there is some motive suggested for his being untruthful, such evidence should be accepted as sufficient to allow secondary evidence.[4] Evidence, a person deposing to the loss of the document in his custody is sufficient. In this connection, illustration (b) to section 104 of the Act has relevance. Where a document has not been seen for many years, the statement by person alleged to be in possession of it to the effect that it was never with him nor was it with him then, is sufficient.[5]

Even where secondary evidence is allowed, the execution of the original document has to be proved as required by section 67 read with section 47.

In criminal cases, even if original case diary statements were not produced as required in section 173(5)(b) of Criminal Procedure Code, section 65 is wide enough to enable the accused to use the copies delivered to him, as secondary evidence for the purpose of contradicting witnesses.[6] On proof of loss of original declaration, secondary evidence can be allowed.[7] Where the original FIR written by a police constable was missing and the constable proved the carbon copy and also the loss of the original, the copy would be admissible as secondary evidence.

18. CLAUSE (D):

This clause relates to case where the original is not easily movable, that is, physically impossible or highly inconvenient. Examples are fixed tablets, monuments, gravestones, survey marks, notices fixed on boards etc., any secondary evidence is allowable.

---

1. *Pearey Lal* v. *Nanak Chand*, AIR 1948 PC 108: 1948 ALJ 231: 61 MLW 437: 52 CWN 785: 50 BLR 643.
2. *Aher Rama Gova* v. *State of Gujarat*, AIR 1979 SC 1567: 1979 Cr LJ 1081: (1979) 4 SCC 500; *Harijiwan Sahu* v. *Jairam Sahu*, AIR 1989 Pat 96; ILR 6 Cal 720 (PC).
3. *Bibi Aisha* v. *Bihar Subai Sunni Majlis Avaqaf*, AIR 1969 SC 253: (1969) 1 SCR 417: (1969) 1 SCJ 347: 1969 All LJ 290.
4. *Jhtisham Ali* v. *Jamna Prashad*, AIR 1922 PC 56: 48 IA 365: 64 IC 299; *Basant Singh* v. *Brij Raj Saran Singh*, AIR 1935 PC 132: 62 IA 180: 57 A 494: 156 IC 864 (PC).
5. *Basant Singh* v. *Brij Raj Saran Singh*, AIR 1935 PC 132: 62 IA 180: 57 A 494: 156 IC 864 (PC).
6. *State of Kerala* v. *Raju*, 1982 Cr LJ 304.
7. *Aher Rama Gova* v. *State of Gujarat*, AIR 1979 SC 1567: 1979 Cr LJ 1081: (1979) 4 SCC 500.

19. CLAUSE (E):

Certified copy of a public document is admissible. In the case of public document, no other kind of secondary evidence is admissible. Section 74 indicates what are public documents.

The intention is to protect public documents from danger of exposure, or loss by constant production. An uncertified copy is inadmissible.[1] Other kind of secondary evidence can be allowed if the case falls under the other clauses.

20. CLAUSE (F):

Certified copy is the only secondary evidence admissible in case of documents of which certified copy is permitted by this or any other law (Bankers Book Evidence Act, Power of Attorney Act, Order XI rule 19 C.P.C.), section 86 is an illustration.

This clause does not dispense with proof of contents of the original.[2] If the original of such a document is lost or destroyed and hence no certified copy can be obtained, clause (c) is also attracted. Clause (f) does not control clause (a).[3]

21. CLAUSE (G):

This clause deals with cases where there are too many documents, and it is not convenient to the court to examine the mass of documents. The documents must be available. Court can call for the documents.[4] The underlying object is to save public time. Secondary evidence is evidence as to the general result of the documents given by the person who has examined them and is skilled in such examination. Example, Chartered Accountant in case of Voluminous Accounts.[5] In L.A. case, if there are numerous sale deeds, all examined by an expert, he can give evidence about the general result of his examination.[6] Last four paragraphs of the section indicate the kind of secondary evidence to be given in the difference contingences.

clauses (a), (c), (d)	– any kind of secondary evidence
clause (b)	– written admission
Clause (e), (f)	– certified copy and no other kind
clause (g)	– evidence of general result of the document by any person who has examined them and who is skilled in the examination of such document.

22. SECTION 65A: The contents of electronic records may be proved in accordance with the provisions of Section 65B.

23. SECTION 65B: Any information contained in an electronic record which is printed on paper, stored, recorded or copied in optical or magnetic media produced by a computer (*i.e.*, computer output) shall be deemed to be also a document, if the conditions mentioned in this section are satisfied in relation

1. *Kalyan Singh* v. *Chhoti*, AIR 1973 Raj 263: 1973 Raj LW 473: ILR (1973) 23 Raj 634.
2. *Bhaskar Sahu* v. *Anama Swara*, AIR 1987 Ori 138: (1986) 2 Ori LR 410; *Subudhi Padhan* v. *Raghu Bhuvan*, AIR 1962 Ori 40.
3. *Bibi Aisha* v. *Bihar Subai Sunni Majlis Avaqaf*, AIR 1969 SC 253: (1969) 1 SCR 417: (1969) 1 SCJ 347: 1969 All LJ 290.
4. *Kishan Lal* v. *Sohanlal*, AIR 1955 Raj 45: 1955 Raj LW 338: ILR (1955) 5 Raj 191.
5. *Krishna Dayal* v. *E.*, AIR 1946 All 227; AIR 1924 All 625; *Sher Muhammad* v. *Dost Muhammad*, AIR 1925 Lah 231: 78 Ind Cas 451.
6. *Collector, Raigarh* v. *Chaturbhuj Panda*, AIR 1964 MP 196: 1964 MPLJ 220: ILR 1963 MP 887.

to the information and computer in question and shall be admissible in any proceedings, without further proof or production of the original, as evidence of any contents of the original or of any fact stated therein of which direct evidence would be admissible.

(2) The conditions referred to in sub-section (1) in respect of a computer output shall be the following, namely—

(a) the computer output containing the information was produced by the computer during the period over which the computer was used regularly to store or process information for the purposes of any activities regularly carried on over that period by the person having lawful control over the use of the computer;

(b) during the said period, information of the kind contained in the electronic record or of the kind from which the information so contained is derived was regularly fed into the computer in the ordinary course of the said activities;

(c) throughout the material part of the said period, the computer was operating properly or, if not, then in respect of any period in which it was not operating properly or was out of operation during that part of the period, was not such as to affect the electronic record or the accuracy of its contents; and

(d) the information contained in the electronic record reproduces or is derived from such information fed into the computer in the ordinary course of the said activities.

(3) Where over any period, the function of storing or processing information for the purposes of any activities regularly carried on over that period as mentioned in clause (a) of sub-section (2) was regularly performed by computers, whether—

(a) by a combination of computers operating over that period; or

(b) by different computers operating in succession over that period; or

(c) by different combinations of computers operating in succession over that period; or

(d) in any other manner involving the successive operation over that period, in whatever order, of one or more computers and one or more combinations of computers,

all the computers used for that purpose during that period shall be treated for the purposes of this section as constituting a single computer; and references in this section to a computer shall be construed accordingly.

(4) In any proceedings where it is desired to give a statement in evidence by virtue of this section, a certificate doing any of the following things, that is to say,—

(a) identifying the electronic record containing the statement and describing the manner in which it was produced;

(b) giving such particulars of any device involved in the production of that electronic record as may be appropriate for the purpose of showing that the electronic record was produced by a computer;

(c) dealing with any of the matters to which the conditions mentioned in sub-section (2) relate, and purporting to be signed by a person occupying a responsible official position in relation to the operation of the relevant device or the management of the relevant activities (whichever is appropriate) shall be evidence of any matter stated in the certificate; and for the purposes of this sub-section it shall be sufficient for a matter to be stated to the best of the knowledge and belief of the person stating it.

(5) For the purposes of this section,—

(a) information shall be taken to be supplied to a computer if it is supplied thereto in any appropriate form and whether it is so supplied directly or (with or without human intervention) by means of any appropriate equipment;

(b) whether in the course of activities carried on by any official, information is supplied with a view to its being stored or processed for the purposes of those activities by a computer operated otherwise than in the course of those activities, that information, if duly supplied to that computer, shall be taken to be supplied to it in the course of those activities;

(c) a computer output shall be taken to have been produced by a computer whether it was produced by it directly or (with or without human intervention) by means of any appropriate equipment.

Explanation.—For the purposes of this section any reference to information being derived from other information shall be a reference to its being derived therefrom by calculation, comparison or any other process.

24. Sections 65A and 65B have been introduced by the Information Technology Act, 2000. Section 65A provides that the contents of electronic records may be proved in accordance with provisions in section 65B. The method of proof by secondary evidence would apply to any computer output as the same has been deemed to be a document for the purposes of proof. By these and other provisions introduced by the Act of 2000, the law of evidence has been adapted to the realities of contemporary business practice. Computers of different sizes or capacities play an important role in modern society. Many a time, the only record of a transaction, will be in the memory of a computer. Detection and proof of crime will be adversely affected if computer output cannot be used by investigation and courts. Yet one must realize that computers can malfunction and face phenomenon of "bugs" and 'Virus". Hence, they are not perfect devices.

Court has power to require oral evidence of any thing of which evidence could be given by a certificate under section 65B(4). Evidence by certificate is only one method of proof. The conditions of admissibility may be proved by oral evidence from the person familiar with the operation of the computer who can give evidence of it's reliability; he need not be a computer expert or someone qualified to sign a certificate. If it is admitted or shown that the computer was malfunctioning, section 65B cannot be invoked.[1] This section deals with admissibility and not weight to be attached to the certified. In estimating the weight to be attached, court must have regard to whether the computer provides information that was supplied contemporaneously to the computer, recorded

1. *P. Padmanabh* v. *Syndicate Bank Ltd.*, AIR 2008 Kant 42: 2008 AIHC 1609: 2008 (2) ALJ (NOC) 510.

contemporaneously for the purpose of being so supplied and whether anyone concerned with the supply of the information or the operation of the computer had a motive or incentive to conceal or misrepresent the facts.[1]

Though the matter does not fall within the parameters of section 65A and 65B, the progressive attitude of courts in the matter of examination of witnesses by way of video conferencing deserves mention, though certain safeguards are required to be taken for that purpose.[2] The Supreme Court has observed that if courts of law do not permit technology developments to be adopted in Court proceedings, it would be lagging behind compared to other sectors and technology is definitely a tool.[3] Supreme Court approved this innovative step, subject to certain safeguards.

25. SECTION 66: Secondary evidence of contents of documents referred to in clause (a) of Section 65 shall not be given unless the party proposing to give such secondary evidence has previously given to the party in whose possession or power the document is or to his attorney or pleader, such notice to produce it as is prescribed by law and if no notice is prescribed by law, then such notice as the court considers reasonable under the circumstances of the case:

Provided that such notice shall not be required in order to render secondary evidence admissible in any of the following cases, or in any other case in which the court thinks fit to dispense with it:—

(1) When the document to be proved is itself a notice;

(2) When, from the nature of the case, the adverse party must know that he will be required to produce it;

(3) When it appears or is proved that the adverse party has obtained possession of the original by fraud or force;

(4) When the adverse party or his agent has the original in Court;

(5) When the adverse party or his agent has admitted the loss of the document;

(6) When the person in possession of the document is out of reach of, or not subject to, the process of the Court.

Provisions of Order XI rule 5 C.P.C. also may be seen.

The word "party" in section 66 means not only the adverse party in the specific litigation, but also a stranger legally bound to produce the document. Section 66 refers to secondary evidence of only the "contents" of documents unlike section 65 which refers to secondary evidence of "existence, condition or contents" of a document. The object of this section is to enable the party in possession of the original to produce it in court so that the best evidence is made available.[4] Notice is unnecessary in the six contingencies contemplated in clause (1) to (6) of the proviso or in any other case as the court considers reasonable under the circumstances of the case.

---

1. (Phipson on Evidence, 15th Edition, Pages 696-701).
2. *Amitabh Bagchi* v. *Ena Bagchi*, AIR 2005 Cal 11: 2004 (3) Cal LT 263: 2005 (2) Civ LJ 281.
3. *State of Maharashtra* v. *Praful B. Desai*, (2003) 1 SCW 1885: 2003 Cr LJ 2033: (2003) 4 SCC 601: AIR 2003 SC 2053.
4. *Surendra Krishna Roy* v. *Mirza Mohammaed Syed Ali Mutawali*, AIR 1936 PC 15: 63 IA 85: 160 IC 29.

The court may, in other cases, dispense with notice, say, where notice is a mere formality or where the party had already denied existence of the document.[1]

26. SECTION 67: Handwriting or signature in a document must be proved to be of the person whose handwriting, signature they purport to be. Sections 67 to 73A have relevance in this regard. For proof of disputed handwriting or signature recourse may be taken to sections 45 or 47 also besides the sections succeeding section 67.[2]

The normal methods of such proof are the following:—

(1) By calling the person who signed or wrote the document.

(2) By calling the person in whose presence the document was signed and written (attestor).

(3) By calling an expert.

(4) By calling the person who is acquainted with the handwriting of the person or persons by whom the document was purported to be written or signed.

(5) By the admission of the person who was alleged to have written or signed.

(6) By comparison of the signature or writing on the document with the admitted or proved signature or writing of the person who purported to have signed or written the document.

(7) By other circumstantial evidence.

Definition of "proved" in section 3 has to be borne in mind.

27. This section applies only where the handwriting or signature are disputed. Proof must of handwriting and signature.[3] This section refers to documents other than documents required by law to be attested.[4] Documents required by law to be attested are required to be proved in terms of section 68. Method No. (1) in the previous paragraph provides the best evidence. When the person who wrote or signed is available, depending on the circumstances of the case, an adverse inference could be drawn if he is not examined.[5] Proof of truth of contents is generally offered by the author.[6] Proof of contents is covered by sections 61 to 66. Proof of genuineness is covered by sections 67 to 73. This section prescribes no particular method of proof.[7] Mere identification of signatures does not amount

---

1. *Antonio Dias Caldeira* v. *Frederick Augustus Gray*, AIR 1936 PC 15; *Gopal Das* v. *Thakurji*, AIR 1943 PC 83: ILR (1943) Kar PC 69: 1943 All LJ 292 (PC): 47 CWN 607; *Mira Bai* v. *Jai Singh*, AIR 1971 Raj 303: 1971 Raj LW 319; *Dinanath Raj* v. *Rama Raj*, AIR 1926 Pat 512: ILR 6 Pat 102: 1926 PHCC 286.
2. *H. Venkatachala Iyengar* v. *B.N. Thimmajamma*, AIR 1959 SC 443: 1959 SCJ 507: (1959) 2 SCA 1: 1959 SCR Supp (1) 426; *Gulzar Ali* v. *State of Himachal Pradesh*, (1998) 2 SCC 192: JT 1998 (4) SC 342: 1997 (2) Andh LD (Cri) 680.
3. AIR 1990 SC 1372; *Hasan Abdulla* v. *State of Gujarat*, 1962 Guj LR 107: AIR 1962 Guj 214: (1962) 2 Cr LJ 55; *Ram Chandra* v. *Jaithmal*, AIR 1934 All 990: 4 All WR 676.
4. AIR 1968 Bom 81.
5. *Muddasani Sarojana* v. *Muddasani Venkat Narsaiah*, AIR 2007 AP 50: 2007 (50) All Ind Cas 813.
6. *Bishwanath Rai* v. *Sachidanand*, AIR 1971 SC 1949: 1971 (2) Civ App J (SC) 245: (1972) 4 SCC 707; *Om Prakash Berlia* v. *Unit Trust of India*, AIR 1983 Bom 1: (1982) 3 Com LJ 89: (1983) 54 Com Cas 136.
7. *S. Gopal Reddy* v. *State of Andhra Pradesh*, AIR 1996 SC 2184: (1996) 4 SCC 596: 1996 Cr LJ 323.

to proof of execution.[1] General mode of proof is through the executant, attestor, person present, expert, person acquainted with handwriting or by comparison, by proof of admission by statement of deceased scribe. Where signature is admitted, no further evidence is necessary.[2]

Mere marking does not dispense with proof of document.[3] Marking by consent dispenses proof.[4]

Registration endorsement proves only admission of execution made by the executant to the registrar of the execution. It is not proof of execution.[5] The effect of admission is a separate question. Fact of registration may be useful in deciding whether presumption under section 90 should be drawn.[6] Mere production of a registered deed is not, by itself, sufficient to prove it; the identity of the executant has to be established by oral evidence. Certificate of registration is *prima facie* proof of execution, in the absence of other evidence.[7]

28. Evidence of due registration may in itself be some evidence of execution.[8] Court is not bound to treat registration endorsement as conclusive proof of execution, particularly in the presence of suspicious circumstances.[9] The endorsement and the admission contained therein is a relevant piece of evidence which can be taken along with the other evidence in the case.[10] Registration does not dispense with proof of execution when the same is denied.[11] Evidence of identifying witness and the registration endorsement is sufficient, though not conclusive. There are contradictory nuances in the decisions of various High Courts and parties will be well-advised to follow the strict requirements of law.

If the plea is one of forgery of signature, evidence need not be adduced to show knowledge of contents.[12] If evidence is that contents were read over before the executant and witnesses signed it, it would be sufficient proof of execution; the scribe need not be examined.[13]

1. *Deputy Commissioner of Pratabgarh* v. *Universal Film Co. (India) Ltd.*, AIR 1950 All 696; *Doraiswami* v. *Rathnammal*, AIR 1978 Mad 78: ILR (1978) 2 Mad 1: (1978) 1 Mad LJ 456; *Om Prakash* v. *State*, AIR 1957 All 388: 1957 Cr LJ 695: 1958 All LJ 764; *Bhaiyalal* v. *Ram Din*, AIR 1989 All 130.
2. *Soni Vallabhadas Liladhar* v. *Assistant Collector of Customs, Jamnagar*, AIR 1965 SC 481: 1965 Cr LJ 490: (1965) 1 SCJ 208: 66 BLR 282.
3. *Sait Tarajee Khimchand* v. *Yelamarti Satyam Alias Satteyya*, AIR 1971 SC 1865: 1971 UJ (SC) 644: (1972) 4 SCC 562.
4. *A.V.S. Perumal* v. *Vadivelu Asari*, AIR 1986 Mad 341: (1986) 99 Mad LW 561: (1986) 1 Mad LJ 283.
5. *Ramkrishan Ganpat Futane* v. *Mohammad Kasam*, AIR 1973 Bom 242: 76 Bom LR 104: ILR (1975) Bom 391.
6. *Irudayam Ammal* v. *Salayath Mary*, AIR 1973 Mad 421: (1972) 2 Mad LJ 508: 86 Mad LW 122.
7. *Irudayam Ammal* v. *Salayath Mary*, AIR 1973 Mad 421: (1972) 2 Mad LJ 508: 86 Mad LW 122; *Ramkrishan Ganpat Futane* v. *Mohammad Kasam*, AIR 1973 Bom 242: 76 Bom LR 104: ILR (1975) Bom 391.
8. *Gopal Das* v. *Thakurji*, AIR 1943 PC 83: ILR (1943) Kar PC 69: 1943 All LJ 292 (PC): 47 CWN 607; *Kalu Nimbuji Singne* v. *Bapurao Chinkaji Shingne*, AIR 1950 Nag 6: 1949 NLJ 226: ILR 1949 N 521.
9. *Mallo* v. *Bakhtawari*, AIR 1985 All 160: 1985 All CJ 345.
10. *Ketharaju Rajeshwari* v. *Kanthamraju Varalakshmamma*, AIR 1964 AP 284.
11. *Bhutkani Nath* v. *Kamaleswari Nath*, AIR 1972 Ass&Nag 15: Assam LR (1972) Assam 140.
12. *Dattatraya* v. *Rangnath*, AIR 1971 SC 2548: 1971 SCD 366: (1972) 4 SCC 181.
13. *Noor Jahan Begum* v. *Abrar Ahmad Khan*, AIR 1982 All 489: (1982) 1 DMC 304: (1982) 8 All LR 149.

Certified copy does not establish the truth of the contents of the document.[1]

29. SECTION 67A: Except in the case of a secure electronic signature, if the digital signature of any subscriber is alleged to have been affixed to an electronic record, the fact that such electronic signature is the electronic signature of the subscriber must be proved.

30. SECTION 68: In the case of a document required by law to be attested (will, mortgage deed, (but not charge), gift) it shall not be used as evidence until at least one attesting witness is called for the purpose of proving execution, if there be any attestor alive and subject to the process of court and capable of giving evidence. In the case of any such document (except a will), which is registered, attestor need not be called unless execution by the person by whom it purports to have been executed, is specifically denied by the person against whom the document is sought to be used.[2] Denial must be by a party to the suit against whom the document is sought to be used. If there is a denial of execution within the meaning of the proviso, the requirement of the section springs into existence. Mere denial of the validity of the document will not attract the proviso.[3] Mere statement denying the genuineness of the document is not enough to indicate that execution is denied within the meaning of the proviso.[4] The word "Execution" in the proviso means not only signing by the executant and includes all acts necessary for execution. In AIR 1939 PC 117, it was held that where defendant pleaded that he did not admit execution or receipt of consideration, plaintiff has to prove both execution and passing of consideration. The contention that there was no specific denial of execution was not accepted. Mere proof of signature of a party to a document is not proof of execution. In the case of a will, testamentary capacity also has to be proved. Mere proof of signature of the testator is not sufficient. Attestation must be proved as part of proof of execution. It is not necessary to examine both attestors, if one attestor gives satisfactory evidence. Evidence of propounder and scribe is not a substitute for evidence of an attestor.[5] Registration is not a substitute for proof of execution as required by law.

Whether the scribe who has affixed his signature is an attestor is to be decided as to under what circumstances and in what manner the scribe acted.[6] It is unnecessary to examine the typist who typed the document.

The question is, did he purport to act as an attesting witness?[7]

Identifying witnesses (at the time of registration) appending their signatures to the registration endorsement (not described as attestor) could be attesting

---

1. *Bishwanath Rai* v. *Sachidanand*, AIR 1971 SC 1949: 1971 (2) Civ App J (SC) 245: (1972) 4 SCC 707; *Dattatraya* v. *Rangnath*, AIR 1971 SC 2548: 1971 SCD 366: (1972) 4 SCC 181.
2. *Durgapada Jana* v. *Nemai Charan Jana*, AIR 1986 Cal 23: (1985) 2 Cal HN 357: (1986) 90 Cal WN 95; *Rosammal Issetheenammal Fernandez* v. *Joosa Mariyan Fernandez*, AIR 2000 SC 2857: (2000) 7 SCC 189: 2000 AIR SCW 3006.
3. *Markande* v. *Sudama Chaubey*, AIR 2007 All 70: 2007 AIHC 963: 2007 (1) ALJ 556.
4. *Kumara Narasimhappa* v. *Lakkanna*, AIR 1959 Mys 148.
5. *Janki Narayan Bhoir* v. *Naryan Namdeo Kadam*, (2003) 2 SCC 91: AIR 2003 SC 761: 2003 AIR SCW 177.
6. *M. Venkatasubbaiah* v. *M. Subbamma*, AIR 1956 Andhra 195: 1956 Andh WR 632.
7. *Onkar Pershad* v. *Jagdish Pershad*, AIR 1952 Punj 237: 53 Punj LR 81; *Nirode Mohan Roy* v. *Charu Chandra Mazumdar*, AIR 1950 Cal 401: 54 CWN 455.

witnesses if they had the animus to attest.[1] The signature of registering officer and identifying witness affixed to the registration endorsement under sections 58 and 59 of Registration Act would amount to valid attesting signatures if the conditions for valid attestation under section 3 of T.P. Act have been satisfied and they had the animus to attest.[2] In a Privy Council case it was held that evidence of due registration is some evidence of execution.[3] The registrar before whom the executant admitted execution at the time of registration puts his signature on the document in discharge of his statutory duty under section 59 of the Registration Act, and not for the purpose of attesting it and it was not proved that he or the identifying witnesses put their signatures for the purpose of attesting the document and hence it has been held that they could not be regarded as attesting witnesses since they have no *"animus attestendi"*.[4] Mere registration is not proof of execution. One available attestor atleast must be called.

Presumption under this section will not apply to wills which are governed entirely by section 68.

Execution of an attested document involves the attestors seeing the executant signing the document after understanding the contents (or after the executant acknowledges his signature to the attestors) and the attestors signing the document in the presence of the executant. In the case of a disputed will, evidence of testamentary capacity, *i.e.*, that he was in a sound disposing state of mind is necessary.[5] Proof a will is required not as a ground for reading the will, but to afford the court reasonable assurance of it being what it purports to be.

If one attesting witness turns hostile, the other witness must be called.[6] So also where attestor examined as a witness fails to prove due execution, the other attestor must be examined.[7]

A document creating a charge is not compulsorily attestable.

31. SECTION 69:

If no attesting witness is found or if the document purports to have been executed in United Kingdom, it must be proved that the attestation of one attesting witness at least is in his handwriting and that the signature of the person executing the document is in the handwriting of that person. This section

1. *Girja Datt Singh* v. *Gangotri Datt Singh*, AIR 1955 SC 346; *Sahakari Khand Udyog Mandal Ltd.* v. *Commissioner of Central Excise & Customs*, AIR 2005 SC 189: 2005 AIR SCW 1518: (2005) 3 SCC 738.
2. *Rani Purnima Debi* v. *Kumar Khagendra Narayan Deb*, AIR 1962 SC 567: 1962 (1) SCJ 725: (1962) 3 SCR 195.
3. *Gopal Das* v. *Thakurji*, AIR 1943 PC 83: ILR (1943) Kar PC 69: 1943 All LJ 292 (PC): 47 CWN 607.
4. *M.L. Abdul Jabbar Saheb* v. *H. Venkata Sastri*, AIR 1969 SC 1147: (1969) 3 SCR 513.
5. *H. Venkatachala Iyengar* v. *B.N. Thimmajamma*, AIR 1959 SC 443: 1959 SCJ 507: (1959) 2 SCA 1: 1959 SCR Supp (1) 426; *Rani Purnima Debi* v. *Kumar Khagendra Narayan Deb*, AIR 1962 SC 567: 1962 (1) SCJ 725: (1962) 3 SCR 195; *Shashi Kumar Banerjee* v. *Subodh Kumar Banerjee*, AIR 1964 SC 529; *Gorantla Thataiah* v. *Thotakura Venkata Subbaiah*, AIR 1968 SC 1332: 1968 2 SCJ 744: 1968 Andh WR 109 (SC); *Meenakshiammal* v. *Chandrasekaran*, AIR 2005 SC 52: 2004 AIR SCW 6254: (2005) 1 SCC 280; *Bharpur Singh* v. *Shamsher Singh*, (2009) 3 SCC 687: AIR 2009 SC 1766: 2009 AIR SCW 1338.
6. *Kunwar Surendra Bahadur Singh* v. *Thakur Behari Singh*, AIR 1939 PC 117: (1939) 2 MLJ 762: ILR (1939) Kar PC 222; *Vishnu Ramkrishna* v. *Nathu Vithal*, AIR 1949 Bom 266.
7. *Janki Narayan Bhoir* v. *Naryan Namdeo Kadam*, (2003) 2 SCC 91: AIR 2003 SC 761: 2003 AIR SCW 177.

provides an alternative method of proof of document covered by section 68 and must be read with section 68.[1]

The first part of the section will apply where attestors are dead or insane or out of jurisdiction or cannot be found after diligent enquiry or absent themselves by colluding with the opposite party.[2] All steps must be exhausted in case of a witness "not found".[3] Law of attestation of wills is found in section 63(c) of Indian Succession Act. Section 69 could be made applicable to cases where the attestor, for reasons of physical or mental disability, or for other reason which the court considers sufficient, is no longer a competent witness under section 118 of Evidence Act.[4]

Section requires proof of attestation of at least one attestor and of the executant.[5] Where there was no suspicion that a thirty year old will is unnatural or has been tampered with and the executant and attestors were dead, presumption could be raised regarding due execution and attestation of the will.[6]

32. SECTION 70:

Admission of a party to an attested document of its execution by himself shall be sufficient proof of its execution as against him, though the document is required by law to be attested. In such case, there is no necessity to call the attesting witness.[7] This section applies naturally, only to a document which is duly attested. This section is an exception to the general rule contained in section 68.[8] Such an admission by a party proves execution even if an attestor examined in the case stated that the executant did not sign in his presence.[9]

Admission contemplated is of due execution in the manner in which a document required by law to be attested, is to be executed. There has been conflict of view among various High Courts as to whether the admission should have been made in the course of legal proceedings or not.[10] The admission must be of a party to the document and not his representative. A mere admission of signature does not amount to admission of execution or of attestation.[11] If attestation is put in issue, plaintiff has to prove due attestation before the section can be relied on.[12]

1. *K. Laxmanan* v. *Thekkayil Padmini*, (2009) 1 SCC 354: AIR 2009 SC 951: 2009 AIR SCW 10: 2009 (1) CCC 526; *Bharpur Singh* v. *Shamsher Singh*, (2009) 3 SCC 687: AIR 2009 SC 1766: 2009 AIR SCW 1338.
2. *Doraiswami* v. *Rathnammal*, AIR 1978 Mad 78: ILR (1978) 2 Mad 1: (1978) 1 Mad LJ 456; *Babu Singh* v. *Ram Sahai*, AIR 2008 SC 2485: 2008 AIR SCW 3429: (2008) 7 SCALE 743.
3. *Ban Jassa Kunwa* v. *Sahu Narain Das*, AIR 1946 All 178: 224 IC 125; *Muthuraman* v. *Subramanian*, AIR 1933 Mad 612; *Babu Singh* v. *Ram Sahai*, AIR 2008 SC 2485: 2008 AIR SCW 3429: (2008) 7 SCALE 743.
4. *Ban Jassa Kunwa* v. *Sahu Narain Das*, AIR 1946 All 178: 224 IC 125.
5. *Deorao* v. *Dhondirao*, AIR 1928 Nag 244, *Doraiswami* v. *Rathnammal*, AIR 1978 Mad 78: ILR (1978) 2 Mad 1: (1978) 1 Mad LJ 456.
6. *Haradhan Mahatha* v. *Dukhu Mahatha*, AIR 1993 Pat 129: 1995 (2) CCC 581: 1995 (2) CurCC 322.
7. *Hira Bibi* v. *Ram Hari Lal*, AIR 1925 PC 203: 5 P 58: 52 IA 362: 89 IC 659.
8. *Bharpur Singh* v. *Shamsher Singh*, (2009) 3 SCC 687: AIR 2009 SC 1766: 2009 AIR SCW 1338.
9. *Ramlal* v. *Septi*, AIR 1926 Pat 295.
10. Ratanlal Dhirajlal's Law of Evidence, 23rd Edition, page 987.
11. *Lachman Singh* v. *Surendra Bahadur Singha*, AIR 1932 All 527: ILR 54 All 1051: 1932 All LJ 653 (FB).
12. *Davood Rowther* v. *Ramanathan Chettiar*, AIR 1938 Mad 43: ILR (1938) Mad 523, *Komal Singh* v. *Krishna Bai*, AIR 1946 Bom 304: ILR 1946 Bom 146.

33. SECTION 71:

If the attestor denies or does not recollect execution of the document, execution may be proved by other evidence. This is an exception to section 68. But section 71 cannot be interpreted so as to allow a party to give the go by to the mandate of section 68 regarding the requirement of calling attesting witness.[1] Where attestor deposed that the testator put thumb impression after the attestor signed the document it will amount to denial of execution so as to attract section 71.[2] Section 71 can be invoked where the attestor denies or does not recollect the execution of the document. But in such a case the other attestor should be called as a witness and if that is not done section 71 cannot be invoked.[3] Execution includes attestation.[4] The scribe, identifying witness, Registrar or any person present at the time of execution could be examined. Mere identification of signature is not sufficient to prove execution.[5] Stephen in his Digest (7th Edition P 78) stated that where an attestor denies execution of the document the case stands as if there was no attesting witness, and execution may be proved by other independent evidence.

34. SECTION 72:

An attested document not required by law to be attested, may be proved as if it was unattested.[6] No attestor to a sale deed need be examined to prove execution of sale deed.[7]

35. SECTION 73:

In order to ascertain whether a signature, writing or seal is that of the person by whom it purports to have been written or made, any signature, writing or seal admitted or proved to the satisfaction of the court to have been written or made by that person may be compared with the one which is to be proved, although that signature, writing or seal has not been produced or proved for any other purpose. The court may direct any person present in court to write any words or figures for the purpose of enabling the court to compare the words or figures so written with any words or figures alleged to have been written by such person. This Section also applies, with necessary modification, to finger impressions. The court, as a matter of prudence and caution, should hesitate to or be slow to arrive at its' findings solely on the comparison made by itself.[8]

This is the mode of direct comparison by court. The rule of caution is not to base the decision entirely on the opinion formed as a result of such comparison. This provision does not infringe article 20(3) of the Constitution.[9] Hand-writing can be proved under sections 67, 45, 47 and 73. Comparison may be made by an expert (section 45), or by one familiar with the hand-writing of the person concerned (section 47) or by the court (section 73). Section 73 does

1. *Janki Narayan Bhoir* v. *Naryan Namdeo Kadam*, (2003) 2 SCC 91: AIR 2003 SC 761: 2003 AIR SCW 177.
2. *Benga Behera* v. *Braja Kishore Nanda*, AIR 2007 SC 1975: 2007 AIR SCW 3741: 2007 (3) All WC 3011: 2007 (3) Rec Civ R 240.
3. *Kunwar Surendra Bahadur Singh* v. *Thakur Behari Singh*, AIR 1939 PC 117: (1939) 2 MLJ 762: ILR (1939) Kar PC 222.
4. *Ram Ratan Misra* v. *Bittan Kaur*, AIR 1980 All 395: 1980 All WC 358: (1980) 6 All LR 445.
5. *Doraiswami* v. *Rathnammal*, AIR 1978 Mad 78: ILR (1978) 2 Mad 1: (1978) 1 Mad LJ 456.
6. *Ram Kishore* v. *Ambika Prasad*, 1966 AWR (HC) 57: AIR 1966 All 515.
7. *Karuppiah Mooppanar* v. *Muthukaruppan Servai*, AIR 1975 Mad 221: 88 Mad LW 6.
8. *Kessarbai* v. *Jethabhai Jivan*, AIR 1928 PC 277: 111 Ind Cas 169: 28 Mad LW 737; *G. Madhavayya* v. *G. Achamma*, AIR 1949 PC 325: (1949) 2 Mad LJ 716.
9. *State of Bombay* v. *Kathi Kalu Oghad*, AIR 1961 SC 1808: (1962) 3 SCR 10: (1961) 2 Cr LJ 856: 64 Bom LR 240.

not specifically say by whom comparison is to be made; but obviously it is by the court.[1] Comparison can be made of hand-writing in letters also.[2] Court is competent to make the comparison, though not bound to do so.[3] This will be done only in exceptional circumstances, as ordinarily court is not to play the role of an expert. Comparison ofcourse, can be made to test the opinion of an expert.[4] Comparison can be made even to test the other evidence.[5]

This provision applies to all kinds of courts, but prudent course is to obtain expert opinion.[6] But the competence of the court is unquestionable.[7] If neither side calls an expert, it is the duty of the court to resort to this Section.[8]

The standard writing must be admitted or proved.[9] "Admission" means not the admission of the person whose signature is disputed, but it must be the admission of the person who claims that the disputed signature was genuine.[10] Where the specimen of the handwriting was obtained under directions of a magistrate who was not conducting the enquiry or trial and accused did not give the specimen voluntarily, it cannot be held that the specimen could not used for the purpose of section 73.[11]

36. "Any person present in Court" will cover parties, accused or strangers.[12] The direction can be given *suo moto* or on request.[13] But court cannot ask the accused to go to police station for the purpose. During investigation court cannot direct the accused to give specimen handwriting.[14] A person can be directed under this section, but cannot be forced to give specimen handwriting. Such a direction can be given only if a proceeding is pending in Court. It cannot be given for the purpose of investigation or for other agencies to use it for comparison or for an anticipated necessity in any case which may be instituted later.[15]

---

1. *State (Delhi Administration)* v. *Pali Ram*, 1979 Cr LJ 17: 1978 Cri App R (SC) 374: AIR 1979 SC 14: (1979) 2 SCC 158; *Ajit Savant Majagavi* v. *State of Karnataka*, AIR 1997 SC 3255: 1997 Cr LJ 3964: (1997) 7 SCC 992: 1997 SCC (Cri) 992.
2. *Kumaran Nair* v. *Bhargavi*, (1987) 2 Ker LT 644: 1988 Cr LJ 1000: 1987 (2) Crimes 915; *State of Uttar Pradesh* v. *Ram Babu Misra*, AIR 1980 SC 791: (1980) 2 SCC 343: (1980) 2 SCWR 25.
3. *Himayam Engineers and Builders Represented by its Proprietor P. Ramana Reddy* v. *S. Ravichandran*, 1990 1 MLJ 428; *Bhupendra Narain Mandal* v. *Ek Narain Lal Das*, AIR 1965 Pat 332.
4. *Devi Prasad* v. *State*, AIR 1967 All 64: 1967 Cr LJ 134.
5. *Fazaladdin Mandal* v. *Panchanan Das*, AIR 1957 Cal 92: ILR (1957) 3 Cal 19; *Devi Prasad* v. *State*, AIR 1967 All 64: 1967 Cr LJ 134; *State (Delhi Administration)* v. *Pali Ram*, 1979 Cr LJ 17: 1978 Cri App R (SC) 374: AIR 1979 SC 14: (1979) 2 SCC 158.
6. *State (Delhi Administration)* v. *Pali Ram*, 1979 Cr LJ 17: 1978 Cri App R (SC) 374: AIR 1979 SC 14: (1979) 2 SCC 158.
7. *State of Gujarat* v. *Vinaya Chandra Chhota Lal*, (1967) 1 SCJ 821: 1967 Cr LJ 668: AIR 1967 SC 778; *Sukhvinder Singh* v. *State of Punjab*, (1994) 5 SCC 152: JT 1994 (4) SC 1: 1994 SCC (Cri) 1376.
8. *Murari Lal* v. *State of Madhya Pradesh*, AIR 1980 SC 531: (1980) 1 SCC 704: (1980) 2 SCR 249: 1980 Cr LJ 396; *Fakhruddin* v. *State of Madhya Pradesh*, AIR 1967 SC 1326: (1967) 2 SCJ 885: 1967 Cr LJ 1197: 1967 MPLJ 473: (1967) 1 SCWR 449: 1967 All LJ 303.
9. *Krushna Chandra* v. *Commr. of Endowments*, AIR 1976 Ori 52: ILR (1976) Cut 28: 1976 Hindu LR 353.
10. *Sunil Chowdhury* v. *Arup Kumar Ghosh*, AIR 2006 SC 109.
11. *Amarjit Singh* v. *State of Uttar Pradesh*, (1998) 8 SCC 613.
12. *State* v. *Parameshwar Pillai*, AIR 1952 TC 482; *State (Delhi Administration)* v. *Pali Ram*, 1979 Cr LJ 17: 1978 Cri App R (SC) 374: AIR 1979 SC 14: (1979) 2 SCC 158.
13. *Shri H.D. Vasishtha* v. *Messrs Glaxo Laboratories (I) Private Limited*, AIR 1979 SC 1.
14. *State of Uttar Pradesh* v. *Ram Babu Misra*, AIR 1980 SC 791: (1980) 2 SCC 343: (1980) 2 SCWR 25; *Sukhvinder Singh* v. *State of Punjab*, 1994 SCC (Cri) 1376.
15. *Balavant N. Viswamitra* v. *Yadav Sadashiv Mule (deceased by L.Rs.)*, AIR 2004 SC 4377: 2004 AIR SCW 5051: 2005 (2) Civ LJ 405.

37. Conclusion found on mere comparison is indecisive and must yield to the positive evidence in the case.[1] There is no legal bar to the judge using his own eyes for comparison. However the opinion based on comparison by the court is not conclusive and is liable to err. Hence the court, as a matter of prudence and caution, should hesitate to arrive at its findings solely on comparison made by itself. Nevertheless court can make such comparison.[2] However, no two signatures of the same person can ever be identical in all respects. Discrepancies in such a case will be within natural variations. Differences depend on so many extraneous factors such as the nature of the pen, the ink, the paper, the posture of the body and hand and the general condition in which a person writes. Hence what are to be compared are the general characteristics of the two handwritings.[3] Forged documents may often be good imitations of hand-writing in genuine document and hence court has to look at dissimilarities also.[4]

In *State of Bombay* v. *Kathi Kalu Oghad*[5] (11 Judges) it has been held that giving specimen handwriting is testimonial compulsion violative of article 20(3) of the Constitution. Accused cannot be compelled to do so. But he can voluntarily do so, when asked to do so by the court. Direction can be given to the accused.[6]

Definition of "sign" in section 3(56) of General Clauses Act, includes a thumb impression. This is further strengthened by the last sentence of section 73 according to which the section applies also, with necessary modifications, to finger impression. But the Court has to make a thorough study to ascertain the characteristics, similarities and dissimilarities and give reasons for its conclusion based on comparison of thumb impression, if it chooses to record a finding on that basis.[7] Where the disputed thumb impression is smudgy, vague or very light, court should not hazard a guess by a casual perusal. (*ibid*).

38. SECTION 73A: In order to ascertain whether a digital signature is that of a person by whom it purports to have been affixed, the court may direct—

(a) that person or the controller or the certifying authority to produce the digital signature certificate;

(b) any other person to apply the public key listed in the Digital Signature Certificate and verify the digital signature purported to have been affixed by that person.

***Explanation*:**—For the purpose of this section, "controller' means controller appointed under section 17(1) of the Information Technology Act, 2000.

---

1. *Kishore Chandra Singh Deo* v. *Ganesh Prasad Bhagat*, AIR 1954 SC 316: (1954) 1 Mad LJ 622: 1954 SCR 919: 1954 SCJ 395; *Manindu* v. *Mahalaxmi Bank Ltd.*, AIR 1945 PC 105; *G. Madhavayya* v. *G. Achamma*, AIR 1949 PC 325: (1949) 2 Mad LJ 716.
2. *State of Gujarat* v. *Vinaya Chandra Chhota Lal*, (1967) 1 SCJ 821: 1967 Cr LJ 668: AIR 1967 SC 778.
3. *Bhupendra Narain* v. *EK Narayan Lal*, AIR 1965 Pat 332.
4. *Ravjappa* v. *Nilakanta Rao*, AIR 1962 Mys 53: (1962) 1 Cr LJ 441: ILR (1960) Mys 1206.
5. AIR 1961 SC 1808: (1962) 3 SCR 10: (1961) 2 Cr LJ 856: 64 Bom LR 240.
6. *State (Delhi Administration)* v. *Pali Ram*, 1979 Cr LJ 17: 1978 Cri App R (SC) 374: AIR 1979 SC 14: (1979) 2 SCC 158.
7. *Thiruvengada Pillai* v. *Navaneethammal*, AIR 2008 SC 1541: (2008) 4 SCC 530: 2008 AIR SCW 1684: 2008 (2) CCC 266: 2008 (5) All MR 32 (NOC).

CHAPTER 16
PUBLIC DOCUMENTS (SECTIONS 74 TO 78)

Every person has the right of inspection of public documents in which he is interested for the protection of such interest.[1] This is a common law right and a right created by the Evidence Act. The extent of the right depends on the interest which that person has in the document and on what is reasonably necessary for the protection of such interest. If any such right is conferred by a statute, the provisions of the statute govern the right.[2] Provisions of the Right to Information Act may also be seen.[3] Admissibility and effectiveness of public documents are covered by sections 35 to 38 of the Evidence Act. Words "right to inspect" should not be understood narrowly.[4]

SECTIONS 74 AND 75

"Public Documents" are (1) documents forming the acts or record of the acts (i) of sovereign authority, (ii) of official bodies and tribunals, and (iii) of public officers, legislative, judicial and executive of India of the commonwealth or of a foreign country, and (2) public records kept in any state, of private documents. Documents which do not fall within the above description are private documents. Certain modes of proof are prescribed in regard to public documents as distiniguished from private documents. According to Wigmore, the term "public" is inadequate and ambiguous. The term could be understand in different ways.[5] A private document does not become a public document merely because it is filed in court. Registration of a document does not make it a public document.

Public document does not require to be proved by examining any witness. *See* also section 114(e). Kind of "acts" has been indicated in section 78 *i.e.*, final, completed acts as distinct from acts of preparatory or tentative character.

Acts of sovereign authority are public statements, proclamations, ordinances, state papers, gazetters, agreements between states etc.[6]

"Official Bodies" include Panchayats, Municipalities, Improvement Trust etc.[7]

---

1. *Parashuram Detaram Shamduasami* v. *Sir Hugh Golding cocke*, ILR 1942 Bom 171.
2. Taylor on Evidence, Pages 1480-1522.
3. Ratanlal Dhirajlal on Law of Evidence, 23rd Edn., Page 1022.
4. *A.K. Kaderkutty* v. *Agricultural Income-tax Officer, Tellicherry*, AIR 1961 Ker 32: 1960 Ker LJ 1191: ILR 1960 Ker 1292.
5. Wigmore II Edition Vol. 35, P. 1650.
6. *Kabul Singh* v. *Ram Singh*, AIR 1986 All 75.
7. (1972) 1 Mys LJ 101.

"Public Officers" *See* section 2(17) C.P.C. and section 21 Indian Penal Code. A public servant may not be a public officer. Municipal Commissioner, though a public servant, is not a public officer.[1]

The following have been held to be public officers:—

Collector, Official Trustie, Official Receiver, Military Officer acting as Court Martial, Court Receiver, I.T. Officer, Custodian of Evacuee Property, Government Pleader, Doctor in Medical Service, Inspector of Police, Village Headman, Bombay Sheriff, Army Officer, Court Bench Clerk, Corporation, Government Officer, Visa Officer, Judge, etc. See *Woodroff & Amir Ali's Law of Evidence 18th Edition*, Vol. III Pages 3285 to 3288.

Corporation Commissioner, Sarpanch, Patvari, MLA, Municipal Chairman, Officer of FCI, Corporation Bank Manager have been held to be not public officers. *(See Ibid)*. The section covers Public Documents of foreign Governments also.

Public Documents – Record of Act:

Judgments, orders and decree are public documents, but not pleadings, affidavits filed in court.[2] Depositions,[3] Warrant,[4] Remand Report,[5] Injury report,[6] Medico Legal Case report,[7] Ballot Papers used by Voters,[8] Electoral rolls,[9] Check Memo maintained by an officer at a counting Table,[10] Death Register,[11] Birth Register,[12] Certified copy of a private sale deed, Hindu Marriage register,[13] Admission Register of a Municipal School,[14] Survery and Settlement Report,[15] Records maintained by Revenue Officer relating to Land Revenue, survey settlement,[16] Cultivation Register of Paddy Producers[17] and Registered GP of Attorney are public documents.

There is a distinction between the record of court and the record of act of the court. It is only the record of the act of court which is a public document. Thus, a compromise petition filed by parties in court is not a public document. So also pleadings filed in court are not public documents. But orders, judgments

1. *Narendra Prasad* v. *Janki Kuer*, AIR 1947 Pat 385: 25 Pat 739.
2. *Collector of Gorakhpur* v. *Ram Sunder Mal*, AIR 1934 PC 157 (PC): 56 A 468: 150 IC 545.
3. *Chandreshwar Prasad Narain Singh* v. *Bisheshwar Pratab Narain Singh*, AIR 1927 Pat 61: 101 Ind Cas 289: ILR 5 Pat 777.
4. *Kantilal Ambalal* v. *State of Gujarat*, AIR 1968 Guj 100: 1968 Cr LJ 758, *Easwaramurthi* v. *King Emperor*, AIR 1944 PC 54: 46 Bom LR 844: 45 Cr LJ 721.
5. *C.I. of Police* v. *Velur*, ILR 1973 Ker 50.
6. *Balgopal Panda* v. *State*, 1990 Cr LJ 1848: 1990 (70) Cut LT 1.
7. *Dalip Kumar* v. *State*, 1995 Cr LJ 1742; Contra *State* v. *Gian Singh*, 1981 Cr LJ 538: 1981 (8) Cr LT 73: 1981 (19) DLT 104; *Balgopal Panda* v. *State*, 1990 Cr LJ 1848: 1990 (70) Cut LT 1.
8. *Jildar Ram* v. *Gouri Shankar Pandey*, AIR 1965 Pat 449.
9. *Kirthan* v. *Thakur*, AIR 1972 SC 158.
10. *Banamali Das* v. *Rajendra Chandra Mardaraj Harichandan*, AIR 1975 SC 1863: (1976) 4 SCC 54: (1976) 1 SCR 212.
11. *Gopi Chand Arya* v. *Bedamo Kuer*, AIR 1966 Pat 231: 1965 BLJR 738.
12. *Vanjakshamma* v. *P. Gopalakrishna*, AIR 1970 Mys 305: (1970) 2 Mys LJ 15: 1970 Cr LJ 1584.
13. *Manjula* v. *Mani*, 1998 Cr LJ 1476 (MD): 1997 Mad LJ (Cri) 715.
14. *Ajjarapu Subbarao* v. *Pulla Venkata Rama Rao*, AIR 1964 AP 53: (1963) 2 Andh WR 307: (1963) 2 Andh LT 442.
15. *Raja Brajasunder Deb* v. *Raja Rajindranarain*, AIR 1941 Pat 260: 22 Pat LT 699.
16. *J. Shiva Shankar* v. *Deputy Superintendent of Police*, 2002 Cr LJ 3168: 2002 (2) Andh LT 295.
17. *Chandran Nair* v. *Kunhambu Nair*, AIR 1982 Ker 232.

or decrees passed by courts are public documents as they are records of acts of court.[1]

FIR under section 154 of Code, search order, Register in Bank of Bengal, Jail Register, Public School Register, Assessment orders are public documents. Confession recorded under section 164 of Criminal Procedure Code is not a public document.[2]

Court has to issue certified copies of documents, though not marked.[3] Order of sanction of prosecution is a public document.[4]

CLAUSE (2) – A true copy of election expenses lodged with election officer is a public record of private document.[5] Certified copy of a registered document is another instance of such a document.[6] So also a memorandum of association, a return submitted to Registrar of J.S. companies are documents falling under clause (2).[7] The original receipt executed by a private individual has to be handed over to the party entitled to custody and does not attract this clause.[8]

SECTION 75: All other documents are private.

SECTION 76: Every public officer having custody of public document which any person has a right to inspect, shall give that person on demand a copy of it on payment of the legal fees together with a certificate at the foot of such copy that it is a true copy of such document or part thereof, as the case may be, and such certificate shall be dealt and subscribed to by such officer with his name and official title, and shall be sealed, whenever such officer is authorised by law to make use of a seal and such copies so certified shall be called certified copies. An officer who, by the ordinary course of official duty, is authorised to deliver such copies, shall be deemed to have the custody of such documents within the meaning of this section.

The purpose is, to avoid as far as possible, the production of the original in court. Such frequent production would be highly inconvenient and expose it to be lost and endangered. This section applies only to public documents.[9] Copies issued otherwise than in accordance with this section are not admissible.[10] Certified copy of a document which was registered, but in a wrong book is admissible as the registration is not invalid.[11] Certified copy of I.T. return can be issued to the assesse as confidentiality is his privilege.[12]

1. *Mangat Ram* v. *State*, 1966 Cr LJ 967; *Kantilal Ambalal* v. *State of Gujarat*, AIR 1968 Guj 100: 1968 Cr LJ 758.
2. *Nika Ram* v. *State of Himachal Pradesh*, AIR 1972 SC 2077: (1972) 2 SCC 80: 1972 Cr LJ 1317; *Uttar Pradesh* v. *Singhara Singh*, AIR 1964 SC 358: (1964) 4 SCR 485: 1965 (1) SCJ 184.
3. *A.A. Kilachand* v. *State of Karnataka*, 1991 IV Kar LJ 705.
4. *State* v. *K Narasimhachary*, AIR 2006 SC 628: 2006 Cr LJ 518: 2005 AIR SCW 6275; Ratanlal Dhirajlal Law of Evidence 23rd Edition – pages 1012 to 1018 and Woodroff and Amir Ali on Law of Evidence 18th Edition Vol. II pages 3289 to 3309.
5. *Kandru Maghi* v. *Budnesher Mazhi*, ILR 1972 3 Cal 6.
6. *Subudhi Pradhan* v. *Raghu Bhavan*, AIR 1962 SC 40.
7. *Finani Properties Pvt. Ltd.* v. *M. Gulamali*, AIR 1967 Cal 390.
8. *Gopal das* v. *Thakurji*, AIR 1943 PC 1: 44 Cr LJ 558 (FC).
9. *Krishna Subala Bose* v. *Dhanpati Dutta*, AIR 1957 Cal 59.
10. *Pramatha Nath* v. *Nirode Chandra*, AIR 1940 Cal 187: ILR (1939) 2 Cal 394: (1939) 7 ITR 570. Contra *Venkataramnna* v. *Varahalu*, AIR 1940 Mad 308: (1939) 7 ITR 560.
11. *Vishwanath* v. *Dhapu*, AIR 1960 Cal 494; *Satindra Nath* v. *Jatindra Nath*, AIR 1935 PC 165: 69 Mad LJ 503: 39 Cal WN 1191.
12. *Narasimha Rama Rao* v. *Venkatramayya*, AIR 1940 Mad 768: ILR 1940 Mad 969: (1940) 8 ITR 450 (KB); *Naim Singh* v. *Tikan Singh*, AIR 1955 All 388; *Rasipuram Union Motor Service Ltd.* v. *Commr. of Income Tax, Madras*, AIR 1957 Mad 151: (1956) 2 Mad LJ 604: ILR 1957 Mad 557.

Certified copies must bear seal and signature of the authority using it. There is not particular form of certification prescribed. But it should contain the particulars prescribed.[1] Words "right to inspect" should not be understood narrowly.[2] Right to copy depends on the right to inspect.[3] There is no such right in regard to documents which Government has a right to refuse to show on grounds of state policy, privileged communication etc. One among several heirs of an assessee is not entitled to certified copy of statements made by declared assesse to I.T. officer. All the heirs should concur in the application as one heir is not the agent of other.[4] Evidence Act is silent regarding right to inspect. It is a common law right which recognised the right to inspect generally for all persons who can show that they have an interest for the protection of which it is necessary that liberty to inspect such document should be given[5] System of Public Interest Litigation must be assumed to have expanded this right. Extent of right, in the absence of statutory provision, depends on the extent of the interest and what is reasonably necessary to protect it. Power to regulate does not include power to abrogate.

Right to inspect and copy is fairly wide. For example, records of the case (section 210 of Code), deposition (section 219 of Code), extract of document showing previous conviction, (section 298 of Code) and charge sheet. (Section 173(4) of Criminal Procedure Code.[6]

SECTION 77: Such certified copies may be produced in proof of the contents of public documents or parts thereof which they purport to the copies. Contents can be proved by resorting to sections 77 or 78, as is appropriate. Certified copy of a public document does not require proof by calling a witness.[7] Section 79 raises a presumption of genuineness of such copy.[8] Production of a certified copy of a registered document is not sufficient to raise the presumption under section 90.[9] Under section 51A of Land Acquisition Act, certified copy of a sale deed is admissible, without examining the vendor or vendor.[10]

1. *Thatha* v. *Peru*, AIR 1986 Ker 196: 1985 Ker LT 1069.
2. *A.K. Kaderkutty* v. *Agricultural Income-tax Officer, Tellicherry*, AIR 1961 Ker 32: 1960 Ker LJ 1191: ILR 1960 Ker 1292.
3. *Rasipuram Union Motor Service Ltd.* v. *Commr. of Income Tax, Madras*, AIR 1957 Mad 151: (1956) 2 Mad LJ 604: ILR 1957 Mad 557.
4. *Muniayammal* v. *Third Additional Income-tax Officer, Salem*, AIR 1960 Mad 366: (1960) 2 Mad LJ 96: ILR (1960) Mad 612.
5. *A.K. Kaderkutty* v. *Agricultural Income-tax Officer, Tellicherry*, AIR 1961 Ker 32: 1960 Ker LJ 1191: ILR 1960 Ker 1292; *State of Madras* v. *Krishnan*, ILR 1961 Mad 1.
6. *Purshottam Jethanand* v. *State of Kutch*, AIR 1954 SC 700: 1954 Cr LJ 1751; *Standard Chartered Bank* v. *Andhra Bank Financial Services Ltd.*, (2006) 6 SCC 94: AIR 2006 SC 3626: 2006 AIR SCW 3460.
7. *Madamanchi Ramappa* v. *Muthaluru Bojjappa*, AIR 1963 SC 1633: (1964) 1 Andh LT 1: (1964) 2 SCR 673; *Collector of Gorakhpur* v. *Ram Sunder Mal*, AIR 1934 PC 157 (PC): 56 A 468: 150 IC 545.
8. *Dalim Kumar* v. *Nandarni Dassi*, AIR 1970 Cal 292: 73 Cal WN 877: ILR (1970) 2 Cal 31; *Krishna Rani* v. *Chuni Lal Gulati*, AIR 1981 P &H 119: 1981 (1) Kar LJ 361: 1981 Hindu LR 16 (Tippani); *Rajasthan State Road Transport Corporation* v. *Devilal*, AIR 1991 Raj 29: 1990 ACJ 230: 1990 (2) ACC 535.
9. *Basant Singh* v. *Brij Raj Saran Singh*, AIR 1935 PC 132: 62 IA 180: 57 A 494: 156 IC 864 (PC); *Harihar Prasad Singh* v. *Deo Narain Prasad*, AIR 1956 SC 305: 1956 SCJ 279: 1956 SCR 1; *Gopal Das* v. *Thakurji*, AIR 1943 PC 83: ILR (1943) Kar PC 69: 1943 All LJ 292 (PC): 47 CWN 607.
10. *Cement Corporation of India Ltd.* v. *Purya*, (2004) 8 SCC 270: AIR 2004 SC 4830: 2004 AIR SCW 5534.

SECTION 78: Public documents specified in this section may be proved as indicated in the section. This is a permissive section, not an exclusive one. This method is not compulsory.[1] The section specifies various ways in which the documents referred to can be proved.

Method of proof prescribed in section 78 for various types of public documents:

(1) Acts, orders or notification of Central Government in any of its' departments, or of the crown Representative or of any State Government or any of its' departments,—
   - By the records of the departments, certified by the heads of those departments respectively,
   - Or by any document purporting to be printed by order of any such Government or, as the case may be, of the crown Representative;

(2) the proceedings of the Legislatures—
   - by the journals of those bodies respectively, or by published Acts or abstracts, or by copies purporting to be printed by order of the Government concerned;

(3) proclamation, orders or regulations issued by Her Majesty or by the privy council, or by any department of Her Majesty's Government,—
   - By copies or extracts contained in the London Gazette, or purporting to be printed by the queen's printer;

(4) The Acts of the Executive or the proceedings of the Legislature of a foreign country,—
   - By Journals published by their authority, or commonly received in this country as such, or by a copy entitled under the seal of the country or the sovereign or by a recognition thereof in some Central Act;

(5) The proceedings of a municipal body in a state—
   - By a copy of such proceedings, certified by the legal keeper thereof, or by a printed book purporting to be published by the authority of such body;

(6) Public documents of any other class in a foreign country—
   - By the original, or by a copy certified by the legal keeper thereof, with a certified copy under the seal of a notary public, or of an Indian consul or diplomatic agent, that the copy is duly certified by the officer having the legal custody of the original, and upon proof of the character of the document according to the law of the foreign country.

CLAUSE (1): If the Acts, orders or notifications amount to "law" in force, under section 57, Judicial notice can be taken.[2] A cyclostyled copy of notification attested by a forest officer is not admissible.[3] A copy of a government notification certified by the head of the department which issued the notification can be produced as evidence under section 78 read with section 65.[4]

1. *Sheodayal Khemka* v. *Joharmull Manmull,* AIR 1924 Cal 74: ILR 50 Cal 549.
2. *State of Madhya Pradesh* v. *Ramcharan,* AIR 1977 MP 68: 1977 Cr LJ 597: ILR 1978 MP 601.
3. *Chandra Naik* v. *State,* 1993 Cr LJ 2128: 1993 (3) Crimes 624: 1993 (76) Cut LT 361.
4. *Janu Khan* v. *State,* AIR 1980 Pat 263: 1960 BLJR 12: 1960 Cr LJ 634.

CLAUSE (2): This clause deals with legislative proceedings. They can be proved by journals of such Legislatures or by published Acts or abstracts or by copies purporting to be printed by order of the government concerned. Parliamentary proceedings of India fall under clause (2), each house of parliament publishes it's own journal's. The word "Journal" in clause (2) applies to Journals of State Legislatures also.[1] Newspaper reports are in the nature of hearsay and no notice can be taken of such reports as newspaper is not one of the documents referred to in section 78.[2]

CLAUSE (3) and (4): These clauses deal with documents as described therein and published by or on behalf of British Government or Foreign Legislature, respectively.

CLAUSE (5): Municipal Board proceedings case be proved by a copy thereof certified by the legal keeper or by a printed book purported to have been published under the authority of the municipal body.[3] Where a municipal council by a resolution authorised the commissioner, who in turn, gave authority to sanitary inspectors who would be prosecution witnesses, the commissioner's order is not admissible as evidence of council Resolution.[4] Where there was a resolution of Municipal counsel authorising Asst. Municipal Prosecutor to institute and conduct prosecution under the PFA Act, and the commissioner authorised the head clerk to attest copies, it has to be regarded as a valid attestation, though the head clerk is not the keeper of the records.[5]

CLAUSE 6: Regarding Foreign Law, sections 38, 45 and 84 may be looked into. Apart from the certificate from the legal keeper of the original document and by the counsel general, there shall also be proof of the character of the foreign judgment according to the law of the foreign country, before it can be admitted and this is a condition precedent.[6] Presumption under section 86 may also be seen. The presumption may be drawn before the said judgment is admitted and by virtue of the presumption of genuineness of the copy of judgment arising under section 86, the third condition under section 78(6) that the character of the document according to the law of the foreign country may be said to have been proved and the judgment may be admitted. (*ibid*).

The Section does not say how any fact, historical or otherwise, is to be proved by the parties, but gives the court liberty to resort to appropriate books or documents of reference on matters of public history.[7]

---

1. *Niharendu Dutt Majumdar* v. *Emperor*, AIR 1942 FC 22: 43 Cr LJ 504: (1942) 4 FCR 38.
2. *Laxmi Raj Shetty* v. *State of Tamil Nadu*, AIR 1988 SC 1274: (1988) 3 SCC 319: 1988 SCC (Cri) 633: (1988) 2 Crimes 107.
3. *Akshay Kumar Chand* v. *Comr. of Bogra Municipality*, AIR 1923 Cal 675: 75 Ind Cas 506.
4. *Gopinathannar* v. *Thomas*, ILR 1960 Ker 1449.
5. *Tillo Ram Karam Chand* v. *State*, AIR 1967 Del 71: 69 Pun LR (D) 22: 1967 Cr LJ 1295.
6. *Badat & Co.* v. *East India Trading Co.*, AIR 1964 SC 538: 1965 (1) SCJ 747: (1964) 4 SCR 19: (1964) 2 SCA 1: 66 Bom LR 402.
7. *The Englishman Ltd.* v. *Lagpat Rao*, ILR (1910) 37 Cal 760.

CHAPTER 17

PRESUMPTIONS (SECTIONS 79 TO 90A, 113A, 114)

1. Presumption is an inference of fact drawn from other known or proved facts.[1] Rule of presumption is a rule that courts may or shall draw a particular inference from a particular fact or evidence, unless and until, if so permitted, the truth of such inference is rebutted. Presumption helps in determining the probative force of evidence by subjecting the extent of probative force under precise rules excluding judicial discretion – a rule which treats an unknown fact as proved by proof or admission of certain other facts. It is a device whereby court is entitled to pronounce on an issue notwithstanding that there is no evidence or insufficient evidence about it. It takes effect by way of allocating the burden of proof in relation to that issue to one party or the other, irrespective of which of them bears the general burden of proof.[2]

"Presumption" in its most comprehensive sense, is an inference, affirmative or negative, of the truth or falsehood of a doubtful fact, drawn by a process of probable reasoning from something proved or taken for granted.[3]

There are two classes of presumptions, presumptions of fact or natural presumptions and presumptions of law or artificial presumptions. There is a third classification arising out of presumption, *i.e.*, irrebuttable presumptions of law or conclusive presumption.[4]

2. Presumptions of fact are inferences which the human mind naturally and logically draws from facts, irrespective of their legal effect; not only are they always rebuttable, but the court may refuse to draw the usual or natural inference notwithstanding that there is no rebutting evidence.[5] Such inferences are drawn, not by virtue of any rule of law but by the spontaneous operation of the reasoning faculty; all that the law does for them is to recognise the propriety of their being so drawn if the court thinks fit. The force of a presumption rests altogether on experience and observation of the course of nature, constitution of the human mind, enlightened human knowledge and experience, the springs of human action and the usages and habits of society.[6] Rules of presumption are

1. *P.R. Metrani* v. *Commissioner of Income Tax, Bangalore,* AIR 2007 SC 386: 2006 AIR SCW 6283: (2007) 1 SCC 789.
2. Phipson on Evidence, 14th Edition, page 83.
3. Best on Evidence 12th Edition, Section 299, Page 267; *Kumar Exports* v. *Sharma Carpets,* (2009) 2 SCC 513: AIR 2009 SC 1518: 2009 AIR SCW 1018.
4. *Syad Akbar* v. *State of Karnataka,* 1979 CAR 273: AIR 1979 SC 1848: (1979) 85 Cr LJ 327: (1979) 85 Cr LJ 1374: 1980 ACJ 38: (1980) 1 SCC 30: (1980) 1 SCR 95; *P.R. Metrani* v. *Commissioner of Income Tax, Bangalore,* AIR 2007 SC 386: 2006 AIR SCW 6283: (2007) 1 SCC 789.
5. Phipson on Evidence 14th Edition, page 5.
6. Best on Evidence, 12th Edition, sec. 303.

drawn from the connection, relation and coincidence of facts and circumstances.[1] It is also permissive, discretionary. This is what is laid down in the definition of "May Presume" occurring in section 4 of the Indian Evidence Act, 1872, by stating that the court may regard a fact as proved, unless and until it is disproved or may call for proof of it.[2] In the former case, court draws a presumption; in the latter case, court declines to draw a presumption. Presumptions of fact are generally rebuttable, unless they are conclusive.[3]

Sections 86 to 88A, 90, 90A, 113A and 114 of the Act relate to presumptions of fact.

3. Presumptions of law or artificial presumptions are arbitrary consequences expressly annexed by law to particular facts and may either be conclusive or rebuttable.[4] The "Connection" in this case is not so intimate or so uniform as to be inclusively presumed to exist in every case, yet it is so general that the law itself, infers one fact from the proved existence of the other in the absence of any opposing evidence. Law defines the nature and amount of evidence sufficient to overthrow the burden of proof. If no opposing evidence is adduced, court is bound to adopt the presumption. This presumption is obligatory. This is indicated in the definition of "shall presume" in section 4 which postulates that court shall regard such fact as proved unless and until it is disproved.[2] This presumption is rebuttable and cannot lead to "conclusive proof".[5]

The chief function of such presumptions is to determine (in relation to a factual issue of a given case) upon whom the burden of proof or the evidential burden rests, depending on the nature and effect of the particular presumption.[6] Sections 41, 79 to 85, 85(A), 85(B), 85(C) and 89 of the 1872 Act relate to presumptions of law. In this connection, the chapter on Burden of Proof is relevant.

Sections 41 and 113 refer to totally irrebuttable presumptions while section 112 refers to a presumption which is irrebuttable except to the extent and in the manner provided therein. This is explained in the definition of "conclusive proof" occurring in section 4.[7] Such presumptions have been adopted in those cases in which the long experienced connection has been found so general and uniform as to render it expedient for the common good that this connection should be taken to be inseparable and universal and from motives of public policy.[8]

---

1. *Sodhi Transport Co.* v. *State of Uttar Pradesh*, (1986) 1 SCR 939: (1986) 1 SCALE 489: (1986) 2 SCC 486: (1986) 2 UJ 147: AIR 1986 SC 1099: 1986 SCC (Tax) 410.
2. *State of West Bengal* v. *E.I.T.A. India Ltd.*, AIR 2003 SC 4126: 2003 AIR SCW 2114: (2003) 5 SCC 239.
3. *Somavanti* v. *State of Punjab*, AIR 1963 SC 151: (1963) 2 SCR 774: (1963) 2 SCJ 35.
4. Phipson on Evidence, 14th Edition, page 5.
5. *Union of India* v. *Pramod Gupta*, AIR 2005 SC 3708: 2005 AIR SCW 4645: (2005) 12 SCC 1; *State of Madras* v. *A. Vaidyanatha Iyer*, AIR 1958 SC 61: 1958 SCR 580: 1958 Cr LJ 232: (1958) 2 LLJ 653; *State of Andhra Pradesh* v. *C. Uma Maheswara Rao*, AIR 2004 SC 2042: (2004) 4 SCC 399: 2004 AIR SCW 2192.
6. Phipson on Evidence, 14th Edition at pages 84, 85.
7. *Izhar Ahmad Khan* v. *Union of India*, AIR 1962 SC 1052: (1962) 2 Cr LJ 215: 1962 Supp (3) SCR 235; *Ashok Layland Ltd.* v. *State of Tamil Nadu*, AIR 2004 SC 2836: 2004 AIR SCW 1001: (2004) 3 SCC 1; *Somavanti* v. *State of Punjab*, AIR 1963 SC 151: (1963) 2 SCR 774: (1963) 2 SCJ 35.
8. Taylor on Evidence sec. 71.

Presumptions, other than conclusive presumptions, are merely rules of evidence. Conclusive presumptions can be rules of evidence or substantive law, depending on whether the basic fact upon proof of which a presumption is required to be drawn is inherently relevant in proving the existence of the later fact and has inherently probative or persuasive value in that behalf or not. If it is so inherently relevant, the rule of conclusive presumption would be a rule of evidence. If it is not so inherently relevant or has no inherently probative value, the rule would be a rule of substantive law.[1]

PRESUMPTIONS OF FACT

4. SECTION 86.—Certified copy of a foreign judicial record may be presumed to be genuine and accurate, if it is certified in the manner prescribed by the section. This section is not exhaustive of the modes of proof of such records. *See* section 78(6). Section 86 has to be read with section 14 C.P.C. The admission of a judgment is not a condition precedent for raising a presumption under section 86. The presumption may be drawn before the judgment is admitted.[2]

5. SECTION 87.—Book of reference referring to information on matters of public or general interest, and published map or chart, the statements of which are relevant facts and which are otherwise relevant, and which are produced for inspection, may be presumed to have been written or published by the person and at the time and place, by whom or at which they purport to have been written or published. There is no presumption of accuracy or conclusiveness of the contents. Though great weight may be attached to survey maps, they are not conclusive, but in the absence of evidence to the contrary, they would be presumed to be accurate. Maps prepared after due enquiry are presumed to be correct, unless shown to be wrong.[3] The accuracy as to the information contained in a map must depend upon the source from which the information is obtained.[4]

Section 57 which indicates the facts of which courts shall take judicial notice refers to statutes, legislative proceedings, official gazette etc., official reports may be referred to for gathering historical facts, but opinions expressed therein cannot be treated as conclusive in respect of matters requiring judicial decision. Judicial notice takes the place of proof.[5] Section 57 is not exhaustive.[6] *See* sections 36, 57, 83, 90 and 114 also.

6. SECTION 88:.—Telegraphic message delivered to the addressee may be presumed to correspond with the message delivered for transmission at the telegraphic office of origin. This presumption can be supported by illustrations (i) and (f) of section 114. Section 88 will apply only if there is proof of receipt

1. *Izhar Ahmad Khan* v. *Union of India*, AIR 1962 SC 1052: (1962) 2 Cr LJ 215: 1962 Supp (3) SCR 235.
2. *Badat & Co.* v. *East India Trading Co.*, AIR 1964 SC 538: 1965 (1) SCJ 747: (1964) 4 SCR 19: (1964) 2 SCA 1: 66 Bom LR 402.
3. *Tarakdas Acharjee Choudhury* v. *Secretary of State*, AIR 1935 PC 125: 156 IC 548.
4. *Nana Akpandja* v. *Fiaga Egblomesse*, AIR 1939 PC 143.
5. *Onkar Nath* v. *Delhi Administration*, AIR 1977 SC 1108: (1977) 2 SCC 611: 1977 Cr LJ 957: 1977 SC 1108.
6. *S. Jeet Singh* v. *Union of India*, AIR 1965 SC 1666: 1965 Punj LR (Supp) 231; *State of Assam* v. *Banshidhar Shewbhagavan and Co.*, AIR 1981 SC 1957: (1981) 4 SCC 283; *Onkar Nath* v. *Delhi Administration*, AIR 1977 SC 1108: (1977) 2 SCC 611: 1977 Cr LJ 957; *Atam Prakash* v. *State of Haryana*, AIR 1986 SC 859: (1986) 2 SCC 249: 1986 Pun LJ 191; *Rattan Arya* v. *State of Tamil Nadu*, AIR 1986 SC 1444: (1986) 3 SCC 385: 1986 (2) SCJ 429.

of the message by the addressee. The form handed over at the post office by the sender and not the form delivered by the post office to the addressee is the original of the message.

There cannot be any presumption regarding the identity of the sender of the telegram and that requires independent proof, direct or circumstantial.[1] Where the original message is not proved to be in the handwriting of the alleged sender, there is no presumption regarding the identity of the sender.

If a telegram is shown to have been correctly addressed and handed over at the office of origin, section 114 enables a presumption to be drawn of it's having been delivered to the addressee residing at the address. Marks affixed at the post/telegraph office are evidence of the dates and places mentioned. The presumption under section 88 would also apply to radio messages. Contents of a telegram in the context of chain of correspondence may furnish proof of authority.[2]

7. SECTION 88A.—The court may presume that an electronic message, forwarded by the originator through an electronic mail server to the addressee to whom the message purports to be addressed corresponds with the message as fed into his computer for transmission; but the court shall not make any presumption as to the person by whom such message was sent.

Explanation.—For the purpose of this section, the expressions "addressee" and "originator" shall have the same meanings respectively assigned to them in clauses (b) and (za) of sub-section (1) of section 2 of the Information Technology Act, 2000.

This section was inserted by Act, 21 of 2000.

8. SECTION 90.—Where a thirty year old document is produced from "proper" custody, court may presume that the signature and every other part of the document which purports to be in the handwriting of any particular person is in that person's handwriting. In the case of a document executed or attested, Court may presume that it was duly executed or attested by the persons by whom it purports to have been executed and attested. A document is regarded as being in proper custody, if it is in the place in which and under the care of the person with whom it would naturally be. No custody is improper if it is shown to have had a legitimate origin or if the particular circumstances are such as to render such an origin probable. This is what is stated in the explanation to the section. The section is based on the principle of necessity and convenience.

Documents, thirty years old, produced from proper custody, and otherwise free from suspicion, prove themselves and no evidence of the handwriting, signature, sealing or delivery need be insisted upon. This rule of convenience is based on the difficulty in producing relevant oral evidence after a long lapse of time.

The period of thirty years is to be reckoned, not from the date on which the document is filed in court, but from the date on which it's genuineness becomes the subject of proof.[3] This rule applies to letters, entrees, receipts, settlement

1. *Kishore Chandra Singh Deo* v. *Ganesh Prasad Bhagat*, AIR 1954 SC 316: (1954) 1 Mad LJ 622: 1954 SCR 919: 1954 SCJ 395; *Mobarik Ali Ahmed* v. *State of Bombay*, AIR 1957 SC 857: 1957 Cr LJ 1346: 1958 SCR 328: (1957) 61 Bom LR 58: 1958 SCJ 111.
2. *Baman Chandra Acharya* v. *Balaram Acharya*, AIR 1966 Ori 160: ILR 1965 Cut 799.
3. *Antonio Dias Caldeira* v. *Frederick Augustus Gray*, AIR 1936 PC 15; *G. Konda Reddi* v. *P Pichireddi*, AIR 1925 Mad 184.

certificates, school registers, books of account, deeds requiring or not requiring attestation and other documents, public or private. The Act applies to probate proceedings and hence this rule applies to a will produced in probate court and as foundation of a party's right and not merely as a piece of evidence in a court.[1] Presumption of "due execution" can lead to presumption of testamentary capacity also.[2]

Custodial propriety must be established, not on general principles, but on the facts of a particular case. A document can be said to be in proper custody if it is found with a person or at a place where, if authentic, it might naturally and reasonably be expected to be found. Illustrations to the section clarify the matter. The surrounding circumstances tending to establish the connection of the party producing the document with the person with whom the document should naturally be are to be looked into. "Proper custody" is one shown to have had a legitimate origin, the legitimacy being rendered by the circumstances.

9. This presumption must be applied with proper care and caution. Court will ordinarily consider age, proper custody, innocent appearance (as against suspicious appearance) of the document, internal and external evidence and surrounding circumstances in deciding whether the presumption is to be drawn in a particular case. Apparently suspicious circumstances such as unacknowledged overwriting, writing on folds, ink being new and other tell-tale circumstances influence Courts in not drawing the presumption.[3] The discretion granted by section 90 is to be exercised not arbitrarily or capriciously, but judiciously. The presumption is easily drawn in certain cases, for example, cases of registered documents, or where attester and scribe are dead or unavailable or where the documents have been acted upon. The power of the court under this section is discretionary.[4] If there are reasonable grounds for suspecting its genuineness and the party who relies on the document fails to satisfy the court of its due execution, the court will not invoke the presumption.

Courts have refused to draw the presumption in cases where evidence in proof of document has been produced but disbelieved or where there is reason to believe the document to be fabricated or grave suspicion attaches to the document on account of erasures and rewriting. Presumption can be drawn even if the witnesses are alive.[5] The presumption is rebuttable.[6]

This presumption arises in respect of the original document and not a copy.[7] However, it applies to a copy as a copy.[8]

1. *Alfred William Luddit* v. *Ginger Coote Airways Ltd.*, AIR 1947 PC 151: 51 Cal WN 498: (1947) 1 All ER 328; *Sarat Chandra Mondal* v. *Panchanan Mondal*, 58 Cal WN 271: AIR 1953 Cal 471; *Harihar Prasad Singh* v. *Deo Narain Prasad*, AIR 1956 SC 305: 1956 SCJ 279: 1956 SCR 1.
2. *Alfred William Luddit* v. *Ginger Coote Airways Ltd.*, AIR 1947 PC 151: 51 Cal WN 498: (1947) 1 All ER 328.
3. *Kapur Chand* v. *Lal Chand*, AIR 1975 Raj 178: 1974 Raj LW 579.
4. *Sital Das* v. *Sant Ram*, AIR 1954 SC 606.
5. *Rao Raja Tej Singh* v. *Hastimal*, AIR 1972 Raj 191: 1972 Raj LW 133.
6. *Sarat Chandra Mondal* v. *Panchanan Mondal*, 58 Cal WN 271: AIR 1953 Cal 471.
7. *Basant Singh* v. *Brij Raj Saran Singh*, AIR 1935 PC 132: 62 IA 180: 57 A 494: 156 IC 864 (PC); *Alfred William Luddit* v. *Ginger Coote Airways Ltd.*, AIR 1947 PC 151: 51 Cal WN 498: (1947) 1 All ER 328; *Sital Das* v. *Sant Ram*, AIR 1954 SC 606; *Harihar Prasad Singh* v. *Deo Narain Prasad*, AIR 1956 SC 305: 1956 SCJ 279: 1956 SCR 1; *Kalidindi Venkata Subbaraju* v. *Chintalapati Subbaraju*, AIR 1968 SC 947: (1968) 2 SCJ 513: (1968) 2 SCR 292; *Shiv Lal* v. *Chetram*, (1971) 2 SCJ 8: AIR 1971 SC 2342: (1971) 2 SCR 104.
8. *Kalyan Singh* v. *Chhoti*, AIR 1973 Raj 263: 1973 Raj LW 473: ILR (1973) 23 Raj 634.

Certified copy of a statement given in mutation proceedings for purpose of showing acknowledgement of a mortgage does not attract this provision unless foundation is laid for reception of secondary evidence under section 65.[1] Registration copies are governed by section 57(5) of Registration Act.

There is no presumption regarding the truth of the contents of ancient documents; nor does it have a bearing on the evidentiary value of the documents. Their value as evidence must depend upon the circumstances available in each case. The presumption relates only to signature and handwriting.[2] The presumption regarding handwriting can apply only if the document itself shows in whose handwriting the document is; it cannot apply to an anonymous document (the writer of which is not known).[3] A mark representing a signature and a thumb impression of the signatory is covered by this presumption, in the absence of proof to the contrary. The section makes no provision to regard a seal as a signature; nor is it to be treated as a signature under the General Clauses Act.[4] Where this presumption is raised, the correctness of the recitals are not to be presumed.[5] This section will not apply in the case of a will governed by the proviso to section 68 of the Evidence Act.

10. SECTION 90A.—Where any electronic record, purporting or proved to be five years old, is produced from any custody which the Court in the particular case considers proper, the Court may presume that the digital signature which purports to be the digital signature of any particular person was so affixed by him or any person authorised by him in this behalf.

This Section has an explanation similar to the explanation to section 90.

11. SECTION 113A.—(Inserted by amending Act 43 of 1983) – This section relates to a situation where the question is whether the commission of suicide by a woman had been abetted by her husband or any other relative of her husband and it is shown that (a) she committed suicide within a period of seven years from the date of her marriage, and (b) her husband or such relative of her husband had subjected her to cruelty. On these facts having been shown, the court having regard to all the other circumstances of the case, may, draw the presumption that such suicide had been abetted by her husband or such relative of her husband. By "Cruelty" is meant "Cruelty" as defined in section 498A of Indian Penal Code (I.P.C.).[6]

This provision is the legislative reflection of societal concern at the increasing menace of atrocities on married women. Section 113B of the Act and section

---

1. *Shiv Lal* v. *Chetram*, (1971) 2 SCJ 8: AIR 1971 SC 2342: (1971) 2 SCR 104; *Lakhi Baruah* v. *Padma Kanta Kalita*, AIR 1996 SC 1253: (1996) 1 CCC 352: (1996) 2 SCALE 644: (1996) 8 SCC 357; *Dayamathi Bai* v. *K.M. Shaffi*, (2004) 7 SCC 107: 2004 AIR SCW 4419: AIR 2004 SC 4082.
2. *Ganesh Prasad Ray* v. *Narendra Nath Sen*, AIR 1953 SC 431: 17 Cut LT 73: 1951 Ker LT (SC) 28.
3. *Kanhiya Lal* v. *Jamna Lal*, AIR 1950 Raj 47: 1950 Raj LW 199.
4. *Krishna Pillai* v. *Raman Charan*, AIR 1955 Cal 194; *Maheswar Naik* v. *Tikayet Sailendra Narayan Bhanj Deo*, AIR 1951 Ori 327: (1949) 1 Cut 312.
5. *Shalinibai* v. *Narayan*, (2005) 9 SCC 359.
6. *Bhagwant Singh* v. *Commissioner of Police Delhi*, AIR 1983 SC 826: (1983) Cr LJ 1081: (1983) 3 SCC 344; *Hans Raj* v. *State of Haryana*, 2004 AIR SCW 1283: AIR 2004 SC 2790: 2004 Cr LJ 1759; *State of Andhra Pradesh* v. *Raj Gopal Asawa*, AIR 2004 SC 1933: (2004) 4 SCC 470: 2004 Cr LJ 1791; *Kunhiabdulla* v. *State of Kerala*, AIR 2004 SC 1731: 2004 AIR SCW 1337: 2004 Cr LJ 5005 (SC): (2004) 4 SCC 13; *Baljeet Singh* v. *State of Haryana*, AIR 2004 SC 1714: 2004 AIR SCW 1230: (2004) 3 SCC 122: 2003 Cr LJ 3711.

304B of Indian Penal Code also serve a similar purpose. The woman must have committed suicide within seven years of her marriage.[1] This provision is permissive and is not mandatory. If there is a charge under section 302 I.P.C., section 113A cannot be invoked.[2]

This presumption arises only in the context of abetment in case of suicide by a married woman. This provision is merely procedural in character and has retrospective effect.[3] In view of the provision, it is open to Courts to look into the past conduct even before 1983. In the absence of proof of past cruelty, no presumption can be raised. The factum of suicide must be proved. The requirement of proof of guilt beyond reasonable doubt is not altered by this provision.[4] Before drawing the presumption, the court is required to consider all the other circumstances of the case. This may be necessary to see if cause and effect relationship existed between the cruelty and the suicide.[5] One of the circumstances to be considered is whether the alleged cruelty was of such a nature as was likely to drive the woman to commit suicide.

12. SECTION 114.—This is a section of crucial importance to courts. The court may presume the existence of any fact which it thinks likely to have happened, having regard to—

(a) Common course of natural events,

(b) Human conduct, and

(c) Public and private business,—

in their relation to the facts of the particular case.

Provisions regarding burden of proof indicate on which party lies the burden of proving disputed facts. Section 114 means that the court is not bound in every instance to presume against the party on whom the burden of proof lies. But there are certain presumptions where room is left for the court to exercise its power of drawing inference so that the court can throw the burden of proof on one party or the other by using or not using permissive presumptions or presumptions of fact. When a court draws a presumption of fact in favour of one party, burden of proof is thrown on the opposite party.[6] The requirement of this section is that court is to use its own common sense and experience in gauging the effect of particular facts. A presumption is not evidence or proof, it only shows on whom the burden of proof lies. They may be rebutted not only by evidence but also by presumptions.[7] Where the facts are ascertained, presumptions arising

1. *Ashok Kumar* v. *State of (NCT of Delhi)*, (2007) 5 SCC 712: AIR 2007 SC 2311: 2007 AIR SCW 4008.
2. *Ramesh Kumari* v. *State (NCT of Delhi)*, AIR 2006 SC 1322: 2006 AIR SCW 1021: 2006 Cr LJ 1622.
3. *Gurbachan Singh* v. *Satpal Singh*, AIR 1990 SC 209: (1990) 1 SCC 445: 1990 Cr LJ 562.
4. *State of West Bengal* v. *Orilal Jaiswal*, (1994) 1 SCC 73: AIR 1994 SC 1418: 1994 AIR SCW 844.
5. *Ramesh Kumar* v. *State of Chhattisgarh*, 2001 Cr LJ 4724: AIR 2001 SC 3837: 2001 AIR SCW 4282; *Rajbabu* v. *State of Madhya Pradesh*, AIR 2008 SC 3212: 2008 Cr LJ 4301: 2008 AIR SCW 5435; *M. Sreedevi* v. *University of Health Services, A.P.*, (2002) 10 SCC 76.
6. *T. Shankar Prasad* v. *State of Andhra Pradesh*, AIR 2004 SC 1242: 2004 AIR SCW 262: 2004 Cr LJ 884.
7. *Kundan Lal Rallaram* v. *Custodian, Evacuee Property, Bombay*, AIR 1961 SC 1316: 1963 1 SCJ 347: 1963 1 MLJ (SC) 85.

from conduct cannot establish a right which the facts themselves disprove.[1] This section deals with presumptions of facts which are inferences of certain fact patterns drawn from experience and observation of common course of nature, the constitution of the human mind, the springs of human action, the usages and habits of society and ordinary course of human affairs.[2] A presumption can be drawn only from the facts and not from other presumptions.[3] The court has absolute discretion to presume the existence of any fact which it thinks likely to have happened.[4] But it is unsafe to use a presumption to draw yet another discretionary presumption unless there is statutory compulsion (*ibid*). There can be no presumption in favour of a fact which offends a statutory principle. There is no scope for presumption when facts are known.

A presumption is a factual assumption drawn from the existence of certain facts.[5] A presumption once drawn is rebuttable.[6] Care must be taken to ensure that the presumption under this section is not stretched to such an extent as to permit suspicion taking the place of proof. In appropriate cases, on the strength of the presumption, the court may dispense with direct proof of certain facts which can be safely presumed to be necessarily existing. There are other statutes which prescribe presumptions, for example, sections 118-122 and 137 of the Negotiable Instruments Act, sections 53 and 101 of the Transfer of Properties Act, section 6 of Land Acquisition Act.

A fact is said to be proved when, the court either believes it to exist or considers it's existence so probable that a prudent person, ought, under the circumstances of the particular case, to act upon the supposition that it exists. *See* also definition of "disproved" and "not proved" in section 3. Presumption of existence of a fact, dispensing with proof thereof may be drawn under section 114 provided the court concludes such fact as likely to have happened, having regard to one of the the aspects mentioned in the section.

13. Common Course of Natural Events.—Court is to be guided by its' own experience and knowledge of common course of natural events, besides human conduct and public and private business. Some examples from decided cases may be seen:

In a case under P.C. Act, where the accused look out currency notes and flung them across the wall, it was held that court may presume that he must have obtained the money from the witness, who, a short while earlier, was shown to have been in possession of the notes.[7] Where the accused (terrorist), short of participating in the actual attack on Parliament, did everything to set

1. *Kishorilal* v. *Chaltibai*, AIR 1959 SC 504: 1959 SCJ 560: 1959 Supp (1) SCR 698.
2. *Syad Akbar* v. *State of Karnataka*, 1979 CAR 273: AIR 1979 SC 1848: (1979) 85 Cr LJ 327: (1979) 85 Cr LJ 1374: 1980 ACJ 38: (1980) 1 SCC 30: (1980) 1 SCR 95; *M. Narsinga Rao* v. *State of Andhra Pradesh*, (2001) 1 SCC 691: AIR 2001 SC 318: 2000 AIR SCW 4427: 2001 Cr LJ 515.
3. *Suresh Budharmal Kalani* alias *Pappu Kalani* v. *State of Maharashtra*, AIR 1998 SC 3258: 1998 SCC (Cri) 1625: (1998) 7 SCC 337: 1998 Cr LJ 4592; *T. Shankar Prasad* v. *State of Andhra Pradesh*, AIR 2004 SC 1242: 2004 AIR SCW 262: 2004 Cr LJ 884; *State of Andhra Pradesh* v. *Vasudeva Rao*, AIR 2004 SC 960: 2004 Cr LJ 620: 2003 AIR SCW 6555.
4. *M. Narsinga Rao* v. *State of Andhra Pradesh*, (2001) 1 SCC 691: AIR 2001 SC 318: 2000 AIR SCW 4427: 2001 Cr LJ 515.
5. *M.S. Narayana Menon* v. *State of Kerala*, (2006) 6 SCC 39: AIR 2006 SC 3366: 2006 Cr LJ 4607.
6. *V.S. Krishnan* v. *Westfort Hi-Tech Hospital Ltd.*, (2008) 3 SCC 363.
7. *Calcutta Chromotype Ltd.* v. *CCE*, (1998) 3 SCC 681: AIR 1998 SC 1631: 1998 AIR SCW 1379; *Tata Engineering and Locomotive Co. Ltd.* v. *State of Bihar*, AIR 1965 SC 40: 1964 (1) SCJ 666: (1964) 6 SCR 885; Contra *C.C.E.* v. *Abex Rubber Co.*, (1998) 9 SCC 400.

in motion the mission, the court could presume that he had nexus with the co-conspirators who were killed and all of them together hatched the conspiracy.[1] The legitimacy of a child may have to be decided by reference to the term during which, in the ordinary course of nature, gestation may continue. A case of adultery may have to be judged having regard to the social conditions and the manner in which the parties are accustomed to live.[2] From the fact that a man and a woman lived together for a number of years under the same roof, a presumption may be drawn that they lived as husband and wife and their children are legitimate.[3] Such presumption of marriage can be repelled only by evidence of clearest character.[4] A presumption may be drawn from omission to contradict a witness.[5] Where a government employee was found in possession of assets disproportionate to his earnings and was unable to explain it, there can be a presumption of corruption.[6] Where a litigant who makes a serious allegation against the opposite party is unable to produce good evidence in support of the allegation, court may presume the allegation to be false.[7] The statement of a judge as to what happened in court is generally presumed to be correct.[8] When a I.T. Officer extended time for filing a return it must be presumed that extension was granted after satisfying himself that a case for extension was made out.[9]

14. Human Conduct.—Court may draw presumption based on its experience of human conduct.

Court could prefer to accept evidence of villagers which fits in with normal conduct of villagers.[10] Where a father is attacked in the presence of his sons, according to normal human conduct, the sons would intervene and retaliate in self-defence.[11] It would be inconsistent with normal conduct for a person to share a plan of murder and to choose a busy place for committing murder or for an assailant to continue to wear his bloodstained clothes for four days after the murder.[12] So also the conduct of a first informant who has a scooter and a tractor, to go on foot to the police station to give information particularly if he is an interested witness and the police station is about six to seven kilometers away.[13]

1. *State (NCT of Delhi)* v. *Navjot Sandhu @ Afasan' Guru*, AIR 2005 SC 3820: 2005 AIR SCW 4148: (2005) 11 SCC 600: 2005 Cr LJ 3950 (SC): 122 (2005) DLT 194 (SC).
2. Ratanlal Dhirajlal on Law of Evidence, 23rd Edition, Pages 1325, 1326.
3. *S.P.S. Balasubramanyam* v. *Suruttayan*, AIR 1992 SC 756: 1992 AIR SCW 441: 1992 (3) SCJ 468.
4. *Badri Prasad* v. *Dy. Director of Consolidation*, AIR 1978 SC 1557: (1978) 3 SCC 527: 1978 Hindu LR 697.
5. *Virendra Singh* v. *Vimal Kumar*, (1976) 2 SCWR 46: (1977) 1 SCR 525: AIR 1976 SC 2169: (1977) 1 SCC 718.
6. *State of Maharashtra* v. *Wasudeo Ramchandra Kaidalwar*, AIR 1981 SC 1186: 1981 Cr LJ 884: (1981) 3 SCC 199.
7. *Virendra Kumar Saklecha* v. *Jagjiwan*, AIR 1974 SC 1957: (1972) 1 SCC 826: (1972) 3 SCR 955.
8. *Union of India* v. *T.R. Verma*, AIR 1957 SC 882: 1958 SCR 499: 60 Punj LR 126: 1958 SCJ 142.
9. *State of Rajasthan* v. *Shamsher Singh*, AIR 1985 SC 1082: 1985 Cri LJ 1348: 1985 SCC (Cri) 421.
10. *Moti* v. *State of Uttar Pradesh*, AIR 2003 SC 1897: 2003 AIR SCW 1372: 2003 Cr LJ 1694.
11. *State of Madhya Pradesh* v. *Mishrilal*, AIR 2003 SC 4089: 2003 Cr LJ 2312: 2003 AIR SCW 2066.
12. *Mousam Singha Roy* v. *State of West Bengal*, (2003) 12 SCC 377; *Khalil Khan* v. *State of Madhya Pradesh*, (2003) 11 SCC 19: AIR 2003 SC 4670: 2003 Cr LJ 5046.
13. *Mohinder Singh* v. *State of Punjab*, AIR 2003 SC 4399: 2003 Cr LJ 5002: 2003 AIR SCW 5033: (2003) 7 SCALE 372.

It would be inconsistent with normal human conduct for anyone on seeing a perfect stranger to straightaway abuse him without any rhyme or reason.[1] No hard and fast rule having universal application with respect to human reaction in various situations can be laid down.[2]

15. Public and private business: Court may presume that the common course of business has been followed in particular cases, provided the existence of course of business is proved or admitted. When the question is whether a particular act was done, the existence of any course of business according to which it naturally would have been done, is a relevant fact. There are various *prima facie* presumptions which are founded upon the experience of human conduct in the ordinary course of business.[3] Where a document was executed *ex facie* by a government official on behalf of the Court of wards and it was not challenged for eighty years, court can presume that the official was duly authorized to act on behalf of the Court of wards.[4] When a person signs a document, he ordinarily does so with a view to execute it; that is the common course of human conduct in private and public business.[5] Several presumptions are made from the regular course of business in public offices, including post offices. Several presumptions are drawn from the usual course of men's private business and offices, where primary evidence of the fact is lacking.[6] Where the general diary of a police station showed the time at which an FIR was sent to a magistrate but it did not contain the magistrate's endorsement and the H.C. of Police deposed that the report was sent to the magistrate, presumption of ante-dating of FIR cannot be drawn.[7]

16. The illustrations to section 114 are not exhaustive. Analogous cases in which facts are distinguishable can also be dealt with hereunder. The illustrations to any section merely exemplify the application of the provision to which it is appended.[8] The general presumptions under section 114 must yield place to presumptions under special statutes.[9] Court is governed by it's own experience and knowledge of common course of natural events, of human conduct and of public and private business. One's personal experience grows with experience and one's own attitude to life, fellow beings and events; it can, however, be supplemented, strengthened and improved by wide reading habits. Judgments of experienced judges must naturally reflect the maturity gained by them from their experience and reading habits. There may be circumstances which weaken or destroy the presumption.[10] The presumption can be rebutted.

1. *Management of Madurantakam Co-op. Sugar Mills Ltd.* v. *S. Viswanathan*, 2005 AIR SCW 1418: AIR 2005 SC 1954: 2005 Lab IC 2271.
2. *Dinesh Borthakur* v. *State of Assam*, AIR 2008 SC 2205: 2008 AIR SCW 3301: (2008) 5 SCC 697.
3. Taylor on Evidence, sections 176 to 178.
4. *Maharaja Prathap Singh* v. *Thakur Manmohan Dey*, AIR 1966 SC 1931: 1967 (2) SCJ 352: (1966) 3 SCR 663.
5. *O.P. Verma* v. *Lala Gehrilal*, AIR 1962 Raj 231: ILR (1961) 11 Raj 103.
6. Taylor on Evidence, sections 181, 182.
7. *Subash and Shiva Shankar* v. *State of Uttar Pradesh*, AIR 1987 SC 1222: 1987 Cr LJ 991: (1987) 3 SCC 331.
8. *Chimna* v. *State*, AIR 1961 Raj 35: ILR (1960) 10 Raj 921: (1961) 1 Cr LJ 310.
9. *Mangi Lal* v. *State of Maharashtra*, AIR 1970 SC 1829: (1970) 2 SCR 270: (1970) Cr LJ 1644.
10. *Gokul Chand* v. *Pravin Kumari*, AIR 1952 SC 231: 1952 SCJ 331: 1952 SCR 825; *Badri Prasad* v. *Dy. Director of Consolidation*, AIR 1978 SC 1557: (1978) 3 SCC 527: 1978 Hindu LR 697.

17. Illustration (a).—Court may presume that a person who is in possession of stolen goods soon after theft is either the thief or received the goods knowing them to be stolen, unless he can account for his possession. Court may, and is not bound to raise the presumption in any given case. Three facts required to be proved before the question of invoking the presumption arises namely,—

(a) the property is stolen property,

(b) the person is in possession of such property, and

(c) such possession is "soon after theft", that is, "recent".

Once these facts are proved, the person found in possession has to account for his possession. If his explanation is reasonable and satisfactory, the presumption cannot be invoked as the illustration is inapplicable; if not, there is judicial discretion in the court to draw one of the two presumptions contemplated in the illustration, namely—

(a) either that he is the thief, or

(b) that he received the goods knowing them to be stolen.

Which of the two presumptions is to be drawn in a particular case depends upon the court's appreciation of the totality of the circumstances of the case. *Onus* to prove guilt of the accused beyond reasonable doubt is always on the prosecution, but under certain conditions, presumptions may alleviate the burden. Possession is presumptive evidence of ownership, but where the property is proved to be stolen, the possessor has to prove that he came by it honestly. The question whether the presumption is to be raised in a particular case depends upon the evidence and circumstances of the case. The nature of the article, the manner of it's acquisition by the owner, the nature of evidence about it's identification, the manner in which it was dealt with by the accused, the place and circumstances of recovery, the length of the intervening period, free availability or transferability or of being hidden for a long time on account of the incriminating effect, and his ability or otherwise to account for possession are factors which have to be considered.[1] Where the article is one which may change hands quite frequently and is commonly available and the recovery was made several months after theft, this presumption cannot be raised. Where property stolen in dacoity was recovered from the accused soon after the incident, inference as to the commission of dacoity could be drawn against them.[2]

18. Possession.—The generally accepted view is that possession must be shown to be exclusive. Possession has two elements, *animus* or intention and *corpus*; hence the person said to be in possession must have knowledge or consciousness of his possession of the property. In other words, possession must be conscious possession. It implies dominion, and consciousness of his dominion and that he can exercise it.[3] Possession must be exclusive.[4] If the property is found on the person or in personal custody of a person, he is in possession thereof. If

1. *Baiju* v. *State of Madhya Pradesh,* AIR 1978 SC 522: 1978 Cr LJ 646: (1978) 1 SCC 588; *Earabhadrappa* v. *State of Karnataka,* AIR 1983 SC 446: 1983 Cr LJ 846: (1983) 1 SCC 330: 1983 SCC (Cri) 447: (1983) 2 SCR 552; *A. Deivendran* v. *State of Tamil Nadu,* AIR 1998 SC 2821: 1998 AIR SCW 285: 1998 Cr LJ 814.

2. *Gulab Chand* v. *State of Madhya Pradesh,* AIR 1995 SC 1598: (1995) 3 SCC 574: 1995 SCC (Cri) 552; *Limbaji* v. *State of Maharashtra,* (2001) 10 SCC 340: AIR 2002 SC 491: 2002 AIR SCW 22.

3. *Pachiripali Satyanarayana (in re:),* AIR 1953 Mad 534: (1953) 1 Mad LJ 175: 1953 Cr LJ 1048; *In re: Wahib Basha,* AIR 1961 Mad 162: (1961) 1 Cr LJ 533.

4. *Apparama Mali* v. *Emperor,* AIR 1934 Bom 16: 35 Cr LJ 523.

it is found in a locked up house or room or box of which he keeps the key, it is fair to say he is in possession thereof.[1] If a person is not aware of the existence of the property, he cannot be said to be in possession, as consciousness is absent. If an article is found in the house of a person, he must be deemed to be aware of it's existence, provided no other person in the house had access to the particular place (ibid). Presence of stolen article in the house of a person which has other inmates capable of committing theft, will not by itself be sufficient to prove his possession, though, coupled with proof of other suspicious circumstances, it may justify the invocation of the presumption. In cases of buildings under plurality of occupation, the invocation of the presumption depends on the circumstances of each case, keeping in view the nature of the article, the place from where it was found, the nature of concealment, if any. Depending upon varied circumstances, all the inmates or only one of them or the head of the family or none of them can be said to be in possession. In some decisions it has been ruled that ordinarily the presumption cannot be invoked against the head of the family.[2] If it is not possible to fix the liability on any particular individual, court is not bound to presume that the article is in the possession of the head of the family.[3] In all such cases, a careful sifting and appreciation of the totality of the circumstances is necessary. Strength of the presumption against head of family depends on the size and noticeability of the article, nature of occupation, etc. Awareness of the article and control over it is sufficient. Where an almirah of which the key was with the father of the accused contained stolen articles it cannot be said to be in the exclusive or joint possession of the accused.[4]

If several persons are shown to be in joint possession of an article, a presumption may arise against all of them. Such "Joint Possession" means that each of them had either physical or constructive possession of the article or any part of it or that one or more of them had possession on behalf of themselves and others and to their knowledge.[5] Joint possession cannot be automatically inferred. Possession of a husband does not necessarily involve liability of wife.

If the place from where the article is recovered is an open place accessible to all, it may be difficult to hold positively that it was in the possession of the accused. If the article is found concealed at a particular spot, though in a larger area accessible to all, different considerations may arise. If it is a case of "discovery" of a fact under section 27, he may be guilty or innocent, depending upon the circumstances of the given case and the "information" proved under section 27. When an article is kept concealed under a bridge or any other place not ordinarily accessible to any person without prior knowledge, it cannot be said that the place is accessible to all.[6] In the case of the accused pointing out the article or place of concealment, the question is not so much whether he was in physical possession as whether he was the author of concealment, for a person

1. Best on Evidence, 12th Edition, Page 197.
2. *Pachiripali Satyanarayana (in re:)*, AIR 1953 Mad 534: (1953) 1 Mad LJ 175: 1953 Cr LJ 1048; In Re Wahib Basha, AIR 1961 Mad 162: (1961) 1 Cr LJ 533; *D. Weston* v. *Peary Mohun Das*, AIR 1914 Cal 396: ILR 40 Cal 898 (SB); *In re: Kodur Thimma Reddi*, 1957 Cr LJ 1091: AIR 1957 AP 758: (1957) 2 Andh WR 156.
3. *E.* v. *Santa Singh*, (1945) 46 Cr LJ 1: AIR 1944 Lah 339: 215 IC 161 (FB).
4. *Radha Kishan* v. *State of Uttar Pradesh*, AIR 1963 SC 822: 1963 All LJ 397: 1963 BLJR 353.
5. *Pachiripali Satyanarayana (in re:)*, AIR 1953 Mad 534: (1953) 1 Mad LJ 175: 1953 Cr LJ 1048; *E.* v. *Santa Singh*, (1945) 46 Cr LJ 1: AIR 1944 Lah 339: 215 IC 161 (FB).
6. *Lachman Ram* v. *State of Orissa*, AIR 1985 SC 486: 1985 Cr LJ 753: (1985) 1 Crimes 611.

who buries the article in a spot unknown to others is really in possession and it does not matter whether the place of concealment is not in his occupation or not.[1]

19. "Soon after the theft", "recent".—Possession is incriminating only if it is soon after the theft and not long after the theft.[2] No fixed time limit can be laid down to determine whether possession is recent or otherwise. Every case must be judged on its own facts. The presumption of guilt varies according to whether the stolen article is or is not capable of being passed readily from hand to hand; hence the importance to be attached to possession must vary with the circumstances of each individual case.[3] Court has to consider the time factor, nature of the article, number of articles, seriousness of the charge and other circumstances.[4]

20. Account for possession.—The presumption can be raised only if the possessor is unable to account for his possession. Failure to account or false account or contradictory accounts are circumstances which require consideration. This is not to say that the onus which rests on the prosecution to prove guilt beyond reasonable doubt is shifted. Law does not require the accused to positively prove his claim to the article or how he came by it. However, it is his duty to offer an explanation, which in the circumstances of the case, can be accepted as reasonable. Mere denial of theft or possession is not sufficient. Where the accused gives a fairly acceptable explanation and prosecution is unable to repel the effect of the same, accused would get the benefit of reasonable doubt. If the explanation is "probably true", it must be accepted, unless it is shown to be untrue and improbable.[5] Failure to explain or false explanation may persuade court to draw the presumption against accused.[6] A satisfactory explanation may raise serious doubt the tenability of the charge.[5]

21. Thief or Receiver.—Whether the possessor is to be presumed to be the thief or receiver depends on the facts of each case. Illustration (a) contemplates a wide discretion to court. Every discretion has to be exercised judiciously. Whether the presumption to be drawn in a given case is that of being a thief or a receiver, depends on the totality of circumstances available in each case. In order to draw the presumption that the accused is the thief, it may be safer to look for some circumstances, in addition to being in possession of the stolen article.[7] If the interval of time is very small, the presumption can be that he is the thief; if the interval is relatively long, the presumption can be that he is the receiver. If the interval is very large, court may be reluctant to draw any

1. *Limbaji* v. *State of Maharashtra*, (2001) 10 SCC 340: AIR 2002 SC 491: 2002 AIR SCW 22.
2. *Ganesh Lal* v. *State of Rajasthan*, (2002) 1 SCC 731: 2002 Cr LJ 967: 2001 AIR SCW 5251; *Amar Singh* v. *State of Madhya Pradesh*, AIR 1982 SC 129: 1982 Cr LJ 610: (1982) 3 SCC 214; *Virumal Mulchand* v. *State of Gujarat*, AIR 1974 SC 334: 1974 Cr LJ 277: (1974) 3 SCC 565.
3. *Earabhadrappa* v. *State of Karnataka*, AIR 1983 SC 446: 1983 Cr LJ 846: (1983) 1 SCC 330: 1983 SCC (Cri) 447: (1983) 2 SCR 552.
4. *Reoti* v. *Emperor*, AIR 1933 All 461: 34 Cr LJ 1018; *Jagnarain Tewari* v. *Emperor*, AIR 1935 Cal 680: 36 Cr LJ 1466, *Amdumiyan* v. *Emperor*, AIR 1937 Nag 17 (FB); *Mavji Nanji* v. *Emperor*, AIR 1941 Bom 325.
5. *Karnal Singh Uttam Singh* v. *State of Maharashtra*, AIR 1976 SC 1097: (1976) 1 SCC 882: (1976) 2 SCR 747.
6. *Maloji Rao Narsingh Rao* v. *Sankar Saran*, AIR 1955 All 490; *Sunderlal* v. *State of Madhya Pradesh*, AIR 1954 SC 28: 1954 Cr LJ 257.
7. *Mahabir Singh* v. *State*, AIR 1951 Pat 296: 52 Cr LJ 154.

presumption.[1] But regard must be had to the other circumstances in the case, including the nature and number of articles, circumstances of the theft and other evidence, if any, against the accused.[2]

Some of the circumstances are, the nature of the recovered articles, the manner of their acquisition by the owner, the nature of the evidence about their identification, the manner in which the articles are dealt with by the accused, the place and circumstances of their recovery, the length of the intervening period and the ability or otherwise of the accused to explain the recovery.[3]

22. Graver charge.—The illustration being no more than illustrative, the presumption is not confined to cases of mere theft, but extends even to serious charges such as murder, dacoity, etc. The general presumption is that a person found to be in recent possession of fruits of a crime is the criminal, unless he can account for his possession. If robbery or theft on the one hand and murder or arson on the other, form part of the same transaction, there can be presumption that the possessor has participated in both the crimes, though in such cases the time factor is crucial.[4] Which circumstance assumes importance depends upon the facts of each case. In the case of murder away from the victim's residence, court may look to evidence that the article of jewellery was habitually worn by the victim or was worn by her shortly before murder. In the case of murder in the victim's residence, court may look for evidence regarding motive or opportunity, such as the presence of accused near the scene of occurrence. It is open to court to look for something more to connect the accused to the graver offence.[5] In *Gilbert Pereira* v. *State of Karnataka*,[6] it was held that unexplained injuries on hand of accused, blood of the same group being found on clothes of accused gave rise to the further presumption that removal of gold ornament and the fatal attack on the deceased should have taken place as part of the same transaction. In *Sardar Khan* v. *State of Karnataka*,[7] it was held that accused pawning jewellery of his deceased wife, cruelty practiced by him on her for obtaining financial benefits from her parents, and absence of any indication to show that any outsider broke into the house and killed her, would be sufficient to establish guilt of the husband regarding the charge under section 302 I.P.C. Where one of the accused is sought to be roped in by invoking section 34 or 149 of IPC, court will take great care not to assume that common object or common intention to commit murder can be attributed to a mere possessor.

---

1. *Maloji Rao Narsingh Rao* v. *Sankar Saran*, AIR 1955 All 490.
2. *Sheo Nath* v. *State of Uttar Pradesh*, AIR 1970 SC 535: 1970 Cr LJ 601: 1970 All Cri R 208; *Baiju* v. *State of Madhya Pradesh*, AIR 1978 SC 522: 1978 Cr LJ 646: (1978) 1 SCC 588; *Mohan Lal* v. *Ajit Singh*, AIR 1978 SC 1183: (1978) 3 SCC 279: 1978 Cr LJ 1107.
3. *Ghanshyam Das Srivastava* v. *State of Madhya Pradesh*, AIR 1973 SC 1183: (1973) 1 SCWR 391: (1973) 1 SCC 656; *Baiju* v. *State of Madhya Pradesh*, AIR 1978 SC 522: 1978 Cr LJ 646: (1978) 1 SCC 588; *A. Deivendran* v. *State of Tamil Nadu*, AIR 1998 SC 2821: 1998 AIR SCW 285: 1998 Cr LJ 814.
4. *Tulsi Ram Kanu* v. *State*, AIR 1954 SC 1: 1953 SCJ 612: 1954 Cr LJ 225; *Sunderlal* v. *State of Madhya Pradesh*, AIR 1954 SC 28: 1954 Cr LJ 257; *Earabhadrappa* v. *State of Karnataka*, AIR 1983 SC 446: 1983 Cr LJ 846: (1983) 1 SCC 330: 1983 SCC (Cri) 447: (1983) 2 SCR 552; *Lachman Ram* v. *State of Orissa*, AIR 1985 SC 486: 1985 Cr LJ 753: (1985) 1 Crimes 611.
5. *Sanwat Khan* v. *State of Rajasthan*, AIR 1956 SC 54: 1956 Cr LJ 150; *Hukam Singh* v. *State of Rajasthan*, AIR 1977 SC 1063: 1977 Cr LJ 639: (1977) 2 SCC 99; *Nagappa Dondiba Kalal* v. *State of Karnataka*, AIR 1980 SC 1753: 1980 Cr LJ 1270.
6. AIR 2004 SC 4454: 2004 Cr LJ 4837: 2004 AIR SCW 4727.
7. (2004) 2 SCC 442: 2004 Cr LJ 910: AIR 2004 SC 1695.

As a general rule of caution, court may insist on something more than mere possession of the article, such as some kind of connecting link.[1] In all cases it is for the prosecution to marshal circumstances justifying the presumption regarding the graver crime.[2] The question, ultimately, is whether the theft and the graver crime such as murder were part of the same transaction or not.[3] In certain cases, the question may arise whether the stolen articles were removed from the possession of the victim of murder during his life time or after his death.[4] Resolution of this question may depend on another question, namely, whether the theft and murder were part of the same transaction.[5]

23. Illustration (b).—This illustration may be read with section 133. Court may presume that an accomplice is unworthy of credit, unless he is corroborated in material particulars. It is important to remember that the principle underlying the illustration is an enabling one and not necessarily of invariable application. This rule of caution has been generally acted upon so that it can be said to have become a rule of law.[6] At the same time, it has to be noticed that an accomplice is a competent witness and conviction based on his uncorroborated evidence is not illegal (section 133). An accomplice is one who is a guilty associate in crime; he was a party to the crime charged and someone who aided and abetted the commission of the crime.[7] Corroborative evidence shows or tends to show that the evidence of the accomplice against the accused is true, in the opinion of a prudent person. Yet, it has to be seen that the illustration indicates that court "may" draw the presumption and not that court "must" in every case draw the presumption. It ultimately depends on the court's view as to the credibility of the evidence of an accomplice in a given case.[8] One accomplice cannot corroborate the evidence of another accomplice.[9] Corroboration is to show that witness is

---

1. *Surjit Singh* v. *State of Punjab*, AIR 1994 SC 110: 1993 AIR SCW 3741: 1993 Cr LJ 3901; *Singaram (in re:)*, AIR 1954 Mad 152: (1953) 2 MLJ 526: 1954 Cr LJ 115: 1953 MWN 572: 66 MLW 795.
2. *Alisher* v. *State of Uttar Pradesh*, AIR 1974 SC 1830: (1974) 4 SCC 254: 1974 Cr LJ 897; *Virumal Mulchand* v. *State of Gujarat*, AIR 1974 SC 334: 1974 Cr LJ 277: (1974) 3 SCC 565; *Wasim Khan* v. *State of Uttar Pradesh*, 1956 Cr LJ 790: AIR 1956 SC 400: 1956 SCA 549; *Shivappa* v. *State of Mysore*, AIR 1971 SC 196: 1971 Cr LJ 260: (1970) 1 SCC 487.
3. *Ronny* alias *Ronald James Alwaries* v. *State of Maharashtra*, AIR 1998 SC 1251: (1998) 3 SCC 625: 1998 Cr LJ 1638: 1998 SCC (Cri) 859; *Mukund @ Kundu Mishra* v. *State of Madhya Pradesh*, AIR 1997 SC 2622: 1997 Cri LJ 3182: 1997 AIR SCW 2580.
4. *Guman* v. *State of Madhya Pradesh*, 1989 Cr LJ 1425.
5. *Sanwat Khan* v. *State of Rajasthan*, AIR 1956 SC 54: 1956 Cr LJ 150; *Sunderlal* v. *State of Madhya Pradesh*, AIR 1954 SC 28: 1954 Cr LJ 257; *Tulsi Ram Kanu* v. *State*, AIR 1954 SC 1: 1953 SCJ 612: 1954 Cr LJ 225; *Lachman Ram* v. *State of Orissa*, AIR 1985 SC 486: 1985 Cr LJ 753: (1985) 1 Crimes 611; *Shivappa* v. *State of Mysore*, AIR 1971 SC 196: 1971 Cr LJ 260: (1970) 1 SCC 487; *Sheo Nath* v. *State of Uttar Pradesh*, AIR 1970 SC 535: 1970 Cr LJ 601: 1970 All Cri R 208.
6. *K.I. Pavunny* v. *Assistant Collector (Hq.), Central Excise Collectorate*, (1997) 1 Crimes 210: (1997) 1 SCALE 640: (1997) 3 SCC 721: (1997) 9 ELT 241: 1997 SCC (Cr) 444; *K. Hashim* v. *State of Tamil Nadu*, (2005) 1 SCC 237: AIR 2005 SC 128: 2004 AIR SCW 6372: 2005 Cr LJ 143; *Sitaram Sao* v. *State of Jharkhand*, JT 2007 (13) SC 157: AIR 2008 SC 391: 2008 (1) AIR Jhar R 993: 2007 AIR SCW 7126 (SC); *Francis Stanley @ Stalin* v. *Intelligence Officer, Narcotic Control Bureau*, AIR 2007 SC 794: 2007 Cr LJ 1157: 2007 AIR SCW 497; *Rampal Pithwa Rahidass* v. *State of Maharashtra*, 1994 Cr LJ 2320: 1994 AIR SCW 1500: (1994) 2 SCR 179.
7. *R.K. Dalmia* v. *Delhi Administration*, AIR 1962 SC 1821: (1962) 2 Cr LJ 805: (1963) 1 SCR 253; *Sheshanna Bhumanna Yadav* v. *State of Maharashtra*, AIR 1970 SC 1330: 1970 Cr LJ 1158: 1970 Ker LJ 669.
8. *K. Hashim* v. *State of Tamil Nadu*, (2005) 1 SCC 237: AIR 2005 SC 128: 2004 AIR SCW 6372: 2005 Cr LJ 143.
9. *Mohd. Hussain Umar* v. *K.S. Dalipsinghji*, 1970 Cr LJ 9: AIR 1970 SC 45: (1970) 1 SCR 130.

creditworthy; corroboration must be in material particulars, of commission of crime and complicity of accused. The need for corroboration arises because he is likely to swear falsely in order to shift the guilt from himself, because he is admittedly a participant in crime and hence is likely to disregard the sanctity of oath and because he gives evidence under promise or expectation of pardon, if he discloses all he knows against his co-criminals and such hope may lead him to help the prosecution. However, if credit is given to his evidence it requires no confirmation from another witness.

24. Nature and extent of corroboration required must necessarily vary with the circumstances of each case and particular circumstances of the offence alleged in each case.[1] There need not be independent confirmation of every material circumstance in the sense that the independent evidence in the case, apart from the evidence of the accomplice, should, in itself, be sufficient to sustain conviction. What is required is there must be some additional evidence rendering it probable that the evidence of the accomplice is true and it is reasonably safe to act upon it to hold that the crime was committed and to hold that accused is connected with the crime.[2] Corroboration must be from an independent source; however it can spring from direct or circumstantial evidence.[3] Where his evidence is not totally unsupported by re-assuring circumstances, accused could be convicted on the basis of his evidence.[4] Even where he assigned a bigger role to the accused than to himself, his evidence can be acted upon.[5]

25. All "accomplices" cannot be treated on the same footing. Nature of the offence and the circumstances under which they make their statements must always be considered. A person who may be guilty only of the offence under section 201 or 202 I.P.C. is not an accomplice of the person accused under section 302 I.P.C.

There can be conviction even on the uncorroborated testimony of an accomplice in appropriate cases where the court is satisfied, having regard to the particular circumstances, motivation, nature of the offence, extent of complicity etc., that the evidence is truthful.[6]

The rule is not applicable in the case of an accomplice who is merely a youthful tool in the hands of one who stood to him in *loco parentis* or where the offence is merely technical. The evidence of bribe-giver who is not a willing participant in the crime, but is really a victim of that offence, cannot be subjected to this presumption.

---

1. *Rameshwar* v. *State of Rajasthan,* AIR 1952 SC 54: 1952 SCJ 46: 1952 Cr LJ 547: (1952) 3 SCR 377; *Vemireddy Satyanarayan Reddy* v. *State,* AIR 1956 SC 379: 1956 Cr LJ 777: (1956) SCC 227; *Haroon Haji Abdulla* v. *State of Maharashtra,* 70 Bom LR 540: 1968 Cr LJ 1017: AIR 1968 SC 832: (1968) 2 SCR 641: (1968) 1 SCWR 243: (1968) 2 SCJ 534.
2. *Ramanlal Mohanlal Pandya* v. *State of Bombay,* AIR 1960 SC 961: 1960 Cr LJ 1380; *Sheshanna Bhumanna Yadav* v. *State of Maharashtra,* AIR 1970 SC 1330: 1970 Cr LJ 1158: 1970 Ker LJ 669; *Lachhi Ram* v. *State of Punjab,* AIR 1967 SC 792: (1967) 1 SCWR 310: 1967 Cr LJ 671; *A. Deivendran* v. *State of Tamil Nadu,* AIR 1998 SC 2821: 1998 AIR SCW 285: (1997) 11 SCC 720.
3. *Rameshwar* v. *State of Rajasthan,* AIR 1952 SC 54: 1952 SCJ 46: 1952 Cr LJ 547: (1952) 3 SCR 377; *Tribhuvan Nath* v. *State of Maharashtra,* AIR 1973 SC 450: 1972 Cr LJ 1277: (1972) 3 SCC 511.
4. *State of Tamil Nadu* v. *Suresh,* (1998) 2 SCC 372: AIR 1998 SC 1044: 1998 Cr LJ 1416.
5. *A. Deivendran* v. *State of Tamil Nadu,* AIR 1998 SC 2821: 1998 AIR SCW 285: (1997) 11 SCC 720.
6. *Prakash Chand* v. *State (Delhi Administration),* AIR 1979 SC 400: (1979) 3 SCC 90: 1979 Cr LJ 329: 1979 MLJ (Cri) 419.

The degree of suspicion which will attach to the evidence of an accomplice must vary according to the extent and nature of his complicity.[1]

26. In *Shamsher Bahadur Saxena* v. *State of Bihar* (at page 412),[2] it has been stated as follows:

> "The rule, which according to the cases has hardened into one of law, is not that corroboration is essential before there can be conviction but that the necessity of corroboration, as a matter of prudence, except where the circumstances make it safe to dispense with it, must be present in the mind of the judge .... before conviction without corroboration can be sustained."[3]

Corroboration may be by direct or circumstantial evidence. Such evidence could be in the form of admissible confession, even retracted one, finger impressions, "last seen alive" in the company of the accused and approver, the prior conduct of the accomplice or the accused, tell-tale blood stains on the person or clothes of accused, injury received by the accused in the occurrence, possession of stolen goods, etc.

In the early years of the Supreme Court, it was observed that though a rape victim is not an accomplice, a large volume of case law has grown up which treated her evidence somewhat along the same lines as accomplice evidence though often for widely differing reasons and the position was that the rule about the need for corroboration of her evidence has hardened into one of law save in exceptional cases.[4] The Supreme Court observed in paragraph 19 that in the case of a young girl, that her tender years, coupled with other circumstances, such as, for example, her demeanour, unlikelihood of tutoring etc., may render corroboration unnecessary, but that is a question of fact in each case and that the only rule of law is that this rule of prudence must be present to the mind and be understood and appreciated by the judge and also that there is no rule of practice that there must, in every case, be corroboration before a conviction can be allowed to stand. A Constitution Bench while approving the earlier dicta regarding evidence of an accomplice, indicated that the judgment should contain some indication that the judge has the rule of corroboration in mind and should proceed to give reasons for considering it unnecessary to require corroboration on the facts of the particular case and show why he considers it safe to convict without corroboration in that case.[5]

This decision, however, did not advert to the "status" of a rape victim as the case was not one of rape, but one of corruption. But, in a decision reported in the same year, the Supreme Court observed that the girl who is the victim of an outrageous act is, generally speaking, not an accomplice, though the rule of prudence requires that her evidence should be corroborated, the nature

1. *In re Amir Sultan*, AIR 1957 Mad 796: 1957 1 Mad LJ (Cri) 209: 1957 Cr LJ 1424.
2. AIR 1956 Pat 404: 1955 BLJR 537: 1956 Cr LJ 1220.
3. *State of Bihar* v. *Basawan Singh*, AIR 1958 SC 500: 1958 Cr LJ 976: 1959 SCR 195; *Dagdu* v. *State of Maharashtra*, AIR 1977 SC 1579: 1977 Cr LJ 1206: 1977 SCC (Cri) 421: (1977) 3 SCC 68; *Sheikh Zakir* v. *State of Bihar*, AIR 1983 SC 911: (1983) 4 SCC 10: 1983 Cr LJ 1285; *K. Hashim* v. *State of Tamil Nadu*, (2005) 1 SCC 237: AIR 2005 SC 128: 2004 AIR SCW 6372: 2005 Cr LJ 143.
4. *Rameshwar* v. *State of Rajasthan*, AIR 1952 SC 54: 1952 SCJ 46: 1952 Cr LJ 547: (1952) 3 SCR 377; *Sheikh Zakir* v. *State of Bihar*, AIR 1983 SC 911: (1983) 4 SCC 10: 1983 Cr LJ 1285.
5. *State of Bihar* v. *Basawan Singh*, AIR 1958 SC 500: 1958 Cr LJ 976: 1959 SCR 195.

and extent of which will vary with the circumstances of each case and this requirement is to lend assurance that her evidence can be safely acted upon.[1]

In *Sheikh Zakir* v. *State of Bihar*,[2] the Supreme Court, while observing that a rape victim cannot be treated as an accomplice, held that her evidence, on account of a long time of decisions in our country, is treated almost like the evidence of an accomplice requiring corroboration. This decision referred to *Rameshwar* v. *State of Rajasthan* and *Gurcharan Singh* v. *State of Haryana*,[3] but did not refer to the Constitution Bench decision in *State of Bihar* v. *Basawan Singh*[4] or to the subtle distinction drawn in *Rameshwar* v. *State of Rajasthan*,[5] between the status of the victim (describing her as not an accomplice) and the status of the victim's evidence (somewhat along the lines as accomplice evidence). In *Bhogibhai Hirjibhai* v. *State of Gujarat*,[6] the Supreme Court held as follows:—

"In the Indian setting, refusal to act on the testimony of a victim of sexual assault in the absence of corroboration as a rule is adding insult to injury. Why should the evidence of the girl or the woman who complains of rape or sexual molestation be viewed with the aid of spectacles fitted with lenses tinged with doubt, disbelief and suspicion? To do so is to justify the charge of male chauvinism in a male dominated society?

In *Aman Kumar* v. *State of Haryana*,[7] the Supreme Court observed:

"It is well-settled that a prosecutrix is not an accomplice - - - she stands at a higher pedestal than an injured witness - - - if the Court of facts finds it difficult to accept the version of the prosecutrix on its' face value, it may search for evidence, direct or circumstantial, which could lend assurance to her testimony. Assurance, short of corroboration as understood in the context of an accomplice would suffice".[8]

The same view has been expressed in *State of Maharashtra* v. *Chandraprakash Jain*[9] and *Narayan Saa* v. *State of Tripura*.[10] In *State of Himachal Pradesh* v. *Asha Ram*,[11] the Supreme Court observed that the evidence of a prosecutrix is more reliable than that of an injured witness and her evidence is vital unless there are compelling reasons which necessitate looking for corroboration of her statement and further that courts should find no difficulty in acting on the testimony of the victim of sexual assault alone to convict an accused where her evidence inspires confidence and is found reliable. The rule of corroboration, however, must be present in the mind of court and court must give reasons for dispensing with the necessity for corroboration.[12] The perspectives of courts may require

1. *Sidheswar Ganguly* v. *West Bengal*, 1958 Cr LJ 273: AIR 1958 SC 143: 1958 SCR 749.
2. AIR 1983 SC 911: (1983) 4 SCC 10: 1983 Cr LJ 1285.
3. AIR 1952 SC 54: 1952 SCJ 46: 1952 Cr LJ 547: (1952) 3 SCR 377; (1973) 2 SCR 197: 1973 Cr LJ 179: AIR 1972 SC 2661.
4. AIR 1958 SC 500: 1958 Cr LJ 976: 1959 SCR 195.
5. AIR 1952 SC 54: 1952 SCJ 46: 1952 Cr LJ 547: (1952) 3 SCR 377.
6. AIR 1983 SC 753: 1983 Cr LJ 1096.
7. AIR 2004 SC 1497: 2004 AIR SCW 827: 2004 Cr LJ 1399.
8. *S. Ramakrishna* v. *State*, (2009) 1 SCC 133: AIR 2009 SC 885: 2008 AIR SCW 8201.
9. AIR 1990 SC 658: (1990) 1 SCC 550: JT 1990 (1) SC 61: 1990 Cr LJ 889.
10. AIR 2005 SC 1452: 2004 AIR SCW 7361: (2004) 7 SCC 775.
11. 2006 Cr LJ 139 (SC): AIR 2006 SC 381.
12. *Bodhisattwa Gautam* v. *Subhra Chakraborty*, AIR 1996 SC 922: 1996 AIR SCW 325: 1996 (1) SCJ 338.

some reappraisal in view of incorporation of section 114A in the Evidence Act.

27. Illustration (c).—Court may presume that a bill of exchange, accepted or endorsed, was accepted or endorsed for good consideration. This is an exception to the general rule that consideration for a contract should be the subject of plea and proof. This presumption as well as presumption under section 118(1)(a) of the Negotiable Instruments Act are rebuttable. The former is an enabling presumption while the latter is a mandatory one. Once the presumption is raised, there is no difference between the two cases in the matter of effect thereof or the manner of rebutting the same. The former is of a general nature and applies to all bills of exchange even though the dispute is not between the parties thereto or persons claiming under them, while the latter is a special rule of evidence intended to operate between the parties or persons claiming under them. The former relates only to acceptance or endorsement, while the latter applies to making or drawing also. Before any such presumption can be raised, there must be admission or proof of execution of the bill of exchange. Mere admission of signature (on the ground it was taken on a blank paper or as a witness etc.) does not amount to admission of the bill of exchange.

The law raises such a presumption in favour of these instruments, partly because it is important to preserve their negotiability intact and partly because the existence of a valid consideration may reasonably be inferred from the solemnity of the instruments themselves and the deliberate mode in which they were executed.[1] The effect of the presumption is that the burden is on the opposite party.[2] Sections 118 and 119 of N.I. Act lay down other presumptions, mandatory in nature. Section 118 of N.I. Act does not effect the rule contained in section 118 of the Evidence Act in cases not falling under the former.[3]

28. There is no presumption, under these two provisions, regarding the quantum of consideration. That has to be gathered from the recitals in the light of the entirety of evidence.[4] Recitals are *prima facie* evidence against the parties to the instruments and may operate to shift on the party pleading the contrary, the burden of rebutting the inference raised by them. But the weight due to the recitals may vary according to the circumstances.[3]

Court is not obliged to invoke the presumption under section 114, illustration (c) in all cases.[3]

29. Illustration (d).—Court may presume that a thing or state of things which has been shown to be in existence within a period shorter than that within which such things or state of things usually cease to exist, is still in existence. The ordinary presumption is that things remain in their original state, that is, *status quo persists*. Things remain in their original state, until the contrary is proved. The time limit within which the inference of continuance has sufficient probative force to be relevant, must vary with each case. Strongest always in the beginning, the force of inference declines in force with lapse of time and ceases

1. Taylor on Evidence, 12th Edition, P 139.
2. *Mohd. Shakeel Wahid Ahmed* v. *State of Maharashtra*, AIR 1983 SC 541: 1983 Cr LJ 967: (1983) 2 SCC 392.
3. *Official Receiver, Kanpur* v. *Abdul Shakoor*, AIR 1965 SC 920: 1965 (2) SCJ 691: (1965) 1 SCR 254.
4. *Narasamma* v. *Veerraju*, AIR 1935 Mad 769: 42 Mad LW 321: ILR 58 Mad 841; *Thirumalai Iyengar* v. *Subba Raja*, AIR 1962 Mad 219: (1962) 1 Mad LJ 193.

to exist till such facts usually cease to exist.[1] *See* the examples of soap bubble, Mount Everest, tree cited by Wigmore on Evidence (section 437). A member of a joint hindu family is presumed to continue to be a member of such family unless the contrary is proved. Presumption should be in favour of the existing state of things.

This probability may also operate retrospectively;[2] but not in cases of marriage or like relationship or mental condition, holding of office etc., from proof of its present existence. However, future, unlike present continuance, is never presumed. If a thing is shown to exist, an inference of its continuity within a reasonably proximate time both forwards and backwards may sometimes be drawn. How far the prescription backwards and forwards may be drawn depends on the nature of the thing and surrounding circumstances.[3]

Sections 107 to 109 deal with specific application of the general principle in illustration (d).

30. Possession and ownership once proved to exist may be presumed to continue until the contrary is shown. There is presumption of the continuance of possession with the person in whom there is title, particularly in regard to vacant land or land incapable of specific acts of possession.[4] But this presumption cannot be drawn in favour of one who is bound to prove his being in possession within 12 years before suit.[5]

Continuance of undivided status of Hindu Undivided Family or partnership may be presumed.[6]

31. Illustration (e).—If it is proved that a judicial or official act has been performed, court may presume that it has been performed "regularly", that is, in accordance with the requirements of law.[7] The presumption arises on the basis that persons holding public office do their duty.[8] The illustration receives support from the maxim that all such acts are presumed to have been rightly and regularly done.[9] The principle is that courts generally uphold such acts, rather than render them inoperative and hence where there is general evidence of acts having been legally and regularly done, courts dispense with proof of circumstances strictly essential to the validity of those acts.[10] Where a police officer deposed that telephonic first information was recorded in the general diary and defence did not summon the general diary to show the contrary, it was held that court may accept the evidence of the police officer as true.[11] The

1. *Ambika Prasad Thakur* v. *Ram Ekbal Rai*, (1966) 1 SCA 35: AIR 1966 SC 605: (1966) 1 SCR 758; *Bibi Tahzibunnisa* v. *Syed Azizur Rahman*, AIR 1980 Pat 89: 1979 BBCJ (HC) 584: 1979 BLJ 619.
2. *Ambika Prasad Thakur* v. *Ram Ekbal Rai*, (1966) 1 SCA 35: AIR 1966 SC 605: (1966) 1 SCR 758; *Murasoli Maran* v. *Union of India*, (1971) 2 MLJ 57: AIR 1972 Mad 40: ILR (1971) 3 Mad 18.
3. *Ambika Prasad Thakur* v. *Ram Ekbal Rai*, (1966) 1 SCA 35: AIR 1966 SC 605: (1966) 1 SCR 758.
4. *Uthamaram Nathusam Sait* v. *Hude Gopalakrishnayya*, AIR 1957 Mad 463.
5. *Ramyad Singh* v. *Pan Kuer*, AIR 1958 Pat 562.
6. *State of Kerala* v. *Saroja*, AIR 1987 Ker 239: 1987 Ker LJ 205.
7. *Sheikh Minzar Hussain* v. *Mohd. Asghar*, AIR 1978 All 413: 1978 All LJ 629: (1978) 4 All LR 564; *Somasudarshan Goud* v. *District Collector*, AIR 1978 AP 420: (1978) 2 Andh WR 443.
8. *Miss Zeenat Tej* v. *Principal of the Prince of Wales Medical College, Patna*, AIR 1971 Pat 43; *Lalji Sah* v. *Sat Narain Bhagat*, AIR 1962 Pat 182.
9. *Madan Lal Lohia* v. *Assistant Controller*, AIR 1977 SC 1871: (1978) 2 ITJ 37: 1978 (2) SCJ 57.
10. Best on Evidence S. 353.
11. *Appu* v. *State of Kerala*, 1989 (2) Kerala Law Times 320.

presumption applies to report of a public analyst.[1] Supreme Court evolved this principle in regard to compliance with rule 18 of PFA Rules.[2] In order that a presumption may be drawn, the official act must be proved to have been done. There could not be any presumption that the act was done.[3] Where a judgment states that a particular thing happened or did not happen in court, ordinarily, the statement cannot be allowed to be challenged by a party unless both the parties agree that the statement is wrong or the court itself admits so.[4]

The appointment of certain teachers under a statutory regulation is an official act and presumption of regularity attaches to it.[5] Where property is attached in execution of a decree, it can be presumed that the attachment was in accordance with law.[6] Where an act is to be performed in a particular manner, and there is no evidence to the contrary, there is a presumption the act has been performed in the manner provided in law.[7] Official work is presumed to be done correctly until disproved by cogent evidence.[8]

Where a person has acted as an officer, it may be presumed that he had been duly appointed.[9] It is for the party who challenges such regularity to plead and prove his case.[10] However Court will not draw the presumption when the act itself is shown, on the face it, to be not legal.[11]

Presumption of regularity may be drawn, if court is satisfied that an action taken by a statutory authority is traceable to statutory power even if the authority has omitted to recite or committed an error in reciting the correct provision of law.[12] Legislature must be presumed to know the facts and conditions rendering

1. *State of Madhya Pradesh* v. *Chhotekhan Nannekhan*, AIR 1970 MP 29: 1970 Cr LJ 238: ILR 1971 MP 197 (FB); *Food Inspector, Cannanore Municipality Cannanore* v. *Pandavalappil Kannan*, AIR 1966 Ker 70: ILR (1965) 2 Ker 301:1966 Cr LJ 416; *Krishna Rajaram Wani* v. *M.V. Koranne and the State of Maharashtra*, AIR 1968 Bom 247: ILR (1967) Bom 729: 1968 Cr LJ 1156; *Food Inspector, Corporation of the City of Mangalore* v. *A.G. Suvarna*, 1985 (1) KLJ 1 (FB); *Chacko* v. *Food Inspector*, 1989 (2) KLT 620; *State of Haryana* v. *Hari Ram Yadav*, AIR 1994 SC 1262: 1994 AIR SCW 606: (1994) 1 SCR 168; *Sadhu Singh* v. *State of Uttar Pradesh*, AIR 1978 SC 1506: 1978 All LJ 887: 1978 SC Cri R 403; *Sone Lal* v. *State of Uttar Pradesh*, AIR 1978 SC 1142: 1978 Cr LJ 1122: (1978) 4 SCC 302; *Srinivas Mall* v. *Emperor*, AIR 1947 PC 135: 49 Bom LR 688.
2. *State of Himachal Pradesh* v. *Narendra Kumar*, AIR 2004 SC 2711: (2004) 4 SCC 567: 2004 AIR SCW 1168.
3. *Maharaja Prathap Singh* v. *Thakur Manmohan Dey*, AIR 1966 SC 1931: 1967 (2) SCJ 352: (1966) 3 SCR 663.
4. *State of Bihar* v. *Mahabir Lal*, AIR 1964 SC 377: (1964) 1 SCR 842: 1964 (2) SCJ 611.
5. *Naseem Bano* v. *State of Uttar Pradesh*, AIR 1993 SC 2592: 1993 AIR SCW 3280: JT 1993 (4) SC 553.
6. *Tika Ram* v. *State*, AIR 1960 All 453: 1960 Cr LJ 1040: ILR (1960) 1 All 53.
7. *Polyglass Acrylic Mfg. Co. Ltd.* v. *Commissioner of Customs, Vishakhapatnam*, AIR 2003 SC 3419: (2003) 4 SCC 762: (2003) 3 SCR 188.
8. *State of Assam* v. *Keshab Prasad Singh*, AIR 1953 SC 309: 1953 SCJ 429: 1953 SCR 865; *Kartar Singh* v. *Delhi Development Authority*, AIR 2000 Del 184: 2000 (83) DLT 529: 2000 (52) DRJ 496.
9. *Ajit Singh* v. *State of Punjab*, AIR 1967 SC 856.
10. *P.J. Ratnam* v. *D. Kanikaram*, AIR 1964 SC 244: (1964) 1 Cr LJ 146: (1964) 3 SCR 1; *Ramakrishna Ganapayya Hegde* v. *Lakshminarayana Timmayya Hegde*, AIR 1984 Kant 45: (1983) 2 Kant LJ 409.
11. *Surat Singh* v. *Municipal Corporation of Delhi*, AIR 1989 Del 51: (1988) 1 DL 364: (1989) 1 Rec Cri R 361.
12. *B.S.E. Brokers Forum, Bombay* v. *Securities and Exchange Board of India*, AIR 2001 SC 1010: 2001 AIR SCW 628: JT 2001 (2) SC 242: (2001) 3 SCC 482.

a statute expedient and beneficial.[1] Unless the contrary is proved, court has to presume that a statute has been validly enacted and all necessary formalities for it's enactment have been duly complied with.[2] Where the government issues a notification that a certain land is urgently needed for public purpose, it may be presumed that the government's decision on the aspect of urgency is properly made.[3] Where delivery of the allotted land under a statute was the official act of the revenue authority, a presumption has to be raised that all antecedent formalities were duly complied with.[4] A presumption can be raised that a Registrar registering a document has discharged his official duties in accordance with law. The presumption that a person acts honestly, applies as much to police officers as to other persons and it is not a judicial approach to distrust or suspect them without good grounds.[5] When a letter intimating that sanction has been granted is received, presumption may be drawn that sanction had in fact been accorded and such official act was regularly performed.[6]

Existence of an acknowledgement regarding a registered article in post office would raise a presumption that the article was delivered to the addressee.[7] Presumption cannot stand rebutted by bare denial.[8] Refusal to receive may lead to presumption of service.[9] Ordinarily a statement of the addressee on oath that the postal cover with such an endorsement was never tendered to him would be sufficient to discharge the presumption of service and shift the onus on the opposite party to establish by evidence that service had been effected.[10] Where a letter of appointment was sent by ordinary post, it was held that a statutory presumption regarding due delivery would arise.

Entries in Record of Rights can be presumed to be correct until the presumption is rebutted.[11] Genuine entries in revenue records are to be generally accepted at their face value, though they are open to attack on the ground that they were made fraudulently and surreptiously.[12] A revenue document is not a document of title; it merely raises a presumption in regard to

1. *Raval and Co.* v. *K.G. Ramachandran*, AIR 1967 Mad 57: (1966) 2 Mad LJ 68: ILR (1966) 2 Mad 437.
2. *Engineering Kamgar Union* v. *Electro Steels Castings Ltd.*, AIR 2004 SC 2401: 2004 AIR SCW 2918: (2004) 6 SCC 36.
3. *Ishwarlal Girdharlal Joshi* v. *State of Gujarat*, AIR 1968 SC 870: (1968) 1 SCA 569: (1968) 2 SCR 267.
4. *Krishna Kumari* v. *State of Haryana*, (1999) 1 SCC 338: AIR 1999 SC 854: 1998 AIR SCW 3958.
5. *Devender Pal Singh* v. *State of N.C.T. of Delhi*, AIR 2002 SC 1661: 2002 AIR SCW 1586: 2002 Cr LJ 2034; *Aher Raja Khima* v. *State of Saurashtra*, AIR 1956 SC 217: (1955) 2 SCR 1285: 1956 Cr LJ 421: 1956 SCJ 24; *Karamjit Singh* v. *State (Delhi Administration)*, AIR 2003 SC 1311: (2003) 5 SCC 291: 2003 Cr LJ 2021.
6. *Tulsi Ram* v. *State of Uttar Pradesh*, AIR 1963 SC 666: (1963) 1 Cr LJ 623: 1963 (2) SCJ 274.
7. *Radha Kishan* v. *State of Uttar Pradesh*, AIR 1963 SC 822: 1963 All LJ 397: 1963 BLJR 353.
8. *Vijay Kumar Agarwal* v. *Bihar State Electricity Board*, AIR 2004 SC 3285: 2003 (2) JLJR 99: (2003) 4 SCALE 371.
9. *Kailash Rani Dang* v. *Rakesh Bala Aneja*, (2009) 1 SCC 732: AIR 2009 SC 1662: 2009 AIR SCW 1188.
10. *Jagat Ram Khullar* v. *Battu Mal*, AIR 1976 Del 111: (1976) 12 DLT 127: 1976 Ren CR 151.
11. *Raja Rajinder Chand* v. *Sukhi*, AIR 1957 SC 286: 1957 SCJ 119: 1956 SCR 889; *Avadh Kishore Das* v. *Ram Gopal*, AIR 1979 SC 861: 1979 UJ (SC) 251: (1979) 4 SCC 790; *Commissioner of Wealth-tax* v. *Officer-in-charge, Court of Wards*, AIR 1977 SC 113: (1976) 3 SCC 864: (1977) 1 SCR 146; *S. Venkatappa* v. *Narayanappa*, AIR 2001 SC 2148: 2001 AIR SCW 1850: (2001) 4 SCC 705.
12. *Sonawati* v. *Sri Ram*, AIR 1968 SC 466: 1968 (2) SCJ 225: (1968) 1 SCR 617; *Karewwa* v. *Hussensab Khansaheb Wajantri*, AIR 2002 SC 504: 2002 AIR SCW 40: (2002) 10 SCC 315.

possession.[1] Presumption arising from several entries in revenue records of a large number of years in respect of ownership and possession of land with a certain person is not rebutted by mere stray entries in favour of another when evidence is of uncertain character and inadequate.[2] All formalities regarding mutations may be presumed to have been complied with. No proof of compliance is necessary. It is for the opposite party to rebut the presumption.[3] Revenue entries could be rebutted only by leading evidence as to the correctness and not by mere denial.[4]

Report of a public analyst is admissible in evidence without formal proof.[5]

Court will not lightly assume abuse or misuse of power in regard to powers conferred on the President by Article 356 of the Constitution. Interference is called for only when there is fraud on power.[6]

32. Illustration (f).—Court may presume that common course of business has been followed in a particular case, provided the course of business is admitted or proved. Where there is a question whether a particular act was done, the existence of any course of; business according to which it naturally would have been done is a relevant fact. This presumption of the course of business having been followed is strong in the case of public officers, *E.g.* From certificate of posting delivery can be presumed. Where a notice is sent by post card correctly addressed, there can be presumption that there was proper service of notice.[7] The presumption of due service arises if a registered letter is returned back with a postal endorsement of refusal.[8] Postal date seals could give rise to presumption that the letter must have been posted and presented to the addressee on the respective dates seen in the seals. The presumption is rebuttable. Mere denial will not invariably lead to rebuttal.[9] Where service is effected by "refusal" of a postal communication, addressee must be imputed with the knowledge of

---

1. *Gurunath Manohar Pavaskar* v. *Nagesh Sidappa Navalgund*, AIR 2008 SC 901: 2008 AIR SCW 298: 2008 (2) AIR Kar R 146.
2. *M.T.W. Tenzing Namgyal* v. *Motilal Lakhotia*, (2003) 5 SCC 1: AIR 2003 SC 1448: 2003 AIR SCW 784.
3. *Ram Sarup* v. *State of Punjab*, 1987 Cr LJ 928: 1986 (2) All Cri LR 387; *State of Himachal Pradesh* v. *Keshav Ram*, AIR 1997 SC 2181: 1997 AIR SCW 2041; *Navalshankar Ishwarlal Dave* v. *State of Gujarat*, 1994 AIR SCW 956: AIR 1994 SC 1496: 1994 Cr LJ 2170; *Sawarni* v. *Inder Kaur*, AIR 1996 SC 2823: 1996 AIR SCW 3613: (1996) 6 SCC 223.
4. *Karewwa* v. *Hussensab Khansaheb Wajantri*, AIR 2002 SC 504: 2002 AIR SCW 40: (2002) 10 SCC 315.
5. *Babulal Hargovindas* v. *State of Gujarat*, AIR 1971 SC 1277: 1971 Cr LJ 1075: 1971 UJ (SC) 500; *State of Himachal Pradesh* v. *Narendra Kumar*, AIR 2004 SC 2711: (2004) 4 SCC 567: 2004 AIR SCW 1168; under PFA Act, 1954.
6. *Rameshwar Prasad* v. *Union of India*, AIR 2006 SC 980: 2006 AIR SCW 494: (2006) 2 SCC 1.
7. *Maharaja Prathap Singh* v. *Thakur Manmohan Dey*, AIR 1966 SC 1931: 1967 (2) SCJ 352: (1966) 3 SCR 663; *Har Charan Singh* v. *Shiv Rani*, AIR 1981 SC 1284: (1981) 2 SCC 535: (1981) 2 SCR 962; *Green View Radio Service* v. *Laxmibai Ramji*, (1990) 4 SCC 497: AIR 1990 SC 2156; *Puwada Venkateswara Rao* v. *C.V. Ramana*, AIR 1976 SC 869: (1976) 2 SCC 409: (1976) 3 SCR 551; *D. Vinod Shivappa* v. *Nanda Belliappa*, AIR 2006 SC 2179: 2006 AIR SCW 2757: 2006 Cr LJ 2897; *C.C. Alavi Haji* v. *Palapetty Muhammed*, 2007 Cr LJ 321: (2007) 6 SCC 555: 2007 AIR SCW 3578.
8. *Gujarat Electricity Board* v. *Atmaram Sungomal Poshani*, AIR 1989 SC 1433: (1989) 2 SCC 602: JT 1989 (3) SC 20.
9. *Dr. Mrs. Sumati P. Shere* v. *Union of India*, (1989) 3 SCC 311: AIR 1989 SC 1431: JT 1989 (2) SC 143; *Har Charan Singh* v. *Shiv Rani*, AIR 1981 SC 1284: (1981) 2 SCC 535: (1981) 2 SCR 962; *Puwada Venkateswara Rao* v. *C.V. Ramana*, AIR 1976 SC 869: (1976) 2 SCC 409: (1976) 3 SCR 551.

the contents of the letter, following the presumption under section 114 of Act 1872 and section 27 of General Clauses Act, 1897.[1] Evidence of posting of letter correctly addressed must be coupled with evidence that it was not received back through the dead letter office. The presumption can be raised even without examining the postman.[2] In commercial transactions the presumption is that the usual course of business was followed by the parties thereto, though court is not bound to draw the presumption in every case. Where two sets of accounts were seized, the account books showing less turnover would not be presumed to be correct.[3] In case of joint tenants, service of notice to quit upon a joint tenant is *prima facie* proof of service of notice on the other joint tenants.

33. Illustration (g).—Court may presume that evidence which could be and is not produced, would, if produced, be unfavourable to the party who withholds it.[4] This rule applies to oral as well as documentary evidence. In the latter case, existence and custody of the document has to be proved.[5] If such evidence is not produced by either party, no adverse inference can be drawn against the plaintiff alone.[6] The rule requiring best evidence cannot be got over by relying on abstract doctrine of burden of proof or that he was not called upon to produce it.[7] The conduct of the person withholding evidence may be attributed to a supposed consciousness that the evidence, if produced, would go against him.[8] *Best on Evidence* (section 411) states that this rule of presumption is based on the principle that no one shall be allowed to take advantage of his own wrong. According to *Wigmore on Evidence*, (section 285), the inference to be drawn is that the tenor of such evidence not produced is unfavourable to the party's case. When best evidence is withheld, adverse inference can be drawn.[9] This adverse inference cannot displace the contrary inference supported by adequate evidence.[10] It is not obligatory to draw an adverse inference. It is

1. *Har Charan Singh* v. *Shiv Rani*, AIR 1981 SC 1284: (1981) 2 SCC 535: (1981) 2 SCR 962.
2. *Puwada Venkateswara Rao* v. *C.V. Ramana*, AIR 1976 SC 869: (1976) 2 SCC 409: (1976) 3 SCR 551.
3. *State of Kerala* v. *M.M. Mathew*, AIR 1978 SC 1571: (1978) 4 SCC 65: 1978 Cr LJ 1690; *Khushalbhai Mahijibhai Patel* v. *A. firm of Mohamadhussain Rahimbux*, AIR 1981 SC 977: (1980) 3 SCR 22: 1980 Supp SCC 1.
4. *Darya Singh* v. *State of Punjab*, AIR 1965 SC 328: (1965) 1 Cr LJ 350: 1964 (2) SCJ 319; *Srichand K. Khetwani* v. *State of Maharashtra*, (1967) 1 SCJ 178: AIR 1967 SC 450: 1967 Cr LJ 414; *Sharada* v. *Dharampal*, AIR 2003 SC 3450: 2003 AIR SCW 1950: (2003) 4 SCC 493.
5. *Bhoolchand* v. *Kay Pee Cee Investments*, (1991) 1 SCC 343: AIR 1991 SC 2053: JT 1991 (1) SC 186; *Devidas* v. *Shrishailappa*, AIR 1961 SC 1277: (1961) 3 SCR 896: 1962 (1) SCJ 557; *Surendranagar District Panchayat* v. *Dahyabhai Amarsinh*, (2005) 8 SCC 750: 2005 Lab IC 4308: 2005 AIR SCW 5562.
6. *Ramrati Kuer* v. *Dwarika Prasad Singh*, AIR 1967 SC 1134: (1967) 2 SCJ 789: (1967) 1 SCR 153.
7. *Gopal Krishnaji Ketkar* v. *Mahomed Haji Latif*, AIR 1968 SC 1413; *Hiralal* v. *Badkulal*, AIR 1953 SC 225: 1953 SCR 758: 1953 SCJ 315.
8. *Srichand K. Khetwani* v. *State of Maharashtra*, (1967) 1 SCJ 178: AIR 1967 SC 450: 1967 Cr LJ 414; *Puneeth Rai* v. *Dinesh Choudhury*, AIR 2003 SC 435; *Sushil Kumar* v. *Rakesh Kumar*, AIR 2004 SC 230: 2003 AIR SCW 6005: (2003) 8 SCC 673; *Sharada* v. *Dharampal*, AIR 2003 SC 3450: 2003 AIR SCW 1950: (2003) 4 SCC 493; *Bharat Heavy Electrical Ltd.* v. *State of Uttar Pradesh*, AIR 2003 SC 3024: 2003 AIR SCW 3469: (2003) 6 SCC 528.
9. *Patel Naranbhai Marghabhai* v. *Deceased Dhulabhai Galbabhai*, AIR 1992 SC 2009: 1992 AIR SCW 2377: (1992) 4 SCC 264; *Bhimshingh* v. *State of Haryana*, 2003 AIR SCW 5188: AIR 2003 SC 4382: (2003) 10 SCC 529.
10. *Ramachandrudu* v. *D. Janaki Ramanna*, AIR 1920 PC 84.

one of fact, depending on a whole set of facts.[1] Where FIR was not produced inspite of direction issued by the Sessions Judge, it could raise a doubt against the prosecution case.[2] If letters threatening the deceased and in the custody of police are not produced in court, it could lead to an adverse inference.[3] Production of the daily diary of the police station is not a matter of course in every case and hence no adverse inference can be drawn on its non-production.[4] Non-production of available evidence need not lead to adverse presumption if other circumstances exist upon which such non-production may be found justifiable on reasonable grounds.[5] Where accused did not file an application for production of case diary and general diary, no adverse inference can be drawn against the prosecution for non-production of the diaries.[6]

Where the prosecution witness specifically stated that the bus tickets he had purchased for himself and others for travelling on a bus were lost when he was being chased by the accused persons, there would be justification for drawing an adverse inference against prosecution for non-production of the tickets.[7] Where an employee disappeared and the employer, after due enquiry, passed an order of dismissal and he reappeared after twenty years demanding he should be taken back and approached court and the employer did not have and could not produce the records of enquiry and the dismissal order, it was held that no adverse inference could be drawn against the employer for non-production of records.[8] Where the government which was directed to produce in court the note put up for release of an item of property on the basis of which the cabinet took a decision and the government failed to produce the note, it was held that the failure of the government showed its *mala fide* intention.[9] In a case of alleged illegal termination of services of a workman, the employer did not produce the muster roll but produced other reliable documents against the employee's case, it was held that no adverse inference could be drawn against the employer for non-production of the muster roll.[10] Where certain records demanded by accused were not produced on the allegation that they had been destroyed, but the destruction register was not produced and no evidence was produced to show records had been destroyed, adverse inference could be drawn against the prosecution.[11]

---

1. *Indira Nehru Gandhi* v. *Shri Raj Narain*, AIR 1975 SC 2299: 1976 2 SCR 347: 1975 Supp SCC 1.
2. *Sheikh Mehboob* v. *State of Maharashtra*, AIR 2005 SC 1805: 2005 AIR SCW 1595: 2005 Cr LJ 2136.
3. *Sawal Das* v. *State of Bihar*, AIR 1974 SC 2276: (1975) 3 SCC 156: (1975) 1 SCR 607.
4. *Kalpnath Rai* v. *State (through CBI)*, 1997 AIR SCW 4166: (1997) 8 SCC 732: 1998 Cr LJ 369: AIR 1998 SC 201.
5. *Municipal Corporation* v. *Siri Niwas*, AIR 2004 SC 4681: 2004 AIR SCW 5184: (2004) 8 SCC 195; *Manager R.B.I.* v. *S. Mani*, 2005 AIR SCW 1729: AIR 2005 SC 2179: 2005 Lab IC 2598.
6. *Ashok Kumar* v. *State of Tamil Nadu*, (2006) 10 SCC 157: AIR 2006 SC 2419: 2006 Cr LJ 2931.
7. *Kamma Otukunta Ram Naidu* v. *Chereddy Pedda Subba Reddy*, AIR 2003 SC 3342: 2003 Cr LJ 4967: 2003 AIR SCW 4747.
8. *C. Jacob* v. *Director of Geology and Mining*, (2008) 10 SCC 115: AIR 2009 SC 264: 2008 AIR SCW 7233.
9. *Union of India* v. *Raja Mohammed Amir Mohammad Khan*, AIR 2005 SC 4383: 2005 AIR SCW 5303: (2005) 8 SCC 696.
10. *Director of V.E. & T.* v. *Nashin Sheikh Chand*, (2006) 10 SCC 301.
11. *Aloke Nath Dutta* v. *State of West Bengal*, (2007) 12 SCC 230: (2006) 13 SCALE 467.

An adverse inference can be drawn against a party if he withholds evidence, but not so if he merely fails to produce evidence.[1] Where FIR named only two eyewitnesses, but investigation revealed presence of two more eyewitnesses who were not questioned during investigation, an adverse inference could be drawn against the prosecution.[2]

34. A party's deliberate avoidance of the witness box raises a presumption against his case and leads to an adverse inference against him. Failure to call material witnesses to give evidence calls for an adverse inference.[3] Where one of the attestors of will was examined and there was no infirmity in his evidence, no adverse inference can be drawn for non-examination of the other attestors.[4] If the presence at the scene of the eye-witness examined in court does not appear to be in serious doubt, non-examination of other eye-witnesses does not call for an adverse inference.[5] The correct principle of law as to the proper effect of non-examination of a witness cannot be decided in the abstract. It is a question which has to be decided on a consideration of the circumstances of the particular case after considering the following aspects:

(a) Whether the witness is in a position to give relevant and material evidence.
(b) Whether he is within easy reach of the prosecution or not or whether circumstances exist justifying his non-examination, as for example, he is likely to be hostile to the prosecution.
(c) The nature and intensity of the controversy raised by the defence on a particular issue on which the witness is expected to give evidence.
(d) Persuasiveness of the evidence on record.

If the prosecution fails to examine a material witness, an adverse inference can be raised.[6] But then, there must be other circumstances also to facilitate the drawing of an adverse inference. Drawing an inference should not be made in a mechanical way.[7] Where prosecution examined only interested eye-witnesses

1. *Srichand K. Khetwani* v. *State of Maharashtra*, (1967) 1 SCJ 178: AIR 1967 SC 450: 1967 Cr LJ 414; *Capital Multi-Purpose Co-operative Societies, Bhopal* v. *State of Madhya Pradesh*, AIR 1967 SC 1815: (1968) 1 SCR 138: 1968 (1) SCJ 444; *Commissioner of Collegiate Education* v. *M. Madhusudhan Reddy*, (2005) 11 SCC 180.
2. *Pratap Singh* v. *State of Madhya Pradesh*, (2005) 13 SCC 624: AIR 2006 SC 514: 2005 AIR SCW 6158.
3. *Manak Lal* v. *Prem Chand*, AIR 1957 SC 425: 1957 SCJ 359: 1957 SCR 575; *Ritesh Chakravarthy* v. *State of Madhya Pradesh*, (2006) 12 SCC 321; *Seth Magan Mal* v. *Darbari Lal Chowdhry*, AIR 1928 PC 39: 107 IC 113; *Thulia Kali* v. *State of Tamil Nadu*, AIR 1973 SC 501: (1972) 3 SCC 393: (1972) 3 SCR 622; *Virendra Kumar Saklecha* v. *Jagjiwan*, AIR 1974 SC 1957: (1972) 1 SCC 826: (1972) 3 SCR 955; *Enuga Lakshmamma* v. *Vennapusa Chinna Mulla Reddy*, AIR 1985 SC 658: (1985) 2 SCC 100: 1985 UJ (SC) 585.
4. *P.S. Sairam* v. *P.S. Rama Rao Pisey*, AIR 2004 SC 1619: 2004 AIR SCW 911: (2004) 11 SCC 320.
5. *Hem Raj* v. *State of Haryana*, AIR 2005 SC 2110: 2005 AIR SCW 1885: 2005 Cr LJ 2152; *Takhaji Hiraji* v. *Thakore Kubersing Chamansing*, AIR 2001 SC 2328: 2001 AIR SCW 2077: 2001 Cr LJ 2602.
6. *Sawal Das* v. *State of Bihar*, AIR 1974 SC 778: (1974) 4 SCC 193: (1974) 3 SCR 74; *Karnesh Kumar Singh* v. *State of Uttar Pradesh*, AIR 1968 SC 1402: 1968 Cr LJ 1655; *Habeeb Mohammad* v. *State of Hyderabad*, AIR 1954 SC 51: 1953 SCJ 678: 35 Cr LJ 338: 1954 SCR 475; *Gulam Mahmood A. Malek* v. *State of Gujarat*, AIR 1980 SC 1558: 1980 Cr LJ 1096: 1980 Cri LR (SC) 504; *Thulia Kali* v. *State of Tamil Nadu*, AIR 1973 SC 501: (1972) 3 SCC 393: (1972) 3 SCR 622.
7. *Harapal Singh* v. *Devinder Sing*, AIR 1997 SC 2914: 1997 AIR SCW 2926: 1997 Cr LJ 3561; *State of Maharashtra* v. *Krishnamurthy Laxmipati Naidu*, AIR 1981 SC 617: 1981 Cr LJ 9: 1981 SCC (Cri) 364 (SC): (1980) Supp SCC 455; *Ram Kumar* v. *State of Haryana*, AIR 1996 SC 3185: 1996 Cr LJ 2441: 1996 AIR SCW 1904.

but failed to examine an independent eye-witness who was available to give evidence, an adverse inference can be drawn.[1] But an oblique motive cannot be attributed to the prosecution which gave up an independent eye-witness after examining the injured witnesses.[2] Where the CD statement of an independent witness was found to be not against the prosecution, no adverse inference can be drawn by his non-examination.[3] Where independent persons of the locality were not willing to tell the police that they had seen the occurrence, veracity of others examined as eye-witnesses cannot be doubted merely on the ground of non-examination of such independent persons.[4] Prosecution has the discretion to decide as to which witness should be examined. It is not necessary to call all the witnesses to prove the same fact and the Court will not interfere with such discretion exercised by the prosecutor unless it can be shown that was influenced by some oblique motive.[5] Where the question was whether a particular person was a minor on a particular date, non-examination of the father and brother of the alleged minor can lead to an adverse inference.[6] In some situations failure to produce police diary and register may call for an adverse inference.[7] Where the accused police officer was charged with the act of giving order to fire and a police officer who accompanied the accused was not examined as a witness by the prosecution, it was held that failure to examine the officer led to an adverse inference against the prosecution and cast serious reflection on the fairness of the trial.[8]

35. Failure of prosecution to explain the injuries sustained by the accused during the occurrence can lead to the following inferences in certain circumstances:

(1) That the prosecution has suppressed the real or full nature of the occurrence.
(2) That the eye-witnesses who denied the injuries, deposed falsely.
(3) That the defence case (if any) that it was a case of self-defence becomes more plausible, shifting the burden on the prosecution.[9]

Prosecution case based on documentary evidence does not become infirm on the ground that witnesses were not examined.[10] If selection of certain eye-witnesses to be examined in court is made fairly and honestly and not with a

1. *Amar Singh* v. *State of Haryana*, AIR 1973 SC 2221: 1973 SCC (Cri) 789: 1973 Cr LJ 1409; *Mangal Singh* v. *State of Madhya Bharat*, AIR 1957 SC 199: 1957 Cr LJ 325; *Gulam Mahmood A. Malek* v. *State of Gujarat*, AIR 1980 SC 1558: 1980 Cr LJ 1096: 1980 Cri LR (SC) 504; *Bir Singh* v. *State of Uttar Pradesh*, AIR 1978 SC 59: (1977) 4 SCC 420: 1978 Cr LJ 177.
2. *Chacko @ Jacob* v. *State of Kerala*, AIR 1998 SC 2250: 1998 Cr LJ 3281: 1998 AIR SCW 2144.
3. *Collector of Customs, Bombay* v. *Messrs Dai-Ichi Karkaria Limited*, (1998) 9 SCC 23.
4. *State of Bihar* v. *Ram Padarath Singh*, AIR 1998 SC 2606: 1998 Cr LJ 4007: 1998 AIR SCW 2640.
5. *Abdul Gani* v. *State of Madhya Pradesh*, AIR 1954 SC 31: 1954 Cr LJ 323 (SC).
6. *Enuga Lakshmamma* v. *Vennapusa Chinna Mulla Reddy*, AIR 1985 SC 658: (1985) 2 SCC 100: 1985 UJ (SC) 585.
7. *Sevi, Koodakkal Karian* v. *State of Tamil Nadu*, AIR 1981 SC 1230: 1981 Cr LJ 736: 1981 SCC (Cri) 679.
8. *Habeeb Mohammad* v. *State of Hyderabad*, AIR 1954 SC 51: 1953 SCJ 678: 35 Cr LJ 338: 1954 SCR 475; *State of Uttar Pradesh* v. *Punni*, AIR 2008 SC 932: 2008 Cr LJ 1028: 2008 AIR SCW 376; *Ram Prasad* v. *State of Uttar Pradesh*, (1974) 3 SCC 388: AIR 1973 SC 2673: 1973 Cr LJ 1807.
9. *Lakshmi Singh* v. *State of Bihar*, (1976) 4 SCC 394: 1976 SCC (Cri) 671: AIR 1976 SC 2263: 1976 Cr LJ 1736.
10. *Bali Ram Prasad* v. *State of Mysore*, AIR 1973 SC 506: 1973 Cr LJ 3: (1972) 3 SCC 681.

view to suppress inconvenient witnesses, no adverse inference can be drawn against the prosecution.[1] That a witness was won over by the accused, if shown to be true, is an acceptable explanation.[2] The duty of the prosecution is only to examine those witnesses who are essential to the unfolding of the prosecution story.[3]

Court must have regard to other circumstances present in the case. Non-production of a document, which, if produced, might also injure the feelings and reputation of his own family cannot enable court to draw an adverse inference if the contract on which he is sued is of small importance. So also where non-production may be justifiable on some reasonable grounds. Where no other case is apparent or proved, court will be entitled to draw adverse inference. Duplication of evidence is one such justifying ground.[4] No adverse inference can be drawn if the question of non-production of relevant evidence was not raised at the trial, when possibly an explanation might have been offered.

36. The presumption cannot displace a contrary inference supported by adequate evidence. A party asking the court to draw an adverse inference against another party by reason of non-examination of a witness, must show that the witness was available to the other party at the time of the hearing; such evidence could be elicited during cross-examination of other witnesses or by leading evidence to that effect.[5] In an Election Petition, it has been held that there is no *onus* on the successful candidate to prove particular facts and his non-examination of a witness who can contradict the facts stated by the opposite party's witness does not lead to adverse inference.[6] If a principal witness is not examined and no explanation is forthcoming, an adverse inference can be drawn. Where a party fails to appear as a witness, an adverse inference can be drawn. So also in a case of serious challenge of an attested document, the non-examination of the attestor.[7] That in case of rival village factions, the average villager is reluctant to appear as witness is an aspect which has to be borne in mind.[8] When independent eye-witness available are given up and only interested eye-witness is examined and no explanation is forthcoming, an adverse inference can be drawn, having regard to all relevant aspects.[9] Where a witness is absconding or untraceable or is not forthcoming on account of village faction fighting or

1. *Pal Singh* v. *State of Uttar Pradesh*, AIR 1979 SC 1116: (1979) 4 SCC 345: 1979 Cr LJ 917.
2. *A. Deivendran* v. *State of Tamil Nadu*, AIR 1998 SC 2821: 1998 AIR SCW 285: 1998 Cr LJ 814; *Allauddin Mian* v. *State of Bihar*, AIR 1989 SC 1456: (1989) 3 SCC 5: 1989 Cr LJ 1466.
3. *Stephen Seneviratne* v. *King*, AIR 1936 PC 289: 37 Cr LJ 963 (PC); *Narain* v. *State of Punjab*, AIR 1959 SC 484: 1959 Supp (1) SCR 724: 1959 Cr LJ 537.
4. *Madan Lal* v. *State of Punjab*, 1974 Cr LJ 1225: (1974) Cur LJ 348.
5. *Jagdishprasad Kashiprasad* v. *State of Maharashtra*, AIR 1970 Bom 166: ILR (1969) Bom 1191: 1970 Cr LJ 660.
6. *Moti Lal* v. *Chandra Pratap Tiwari*, AIR 1975 SC 1178: 1975 UJ (SC) 333: (1975) 4 SCC 862; *Khaje Khanavar Khadskhan Hushenkhan* v. *Siddavanhalli Nijalingappa*, AIR 1968 Mys 18: 13 Law Rep 153.
7. *Enuga Lakshmamma* v. *Vennapusa Chinna Mulla Reddy*, AIR 1985 SC 658: (1985) 2 SCC 100: 1985 UJ (SC) 585.
8. *Raghubir Singh* v. *State of Uttar Pradesh*, AIR 1971 SC 2156: 1971 Cr LJ 1468: 1971 U J (SC) 762.
9. *Bir Singh* v. *State of Uttar Pradesh*, AIR 1978 SC 59: (1977) 4 SCC 420: 1978 Cr LJ 177; *Awadhesh* v. *State of Madhya Pradesh*, (1988) 2 SCC 557: AIR 1988 SC 1158: JT 1988 (2) SC 72.

has turned hostile or is not available, or has been won over by the accused, no inference may be drawn.[1] A party has the right to choose his own witness. In a criminal case, witnesses essential to the unfolding of the narrative on which prosecution is based must be called by the prosecution.[2] *Bona fide* exercise of prosecutorial discretion must be respected.[3] If a material witness is deliberately or unfairly held back, it reflects on the prosecution case.[4] This applies to the defence also.[5] Where both parties can produce some evidence but neither does so, its' non-production is inconclusive.[6]

37. Adverse inference will be drawn against a party not giving evidence as a witness when no other material evidence is produced by him.[7] It is the duty of a party personally knowing all the circumstances of the case to give evidence; failure to do so could lead to an adverse inference. This is more so where there is a previous admission made by that party,[8] or where he does not give evidence in support of entries in books of account sought to be relied on by him.[9] So also in the case of a party who withholds relevant documents admitted to have been in existence,[10] though not in a case where he merely fails to obtain evidence.[11] Where the burden of proof is entirely on one party, non-production of relevant documents by the opposite party cannot give rise to an adverse inference.[12] Where a party has not produced the registered cover received by him which would have shown the actual date of receipt of the cover by him, an adverse inference can be drawn against him.[13] It is not sound practice for parties desiring to rely upon a state of facts to withhold from the court documents in

---

1. *Ram Avtar Rai* v. *State of Uttar Pradesh*, AIR 1985 SC 880: 1985 Cr LJ 902: (1985) 2 SCC 61; *Dalbir Kaur* v. *State of Punjab*, AIR 1977 SC 472: (1976) 4 SCC 158: 1977 Cr LJ 273; *Allauddin Mian* v. *State of Bihar*, AIR 1989 SC 1456: (1989) 3 SCC 5: 1989 Cr LJ 1466.
2. *Stephen Seneviratne* v. *King*, AIR 1936 PC 289: 37 Cr LJ 963 (PC).
3. *Pal Singh* v. *State of Uttar Pradesh*, AIR 1979 SC 1116: (1979) 4 SCC 345: 1979 Cr LJ 917; *Dilafroz* v. *Raja Gauhar Zamir Khan*, AIR 1946 PC 16; *Sevi, Koodakkal Karian* v. *State of Tamil Nadu*, AIR 1981 SC 1230: 1981 Cr LJ 736: 1981 SCC (Cri) 679.
4. *Habeeb Mohammad* v. *State of Hyderabad*, AIR 1954 SC 51: 1953 SCJ 678: 35 Cr LJ 338: 1954 SCR 475.
5. *Deonath Dudhnath Mishra, Amravati* v. *State of Maharashtra*, AIR 1967 Bom 1: 1965 Mah LJ 565: 1967 Cr LJ 21.
6. *Ramrati Kuer* v. *Dwarika Prasad Singh*, AIR 1967 SC 1134: (1967) 2 SCJ 789: (1967) 1 SCR 153.
7. *Pandurang Jivaji Apte* v. *Ramchandra Gangadhar Ashtekar*, AIR 1981 SC 2235: (1981) 4 SCC 569; *Kalappa Dyanappa* v. *Venkatesh alias Ramachandra Ganesh Padaki*, AIR 1962 Mys 260; *Bijoy Kumar Karnani* v. *Lahori Ram Prasher*, AIR 1973 Cal 465.
8. *Prakash Chand Sharma* v. *Narendra Nath Sharma*, AIR 1976 SC 2456: 1975 UJ (SC) 848: (1976) 3 SCC 215.
9. *Chandrakantaben* v. *Vadilal Bapalal*, AIR 1989 SC 1269: (1989) 1 APLJ (SC) 76: (1989) 2 SCC 630.
10. *Mohan Singh* v. *Bhanwarlal*, (1964) 5 SCR 12: AIR 1964 SC 1366: 1964 MPLJ 249; *Manasarovar Agencies* v. *Governor-General in Council, Dominion of India, New Delhi*, AIR 1955 Mys 123: ILR 1955 Mys 444; *Kumar Harish Chandra Singh Das Deo* v. *Bansidhar Mohanty*, AIR 1965 SC 1738: 1966 (1) SCJ 145: (1966) 1 SCR 153; *Khushalbhai Mahijibhai Patel* v. *A. firm of Mohamadhussain Rahimbux*, AIR 1981 SC 977: (1980) 3 SCR 22: 1980 Supp SCC 1.
11. *Srichand K. Khetwani* v. *State of Maharashtra*, (1967) 1 SCJ 178: AIR 1967 SC 450: 1967 Cr LJ 414.
12. *Bihar State Board Religious Trust, Patna* v. *Mahant Sri Biseshwar Das*, AIR 1971 SC 2057: 1972 Pat LJR 16: (1971) 3 SCR 680.
13. *Binod Bihari Singh* v. *Union of India*, AIR 1993 SC 1245: 1993 AIR SCW 475: (1992) 3 SCR 468.

their possession which would throw light upon the proposition.[1] But where neither party produced relevant documents, the absence of such evidence is inconclusive.[2] Where a party in possession of best evidence withholds it, the Court may draw an adverse inference against him even though the *onus* of proof does not lie on him.[3] This principle applies to cases before other authorities also.[4] Where the government withholds a document under an untenable plea of privilege, an adverse inference can be drawn. This principle has been applied in cases of negligence also.[5] Non-production of relevant account books may give rise to adverse inference.[6] Where there is no evidence that a relevant document is with a party or within his power, court would refuse to draw an adverse inference against him.[7] It is not incumbent on a party to produce documents, which, he believes, have no bearing on a dispute. It is for the opposite party to apply for inspection of document and if he fails to do so, court cannot draw any presumption regarding the contents of the document. If the opposite party did not question the party in possession of certain documents, no adverse inference can be drawn who did not produce the documents. But, court could in weighing the evidence, take into consideration, non-production of the documents.[8]

38. The rule applies to the State also.[9] If there is no cross-examination of a party regarding documents which he failed to produce, adverse inference may not be drawn against him.[10] To draw an adverse inference on the non-examination of a witness, it must be shown that he is a material witness.[11]

Where the accused has a particular version and he does not examine material witnesses, an adverse inference may arise against him.[12]

---

1. *Murugesam* v. *Gnana Sambanda Pandara*, AIR 1917 PC 6: 44 IA 98: 40 M 402: 39 IC 659; *Hiralal* v. *Badkulal*, AIR 1953 SC 225: 1953 SCR 758: 1953 SCJ 315; *Gopal Krishnaji Ketkar* v. *Mahomed Haji Latif*, AIR 1968 SC 1413.
2. *Ramrati Kuer* v. *Dwarika Prasad Singh*, AIR 1967 SC 1134: (1967) 2 SCJ 789: (1967) 1 SCR 153.
3. *Devidas* v. *Shrishailappa*, AIR 1961 SC 1277: (1961) 3 SCR 896: 1962 (1) SCJ 557; *Gopal Krishnaji Ketkar* v. *Mahomed Haji Latif*, AIR 1968 SC 1413; *Virendra Kumar Saklecha* v. *Jagjiwan*, AIR 1974 SC 1957: (1972) 1 SCC 826: (1972) 3 SCR 955; *Atyam Veerraju* v. *Pechetti Venkanna*, AIR 1966 SC 629: (1966) 1 SCR 831: 1967 (1) SCJ 17; *Ramdas Oil Mills* v. *Union of India (Military Deptt.)*, AIR 1977 SC 638: (1977) 1 SCC 592; *State Inspector of Police* v. *Surya Sankaram Karri*, (2006) 7 SCC 172: AIR 2007 SC (Supp) 1860: 2006 AIR SCW 4576; *Jagmodhan Mehatabsing Gujaral* v. *State of Maharashtra*, (2006) 8 SCC 629.
4. *Capital Multi-Purpose Co-operative Societies, Bhopal* v. *State of Madhya Pradesh*, AIR 1967 SC 1815: 1968 (1) SCJ 444: 1968 All LJ 189; *Commissioner of Income-tax, Madras* v. *Best and Co. (Private) Ltd. Madras*, AIR 1966 SC 1325: 1966 (1) SCJ 542: (1966) 2 SCR 480.
5. *Kumar Harish Chandra Singh Das Deo* v. *Bansidhar Mohanty*, AIR 1965 SC 1738: 1966 (1) SCJ 145: (1966) 1 SCR 153; *Union of India* v. *Mahadeolal Prabhu Dayal*, AIR 1965 SC 1755: (1966) 1 SCJ 505: (1965) 3 SCR 145.
6. *Goswami Shri Mahalaxmi Vahuji* v. *Shah Ranchhoddas Kalidas*, AIR 1970 SC 2025: (1970) 2 SCA 143: (1970) 2 SCR 275; *Khushalbhai Mahijibhai Patel* v. *A. firm of Mohamadhussain Rahimbux*, AIR 1981 SC 977: 1980 3 SCR 22: 1980 Supp SCC 1; *Ramdas Oil Mills* v. *Union of India (Military Deptt.)*, AIR 1977 SC 638: (1977) 1 SCC 592; *Hiralal* v. *Badkulal*, AIR 1953 SC 225: 1953 SCR 758: 1953 SCJ 315.
7. *Devidas* v. *Shrishailappa*, AIR 1961 SC 1277: (1961) 3 SCR 896: 1962 (1) SCJ 557.
8. *Mahant Shri Srinivas Ramanuj Das* v. *Surjanarayan Das*, AIR 1967 SC 256: 33 Cut LT 105: 1966 Supp SCR 436.
9. *Baljit Singh* v. *State of Uttar Pradesh*, AIR 1976 SC 2273: (1976) 4 SCC 590: 1976 Cr LJ 1745.
10. *Indira Kaur* v. *Sheo Lal Kapoor*, AIR 1988 SC 1074: (1988) 2 SCC 488: JT 1988 (1) SC 652(2).
11. *Pattad Amarappa* v. *State*, AIR 1989 SC 2004: 1989 Supp (2) SCC 389: 1989 Cr LJ 1267.
12. *Gajendra Singh* v. *State of Uttar Pradesh*, AIR 1975 SC 1703: 1975 Cr LJ 1494: (1975) 4 SCC 241.

39. Illustration (h).—Court may presume that if a person refuses to answer a question which he is not compelled to answer by law, the answer would be unfavourable to him, except in cases where the answer might cause loss to him in matters unconnected with the matter in relation to which the question is asked. section 313 of the Code of Criminal Procedure empowers the court to examine the accused, but he does not render himself liable to punishment by refusing to answer or gives false answers. The provision enabling an adverse inference available in section 313(2) of the 1898 Code has been omitted in new Code. *See* sections 132, 147 and 148 of the Act 1872.

40. Illustration (i).—Court may presume that when a document creating an obligation is in the hands of the obligator, the obligation has been discharged, though not in a case where the circumstances are such that he may have stolen it. The basis of the presumption is that people are usually vigilant in guarding their property, prompt in asserting their rights and diligent in claiming and collecting their dues.[1] The strength of the presumption which might be raised varies in different circumstances. Presumption is weakened in a case where the defendant produces such a document, but not the title deeds which were deposited with the creditor.

41. The illustrations to section 114, being merely illustrations, are not exhaustive. Other presumptions may also be raised under this provision under proper circumstances, *e.g.*, genuiness of old accounts, what is admitted by a party must be true, presumption against misconduct, illegality and immorality, condonation of adulterous act, existence of an agency, character of agency (that it is general and not special), acting within the scope of authority, conduct approving an unauthorised act of an agent, alteration in a document being made prior to the execution of the deed (not material alteration), child bearing age, possession of one co-owner being on behalf of all co-owners, consideration for a document admitted or proved, continuance of state of things, undue influence in case of special relationship of parties to a document, presumption of innocence, good faith except in special cases, *res ipsa loquitor, mens rea* (every person knows and intends the natural, probable but not the remote or incidental consequences of his voluntary words of acts), knowledge of law, contents of deed duly executed, once a mortgage always a mortgage, possession follows title in certain cases, possession indicates title, marriage and legitimacy etc. But in criminal cases, no presumption can ordinarily be raised which has no origin in any statute.[2] There were and are statutes providing for *mens rea* on certain facts being established. However, a presumption of innocence is regarded as a human right.[3] No presumption can be drawn against an accused for not examining himself as a witness.[4]

In considering the application of the various illustrations to section 114, the court shall have regard to certain specific factors referred to in the section at the end of illustration (i). Such factors are as follows:

---

1. Woodrooffe and Amir Ali on Law of Evidence Vol. 3, Page 2846.
2. *Harendra Sarkar* v. *State of Assam*, AIR 2008 SC 2467: 2008 AIR SCW 3785: (2008) 9 SCC 204.
3. *Narendra Singh* v. *State of Madhya Pradesh*, AIR 2004 SC 3249: (2004) 10 SCC 699: 2004 AIR SCW 3094.
4. *Baidya Nath Prasad Srivastava* v. *State of Bihar*, AIR 1968 SC 1393: (1968) Cr LJ 1650: (1969) 1 SCR 172; Ratanlal and Dhirajlal on Evidence, 23rd Edition, Pages 1387 to 1424.

As to illustration (a).—A shopkeeper has in his till a marked rupee soon after it was stolen, and cannot account for its possession specifically, but is continually receiving rupees in the course of his business;

As to illustration (b).—*A*, a person of the highest character, is tried for causing a man's death by act of negligence in arranging certain machinery. *B*, a person of equally good character, who also took part in the arrangement, describes precisely what was done, and admits and explains the common carelessness of A and himself;

As to illustration (b).—A crime is committed by several persons. *A*, *B* and *C*, three of the criminals, are captured on the spot and kept apart from each other. Each gives an account of the crime implicating *D* and the accounts corroborate each other in such a manner as to render previous concert highly improbable;

As to illustration (c).—*A*, the drawer of a bill of exchange, was a man of business. B, the acceptor was young and ignorant person, completely under *A*'s influence;

As to illustration (d).—It is proved that a river ran in a certain course five years ago, but it is known that there have been floods since that time which might change its course;

As to illustration (e).—A judicial act, the regularity of which is in question, was performed under exceptional circumstances;

As to illustration (f).—The question is, whether a letter was received. It is shown to have been posted, but the usual course of the post was interrupted by disturbances;

A to illustration (g).—A man refuses to produce a document which would bear on a contract of small importance on which he is sued, but which might also injure the feelings and reputation of the family;

As to illustration(h).—A man refuses to answer a question which he is not compelled by law to answer, but the answer to it might cause loss to him in matters unconnected with the matter in relation to which it is asked;

As to illustration (i).—A bond is in possession of the obligor, but the circumstances of the case are such that he may have stolen it.

LEGAL PRESUMPTIONS

42. SECTION 79.—Court shall presume to be genuine, every document purporting to be a certificate, certified copy or other document, which is by law declared to be admissible as evidence of any particular fact and which purports to be duly certified by any officer of Central or State Government or by any officer in the State of Jammu and Kashmir who is duly authorised thereto by the Central Government: provided that such document is substantially in the form and purports to be executed in the manner declared by law in that behalf.

Court shall also presume any officer by whom any such document purports to be signed or certified, held, when he signed it, the official character which he claims in such paper.

The section applies only to certified copies and not to original documents. In the case of a registered document, the certificate of registration requires no proof. Certified copy under the first part must be executed substantially in the prescribed form and manner.[1] Law does not insist on the maker of the entries

1. *Bhinka* v. *Charan Singh*, 1959 ALJ 557: AIR 1959 SC 960: 1959 Cr LJ 1223.

in the original to be examined as a witness. Probative value of such entries depends on a variety of circumstances, including the other evidence in the case. This presumption is only a *prima facie* presumption. If the certificate etc., is not correct, such incorrectness can be shown. It is an old principle of law that where a person acts in an official capacity it shall be presumed that he was duly appointed. This presumption is mandatory. Under this section, a court is bound to presume that a certified copy of a document is genuine and also that the officer signed it in the official character which he claimed in the said document.[1] Government records produced in evidence must be presumed to be genuine. Statement of parties recorded in mutual proceedings are public documents and attract the operation of this Section.

43. SECTION 80.—Where any document is produced before any court—

(a) purporting to be a record or memorandum of evidence or of any part of the evidence given by a witness in a judicial proceeding or before any officer authorised by law to take any such evidence, or

(b) purporting to be a statement or confession by any prisoner or accused taken in accordance with law and purporting to be signed by any judge or Magistrate or by any such officer as aforesaid.

Court shall presume that:—

(i) the document is genuine;

(ii) that any statement as to the circumstances under which it was taken, purporting to be made by the person signing, are true; and

(iii) that any such evidence, statement or confession was duly taken.

This provision dispenses with formal proof.[2] Section 161 statements (Cr.P.C.), memo of TIP are not covered by this Section. Heading of a deposition descriptive of the witness forms no part of the evidence given by him. A confession recorded by a second class magistrate not specifically empowered in that behalf, does not attract this provision.[3] Endorsement on a deposition or Memo of TIP has to be accepted as correct until the contrary is proved.[4] The practice of handing over the deposition to a witness who can read and understand it is a sufficient compliance with the rule which requires the deposition to be read over to him. There is no general presumption that every officer is authorized by law to record evidence. An affidavit is not evidence. This section will not apply to any statement failing to satisfy the provisions of section 33. Presumption regarding confession will arise only when it was recorded strictly in accordance with law. Section 80 will not apply to a confession recorded by a Tahsildar having powers of a second class magistrate and who was not specifically empowered to record any statement during investigation.[3] A confession recorded in gross disregard of the precautions prescribed in section 164 Cr.P.C. cannot attract the operation of this section.[5]

1. *Bhinka* v. *Charan Singh*, 1959 ALJ 557: AIR 1959 SC 960: 1959 Cr LJ 1223.
2. *Madi Ganga* v. *State of Orissa*, AIR 1981 SC 1165: 1981 Cr LJ 625: (1981) 2 SCC 224.
3. *Nika Ram* v. *State of Himachal Pradesh*, AIR 1972 SC 2077: (1972) 2 SCC 80: 1972 Cr LJ 1317.
4. *Kashmira Singh* v. *State of Madhya Pradesh*, AIR 1952 SC 159: 1952 SCR 526: 1952 SCJ 201: 1952 Cr LJ 839.
5. *Nazir Ahmad* v. *King-Emperor*, AIR 1936 PC 253: 37 Cr LJ 897: 1936 ILR 17 Lah 629: 63 IA 372.

Evidence must be given of the identity of the person making the deposition or statement.[1]

44. SECTION 81.—Court shall presume the genuineness of every document purporting to be—

(a) the London Gazette or any Gazette official or government gazette of a colony, or

(b) to be a newspaper or journal, or

(c) to be a copy of a private Act of Parliament of UK, or

(d) a document directed by any law to be kept by a person if it is kept substantially in the form required by law and is produced from proper custody.

See also sections 37 and 57(7).

Statements in gazetteers cannot be relied on as evidence of title, but they provide historical materials and practices followed by institutions.[2]

Presumption of genuineness of a newspaper does not mean reports therein are admissible. Such supports are merely hearsay.[3] Reports of legislative debates are evidence of speeches made, but not of any facts contained in the speeches.[4] What is published in a government owned paper may be presumed to correctly represent the actual state of affairs relating to government business until the contrary is shown.[5] The last part of this section refers to and includes documents mentioned in section 35, most of which are declared to be public documents by section 74.

45. SECTION 81A.—Court shall presume the genuineness of every electronic record purporting to be the official gazette, or purporting to be electronic record directed by any law to be kept by any person, if such electronic record is kept substantially in the form required by law and produced from proper custody.

This is a mandatory presumption regarding genuineness of the electronic records purporting to be the official gazette or electronic record kept in accordance with the form required by law and produced from proper custody.

46. SECTION 82.—In case of documents admissible in proof of any matter in any court of England or Ireland without proof of the seal or stamp or signature authenticating it or of the judicial or official character claimed by the person by whom it purports to be signed, Courts in India shall presume that such seal, stamp or signature is genuine and the person signing it held such office which he claimed. The document would be admissible for the same purpose for which it would be admissible in England or Ireland.

1. *Gopal Das* v. *Thakurji*, AIR 1943 PC 83: ILR (1943) Kar PC 69: 1943 All LJ 292 (PC): 47 CWN 607.
2. *Mahant Shri Srinivas Ramanuj Das* v. *Surjanarayan Das*, AIR 1967 SC 256: 33 Cut LT 105: 1966 Supp SCR 436.
3. *Laxmi Raj Shetty* v. *State of Tamil Nadu*, AIR 1988 SC 1274: (1988) 3 SCC 319: 1988 SCC (Cri) 633: (1988) 2 Crimes 107; *Samant N. Balakrishna* v. *George Fernandez*, AIR 1969 SC 1201: (1969) 3 SCR 603: (1970) 1 SCA 376.
4. *Rt. Hon. Gerald Lord Strickland* v. *Carmelo Mifsud Bonnici*, AIR 1935 PC 34: 153 IC 1.
5. *R.S. Nayak* v. *A.R. Antulay*, AIR 1986 SC 2045: 1986 Cr LJ 1922: (1986) 2 SCC 716.

47. SECTION 83.—Maps or plans purporting to be made by Governmental Authority shall be presumed to be so made and to be accurate. But maps or plans made for the purpose of any cause must be proved to be accurate.[1] Section 36 provides for relevancy of maps, plans and charts. This Section deals with maps or plans made for public purpose as distinct from private purpose. There is no presumption in favour of accuracy of maps prepared by private persons.[2]

Plan prepared by a court Commissioner appointed in a litigation must be proved to be accurate. No importance attaches to a plan prepared by a party himself.

48. SECTION 84.—There shall be a presumption of genuiness of every book purporting to be printed or published under Governmental Authority of any country and purporting to contain any of the laws of that country. So also every book containing reports of decisions of courts of that country. *See* section 35 regarding relevancy. A newspaper report of a case is, strictly speaking, not covered by sections 38 and 84.

The effect of this section is that court may take judicial notice of a publication containing foreign law. There is no presumption that any such book contains the whole law of that country.

49. SECTION 85.—This section raises a presumption regarding execution and authentication of every document purporting to be a power of attorney executed before and authenticated by a specified official. *See* Order III rule 2 C.P.C., section 2(21) of Indian Stamp Act and Section 69 of Registration Act. Under section 57(b) of the Evidence Act, Court shall take judicial notice of seals of notary public. Contents of the document are required to be proved like any other fact.

50. SECTION 85A.—The court shall presume that every electronic record purporting to be an agreement containing the electronic signature of the parties, was so concluded by affixing the electronic signature of the parties.

51. SECTION 85B.—(1) In any proceedings involving a secure electronic record, the Court shall presume unless the contrary is proved, that the secure electronic record has not been altered since the specific point of time to which the secure status relates.

(2) In any proceedings, involving secure electronic signature, the Court shall presume until the contrary is proved that—

(a) the secure electronic signature is affixed by subscriber with the intention of signing or approving the electronic record;

(b) except in the case of a secure electronic record or a secure electronic signature, nothing in the Section shall create any presumption relating to authenticity and integrity of the electronic record or any electronic signature.

52. SECTION 85C.—Court shall presume, unless contrary is proved, that the information listed in a electronic signature certificate is correct, except for the information specified as subscriber information which has not been verified, if the certificate was accepted by the subscriber.

---

1. *Kesho Prasad Singh* v. *Bhagjogna Kuer*, AIR 1937 PC 69: 41 Cal WN 577: ILR 16 Pat 258; *Ram Kishore Sen* v. *Union of India*, AIR 1966 SC 644: (1966) 1 SCR 430.
2. *Ram Kishore Sen* v. *Union of India*, AIR 1966 SC 644: (1966) 1 SCR 430.

53. SECTION 89.—Every document called for and not produced by a party after notice to produce shall be presumed to have been attested, stamped and executed in the manner required by law. (Presumed proof).

This presumption is quite different from the presumption under illustration (g) to section 114. This section is applicable in cases falling under sections 65(a) and 66.[1] Notice to produce is mandatory, though it is redundant in a case where the party excuses himself from the production of the original document on the plea that it is not traceable or is lost.[2] Order XVI rule 6 of C.P.C. may also be seen. The presumption will not arise in favour of a party where notice to produce has not been given to the opposite party.[3] Giving notice to produce does not arise once a party pleads that the document is not traceable.[4]

---

1. *Kashibai Martand* v. *Vinayak Ganesh*, AIR 1956 Bom 65: 57 Bom LR 918: ILR (1955) Bom 999.
2. *Patel Manilal Chhaganlal* v. *Municipal Corporation, Surat*, AIR 1978 Guj 193: 19 Guj LR 412.
3. *Mira Bai* v. *Jai Singh*, AIR 1971 Raj 303: 1971 Raj LW 319.
4. *Patel Manilal Chhaganlal* v. *Municipal Corporation, Surat*, AIR 1978 Guj 193: 19 Guj LR 412.

CHAPTER 18
EXCLUSION OF ORAL BY DOCUMENTARY EVIDENCE (SECTIONS 91-100)

Section 91.—This Section applies in two situations, namely—

(i) When the terms of a contract or grant, or of any other disposition of property have been reduced to the form of a document, and

(ii) in all cases in which any matter is required by law to be reduced to the form of a document—

In such cases no evidence shall be given in proof of the terms of such contract, grant or other disposition of property or of such matter except:—

(a) the document itself, or

(b) secondary evidence of its' contents in cases in which secondary evidence (is admissible under the provisions) herein before contained.

Exception 1.—When a public officer is required by law to be appointed in writing, and when it is shown that any particular person has acted as such officer, the writing by which he is appointed need not be proved.

Exception 2.—Wills admitted to probate in India may be proved by the probate.

Explanation 1.—This section applies equally to cases in which contracts, grants or dispositions of property referred to are contained in one document, and to cases in which they are contained in more documents than one.

Explanation 2.—Where there are more originals than one, one original only need be proved.

Explanation 3.—The statement in any document whatever, of a fact other than the facts referred to in this section, shall not preclude the admission of oral evidence as to the same fact.

2. Document is the best evidence of its contents.[1] This is the best evidence rule. Section 91 bars evidence other than primary or secondary evidence (where it is permitted) of the terms of a contract, grant, disposition reduced to writing and in all cases in which any matter is required by law to be reduced to the form of a document. Proof of oral sale is admissible even if there be an unregistered sale deed which was not produced in court.[2] To prove the contents of a document, the document itself must be produced. All other contemporaneous utterances at the time of the execution are merged in the deed and are legally immaterial to determine the terms of the deed, as otherwise mischief will result; this rule binds a third party to the deed also.[3] The policy behind this rule is to

1. *Bai Heera Devi* v. *Official Assignee, Bombay*, AIR 1958 SC 448: 1958 SCJ 766: (1958) 1 SCR 1384.
2. *Deopato Kuer* v. *Kamat Prasad Singh*, AIR 1976 Pat 18: 1976 BLJR 378.
3. *Roop Kumar* v. *Mohan Thedani*, AIR 2003 SC 2418: 2003 AIR SCW 2425: (2003) 6 SCC 595.

bar collateral evidence which can create mischief. 'The principle is that in all proceedings in which contents of a document are to be proved, the document itself must be produced in Court or its' absence accounted for before evidence of contents is admitted. (*Ibid*). Any other evidence is excluded from being used either as a substitute or to contradict or alter them. (*Ibid*). The primary evidence from which the intention of the parties is to be gathered is the document itself and surrounding circumstances, but not the subsequent conduct. If the original document is inadmissible in evidence for any reason, copy of the document or oral evidence cannot be any substitute.[1]

3. There is no bar to prove that a document was never intended to be acted upon and was created for the purpose of creating evidence about some other matter.[2] There is no bar to prove that the contract was a fictitious or a colourable device. It is open to any of the parties to a document to adduce oral evidence to show that his signature in the document was a forgery.[3] In the case of mortgage, one mortgagor can show that he was only a surety for other mortgagors.[4]

4. Sections 91 and 92 apply only to contracts, grants and other dispositions of property. A Will does not fall within the expression "Contract or Grant". It is not a disposition till the death of the maker. Hence, the sections do not apply to Wills. Divorce is not a disposition. A unilateral divorce is not a contract.

5. Where a matter is one not required by law to be in writing, oral evidence is not excluded unless the transaction to an action has been reduced to writing.[5] The document is the sole repository of the terms of the contract. A mortgage by unregistered instrument is inadmissible and cannot be used in evidence. The transaction cannot be proved by oral evidence, by reason of section 49 of Registration Act and the present section. Before evidence is excluded under this Section (or under section 92), it must be shown that the document purports to record all the terms of the contract between the parties.[6] Hence, it is clear that when all the terms have not been reduced to writing, oral evidence is not excluded.[7]

6. "Terms" in this section and section 92 relates to statements, assertions or representations in the document which relate to the subject-matter of the contract and something to be done or not to be done under the contract. "Term" does not include a condition precedent to the formation of the contract.[8]

This bar applies to strangers to the contract also.[9] This section deals only with mode of proof. Mode of proof is a question of procedure and can be waived.[10]

1. *Fort Gloster Industries* v. *Sethia Mercantile (Pvt.) Ltd.*, AIR 1971 SC 2289: (1972) 4 SCC 252: (1971) 2 Civ App J (SC) 52.
2. *Yadav Ram* v. *Laman Singh Bisht*, AIR 1978 All 123; *Chanderwati* v. *Lakhmi Chand*, AIR 1988 Del 13: (1987) 5 Reports 507: (1987) 13 DRJ 248.
3. *Thyagaraja Mudaliar* v. *Vedathanni*, AIR 1936 PC 70: ILR 59 Mad 446.
4. *Sultan Md. Mohiuddeen* v. *Amthual Jalal*, AIR 1927 Mad 110; *Lakshmane Sahu* v. *S Patra*, AIR 1941 Pat 211.
5. (Obla) *Sundarachariar* v. *Narayana Ayyar*, AIR 1931 PC 36: 58 Ind App 68: ILR 54 Mad 257.
6. *Mohammad Akbar Khan* v. *Attar Singh*, AIR 1936 PC 171: 17 L 557.
7. *Jamna Dad* v. *Srinath Roy*, ILR (1989) 17 Cal 176.
8. *B.B. Bhat* v. *V.R. Thakur*, (1972) 74 Bom LR 509.
9. *Meenakshisundaram Pillai* v. *Stchenchu Mudaliar*, AIR 1928 Mad 459: 109 Ind Cas 18.
10. *Binani Properties Private Ltd.* v. *M. Gulamaji Abdul Hossain and Co.*, AIR 1967 Cal 390.

"Contract" includes contract of service, arbitration agreement, compromise agreement, agreement to sell, etc.[1] "Any other disposition" includes Sale, Mortgage, Lease, Partition, Wakf, etc. A receipt is not covered by the section.

An agreement that a sale deed was not to be operative as such and was to remain with the party for a different purpose is admissible.[2] Section 91 does not shut out oral evidence to show that the document was brought about for the purpose of showing that there was no agreement between the parties and was never intended to operate as an agreement. The section does not preclude a party from proving that the real contract is different from what was found in that document.[3]

7. A collateral agreement that a sale deed executed by one of the parties is nominal is not covered by the section. So also a colourable device.[4] When a tenancy was created by a rent-note, oral evidence is admissible to prove that the real tenant was someone other than the person shown in the document as a tenant.[5] Oral evidence is admissible to show that a written agreement executed was never intended to operate an agreement, but was brought about solely for creating evidence about some other matter.[6] Where a document purports to be an agreement for sale of land, one of the parties can lead evidence to show the real nature of the transaction was a loan for which the document was a security.[7] A collateral agreement that the sale deed between the parties was a nominal one and will not be acted upon is not affected by section 91 or 92 and can be proved by other evidence.[8]

A clause in an agreement may embody a trade practice and it may constitute a restrictive trade practice under the Monopolies and Restrictive Trade Practice Act, 1961 and oral evidence is admissible to show that the particular trade practice is a restrictive trade practice.[9]

8. Liability of the insurer has to be ascertained from the express terms of the agreement, if it is a written agreement and no other evidence would be admitted.[10] Where an industrial dispute was settled in writing, the same could not be varied by oral evidence.[11] A bank guarantee has to be construed on its' own terms and contemporaneous documents have no relevance in this regard.

---

1. *Radha Kishan* v. *Sapattar Singh*, AIR 1957 All 406.
2. *Bhuralal s/o Kaluram Marwada* v. *Bhiriya s/o Roopsingh Deshwali*, AIR 1963 MP 210: 1962 Jab LJ 433: 1962 MPC 450.
3. *Arumoorthi* v. *S.E. Committee*, AIR 1962 Mad 360.
4. *Sonar Bangla Bank Ltd.* v. *Calcutta Engineering College*, AIR 1960 Cal 409; *Sukumar Bysack* v. *Sushil Kanta Banerjee*, AIR 1972 Cal 207: 76 Cal WN 116; *Thyagaraja Mudaliar* v. *Vedathanni*, AIR 1936 PC 70: ILR 59 Mad 446.
5. *Niranjan Kumar* v. *Dhyan Singh*, AIR 1976 SC 2400: 1976 RCJ 814: 1976 UJ 802: (1976) 4 SCC 89.
6. *Yadav Ram* v. *Laxman Singh*, AIR 1978 All 123; *Thyagaraja Mudaliar* v. *Vedathanni*, AIR 1936 PC 70: ILR 59 Mad 446.
7. *Sukumar Bysack* v. *Sushil Kanta Banerjee*, AIR 1972 Cal 207: 76 Cal WN 116.
8. *Pandit Ramjilal Tiwari* v. *Shri Vijai Kumar*, 1970 Cr LJ 1176: 1970 Jab LJ 20: 1970 MPLJ 50.
9. *Mahindra and Mahindra Ltd.* v. *Union of India*, AIR 1979 SC 798: (1979) 2 SCC 529: (1979) 2 SCR 1038.
10. *New India Assurance Company Ltd.* v. *Kusumanchi Kameshwara Rao*, (1997) 9 SCC 179: JT 1996 (10) SC 779.
11. *Fabril Gasosa* v. *Labour Commissioner*, AIR 1997 SC 954: 1997 LabIC 912: 1997 AIR SCW 890.

Surrounding circumstances are relevant for construction only if any ambiguity exists in the document and not otherwise.[1]

9. A grant, as distinct from its terms, can be proved by admission.[2] Oral evidence to vary terms is not admissible.[3] There is no bar to prove the existence of a contract or the relationship of landlord – tenant brought about by possession and payment of rent.[4] Evidence can be lead to show that vendee under sale deed had prior possession. Oral evidence of fact of partition is allowed even where the partition deed is inadmissible for want of registration.[5]

10. The section deals with terms of a document and not with recitals other than terms. They can be contradicted by oral evidence.[6] Oral evidence can be given to show that though there was a recital in the document about passing of consideration, that consideration was actually not paid.[7] Evidence to explain or contradict recitals may be given.[8] Want or failure of consideration or condition precedent to the transfer can be proved by oral evidence. Want or failure of consideration can also be so proved.[9] Improvements which led to enhanced rent can be proved.[10] Where a gift deed recited there was no consideration, parties to the document cannot lead evidence to show there was consideration, but strangers to the document can lead such evidence.[11] If Plaintiff has made alterations or interpolations it is not the original document and he will not be allowed to adduce secondary evidence of it's contents.

11. Indian Registration Act only requires certain documents to be registered on pain of the consequence entailed in Section 49 of that Act while the Transfer of Property Act (Section 54) enacts that with a limited exception, the sale of immovable property can only be made by a registered instrument. Registration Act, by itself, does not make a mere oral sale invalid.[12]

---

1. *State Bank of India* v. *Mula Sahakari Sakhar Karkhana Ltd.*, (2006) 6 SCC 293: AIR 2007 SC 2361: 2007 AIR SCW 4182.
2. *Deep Chandra* v. *Sajjad Ali Khan*, AIR 1951 All 93: 1951 ALJ 81: ILR 1950 A 1033 (FB); *Parmanand* v. *Laxminarain*, AIR 1955 MB 129: Madh BLJ 1955 HCR 718: Madh BLR 1955 Civil 411; *Tejraj* v. *Mohanlal*, AIR 1955 Raj 157: ILR (1955) 5 Raj 476; *Nand Singh* v. *Sewa Singh*, AIR 1959 Punj 609: 60 Pun LR 139.
3. *Motilal Singh* v. *Fulia*, AIR 1958 Pat 61; *Sham Singh* v. *Waryam Singh*, AIR 1971 All 494.
4. *Mt. Ugni* v. *Chowa Mahto*, AIR 1968 Pat 302: 1968 BLJR 93: ILR 46 Pat 1315.
5. *Tara Pada Ray* v. *Shyama Pada Ray*, AIR 1952 Cal 579; *Sikhari Lakshmaiah* v. *Sikhari Peddamallaiah (died)*, AIR 1979 AP 275.
6. *Bhaskar Waman Joshi* v. *Shrinarayan Rambilas Agarwal*, AIR 1960 SC 301: (1960) 2 SCR 117: 1960 SCJ 327; *Ganesh Prasad* v. *Deo Nandan Raut*, AIR 1985 Pat 94: 1984 Pat LJR 659: 1985 BLJR 736; *State Bank of India* v. *Premco Saw Mill*, AIR 1984 Guj 93: 1983 Guj LH 829: (1983) 2 Civ LJ 465; *Krishnabai Ganpatrao Deshmukh* v. *Appasaheb Tuljaramrao Nimbalkar*, AIR 1979 SC 1880: 1979 UJ (SC) 646: (1979) 4 SCC 60.
7. *Bhawanbhai Premabhai* v. *Bai Vahali*, AIR 1955 Bom 320: 57 Bom LR 250.
8. *Bhaskar Waman Joshi* v. *Shrinarayan Rambilas Agarwal*, AIR 1960 SC 301: (1960) 2 SCR 117: 1960 SCJ 327.
9. *Ganesh Prasad* v. *Deo Nandan Raut*, AIR 1985 Pat 94: 1984 Pat LJR 659: 1985 BLJR 736.
10. *State Bank of India* v. *Premco Saw Mill*, AIR 1984 Guj 93: 1983 Guj LH 829: (1983) 2 Civ LJ 465.
11. *Bai Heera Devi* v. *Official Assignee, Bombay*, AIR 1958 SC 448: 1958 SCJ 766: (1958) 1 SCR 1384.
12. *M.E. Moolla and Sons Ltd.* v. *Official Assignee Rangoon*, AIR 1936 PC 230: ILR 14 Rang 400.

A document is inadmissible for want of registration; yet it may be admissible for a collateral purpose.[1] Collateral purposes are, possession, its character, severance-in-status, use of admission therein, refreshing memory, starting point of adverse possession, etc. A family arrangement may be even oral in which case no registration is necessary. Registration would be necessary only if the terms of the family arrangement are reduced to writing. A mere memorandum prepared after the family arrangement had already been made for the purpose of the record or for information does not create or extinguish any right in immovable property and hence is not compulsorily registrable.[2] A subsequent memorandum of partition embodying the factum of partition is only a family arrangement and its' registration is unnecessary.[3] If parties creating security by deposit of title deeds intend to reduce the contract to writing, such a document must be registered. If not registered, the document cannot be used in evidence and the transaction cannot be proved by oral evidence.[4] The test is whether the memorandum in question is the bargain between the parties and if so, if it is not registered, no evidence is allowed. That is because the parties tacitly considered the document as the only repository and evidence of their agreement.[5] Where a mortgage was already affected by deposit of title deeds, and the subsequent memorandum was only a record of the completed transaction, no registration was necessary and oral evidence could be adduced in respect of the debt.[6] If a D.P. Note and loan transaction took place simultaneously and note is merely collateral security and hence section 91 does not apply. If the D.P. note refers to rate of interest or date of maturity, oral evidence cannot be given to prove those aspects. The terms in the D.P. note cannot be proved by oral evidence.[7]

12. A party to a deed inadmissible for want of registration, examined as a witness, may be cross-examined regarding a recital without showing it to him. (*See 145, I part*). But he cannot be contradicted by it. (*See 145, II part*). An instrument which effects partition is registerable. A deed which merely recites a past partition is not compulsorily registerable. In the former case, the document is inadmissible, if there was no registration and secondary evidence of the factum of partition cannot be allowed. In the latter case, the unregistered document relating a past partition is admissible. A mere list of properties allotted to various sharers is not an instrument of partition requiring registration.[3] The same principle applies to other types of documents. The fact of partnership

---

1. *Roshan Singh* v. *Zile Singh*, AIR 1988 SC 881; *Mattapalli Chelamayya* v. *Mattapalli Venkataratnam*, AIR 1972 SC 1121: 1972 SCD 783; *Nagarmal Tekriwal* v. *State of Bihar*, (1970) 1 SCC 587; *N. Varda Pillai* v. *Jeevaratnammal*, AIR 1919 PC 44: 49 Ind App 285: ILR 43 Mad 244; *Ram Rattan* v. *Parma Nand*, AIR 1946 PC 51: 1946 Oudh WN 216: 73 IA 28; *Satish Chand Makhan* v. *Govardhan Das Byas*, AIR 1984 SC 143: (1984) 1 SCC 369: (1984) 1 Ren CR 264; *Sita Manharani* v. *Chhedi Mahto*, AIR 1955 SC 328; *Bhaiya Ramanuj Pratap Deo* v. *Lalu Maheshanuj Pratap Deo*, AIR 1981 SC 1937: (1982) 1 SCR 417; *Satish Chand Makhan* v. *Govardhan Das Byas*, AIR 1984 SC 143: (1984) 1 SCC 369: (1984) 1 Ren CR 264.
2. *Kale* v. *Deputy Director of Consolidation*, AIR 1976 SC 807: (1976) 2 All LR 173: (1976) 3 SCC 119.
3. *Roshan Singh* v. *Zile Singh*, AIR 1988 SC 881.
4. *Veeramachineni Gangadhara Rao* v. *The Andhra Bank Ltd.*, AIR 1971 SC 1613: (1972) 1 Andh LT 8: 1971 (Supp) SCR 209.
5. *Subramanian* v. *Lutchman*, AIR 1923 PC 50: (1923) 50 Ind App 77; *Hari Sanker Paul* v. *Kedarnath Saha*, AIR 1939 PC 167: 66 Ind App 184.
6. *Rachpal Mahraj* v. *Bhagwandas Daruka*, AIR 1950 SC 272: 1950 SCJ 361: 1950 SCR 548.
7. *Ganga Ram* v. *Keshava Deo*, AIR 1960 Raj 10: ILR (1958) 8 Raj 1085: 1959 Raj LW 6672.

may be proved by parole evidence of the acts of parties without producing the deed. Parole evidence is admissible if the writing amounted only to unaccepted proposals.[1] For section 91 to apply, there must be concluded contract, reduced to writing.

13. Conduct of Parties.—The form in which a deed is clothed is not decisive. Where there is a dispute whether a document evidenced a sale coupled with an agreement to repurchase or a mortgage by conditional sale, the question is as to the character of the transaction to be ascertained from the provisions of the deed viewed in the light of the surrounding circumstances. If the language of the deed is ambiguous, the intention may be ascertained from the contents of the deed with such extrinsic evidence as is permitted by law to show in what manner the language of the deed was related to the existing facts. Oral evidence of intention is not admissible in interpreting the covenants in the deed, but evidence to explain or even contradict the recitals as distinguished from the terms of the deed may be given. Evidence of contemporaneous conduct is always admissible as surrounding circumstance, but evidence of subsequent conduct of the parties is not admissible.[2] Where the terms of the deed are unambiguous and envisage an out and out sale, no oral evidence of conduct of parties or surrounding circumstances could be admitted to vary or contradict the terms.[3] Section 91 requires the "terms" to be reduced to writing. If some terms are oral and some are in writing, section 91 will not apply. The document, even if not stamped, can be looked into to see if it constitutes the sole contract between the parties and contains all its' terms. If all the terms are not seen, oral evidence is not excluded. If the document is not intended to replace the original contract, section 91 will not apply.[4]

14. Section 35 of Indian Stamp Act says no instrument chargeable with duty shall be admitted for any purpose unless it is duly stamped. "Any purpose" includes collateral purpose.[5] A promissory note may come into existence for a pre-existing debt or a past liability in which case the document would be only a conditional discharge or payment of the loan and it is reduced to writing and if the document is inadmissible, no suit would lie on the original cause of action for the loan.[6] In view of sections 35 and 36 of the Stamp Act, secondary evidence of the contents of an inadmissible document which is insufficiently stamped, by producing a copy is not admissible.[7]

15. Where the original has been lost and copy has been admitted as secondary evidence, section 36 of Stamp Act will not apply. It applies only to a document produced in court.[8] If plaintiff's suit is based on unstamped lease but defendant

1. *Seetharama Naidu* v. *Govindasami Chettiar*, AIR 1926 Mad 35.
2. *Bhaskar Waman Joshi* v. *Shrinarayan Rambilas Agarwal*, AIR 1960 SC 301: (1960) 2 SCR 117: 1960 SCJ 327; *Raja Bahadur Narasingerji Gyanagerji* v. *Raja Panuganti Parthasaradhi Rayanim Garu*, AIR 1924 PC 226: 51 IA 305: 47 M 729: 82 IC 993; *Godhra Electricity Co. Ltd.* v. *State of Gujarat*, AIR 1975 SC 32: (1975) 1 SCC 199: (1975) 2 SCR 42.
3. *Maung Kyin* v. *Ma Shwe Law*, AIR 1917 PC 207: 44 IA 236: 45 C 320: 42 IC 642.
4. *Lakshmi Narain* v. *Mst. Aparna Devi*, AIR 1953 All 535.
5. *Ram Rattan* v. *Parma Nand*, AIR 1946 PC 51: 1946 Oudh WN 216: 73 IA 28.
6. Ratanlal and Dhirajlal on Law of Evidence, 23rd Edition, Page 1090.
7. *Jupudi Kesava Rao* v. *Pulavarthi Venkata Subbarao*, AIR 1971 SC 1070: (1971) 1 SCC 545: 1972 (1) SCJ 643: (1971) 3 SCR 590.
8. *Chinmoyee Baxi* v. *Raja Sankari Prosad Singh*, AIR 1955 Cal 561: ILR (1956) 2 Cal 45: 95 Cal LJ 205.

admitted contents of the lease, the admission is primary evidence. There cannot be penalty on lost documents. Unstamped original document is inadmissible and secondary evidence cannot be given.[1] Where after settlement of accounts, a bond was made with the intention of consolidating and securing the debt, but the same is inadmissible for want of stamp, the new contract supercedes the old one and the money cannot be recovered on accounts stated (original consideration). In a suit on inadmissible D.P. Note, decree can be given on original consideration. This cannot be done where the advance of money and execution of D.P. Note constitute one transaction and are inseparable.[2] Where D.P. Note has been executed in respect of an anterior claim, plaintiff can fall back on the original cause of action if it is within limitation.[3] In the case of loan and D.P. Note being contemporaneous, there has been conflict of opinion. "Contemporaneous" does not necessarily mean that there is no obligation apart from the D.P. Note. If the loan and D.P. Note form part of an integral transaction, original cause of action has no independent existence and there is merger.[4] If D.P. Note is the only document containing the terms of the contract, and if it is otherwise inadmissible, creditor can make no recovery. (*See* section 91 Illustration (b)).[5] In every case, it is a question of fact whether the D.P. Note was intended to constitute the contract or for some collateral purpose.[6] D.P. Note may be taken in supersession or discharge of an antecedent debt, in which case, the document alone can be used in court to prove the terms. This is a case where the debt has been reduced to the form of a document. If the D.P. Note does not embody all the terms of the contract, it's true nature can be proved. When it has been given as collateral security or by way of conditional payment, suit on the debt will lie.[7]

16. If D.P. Note is taken in satisfaction of a pre-existing liability, the latter can be proved if D.P. Note is inadmissible. That a D.P. Note has been executed as collateral security for defaulted installments of a chit fund can be proved by oral evidence. If the D.P. Note and loan are contemporaneous, where the cause of action on the D.P. Note fails, plaintiff's cause of action on the debt survives, in the absence of special circumstances.[8]

17. Where a document is materially altered and hence cannot be the basis of a valid claim, suit cannot be filed, apart from the document.[9] The alteration invalidates the document. Public policy and equity dictate this rule.

---

1. *Chinmoyee Baxi* v. *Raja Sankari Prosad Singh*, AIR 1955 Cal 561: ILR (1956) 2 Cal 45: 95 Cal LJ 205.
2. *K. Anantharamiah* v. *Shivuramaiah*, AIR 1968 Mys 148: (1967) 2 Mys LJ 369.
3. *Ganga Ram* v. *Keshava Deo*, AIR 1960 Raj 10: ILR (1958) 8 Raj 1085: 1959 Raj LW 6672.
4. *K. Panduranga Pai* v. *State*, AIR 1985 AP 268; *Lothamasu Sambasiva Rao* v. *Thadwarthi Balakotiah*, AIR 1973 AP 342: (1974) 1 Andh WR 235: ILR (1974) AP 1 (FB).
5. *Lakshmi Narain* v. *Aparna Devi*, AIR 1953 All 535.
6. *Rangaswami Reddi* v. *K. Doraiswami Reddi*, AIR 1957 Mad 715: (1957) 2 Mad LJ 196: ILR (1957) Mad 987.
7. *Firm of Shamlal and Co.* v. *V.R.C. Rajagopala Chettiar*, AIR 1977 Mad 340: 90 Mad LW 555: (1977) 2 Mad LJ 235; *Lothamasu Sambasiva Rao* v. *Thadwarthi Balakotiah*, AIR 1973 AP 342: (1974) 1 Andh WR 235: ILR (1974) AP 1 (FB); *S. Chattanatha Karayalar* v. *Central Bank of India Ltd.*, AIR 1965 SC 1856: 1966 (2) SCJ 317: (1965) 3 SCR 318.
8. *Lakshmi Narain* v. *Mst. Aparna Devi*, AIR 1953 All 535; *K. Panduranga Pai* v. *State*, AIR 1985 AP 268.
9. *Suresh Chandra* v. *Satish Chandra*, AIR 1983 All 81: 1982 All WC 795.

18. "Matters required by law to be reduced to form of document". If the law requires a deed, no other proof can be substituted so long as the document exists. *e.g.*, Judgments, Depositions, Confession to a Magistrate.[1]

19. Sections 91 and 92—A comparison:—The two conditions for applicability of the provisions are common, that is, "When the terms of a contract, grant or any other disposition of property have been reduced to the form of a government or wherever any matter is required by law to be reduced to the form of a document". The difference in the two sections relates to their consequence. In the case of section 91, the consequence is that no evidence shall be given in proof of the terms of such contract, grant or other disposition of property or of such matter, except the document itself or secondary evidence of its' contents in cases in which secondary evidence is admissible under the earlier provisions of the Act. The consequence under the section 92 is that no evidence of any oral agreement or statement shall be admitted, as between the parties to the instrument or their representatives in interest, for the purpose of contradicting, varying, adding to or subtracting from, its' terms, that is, of altering the terms in any manner. The bar under section 92 applies as between the parties to the contract, while there is no such limitation under section 91 so that the bar thereunder applies to a person who was not a party to the contract. Section 92 applies to documents which can be described as dispositive while section 91 applies to all documents whether they are dispositive or not. Section 91 applies to documents which are bilateral and also unilateral, while section 92 which applies only to bilateral documents.[2] Where matters are reduced to writing after deliberation and consideration and which show the truth of the agreement between the parties thereto, it would be wrong to permit such agreement to be controlled by averments of parties to be proved by the uncertain or unreliable testimony based on slippery memory. (*Ibid*). When parties have deliberately put their agreement into writing, the presumption is that, between themselves and their privies, they intended the writing to form a full and final statement of their intentions and which should be placed beyond the reach of future controversy, bad faith or deceptive memory. (*Ibid*).

20. The bar relates to contracts, grants and other dispositions of property embodied in documents, whether by consent or by requirement of law. Intention of the parties to the transaction is to be gathered from the averments in the document in question and by other attendant circumstances, subject to provisions of section 92.[3] The rule underlying section 92 is based on the best evidence rule as also principle of estoppel. Where the transaction is contained in more than one document, the documents must be read and understood together and section 92 is not applicable.[4] When the true character of a document is in dispute, extrinsic evidence is admissible.[5] Even a stranger to a contract is subject to provisions of

1. *Nazir Ahmad* v. *King-Emperor*, AIR 1936 PC 253: 37 Cr LJ 897: 1936 ILR 17 Lah 629: 63 IA 372.
2. *Roop Kumar* v. *Mohan Thedani*, AIR 2003 SC 2418: 2003 AIR SCW 2425: (2003) 6 SCC 595.
3. *Bishun Deo Narain Rai* v. *Anmol Devi*, AIR 1998 SC 3006: 1998 AIR SCW 2860: (1998) 7 SCC 498.
4. *S. Chattanatha Karayalar* v. *Central Bank of India Ltd.*, AIR 1965 SC 1856: 1966 (2) SCJ 317: (1965) 3 SCR 318.
5. *R. Janakiraman* v. *State*, (2006) 1 SCC 697: 2006 Cr LJ 1232: AIR 2006 SC 1106; *Roop Kumar* v. *Mohan Thedani*, AIR 2003 SC 2418: 2003 AIR SCW 2425: (2003) 6 SCC 595; *Vimal Chand Ghevarchand Jain* v. *Ramakant Eknath Jadoo*, (2009) 5 SCC 713: AIR 2009 SC (Supp) 1550.

Section 91.[1] That a document was sham and never intended to be acted upon can be shown. If a document merely records a certain fact and does not bring a transaction into existence, it is only a piece of evidence and in the absence of the document, oral evidence is admissible. Adoption changes status of a person and not the deed of adoption. In the absence of the deed, oral evidence of adoption can be given.[2] Arbitration proceedings are not governed by these sections. But the principles therein as principles of natural justice are applicable.

If the terms of a written transaction are in dispute between a party to it and a stranger, Section 92 does not prevent either of them from leading oral evidence to vary the terms.[3]

21. Contradicting, varying.—"Oral evidence" referred to in section 92 (also section 91) refers not only to the chief-examination of the party opposing the document and his witnesses, but also the cross examination of the opposite party and his witness.[4] If the language of the document admits of several meanings, Court can consider the subsequent conduct of the parties.[5] Oral evidence is inadmissible to prove that a document purporting to be an absolute sale deed is really a gift.[6] Similarly evidence to show that a deed of possessory mortgage in reality created a simple mortgage is not allowed.[7] Where the plaintiff and his father executed an outright sale deed in favour of the purchaser and on the same day the purchaser leased the property in favour of plaintiff's father in law and there was an oral agreement of sale to the effect that if plaintiff pays the price within five years, the purchaser will reconvey the property and plaintiff filed a suit for reconveyance, Privy Council held that the oral agreement of sale did not attract the bar under section 92 and hence could be proved by evidence and the oral agreement of sale did not "contradict", "vary" or "add to" or "subtract" from the terms of the document.[8]

Contradicting recitals is not "varying". For example, description of village, date, consideration, etc.[9] Oral agreement contradicting recitals is admissible. Evidence to show the contractual relationship is other than the one expressed in the document is not admissible. Purpose of loan can be shown. Legal necessity can be so proved. Express covenant for title or for freedom from encumbrance is not a recital, but a term. A separate oral agreement on a collateral matter can be proved, though it may have the effect of adding another distinct term to the contract on a collateral matter.[10] Where an agreement has been admitted by all parties, it is not necessary to prove it and hence sections 91 and 92 have no application. Parole evidence is allowed in the cases covered by the provisos.

---

1. *Roop Kumar* v. *Mohan Thedani,* (2003) 6 SCC 595: AIR 2003 SC 2418: 2003 AIR SCW 2425.
2. *Jahuri Sah* v. *Dwarika Prasad Jhunjhunwala,* AIR 1967 SC 109: (1966) 2 SCWR 184: 1968 (1) SCJ 315.
3. *Bai Heera Devi* v. *Official Assignee, Bombay,* AIR 1958 SC 448: 1958 SCJ 766: (1958) 1 SCR 1384.
4. *Hindusthan Fasteneres Ltd.* v. *Nasik Workers' Union,* (2007) 11 SCC 660.
5. *Raj Kumar Rajendra Singh* v. *State of Himachal Pradesh,* AIR 1990 SC 1833.
6. *Hanifunnissa* v. *Faijunissa,* (1911) ILR 33 All 340: 38 Ind App 85 (PC).
7. *Feroz Shah* v. *Sobhat Khan,* AIR 1933 PC 178: ILR 14 Lah 466: 1933 All LJ 1193.
8. *Sara Veeraswami* v. *Tallure Narayya,* AIR 1949 PC 32: ILR 1949 Mad 487: 75 Ind App 252.
9. *Krishnabai Ganpatrao Deshmukh* v. *Appasaheb Tuljaramrao Nimbalkar,* AIR 1979 SC 1880: 1979 UJ (SC) 646: (1979) 4 SCC 60.
10. *Lok Nath* v. *Jagbir Suri,* 1982 Cr LJ 1328: 1982 Sri LJ 80 (J&K).

22. Adding to.—These words do not exclude any oral agreement to reconvey a property sold outright. Such an oral agreement merely adds a stipulation quite unconnected with the terms of the sale deed; it does not "add" to the terms of the sale deed.[1] Any agreement as to the implied warranty regarding the correctness of the extent of the property sold should be established on the terms of the sale deed and it is not open to a party to travel outside the sale deed and adduce evidence of to prove a warranty *de hors* the deed.[2]

23. The question whether oral evidence can be admitted to explain the contents of a document depends upon the degree of formality of the document.[3] The Section does not apply to a statement contained in a writing which is in the nature of a condition precedent to the very formation of that contract.[4]

A lessee is not barred from showing that despite the recital to the contrary in the deed to which he is a party, he was not actually put in possession of the land which he took under the document. Equally, the lessor is not precluded from showing that he did not receive the advance amount recited in the document as having been received by him.[5] In the case of a contract for purchase of agricultural land for building purposes which contains a recital of a representation of the seller that permission of the authorities for conversion of the land was expected shortly, the representation cannot be regarded as a "term" of the contract and hence oral evidence as to the correctness of the representation can be received.[6] Similarly, a recital regarding encumbrances is not a term of the sale deed.[7]

24. These sections apply only where the document produced is the whole disposition *i.e.* parties intended that the whole of it to be embodied thereon. If the deed does not contain the whole of the agreement and there is ambiguity, oral evidence consistent with written agreement is permissible.

25. Nature of document.—If parties to a written agreement desire to prove that they did not agree to a contract on the terms recited in the document or that they did not intend to act upon the document, oral evidence to that effect is not barred.[8] Under the old law relating to benami transactions, it was open to the executant of a sale deed to adduce evidence to prove that sale deed was executed in order to defeat the claims of a creditor and that it was a benami transaction. Such a plea cannot be met with the plea of bar under section 92 since the plea really would be that the executant did not intend to dispose of the beneficial interest in the property to the transferee.[9] It is open to the parties to show that the real nature of the transaction was different from what the document purports to show.[10] It is open to a party to show that a transaction did not have his consent.[8]

---

1. *Sara Veeraswami* v. *Tallure Narayya*, AIR 1949 PC 32: ILR 1949 Mad 487: 75 Ind App 252.
2. *M. Delli Gramani* v. *C.R. Ramachandran*, AIR 1953 Mad 769: (1952) 65 Mad LW 82: ILR 1952 Mad 682.
3. *N. Chellaperumal Chetty* v. *N.M. Jayarathnam Chettiar*, AIR 1960 Mad 314: (1960) 1 Mad LJ 237: 73 Mad LW 233.
4. *P.B. Bhat* v. *V.R. Thakkar*, AIR 1972 Bom 365: 74 Bom LR 509: 1972 Mah LJ 756.
5. *Purna Nand Puri* v. *Kamala Sinha*, AIR 1965 Pat 39.
6. *Ananth Sham Rao* v. *N.B. Kucheriya*, AIR 1956 Bom 252.
7. *R. Muninarayana Reddy* v. *C.P. Chinna Swamy*, AIR 1952 Mys 120.
8. *Tyagaraja Mudaliar* v. *Vedathanumi*, AIR 1936 PC 70: 63 Ind App 126: ILR 59 Mad 446.
9. *A. Rakkiyana Gounder* v. *Chinnu Goundan*, AIR 1954 Mad 84: (1953) 2 Mad LJ 450: ILR 1954 Mad 271; *Thyagaraja Mudaliar* v. *Vedathanni*, AIR 1936 PC 70: ILR 59 Mad 446; *Gangabai* v. *Chhabubai*, AIR 1982 SC 20: (1982) 1 SCC 4: (1982) 2 SCWR 53.
10. *Arumoorthi Chetiyar* v. *SEC of Vadugapatti*, AIR 1962 Mad 360.

26. A consent decree is in effect a contract between the parties with seal of the court superadded to it. To find the meaning of the words employed in the decree, Court has to ascertain the circumstances under which those words came to be used. If there is any vagueness, the words must be construed having regard to surrounding and attendant circumstances and the evidence led by the parties.[1] Where a consent decree does not refer to the entire dispute between the parties and some vagueness remains, the factual background as also the manner in which existence of rights have been claimed by the parties would be relevant. *(Ibid)*

27. Where the contract was intended to serve some other purpose, evidence can be adduced to prove it to be so.[2] Evidence can be adduced to show the document was illusory, fictitious, colourable device, which cloaked something else, and the apparent state of affairs is not real one.[3] Court is entitled to go into the real nature of the transaction, look behind the façade and identify the essence and reality of the transaction. An example is benami transaction.[4] It is always permissible to look to the surrounding circumstances to see in what manner the language of a document was related to existing facts. Court's power to arrive at the true meaning in the light of all the surrounding circumstances is not fettered. Oral evidence of circumstances is admissible.[5] In the case of a mortgage, extraneous evidence is admissible to show that the property ostensibly mortgaged was not in fact intended to be mortgaged or within the scope of the security.[6] In the case of registered lease deed, oral variation of rent cannot be proved.[7]

28. Intention.—No oral evidence can be allowed to ascertain the intention contrary to the terms of the document.[8] Evidence is allowable of fraud or mistake. Evidence may supplement, but not supplant or contradict. Evidence of acts done under an instrument is a guide to the intention of the parties where there is of a doubt about their intention.[9] If the words are clear, there is very little that the court can do about it.[10] Intention of the parties has to be gathered from the language used by them in the document, considered in the light of the

1. *Parayya Allayya Hittalamani* v. *Parayya Gurulingayya Poojari*, AIR 2008 SC 241: (2007) 14 SCC 318: 2007 AIR SCW 6654.
2. *Thyagaraja Mudaliar* v. *Vedathanni*, AIR 1936 PC 70: ILR 59 Mad 446.
3. *Ibid, Gangabai* v. *Chhabubai*, AIR 1982 SC 20: (1982) 1 SCC 4: (1982) 2 SCWR 53; *Krishnabai Ganpatrao Deshmukh* v. *Appasaheb Tuljaramrao Nimbalkar*, AIR 1979 SC 1880: 1979 UJ (SC) 646: (1979) 4 SCC 60; *Bhagwan Dayal* v. *Reoti Devi*, AIR 1962 SC 287: (1962) 3 SCR 440: 1962 (1) SCJ 348.
4. *Savitri Devi* v. *State*, AIR 1989 Pat 327: 1989 Pat LJR (HC) 772: 1989 BLT (Rep) 313.
5. *Sait Balumal Dharumdas* v. *Gollapudi Venkata Chelpathi Rao*, AIR 1955 Mad 78: 67 Mad LW 889: 1954 Mad WN 794.
6. *(Sri Raja) Inuganti Venkatarama Rao* v. *(Sri Raja) Sobhanadri Appa Rao Bahadur Garu*, AIR 1936 PC 91: 1936 All LJ 258: 63 Ind App 169.
7. *Raval and Company* v. *K.C. Ramachandran*, AIR 1974 SC 818: (1974) 1 SCC 424: (1974) 2 SCR 629.
8. *Sait Balumal Dharamdas* v. *Gollapudi Venkata Chelpathi Rao*, AIR 1955 Mad 78: 67 Mad LW 889: 1954 Mad WN 794; *Sait Bolumal Dharmdas Firm, Bankers* v. *Gollapudi Venkatachelapathi Rao*, AIR 1959 AP 612: (1959) 2 Andh WR 23: ILR 1959 AP 929; *Satyanarayan Shah* v. *Star Company Ltd.*, AIR 1984 Cal 3994.
9. *Abdulla Ahmed* v. *Animendra Kissen Mitter*, AIR 1950 SC 15: 1950 SCJ 153: 1950 SCR 30; *Hindu Public* v. *Rajdhani Puja Samiti*, AIR 1999 SC 964: (1999) 2 SCC 583: 1999 AIR SCW 582.
10. *Madhya Pradesh Housing Board* v. *Progressive Writers*, (2009) 5 SCC 678: 2009 AIR SCW 2484: AIR 2009 SC 1585.

surrounding circumstances and object the contract.[1] Where a document does not amount to an agreement, oral evidence can be allowed to prove that the real intention was different from that expressed by the terms of the document.[2]

29. Does the writing contain the whole contract?.—Section 92 applies only where, upon the face of it, the document appears to contain the whole contract. If, on the face of it, it appears that there are other conditions, oral or otherwise, which go to make up the entire contract, such conditions, if oral, can be orally proved.[3] The inference that the document does not contain the whole contract may be drawn from the document itself as well as from extrinsic evidence.[4] Even in the case indicated above, such oral evidence should not lead to varying the terms of the document.[5] Whether an agreement is a completed bargain or a provisional agreement depends on the intention of the parties deducible from the language used by them on the occasion. Where a document is signed only by one party, it is not a written agreement between the parties.

30. Collateral Oral Agreement.—A separate oral agreement regarding which the document is silent, which is not inconsistent with its terms, can be proved, for example, a collateral warranty. This is covered by second proviso. Oral evidence is admissible to show the time at which a document becomes a contract, for example, time of commencement of a lease. If the document is merely a record of an already completed transaction, sections 91, 92 will not apply.[6]

31. As between the parties.—Section 92 does not apply to strangers.[7] Where a sale deed is executed by *A* and *B* in favour of *C* and *D*, in a suit between only *C* and *D* (*A* and *B* not being parties) Section 92 has no application.[8] Section will not also apply in a suit between representatives of only one party to the document.[9] Where a Karta of HUF executes sale deed, all the members must be treated as parties to the sale deed within the meaning this section.[10] If a document is taken in the name of one member, other members can show that the deed was taken for the benefit of the family.

32. Evidence of Conduct:—If evidence of conduct or subsequent acts do not establish an agreement other than that appearing on the face of the document, it is irrelevant. If it does, it is excluded by sections 91 and 92. Such evidence of conduct is admissible only to the extent oral evidence is admissible, as indicated earlier. It is admissible to show the real nature of the transaction or if the terms are ambiguous. But conduct leading to the inference of conflicting contemporaneous oral agreement is not admissible. Subsequent conduct may

1. *Bank of India* v. *K. Mohandas*, (2009) 5 SCC 313: AIR 2009 SC (Supp) 2783.
2. *Egged Co-operative Society* v. *Levy Geffen*, AIR 1947 PC 32: (1947) 15 ITR 302: 48 Cr LJ 791; *Thyagaraja Mudaliar* v. *Vedathanni*, AIR 1936 PC 70: ILR 59 Mad 446.
3. *Balaram Agasti* v. *Ramesh Chandra Mohanty*, AIR 1973 Ori 13.
4. *Mohammad Akbar Khan* v. *Attar Singh*, AIR 1936 PC 171: 17 L 557; *Leena Roy Choudhary* v. *Indumati Bose*, AIR 1980 Pat 120: 1980 BBCJ (HC) 123: 1980 BLJR 255.
5. *Ram Kumar Himatsingha* v. *Gajendra Chandra Bora*, AIR 1957 Assam 68: ILR (1956) 8 Assam 503.
6. *Velamakanya Krishnayya* v. *S. Ponnuswami Iyer*, AIR 1924 Mad 547: ILR 47 Mad 398.
7. *In re: P. Ramamoorthi*, AIR 1953 Mad 94: (1952) 2 Mad LJ 671.
8. *Muhammad Sultan Mohideen Ahmed Ansari* alias *Chand Badsha* v. *Amathul Jalal* alias *Achi Bibi Saheba*, AIR 1927 Mad 1102; (Illur) *Ramayya Chetti* v. *Mannaru Chetti*, AIR 1930 Mad 590; *Mohan Lal* v. *Board of Revenue, U.P. Allahabad*, AIR 1982 All 273: 1982 All CJ 174.
9. *Vijay Kumar Prasad* v. *State of Bihar*, AIR 1963 SC 1.
10. *Nagaswami Iyer* v. *Ramaswami Aiyar*, AIR 1925 Mad 288: 85 Ind Cas 212: 47 Mad LJ 755.

be relevant to show the nature of the transaction or the intent of the transferor. Where subsequent conduct arose as a result of subsequent change in design, such conduct will not affect the validity and genuineness or operate to nullify the effect of a *bona fide* transaction made earlier.[1] There is limitation on the power of court to arrive at the true meaning of a document in the light of the surrounding circumstances.[2] Extrinsic evidence to determine the effect on intention is allowed where these remains a doubt as to its' true meaning and evidence of acts done under it is a guide to the intention of the parties.[3]

33. The following have been held to amount to contradicting or varying the terms:—Modification of terms of sale deed, gift deed, partition deed, lease.[4] Plea of variation of terms in contract of service. Oral agreement for renewal of lease. Oral agreement that one of the items of property included in a lease deed is to be held free of rent though the deed stipulates rent for each of the items separately. Contradicting arrangement regarding possession where the lease deed shows tenant was to get actual possession. Oral agreement that D.P. Note was not to be enforced till the happening of a certain contingency; contention that D.P. Note was not really for a loan but was advance for purchase of paddy; oral agreement that mortgage money would be repayable in installments though the deed stipulated lump sum repayment on demand; oral agreement stipulating method of payment otherwise than on demand;[5] contention that mortgagee did not owe a certain sum to a particular individual as clearly admitted in the mortgage deed;[6] Oral evidence is admissible to show that after a conveyance creating a joint tenancy, purchasers subsequently dealt with the property as tenants-in-common, to show that though lease deed shows only one lessee, another person is co-sharer with him, to show that an apparent usufructuary mortgage is really a simple mortgage for the purpose of Mysore Agriculture Debt Relief Act,[7] and to show full particulars of building insured under a policy which gives a vague and not exhaustive description.[8]

34. Preliminary Negotiations.—Where the mortgage clearly stipulates that income shall belong to mortgagee in lieu of interest, it cannot be contradicted by reference to preliminary negotiations. Where the contract is clear and it's meaning is expressed in clear language, evidence of prior negotiations is not admissible. Antecedent documents can be looked into for identifying the property dealt with by the contract. If the preceding correspondence and the subsequent agreement constitute a single contract, correspondence would be admissible, not otherwise. Prior correspondence could be looked into to see the circumstances under which a compromise was arrived at.

---

1. *Md. Sabir Ali* v. *Tahir Ali*, AIR 1957 All 94: ILR (1954) 2 All 556.
2. *Baijnath* v. *Hajee Valley Md.*, AIR 1933 PC 178; *P.L. Bapuswami* v. *N. Pattay Gounder*, AIR 1966 SC 902: (1966) 2 SCR 918: 1967 (1) SCJ 842.
3. *Godhra Electricity Co. Ltd.* v. *State of Gujarat*, AIR 1975 SC 32: (1975) 1 SCC 199: (1975) 2 SCR 42; *Abdulla Ahmed* v. *Animendra Kissen Mitter*, AIR 1950 SC 15: 1950 SCJ 153: 1950 SCR 30.
4. *Bhola Nath Rastogi* v. *Santosh Prakash Arya*, AIR 1975 Pat 336: ILR (1975) 54 Pat 415; *Ram Chander* v. *Mangal Singh*, AIR 1981 P&H 94: (1981) 1 Rent LR 277.
5. *K. Appukuttan Panicker* v. *S.K.R.A.K.R. Athappa Chettiar*, 1966 Ker LT 1145: AIR 1966 Ker 303: ILR (1966) 2 Ker 475.
6. *Janki* v. *Ganesh Ram*, AIR 1984 All 219: 1984 All CJ 185.
7. *Narasimiah* v. *Venkatappa*, AIR 1957 Mys 86.
8. *General Assurance Society Ltd.* v. *Mohd. Salim*, AIR 1965 All 561.

Evidence to show that property ostensibly mortgaged was in fact not intended to be mortgaged is admissible. Sale deed cannot be allowed to be shown to be a mortgagee.

35. In the case of sale deed coupled with an oral agreement to reconvey the property, it was held in[1] that the agreement did not contradict, vary, etc., the terms of the sale deed. Nor did it "add to" such terms. To be excluded, the oral agreement must bear, in some one or more of the ways specified in the section, upon the terms of the sale as contained in the instrument. To add a stipulation which is quite unconnected with the terms of sale is not an addition of the kind barred by the section. The addition contemplated must be an addition to the terms and not of a collateral matter. An out and out gift cannot be allowed to be altered by oral evidence into a Will. But such evidence is allowed to show that parties never intended to act upon the document.[2] A party can prove that a condition precedent not mentioned in the document should be established before the written contract can be given effect to.[3] Oral evidence to show that one of the executants of a D.P. Note signed it only as surety is inadmissible. Some decisions have taken a contra view. In the case of a benami transaction, that is, sale deed taken in the name of a nominal purchaser, that contract is between the parties thereto, and the dispute in court would be, ordinarily between the nominal purchaser and the real purchaser and between them there is no writing and therefore section 92 has no place.[4] Where *A* executes a sale deed in the name of *B* to shield the property from his own creditors, and pleads so in court, section 92 will apply. But in such a case absence of consideration for the sale deed can be proved by oral evidence, in which case, the transaction would fail for want of consideration (*Proviso I*).[5] Another way of looking at the problem is to say that *A* is really contending that the sale deed is sham, not intended to be acted upon and this is allowed to be proved.[6]

36. Implied terms, whether by construction or by implication of law, cannot be varied by oral evidence.[7]

37. Section 108 of T.P. Act sets out covenants which are implied, in the absence of contract or local usage. Oral evidence of such contracts are admissible.[8]

38. Where, in a suit on a D.P. Note, defendant pleaded a collateral agreement to receive the income of certain land in repayment of the debt, it was held that oral evidence of such agreement in discharge of liability is admissible.[9] If a separate agreement does not vary or contradict or add to the terms of the deed, oral evidence is permissible to show such agreement.[10]

1. *Gannamaneedi Madhavayya* v. *Gannamaneedi Achamma (Since deceased)*, AIR 1949 PC 32.
2. *Thyagaraja Mudaliar* v. *Vedathanni*, AIR 1936 PC 70: ILR 59 Mad 446.
3. *Rowland Ady* v. *Administrator-General, Burma*, AIR 1938 PC 198: 32 Sind LR 810: (1938) 2 Mad LJ 469.
4. *Indian Cable Co. Ltd.* v. *Sumitra Chakraborty*, AIR 1985 Cal 248: (1985) 89 Cal WN 559: (1985) 1 Cal HN 428.
5. *Laxmibai* v. *Keshav Annaji Pokharkar*, AIR 1916 Bom 239.
6. *A. Rakkiyana Gounder* v. *Chinnu Goundan*, AIR 1954 Mad 84: (1953) 2 Mad LJ 450: ILR 1954 Mad 271.
7. *Nannapaneni Subayya Chowdary* v. *Garikapati Veeraya*, AIR 1957 AP 307: 1955 Andh LT 713: ILR 1955 Andh 170.
8. *Leena Roy Choudhary* v. *Indumati Bose*, AIR 1980 Pat 120: 1980 BBCJ (HC) 123: 1980 BLJR 255.
9. *Ram Jatan* v. *Chandra Bali*, AIR 1960 All 746; *Chaganlal* v. *Jaggiwandas*, AIR 1940 Bom 54: 187 Ind Cas 41.
10. *Punit Mahton* v. *Mahabir Mahton*, AIR 1959 Pat 531: 1959 BLJR 397.

39. Proviso (1).—Any fact may be proved which would invalidate any document, or which would entitle any person to any decree or order relating thereto; such as fraud, intimidation, illegality, want of due execution, want of capacity in any contracting party, want or failure of consideration, or mistake in fact or law, that is, in circumstances where the contract is void or voidable, or subject to reformation, upon ground of fraud, illegality etc. in it's inception. Illustrations (d) and (e) may be seen. The rule contained in the section is not infringed by the reception of oral evidence showing that the document is void or never had any legal existence or binding force.[1] Extrinsic evidence is admissible to prove any matter which by substantive law affects the validity of a document or entitles a party to relief in respect thereof, even if such evidence tends to vary, add to, or, in some cases contradict the writing.[2] Validity of the transaction can be impeached on the grounds mentioned in the proviso. There can be a suit for rectification under section 26, Specific Relief Act.[3] Section 92 does not apply in relation to a contention that the transaction is a sham one.[4]

40. The proviso is not exhaustive of the grounds as is evident from the words "such as". Any fact which would invalidate a document can be proved. But a person who wants to stand by a document cannot seek to challenge it under the proviso.

Evidence is admissible to show the real nature of a transaction. What is ostensibly a sale deed can be shown to be a gift. Evidence is admissible to show real consideration was different from what is mentioned in the document. Where the document did not contain all the agreed terms, this proviso would apply. Evidence can be adduced to show that a document did not relate to the land within the jurisdiction of the sub-registrar who registered it as such evidence tends to invalidate the document.[5]

41. Fraud arises where there has been a promise made without any intention of performing it or where there has been a concealment of fact by one having knowledge or belief of the fact.[6] Where a contract has been induced' on the faith of a representation made which is untrue, the contract has to be considered as obtained fraudulently.[7] "Fraud" must be fraud within the meaning of the definition in section 17(3) of the Contract Act. Fraud as contemplated by the proviso (1) is, at the very inception, fraud which vitiates the transaction and not by any subsequent conduct or representation of any party.[8]

Oral evidence is admissible to prove that the real object or consideration of an agreement in writing is unlawful and therefore the agreement is void. *See* section 23 of the Indian Contract Act.[9] Want of due execution of a document

---

1. Taylor on Evidence, 10th Edn., P 814.
2. Phipson on Evidence, 15th Edn. P 1182.
3. *Sateri Shiddappa Gadkari* v. *Rudrappa Shetteppa Bachenhatti*, AIR 1954 Bom 463: 56 Bom LR 394: ILR 1954 Bom 930.
4. *Gangabai* v. *Chhabubai*, AIR 1982 SC 20: (1982) 1 SCC 4: (1982) 2 SCWR 53; *R. Janakiraman* v. *State*, (2006) 1 SCC 697: 2006 Cr LJ 1232: AIR 2006 SC 1106.
5. *Venkata Rama Rao* v. *Appa Rao*, AIR 1936 PC 91: 63 Ind App 169.
6. *Yeshwant Deo Rao* v. *W. Ramchand*, AIR 1951 SC 16: 1951 SCJ 19: 1951 SCR 852; *Shiva Nath Prasad* v. *State of West Bengal.*, AIR 2006 SC 1181: 2006 AIR SCW 828: 2006 Cr LJ 1258.
7. *Abaji* v. *Laxman*, ILR (1906) 30 Bom 426.
8. *Narsingdas Takhatmal* v. *Radhakisan Rambakas*, AIR 1952 Bom 425: 54 BLR 492.
9. *Kashinath Chukerbati* v. *B. Chukerbati*, ILR (1884) 10 Cal 640.

may be proved. Want or failure of consideration or difference in the kind of consideration may be proved. But oral evidence to vary the consideration is not permitted.[1] A mutual mistake relating to the survey number shown in a document can be proved.[2] It is open to a plaintiff or a defendant to plead and prove a mistake.

42. Proviso (2).—A separate oral agreement on a distinct and collateral matter, and which is not inconsistent with its' terms, may be proved, if the original deed is silent on the point dealt with by the oral agreement. In considering whether or not the proviso applies, Court shall have regard to the degree of formality of the document. This proviso has to be read with illustrations (f), (g), (h).

The rule as to the inadmissibility of parole evidence to vary the terms of a document is not violated by proof of any collateral parol agreement, which does not interfere with the terms of the written contract, though it may relate to the same subject-matter. Parties can prove that contemporaneously or as a preliminary measure, they entered into a distinct oral agreement on some collateral matters.[3] The only case in which oral evidence can be admitted under this proviso is where the document is silent on the matter sought to be proved and the agreement to be proved is consistent with the terms of the document. The purpose is to allow proof of the real intention of the parties. Where the document does not record all the terms of a contract, oral evidence is admissible to explain the real nature of the transaction.[4] If the transaction is required to be in writing, the separate agreement must also be in writing.

Such an agreement regarding quality of goods in a contract of sale could be proved.[5] The collateral agreement may relate to the same subject-matter, but not interfere with the terms of the writing and it could be contemporaneous or preliminarily.[6] *See* Illustrations (f) to (h). In deciding this aspect, court shall have due regard to formality of the document. *See* Illustration (h). But oral agreement, if it is inconsistent with the written terms, is shut out. The more formal the deed is, the less is the scope of admissibility of oral agreement. D.P. Note is not a formal document, but a document required by law to be reduced to writing is a formal document.

If D.P. Note is silent regarding interest, a verbal agreement made subsequently is provable. Regarding Bond, it has been held that agreement can be proved.[7] Even in the case of a mortgage, a formal deed, later agreement to pay compound interest is provable if the deed is silent.[8] An agreement under which mortgagee was to take the mortgage property in full satisfaction of entire amount due can be proved. Such an agreement cannot be said to vary the terms of the mortgage

1. *Motilal Singh* v. *Mt. Fulia*, AIR 1958 Pat 61; *K.S. Narasimhachari* v. *The Indo Commercial Bank Ltd., G.T. Madras, represented by the Punjab National Bank Ltd*, AIR 1965 Mad 147: ILR (1964) 2 Mad 841: (1965) 1 Mad LJ 371.
2. *Baluswami Aiyar* v. *Lakshmana Aiyar*, AIR 1921 Mad 172: ILR 44 Mad 605 (FB).
3. Taylor on Evidence, 10th Edition, Page 929.
4. *Sir Md. Akbar Khan* v. *Atta Singh*, AIR 1936 PC 71.
5. *Indian Textiles Company Ltd.* v. *Kanhaiya Lal Agarwalla*, AIR 1959 Pat 378: 1958 BLJR 108.
6. *Jehangir Shapoorji Taraporevala* v. *Reverend , Secretary of the Bombay Tract and Book Society Savarkar*, AIR 1932 PC 231.
7. *Radhasoami Satsang Sabha Dayalbag* v. *Hanskumar Kishanchand*, AIR 1959 MP 172: 1959 MPC 102: 1959 MPLJ 301.
8. *Sital Prasad Jagmohan Singh* v. *Kurhan Hussain*, AIR 1952 Nag 25: ILR 1951 Nag 858.

deed. An oral arrangement between the parties to a mortgage deed to the effect that the mortgagee was to be put in possession and the income to be taken in satisfaction of interest is admissible.[1]

43. Oral agreement is admissible only on collateral matters on which the deed is silent. Where a sale deed clearly specifies consideration, a separate oral agreement that the purchaser to pay something more is barred. Want of consideration is not hit by the section. Oral agreement to the effect that a part of the consideration of a mortgage was reserved to pay off debts of the mortgagor (mortgagor admitted only a part was paid in cash, though document recited payment of entire consideration) can be proved.[2] The basis is that the document was not intended to contain the whole agreement between the parties, but only the principal terms. Where in an agreement to sell by one member of a HUF, oral evidence to show that he would obtain signatures of other members in the sale deed is barred.[3] Where the later agreement seeks merely to lay down the means by which the original contract was to be implemented, it is not barred. An agreement to set-off rent due for certain land by the tenant towards interest due on simple mortgage executed by him to the landlord is admissible. On the question whether an oral agreement to release the whole or part of the claim under a mortgage is admissible, there are conflicting decisions.[4] If a lease deed is silent as to the place of payment of rent, later agreement specifying the place is admissible.[5] A lessee under a registered lease can prove an oral agreement regarding his preferential right to purchase the leased property if it is brought to sale since the lease deed was silent on the point.[6]

In the case of a mortgage by conditional sale, separate oral agreement for absolute sale is inadmissible. Oral warranty of title in the case of sale deed is barred.[7] In the case of a D.P. Note executed by two persons, a subsequent oral agreement that the liability of one would cease on a certain date, a simple acknowledgment by the other executant being substituted for the D.P. Note, was held to be admissible. It can be shown that an instrument was not meant to operate until the happening of a given condition, but not that contract was to be defeated by such a happening. Agreement altering an unconditional promise to pay into a conditional de-feasible one is inadmissible.

44. Proviso (3).—The existence of any separate oral agreement, constituting a condition precedent to the attaching of any obligation under any such contract, grant or disposition of property, may be proved. *See* Illustration (i) and section 46 of Negotiable Instruments Act. Distinction must be made between an agreement that no obligation shall be attached to a written transaction and an agreement that though such obligation does attach, it shall be postponed to a future date. It can be shown that an instrument apparently a deed had really been delivered

1. *Bal Govind Babu* v. *Registrar Administration*, AIR 1946 All 283.
2. *Ram Rup Singh* v. *Jang Bahadur Singh*, AIR 1951 Pat 566: ILR 30 Pat 391.
3. *Hari Singh* v. *Umrao Singh*, AIR 1979 All 65.
4. *Punit Mahton* v. *Mahabir Mahton*, AIR 1959 Pat 531: 1959 BLJR 397.
5. *J.N. Sahni* v. *State of Madhya Bharat*, Madh BLJ 1954 HCR 739: ILR 1954 MB 343: AIR 1954 MB 184 (FB).
6. *Jehangir Shapoorji Tarapouwala* v. *Rev Swarkar*, AIR 1932 PC 231; *Secretary of Bombay* v. *Tract and Book Society*, AIR 1932 PC 231.
7. *M. Delli Gramani* v. *C.R. Ramachandran*, AIR 1953 Mad 769: (1952) 65 Mad LW 82: ILR 1952 Mad 682.

as an escrow that is deposited with a third person to be delivered by him to the person to whom it purports to benefit upon the performance of some condition upon which only the writing is to have effect. It neither varies nor alters but merely suspends the commencement of the obligation.[1] An agreement that if the sale deed was not registered on the date of execution and if consideration was not paid at the time of registration, the deed stood cancelled does not attract this proviso. Parties are not estopped from showing that a paper purporting to be a signed agreement, was in fact signed by mistake or that it was signed on the terms that it should not be an agreement till money was paid or something else was done or that it was intended to be sham and not operative.[2] The condition precedent referred to in this proviso is a condition the subject-matter of which is *de hors* the contents of the instrument and hence it cannot affect its terms. But it is open to adduce oral evidence to show that the arrangement as embodied in the deed is not what it purports to be but something different.[3] The condition precedent must be extraneous to the instrument itself. An oral agreement that consideration was not to be paid until the happening of a particular contingency can be proved; but not an agreement that a part of the consideration was not payable until the vendee got possession of the entire land sold as it is inconsistent with the terms of the sale deed.[4] The agreement regarding condition precedent does not require any new consideration. Such condition in respect of a sale deed can be proved only by the vendor or his representative. Evidence is admissible to show that deed was not intended to operate as a contract until approved by a third party.[5] The oral agreement must be in suspension and not in defeasance of the written deed.

45. Condition Precedent.—An agreement in defeasance of the contract is different from an agreement suspending the coming into force of the contract.[6] It cannot be shown by oral evidence that the contract was to be defeated on the happening of an event. It may be shown that the contract or instrument was not meant to operate until the happening of a given condition.[7] Rule in this proviso does not apply to a case where the written contract had not only become binding, but had actually been performed as to a large part of it's obligations. The proviso does not apply where the obligation has already attached. If a contract has come into force forthwith and has been partly acted upon there is no condition precedent at all and the proviso will not apply.[8] In a suit for specific performance of a contract for sale of property which was subject to a mortgage, oral agreement that the ascertainment of the exact amount due thereunder was a condition precedent to the execution of the sale deed, can

1. *H.S. Shama Rao* v. *Patel Kanake Gowda*, AIR 1962 Mys 203; *Rowland Ady* v. *Administrator-General, Burma*, AIR 1938 PC 198: 32 Sind LR 810: (1938) 2 Mad LJ 469.
2. *Gangabai* v. *Chhabubai*, AIR 1982 SC 20: (1982) 1 SCC 4: (1982) 2 SCWR 53.
3. *Ram Jatan* v. *Chandra Bali*, AIR 1960 All 746.
4. *Muthusami Iyer* v. *Dharma Raja*, AIR 1926 Mad 495.
5. *Thyagaraja Mudaliar* v. *Vedathanni*, AIR 1936 PC 70: ILR 59 Mad 446.
6. *Rowland Ady* v. *Administrator-General, Burma*, AIR 1938 PC 198: 32 Sind LR 810: (1938) 2 Mad LJ 469.
7. *Sahadeo Shrawan* v. *Namdeo Atmaram*, AIR 1949 Nag 15: ILR 1948 Nag 900; *T.V. Kochuvareed* v. *P. Mariappa Gounder*, AIR 1954 TC 10: (1953) 23 Com Cas 468; *Narandas Morardas Galiwala* v. *S.P.A.M. Papammal*, AIR 1967 SC 333: (1966) 2 SCWR 239: 1967 (2) SCJ 8; *Rowland Ady* v. *Administrator-General, Burma*, AIR 1938 PC 198: 32 Sind LR 810: (1938) 2 Mad LJ 469.
8. *Palaniappa* v. *P.T. Kandaswamy*, 1971 I Mys LJ 258.

be proved.[1] The condition must be *de hors* the contents of the contract. Oral evidence to show one of the executants of a D.P. Note was only a surety for one month cannot be adduced as the liability got attached from the date of D.P. Note and ceased on the expiry of one month. An oral agreement that the D.P. Note was not enforceable until the happening of a particular event cannot be proved. A collateral agreement that alters the legal effect of an instrument must be excluded.[2] Such an agreement, if it forms part of the same transaction and not in derogation of the D.P. Note is provable.[3]

46. There is conflict of view on the question of an oral agreement that D.P. Note was not to be enforced till certain accounts were reopened and settled.

47. Proviso 4.—The existence of any distinct subsequent oral agreement to rescind or modify any such contract, grant or disposition of property, may be proved, except in cases in which such contract, grant or disposition of property is by law required to be in writing, or has been registered according to the law in force for the time being as to the registration of documents. After an agreement has been reduced to writing, it is competent for the parties, at any time before the breach of it, by a new contract not in writing, either altogether to waive, dissolve or annul the former agreement, or in any manner to add to, or subtract from, or vary or qualify the terms of it, and thus to make a new contract, which is to be proved, partly by the written agreement, and partly by the subsequent varied terms, engrafted upon what will thus be left of the written agreement. The rule against varying or contradicting a written instrument by oral evidence, does not exclude verbal evidence adduced to prove that the written agreement has been totally waived or discharged.[4]

Subsequent waiver or discharge can be proved. But the new contract cannot be verbal one in cases in which the old contract was by law required to be in writing or had been registered. Such an agreement must be made subsequently and not contemporaneously. It must be complete in itself and embody distinctly the terms of the new contract. If a mortgagee becomes a tenant of mortgager, subsequent oral agreement for adjustment of rent towards interest can be proved as it merely creates machinery for discharge of interest.[5] But if the rent is either less or more than the interest, the agreement either limits or enhances or creates an interest in the mortgage security and would be hit by the proviso.

48. This proviso applies to subsequent agreement which directly (and not indirectly) affects the terms of the prior instrument. Oral evidence is admissible to prove discharge of mortgage. Oral agreement to pay a lesser sum cannot be proved in view of this proviso and section 17(b) of Registration Act.[6] Evidence can be received to show that there was, apart from the rent note, a distinct subsequent oral agreement under which the terms of the oral contract were modified and that partners of the firm, both before and after its' recomposition were the real tenants of the shop.[7] The proviso does not bar a subsequent oral

1. *Syed Noor* v. *Qutbuddin*, AIR 1956 Hyd 114: ILR 1956 Hyd 328.
2. *Ram Jatan* v. *Chandra Bali, Opposite Parties*, AIR 1960 All 746.
3. *S. Chattanatha Karayalar* v. *Central Bank of India Ltd.*, AIR 1965 SC 1856: 1966 (2) SCJ 317: (1965) 3 SCR 318.
4. Taylor on Evidence, 10th Edition, Page 820.
5. *Patel Kempegowda* v. *Channaveeriah*, AIR 1958 Mys 43.
6. *In Re: Donepudi Rangayya*, AIR 1927 Mad 1111.
7. *Niranjan Kumar* v. *Dhyan Singh*, AIR 1976 SC 2400: 1976 RCJ 814: 1976 UJ 802: (1976) 4 SCC 89.

agreement substituting a new contract for one reduced to writing and registered, that is, novation. An unregistered mortgage is inadmissible in evidence. But if it is considered as a mere memorandum evidencing the deposit of total deeds in pursuance of an earlier contract, the correctness of the recitals therein can be gone into irrespective of sections 91 and 92.[1] Oral variation of rent fixed in a registered lease deed cannot be proved.[2]

49. Exception to the proviso relates to cases where the contract is required by law to be in writing or has been registered (though it may not require registration). In such cases the prohibition contained in the main section will apply. Examples of contract required to be in writing are those covered by sections, 54, 118, 59, 123, 107, 130 of T.P. Act, section 63 of Indian Succession Act and Section 5 of Indian Trusts Act.[3] Where a lease deed has been registered, though law does not require it to be in writing, it is covered by this exception.[4] Oral discharge of mortgage can be proved. In such a case there is no contradicting or varying etc. When payment is made, mortgager is carrying out the terms of the mortgage and not varying them. But an executory agreement for payment of a lesser sum is not saved.[5]

Normally title will pass to the buyer on registration of the sale deed with effect from the date of execution of the sale deed, unless payment of entire consideration is a condition precedent, in which case, the intention of the parties is primarily to be gathered from the recitals in the deed, which, if ambiguous, require the surrounding circumstances and conduct of the parties to be looked into, subject to the limitations prescribed by section 92.[6] Registration of a deed, whether compulsorily registrable or not, is a bar to reception of oral evidence in proof of its modification. Such a contract can be modified or rescinded only by a registered document and no evidence of subsequent oral agreement to such an effect is permissible. Contract must be read as a whole to ascertain the true meaning of its' several clauses and the words of each clause should be understood so as to bring them in harmony with the other provisions.[7] Terms of a registered settlement cannot be varied or modified by any subsequent arrangement.[8]

50. Proviso (5).—Any usage or custom by which incidents not expressly stated in any contract are usually annexed to contracts of that description, may be proved. But the annexing of such incidents would not be repugnant to or inconsistent with, the express terms of the contract. Reception of evidence of usage is often not only justified in principle, but absolutely necessary, and without it, the intention of the parties would be defeated. But the proposed

1. *Veeramachineni Gangadhara Rao* v. *The Andhra Bank Ltd.*, AIR 1971 SC 1613: (1972) 1 Andh LT 8: 1971 (Supp) SCR 209.
2. *Raval and Company* v. *K.C. Ramachandran*, AIR 1974 SC 818: (1974) 1 SCC 424: (1974) 2 SCR 629.
3. *Kamta Singh* v. *Chaturbhuj Singh*, AIR 1934 PC 98: 61 Ind App 185.
4. *Raval and Company* v. *K.C. Ramachandran*, AIR 1974 SC 818: (1974) 1 SCC 424: (1974) 2 SCR 629.
5. *Kashinath Bhaskar Datar* v. *Bhaskar Vishweshwar*, AIR 1952 SC 153: 1952 SCJ 150: 1952 SCR 491.
6. *Kaliaperumal* v. *Rajagopal*, (2009) 4 SCC 193: AIR 2009 SC 2122: 2009 AIR SCW 2711.
7. *Bank of India* v. *K. Mohandas*, (2009) 5 SCC 313: AIR 2009 SC (Supp) 2783.
8. *S. Saktivel (Dead) by Lrs.* v. *M. Venugopal Pillai*, AIR 2000 SC 2633: (2000) 7 SCC 104: 2000 AIR SCW 2849.

evidence should not be repugnant to or inconsistent with the terms of the written contract.[1]

51. Oral evidence can be given to show that, by the usage or custom, an incident, not expressly mentioned in the contract, is a term of the contract. Usage is admissible to prove unexpressed incidents. The proviso has wide application in commercial contracts as the field is covered by trade usages. Parties knew or may be reasonably presumed to have known usage of the trade. It is accepted that the contract was itself framed with reference to the usage. The usage should not be repugnant to or inconsistent with the terms of the contract.

52. Proviso (6).—Any fact may be proved which shows in what manner the language of a document is related to existing facts. Such facts are an aid to construction of a document.[2]

To ascertain the identity or extent of the subject referred to in a document or the sense in which particular terms have been used or to clear up any other doubt that may arise in applying the document to the case, oral evidence is admissible. If a contract is doubtful in it's meaning, surrounding circumstances existing at the time of the contract can be looked into. If there is no dispute as to how the contents of the document are related to the existing facts, no oral evidence is admissible.[3] If a grant purports to deal with all land of the grantor situated at a particular place, oral evidence is allowed to show the correct description of the items of land. Where the meaning of a contract is expressed in a perfectly understandable language and can apply to existing facts, prior conduct or negotiations cannot be used to add to the meaning so expressed. If the language is ambiguous and admits of a variety of meanings, this proviso can be invoked.[4] Surrounding circumstances may be considered to ascertain the true meaning, especially when there is ambiguity.[5] Nomenclature and amount of stamp duty are not conclusive.[6] An earlier registered document cannot be construed in the light of a later unregistered deed.[7] Extrinsic evidence is allowed to show the true nature of the transaction. This proviso is more a substantive provision than a proviso.[8] If the language is capable of being applied to a number of things or persons, oral evidence may be given to show what was the thing or who was the person intended.[9] A party will not be allowed to say that when he wrote one thing he meant something different.[10]

1. Best on Evidence, 9th Edition, Page 211.
2. *Belapur Co. Ltd.* v. *Maharashtra State Farming Corporation*, AIR 1969 Bom 231; *P.B. Bhat* v. *V.R. Thakkar*, AIR 1972 Bom 365: 74 Bom LR 509: 1972 Mah LJ 756.
3. *Radha Sundar Dutta* v. *Mohd. Jahadur Rahim*, AIR 1959 SC 24: 1959 SCJ 212: 1959 SCR 1309.
4. *Godhra Electricity Co. Ltd.* v. *State of Gujarat*, AIR 1975 SC 32: (1975) 1 SCC 199: (1975) 2 SCR 42; *Raj Kumar Rajindra Singh* v. *State of Himachal Pradesh*, AIR 1990 SC 1833.
5. *A. Sreenivasa Pai* v. *Saraswathi Ammal* alias *G. Kamala Bai*, AIR 1985 SC 1359: (1985) 4 SCC 85.
6. *Thayyil Mammo* v. *Kottiath Ramunni*, AIR 1966 SC 337: 1966 (1) SCJ 138.
7. *Raghunath* v. *Kedarnath*, AIR 1969 SC 1316: (1970) 2 SCD 28: (1969) 3 SCR 497.
8. *S. Sundaram Pillai* v. *V.R. Pattabiraman*, AIR 1985 SC 582: (1985) 1 SCC 591: (1985) 1 Ren CJ 267; *Belapur Co. Ltd.* v. *Maharashtra State Farming Corporation*, AIR 1969 Bom 231.
9. *Gurubasappa* v. *Gurulingappa*, AIR 1962 Mys 246: ILR 1961 Mys 878; *Sait Bolumal Dharmdas Firm, Bankers* v. *Gollapudi Venkatachelapathi Rao*, AIR 1959 AP 612: (1959) 2 Andh WR 23: ILR 1959 AP 929.
10. *Afshar M.M. Tacki* v. *Dharamsey Tricamdas*, AIR 1947 Bomb 98.

Section 92 is only a rule of evidence; it does not fetter the court's power to arrive at the true meaning and effect of a transaction in the light of all surrounding circumstances. Extraneous evidence, oral or otherwise, is barred to prove a different intention from what they reduced to writing. In the case of a sale deed and a deed of agreement for repurchase, oral evidence cannot be let into show that the transaction was a mortgage by condition sale. The case must be decided on a consideration of the contents of the deeds with assistance of admissible surrounding circumstances.[1] In the case of an ambiguous instrument, subsequent conduct or statement is admissible to ascertain true nature of the transaction.[2]

In construing wills, it is the primary duty of court to ascertain intention from the language of the will. In doing so, court is bound and entitled to bear in mind matters other than merely the words used, such as surrounding circumstances, the position of the testator, his family relationships etc.[3]

53. SECTION 93.—When the language used in a document is, on its' face, ambiguous or defective, evidence may not be given of facts which would show its' meaning or supply its' defects. Sections 93 to 98 deal with rules for construction of documents with the aid of extrinsic evidence. The defect could be patent ambiguity or latent ambiguity. According to section 93, in the case of patent ambiguity in the language of a document, extrinsic evidence cannot be given to show its meaning or supply it's defects. Sections 95 to 97 deal with latent ambiguity. Section 93 does not apply in relation to latent ambiguity. This section will not apply to wills. Patent ambiguity is that which appears upon the document while latent ambiguity is that which seems certain and without any ambiguity on the basis of that which appears upon the deed but there is some collateral matter out of the deed that spells out ambiguity. In the case of latent ambiguity perusal shows no ambiguity but there is uncertainty as to its' application while patent ambiguity is detected from merely reading the deed. If the ambiguity is patent, no evidence can be given to make it certain; that is where the words of a deed are so defective or ambiguous as to have no meaning and this section bars evidence to show what the author of the deed intended to say.[4] The language is ambiguous only if found to be of uncertain meaning to persons of competent skill and information. Ambiguity of language does not mean inaccuracy of language. According to section 100 of Evidence Act, Sections 91 to 99 do not apply to the construction of wills under the provisions of the Indian Succession Act, 1865.

54. SECTION 94.—When the language of a deed is plain in itself or when it applies accurately to existing facts, evidence may not be given to show that it was not meant to apply to such facts.[5] Compare sections 94 and 95 with proviso 6 to section 92. Sections 94 and 95 define the sphere of operation of the proviso. Section 94 accepts the plain and grammatical meaning of a deed when the language is not ambiguous and applies to existing facts and no evidence is allowed to show that it was not meant to apply to such facts. Surrounding

1. *Rambujhawan Prasad Singh* v. *Jugal Singh*, AIR 1957 Pat 126: 1956 BLJR 83.
2. *Godhra Electricity Co. Ltd.* v. *State of Gujarat*, AIR 1975 SC 32: (1975) 1 SCC 199: (1975) 2 SCR 42; *Shyam Lal* v. *Shyam Narain*, AIR 1973 All 234.
3. *Manikam Pillai* v. *Venkatesa Chetti*, AIR 1927 Mad 494.
4. Stephen's Digest, Article 91.
5. *Chunchun Jha* v. *Ebadat Ali*, AIR 1954 SC 345: 1954 SCJ 469: (1955) 1 SCR 174.

circumstances are to be looked into only for the purpose of finding out whether the words apply to existing facts.[1] Even if the words are plain, but do not fit in with the admitted facts and a doubt arises, extrinsic evidence is admissible (section 95, 97).[2] This section does not speak of any patent or latent ambiguity. When the language in its' ordinary sense applies to the facts without any difficulty, evidence to show that it bears a different meaning will not be accepted as it contradicts the document.[1] Evidence to show that common words, whose meaning is plain, not appearing from the context to have been used in a peculiar sense, have been in fact so used, is not admissible.[3] In the case of property, where the subject-matter has been described properly, evidence cannot be given to show the something more or less has been intended.[4] If a person known to the testator, accurately fulfills the words in a will, evidence cannot be given to show that such person was not intended. Where a deed showed a particular land having been sold to a person and the language is plain and clear no evidence will be allowed to show that the land sold was some other land. Ordinarily the document must be allowed to speak for itself.

55. SECTION 95.—When language used in a document is plain in itself, but is unmeaning in reference to existing facts, evidence may be given to show that language was used in a particular sense. The Illustration refers to a sale deed by *A* to *B* of "my house in Calcutta". *A* had no house in Calcutta, but had a house in Howrah, of which *B* had been is possession since the execution of the sale deed. These facts may be proved to show that the deed related to the house in Howrah. Sections 95 to 97 deal with latent ambiguities. Section 95 is based on the maxim *Falsa demonstratio non nocit*. In a sale deed, if there is a conflict between the boundaries and the extent, there is a latent ambiguity since both descriptions are plain and clear and hence extrinsic evidence is admissible to show whether whole land lying within the boundaries was given possession of and enjoyed.[5]

Latent ambiguity arises, ordinarily, from the existence of facts external to the instrument and the creation, by these facts, of a question not solved by the document itself. It arises when the words are clear but their application to circumstances is doubtful. Here, ambiguity being raised by extrinsic evidence, it is allowed to be removed by the same means. *See* section 80, Indian Succession Act. For example, a will leaves property to "my nephew" and there are two nephews. Extrinsic evidence is admissible to show which nephew was intended. *See* also sections 78, 79 of the Indian Succession Act.

56. SECTION 96.—Sections 95 and 97 deal with imperfect descriptions while Section 96 deals with equivocal description. Here, description is partly correct and partly incorrect. This section covers cases of conflicting descriptions of property in deeds.

Extrinsic evidence is admissible for explaining apparently conflicting statements in the body of a deed and in the schedule thereto.[6]

1. *Kamla Devi* v. *Takhatmal*, AIR 1964 SC 859: 1963 Mah LJ 730: (1964) 2 SCR 152.
2. *Basudev Das* v. *Somenath Das*, AIR 1964 Ori 63: ILR (1963) Cut 189: 29 Cut LT 666.
3. Stephen's Digest, Article 91.
4. Phipson on Evidence, 15th Edition, Page 1232.
5. *Alla Basavapunnareddy* v. *Kalaga Krishnayya*, AIR 1966 AP 260: (1965) 2 Andhra WR 366; *Palestine Kupat Am. Bank Co-operative Society Ltd.* v. *Govt. of Palestine*, AIR 1948 PC 207: 62 Mad LW 21: 52 Cal WN 719.
6. *Hussanally* v. *Mangaldul*, AIR 1921 PC 40.

57. SECTION 97.—When the language used applies partly to one set of existing facts, and partly to another set of existing facts, but the whole of it does not apply correctly to either, evidence may be given to show to which of the two it was meant the apply. The illustration refers to a case where *A* agrees to sell *B* "my land at *X* in the occupation of *Y*". *A* has land at but not in the occupation of *Y*, and he has land in the occupation of *Y* but it is not at *X*. Evidence may be given of facts showing which he meant to sell. This section is an extension of the rule in Section 95. Where land within certain boundaries is sold and is wrongly described as containing a certain area, the error in the area is generally regarded as a mere mis-description and is rejected.[1] Parol evidence is also admissible to reconcile the conflicting descriptions.[2]

58. SECTION 98.—Evidence may be given to show meaning of llegible or not commonly intelligible characters, of foreign, obsolete, technical, local and provincial expressions, of abbreviations and of words used in a peculiar sense. *See* also sections 45, 49, 57(1) and 92 proviso (5). Doubt may arise either because the language is unintelligible to the court or be susceptible to two or more meanings or because the persons or things mentioned may require to be identified. This section allows evidence of two varieties. If the characters are in shorthand or otherwise difficult to be deciphered or if the language, whether as being foreign, obsolete, technical, local, is either not understood or is capable of bearing two or more meanings, the evidence of those skilled in deciphering writings or understanding the language or the meaning of the peculiar terms is admissible.[3] Notes in shorthand are not "commonly intelligible characters and abbreviations", but the report of a short hand writer is, strictly speaking, not substantive evidence and can be used only as part of oral evidence.[4]

59. SECTION 99.—Persons who are not parties to a document, or their representatives in interest, may give evidence of any facts tending to show a contemporaneous agreement varying the terms of the document. The principle of section 92 does not apply to third persons.[5] The right under section 99 applies not only to "varying" but to all processes contemplated in section 92. *(Ibid).*

60. SECTION 100.—Nothing in this chapter VII of the Evidence Act shall be taken to affect any of the provisions of the Indian Succession Act, 1865 as to the construction of wills.

---

1. *Palestine Kupat Am. Bank Co-operative Society Ltd.* v. *Govt. of Palestine*, AIR 1948 PC 207: 62 Mad LW 21: 52 Cal WN 719.
2. *Hussanally* v. *Mangaldas*, AIR 1921 PC 40.
3. *A. Pleader* v. *Judges of the High Court of Madras*, AIR 1930 PC 144: 31 Cr LJ 489; *State of Rajasthan* v. *Bundi Electric Supply Co., Ltd., Bundi*, AIR 1970 Raj 36: ILR (1969) 19 Raj 340: 1969 Raj LW 473.
4. *Laxminarayan* v. *Returning Officer*, AIR 1974 SC 66: (1974) 3 SCC 425: (1974) 1 SCR 822.
5. *Bai Heera Devi* v. *Official Assignee, Bombay*, AIR 1958 SC 448: 1958 SCJ 766: (1958) 1 SCR 1384.

CHAPTER 19
BURDEN OF PROOF
(SECTIONS 101 TO 113, 114A AND 114B)

Law regarding burden of proof deals with the questions by whom and in what manner evidence must be produced and by which party any fact is to be proved. It determines the right and liability to lead evidence and of the right of rebuttal. It assumes importance if both parties fail to adduce evidence or if both parties adduce evidence but the evidence is evenly balanced and the same leaves the court in doubt.

2. Provisions regarding burden of proof imply certain presumptions. When it is said that burden of proof in regard to any state of things is on a party, it means that there is an initial presumption in favour of the absence of such state of things.

3. Proof means anything which serves, either mediately or immediately to convince the mind of the truth or falsehood of a fact or proposition. A fact is said to be proved, according to the definition in section 3 of the Act, when, after considering the matters (not necessarily evidence, *e.g.*, burden of proof, inferences, presumptions, charge, section 313 answers, pleadings, taking judicial notice etc.) before it, the court either believes it to exist, or considers it's existence so probable that a prudent man ought, under the circumstances of the particular case, to act upon the supposition that it exists. A fact is said to be disproved when after considering the matters before it, the court either believes that it does not exist or consider its non-existence so probable that a prudent man ought to act upon the supposition that it does not exist. A fact is said to be 'not proved' when it is neither proved nor disproved (*See* definitions in section 3). Test of proof is the test of probabilities upon which a prudent man may base his opinion; in other words, it is the estimate which a prudent man makes of the probabilities, having regard to what must be his duty as a result of his estimate. Proof to rigid mathematical demonstration is impossible. Absolute certainty and perfect evidence are seldom possible. Such degree of probability as would satisfy the mind of a reasonable man as to the existence of a fact *i.e.*, preponderance of probabilities – that is the approach in a civil case.

4. The approach is somewhat different in a criminal case. Proof does not rest on mere preponderance of probability so far as the guilt of the accused is concerned. Prosecution has to discharge this burden to a greater degree *i.e.*, proof beyond reasonable doubt. In a civil case, interests of two parties are in conflict, and the court is called upon to decide the issue of conflict. Court must decide one way or the other and cannot decide either way except upon the balance of probabilities. The facts may be so balanced that each case seems equally probable or improbable, and then it is said that plaintiff has not satisfied the court that he has made out his case. But if there is a substantial preponderance of probability on either side, though the case still be full of doubt, the court must decide as the scale inclines. In a criminal case, apparently no conflict exists. The State does not wish to convict the accused at any cost. It is in the interest of justice that if he is guilty he should be convicted; but it is not in the interest of justice that he should be convicted unless his guilt is fully and clearly made out. Court cannot insist on such a degree of probability as to amount to absolute certainty as will exclude every possible doubt, and negative every possible theory; but the court should have arrived at such a degree of moral certainty as will warrant it, in the interest of justice, in taking the risk of being mistaken. That risk, under our system is negligible. The distinction in this behalf between civil cases and criminal cases is one drawn by courts and not by any statutory provision. This principle has been adopted from the common law of England and has become part of the common law of India.

5. Consequence of an erroneous conviction is serious for the accused and society. Hence persuasion of guilt must amount to such a moral certainty as convinces the mind of the judge, as a reasonable man, beyond reasonable doubt. We must keep in mind the dividing line between legal proof and moral certainty. But once evidence comes before court and stands the test of severe legal scrutiny, the effect of that evidence constitutes the legal proof. Then the dividing line vanishes. Test of proof is not the absence of reasonable doubt, though that is often a convenient way of expressing what is meant by proof. The test is really the estimate which a prudent man makes of the probabilities having regard to what must be his duty as a result of the estimate.

6. Kenny in '*Outlines of Criminal Law*' says "If the scales of evidence hang like even, throw into them some grams of mercy; or as is more commonly put, give the prisoner benefit of any reasonable doubt – not be it noted – of every doubt, but only of a doubt for which reasons can be given; for everything relative to human affairs and dependent on human evidence is open to some possible imaginary doubts; it is a condition of mind which exists when the jurors cannot say they feel an abiding conviction, a moral certainty of the truth of the charge; for it is not sufficient for the prosecution to establish a probability, even though a strong one according to the doctrine of chances; it must establish the fact to a moral certainty, a certainty that convinces the understanding, satisfies the reason and directs the judgment................to warrant an acquittal, the doubt must not be light or capricious, such as timidity or passion prompt or weakness or corruption readily accepts".

Wharton in "Criminal Law of Evidence" said: "Reasonable doubt is that which makes you hesitate as to the correctness of the conclusion which you reach. If under your oath or upon your conscience, after you have fully investigated the evidence and compared it in all it's aspects, you say to yourself "I doubt if he is guilty", then it is reasonable doubt. It is a doubt which settles in your judgment and finds a resting place there. It must be such a doubt as in the graver transactions of life, would cause a reasonable man to hesitate and pause in passing a final judgment on the question before him. A reasonable doubt must be one arising from the evidence or from the want of evidence, and cannot be an imaginary doubt or conjecture unrelated to evidence". Reasonable doubt is real, substantial, serious, actual doubt arising out of the evidence and existing after consideration of all evidence.

7. Sankey L.C. in 1983 AC 462 (explained in 1942 AC 1) said: "Throughout the Web of English Criminal Law one golden thread is always to be seen, that it is the duty of the prosecution to prove the prisoner's guilt subject to statutory exception. If at the end of the trial and on the whole of the case, there is a reasonable doubt created by the evidence given either by the prosecution or the prisoner, as to whether the prisoner killed the deceased with a malicious intent, the prosecution has not made out the case and the prisoner is entitled to acquittal. No matter what the charge and where the trial, the perception that the prosecution must prove the guilt of the prisoner is part of the common law of England and no attempt to whittle it down can be entertained".

8. 'That it is better that ten guilty men should escape than that one innocent man should suffer' is said to be a maxim of English Law. This maxim is often misunderstood. It means only that the great care should be taken by the court in convicting the accused. The presumption is that he is innocent till the contrary is clearly established. The burden of proof that the accused is guilty is always on the prosecution. If there is reasonable doubt about the guilt of the accused, benefit of the doubt must go to him. Cockburn, C.J. said "the doubt the benefit of which the accused is entitled must be such as rational, thinking, sensible man may fairly and reasonably entertain, not the doubts of a vacillating mind that has not the moral courage to decide but shelters itself in a vain and idle skepticism. There must be doubt which a man may honestly and conscientiously entertain".

9. Academicians and Judges have tried to define 'reasonable doubt', but that has not been done satisfactorily yet. Here is an attempt[1] 'That degree is not well-settled. It need not reach certainty but must carry a high degree of probability. Proof beyond reasonable doubt does not mean proof beyond the shadow of doubt. The law would fail to protect the community if it admitted fanciful possibilities to deflect the course of justice. If the evidence is strong against a man as to leave only a remote possibility in his favour that can be dismissed with the sentence'. "Of course it is possible, but not in the lest probable, the case is proved beyond reasonable doubt, but nothing short of that will suffice". The 'remote possibility' theory was adopted by Jaganmohan Reddy, J. in *Himachal Pradesh Administration* v. *Om Prakash*.[2] This view has been sharply criticized by writers. It is said even a remote possibility has to be considered, though it has to be rejected if the court is reasonably sure that it is so remote that it can be safely disregarded. The phrase 'reasonable doubt' can therefore be left undefined and speak for itself. Standard of proof is a high one, but not to be confused with absolute certainty or perfect evidence.[3]

10. In[4] it is observed: "A criminal trial is not like a fairy tale wherein one is free to give flight to one's imagination and fantasy. It concerns itself with the question as to whether the accused arraigned at the trial is guilty of the crime with which he is charged. Crime is an event in real life and is the product of interplay of different human emotions. In arriving at the conclusion about the guilt of the accused charged with the commission of a crime, the court has to judge the evidence by yardstick of probabilities, its intrinsic worth and the animus of witnesses. Every case in the final analysis would have to depend

---

1. Lord Denning's attempt in *Miller* v. *Minister of Pensions*, 1947 (2) All ER 372 (373): 177 LT 536: 63 TLR 474.
2. AIR 1972 SC 975: (1972) 1 SCC 249: 1972 SCC (Cri) 88: (1972) 1 SCJ 691.
3. *R. Balakrishna Pillai* v. *State of Kerala*, 1987 (1) KLT 928 FB; *State of Uttar Pradesh* v. *Pussu* alias *Ramkishore*.
4. *State of Punjab* v. *Jagir Singh*, 1973 Cr LJ 1589: (1974) 3 SCC 277: AIR 1973 SC 2407: 1973 SCC (Cri) 886.

upon its own facts. Although the benefit of every reasonable doubt should be given to the accused, the courts should not at the same time reject evidence which is *ex facie* trustworthy on ground which are fanciful or in the nature is conjectures".

11. In[1], the Supreme Court observed:

"Even at this stage we may remind ourselves of a necessary social perspective in criminal cases which suffers from insufficient forensic appreciation. The dangers of exaggerated devotion to the rule of benefit of doubt at the expense of social defence and to the soothing sentiment that all acquittals are always good regardless of justice to the victim and the community, demand a special emphasis in the contemporary context of escalating crime and escape. The judicial instrument has a public accountability. The cherished principles or golden thread of proof beyond reasonable doubt which runs through the web of our law should not be stretched morbidly to embrace every hunch, hesitancy and degree of doubt. The excessive solicitude reflected in the attitude that a thousand guilty men may go but one innocent martyr shall not suffer is a false dilemma. Only reasonable doubts belong to the accused. Otherwise, any practical system of justice will then break down and lose credibility with the community. The evil of acquitting a guilty person lightheartedly as a learned author (Glanville in Proof of Guilt) has saliently observed, goes much beyond the simple fact that just one guilty person has gone unpunished. If unmerited acquittals become general, they tend to lead to a cynical disregard of the law, and this in turn leads to a public demand for harsher legal presumptions against indicted persons and more severe punishment of those who are found guilty. Thus, too frequent acquittals of the guilty may lead to a ferocious penal law, eventually eroding the judicial protection of the guiltless. For all these reasons it is true to say, with Viscount Simon, that "miscarriage of justice may arise from the acquittal of the guilty no less than from the conviction of the innocent". In short our jurisprudential enthusiasm for presumed innocence must be moderated by the pragmatic need to make criminal justice potent and realistic".

In[2] the Supreme Court cautioned that the above observations do not affect the well-established principles of presumption of innocence and the burden of proof beyond reasonable doubt. However, it has to be noticed that the observations in the decisions noticed above have been quoted with approval in AIR 1983 SC 867.[3]

12. The principle of proof beyond reasonable doubt is applicable in the matter of testing the guilt of the accused. It has no operation in the area of proof of primary facts, particularly in cases where the guilt of the accused is sought to

1. *Shivaji Sahabrao Babade* v. *State of Maharashtra*, (1974) 1 SCR 489: (1973) 2 SCC 793: AIR 1973 SC 2622: 1973 Cr LJ 1783.
2. *Kali Ram* v. *State of Himachal Pradesh*, AIR 1973 SC 2773: 1973 Cr LR 705: (1973) 2 SCC 808: 1974 CAR 1: (1974) 1 SCR 722: 1974 Cr LJ 1.
3. *State of Uttar Pradesh* v. *Pussu*, AIR 1983 SC 867: 1983 Cr LJ 1356: (1983) 3 SCC 502; *State of Uttar Pradesh* v. *Krishna Gopal*, AIR 1988 SC 2154: 1989 Cr LJ 288: (1988) 4 SCC 302: JT 1988 (3) SC 544; *Gangadhar Behera* v. *State of Orissa*, AIR 2002 SC 3633: 2002 Cr LJ 41: 2002 AIR SCW 4271: 2002 (7) Supreme 276; *Sucha Singh* v. *State of Punjab*, 2003 AIR SCW 3984: AIR 2003 SC 3617: (2003) 7 SCC 643: 2003 Cr LJ 3876; *State of Punjab* v. *Karnail Singh*, 2003 Cr LJ 3892: AIR 2003 SC 3609: 2003 AIR SCW 4065 (SC).

be established by circumstantial evidence. Proof of primary facts is one thing and inference of facts to be drawn from primary facts is another thing. In regard to proof of basic or primary facts, court has to judge evidence in the ordinary way and in the appreciation of evidence in respect of proof of these basic or primary facts, there is no scope for the application of the principle of benefit of doubt. The Court considers evidence and decides whether that evidence proves a particular fact or not. When it is held that certain fact is proved the question arises whether that fact leads to an inference of the guilt of the accused or not and in dealing with this aspect of the problem, doctrine of benefit of doubt would apply and inference of guilty of accused can be drawn only if proved fact is incompatible with his innocence and is compatible only with guilt of accused.[1]

13. Proof is to be attempted by producing oral and documentary evidence, material objects, materials gathered at local inspection, marshalling probabilities, highlighting of surrounding circumstances and relying on admissions and presumptions.

14. "Burden of proof" has two distinct meanings the burden of establishing a case and the burden of introducing evidence. The burden of establishing a case is a burden cast on the pleadings. It remains always where the pleadings originally rest it and never shifts. "Burden of proof" in the sense of burden on evidence (called onus of proof) may shift constantly as evidence is introduced by one side or the other or as the one or the other preponderates over the other (AIR 1964 SC 136). The party succeeds on whose side the scale finally preponderates to a definite extent. Burden of proof may be affected by presumptions or admissions in pleadings. The phrase "Burden of Proof" is used in three different ways:—(a) to indicate the duty of bringing forward evidence in support of a proposition at the beginning or later, (b) to make clear the duty of establishing a proposition as against all counter evidence, and (c) an indiscrimate use in which it may mean either or both the above.[2] According to Phipson, the phrase "burden of proof" has three meanings:

(1) the persuasive burden, the burden of proof as a matter of law and pleading, the burden of establishing a case,

(2) the evidential burden, *i.e.*, burden of proof in the sense of adducing evidence, and

(3) in burden of establishing admissibility of evidence.[3] The *onus probandi* is important in the early stages of a case. It may also assume importance where no evidence at all is led on a disputed question by either side; in such a case, the party on whom the *onus* lies must fail. Where both sides adduce evidence, abstract notions of *onus* are out of place. Truth or otherwise of the case must always be judged on such evidence.[4] Even a

1. *M.G. Agarwal* v. *State of Maharashtra*, AIR 1963 SC 200: 1963 (1) Cr LJ 235: 64 Bom LR 773: (1963) 2 SCR 405.
2. *Anil Rishi* v. *Gurbaksh Singh*, (2006) 5 SCC 558: AIR 2006 SC 1971: 2006 AIR SCW 2394.
3. Phipson on Evidence, 13th Edition, Page 44.
4. *Prem Lata* v. *Arhant Kumar Jain*, AIR 1973 SC 626: (1973) 3 SCC 718: 1973 All WR (HC) 310; *Rani Laxmibai Kshetriya Gramin Bank* v. *Chand Behari Kapoor*, AIR 1998 SC 3104: 1998 AIR SCW 3016: (1998) 7 SCC 469; *Trichinopoly Mills, Limited* v. *National Cotton Textile Mills Workers Union*, AIR 1960 SC 1003: (1960-61) 18 FJR 99: (1960) 2 Lab LJ 46; *Moran Mar Basselios Catholicos* v. *Thukalan Paulo Avira*, AIR 1959 SC 31: 1958 Ker LT 721: 1958 Ker LJ 874; *Kalwa Devadattam* v. *Union of India*, AIR 1964 SC 880: 1963 (2) SCJ 256: (1964) 3 SCR 191; *Standard Chartered Bank* v. *Andhra Bank Financial Services Ltd.*, (2006) 6 SCC 94: AIR 2006 SC 3626: 2006 AIR SCW 3460; *Chet Singh* v. *State of Punjab*, (1977) 2 SCC 499: AIR 1977 SC 1494: (1977) 3 SCR 369.

party on whom the burden of proof lies can be excused from producing evidence in his control.[1] A party in possession of best evidence cannot withhold it on the ground that the onus of proof did not lie on him or that he was not called upon to produce it and hence court ought to draw adverse inference against him.[2]

15. SECTION 101.—Chapter VII of the Evidence Act deals with burden of proof. According to section 101, whoever desires any court to give judgment as to any legal right or liability dependent on the existence of facts which he asserts, must prove that those facts exist. According to second para of the section, when a person is bound to prove the existence of any fact, it is said that the burden of proof lies on that person. The expressions "proved", "disproved" and "not proved" are defined in section 3. To decide whether a disputed fact is proved, court has to consider the "Matters" before it. It follows that "Proof" is based on "Matters" from which the court decides whether a preponderance of probability regarding the existence or non-existence of a disputed fact has been established. The *onus* to prove a fact is on the party who asserts it.[3] Section 101 as also section 102 deal with general propositions while sections 103 to 113B deal with specific situations. *Onus probandi,* properly means that if a fact has to be proved, the person whose interest it is to prove it, should adduce evidence in proof thereof. Burden of proof lies on the party who substantially asserts the affirmative of the issue and not upon the opposite party. The party on whom the burden lies must prove his case and cannot rely on the weakness of his opponent's case. A party, on whom the burden of proof lies, if he fails to discharge it, has to fail.[4] When the whole of the evidence is before the court, the duty of the court is to consider the evidence and arrive at a conclusion without entering into a discussion on the question of burden of proof, provided such a conclusion is possible.[5] If the evidence adduced by the rival parties is so evenly balanced that it can arrive at no definite conclusion, the issue has to be decided against the party on whom the burden of proof lies.[6] *Onus* of proof will assume importance when neither of the rival parties adduce any evidence; in such a case, the party on whom the onus lies looses his case.[7] Where the party on whom *onus* of proof lies makes a significant admission regarding a disputed fact, the burden of proof shifts.

1. *Hiralal* v. *Badkulal,* AIR 1953 SC 225: 1953 SCR 758: 1953 SCJ 315.
2. *Gopal Krishnaji Ketkar* v. *Mahomed Haji Latif,* AIR 1968 SC 1413.
3. *Binani Industries Ltd., Kerala* v. *Assistant Commissioner of Commercial Taxes, VI Circle, Bangalore,* (2005) 11 SCC 149; *Anil Rishi* v. *Gurbaksh Singh,* (2006) 5 SCC 558: AIR 2006 SC 1971: 2006 AIR SCW 2394.
4. *Trichinopoly Mills, Limited* v. *National Cotton Textile Mills Workers Union,* AIR 1960 SC 1003: (1960-61) 18 FJR 99: (1960) 2 Lab LJ 46; *C. Abdul Shukoor Saheb* v. *Arji Papa Rao,* AIR 1963 SC 1150: 1964 (1) SCJ 168: 1963 SUPP (2) SCR 55; *Kalwa Devadattam* v. *Union of India,* AIR 1964 SC 880: 1963 (2) SCJ 256: (1964) 3 SCR 191.
5. *Mohammad Aslam Khan* v. *Feroze Shah,* AIR 1932 PC 228: 59 IA 386: 13 L 687: 138 IC 770; *Kumbhan Lakshmanna* v. *Tangirala Venkateswarlu,* AIR 1949 PC 278: ILR (1950) Mad 567; *Kalwa Devadattam* v. *Union of India,* AIR 1964 SC 880: 1963 (2) SCJ 256: (1964) 3 SCR 191; *Jagan Nath* v. *Jagdish Rai,* AIR 1998 SC 2028: 1998 AIR SCW 1883: (1998) 5 SCC 537.
6. *Harmes* v. *Hinkson,* AIR 1946 PC 156: 1946 2 Mad LJ 156: 227 IC 295: 50 Cal WN 895; *Kumbhan Lakshmanna* v. *Tangirala Venkateswarlu,* AIR 1949 PC 278: ILR (1950) Mad 567; *Prem Lata* v. *Arhant Kumar Jain,* AIR 1973 SC 626: (1973) 3 SCC 718: 1973 All WR (HC) 310; *Ram Kishore Sen* v. *Union of India,* AIR 1966 SC 644: (1966) 1 SCR 430; *Ramji Dayawala and Sons (P) Ltd.* v. *Invest Import,* AIR 1981 SC 2085: (1981) 1 SCC 80: (1981) 1 SCR 899.
7. *Harmes* v. *Hinkson,* AIR 1946 PC 156: 1946 2 Mad LJ 156: 227 IC 295: 50 Cal WN 895.

Several statutes contain provisions according to which on the burden bearer in a civil or criminal case proving certain facts, the opposite party has the reverse burden, that is, duty of proving certain other facts to exonerate him from liability. For example, Negotiable Instruments Act, Prevention of Corruption Act. A presumption is raised against the defendant or the accused as the case may be, on certain foundational or basic facts being proved by plaintiff or the prosecution respectively.

15A. SECTION 102.—According to section 102, the burden of proof in a suit or proceeding lies on that person who would fail if no evidence at all were given on either side. There are two illustrations given for this section. A plaintiff sues for recovery of possession of a piece of land from the defendant, admitted to be in possession. If no evidence is adduced by either party, defendant would be entitled to retain possession, and hence the burden to prove that plaintiff has title and consequently is entitled to secure possession is on the plaintiff. Plaintiff sues defendant for recovery of money due under a promissory note and defendant contends that the document was obtained by fraud or that he has paid back the money, which plaintiff denies. If no evidence were given on either side, plaintiff would succeed as the promissory note is not disputed and fraud or non-passing of consideration, as the case may be, is not proved.

If on the pleadings, the *onus* is on the plaintiff and he discharges the *onus* and makes out a case which entitles him to relief, the *onus* shifts to the defendant to prove those circumstances which would disentitle the plaintiff to any relief.[1]

The following illustrative cases may be seen:

1. In a suit for recovery of money due on the basis of adjustment signed by the defendant who denies the correctness of the amount found due, the defendant who is in possession of account books from which the balance could be ascertained, should produce them before the court. He cannot be allowed to say, relying on the abstract doctrine of burden of proof, that he is not required to produce the books unless called upon to do so.[2]
2. The *onus* is on the party who pleads estoppel.[3]
3. The *onus* is on the insurer to show the breach of conditions of policy for avoiding its' liability.[4]
4. Plaintiff who claims title to the suit property has the burden to prove the same.[5]
5. In a suit for recovery of possession on title, once the plaintiff has been able to create a high degree of probability so as to shift the *onus* on the defendant, it is for the defendant to discharge his *onus* and in the absence thereof, plaintiff's case has to be uphold.[6]
6. Plaintiff who claims to have a share in a property should prove the same.[7]

---

1. *Anil Rishi* v. *Gurbaksh Singh*, (2006) 5 SCC 558: AIR 2006 SC 1971: 2006 AIR SCW 2394.
2. *Hiralal* v. *Badkulal*, AIR 1953 SC 225: 1953 SCR 758: 1953 SCJ 315.
3. *Mitra Sen Singh* v. *Janki Kuar*, AIR 1924 PC 213: 51 IA 326: 46 A 728: 82 IC 946.
4. *Union of India* v. *Sohanlal Sampatlal*, (1971) 2 SCR 706: AIR 1971 SC 432: 41 Com Cas 136.
5. *Rangammal* v. *Kuppuswami*, (2008) 11 SCC 306.
6. *Mohan Singh* v. *Bhanwarlal*, (1964) 5 SCR 12: AIR 1964 SC 1366: 1964 MPLJ 249.
7. *Janki Vashdeo Bhojwani* v. *Industrial Bank Ltd.*, AIR 2005 SC 439: 2004 AIR SCW 7064: (2005) 2 SCC 217.

7. Where co-heirs (co-owners) seek to establish their right, the burden of proof is on the person who pleads adverse possession.[1]
8. If an agreement is challenged as being in restraint of trade, the onus of proving that the restrictions were reasonably necessary for the interest of the person claiming under the agreement is on that person.[2]
9. Where debutter property was alienated, it is for the party who supports the alienation to show that the alienation was made for legal necessity.[3]
10. In a contract for work involving transfer of contracted goods, burden of showing that the transfer constituted taxable sale is on the taxing authority.[4]
11. When adequate evidence is disclosed by the taxing authority but the assese fails to produce before the authority materials in his possession, adverse inference can be drawn against him.[5]
12. Burden to show that the transferee was acting in good faith is on the transferee.[6]
13. Where a party justifying a transaction shows that it was a *bona fide* one, the opposite party has to show that it was sham or bogus.[7] A person who alleges *mala fides* has to prove it.[8]
14. A party setting up a case of bias has to prove it.[9]
15. Where plaintiff claimed succession to the property of a person who was not heard of for over seven years, he has the *onus* to prove the date of death. It cannot be considered that the person was dead on the date of the plaint.[10]

---

1. *P. Lakshmi Reddy* v. *L. Lakshmi Reddy*, AIR 1957 SC 314: 1957 SCJ 248: 1957 SCR 195; *Konda Lakshmana Bapuji* v. *Govt. of Andhra Pradesh*, AIR 2002 SC 1012: (2002) 3 SCC 258: 2002 (1) SCJ 508; *Mt. Allah Rakhi* v. *Shah Mohammad Abdur Rahim*, AIR 1934 PC 77: 61 Ind App 50; *Gurbinder Singh* v. *Lal Singh*, AIR 1965 SC 1553: (1965) 1 SCWR 670: (1965) 3 SCR 63.
2. *Vancouver Malt & Sake Brewing Co. Ltd.* v. *Vancouver Breweries, Ltd.*, AIR 1934 PC 101; *Niranjan Shankar Golikari* v. *Century Spinning and Manufacturing Company Limited*, AIR 1967 SC 1098: 1967 (2) SCJ 317: (1967) 2 SCR 378.
3. *Ramsumranprasad* v. *Mt. Shyamkumar*, AIR 1922 PC 356; *Palaniappa Chetty* v. *Devasikamony Pandara Sannadhi*, AIR 1917 PC 33: 44 Ind App 147.
4. *Government of Andhra Pradesh* v. *Guntur Tobaccos Ltd.*, AIR 1965 SC 1396: (1965) 1 SCWR 494: (1965) 2 SCR 167.
5. *Commissioner of Income-tax, Madras* v. *Best and Co. (Private) Ltd. Madras*, AIR 1966 SC 1325: 1966 (1) SCJ 542: (1966) 2 SCR 480; *Commissioner of Income Tax, West Bengal* v. *Anwar Ali*, AIR 1970 SC 1782: 76 ITR 696; *Principal, Patna College, Patna* v. *Kalyan Srinivas Raman*, AIR 1966 SC 7: (1966) 1 SCR 974: 1967 (1) SCJ 260; *M. Ct. M. Chidambaram Chettiar (dead)* v. *The Commissioner of Income-tax, Madras* AIR 1966 SC 1453: 1966 (1) SCJ 590: (1966) 2 SCR 761; *Commissioner of Income-tax, Bombay City I Bombay* v. *Chugandas and Co., Bombay*, AIR 1965 SC 568: 1965 (1) SCJ 49: (1964) 8 SCR 332; regarding taxation matters).
6. *C. Abdul Shukoor Saheb* v. *Arji Papa Rao*, AIR 1963 SC 1150: 1964 (1) SCJ 168: 1963 SUPP (2) SCR 55.
7. *Subhra Mukerjee* v. *Bharat Coking Coal Ltd.*, AIR 2000 SC 1203: (2000) 3 SCC 312: 2000 AIR SCW 865.
8. *E.P. Royappa* v. *State of Tamil Nadu*, AIR 1974 SC 555: (1974) 4 SCC 3: 1974 Lab IC 427; *Ashutosh Lahiry* v. *State of Delhi*, AIR 1953 SC 451: 1950 SCJ 433: 1953 Cr LJ 1921; *C.K. Gangadharan* v. *Commissioner of Income Tax, Cochin*, (2008) 8 SCC 739: (2008) 228 ELT 497.
9. *Vijay Kumar Prasad* v. *State of Bihar*, AIR 1963 SC 1.
10. *Darshan Singh* v. *Gujjar Singh*, (2002) 2 SCC 62: AIR 2002 SC 606: 2002 AIR SCW 201.

16. Where a document recites passing of full consideration, it is for the party who controverts the passing of full consideration, to prove his contention.[1] If there is an admission in another deed, the party disputing has to prove his case.[2]
17. In a suit for specific performance of an agreement of sale, burden is on a subsequent purchaser from the owner to prove that he is a *bona fide* purchaser for value without notice.[3]
18. If a person pleads a specific custom, he must prove it.[4]
19. A party who pleads that a general custom has been varied by a special custom, has the onus to prove the special custom.[5]
20. A Motor vehicle insurer who seeks to avoid liability by contending that the driver did not have a valid driving license, has to prove that case.[6]
21. Where a defendant pleads discharge by him of the debt due to plaintiff, burden is on him to prove discharge.[7]
22. Once defendant admits the mortgage executed by him, burden is on him to show that it was extinguished lawfully, say by execution of a subsequent sale deed.[8]
23. Where a party sought to sustain a transaction entered into with a *pardanashin* lady, he has to prove that she executed the document after clearly understanding the nature of the transaction.[9] Depending on the circumstances of the case, court may insist on proof that the lady had independent advice.
24. A party who pleads fraud must prove it.[10] So also in the case of allegation of misrepresentation.[11]
25. Burden of proof that any particular property is joint family property, in the first instance, is on the party who pleads so. It is only when existence

---

1. *Thakur Bhagwan Singh* v. *Bishambar Nath (minor)*, AIR 1940 PC 114; *Kishore Chandra Singh Deo* v. *Ganesh Prasad Bhagat*, AIR 1954 SC 316: (1954) 1 Mad LJ 622: 1954 SCR 919: 1954 SCJ 395.
2. *Kishore Chandra Singh Deo* v. *Ganesh Prasad Bhagat*, AIR 1954 SC 316: (1954) 1 Mad LJ 622: 1954 SCR 919: 1954 SCJ 395.
3. *Bhup Narain Singh* v. *Gokul Chand Mahton*, AIR 1934 PC 68: 61 IA 115: 13 P 242: 147 IC 1134.
4. *Kochan Kani Kunjuraman Kani* v. *Mathevan Kani Sankaran Kani*, AIR 1971 SC 1398: 1971 Ker LT 458: 1971 (Supp) SCR 786; *Munshi Dass* v. *R. Mal Singh*, AIR 1977 SC 2002: 1977 UJ (SC) 555: (1977) 4 SCC 65; *Salekh Chand* v. *Satya Guptha*, (2008) 13 SCC 119: AIR 2009 SC (Supp) 418: 2008 AIR SCW 4211.
5. *Kehar Singh* v. *Chanan Singh*, AIR 1968 SC 806: 1968 (2) SCJ 608: (1968) 2 SCR 651; *Salig Ram* v. *Maya Devi*, AIR 1955 SC 266: (1955) 1 SCR 1911: ILR 1955 Punj 167: 1955 FCJ 248 (SC).
6. *Narchinva V. Kamat* v. *Alfredo Antonio Deo Martins*, AIR 1985 SC 1281: (1985) 2 SCC 574: 1985 ACJ 397.
7. *Madan Lal* v. *State of Punjab*, AIR 1967 SC 1590: 1967 Cr LJ 1401: (1967) 3 SCR 439.
8. *Wali Mohammed* v. *Mohammad Baksh*, AIR 1930 PC 91: 57 Ind App 86.
9. *Krishna Mohan Kul @ Nani Charan Kul* v. *Pratima Maity*, AIR 1963 SC 1203; *Hem Chandra Roy Chaudhury* v. *Suradhani Debya Chaudhurani*, AIR 1940 PC 134: ILR (1940) 2 Cal 436.
10. *Narayanan* v. *Official Assignee, Rangoon*, AIR 1941 PC 93: (1941) 31 NY Supp 2(d) 631.
11. *Kuppuswami Chettiar* v. *A.S.P.A. Arumugam Chettiar*, AIR 1967 SC 1395: 1967 (2) SCJ 5: (1967) 1 SCR 275.

of adequate nucleus is shown for the acquisition of the property that the *onus* shifts to other party who claims that the property is self-acquired without aid from family nucleus or property.[1]

26. Where a Hindu (Mitakshara) son, who is bound to discharge the personal debts of his father, pleads that the debts were not true or were incurred for immoral or immoral purposes, the burden is on him to prove such averments.[2] In the case of alienation by the Karta of HUF, the burden of proving legal necessity or benefit to the family is on the alienee.[3] A party who pleads that a HUF has severed in status, has to prove it.[4]
27. In a suit by landlord for eviction of tenant on the ground of denial of landlord's title by the tenant, burden is on the landlord to prove the factum of denial and that the denial was not *bona fide*.[5]
28. The standard of proof required for proving non-access between husband and wife must at least be of a degree between proof beyond reasonable doubt and test of preponderance of probability.[6]
29. It is for the plaintiff or applicant to show that his plaint or application is within time.[7]
30. Where the plaintiff's suit was to be filed within three years of his acquiring knowledge of a fact, defendant has to prove that plaintiff had knowledge of the fact more than three years back prior to filing of the suit.[8]
31. The burden to bring the case under section 14, Limitation Act rests with plaintiff.[9]
32. In an action for divorce, the burden to prove adultery is on the person who alleges it.[10]
33. Prosecution must prove common intention of the accused by leading evidence of relevant facts, circumstances and conduct of accused.[11]

---

1. *Mudigowda Gowdappa Sankh* v. *Ramchandra Revgowda Sankh*, AIR 1969 SC 1076: (1969) 3 SCR 245: 1970 Mah LJ 392; *D.S. Lakshmaiah* v. *L. Balasubramanyam*, AIR 2003 SC 3800: 2003 AIR SCW 4347: (2003) 10 SCC 310.
2. *Sita Ram* v. *Radha Bai*, AIR 1968 SC 534: (1967) 2 SCWR 838: 1968 (2) SCJ 231; *Appasaheb Peerappa Chandgade* v. *Devendra Peerappa*, (2007) 1 SCC 521: AIR 2007 SC 218: 2006 AIR SCW 5562.
3. *Pandurang Mahadeo Kavade* v. *Annaji Balwant Bokil*, AIR 1971 SC 2228: 1971 UJ (SC) 311: 1971 1 Civ App J (SC) 318.
4. *Chinthamani Ammal* v. *Nandagopal Gounder*, (2007) 4 SCC 163: AIR 2007 SC (Supp) 593: 2007 AIR SCW 1629.
5. *J.J. Lal Pvt. Ltd.* v. *M.R. Murali*, AIR 2002 SC 1061: 2002 AIR SCW 794: (2002) 3 SCC 98.
6. *Kamti Devi* v. *Poshi Ram*, AIR 2001 SC 2226: 2001 AIR SCW 2100: (2001) 5 SCC 311.
7. *Panna Lal* v. *Murari Lal*, AIR 1967 SC 1384: 1968 (1) SCJ 355: (1967) 2 SCR 757.
8. *K.S. Nanji and Company* v. *Jatashankar Dossa*, AIR 1961 SC 1474: 1961 BLJR 514: (1962) 1 SCR 492.
9. *Madhavrao Narayanrao Patwardhan* v. *Ram Krishna Govind Bhanu*, AIR 1958 SC 767: 1958 SCJ 963: 1959 SCR 564.
10. *Chandra Mohini Srivastava* v. *Avinash Prasad Srivastava*, AIR 1967 SC 581: (1967) 1 SCR 864: 1967 (1) SCJ 42.
11. *Maqsoodan* v. *State of Uttar Pradesh*, AIR 1983 SC 126: (1983) 1 SCC 218: 1983 Cr LJ 218: 1982 ALJ 1524; *Bhaba Nanda Sarma* v. *State of Assam*, AIR 1977 SC 2252: 1978 (1) SCJ 460: (1978) 1 SCR 714; *Ramprasad Tukaram Gadade* v. *State of Maharashtra*, (2003) 12 SCC 306.

34. Where the disputed property has been for a long period treated as trust property, *onus* is on the trustee to show that the property belonged to him personally.[1]
35. Onus of proof that the testator was a major when he made the will and was competent to execute the will is on the party relying on the will.[2]
36. The propounder of a will has the duty to explain the suspicious circumstances surrounding the terms and execution of the will. If the caveator alleges undue influence, fraud or coercion, onus is on him to prove the same.[3] Mere presence of motive and opportunity are not enough to prove undue influence.[4] If the propounder of the will was the principal beneficiary under the will and had taken active part in its' execution and registration, it would give rise to suspicion which has to be taken into consideration by the Court which will uphold the will only if it is clearly proved that the testator approved the terms of the will and that the suspicious circumstances had been explained satisfactorily.[5]

Further illustrations may be seen in pages 1188 to 1240 of Ratanlal.[6] In deciding where the burden or onus of proof on a particular disputed fact lies, Court has to look at the pleadings as also the principles of law relating to the substantive law relating the matter covered by the disputed fact.

Examples of "other Laws" are sections 118, 112 of N.I. Act, section 16(1)(a) of PFA Act, section 12 of Protection of Civil Rights Act, sections 123A, 138A and 139 of Customs Act, section 89 of Stamp Act, section 4(2) of SIT Act, sections 8(3), 35, 36 of the Arms Act, section 128(c) of M.V. Act, sections 10(c), 12 and 14 of E.C. Act, section 68 of Indian Contract Act, provisions of Bankers Book Evidence Act etc.

16. SECTION 103.—The burden of proof as to any particular fact lies on that person who wishes the court to believe in its existence, unless it is provided that the proof of that fact shall lie on any particular person. The two illustrations to the Section indicate that the party who relies on a previous admission of the opposite party or pleads *alibi,* has the burden of proving such facts.

Where in a matrimonial case, the husband raises the plea that an earlier marriage subsists, burden of proving that particular fact lies on him.[7] Accused who raises a plea of *alibi* is required to prove that particular fact.[8]

1. *Trichinopoly Mills, Limited* v. *National Cotton Textile Mills Workers Union,* AIR 1960 SC 1003: (1960-61) 18 FJR 99: (1960) 2 Lab LJ 46.
2. *Kalidindi Venkata Subbaraju* v. *Chintalapati Subbaraju,* AIR 1968 SC 947: (1968) 2 SCJ 513: (1968) 2 SCR 292.
3. *Shashi Kumar Banerjee* v. *Subodh Kumar Banerjee,* AIR 1964 SC 529; *Gurdial Kaur* v. *Kartar Kaur,* (1998) 4 SCC 384: AIR 1998 SC 2861: 1998 AIR SCW 1695; *Daulat Ram* v. *Sodha,* AIR 2005 SC 233: 2004 AIR SCW 6523: (2005) 1 SCC 40; *Gorantla Thataiah* v. *Thotakura Venkata Subbaiah,* AIR 1968 SC 1332: 1968 2 SCJ 744: 1968 Andh WR 109 (SC); *Bharpur Singh* v. *Shamsher Singh,* (2009) 3 SCC 687: AIR 2009 SC 1766: 2009 AIR SCW 1338.
4. *Naresh Charan Das Gupta* v. *Paresh Charan Das Gupta,* AIR 1955 SC 363: 1955 SCJ 293: 1955 SCR 1035.
5. *Cora Lillian Mc. Pherson* v. *Oron Leo McPherson,* AIR 1936 PC 246; *Benga Behera* v. *Braja Kishore Nanda,* AIR 2007 SC 1975: 2007 AIR SCW 3741: 2007 (3) All WC 3011: 2007 (3) Rec Civ R 240; *Venkat Rao* v. *Namdeo,* AIR 1931 PC 285.
6. Law of Evidence by Ratanlal and Dhirajlal, 23 Edition.
7. *Savitaben Somabhai Bhatiya* v. *State of Gujarat,* (2005) 3 SCC 636: 2005 AIR SCW 1601: AIR 2005 SC 1809.
8. *Jayantibhai Bhenkaarbhai* v. *State of Gujarat,* AIR 2002 SC 3569: (2002) 8 SCC 165: 2002 SCC (Cri) 1873: 2002 Cr LJ 4734: 2002 AIR SCW 4187.

17. SECTION 104.—The burden of proving any fact necessary to be proved in order to enable any person to give evidence of any other fact is on the person who wishes to give such evidence. The two illustrations to the section indicate that where *A* desires to prove a dying declaration by *B*, he must prove *B's* death and where *A* desires to prove by secondary evidence the contents of a lost document, he must prove that the document has been lost.

Where plaintiff took no steps to produce an original sale deed or to prove that it was lost or to establish the source from which the certified copy filed by him was obtained, or, in other words failed to take steps to lay the foundation to adduce secondary evidence, the purported secondary becomes inadmissible.[1]

18. SECTION 105.—Burden of proving applicability of any of the general exceptions in the I.P.C. or special exceptions or provisos in I.P.C. or in any other penal law is upon the accused and the court shall presume the absence of any such circumstances. This rule is an extension of the rule in section 103 and constitutes an important qualification to the general rule in Criminal Law that *onus* of proving everything essential to the establishment of the charge against the accused rests on the prosecution. But the burden on the accused of proving any specific defence is not so onerous as it is on the prosecution, but is only as in a civil case, that is, preponderance of probabilities.[2] Defence may adduce evidence or merely rely on the circumstances brought out from and admissions made by prosecution witnesses, presumptions, defence statements and probabilities.[3] If upon consideration of the evidence in the case, a reasonable doubt is created in the mind of the court about the existence of the ingredients of the offence, the accused is entitled to the benefit of the doubt.[4] Accused can argue

---

1. *Dayamathi Bai* v. *K.M. Shaffi*, (2004) 7 SCC 107: 2004 AIR SCW 4419: AIR 2004 SC 4082.
2. *State of Madhya Pradesh* v. *Ahmadullah*, AIR 1961 SC 998: 1961 (2) SCJ 197: (1961) 3 SCR 583; *Harbhajan Singh* v. *State of Punjab*, AIR 1966 SC 97: 1966 (1) SCJ 753: (1965) 3 SCR 235; *Dahyabhai* v. *State of Gujarat*, AIR 1964 SC 1563: (1964) 2 Cr LJ 472: (1964) 1 SCWR 831: (1964) 7 SCR 361; *Onkarnath Singh* v. *State of Uttar Pradesh*, AIR 1974 SC 1550: (1975) 3 SCC 276: (1975) 1 SCR 80; *Pratap* v. *State of Uttar Pradesh*, AIR 1976 SC 966: 1976 Cr LJ 697: (1976) 2 SCC 798; *P.C. Sethi* v. *Union of India*, (1975) 3 SCR 201: AIR 1975 SC 2164: (1975) 4 SCC 67; *S.L. Goswami* v. *State of Madhya Pradesh*, AIR 1972 SC 716: (1972) 2 SCR 948: 1974 (1) SCJ 35; *Mahomed Ramzani* v. *State of Delhi*, AIR 1980 SC 1341: 1980 Cr LJ 1010: 1980 Supp SCC 215; *Bhupendra Singh A. Chudasama* v. *State of Gujarat*, AIR 1997 SC 3790: 1997 AIR SCW 3938: (1998) 2 SCC 603; *Laxman Singh* v. *Poonam Singh*, 2003 AIR SCW 4566: AIR 2003 SC 3204: (2004) 10 SCC 94: 2003 Cr LJ 4478; *Kulwant Singh* v. *State of Punjab*, (2004) 9 SCC 257: AIR 2004 SC 2875: 2004 AIR SCW 778; *V. Subramani* v. *State of Tamil Nadu*, 2005 AIR SCW 1311: AIR 2005 SC 1983: 2005 Cr LJ 1727; *State of Madhya Pradesh* v. *Ramesh*, 2005 Cr LJ 652: AIR 2005 SC 1186: 2004 AIR SCW 6663 (SC); *Krishna* v. *State of Uttar Pradesh*, AIR 2007 SC 2452: 2007 Cr LJ 3525: 2007 AIR SCW 4372; *Vijayee Singh* v. *State of Uttar Pradesh*, AIR 1990 SC 1459: (1990) 3 SCC 190: 1990 Cr LJ 1510; *Yogendra Morarji* v. *State of Gujarat*, AIR 1980 SC 660: (1980) 2 SCC 218: 1980 Cr LJ 459; *Mahomed Ramzani* v. *State of Delhi*, AIR 1980 SC 1341: 1980 Cr LJ 1010: 1980 Supp SCC 215; *K.M. Nanavati* v. *State of Maharashtra*, AIR 1962 SC 605: (1962) 1 Cr LJ 521: 1962 (2) SCJ 347.
3. *Bahadur Singh* v. *State of Punjab*, (1992) 4 SCC 503: AIR 1993 SC 70: 1992 Cr LJ 3709; *Ratan Lal* v. *State of Madhya Pradesh*, AIR 1971 SC 778: (1971) 3 SCR 251: 1971 Cr LJ 654.
4. *K.M. Nanavati* v. *State of Maharashtra*, AIR 1962 SC 605: (1962) 1 Cr LJ 521: 1962 (2) SCJ 347; *State of Madhya Pradesh* v. *Ahmadullah*, AIR 1961 SC 998: 1961 (2) SCJ 197: (1961) 3 SCR 583; *Dahyabhai* v. *State of Gujarat*, AIR 1964 SC 1563: (1964) 2 Cr LJ 472: (1964) 1 SCWR 831: (1964) 7 SCR 361; *Jai Lal* v. *Delhi Administration*, AIR 1969 SC 15: (1969) 1 SCR 140; *D. Satyanarayana* v. *P.T. Reddy*, AIR 1974 SC 2164: 1974 Lab IC 1421: 1972 4 SCC 745; *Oyami Ayatu* v. *State of Madhya Pradesh*, AIR 1974 SC 216: 1974 Cr LJ 305: (1974) 3 SCC 299; *State of Uttar Pradesh* v. *Ram Swarup*, AIR 1974 SC 1570: 1974 Cr LJ 1035: (1974) 4 SCC 764.

for acquittal giving him the benefit of right of private defence, even without raising a specific plea of right of private defence.[1] This is so even though he had specifically raised the plea of *alibi*, an apparently contrary plea.[2] The question of plea of private defence or other exception arises only after the initial burden resting on the prosecution is discharged.[3] Even when accused totally denies the act alleged against him in the charge and does not specifically raise a plea based on any exception, if the evidence of the existence of circumstances bringing the case within a general or special exception is found in the evidence on record, the court must review the entire evidence and if so satisfied, either acquit the accused or convict him of a lesser offence, as the case may be.[4] Proof of defence raised by accused is based on the standard in the definition of "Proved" in section 3 of the Act.[5]

19. SECTION 106.—When any fact is specially within the knowledge of any person, the burden of proving that fact is on him. There are two illustrations given under the section and both are important. One is that when a person does an act with some intention other than that which the character and circumstances of the act suggest, the burden of proving that intention is upon him. The second is that if he is charged with travelling on a railway without a ticket, the burden of proving that he had a ticket, is on him.

Section 106 is an exception to the general rule contained in section 101, namely, that the burden is on the person who asserts a fact. The principle of section 106 applies only to such matters as are supposed to be specially within the knowledge of a party. But section 106 is not intended to relieve the prosecution of the burden of proving the charge. Section 106 is intended to meet certain exceptional situations in which it would be impossible or at any rate, disproportionality difficult for the prosecution to establish facts which are specially within the knowledge of the accused and which he could prove without much difficulty or inconvenience. The word "especially" indicates that it means facts which are preeminently within a person's knowledge.[6] But it cannot be argued that facts of a case are known to the accused and hence in every case he has to disprove the charge.[7] In applying the principle underlying this section, consideration by the court must be in a common sense way and balance of convenience and disproportion of the labour that would be involved in finding out and proving certain facts balanced against the triviality of the issue at stake and the ease with which the accused could prove them, are all matters which must be considered. The section cannot be applied in such a

---

1. *Gottipulla Venkata Siva Subbrayanam* v. *State of Andhra Pradesh*, AIR 1970 SC 1079: 1970 Cr LJ 1004: 1970 (2) SCJ 560.
2. *State of Mysore* v. *Raju Shetty*, AIR 1961 Mys 74: (1961) 1 Cr LJ 403: ILR (1960) Mys 1126.
3. *Yogendra Morarji* v. *State of Gujarat*, AIR 1980 SC 660: (1980) 2 SCC 218: 1980 Cr LJ 459; *Narain Singh* v. *State of Punjab*, (1964) 1 Cr LJ 730: (1963) 1 SCWR 29: 1963 (2) SCJ 324 (SC).
4. *State of Uttar Pradesh* v. *Lakhami*, AIR 1998 SC 1007: 1998 Cr LJ 1411: (1998) 4 SCC 336; *Bisna* v. *State of West Bengal*, (2005) 12 SCC 657: AIR 2006 SC 302: 2005 AIR SCW 5798.
5. *Dahyabhai* v. *State of Gujarat*, AIR 1964 SC 1563: (1964) 2 Cr LJ 472: (1964) 1 SCWR 831: (1964) 7 SCR 361; *Vareed Jacob* v. *Sosamma Geevarghese*, AIR 1966 SC 1; *State of Uttar Pradesh* v. *Ram Swarup*, AIR 1974 SC 1570: 1974 Cr LJ 1035: (1974) 4 SCC 764; *Ranjeet Mal* v. *General Manager, Northern Railway, New Delhi*, AIR 1977 SC 1701: (1978) 1 Lab LN 10; *Mahomed Ramzani* v. *State of Delhi*, AIR 1980 SC 1341: 1980 Cr LJ 1010: 1980 Supp SCC 215.
6. *Mohd. Usman* v. *State of Bihar*, AIR 1968 SC 1273: 1968 Cr LJ 1475: (1968) 2 SCJ 730.
7. *Stephen Seneviratne* v. *King*, AIR 1936 PC 289: 37 Cr LJ 963 (PC).

manner as to undermine the well-established rule that, save in very exceptional circumstances, the burden is on the prosecution and that burden never shifts.[1] In the second illustration to the section, if the accused had purchased a ticket he would instantly know from where he purchased the ticket and take steps to prove it.

In a case resting on circumstantial evidence, if the accused fails to offer a reasonable explanation in discharge of the burden placed on him, that itself provides an additional link in the chain of circumstances proved against him.[2]

Sections 103 and 106 do not absolve the prosecution from the duty of discharging its general or primary burden of proving the charge beyond reasonable doubt. It is only when the prosecution has led evidence which, if believed, will sustain a conviction or which makes out a *prima facie* case, that the question arises of considering facts of which the burden of proof may lie on the accused. There may be exceptions to this principle of law, for example, where burden of proof may be imposed on the accused by reason of a statute.[3] Section 106 cannot apply to facts capable of being known also by persons other than the accused.[4] The burden of proving *alibi* is on the accused, even so, the burden of proving the prosecution case is on the prosecution, irrespective of whether or not accused has made out a plausible defence.[5] Unless a statute rules out *mens rea* as a constituent part of an offence, an accused cannot be found guilty unless his guilty mind (*mens rea*) is proved. When the accused and his wife were last seen together in premises to which an outsider may not have access, it is for the husband to explain the reason for the unnatural death of his wife.[6] The burden to establish that the offence took place within the jurisdiction of the particular magistrate is on the prosecution and such knowledge cannot be said to be specially within the knowledge of accused.[7]

20. Customs authorities are not covered by the provisions of the Evidence Act; nevertheless, they are to be guided by section 106 as also principles of natural justice, which means that those authorities would be deemed to have discharged their burden if they adduce so much evidence as is sufficient to raise a presumption in their favour regarding the existence of the facts sought to be proved,[8] *dissenting from*[9] *and following.*[10] Burden of proving receipt of goods under

1. *Amba Lal* v. *Union of India*, AIR 1961 SC 264: (1961) 1 Cr LJ 326: (1961) 1 SCR 933.
2. *Bhandari Construction Co.* v. *Narayan Gopal Upadhye*, AIR 2007 SC 1441: 2007 AIR SCW 1846: (2007) 3 SCC 163.
3. *Vikramjit Singh* v. *State of Punjab*, (2006) 12 SCC 306: 2006 AIR SCW 6197: 2007 Cr LJ 1000.
4. *Rajik Ram* v. *Jaswant Singh Chauhan*, AIR 1975 SC 667: (1975) 4 SCC 769.
5. *Gurucharan Singh* v. *State of Punjab*, AIR 1956 SC 460: 1956 Cr LJ 827 (SC).
6. *Dnyaneshwar* v. *State of Maharashtra*, (2007) 10 SCC 445: AIR 2007 SC (Supp) 686; *Swamy Shraddananda* v. *State of Karnataka*, AIR 2007 SC 2531: 2007 AIR SCW 4513: 2007 (5) AIR Kar R 132; *Rohit Singh* v. *State of Bihar*, (2006) 12 SCC 734: AIR 2007 SC 10: 2006 AIR SCW 5385; *Bhandari Construction Co.* v. *Narayan Gopal Upadhye*, AIR 2007 SC 1441: 2007 AIR SCW 1846: (2007) 3 SCC 163.
7. *Krishna Kumar* v. *Union of India*, AIR 1959 SC 1390: 1959 Cr LJ 1508: (1960) 1 SCR 452.
8. *Collector of Customs, Madras* v. *D. Bhoormull*, AIR 1974 SC 859: 1974 (2) SCJ 238: (1974) 2 SCC 544.
9. *Amba Lal* v. *Union of India*, AIR 1961 SC 264: (1961) 1 Cr LJ 326: (1961) 1 SCR 933.
10. *Issardas Daulat Ram* v. *Union of India*, AIR 1966 SC 1867: (1962) Supp 1 SCR 358: 1966 Cr LJ 1507; *Kanungo and Co.* v. *Collector of Customs, Calcutta*, AIR 1972 SC 2136: 1973 (2) SCJ 219: (1973) 2 SCC 438.

the customs Act is on the accused.[1] Where the question is whether accused had a valid permit to export a particular kind of goods, burden is on the prosecution to prove that the goods being exported was the particular kind of goods.[2] Where foreign goods were seized under the Customs Act and accused pleaded that goods were sent to him by a broker in Bombay, he has to prove the fact which is within his knowledge.[3] The burden of proving that goods seized are not smuggled goods is on the accused as section 123(1) of the Customs Act is similar to section 106 of the Evidence Act. Where gold with foreign markings was seized, the burden lay upon the person from whom the gold was seized to account for his possession. (*Ibid*).

Where psychotropic substance was seized from a factory belonging to the accused, burden would be on him to prove how the substance came to be found in his factory.[4] In the case of dishonor of a cheque issued by a company, the drawee would not be expected to know whether the signatory of the cheque was instructed to do so or whether he has been deprived of such authority and these matters are particularly within the knowledge of the company and those in charge of the company have the duty to establish the same.[5] A person who claims to be a citizen of a particular country is required to prove the correctness of what he asserts. This is generally done by producing evidence of his date and place of birth, name of his parents, their place of birth and citizenship or even, sometimes, place of birth of grand-parents, which facts would necessarily be within the personal knowledge of claimant and not the state authorities. Once he discloses these facts, the state authorities are in a position to verify the alleged facts and lead contra evidence.[6]

If the dead body of a rape victim is found on the cot inside the house of the accused, burden would be on him to explain how the dead body happened to be there.[7] Where the dead body and severed head of victim were found in the field and near the tubewell of the accused which were in the vicinity of the house of the accused, it was for him to explain how they came to be at the spot and if he failed to do, though it would not be sufficient to fasten guilt on him, it would be a relevant circumstance against him while considering the totality of the circumstances against him.[8] Where a person was abducted and killed, the

1. *Gandhi Faizeam College Shahajahanpur* v. *University of Agra*, (1975) 3 SCR 810: AIR 1975 SC 1821: (1975) 2 SCC 283.
2. *Shrinivas Pannalal Chokhani* v. *State of Madhya Pradesh*, AIR 1954 SC 23: 1954 Cr LJ 253.
3. *Shah Guman Mal* v. *State of Andhra Pradesh*, AIR 1980 SC 793: (1980) 2 SCC 262: 1980 Cr LJ 557.
4. *Jagdish Budhroji Purohit* v. *State of Maharashtra*, (1998) 7 SCC 270: AIR 1998 SC 3328: 1998 Cr LJ 4626; *Avtar Singh* v. *State of Punjab*, AIR 2002 SC 3343: 2002 AIR SCW 3891: 2002 Cr LJ 4330; *Madan Lal* v. *State of Himachal Pradesh*, AIR 2003 SC 3642: 2003 AIR SCW 3969: 2003 Cr LJ 3868.
5. *N. Rangachari* v. *Bharat Sanchar Nigam Ltd.*, AIR 2007 SC 1682: 2007 AIR SCW 2591: 2007 Cr LJ 2448.
6. *Sarbananda Sonowal* v. *Union of India*, AIR 2005 SC 2920: 2005 AIR SCW 3393: (2005) 5 SCC 665; *Sanjay @ Kaka* v. *State (N.C.T. of Delhi)*, AIR 2001 SC 979: (2001) 3 SCC 190: 2001 SCC (Cri) 449: 2001 Cr LJ 1231: 2001 AIR SCW 767; *Ezhil* v. *State of Tamil Nadu*, (2002) 9 SCC 189: AIR 2002 SC 2017: 2002 Cr LJ 2799.
7. *State of Andhra Pradesh* v. *Gagula Satya Murthy*, AIR 1997 SC 1588: (1997) 1 SCC 272: 1997 Cr LJ 774: (1996) 4 Crimes 203: (1996) 8 SCALE 391.
8. *State of Punjab* v. *Karnail Singh*, 2003 Cr LJ 3892: AIR 2003 SC 3609: 2003 AIR SCW 4065 (SC).

presumption would be justified that the abductors themselves killed the victim unless they explained otherwise as to what they did with the victim of the abduction.[1] Where a housewife died of drowning in the well in the courtyard of the house of the in-laws, and at the time of the incident only the in-laws, namely, the accused persons were in the house, burden would be on them to prove what happened on that night which resulted in her death.[2] Where accused admitted he was found in possession of contraband gold but that his possession was not conscious possession, he has to establish the alleged fact because how he came to be in possession must be within his knowledge.[3] Prosecution is not required to explain why the accused chose to make a confession as that would be within his exclusive knowledge, unlike motive for the crime which, at times, would be known to others also.[4] In a prosecution under P.C. Act for accumulating wealth beyond the known sources of income of the accused, such sources would be within the knowledge of the accused.[5]

21. SECTIONS 107 and 108.—Section 107 states that when the question is whether a man is alive or dead and it is shown that he was alive within thirty years, the burden of proving that he is dead is on the person who affirms.

According to section 108 which is a proviso to section 107, when the question is whether a man is alive or dead, and it is proved that he has not been heard of for seven years by those who would naturally have heard of him if he had been alive, the burden of proving that he is alive is shifted to the person who affirms it.

There is generally no presumption of law by which the fact that a person was alive or dead on a given date can be established and the question must be decided on the facts of the particulars case.[6] Section 107 is almost similar to illustration (d) of section 114 which refers to a presumption of existence of a state of things. Sections 107 and 108 must be read together since the latter is only a proviso to the former and both constitute one rule when read together.[7] Section 107 deals with a presumption of continuance of life, while section 108 lays down a contrary principle.[8] Where the question was whether a person was alive on a particular date and there was evidence to show he was alive one

---

1. *State of West Bengal* v. *Mir Mohammad Omar*, 2000 AIR SCW 3230: 2000 SCC (Cri) 1516: (2000) 8 SCC 382: AIR 2000 SC 2988: 2000 Cr LJ 4047; *Sucha Singh* v. *State of Punjab*, AIR 2001 SC 1436: (2001) 4 SCC 375: 2001 AIR SCW 1292: 2001 Cr LJ 1734; *Ram Gulam* v. *State*, AIR 2001 SC 2842: (2001) 8 SCC 311: 2001 Cr LJ 4632; *Trimukh Maroti Kirkan* v. *State of Maharashtra*, (2006) 10 SCC 681: 2006 AIR SCW 5300: 2007 Cr LJ 20: JT 2006 (9) SC 50.
2. *Balram Prasad Agrawal* v. *State of Bihar*, AIR 1997 SC 1830: (1997) 9 SCC 338: 1997 Cr LJ 1640; *Trimukh Maroti Kirkan* v. *State of Maharashtra*, (2006) 10 SCC 681: 2006 AIR SCW 5300: 2007 Cr LJ 20: JT 2006 (9) SC 50; *Harishankar Gupta* v. *State of Chhattisgarh*, 2007 Cr LJ 1009: 2007 Cg LJ 66: 2007 (1) Crimes 441; *Ujjagar Singh* v. *State of Punjab*, (2007) 13 SCC 90: AIR 2008 SC (Supp) 190 : 2008 AIR SCW 33; *State of Rajasthan* v. *Jaggu Ram*, (2008) 12 SCC 51: AIR 2008 SC 982: 2008 AIR SCW 521.
3. *Murlidhar* v. *State of Rajasthan*, 2005 AIR SCW 2596: AIR 2005 SC 2345: 2005 Cr LJ 2608.
4. *Devender Pal Singh* v. *State of N.C.T. of Delhi*, AIR 2002 SC 1661: 2002 AIR SCW 1586: 2002 Cr LJ 2034.
5. *State of Madhya Pradesh* v. *Awadh Kishore Gupta*, AIR 2004 SC 517: 2003 AIR SCW 6501: 2004 Cr LJ 598.
6. Halsbury's Law of England, 4th Edition, Vol. 17, Page 85.
7. *Life Insurance Corporation of India* v. *Anuradha*, (2004) 10 SCC 131: AIR 2004 SC 2070: 2004 AIR SCW 2017.
8. *Badshah* v. *State of Uttar Pradesh*, (2008) 3 SCC 681: AIR 2008 SC (Supp) 1476.

year earlier on that date, the party who alleges that the person was dead on the relevant date has to *onus* to prove it.

Any provision laying down a rule of burden of proof, necessarily, by implication, lays down a principle of presumption. Presumptions under there two sections are rebuttable. If a person has not been heard of for seven years, there is a presumption of law that he is dead under section 108 and the burden shifts to the other side of proving that person is alive.[1] The presumption does not extend to the date of death.[2] There is no presumption that he died at the end of first seven years or at any particular date or at any subsequent period. Date of death is a matter of inference on the basis of evidence, factual or circumstantial. *Onus* of proving that a particular person was alive or dead on a particular date lies on the person who asserts it.[3] There is no presumption as to how long a person was alive or at what time he died. It cannot be presumed that a person had died seven years prior to the date of institution of the suit.[4]

Close relations and friends are persons who would have naturally heard from the person concerned.

The presumption of death would be the date on which the question was raised and not on any antecedent date. If so, the natural inference is that he was alive till the question was raised. To a case where section 108 is attracted, Section 107 does not apply. The earliest date to which death can be presumed can only be the date when the suit or claim of right is filed. The exact date of actual death is a matter of proof. Where two persons die in a common calamity, there is no presumption that the older person died first. As to which of them died first is a pure question of fact, the *onus* of proving which lies on the party who asserts the affirmative.[5] Section 21 of the Hindu Succession Act may be seen in this connection.

22. SECTION 109.—When the question is whether persons are partners, landlord and tenant, or principal and agent, and it has been shown that they have been acting as such, the burden of proving that they do not stand, or have ceased to stand, to each other in those relationships respectively, is on the person who affirms it.

When the existence of a personal relationship or a state of things is once proved, law presumes that it continues to exist as before, till the contrary is shown or till a different presumption is raised, from the nature of the subject in question. Cases other than the three cases mentioned in the section can be covered by the illustration (d) to section 114 of this Act. When a person, allegedly a partner is to be made liable, plaintiff has to prove that such a person is a partner and continues to be a partner or has been acting as a partner of the firm.[6] Partnership once shown to exist is presumed to continue until the contrary

1. *Ramrati Kuer* v. *Dwarika Prasad Singh*, AIR 1967 SC 1134: (1967) 2 SCJ 789: (1967) 1 SCR 153; *Rubabbuddin Sheikh* v. *State of Gujarat*, (2007) 4 SCC 404: AIR 2007 SC 1914: 2007 Cr LJ 3206.
2. *N. Jayalakshmi Ammal* v. *R. Gopal Pathar*, AIR 1995 SC 995: 1995 AIR SCW 983: 1995 Supp (1) SCC 27; *Darshan Singh* v. *Gujjar Singh*, (2002) 2 SCC 62: AIR 2002 SC 606: 2002 AIR SCW 201.
3. *Life Insurance Corporation of India* v. *Anuradha*, (2004) 10 SCC 131: AIR 2004 SC 2070: 2004 AIR SCW 2017.
4. *Saroop Singh* v. *Banto*, AIR 2005 SC 4407: 2005 AIR SCW 5314: (2005) 8 SCC 330.
5. *Agha Mir Ahmad Shah* v. *Mir Mudassir Shah*, AIR 1944 PC 100: 71 IA 171.
6. *Bharat Spinning & Weaving Co. Ltd.* v. *Manilal Lallubhai*, AIR 1935 PC 175.

is proved. Once a person is shown to be acting as a partner, the presumption is that he is a partner and continues to be such. Similar is the case in regard to landlord-tenant and principal-agent. Once such relationship is shown to exist, it is for the person concerned to show that such relationship ceased to exist. While the presumption under this section is mandatory but rebuttable, the presumption under section 114, illustration (d) is optional.

Under Hindu law, a joint family is presumed to remain so, until evidence of severance in status is given.

23. SECTION 110.—When the question is whether any person is owner of anything of which he is shown to be in possession, the burden of proving that he is not the owner is on the person who affirms that he is not the owner.

Though the law of property has to deal with notions of ownership and possession, they are not the same. A person may possess a right without owning it. Possession is *de facto* while ownership is *de jure*.[1] Possession is good title against all except the true owner and entitles the possessor to protect his possession against all except the owner. Even the owner can dispossess him only by recourse to law.[2] The principle underlying this section is that possession is *prima facie* evidence of title.[3] Anyone who seeks to oust the possessor must establish his right to do so. This is to be presumed from lawful possession until the want of title or better title is proved. (*Ibid*). A plaintiff who seeks to dispossess the defendant who is in possession, must recover on the strength of his own title and cannot, in the first instance, call upon the defendant to show the title under which he holds.[4] According to this section, possession is *prima facie* evidence of title because it is the sum of the acts of ownership. Such possession is sufficient, in the eye of law, to maintain a suit against a mere trespasser. Possession is evidence of title and provides a good title as against a wrongdoer. Plaintiff suing for possession must prove subsisting title. This section merely lays down a rule of evidence. The concept of possessory title is based on the principle that possession by itself constitutes a limited title to property, a title which is good against the whole world except the rightful owner.[5] Such possessory title has all the features of an "interest" in land and is presumptive evidence of title. (*Ibid*). There is no corresponding mandatory rule that person having title should be presumed to be in possession, though a permissive presumption may be drawn under section 114. If the evidence of possession produced by rival parties is evenly balanced, such a presumption may, if the circumstance of the particular case require it, be raised. Once it is found that plaintiff having title was in possession, law presumes continuity of that possession.[6] Presumption of possession and/or continuity thereof both forward and backward can also be raised under this section.[7] Where tax receipts for over forty years showed

1. Salmond on Jurisprudence, Page 277.
2. *Lallu Yeshwant Singh* v. *Rao Jagdish Singh*, AIR 1968 SC 620: 1968 (2) SCJ 244: (1968) 2 SCR 203.
3. *Chief Conservator of Forests* v. *Collector*, AIR 2003 SC 1805: (2003) 3 SCC 472: 2003 AIR SCW 1251.
4. *M.T.W. Tenzing Namgyal* v. *Motilal Lakhotia*, (2003) 5 SCC 1: AIR 2003 SC 1448: 2003 AIR SCW 784.
5. *Nair Service society Ltd.* v. *K.C. Alexander*, AIR 1968 SC 1165: (1968) 3 SCR 163: 1968 Ker LJ 176.
6. *Nathoo Lal* v. *Durga Prasad*, AIR 1954 SC 355: 1955 SCR 51: 1954 SCJ 557: 1954 SCA 921.
7. *Gurunath Manohar Pavaskar* v. *Nagesh Siddappa Navalgund*, (2007) 13 SCC 565: AIR 2008 SC 901: 2008 AIR SCW 298.

that the disputed land was the subject-matter of grant of tenancy by the land owner, it was held that a presumption could be raised in regard to possession both backwards and forwards.[1] Where the persons claiming to be pattedars were in possession of the disputed land for a long number of years as pattedars, there was no proof of conferment of patta on anyone else, the facts relating to acquisition of title were not known and the State could not prove its' title to the land, the presumption under this section applied and burden was on the State to prove that the pattedars were not owners of the land.[2] In a regular suit for recovery of possession of property (other than under section 6 of the Specific Relief Act, corresponding to section 9 of the Specific Relief Act, 1877), based on plaintiffs' prior possession without proof of title, plaintiff is entitled to succeed against all persons who do not have title to the property.[3] The defendant cannot succeed in the suit by showing that the title and right to possession are in a third party.[4] If the plaintiff put forward a definite case of possession on the basis of specific evidence which was rejected by court, she cannot fall back on the presumption under this section.[5]

Where one co-owner is in possession of co-ownership land, his possession is on behalf of all the co-owners unless ouster is pleaded and proved.[6]

A Magistrate, under section 145 Cr.P.C. is concerned with the question of actual possession and should not investigate question of title, except where such investigation is necessary in order to ascertain who is in actual possession.[7] Question of title may have relevance under section 145 if the land does not admit of actual physical possession, or where the evidence on both sides does not inspire confidence or is equally balanced or where the question of title has a bearing on the fact of actual possession.[8] A finding of possession recorded by a magistrate affects all persons interested therein, though it is open to challenge before the civil court.[9]

Possession of a part of land within defined boundaries in exercise of a right to claim the whole is evidence of the possession of the whole.[10]

24. SECTION 111.—Where there is a question as to good faith of transaction between parties one of whom stands to the other in a position of active

1. *Patinhare Purayil Nabeesumma* v. *Miniyatan Zacharias*, AIR 2008 SC 1456: 2008 AIR SCW 1502: (2008) 5 SCC 25, and *Ibid.*
2. *Chief Conservator of Forests* v. *Collector*, AIR 2003 SC 1805: (2003) 3 SCC 472: 2003 AIR SCW 1251.
3. *Nair Service society Ltd.* v. *K.C. Alexander*, AIR 1968 SC 1165: (1968) 3 SCR 163: 1968 Ker LJ 176.
4. *Somnath Berman* v. *Dr. S.P. Raju*, AIR 1970 SC 846: 1970 (1) SCJ 889: (1970) 2 SCA 544.
5. *Sevugan* v. *Kannappa*, AIR 1931 Mad. 282: 60 Mad LJ 430: 130 Ind Cas 845.
6. *Wuntakal Yaloi Chenabasavana Gowd* v. *Rao Bahadur Y. Mahabaleshwarappa*, AIR 1954 SC 337: 1954 SCJ 475: 1955 SCR 131; *Karbalai Begum* v. *Mohd. Sayeed*, AIR 1981 SC 77: (1980) 4 SCC 396: (1981) 1 SCR 863.
7. *Bhinka* v. *Charan Singh*, 1959 ALJ 557: AIR 1959 SC 960: 1959 Cr LJ 1223; *Ram Saroop* v. *Darsano*, 21 Cr LJ 748.
8. *Abdul Gafoor* v. *State*, (1961) 2 Cr LJ 426; *S.M. Yaqab* v. *T.N. Basu*, AIR 1949 Pat 146: 27 Pat 1027: 1949 Cr LJ 299 (SB); *Parmeshwar Din* v. *Sheo Moorat*, AIR 1952 All 918: 1952 All LJ 266: 1952 Cr LJ 1650.
9. *Jainath Pati* v. *Ramlakhan Prasad*, AIR 1929 Pat 505: 30 Cr LJ 840: 10 Pat LT 689; *Bhinka* v. *Charan Singh*, 1959 ALJ 557: AIR 1959 SC 960: 1959 Cr LJ 1223.
10. *O.K. Foli* v. *eo Akassee*, AIR 1936 PC 185.

confidence, the burden of proving good faith of the transaction is on the party who is in a position of active confidence. There shall be a presumption of absence of good faith in those cases. Such position of the other party may disable him from proving the *mala fides* of the transaction; hence the burden on the person in a position of active confidence, *e.g.*, will by an old, ailing, illiterate person. The main question will be if the executant had independent advice.[1] "Good faith" indicates that the relationship between the parties must be such that one is bound to protect the interests of the other. This applies to a trustee, executor, guardian, administrator, agent, medical attendant, attorney, etc. This section applies even to other cases where one stands in a confidential relationship with the other whereby his predominating influence exists, for example, *pardanashin* ladies.[2] Section 16 of Contract Act also may be seen.[3] Where a settlement was allegedly executed by an ailing, illiterate woman who was 106 years old, the burden of proving good faith of the transaction would be on the executee, who was the dominant party and in position of active confidence.[1]

This principle is extended to cases where there is proof of a person dependent by virtue of his physical or mental infirmity or disability on another party, and there are circumstances showing that the other party, taking advantage of such position, has secured a deed for his own benefit.[4] This is so even though it is not a case of "fiduciary" relationship. Section 111 applies when the *bona fides* of a transaction is in question.

"Undue influence" is defined in section 16 of the Indian Contract Act. According to section 19A of that Act, when consent to a contract was caused by undue influence, it is voidable at the option of the party whose consent was so caused. This provision is also based on fiduciary relationship. The distinction between the two provisions is that Section 111 of the Evidence Act is of general application to cases of where parties are in a position of active confidence while section 19A of the Contract Act applies only to contracts where one party is in a position to "dominate the will" of the other or where he holds a real or apparent authority over other or in a fiduciary relation to the other or contract is made with a person whose mental capacity is temporarily or permanently impaired by reason of age, illness or mental or bodily distress.[5]

The illustrations to section 111 refer to two instances of such relationship of active confidence, namely, adviser and client and father and child. Relationship between doctor and patient, spiritual advisor and penitent, husband and wife, guardian and ward, agent and principal also attract the provision.

Words "active confidence" indicate that the relationship must be such that one is bound to protect the other.[6] In such cases, it is important to see if the person conferring benefit had competent and independent advice. In individual

---

1. *Krishna Mohan Kul* alias *Nani Charan Kul* v. *Pratima Maity*, (2004) 9 SCC 468: AIR 2003 SC 4351: 2003 AIR SCW 5142.
2. *Nisar Ahmad Khan* v. *Raja Mohan Manucha*, AIR 1940 PC 204: 67 IA 431.
3. *Ladli Prashad Jaiswal* v. *Karnal Distillery Co. Ltd., Karnal*, AIR 1963 SC 1279: (1964) 1 SCR 270: 1964 (1) SCJ 12; *Poosa Trurai* v. *Kannappa Chettiar*, ILR 43 Mad 546: AIR 1920 PC 65 (PC).
4. *Daya Shankar* v. *Bachi*, AIR 1982 All 376.
5. *Ladli Prashad Jaiswal* v. *Karnal Distillery Co. Ltd., Karnal*, AIR 1963 SC 1279: (1964) 1 SCR 270: 1964 (1) SCJ 12.
6. *Anil Rishi* v. *Gurbaksh Singh*, (2006) 5 SCC 558: AIR 2006 SC 1971: 2006 AIR SCW 2394.

cases, age, capacity as also the nature of the benefit also must be considered. Courts have accepted that the provision applies to transactions to which a *pardanashin* (secluded) woman is a party. Court must be satisfied that transaction was explained to her, that she clearly understood the nature and effect of the transaction or that she had independent advice. The rule of special protection of a *pardanashin,* old and illiterate woman is not inflexible and should be applied in the light of facts of each case. Where the beneficiary of the transaction is a stranger who dealt with her at arm's length, there must be evidence of influence. The expression "*pardanashin*" is not to be taken in its strict literal sense. It only means a woman, who, by habit or family usage does not come out in the open to conduct her affairs.[1]

In the case of documents executed by *pardanashin* ladies, he who relies on such documents should satisfy the Court that the contents of the document had been explained to and understood by them.[2] An illiterate and rustic village woman is entitled to the same protection as in the case of a *pardanashin* lady. This is so also in the case of an old woman suffering from infirmity, ignorance, illiteracy, inexperience and dependency. What is necessary is her free and intelligent consent to the transaction.[3]

This special position is accorded also to mentally infirm persons.[4] The extent and character of the explanation or evidence required must depend on the circumstances of each case. Where there was no special relationship between the two, it may be sufficient to show this the executant knew the nature of the transaction. In case of special relationship between the two, Court must be satisfied that the executant understood its nature and really intended it.[5] Independent advice is not a requirement in all cases; whether it is required in a given case depends as the other circumstances present in the case.[6]

In a case of Will executed by the husband in favour of the newly wedded wife, it can be presumed that she was in a position to influence him.[7] Where three sisters executed a D.P. note in favour of the husband of the eldest sister, it was held that the circumstances of the case showed that the eldest sister was in a position to influence the younger sisters and the onus of proving good faith was on her husband.[8] Where an elderly woman depending entirely for food, clothes and management of property on her nephew executed a gift of her property

1. *Shyam Lal* v. *Ranbir Singh,* AIR 1951 All 386: 1951 ALJ 334.
2. *Farid-ud-Nisa* v. *Munshi Mukhtar Ahmad,* AIR 1925 PC 204: 52 IA 342: 47 A 703: 89 IC 749; *Kundan Lal* v. *Musharrafi Begum,* AIR 1936 PC 207: 63 IA 326: 11 Luck 346: 164 IC 156; *Kharbuja Kuer* v. *Jangbahadur Rai,* AIR 1963 SC 1203: (1963) 1 SCR 456: 1963 (2) SCJ 882; *Bank of Khulna* v. *Jyoti Prakash Mitra,* AIR 1940 PC 147: 67 IA 377.
3. *Hem Chandra Roy Chaudhury* v. *Suradhani Debya Chaudhurani,* AIR 1940 PC 134: ILR (1940) 2 Cal 436; *Tungabai* v. *Yeshvant Dinkar Jog,* AIR 1945 PC 8: ILR (1945) Bom 189: 49 Cal WN 55.
4. *Daya Shankar* v. *Bachi,* AIR 1982 All 376; *Sher Singh* v. *Pirthi Singh,* AIR 1975 All 259.
5. *Ramanamma (Valluri)* v. *Marina Virana,* AIR 1931 PC 100: 131 IC 401; *Hem Chandra Roy Chaudhury* v. *Suradhani Debya Chaudhurani,* AIR 1940 PC 134: ILR (1940) 2 Cal 436; *Kharbuja Kuer* v. *Jangbahadur Rai,* AIR 1963 SC 1203: (1963) 1 SCR 456: 1963 (2) SCJ 882.
6. *Kundan Lal* v. *Musharrafi Begum,* AIR 1936 PC 207: 63 IA 326: 11 Luck 346: 164 IC 156.
7. *Surendra Pal* v. *Dr. Saraswati Arora (Mrs.),* AIR 1974 SC 1999: (1974) 2 SCC 600: (1975) 1 SCR 687.
8. *A.V. Palanivelu Mudaliar* v. *Neelavathi Ammal,* AIR 1937 PC 50: 1937 All LJ 575: 167 Ind Cas 5.

in his favour, a presumption of undue influence was raised.[1] A money lender cannot be assumed to be in a position to dominate the will of the borrower.[2] But the helpless condition of a borrower may result in exercising undue influence over the borrower by the money lender. [3]

If there was a fraudulent misrepresentation regarding the character of the transaction, the transaction is void; if it is regarding the contents of the document, the transaction is voidable.[4]

A Will is not a "transaction" within the meaning of this section and hence is not governed by it. But almost similar care and caution would be necessary when a beneficiary under a will was in a position of confidence towards the testator or if there are suspicious circumstances surrounding the execution of the will or the nature of disposition under the will. But if a will has been proved to have been executed by a person of competent understanding and apparently a free agent, the burden of showing that it was executed under undue influence is on the party who alleges it.[5]

25. SECTION 111A.—In case of offences under sections 121 to 123 of I.P.C. or of criminal conspiracy or attempt to commit or abetment of an offence under sections 122 or 123 of I.P.C. in an area declared to be a disturbed area or an area in which there has been over a period of one month extensive disturbance of the public peace and it is shown that the accused had been at a place in such area at a time when fire arms or explosives were used at or from that place to attack or resist the members of any armed forces or forces charged with the maintenance of public order acting with discharge of their duties, it shall be presumed until the contrary is shown that he had committed the offence.

26. SECTION 113B.—In the case of allegation of committing dowry death of a woman, if it is shown that "soon before" her death, the victim had been subjected by the perpetrator, to cruelty or harassment for, or in connection with any demand for dowry, the Court shall presume that such person has caused the dowry death. "Dowry death" shall have the same meaning as in section 304-B I.P.C. Dowry is any property or valuable security given or agreed to be given either directly or indirectly – (a) by one party to the marriage to the other party to the marriage, or (b) by the parents of either party to a marriage or by any other to either party to the marriage or to any person at or before or any time after the marriage in connection with the marriage of the said parties but does not include dowry or mahar in the case of Muslims. "Valuable security" has the same meaning as in section 30 IPC.

According to section 304-B I.P.C., suicide is also a dowry death. Ingredients of section 304-B I.P.C. must be proved before presumption under section 113-B of 1872 Act arises. The husband or other relative of the wife need not be the actual or direct participants in causing death. Where death took place within 7 years of the marriage, the in-laws did not inform the parents about the death

---

1. *Inche Norah Binte Mohamed Thair* v. *Shaik Allie Bin Omar Bin Abdullah Bahaoshuan*, AIR 1929 PC 3: 115 IC 733.
2. *Barakat-un-Nisa Begum* v. *Debi Bakhsh*, AIR 1927 PC 84: 101 IC 29.
3. *M.B. Singh* v. *Shadilal*, ILR 31 All 386 PC.
4. *Ningawwa* v. *Byrappa Shiddappa Hireknrabar*, AIR 1968 SC 956: (1968) 1 SCWR 872: 1968 (2) SCJ 555; *Duleria Devi* v. *Janardhan Singh*, AIR 1990 SC 173.
5. *N.C.D. Gupta* v. *PCD Gupta*, AIR 1956 SC 363; *Surendra Pal* v. *Dr. Saraswati Arora (Mrs.)*, AIR 1974 SC 1999: (1974) 2 SCC 600: (1975) 1 SCR 687.

this section is attracted.[1] Section 113-B, being procedural, is retrospective.[2] If the offence was before the enactment of section 304-B I.P.C., the presumption is not attracted. The presumption arises on proof of dowry demand and cruelty by the husband. In understanding the words "soon before", there is no straight jacket formula. There must be a live link between the cruelty an account of dowry demand and dowry death appearing to exist. "Soon before" is a term of relative import.

27. SECTION 114A:—In a prosecution for rape under clause (a), clause (b), clause (c), clause (e), clause (f), clause (g), clause (h), clause (i), clause (f), clause (k), clause (l), clause (m), or clause (n) of sub-section (2) of section 376 I.P.C., where sexual intercourse by the accused is proved and the question is whether it was without the consent of the woman alleged to have been raped and such woman states in her evidence before the Court that she did not consent, the Court shall presume that she did not consent.

Explanation:—In this section, "sexual intercourse" shall mean any of the acts mentioned in clauses (a) to (d) of section 375 of the I.P.C.

The present section 114A is the new form of section 114A introduced by Amending Act 4 of 2003. In other words, the present section 114A introduced by Amending Act 13 of 2013 substituted section 114A newly introduced by Act 4 of 2003. The earlier section 114A read as follows:

> "In a prosecution for rape under clause (a) or clause (b) or clause (c), or clause (d) or clause (e) or clause (g) of sub-section (2) of section 376 of the IPC (45 of 1860), where sexual intercourse by the accused is proved and the question is whether it was without the consent of the woman alleged to have been raped and she states in her evidence before the Court that she did not consent, the Court shall presume that she did not consent".

28. The presumption is rebuttable on the part of the accused. This section has been applied in several cases.[3]

29. SECTION 41 (Conclusive Proof).—A final judgment, order or decree of a competent court is relevant – (a) if the court is exercising probate, matrimonial jurisdiction, and (b) if the judgment (order or decree) confers upon or takes away from any person any legal character, or which declares any person to be entitled to such character or to be entitled to any specific thing, not as against any particular person, but absolutely. Relevancy relates to existence of any such legal character, or the title of any such person to any such thing. The judgment is conclusive proof that, (a) any legal character which it confers, accrued at the time when such judgment came into operation, (b) that any legal character, to which it declares any such person to be entitled accrued to him at the time when such judgment declares it to have accrued to him, (c) that any legal character which it takes away from any such person, ceased at the time from which such judgment declared that it had ceased or should cease, (d) that anything to which it declares any person to be so entitled was the property of that person from which such judgment declares that it had been or should be his property.

1. *Shanti* v. *State of Haryana*, AIR 1991 SC 1226: 1991 Cr LJ 1713: (1991) 1 SCC 371.
2. *Bhoora Singh* v. *State of Uttar Pradesh*, 1992 Cr LJ 2294: 1992 All LJ 749: 1991 All Cri R 562.
3. *Kuldeep Singh* v. *State of Punjab*, 2003 Cr LJ 3777: 2004 (1) Chand LR (Civ and Cri) 165: 2003 (3) Rec Cri R 455; *Burla Venugopalakrishna* v. *State of Andhra Pradesh*, 2005 Cr LJ 1164: 2005 (3) Andh LT (Cri) 126 AP; *Yedla Srinivasa Rao* v. *State of Andhra Pradesh*, (2006) 11 SCC 615.

The judgment referred to in section 41 is a judgment *in rem*, as distinct from a judgment *in personem*. It merely declares the status of the person or thing. In first part, the section declares relevancy of certain judgments; the second part declares their conclusiveness regarding the time factor. Such a judgment is relevant in all cases whether such judgments are interparties or not.[1] The section is not exhaustive; there may be judgments such as those in suits under section 92 C.P.C. which have the effect of judgment *in rem* and bind the entire worldthough such judgments may not be conclusive.[2] Declaration of "legal character" is different from declaration of "legal right"; it is something more than a mere right and indicative of status with reference to the whole world. The section does not apply to lunacy proceeding. The principle is based on public policy.

30. SECTION 112.—That any person was born – (a) during the continuance of a valid marriage between his mother and any man or (b) within 280 days after the dissolution of the marriage, mother remaining unmarried, shall be conclusive proof that he is the legitimate son of that man. This presumption is allowed to be rebutted only by showing that the spouses had no access to each other at any time when he could have been conceived. This rule is based on prudence, natural justice and public policy. This presumption is a conclusive presumption which can be displaced only by proof of non-access as indicated above.[3] This section refers to the point of time of the birth of the child as he deciding factor. Relevancy of time of conception is only with reference to the aspect of access or non-access.[4]

It assumes the existence of a valid marriage. A person claiming to be the illegitimate child must prove it. Where paternity is admitted, but illegitimacy is alleged, the same has to be proved.[5] Maternity is also a matter of proof.[6]

The section applies irrespective of whether the mother was a married woman or not at the time of conception; that is an aspect covered by the time element in the section. Court leans against illegitimacy. Entry in birth register is not sufficient, in the absence of proof of non-access.[7] The presumption applies to persons of all religions.[8] A child born during the subsistence of the marriage is presumed to be legitimate even if born within a few months of the marriage and this can be rebutted only by proof of non-access at the time of conception, even if at that time, the parents were not married.[9] Evidence of actual intercourse

---

1. *State of Bihar* v. *Radha Krishna Singh*, AIR 1983 SC 684: (1983) 1 SCALE 789: (1983) 2 SCR 808: (1983) 3 SCC 118: 1983 Cur Civ LJ (SC) 273.
2. *Anjuman Islamia* v. *Latafat Ali*, AIR 1950 All 109: 1950 ALJ 776; *Sriram* v. *Prabhu Dayal*, AIR 1972 Raj 180: 1972 WLN 49: 1972 Raj LW 169.
3. *Gautam Kundu* v. *State of West Bengal*, AIR 1993 SC 2295: 1993 AIR SCW 2325: 1993 Cr LJ 3233: (1993) 3 SCC 418; *Banarsi Dass* v. *Teeku Dutta*, (2005) 4 SCC 449: 2005 (A) JT (SC) 627; *Dukhtar Jahan* v. *Mohd. Farooq*, (1987) 1 SCC 624: 1987 SCC (Cri) 237.
4. *Palani* v. *Sindhu*, (2005) 4 SCC 449.
5. *Shivajirao Lagad* v. *Bapurao Lagad*, AIR 1957 MP 174: 1957 MPC 366: 1957 MPLJ 481.
6. *Nand Kishwar Bux* v. *Gopal Bux*, AIR 1940 PC 93: ILR (1940) Kar PC 235: 188 IC 1.
7. *Mohindar Kaur* v. *Narindar Singh*, AIR 1960 Pun 169.
8. *Boramma* v. *Dharmappa*, AIR 1969 Mys 17: (1968) 2 Mys LJ 39: 15 Law Rep 204.
9. *Dukhtar Jahan* v. *Mohammed Farooq*, AIR 1987 SC 1049: 1987 Cr LJ 849: (1987) 1 Crimes 245; *Madan Lal* v. *Sudesh Kumari*, AIR 1988 Del 93: (1987) 1 Hindu LR 384: (1987) 1 DMC 528; *Mahendra Manilal Nanavati* v. *Sushila Mahendra Nanavati*, AIR 1965 SC 364: 66 Bom LR 681: 1965 Mah LJ 365.

is barred. Once marriage is proved, the court can presume its continuance.[1] Under this section, presumption of legitimacy follows the subsistence of a valid marriage.[2]

Access and Non-Access: These words mean existence and non-existence of opportunity for sexual intercourse.[3] It means effective access. Physical incapacity to procreate amounts to non-access.[4] A successful vasectomy operation (with repeated semen tests performed to eliminate errors) indicates non-access to procreate.[5] The fact that another man had intercourse with the wife or that she was leading an immoral life is not sufficient to rebut the presumption. A case of non-access must be a clear and satisfactory probability.[6] Evidence must be compulsive and clinching.[7] Pendency of a case under section 125 of the Criminal Procedure Code cannot constitute proof of non-access.[8] Even proof of adultery by the wife will not have any effect, if the spouses had access to each other at the beginning of period of gestation.

Blood test cannot be compelled by Courts.[9] It is doubtful if voluntary blood test can have any efficiency since result of such test cannot probabalise of improbabilise access.[9] Blood grouping test has its own limitation, it cannot possibly establish paternity, though it can indicate its possibility. The decision in[10] may be seen in relation to blood test. DNA test result must prevail over the presumption under this section.[11]

31. SECTION 113.—Notification in the official gazette regarding cessation to any Princely State shall be conclusive proof that a valid cessation of such territory took place at the date mentioned in such notification.

---

1. *Ismail Ahmed* v. *Momin Bibi*, AIR 1941 PC 11.
2. *Perumal Nadar* v. *Ponnuswami*, (1970) 1 SCC 605: AIR 1971 SC 2352: 1970 (2) SCJ 653.
3. *Karapaya Servai* v. *Mayandi*, AIR 1934 PC 49: 12 R 243: 147 IC 891; *Chilukuri Venkateswarlu* v. *Chilukuri Venkatanarayanan*, AIR 1954 SC 176: 1954 SCR 424: 1954 SCJ 84.
4. *Bhagwan Baksh Singh* v. *Mahesh Bakhsh Singh*, AIR 1935 PC 199: 159 IC 325.
5. *Chiruthakutty* v. *Subramanian*, 1986 Ker LT 1068: AIR 1987 Ker 5: 1986 Ker LJ 744.
6. *Chilukuri Venkateswarlu* v. *Chilukuri Venkatanarayanan*, AIR 1954 SC 176: 1954 SCR 424: 1954 SCJ 84; *Perumal Nadar* v. *Ponnuswami*, (1970) 1 SCC 605: AIR 1971 SC 2352: 1970 (2) SCJ 653.
7. *Dukhtar Jahan* v. *Mohammed Farooq*, AIR 1987 SC 1049: 1987 Cr LJ 849: (1987) 1 Crimes 245.
8. *Boramma* v. *Dharmappa*, AIR 1969 Mys 17: (1968) 2 Mys LJ 39: 15 Law Rep 204.
9. *Hargovind Soni* v. *Ramdulari*, AIR 1986 MP 57: (1986) 1 DMC 457: (1986) 1 Civil LJ 665; *Vasu* v. *Santha*, 1975 Ker LT 533.
10. *Gautam Kundu* v. *State of West Bengal*, AIR 1993 SC 2295: 1993 AIR SCW 2325: 1993 Cr LJ 3233: (1993) 3 SCC 418.
11. *Nandlal Wasudeo Badwaik* v. *Lata Nandlal Badwaik*, (2014) 2 SCC 576.

CHAPTER 20

ESTOPPEL
(SECTIONS 115 TO 117)

SECTION 115.—When one person has, by his declaration, act or omission, intentionally caused or permitted another person to believe a thing to be true and to act upon such belief, neither he nor his representative shall be allowed, in any suit or proceeding between himself and such person or his representative, to deny the truth of that thing.

2. To invoke the above doctrine of estoppel, three conditions must be satisfied, namely,

(a) representation by a person to another,

(b) the other shall have acted upon the said representation, and

(c) such action shall have been detrimental to the interests of the person to whom the representation was made.

All these three conditions must be satisfied to invoke the doctrine of *estoppel*.[1] No cause of action arises from estoppel itself; it only precludes a person from denying the truth of some statement previously made by him.[2] Estoppel does not create interest in property except as provided in section 47 of Transfer of Property Act. (*Ibid*). Principle of estoppel cannot operate against a person who was not in existence at the date when the transaction took place. Where an order of extension of service of an employee was cancelled before it became operative, the question of estoppel did not arise.[3] Complicated questions of estoppel and acquiescence can properly be examined in a title suit, that is, a suit for declaration of title and consequential reliefs and not in a simple suit for injunction.[4] While applying the principle of estoppel or acquiescence, the Court would be concerned with the conduct of the party for determination as to whether he can be permitted to take a different stand in a subsequent proceeding, unless there exists a statutory bar.[5] An estoppel which enables a party as against another party to claim a right of property, which in fact he does not possess, may itself be the foundation of a right as against the person estopped. But estoppel cannot have the effect of conferring upon a person a legal status expressly barred to him by a statute.[6]

---

1. *Gyarsi Bai* v. *Dhansukh Lal*, (1965) 2 SCR 154: AIR 1965 SC 1055: 1965 (2) SCJ 783; *Dhiyan Singh* v. *Jugal Kishore*, AIR 1952 SC 145: 1952 SCR 478: 1952 SCJ 142.
2. *Banwari Lal* v. *Sukhdarshan Dayal*, AIR 1973 SC 814: (1973) 1 SCC 294: (1973) 1 SCWR 19.
3. *State of Uttar Pradesh* v. *Girish Bihari*, AIR 1997 SC 1354: 1997 AIR SCW 1462: (1997) 4 SCC 362.
4. *Anathula Sudhakar* v. *P. Buchi Reddy*, AIR 2008 SC 2033: 2008 AIR SCW 2692: (2008) 4 SCC 594.
5. *Jai Narain Parasrampuria* v. *Pushpa Devi Saraf*, (2006) 7 SCC 756.
6. *B.L. Sreedhar* v. *K.M. Muinreddy*, AIR 2003 SC 578: 2002 AIR SCW 5221: (2003) 2 SCC 355.

3. Rule of estoppel is regarded as a rule of evidence based on equity and good conscience. The object is to prevent fraud and secure justice between the parties by promotion of honesty and good faith.[1] *He who seeks equity must do equity.*[2] Estoppel, being an equitable doctrine, must yield when equity so requires.[3] Though estoppel is often described as a rule of evidence, the concept itself can be more carefully viewed as a rule of substantive law.[4]

4. Sections 115 to 117 are not exhaustive of law of estoppel.[5] Section 234 of Indian Contract Act, section 18 of Specific Relief Act, sections 40 and 41 of Transfer of Property Act, sections 27 and 53 of Indian Sale of Goods Act and section 28 of Indian Partnership Act may be seen.

5. This section deals with estoppel by intentional representation or misrepresentation, express or implied, through act or omission or conduct. What is important is not the motive, but the effect of the representation. Question is, was the other party induced to act on the faith of the representation, act, conduct or omission? Intention to defraud is unnecessary.[6] Representation may have been made innocently or mistakenly.

There must have been a declaration, act, conduct or omission. By the declaration, the declarant must have intentionally caused or permitted another to believe a thing to be true and to act upon his belief. If so, the declarant or his representative cannot be allowed, in a case between the two, to deny the truth of that thing.[7]

Proof of intent may be direct or circumstantial *i.e.*, conduct. The representation must have been the proximate and not the remote cause of leading the other party to his prejudice. The action taken must have been to his detriment.[8] A

---

1. *R.S. Maddanappa* v. *Chandramma*, AIR 1965 SC 1812: 1966 (2) SCJ 310: (1965) 3 SCR 283; *Union of India* v. *Godfrey Philips India Ltd.*, AIR 1986 SC 806: 1985 22 ELT 306: 1986 Tax LR 2002: (1985) 4 SCC 369; *Delhi Cloth and General Mills Ltd.* v. *Union of India*, AIR 1987 SC 2414: JT 1987 (5) 35: 1987 (3) SCJ 328: (1988) 1 SCC 86; *Bollavaram P.N. Reddy* v. *State of Andhra Pradesh*, AIR 1991 SC 1468: 1991 SCC (Cri) 586: 1991 Cr LJ 1833: (1991) 3 SCC 434.
2. *Delhi Cloth and General Mills Ltd.* v. *Union of India*, AIR 1987 SC 2414: JT 1987 (5) 35: 1987 (3) SCJ 328: (1988) 1 SCC 86; *Union of India* v. *Godfrey Philips India Ltd.*, AIR 1986 SC 806: 1985 22 ELT 306: 1986 Tax LR 2002: (1985) 4 SCC 369.
3. *Indira Bai* v. *Nand Kishore*, AIR 1991 SC 1055: (1990) 4 SCC 668: 1991 (1) Civ LJ 1; *See* also *Chhaganlal Keshavlal Mehta* v. *Patel Narandas Haribhai*, AIR 1982 SC 121: (1981) 3 SCALE 1861: 1982 UJ 120: (1982) 1 SCC 223: (1982) 2 SCR 166.
4. *Canada & Dominion Sugar Co. Ltd.* v. *Canadian National (West Indies) Steamships Ltd.*, AIR 1947 PC 40: 1947 AC 46: (1946) 3 WWR 759; *Depuru Veeraraghava Reddi* v. *Depuru Kamalamma*, AIR 1951 Mad 403: (1950) 2 MLJ 575: 1950 MWN 710; *Dawson's Bank Ltd.* v. *Nippon Menkwa Kabushiki Kaisha*, AIR 1935 PC 79: (1935) LR 621: ILR 62 Ind App 100.
5. *Jaikaran Singh* v. *Sita Ram Agarwalla*, AIR 1974 Pat 364: 1974 BLJR 338.
6. *Srirangam Venkataratnam* v. *Perambadur*, AIR 1965 AP 163: (1964) 2 Andh LT 299: (1965) 1 Andh WR 112.
7. *Sales Tax Officer, Banaras* v. *Kanhaiya Lal Mukund Lal Saraf*, AIR 1959 SC 135: 1959 SCJ 53: 1959 SCR 1350.
8. *Ishar Singh Ex Principal Punjab Govt. Dental College and Hospital* v. *State of Punjab Through The Secretary To Government Department of Health*, AIR 1987 SC 808; *P.C. Goswami* v. *Collector of Darrang*, AIR 1982 SC 1214: (1982) 1 SCC 439: (1982) 2 APLJ 29 (SC); *Gyarsi Bai* v. *Dhansukh Lal*, (1965) 2 SCR 154: AIR 1965 SC 1055: 1965 (2) SCJ 783; *R.S. Maddanappa* v. *Chandramma*, AIR 1965 SC 1812: 1966 (2) SCJ 310: (1965) 3 SCR 283; *Mahindra and Mahindra Ltd.* v. *Union of India*, AIR 1979 SC 798: (1979) 2 SCC 529: (1979) 2 SCR 1038; *Hem Nolini Judah* v. *Isolyne Sarojsbashini Bose*, AIR 1962 SC 1471: 1962 All LJ 695: ILR 1962 2 All 683.

party who fails to raise the plea of estoppel and joins issue on the merits, cannot thereafter raise the plea of estoppel.[1]

There is no estoppel when both parties were labouring under a mistake.[2] If the person to whom a representation was made, was aware of the real state of affairs or had means of knowledge, there can be no estoppel.[3] When both parties were under a common error as per the erroneous advice of their lawyers regarding the construction of a document, no estoppel arises.[4] When representation is regarding a position of law, no estoppel arises.[5]

A person can plead estoppel in his own individual character and not as a representative of his assignor.[6]

6. Waiver.—Waiver is a voluntary and intentional relinquishment of a right infavour of another. Essence of waiver is estoppel. Relinquishment must be a conscious one *i.e.*, an intentional one with knowledge. Waiver looks mainly to conduct.[7] Waiver does not depend on misrepresentation. Waiver may be express or implied. Waiver, by itself, does not create any right in the other party.[8] Essential element of waiver is intention to abandon a right.[9] Opportunity for choice is the essence of waiver. In a transfer of a case from a competent court to an incompetent court, there cannot be waiver.[10] Waiver is contractual and may constitute a cause of action. There is no such thing as estoppel by waiver.[11] Rule of waiver cannot apply to matters based on public policy.[12] Benefit of rules of procedure can be waived.[13] Statutory rules cannot be waived by Government.[14] Even if a provision of law is mandatory, if it deals with

---

1. *His Holiness Digya Darshan Rajendra Ram Doss* v. *Devendra Doss*, AIR 1973 SC 268: (1973) 1 SCC 14: 1973 SCD 59.
2. *Sales Tax Officer, Banaras* v. *Kanhaiya Lal Mukund Lal Saraf*, AIR 1959 SC 135: 1959 SCJ 53: 1959 SCR 1350.
3. *Chhaganlal Keshavlal Mehta* v. *Patel Narandas Haribhai*, AIR 1982 SC 121: (1981) 3 SCALE 1861: 1982 UJ 120: (1982) 1 SCC 223: (1982) 2 SCR 166; *R.S. Maddanappa* v. *Chandramma*, AIR 1965 SC 1812: 1966 (2) SCJ 310: (1965) 3 SCR 283.
4. *John Agabog Vertannes* v. *James Goldar Robinson*, AIR 1927 PC 151: 54 IA 276: 5 R 427: 102 IC 639.
5. *Sales Tax Officer, Banaras* v. *Kanhaiya Lal Mukund Lal Saraf*, AIR 1959 SC 135: 1959 SCJ 53: 1959 SCR 1350.
6. *Municipal Corporation of Greater Bombay* v. *Dr. Hakimwadi Tenants Association*, AIR 1988 SC 233: JT 1987 (5) SC 448: 1988 (1) SCJ 78.
7. *Municipal Corporation of Greater Bombay* v. *Dr. Hakimwadi Tenants Association*, AIR 1988 SC 233: JT 1987 (5) SC 448: 1988 (1) SCJ 78; *Dr. Karan Singh* v. *State of Jammu and Kashmir*, AIR 2004 SC 2480: 2004 AIR SCW 2973: (2004) 4 SCALE 418; *Vaishakhi Ram* v. *Sanjeev Kumar Bhatiani*, (2008) 14 SCC 356: AIR 2008 SC 1585: 2008 AIR SCW 1753.
8. *Humayun Properties Ltd* v. *Ferrazzinis Private Ltd.*, AIR 1963 Cal 473.
9. *Basheshwar Nath* v. *Commissioner of Income Tex*, AIR 1959 SC 149: 1959 (35) ITR 190: 1959 SCJ 1207.
10. *A.R. Antulay* v. *R.S. Nayak*, AIR 1988 SC 1531: JT 1988 (2) SC 325: (1988) 2 SCC 602.
11. *Dawson's Bank Ltd.* v. *Nippon Menkwa Kabushiki Kaisha*, AIR 1935 PC 79: (1935) LR 621: ILR 62 Ind App 100.
12. *Abdul Waheedkhan Puthan Soudhagar* v. *Reny Charles Pavey*, AIR 1965 Mys 303: (1951) 1 Lab LJ 361; *Duggirala Balarama Krishnayya* v. *Arokapudi Jagannadha Rao*, AIR 1983 AP 136: (1983) 1 APLJ (HC) 255; *Noor Jahan Begum* v. *Abrar Ahmad Khan*, AIR 1982 All 489: (1982) 1 DMC 304: (1982) 8 All LR 149.
13. *Dalim Kumar* v. *Nandarni Dassi*, AIR 1970 Cal 292: 73 Cal WN 877: ILR (1970) 2 Cal 31.
14. *Nookala Setharamaiah* v. *Kotaiah Naidu*, AIR 1970 SC 1354: (1971) 1 SCR 153.

individual rights of the person concerned, and is for his benefit, he can always waive such a right.[1] Inherent lack of jurisdiction cannot be cured by waiver.[2] Estoppel is not a cause of action. It may assist a plaintiff in enforcing a cause of action. Waiver is contractual and may constitute a cause of action. A right can be waived by the party for whose benefit certain requirements or conditions had been provided by a statute subject to the condition that no public interest is involved. A party pleading waiver has to show that the agreement waiving the right in consideration of some compromise came into being. Statutory right may also be so waived.[3] A person cannot be held bound by waiver unless he is aware of what he is waiving.[4] An order which lacks inherent jurisdiction would be a nullity and hence doctrine of waiver is inapplicable.[5] A unilateral act or conduct of one person, which is not relied on by another to his detriment is only waiver, acquiescence or latches. An act or conduct, amounting to abandonment of his right and inducing another to change his position to his detriment raises bar of estoppel.[6] Plea of invalidity of contract on the ground that it is against public policy can be raised by one of the parties. Estoppel does not arise in such a situation.[7] There is no estoppel against plea of invalidity of a compromise decree on the ground that it contains an illegal contract. Where Rent Control Law bars execution of decree for eviction, failure to raise objection in the suit does not estop the raising of plea of non-excitability. Waiver may be express or implied.

7. There cannot be estoppel against statute or exercise of statutory power.[8] Estoppel, however, would not arise if sanction under a statute had been procured by fraud or collusion.[9] Estoppel cannot render valid a transaction which is invalid under a statute or give court jurisdiction denied by law or oust jurisdiction under statute which precludes parties from contracting out of its provisions. Regarding exemption from attachment of salary (section 60 C.P.C.), there can be no estoppel.[10] Estoppel cannot make government do an act prohibited by law.[11] In the case of provision of a statute which is intended for benefit of public, on

1. *Commissioner of Customs, Mumbai* v. *Virgo Steels, Bombay*, AIR 2002 SC 1745: 2002 AIR SCW 1698: (2002) 4 SCC 316.
2. *Hiralal* v. *Kalinath*, AIR 1962 SC 199: 1961 (2) SCJ 592: (1962) 2 SCR 747; *Sushil Kumar Mehta* v. *Govind Ram Bohra*, (1990) 1 SCC 193: (1990) 1 Rent LR 428: 1989 Supp (2) SCR 149.
3. *Krishna Bahadur* v. *Purna Theatre*, (2004) 8 SCC 229: AIR 2004 SC 4282: 2004 AIR SCW 4758.
4. *Manak Lal* v. *Prem Chand*, AIR 1957 SC 425: 1957 SCJ 359: 1957 SCR 575.
5. *B.S.M.D.C.* v. *Encon Builders (I) Pvt. Ltd.*, AIR 2003 SC 3688: 2003 AIR SCW 4186: (2003) 7 SCC 418.
6. *Bishan Singh* v. *Khazan Singh*, AIR 1958 SC 838: 1958 SCJ 1234: 1959 SCR 878.
7. *Nagappa* v. *Gurudayal Singh*, AIR 1992 SC 248.
8. *A.C. Jose* v. *Sivan Pillai*, (1984) 2 SCC 656: 1984 Ker LT 510: AIR 1984 SC 921; *P.C. Goswami* v. *Collector of Darrang*, AIR 1982 SC 1214: (1982) 1 SCC 439: (1982) 2 APLJ (SC) 29; *Air India* v. *Nergesh Meerza*, AIR 1981 SC 1829: 1981 Lab IC 1313: (1981) 4 SCC 335; *Thakur Amar Singh* v. *State*, AIR 1955 SC 504: 1955 SCJ 523: (1955) 2 SCR 303; *Mathra Parshad and Sons* v. *State of Punjab*, AIR 1962 SC 745: (1962) 13 STC 180: 1962 Supp (1) SCR 913; *Bengal Iron Corporation* v. *C.T.O*, AIR 1993 SC 2414: 1993 AIR SCW 2718: 1994 Supp (1) SCC 310; *S.B. Noronah* v. *Prem Kumari Khanna*, AIR 1980 SC 193: (1980) 1 SCR 281: 1980 (1) SCJ 446.
9. *S.B. Noronah* v. *Prem Kumari Khanna*, AIR 1980 SC 193: (1980) 1 SCR 281: 1980 (1) SCJ 446; *Bollavaram P.N. Reddy* v. *State of Andhra Pradesh*, AIR 1991 SC 1468: 1991 SCC (Cri) 586: 1991 Cr LJ 1833: (1991) 3 SCC 434.
10. *Noor Jahan Begum* v. *Abrar Ahmad Khan*, AIR 1982 All 149: (1982) 1 DMC 304: (1982) 8 All LR 149.
11. *S.B. Noronah* v. *Prem Kumari Khanna*, AIR 1980 SC 193: (1980) 1 SCR 281: 1980 (1) SCJ 446.

the ground of public policy, there can be no estoppel.[1] An assesse who files a return is not estopped from contending that he is not a dealer and not liable to pay tax. University has statutory right to alter its regulations and is not estopped from doing so after admission of students. In the absence of statutory support for cess, it cannot be demanded merely because of condition in excise auction.[2] Principle of equitable estoppel can be invoked to prevent manifest injustice. When University, after taking a long time for declaring a student as having passed, seeks to deny him the degree certificate on the ground he has failed in one subject, relief can be given.[3] A landlord who gives oral consent to subletting (which consent is unlawful) is not estopped from contending so.[4] If permission for transfer of land granted at a person's request is contrary to law, the person who is affected by the transfer is not estopped from challenging the transfer.[1]

8. An admission made in ignorance of correct position of law creates no estoppel.[5] A person who consented to an agreement is not estopped from contending that the agreement is null and void as being opposed to public policy.[6] So also regarding a party obtaining stay order under Arbitration Act from contending that the Arbitration Agreement is illegal and Award is not binding. So also filing and withdrawal of an earlier case by landlord would not estop him from contending that the lease is void.[7] Decision in void proceeding cannot give rise to estoppel.[8] There can be no estoppel against an order without jurisdiction.[9] A person who filed suit in the court of lowest jurisdiction showing the appropriate value, is estopped, after loosing the suit, from contending that the court had no jurisdiction.[10] A party who obtained a benefit under a provision of law is estopped from challenging the validity of the law.[11]

9. There can be no estoppel on a point of law.[12] If an appointment is clearly against law, no question of estoppel arises.[13] Representation under influence of wrong view of his legal rights or law does not lead to estoppel.[14] *See* cases

1. *Maritime Electric Co. Ltd.* v. *General Diaries Ltd.*, 1937 AC 610: AIR 1937 PC 114: 168 IC 616.
2. *State of Mysore* v. *D. Cawasji and Co.*, AIR 1971 SC 152: (1971) 2 SCR 799: 1971 (2) SCJ 363; *K. Ramadas Shenoy* v. *Chief Officers, Town Municipal Council. Udipi*, AIR 1974 SC 2177: (1974) 2 SCC 506: (1975) 1 SCR 680.
3. *T.H. Srinivasa* v. *Bangalore University*, ILR 1985 Kar 2763.
4. *Waman Shriniwas Kini* v. *Ratilal Bhagwandas and Company*, AIR 1959 SC 689: 1959 SCJ 635: 1959 SCR Supp (2) 217.
5. *Shantilal Shiv Kumar* v. *Transport Appellate Tribunal, Rajasthan, Jaipur*, AIR 1967 Raj 138: 1967 Raj LW 468: ILR (1966) 16 Raj 682.
6. *Nagappa* v. *Gurudayal Singh*, AIR 1992 SC 248; *Indira Bai* v. *Nand Kishore*, AIR 1991 SC 1055: (1990) 4 SCC 668: 1991 (1) Civ LJ 1.
7. *Kakubhai and Co.* v. *Nathmal Kisanlal*, AIR 1980 Bom 25: 1979 Mah LJ 450.
8. *Kameshwar Pandey* v. *Deolal Barhi*, AIR 1964 Pat 247: 1962 BLJR 960.
9. *Mathura Prasad Sarjoo Jaiswal* v. *Dossibai N.B. Jeejeebhoy*, (1970) 1 SCC 613: AIR 1971 SC 2355: (1970) 3 SCR 830; *P. Dasa Muni Reddy* v. *P. Appa Rao*, AIR 1974 SC 2089: (1975) 2 SCR 32: 1976 Ren CR 58.
10. *Tata Iron and Steel Co. Ltd.* v. *Arun Chandra Bose*, AIR 1967 Pat 246.
11. *Gulabchandra Kammodlal Jain* v. *State Government of Madhya Pradesh*, AIR 1963 MP 301: 1963 (2) Cr LJ 521: ILR (1964) MP 694.
12. *Baba Kartar Singh Bedi* v. *Dayal Das*, AIR 1939 PC 201: ILR (1939) Kar 350 (PC); *A.C. Jose* v. *Sivan Pillai*, (1984) 2 SCC 656: 1984 Ker LT 510: AIR 1984 SC 921.
13. *Ravinder Sharma* v. *State of Punjab*, AIR 1995 SC 277: 1995 (2) SCJ 86: 1994 AIR SCW 4438.
14. *Sales Tax Officer, Banaras* v. *Kanhaiya Lal Mukund Lal Saraf*, AIR 1959 SC 135: 1959 SCJ 53: 1959 SCR 1350.

of erroneous admissions to college.[1] There is no estoppel regarding an illegal municipal resolution, against a member who was party to it.[2] An admission on a question of law made by the lawyer can be challenged by the party.[3] There can be no estoppel also regarding statement of legal effect of facts or of document.[4] But a tenant who admitted that the *bona fide* need set up by the landlord is genuine and allowed the court to pass an order on that basis is estopped from challenging it.[5] There can be no estoppel against statute.[6] A person who participated in a meeting held for explaining induction of voting machines is not estopped from challenging it if such process is impermissible in law.[7] Statement made under mis-appreciation of law entails no estoppel. (*Ibid*).

10. Estoppel must be specifically pleaded.[8] The onus is on the person who sets up the plea, to prove it. If a person knows that his parents were dead at the time of adoption and hence adoption has no legal force, the conduct of the adoptive mother showing he was her adopted son creates no estoppel. When facts are ascertained, presumption arising from conduct cannot establish a right which the facts disprove.[9] When a right which is not a legal right is transferred, the transferee who obtained benefit there under, is not estopped from challenging validity of the transfer.[10] That is because both made a common mistake of law. The principle of estoppel has no application in Income Tax cases.[11] Income which is not taxable cannot be taxed on the basis of estoppel.[11] Estoppel applies to the same assessment, but not to successive assessments.

11. Estoppel by Election.—A person, having two alternative but mutually exclusive courses of action, chooses to adopt one and rejects the other expressly or impliedly, is said to have elected to choose one. He is later precluded from adopting the other course. He cannot be permitted to approbate and reprobate, blow hot and cold. The principle is that after the election, restitution is impossible.[12] Knowledge of right to election is a condition precedent. Where a person has the choice of two rights either of which he is at liberty to adopt,

1. *Ashok Chand Singhvi* v. *University of Jodhpur*, AIR 1989 SC 823: JT 1989 (1) SC 177: (1989) 1 SCC 399; *Rajendra Prasad Mathur* v. *Karnataka University*, AIR 1986 SC 1448: ILR 1986 Kant 2495: 1986 (3) Supreme 207; *Sanatan Gauda* v. *Berhampur University*, AIR 1990 SC 1075: (1990) 2 SCR 273: JT 1990 (2) SC 57.
2. *C.N. Ramaswamy* v. *Town Municipal Council, Chickmagalur*, AIR 1988 Kant 168: (1987) 1 Kant LJ 356: (1987) 13 Reports 457.
3. *State* v. *B. Chickvenkatappa*, AIR 1965 Mysore 253.
4. *Societe Beige De Bauque* v. *Girdhari Lal*, AIR 1940 PC 90: ILR (1940) Kar PC 208.
5. *R. Raja Konar* v. *Andal Ammal*, AIR 1973 Mad 47.
6. *Workmen of Hindustan Lever Ltd.* v. *Management*, AIR 1984 SC 516: (1984) 2 SCR 307: (1984) 1 SCC 728.
7. *A.C. Jose* v. *Sivan Pillai*, (1984) 2 SCC 656: 1984 Ker LT 510: AIR 1984 SC 921.
8. *Milak Brothers* v. *Union of India*, AIR 1990 SC 2256; *Nagji Vallabhaji and Co.* v. *Meghji Vijpar and Co.*, AIR 1987 Bom 142: (1986) 88 Bom LR 633: (1987) 1 Bom CR 547; *Bakul Oil Industries* v. *State of Gujarat*, AIR 1987 SC 142: (1987) 1 SCC 31: 1987 Tax LR 2059; *Express Newspaper (P) Ltd.* v. *Michael Mark*, AIR 1963 SC 1141: (1963) 3 SCR 405: (1962) 2 Lab LJ 220.
9. *Kishorilal* v. *Chaltibai*, AIR 1959 SC 504: 1959 SCJ 560: 1959 Supp (1) SCR 698.
10. *Sales Tax Officer, Banaras* v. *Kanhaiya Lal Mukund Lal Saraf*, AIR 1959 SC 135: 1959 SCJ 53: 1959 SCR 1350.
11. *Commissioner of Income-Tax* v. *V.M.R.P. Firm Muar*, AIR 1965 SC 1216: (1965) 1 ITJ 683: (1965) 1 SCR 815.
12. *Bhau Ram* v. *Baij Nath Singh*, AIR 1962 SC 1476: 1962 Jab LJ 676; *Prafulla Chandra Sinha* v. *Chotanagpur Banking Association Ltd.*, AIR 1965 Pat 502: 1965 BLJR 558: (1966) 36 Com Cas 845.

but not both, and if he adopts one, he cannot afterwards assert the other.[1] The doctrine against approbation and reprobation is only one application of the doctrine of election.[2] It applies only to conduct; but it cannot operate against provisions of a statute.[3]

12. Admission.—Admission can operate as estoppel only if the conditions of this section are satisfied.[4] A clear admission in pleadings operates as estoppel. If the other person was not induced to change his position, there is no estoppel. A gratuitous admission regarding title of a party who has no title can be withdrawn and shown to be erroneous, provided it does not operate as an estoppel. An admission in writ petition that certain land is pasture land may create estoppel.[5] An admission in a previous suit is admissible, though not conclusive.[6] Admission in an affidavit filed by Government is only an expression of opinion and not a specific assurance and is not binding.[7] An admission made *in terrorem* will not operate as estoppel.[8] Particular value given in the plaint for suit property cannot estop plaintiff from proving correct value later if defendant was aware of correct state of affairs and was not misled nor prejudiced.[9]

13. Estoppel by Negligence:

(1) A party must owe a duty to another;

(2) There must be some relationship of contract or agency;

(3) There must be some reason to think that an act would or would not be done;

(4) Negligence should be the proximate cause or real cause of the result;

(5) Negligence must be in the transaction itself and should be so connected with the result to which it led that it is impossible to treat the two separately.[10] There is a breach of duty if the party concerned has not taken due precautions to avert the risk.[11] To create estoppel, the negligence must be serious as to amount to a breach of duty. (Ibid). Where a forged cheque was paid by a Bank, the Bank is liable for wrong payment and plea of estoppel by negligence of the customer cannot be raised.[12]

---

1. *Lissenden* v. *C.A.V. Bosch Ltd.*, 1940 AC 412: 162 LT 195: (1940) 1 All ER 425 (HL); *National Insurance Company Ltd.* v. *Mastan*, AIR 2006 SC 577: 2005 AIR SCW 6305: (2006) 2 SCC 641.
2. *Bhau Ram* v. *Baij Nath Singh*, AIR 1961 SC 1327: 1961 (2) SCJ 89: (1962) 1 SCR 358.
3. *Commissioner of Income-Tax* v. *V.M.R.P. Firm Muar*, AIR 1965 SC 1216: (1965) 1 ITJ 683: (1965) 1 SCR 815.
4. *Abdul Hameed Khan* v. *Commissioner of Income-Tax, Andhra Pradesh, Hyderabad*, AIR 1967 AP 211: (1967) 1 Andh LT 182: ILR 1967 AP 1499.
5. *Gulabbhai Vallabhbhai Desai* v. *H.A. Khan, Collector of Daman*, AIR 1970 Goa 59.
6. *Basant Singh* v. *Janki Singh*, AIR 1967 SC 341: 1967 All LJ 1: (1967) 1 SLJ 476.
7. *N.C. Singhal* v. *Union of India*, AIR 1980 SC 1255: (1980) 3 SCC 29: 1980 SCC (L&S) 269; *P.C. Sethi* v. *Union of India*, (1975) 3 SCR 201: AIR 1975 SC 2164: (1975) 4 SCC 67; *J.K. Steel Ltd.* v. *Union of India*, AIR 1970 SC 1173: (1969) 2 SCR 481.
8. *Mohd. S. Labbai* v. *Mohd Hanifa*, AIR 1976 SC 1569: (1976) 4 SCC 780: (1976) 3 SCR 721.
9. *Shrinivas Krishnarao Kango* v. *Narayan Devji Kango*, AIR 1971 Mys 174: (1971) 1 Mys LJ 154.
10. *New Marine Coal Co. (Bengal) Private Ltd.* v. *Union of India*, AIR 1964 SC 152; *Standard Chartered Bank* v. *Andhra Bank Financial Services Ltd.*, (2006) 6 SCC 94: AIR 2006 SC 3626: 2006 AIR SCW 3460.
11. *Mercantile Bank of India Ltd.* v. *Central Bank of India Ltd.*, AIR 1938 PC 52: (1938) 1 All ER 52: ILR (1938) Mad 360 (PC).
12. *Canara Bank* v. *Canara Sales Corporation*, AIR 1987 SC 1603: (1987) 2 SCC 666: 1987 Cr LJ 1872.

14. Estoppel by Conduct.—This is where a person by his words or conduct, willfully endeavours to cause another to believe in a certain state of things knowing it to be false, or if a person in express terms or by conduct, makes a representation to another of the existence of a certain state of facts which he intended to be acted upon in a certain way, or if a person, whatever his meaning may be, so conducts himself that a reasonable person would take his conduct to mean a certain representation of facts and that it was a true representation or if by the transaction itself which is in dispute, one has led another into the belief of a certain state of facts, by conduct of culpable negligence calculated to have that result and such culpable negligence has been the proximate cause of leading and has led another to act by mistake upon that belief. In all those cases, the second person believes in a certain state of things and acts upon such belief to his own detriment. In these circumstances, the first person is estopped from denying the existence of such state of things.[1]

Mere execution of decree of trial court by the plaintiff would not amount to such conduct, when his other conduct clearly manifested that he was not prepared to accept the decree.[2] When charged with a liability, if a person states that he will send the goods towards discharge and does not demur, it is conduct leading to estoppel.[3] Where manufacturers accepted the condition in the Industrial License to the effect that the packing of yarn in hank form shall be in accordance with policy in force and commissioners' direction, they were bound by the direction.[4] Acceptance of cost in restoration application does not estop a party from challenging the order.[5] Such acceptance in an amendment application has been held to lead to estoppel. Where a party by his conduct induced another to believe that the latter was in lawful possession of land and had consequently right to construct a building, the party could not later question the legality of the possession or right to construct building. Landlord who did not object to the tenant converting a house into non-residential building is estopped from applying for eviction on the ground of *bona fide* need for residence.[6] An heir who relinquishes his future right of inheritance for consideration is estopped from claiming inheritance.[7] Where the HUF manager alienated family property with the consent of his widowed mother, she is estopped from challenging it on the ground of want of necessity.[8] A party who accepted payment under an award, cannot challenge the award.[9] Where a claimant in L.A. case agreed to receive reduced compensation and waive further claim if compensation is paid within a stipulated period and also received it, he is estopped from claiming interest.[10] Where a teacher served for five years receiving salary without objection by the

---

1. Ratanlal Dhirajlal on Law of Evidence, 23rd Edition, page 1434.
2. *Ramesh Chandra Chandiok* v. *Chuni Lal Sabharwal*, AIR 1971 SC 1238: (1971) 2 SCR 573: 1971 (2) SCJ 619.
3. *Walter Smith* v. *Ahmed Abdeenbhoy Peerbhoy*, AIR 1935 PC 154.
4. *G.T.N. Textiles Ltd.* v. *Assistant Directors, R.O.T. Commr*, AIR 1993 SC 1596: (1993) 3 SCC 438: (1993) 2 SCR 403.
5. *K.R. Singh* v. *A.G. Thakare*, AIR 1991 Bom 296: 1990 Bom LR 623: 1991 (2) Mah LR 99.
6. *Pokuru Vardarajam* v. *State of Andhra Pradesh*, AIR 1976 AP 90: (1975) 2 APLJ (HC) 40.
7. *Gulam Abbas* v. *Haji Kayyam Ali*, AIR 1973 SC 554: (1973) 1 SCC 1: 1973 Jab LJ 1041.
8. *K.C. Kapoor* v. *Radhika Devi*, AIR 1981 SC 2128: 1981 All LJ 1172.
9. *Govindji Jevat and Co.* v. *Shree Saraswati Mills Ltd.*, AIR 1982 Bom 76.
10. *State of Assam* v. *Jitendra Kumar Senapati*, AIR 1981 SC 969: 1981 UJ (SC) 189: (1981) 2 SCC 221.

approving authority, the school and the authority are estopped from terminating her on the ground of their mistake in appointing him.[1] Where the lessor did not object to construction of building by lessee's successors and also received rent, he is estopped from contending that the latter had no right to construct.[1] Villagers who subscribed to a mahazar preceding grant of gomal land for purpose other than pasturage cannot assail the grant later. Where the defendant successfully pleaded before the Tahsildar that what was payable was land revenue and not rent and when plaintiff filed a suit in civil court, sought to contend that section 30 of Mysore Tenancy Act was a bar to the suit, it was held there was estoppel. An admission of Mulageni (permanent) tenancy in a prior suit and acquiescence in a similar finding in that suit is conclusive.

Where the party sought to be estopped had no special knowledge of the correct facts, there can be no estoppel. Plaintiff who had no special knowledge of the income, claimed *mesne* profits at a particular rate, is not estopped from claiming at a higher rate.[2]

If the act or conduct is founded on mistake, there can be no estoppel. Where parties act under a common misapprehension, there can be no estoppel till it is cleared.[3]

Even where estoppel by record, that is *Resj udicata* is not attracted, one can rely on estoppel by conduct.[4] Estoppel by conduct is at the heart of rules embodied in Sections 115 to 117. Where the owner of a property clothes a third person with apparent ownership of property and right of disposition thereof and the latter disposes of that property, the real owner is estopped from asserting this title against the transferee in good faith and for consideration.[5] Where the Revenue Department in an earlier case had accepted the decision that certain items were entitled to MODVAT Credit and did not go in appeal, it cannot be permitted to take a different stand in a later case.[6] Where the plaintiff had availed the remedy of reference under the Land Acquisition Act for enhancement of compensation, he was estopped from challenging the L.A. proceedings by filing a suit subsequently.[7] The party against whom estoppel is pleaded should have made a representation, express or implied, intended to induce a course of conduct by the party to whom it is made.[8] A decree-holder who asked the executing court to secure permission of competent authority for sale of property of the judgment-debtor since the latter belonged to schedule tribe, cannot thereafter be allowed to contend that the judgment-debtor did not belong to S.T. category and hence no such permission was needed.[9] Where a party was receiving deficit grant from the Government on the representation that a certain amount had to be paid on account of house rent for the school building, cannot later contend that

1. *Narendra Bahadur Tandon* v. *Shankar Lal*, AIR 1980 SC 575: (1980) 2 SCR 821: (1980) 2 SCC 253: 1967 All 405.
2. *Magunta Kota Reddy* v. *Pothula Chendrasekhara Reddy*, AIR 1963 AP 42: (1962) 2 Andh WR 18: ILR (1963) AP 1033.
3. *Steuart and Co. Ltd* v. *C. Mackertich*, AIR 1963 Cal 198.
4. *Sunderbai* v. *Devrao Shanker Deshpande*, AIR 1954 SC 82: 1953 SCJ 693: (1953) 2 Mad LJ 782.
5. *Listi Shi* v. *Pong Tsoi Ching*, AIR 1935 PC 208: 159 IC 794.
6. *Birla Corporation Ltd.* v. *Comr. of C.E.*, (2005) 6 SCC 97.
7. *Union of India* v. *Ujagar Singh*, AIR 2003 P&H 297: 2004 (2) PunLR 239.
8. *Palestine Kupat Am. Bank Co-operative Society Ltd.* v. *Govt. of Palestine*, AIR 1948 PC 207: 62 Mad LW 21: 52 Cal WN 719.
9. *Raghunath Pradhani* v. *Damodara Mahapatra*, AIR 1978 SC 1820.

there was no liability to pay rent.[1] Where an employee having been convicted of an offence was removed from service, but after undergoing the sentence, he appealed to the appellate authority against his removal from service, which reduced the punishment to reduction to lower pay-scale denying back-wages, cannot subsequently file a suit for declaration that the punishment was illegal.[2] Where a Muslim father sold a piece of land under a sale deed attested by his son without any objection though it was against his interest, the son would be estopped from challenging the sale deed subsequently by.[3] Where the owner of acquired land accepted the compensation without demur, he is estopped from claiming title over the land.[4]

15. Issue Estoppel.—If an issue of fact was been tried by a competent Court earlier and a finding reached in favour of accused, it constitutes issue estoppel against prosecution.[5] The accused in the two cases must be the same.[6] Both cases must be criminal cases.[7] Rule of issue estoppel relates only to admissibility of evidence which is designed to upset an earlier finding.[8] The earlier trial should have been lawful.[9] The same issue of fact and law must have been decided in the previous litigation.[10] Principle of issue estoppel is that where an issue of fact has been tried by a competent court earlier and a finding has been reached in favour of an accused, such a finding would constitute estoppel or *res judicata* against the prosecution not as a bar to the trial and conviction of the accused for a different and distinct offence but as precluding the reception of evidence to disturb that finding of fact when the accused is tried subsequently even for a different offence which might be allowed by law.[11] The parties and the fact in issue tried in the former trial must be the same. Issue estoppel arises in criminal and civil cases.

When the subsequent case for defalcation related to a different period, the finding of acquittal in the earlier case does not operate as issue estoppel.[10]

---

1. *Management Committee T.K. Ghosh's Academy* v. *T.C. Palit*, AIR 1974 SC 1495: (1974) 2 SCC 354: (1974) 3 SCR 872.
2. *State of Punjab* v. *Krishnan Niwas*, AIR 1997 SC 2379.
3. *Mahboob Sahab* v. *Syed Ismail*, AIR 1995 SC 1205.
4. *M.T.W. Tenzing Namgyal* v. *Motilal Lakhotia*, (2003) 5 SCC 1: AIR 2003 SC 1448: 2003 AIR SCW 784.
5. *Piara Singh* v. *State of Punjab*, (1969) 3 SCR 236: AIR 1969 SC 961: 1969 Cr LJ 1435; *State of Andhra Pradesh* v. *Kokkiligada Meeraiah*, AIR 1970 SC 771: (1969) 2 SCR 1004: 1970 Cr LJ 759; *Lalta* v. *State of Uttar Pradesh*, AIR 1970 SC 1381: (1969) 2 SCR 526: 1970 Cr LJ 1270.
6. *Mohar Rai* v. *State of Bihar*, AIR 1968 SC 1281: (1968) 3 SCR 525: 1968 Cr LJ 1479.
7. *Krishnawati* v. *Hans Raj*, AIR 1974 SC 280: 1975 (1) SCJ 87: (1974) 2 SCR 524; *Bhoor Singh* v. *State of Punjab*, AIR 1974 SC 1256: 1974 Cr LJ 929: (1974) 4 SCC 754.
8. *Bhoor Singh* v. *State of Punjab*, AIR 1974 SC 1256: 1974 Cr LJ 929: (1974) 4 SCC 754; *Pritam Singh* v. *State of Punjab*, 1956 Cr LJ 805: AIR 1956 SC 415; *Jyoti Prokash Mitter* v. *Hon'ble Mr. Justice H.K. Bose, Chief Justice of the High Court, Calcutta*, AIR 1965 SC 961: (1965) 2 SCR 53: (1965) 1 SCWR 524; *Lalta* v. *State of Uttar Pradesh*, AIR 1970 SC 1381: (1969) 2 SCR 526: 1970 Cr LJ 1270.
9. *Assistant Collector of the Customs, Bombay* v. *L.R. Melwani*, AIR 1970 SC 962: (1969) 2 SCR 438: 1970 Cr LJ 885.
10. *Gopal Prasad Sinha* v. *State of Bihar*, AIR 1971 SC 458: (1971) 2 SCR 619: 1972 (1) SCJ 574.
11. *Masud Khan* v. *State of Uttar Pradesh*, AIR 1974 SC 28: 1975 (1) SCJ 129: (1974) 1 SCR 793; *Pritam Singh* v. *State of Punjab*, 1956 Cr LJ 805 (SC): AIR 1956 SC 415; *Manipur Administration, Manipur* v. *Thokchom Bira Singh*, AIR 1965 SC 87: 1965 Cr LJ 120: 1964 7 SCR 123; *Ravinder Singh* v. *State of Haryana*, AIR 1975 SC 856: (1975) 3 SCC 742: (1975) 3 SCR 453; *S.G.P.C.* v. *Mahant Harnam Singh*, AIR 2003 SC 3349: 2003 AIR SCW 4757: (2003) 7 SCALE 565.

Unlike cause of action estoppel, issue estoppel is not an absolute one and in special circumstances such as fresh material or new developments in the law which shows the issue to have been wrongly decided either in fact or law, court would allow the issue to be reopened if that is necessary to work out justice between the parties. Plea of issue estoppel is available even if plea of *res judicata* cannot be established.[1] Cause of action estoppel is that which prevents a party to an action from asserting or denying as against the other party, the existence of a particular cause of action, the non-existence or existence of which has been decided by the competent court in a previous case between the same parties.[2]

16. Inconsistent Positions.—Where a defendant successfully contested the competency of an execution petition on the ground that only a separate suit will lie, he cannot in such a suit filed by decree-holder contend that suit is not the appropriate remedy.[3] Where a party is given option to amend pleading or supply particulars or to strike out paragraphs as being vague and he chooses to amend his pleading, he cannot subsequently chose to adopt the other alternative.[4] There cannot be inconsistent stands on Court's jurisdiction.[5] Where a person allowed to appear for a competitive examination as being duly qualified, is successful, appointed probationer and is discharged after two years as not qualified and meanwhile became over-age, the discharge is hit by estoppel. This principle does not apply to a temporary appointee. That a person without domicile is allowed to appear for a test is no ground to estop the authority from not admitting him to appear for the test.[6] A tenderer is not estopped from challenging the Rules under which tender was called.[7] An adopted son succeeding to the estate cannot challenge the adoption.

17. Abandonment.—Abandonment of right is much more than mere waiver, acquiescence or laches and is something akin to estoppel, if not estoppel itself. Mere waiver short of abandonment of right, does not disentitle the holder of shares vested in him, from challenging the validity of any purported forfeiture of the shares. A person who has a vested right and in whom the legal title lies, does not and cannot, lose that title by mere laches, or mere standing by or even by saying that he has abandoned his right unless there is something more, namely, inducing another party by his words or conduct to believe the truth of that statement and to act upon it to his detriment, that is to say, unless there is estoppel, pure and simple. It is only in such a case that the right can be lost by what is loosely called abandonment or waiver; but it is not even then not abandonment or waiver as such which deprives him of his title but the estoppel which prevents him from asserting that his interest has not been legally extinguished.[8]

1. Halsbury's Laws of England Vol. 16, Page 1030.
2. Ratanlal Dhirajlal on Evidence, 23rd Edition P. 1470.
3. *B.S. Lail* v. *Sardar Mal Lalwani*, AIR 1964 MP 124: 1963 MPLJ 79: 1963 Jab LJ 181.
4. *Amin Lal* v. *Hunna Mal*, AIR 1965 SC 1243: 1966 (1) SCJ 43: (1964) 2 SCWR 713.
5. *Controller of Insurance* v. *Vanguard Insurance Co. Ltd.*, AIR 1966 Mad 437: (1966) 1 Com LJ 85: (1966) 36 Com Cas 119.
6. *Nookavarapu Kanakadurga Devi* v. *Kakatiya Medical College represented by its Principal, Warangal*, AIR 1972 AP 83.
7. *P. Bhooma Reddy* v. *State of Mysore*, AIR 1969 SC 655: (1969) 3 SCR 144.
8. *Sha Mulchand and Co. Ltd.* v. *Jawahar Mills Ltd., Salem*, AIR 1953 SC 98: 1953 SCJ 68: 1953 SCR 351; *Dr. Karan Singh* v. *State of Jammu and Kashmir*, AIR 2004 SC 2480: 2004 AIR SCW 2973: (2004) 4 SCALE 418.

18. Estoppel by silence or acquiescence.—Whenever there is a duty owing by a person towards another to speak or act which he failed to do and the other party has been led thereby to change his position, such silence would operate as estoppel against the former; but where there is no duty to speak, no estoppel can arise.[1] A person is bound to speak out in certain situations and his very silence becomes an expression as if he has openly consented to what is said or done and had become a party to the transaction. A person who applied for a particular post sought to be filled under the relevant recruitment rules and took the chance of being selected, cannot, on his not being selected, challenge the constitutionality of the rules.[2] A party who submits to arbitration proceedings by participating in it for a long time, cannot later contend that the matter was incapable of being referred to arbitration.[3] Where an employee kept quiet on the question of seniority for over twelve years and then sought to challenge the seniority list by overturning the seniority of a number of other employees shown as his seniors in the list, his claim is barred by acquiescence.[4] Where some employees who were entitled to continue in service till 60 years of age but were retired at 58 years, accepted it and did not challenge the same, they were guilty of waiver and acquiescence and had no right to challenge it thereafter.[5] The principle would apply even when both parties were acting under a mistake of law as to their rights.[6] Mode of proof being a matter of procedure, relevant evidence can be brought on record without following the regular procedure if both parties agree.[7] In the matter of jurisdiction, consent or acquiescence cannot give jurisdiction.[8] Supreme Court has relaxed the rigor of this principle in some cases. Where a person acquiesces and submits to the jurisdiction of enquiry committee or officer without raising any objection, he cannot be allowed to challenge such jurisdiction subsequently in a writ petition.[9] An objection as to territorial jurisdiction does not go to the root of jurisdiction and hence a judgement-debtor is not estopped from raising that objection in execution as to the validity of the decree.[10]

19. Standing By.—Where a person stands by while his right is being infringed by another, the rule of estoppel by acquiescence applies under the following conditions:—

(a) The person infringing the legal right must be mistaken as to his legal right,

(b) He must expend money or do some act on the faith of his mistaken belief,

1. *Union of India* v. *Watkins Mayor and Co.*, AIR 1966 SC 275: (1965) 2 SCWR 289: 1967 (1) SCJ 304.
2. *I.L. Honnegouda* v. *State of Karnataka*, AIR 1978 SC 28: 1977 (1) SCJ 524.
3. *Prasum Roy* v. *C.M.D.A.*, AIR 1988 SC 205: (1987) 3 SCR 569: (1987) 4 SCC 217.
4. *State of Punjab* v. *Balkaran Singh*, AIR 2007 SC 641: 2007 AIR SCW 240: 2007 (2) Civ LJ 194.
5. *Chairman, Uttar Pradesh Jal Nigam* v. *Jaswant Singh*, 2007 AIR SCW 672: AIR 2007 SC 924: 2007 (2) ALJ 242.
6. *Jai Narain Paras Rampuria* v. *Puspa Devi Saraf*, (2006) 7 SCC 756.
7. *Kalyan Peoples' Co-operative Bank Ltd. (In both the Appeals)* v. *Dulhanbibi Aqual Aminsaheb Patil*, AIR 1966 SC 1072: 1963 (2) SCJ 176: (1963) 2 SCR 348.
8. *Hiralal* v. *Kalinath*, AIR 1962 SC 199: 1961 (2) SCJ 592: (1962) 2 SCR 747; *S. Sethuraman* v. *R. Venkataraman*, AIR 2007 SC 2499: 2007 AIR SCW 4445: (2007) 6 SCC 382.
9. *National High School, Madras* v. *Education Tribunal*, AIR 1992 SC 717: 1992 Lab IC 574: 1992 AIR SCW 359.
10. *Hiralal* v. *Kalinath*, AIR 1962 SC 199: 1961 (2) SCJ 592: (1962) 2 SCR 747.

(c) The person whose right is infringed must know his own right,

(d) He must know of the mistaken belief of the person infringing his right, and

(e) He must encourage the person in his expenditure of money or other act directly or by abstaining from asserting his legal rights.[1] Where there is no mistaken belief as to ownership of land, much less any such belief known to the other side, there is no basis for the application of the equitable doctrine of estoppel.[2]

20. Estoppel by Record.—Estoppel by record results from the judgment of a competent court. This is what is provided in section 11, C.P.C.[3] There is a slightly different view expressed in another decision. The view is that the effect of the plea of *res judicata* may, in the result, operate like an estoppel by preventing a party to a litigation from denying the accuracy of the former adjudication; but doctrine of *res judicata* prohibits the court from adjudicating a matter already adjudicated upon, while estoppel prohibits a party after the enquiry has already been entered upon from proving anything which would contradict his own previous declaration or act to the prejudice of another party, who, relying on such declaration or act, altered his position.[4] Estoppel by deed is where the person sought to be estopped (or his predecessor in interest) has obtained possession of property or some advantage under the deed.[5] If the deed is fictitious, it has no legal significance and the party is not bound by the contents thereof.

21. Estoppel *in pais*.—Estoppel in pais, as it is known in modern times, arises from agreement or contract and from act or conduct of misrepresentation which has induced a change in position in accordance with the intention of the party against whom the estoppel is alleged. Sections 116 and 117 are instances of estoppel *in pais*.

22. Equitable estoppel.—Equitable estoppel rests on the principle that where a party with full knowledge or with sufficient notice or means of knowledge of his rights and of all the material facts, remains inactive or abstains from impeaching a transaction or freely does what amounts to a recognition thereof or acts in a manner inconsistent with it's repudiation so as to affect the situation of the parties so that the other party is induced to suppose that it is recognized, such conduct amounts to acquiescence.[6]

23. Legitimate (Reasonable) Expectation.—This has its genesis in administrative law. Government is expected to honour it's statements of policy or intention and cannot disregard such policy statements unfairly or apply them selectively. Doctrine of legitimate expectation was evolved in this context and it has become a source of substantive law as also procedural rights. This doctrine can be invoked if the decision which is challenged in court has some person aggrieved either by altering rights or obligations of that person which are enforceable by or against him in private law or by depriving him of some

1. *Sidde Gowda* v. *Nadakala Sidda Naika*, AIR 1952 Mys 117: ILR 1952 Mys 384.
2. *Canadian Pacific Railway Co.* v. *E.*, AIR 1932 PC 108: 138 IC 292.
3. *Sarangapani* v. *V. Narasimhacharlu*, AIR 1953 Mad 384.
4. *Sita Ram* v. *Amir Begum*, ILR (1866) 8 All 324: 1886 All WN 101.
5. *Deb Narayan Shyam* v. *State of West Bengal*, AIR 2005 SC 1167: 2005 AIR SCW 172: (2005) 2 SCC 286.
6. Ratanlal and Dhirajlal on Evidence, 23rd Edition Page 1500.

benefits or advantage which either (a) he had been permitted by the authority to enjoy or which, he can legitimately expect to be permitted to continue to do until there has been communicated to him some rational grounds for withdrawing it or which he has been given an opportunity to comment or (b) he has received assurance from the authority that it will not be done without giving him first an opportunity of advancing reasons for contending that it should not be withdraw. The question whether the expectation or claim is reasonable or legitimate, is a question of fact in each case. This question has to be decided not according to the claimant's perception but in larger public interest.[1] Public interest has to prevail over private interest.[2] The principle of legitimate exception cannot be applicable strictly to the academic courses in the field of education where needs are fast changing. In the absence of any assurance having been given by the authority, this doctrine cannot be applied.[1]

24. Declaration, Act or Omission.—Representation may be by statement or conduct. Conduct includes negligence or silence.[3] There is no estoppel if there is no representation or no change in position, or the causal connection.[4] Form of representation is immaterial. It may be express or implied.

There is no estoppel against cancellation of an appointment made on the basis of supposed qualification professed by the appointee.

Mere attestation of a deed does not involve knowledge of recitals therein. If attestation is with such knowledge of recitals, (recital being that the land belongs to the executant), the attestor may be estopped from setting up title in himself.[5] Mere attestation cannot lead to estoppel if the executant of the will knew the true position.[6] If attestation was made as an acknowledgment, there can be estoppel.

If a person stands by and allows another to advance or expend money on property on which he has a charge, he may be estopped by his conduct of acquiescence. But a duty to speak, which is the ground of liability, arises only where silence can be considered as having an active part, that of misleading. Conduct by negligence or silence, when there is duty to speak the truth, may lead to estoppel.

The representation, whatever be the form, must be clear and unambiguous.[7] It must be susceptible of only one inference. The whole of the representation must be looked into. It must be unequivocal.[8] It must be such as will be reasonably understood in a particular sense by the person to whom it is addressed.

---

1. *Nation Buildings Construction Corporation* v. *S. Raghunathan*, AIR 1998 SC 2779: 1998 Lab IC 3496: 1998 AIR SCW 2954.
2. *Union of India* v. *International Trading Co.*, (2003) 5 SCC 437: AIR 2003 SC 3983: 2003 AIR SCW 282.
3. Halsbury's Laws of England Vol. 16, Page 1069.
4. *Girindra Nath Mukherjee* v. *Soumen Mukherjee*, AIR 1988 Cal 375.
5. *Allam Gangadhara Rao* v. *Gollapalli Gangarao*, AIR 1968 AP 291: ILR 1970 AP 933; *Krishnan Govindan* v. *Chinnamma Chellamma*, AIR 1959 Ker 237: 1958 Ker LT 1062; *Raibhan Laxmanji* v. *Namdeo Punjaji*, AIR 1952 Nag 96: 1952 Ngp LJ 76.
6. *R.S. Maddanappa* v. *Chandramma*, AIR 1965 SC 1812: 1966 (2) SCJ 310: (1965) 3 SCR 283.
7. *Delhi Cloth and General Mills Ltd.* v. *Union of India*, AIR 1987 SC 2414: JT 1987 (5) 35: 1987 (3) SCJ 328: (1988) 1 SCC 86.
8. *State of Bihar* v. *B.L. Agarwalla*, AIR 1966 Pat 410.

One part, though sufficient to create an estoppel cannot be separated from another part connected with it, which takes away it's effect.[1] An ambiguous representation does not lead to estoppel.[2]

Representation must be of an existing fact and material having reference to existing or past state of things and not of mere intention.[3] A promise *defuturo* does not lead to estoppel.[4] Such a promise may give rise to equity and lead to specific performance, but not estoppel.[5] The state also comes within the range of this equity, which is different from estoppel.

Motive or intention is irrelevant. An innocent or ignorant representation also could lead to estoppel.[6]

Where plaintiff showed the value of the property in the plaint, he is not estopped from proving that the correct value is different, since there was no question of defendant changing his position.[7] Failure to raise objection to the nomination for a seat reserved for Scheduled Caste estops the other candidate from contending later that the candidate did not belong to Scheduled Caste[8] provided he knew it. The principle applies to representation of Government also.[9]

25. Intentionally.—The statement or conduct should have been intentional with the object of inducing the other party to change his position.[10] Intention must be actual or reasonably capable of being informed. Intention to deceive is not necessary. It is not necessary that the person who made the representation must have been under no mistake or misapprehension himself.[11] Motive or knowledge of the person representing is immaterial. If a sub-lessor permits sub-lessee to use the premises contrary to the conditions of the main lease, he will be estopped from ejecting sub-lessee on the ground of breach of conditions.[12] The intention must be to produce a particular state of mind in the representee.[13] Defendant should have been misled. An involuntary representation or one made under

1. *Canada & Dominion Sugar Co. Ltd.* v. *Canadian National (West Indies) Steamships Ltd.*, AIR 1947 PC 40: 1947 AC 46: (1946) 3 WWR 759.
2. *Delhi Cloth and General Mills Ltd.* v. *Union of India*, AIR 1987 SC 2414: JT 1987 (5) 35: 1987 (3) SCJ 328: (1988) 1 SCC 86.
3. *Allahabad Dist. Co-op. Ltd.* v. *Hannman Dutt Tewari*, AIR 1982 SC 120: (1981) 4 SCC 431: 1982 All LJ 50; *State of Madras* v. *Madras Electric Tramways (1904) Ltd.*, AIR 1957 Mad 169: (1957) 27 Com Cas 398; *Dawson's Bank Ltd.* v. *Nippon Menkwa Kobushiki Kaisha*, AIR 1935 PC 79: 62 IA 100: 13 R 256: 155 IC 1: 37 PLR 323.
4. *Dhiyan Singh* v. *Jugal Kishore*, AIR 1952 SC 145: 1952 SCR 478: 1952 SCJ 142.
5. *Century Spinning and Manufacturing Company Ltd.* v. *Ulhasnagar Municipal Council*, (1970) 1 SCC 582: AIR 1971 SC 1021: 1970 (2) SCJ 689: (1970) 3 SCR 854.
6. *Union of India* v. *Tarachand*, AIR 1976 MP 101: 1976 MPLJ 156: 1976 Jab LJ 457.
7. *Shrinivas Krishnarao Kango* v. *Narayan Devji Kango*, 1971 I Mys LJ 154: AIR 1971 Mys 174.
8. *Ganpat* v. *Returning Officer*, AIR 1975 SC 420: AIR 1976 SC 2381: (1977) 1 SCR 194.
9. *Union of India* v. *Indo Afghan Agencies Ltd.*, (1968) 2 SCR 366: AIR 1968 SC 718: (1968) 1 SCWR 553; *C. Beepathuma* v. *Velasari Shankararnarayana Kadambolithaya*, AIR 1965 SC 241: (1964) 5 SCR 836; *Union of India* v. *Godfrey Philips India Ltd.*, AIR 1986 SC 806: 1985 22 ELT 306: 1986 Tax LR 2002: (1985) 4 SCC 369; *Motilal Padampat Sugar Mills Co. Ltd.* v. *State of Uttar Pradesh*, AIR 1979 SC 621: 1979 (2) SCJ 185: (1979) 2 SCR 641.
10. *Imperial Bank of Canada* v. *Mary Victoria Begley*, AIR 1936 PC 193: 163 IC 295.
11. *Kamakshya Narain Singh Bahadur* v. *Baldeo Sahai*, AIR 1950 Pat 97: 27 Pat 441; *Harbans Lal Arora* v. *Divisional Supdt. Central Railway, Jhansi*, AIR 1960 All 164.
12. *Faqir Chand* v. *Shri Ram Rattan Bhanot*, AIR 1973 SC 921: (1973) 3 SCR 454.
13. *Baghel Singh* v. *Mihan Singh*, AIR 1953 Punj 171.

compulsion of law is not sufficient. The representation and action taken must be connected together as cause and effect.[1] A person who made a representation must be held to have done so intentionally, if a reasonable person would take the representation to be true and believe that it was meant that he should act upon it.[2] It is not necessary that the person making the representation must be influenced by a fraudulent intention. The determining element is not the motive nor the state of knowledge of the party making the representation, but the effect of the representation.

26. "To Believe".—The representee must believe the representation to be true. He could not believe if he knew it to be false.[3]

27. "A Thing".—A proposition of law is not a thing.

28. "To Act".—The representee must have acted on the representation.[4]

29. "Representatives".—Representatives and persons claiming gratuitous title are bound by estoppel. Privity is necessary. A stranger is not bound nor can take advantage.

30. Minor.—If a minor represents fraudulently or otherwise that he is of age, and thereby induces another to enter into a contract with him, in an action on the contract, the minor is not estopped from setting up his minority.[5] This is so because of another principle of law that a minor is not liable upon a contract nor for a wrong arising out of his action, such as misrepresentation or fraud. Rule of evidence cannot override substantive law. (Section 11 of Contract Act). Any deed executed by a minor representing as a major is a nullity and the plea of estoppel cannot be raised.[6]

But doctrine of restitution (Section 33 of Specific Relief Act) may be applicable. The minor plaintiff may be made to restore *status quo* ante in equity.[7] Section 33 has no application if the minor is a plaintiff. Decree on a minor's mortgage can be passed for foreclosure. No personal decree can be granted.

31. Corporation.—The principle applies to Corporations also. If the act undertaken was *ultra-vires* the corporation, corporation is not estopped from contending that the act is invalid. Estoppel cannot be pleaded against Municipality against taxes fixed under statute.[8] Municipality has no power to

---

1. *Ramankulangare Illath Narayan Nambi* v. *Pilavil Illath Sankaran Nambi*, AIR 1937 Mad 158.
2. *Sarat Chunder Dey* v. *Gopal Chunder Laha*, ILR (1893) 20 Cal 296 19 Ind App 203 (PC).
3. *Canada & Dominion Sugar Co. Ltd.* v. *Canadian National (West Indies) Steamships Ltd.*, AIR 1947 PC 40: 1947 AC 46: (1946) 3 WWR 759; *Kalloo Gaji Bahna* v. *Rishab Kumar*, AIR 1951 Nag 347: 1951 NLJ 544: ILR 1951 Nag 909; *John Agabog Vertannes* v. *James Goldar Robinson*, AIR 1927 PC 151: 54 IA 276: 5 R 427: 102 IC 639; *Kishori Lal* v. *Collector of Etah*, AIR 1934 PC 83; *Swaminadha Aiyar* v. *Swaminatha Aiyar*, AIR 1927 Mad 458: 99 Ind Cas 772; *Jai Prakash Sinha* v. *The Chairman, Bihar School Examination Board*, AIR 1976 Pat 301; *P.C. Goswami* v. *Collector of Darrang*, AIR 1982 SC 1214: (1982) 1 SCC 439: (1982) 2 APLJ (SC) 29; *R.S. Maddanappa* v. *Chandramma*, AIR 1965 SC 1812: 1966 (2) SCJ 310: (1965) 3 SCR 283; *Sales Tax Officer, Banaras* v. *Kanhaiya Lal Mukund Lal Saraf*, AIR 1959 SC 135: 1959 SCJ 53: 1959 SCR 1350.
4. *Rukmini Debi* v. *Mihir Bala Sarkar*, AIR 1977 Cal 161: 81 Cal WN 481: (1977) 1 Cal LJ 125; *R.S. Maddanappa* v. *Chandramma*, AIR 1965 SC 1812: 1966 (2) SCJ 310: (1965) 3 SCR 283; *Mahindra and Mahindra Ltd.* v. *Union of India*, AIR 1979 SC 798: (1979) 2 SCC 529: (1979) 2 SCR 1038; *Hem Nolini Judah* v. *Isolyne Sarojsbashini Bose*, AIR 1962 SC 1471: 1962 All LJ 695: ILR 1962 2 All 683.
5. *Mohiri Bibi* v. *Dhatmodas Ghosh*, (1903) 30 Ind App 114: ILR 30 Cal 539 (PC).
6. *Sadiq Ali Khan* v. *Jai Kishori*, AIR 1928 PC 152: 55 Mad LJ 88.
7. *Johri* v. *Mahila Draupati*, AIR 1991 MP 340: 1991 MPLJ 217.
8. *Maritime Electric Co. Ltd.* v. *General Diaries Ltd.*, 1937 AC 610: AIR 1937 PC 114: 168 IC 616.

grant sanction for building contrary to bylaws; but it would be estopped from withdrawing sanction and requiring demolition.

32. State.—There can be estoppel against State.[1] There is no estoppel against Legislature.[2] Pursuant to an agreement between the Government and a private company, the latter set up plant in a piece of land (on invitation to set up industries). Government had assured them supply of raw material. Subsequently, an Act was passed which obliterated the company's rights and enabled Government to get out of its commitment. Such a subsequent taking away was not permissible by reason of estoppel.[3] Estoppel applies to administrative actions. This principle does not apply at the level of Government policy.[4] The fact that at one time Government disclaimed its rights in minerals does not deprive it of its title. A letter written by an officer which is not in consonance with the subsequent Government direction would not affect the position of the Government nor create estoppel against it.[5] Where a person claiming to be owner of land with trees on it, obtained permission to fell trees, if he is found to be not the owner, Government is not estopped from claiming the value of trees from him. Both acted under mistake.[6] A person who has consented to an agreement can plead that it is a nullity being opposed to public policy.[7] A statutory obligation of an unconditional character cannot be defeated by a plea of estoppel.[8]

33. Principal and Agent.—A person may be estopped by reason of his agent's misrepresentation. But the act of the agent must be within the scope of his agency. (*See* Section 237 of Contract Act). Law recognizes agency by conduct, by estoppel, that is, where the principal allows another to transact with third parties on his behalf and makes them believe that the person is transacting with them on his behalf, he is bound by the acts of the ostensible agent.[9]

If an agent is held out as having limited authority, any person dealing with him does so at his own risk. If the latter was led to believe honestly in the existence of the authority to the extent apparent to him, the principal will be liable. A fraud by the agent acting within the scope of his authority makes the principal liable.

---

1. *Collector of Bombay* v. *Municipal Corpn.*, AIR 1951 SC 469: 1951 SCJ 752: 54 Bom LR 122.
2. *G.H.C. Ariff* v. *Jadunath Majumdar Bahadur*, AIR 1931 PC 79: 58 IA 91; *Commissioner of Income-tax* v. *B.N. Bhattachaijee*, AIR 1979 SC 1725: (1979) 3 SCR 1133: 1979 UPTC 1244: (1979) 4 SCC 121; *Vij Resins Pvt. Ltd.* v. *State of Jammu and Kashmir*, AIR 1989 SC 1629: (1989) 3 SCC 115.
3. *Vij Resins Pvt. Ltd.* v. *State of Jammu and Kashmir*, AIR 1989 SC 1629: (1989) 3 SCC 115; *Rose Educational, Scientific and Cultural Society* v. *D.D.A.*, AIR 1990 Del 75: 1989 (38) DLT 344: (1989) 17 DRJ 132.
4. *K. Ram Mohan Rao* v. *Endowments Commissioner in Karnataka, Bangalore*, AIR 1989 Kant 192: ILR 1989 Kant 3289.
5. *Vijaya Bank* v. *Kishore Chandra Chandulal Patel*, AIR 1987 SC 1790: 1987 Guj LH 37.
6. *Rajkumar Rajindra Singh* v. *H.P. Administration*, AIR 1964 HP 19; *Rai Sunil Kumar Mitra* v. *Thakur Singh*, AIR 1984 Pat 80: 1984 Pat LJR 140: 1984 BLJ 134; *P.C. Goswami* v. *Collector of Darrang*, AIR 1982 SC 1214: (1982) 1 SCC 439: (1982) 2 APLJ (SC) 29.
7. *Union Carbide Corpn.* v. *Union of India*, JT 1991 (6) SC 8: (1991) 4 SCC 584: AIR 1992 SC 248.
8. *State of Kerala* v. *Gwalior Rayon Silk Manufacturing (Wvg.) Co. Ltd.*, AIR 1973 SC 2734: (1973) 2 SCC 713: (1974) 1 SCR 671; *Maritime Electric Co. Ltd.* v. *General Diaries Ltd.*, 1937 AC 610: AIR 1937 PC 114: 168 IC 616.
9. *Moosa Bhoy* v. *Kristiah*, AIR 1952 Hyd 79: ILR 1952 Hyd 341.

Where a person purported to act on his own behalf, he cannot subsequently say he acted as an agent of another. An agent who acted so, also cannot deny his agency.

Implied agency is real or actual authority. Agency by estoppel is not real but only apparent authority.

34. Partners.—*See* section 28 of Indian Partnership Act. A person who holds himself out as partner or allows others to use his name, is a partner by estoppel.

If one partner referred a dispute to arbitrator and other partners who knew it did not come forward to object till the passing of the award, they are estopped from challenging the award on the ground of want of authority.[1]

35. Trustee.—A person who entered possession as a trustee cannot dispute the validity of the trust.[2] An estoppel may be personal to the trustee and not apply to the trust. Ex. Trustees of a private temple under Government management who later accepted posts of temple servants, are estopped from contending that the temple was a denominational one or that they had right to be in management of the temple.[3]

36. Family Arrangement.—Family arrangement may give rise to estoppel. This is so, provided the parties to the case were parties to the arrangement or acted on it or derived some benefit from it and it should have been an honest settlement of an existing dispute. It will hold good even if the parties had misunderstood their situation and mistaken their rights.[4] The consenting parties will be estopped from repudiating it. An arrangement regarding a future right (reversionary right) does not give rise to estoppel. Settlement of doubtful claims or what the parties regarded as doubtful, without worry, fight and expense forms the consideration. Reversioners who joined a partition even during the life time of the widow, believing that reversion had opened and they had right to partition and enjoyed the shares, are estopped from disputing the partition. A presumptive reversioner has only a *spes-successionis* and he may elect to stand by or ratify the alienations by the widow in which case he would be estopped from challenging the same later.[5] Compromise by which widow obtained a part of property absolutely and reversioner immediately obtained a part, estops both from challenging the same thereafter. Minor who on attaining majority, ratifies or acquiesces in a transaction is estopped from challenging it.[6] Where under a family arrangement defendant recognised plaintiff's right under her husband's Will, he cannot be allowed to plead the husband's incompetence to make the Will. Where a father and sons entered into an arrangement to settle a family dispute and even the normal succession was altered, any party to the arrangement cannot later challenge its' legality.[7] Parties taking advantage under

1. *Parmeshwar Lal and Co.* v. *Jai Narain*, AIR 1952 Pun 373.
2. *Pichai Pillai* v. *Lingam Iyer*, AIR 1928 Mad 268: 108 Ind Cas 199.
3. *Nellor Marthandam Vellalar* v. *Commissioner, Hindu Religious and Charitable Endowments*, AIR 2003 SC 4225: 2003 AIR SCW 3925: (2003) 10 SCC 712.
4. *Martin. Cashirt* v. *Peter J. Cashin*, AIR 1938 PC 103: 1939 Mad WN 85: 182 Ind Cas 419.
5. *Seetharamayya* v. *Sarva Chandrayya*, AIR 1955 Andhra 68: (1954) 2 Mad LJ (Andh) 162: 1954 Andh LT (Civil) 135; *S. Shanmugam Pillai* v. *K. Shanmugam Pillai*, AIR 1972 SC 2069: (1973) 2 SCC 312: (1973) 1 SCR 570.
6. *Seetharamayya* v. *Sarva Chandrayya*, AIR 1955 Andhra 68: (1954) 2 Mad LJ (Andh) 162: 1954 Andh LT (Civil) 135.
7. *Chinnathayi* v. *Kulasekara Pandiya Naicker*, AIR 1952 SC 29: 1952 SCJ 1: 1952 SCR 241.

a family settlement cannot resile from it on the ground that the document is not registered.[1] A lady who was married pursuant to some arrangement between her father and father-in-law settling some property on her was given relief on the ground of promissory estoppel.[2] A sharer who sold the property allotted to him under a partition deed and utilized the proceeds for himself cannot challenge the partition deed as nominal.[3]

If a defective notice to quit is accepted by the tenant, he is estopped from challenging his notice.[4] When a judgment-debtor requested court not to advertise sale in newspaper, he is estopped from challenging sale on the ground for want of paper publication.[5] A person who submits himself to the jurisdiction of a forum cannot challenge jurisdiction later.[6] If it is a case of total lack of jurisdiction, it can be raised. If parties to a eviction petition refrain from adducing evidence and persuade the court to pass order on agreement, they are estopped from raising the question in a second application.[7] Where a cheque is sent in full settlement of all dues and the creditor accepts and realises it, he is estopped from claiming anything more.[8]

37. Recitals in Deeds.—Recitals in deeds are in some cases conclusive and in all cases evidence against the parties to the deeds and those who claim under them. If a document clearly showed division of right, its construction cannot be controlled by subsequent conduct.[9] If an arrangement was deliberately made and parties acted upon it, and if recitals are made in the deed on the faith of which the other parties acted, the parties cannot go behind the recitals. A unilateral statement by vendor in sale deed cannot estop the vendee.

A recital in a document is a statement made deliberately and is always evidence against the parties but not against third parties.[10] Where a recital in a deed stated that the land was of a particular category and the parties dealt with on that basis, it is not open to the parties to resile from that position. Where the executant stated that he was the exclusive owner of the property and entitled to execute the document, he cannot later contend that he had no right to execute the same.[11]

Absence of knowledge is not an element in section 43 of T.P. Act.[12] Rule of estoppel is also basic to section 53A of T.P. Act.

1. *Kale* v. *Deputy Director of Consolidation*, AIR 1976 SC 807: (1976) 2 All LR 173: (1976) 3 SCC 119.
2. *N.A. Md. Kasim* v. *Sulochana*, 1995 AIR SCW 2557: AIR 1995 SC 1624: 1995 Supp (3) SCC 128.
3. *Azeez Sait* v. *Aman Bai*, AIR 2003 SC 444: 2003 AIR SCW 5106: (2003) 12 SCC 419.
4. *Dipak Kumar Ghosh* v. *Mira Sen*, AIR 1987 SC 759: (1987) 1 SCC 562: 1987 (1) SCJ 478.
5. *Karnataka Bank Ltd., Bangalore* v. *K. Shamanna*, AIR 1972 Mys 321: (1972) 2 Mys LJ 20.
6. *Nadia District Bus Owners Association* v. *District Magistrate, Nadia*, AIR 1969 Cal 458: 1964 (2) SCJ 518: (1964) 2 SCR 310.
7. *Pulavarthi Venkata Subba Rao* v. *Valluri Jagannadha Rao*, AIR 1967 SC 591: 1964 (2) SCJ 518: (1964) 2 SCR 310; *Autar Singh* v. *Sohan Lal*, AIR 1970 J&K 26: 1969 Kash LJ 238 (FB).
8. *Bhuban Chandra Sadhukhan* v. *Biswanath Dey*, AIR 1962 Cal 34: 65 CWN 437: ILR (1961) 2 Cal 389.
9. *Venkatapathi Raju* v. *Venkatanarasimha Raju*, AIR 1936 PC 264: 63 Ind App 397: ILR 1937 Mad 1.
10. *Darisi Masthanamma* v. *Mandiga Rama Krishna*, AIR 2006 AP 286: 2006 AIHC 334 NOC: 2007 (1) Civ LJ 123.
11. *Lakshmi Devi* v. *Kala Devi*, AIR 1977 All 509: (1978) 2 Ren CR 579.
12. *Veeraswami* v. *Durga Venkata Subbarao*, AIR 1957 AP 288: 1956 Andh WR 1115.

38. Fundamental Rights.—Rule of estoppel cannot apply in respect of fundamental rights.[1] There can be no estoppel against the Constitution.[2]

39. Criminal Trials.—Accused is not estopped in the matter of raising defences. He can plead several defences.[3] Absence of specific defence cannot be a ground for conviction. Estoppel is a rule of civil action and has no application in criminal cases, though in such a case, it would be prejudicial to set up a different story.

40. Feeding the Grant.—This phrase means that where a grantor has purported to grant interest in land which he did not at the time possess, but subsequently acquired the land, the benefit of such subsequent acquisition ensures to the benefit of the earlier grantee.[4] This principle received partial recognition in section 43 of Transfer of Property Act, 1882.

41. Section 41 of Transfer of Property Act.—Section 41 of T.P. Act is similar in principle to section 115 of Evidence Act. When an owner transfers property with apparent ownership and right of disposition, he would be estopped from claiming title against a person to whom his original transferee disposed of the property and who took it in good faith and for consideration.[5] Section 41 will not apply if the transferee had not taken care to ascertain the transferor's title and where ostensible owner was not in possession with the consent of the real owner.[6]

42. Section 53 of the T.P. Act provides for estoppel between the transferor and the transferee which has no operation against third parties who do not claim under those parties.[7]

43. Promissory Estoppel.—When one party has by his words or conduct made to the other a clear and unequivocal promise or assurance which is intended to affect legal relations between them and to be acted accordingly, then once the other party has taken him at his word and acted on it, the promisor cannot be allowed to revert to their previous legal relations as if no promise had been made.[8]

This doctrine is based on equity and fairness in action and not on any vested right. In equity, court has to strike a balance between individual rights and larger public interest. Freedom to contract is a common law right enjoyed by all; but when the Government is contracting with private parties, this freedom is circumscribed by the principles of administrative law which requires larger public interest to be taken into account.[9] But a person who has himself misled the authority by making a false statement cannot invoke this doctrine, if his

1. *State of Maharashtra* v. *Mahalaxmi Stores*, AIR 1986 SC 180; *Basheshwar Nath* v. *Commissioner of Income Tex*, AIR 1959 SC 149: 1959 (35) ITR 190: 1959 SCJ 1207; *Behram Khurshid Pesikaka* v. *State of Bombay*, AIR 1955 SC 123: 1955 SCR 613: 1955 SCJ 73.
2. *Air India* v. *Nergesh Meerza*, AIR 1981 SC 1829: 1981 Lab IC 1313: (1981) 4 SCC 335.
3. *Daungarshi Madanlal Zunzunwala* v. *Deviprasad Omprakash Bajoria*, 1985 Cr LJ 1943.
4. *Renu Devi* v. *Mahendra Singh*, AIR 2003 SC 1608: 2003 AIR SCW 993: (2003) 10 SCC 200.
5. *Listi Shi* v. *Pong Tsoi Ching*, AIR 1935 PC 208: 159 IC 794.
6. *Mahommed Shafi* v. *Mahommed Said*, AIR 1930 All 847: 52 All 248.
7. *S.N. Banerji* v. *K.L. and S. Co.*, AIR 1941 PC 128: ILR (1941) Kar PC 150.
8. Halsbury's Laws of England, 4th Edition, Vol. 16, Page 1017.
9. *M.P. Mathur* v. *DTC*, AIR 2007 SC 414: 2006 AIR SCW 6320: (2006) 12 SCALE 446; *Sharma Transport* v. *Govt. of U.P.*, (2002) 2 SCC 188: AIR 2002 SC 322: 2001 AIR SCW 4958; *Baunari Amman Sugars Ltd.* v. *C.T.O.*, (2005) 1 SCC 625.

misrepresentation misled the authority into taking a decision which on discovery of the misrepresentation, is sought to be cancelled.[1]

In the words of Lord Denning – "A man must keep his word. All the more so when the promise is not a bare promise but is made with the intention that the other party should act upon it. Just as a contract is different from tort and estoppel, so also in the sphere now under discussion, promises may give rise to a different equity from other conduct".[2]

The difference may lie in the necessity of showing detriment where one party deliberately promises to waive, modify or discharge his strict legal rights, intending the other party to act on the faith of the promise, and the other party actually does act on it, then it is contrary not only to equity but also to good faith, to allow the promisor to go back on his promise. It should not be necessary for the other party to show that he acted to his detriment in reliance on the promise. It should be sufficient that he acted on it.[3] According to Lord Denning, this principle does not create cause of action where none existed before and it only prevents a party from insisting upon his strict legal rights, when it would be unjust to allow him to enforce them, having regard to the dealings which have taken place between them.[4] The doctrine of promissory estoppel as laid down in the English cases has been applied in India.[5]

44. The promise must be clear and unequivocal.[6] It is not necessary that the promisee should suffer detriment; it is enough that he acts on the representation and alters his position.[7] The doctrine does not apply where there is a concluded contract between the parties. If the assurance was conditional and the conditions were not fulfilled, the doctrine will not apply. The doctrine should not be reduced to a rule of the thumb.[8] The doctrine is based on the conduct of the party making a representation to the other so as to enable him to arrange his affairs in such a manner as if the said representation would be acted upon. It provides a cause of action and need not necessarily a defence.[9]

45. The following principles have to be borne in mind:—

(a) The legislature cannot be precluded from exercising its' functions to legislate by invoking this doctrine.

(b) The doctrine can be invoked against Government or public authority subject to the following:—

(i) It cannot be invoked to compel the authority to act contrary to the obligation or liability imposed by law.

1. *Central Airmen Selection Board* v. *Surender Kumar Das*, AIR 2003 SC 240: 2002 AIR SCW 4693: JT 2002 (9) SC 401.
2. Modern Law Review, Vol. 15.
3. *Sharma Transport* v. *Government of Uttar Pradesh*, (2002) 2 SCC 188: AIR 2002 SC 322: 2001 AIR SCW 4958.
4. *Combe* v. *Combe*, (1951) 2 KB 215: (1951) 1 All ER 767.
5. *Seth Satnarain* v. *Union of India*, (1968) 2 SCWR 335.
6. *M. Raja* v. *Ceri Educational Society Pilani*, (2006) 2 SCC 636.
7. *Motilal Padampat Sugar Mills Co. Ltd.* v. *State of Uttar Pradesh*, AIR 1979 SC 621: 1979 (2) SCJ 185: (1979) 2 SCR 641; *Delhi Cloth and General Mills Ltd.* v. *Union of India*, AIR 1987 SC 2414: JT 1987 (5) 35: 1987 (3) SCJ 328: (1988) 1 SCC 86.
8. *State of Himachal Pradesh* v. *Ganesh Wood Products*, AIR 1996 SC 149: JT 1995 (6) SC 485: (1995) 6 SCC 363.
9. *L.M.L. Ltd.* v. *State of Uttar Pradesh*, AIR 2008 SC 1032: 2008 AIR SCW 599: (2008) 3 SCC 128.

(ii) The doctrine, if it is established on the facts and circumstances of the case, and if it would be inequitable in the larger public interest to hold the authority to the promise or representation made by it, it will not be enforced.

(iii) The doctrine cannot be invoked when the representation made by the authority is beyond it's powers.

(iv) The doctrine cannot be invoked if it is shown that the representation was obtained by playing fraud.

46. The doctrine is attracted where a person alters his position pursuant to the promise made by the state to grant tax concessions. Such a policy decision shall be expressed under notifications issued under statutory provisions or executive instructions.[1] Executive necessity cannot release the Government from honouring its' solemn promises relying on which citizens have acted.[2] Where a company acted upon the permission granted by the minister in charge in conformity with the master plan with the concurrence of the Delhi Development Authority and constructed a substantial building, it cannot be contended that the minister's order was illegal, improper or invalid.[3] Where the State Government held out certain specific promises as inducement for its' employees to move into a newly created department, and the employees having believed such representations and having acted upon thereon, could not be denied rights and benefits promised to them.[4] Where the state, through its officers who have power to convey appropriate offers, made representations to exempt or abolish a commodity as a taxable commodity, the Government cannot be allowed to go back on its' promise.[5] The doctrine is not based on loss or detriment, but upon alteration of position in response to a representation.[6] Where a customs circular stated that demurrage did not form part of assessment value of imported goods, the same was held binding on the department.[7]

47. Even under section 115, it is open to a party who acted on a representation made by the Government to claim that the latter shall be bound to carry out the promise made by it.[8] Where an incentive was offered to set up an industry

1. *Southern Petrochemical Industries Co. Ltd.* v. *Electricity Inspector and E.T.I.O.*, AIR 2007 SC 1884: 2007 AIR SCW 3752: (2007) 5 SCC 447; *L.M.L. Ltd.* v. *State of Uttar Pradesh*, AIR 2008 SC 1032: 2008 AIR SCW 599: (2008) 3 SCC 128.
2. *Union of India* v. *Indo Afghan Agencies Ltd.*, (1968) 2 SCR 366: AIR 1968 SC 718: (1968) 1 SCWR 553.
3. *Express Newspapers Pvt. Ltd.* v. *Union of India*, AIR 1986 SC 872: (1986) 1 SCC 133: 1986 (29) DLT 131.
4. *Bhim Singh* v. *State of Haryana*, AIR 1980 SC 768: 1980 UJ (SC) 829.
5. *Tata Iron and Steel Co. Ltd.* v. *State of Jharkhand*, (2005) 4 SCC 272: AIR 2005 SC 2871: 2005 AIR SCW 1781.
6. *Motilal Padampat Sugar Mills Co. Ltd.* v. *State of Uttar Pradesh*, AIR 1979 SC 621: 1979 (2) SCJ 185: (1979) 2 SCR 641; *Vividh Marbles Pvt. Ltd.* v. *Commercial Tax Officer*, AIR 2007 SC 861: AIR 2007 SC (Supp) 841; *Uttar Pradesh Power Corpn. Ltd.* v. *Sant Steel and Alloys (P) Ltd.*, 2007 (14) SCALE 36: AIR 2008 SC 693: 2007 AIR SCW 7814; *Union of India* v. *Godfrey Philips India Ltd.*, AIR 1986 SC 806: 1985 22 ELT 306: 1986 Tax LR 2002: (1985) 4 SCC 369.
7. *Commissioner of Customs* v. *Indian Oil Corporation Ltd*, AIR 2004 SC 2799: 2004 AIR SCW 1310: (2004) 3 SCC 488.
8. *Union of India* v. *Indo Afghan Agencies Ltd.*, (1968) 2 SCR 366: AIR 1968 SC 718: (1968) 1 SCWR 553; *Ashok Kumar Maheshwari (Dr.)* v. *State of Uttar Pradesh*, (1998) 2 SCC 502: 1998 AIR SCW 729: AIR 1998 SC 966: (1998) 2 Supreme 100; *State of Orissa* v. *Mangalam Timber Products Ltd.*, (2004) 1 SCC 139: AIR 2004 SC 297: 2003 AIR SCW 6130.

and accordingly a person set up such an industry, Government could not go back on its' promise.[1] Minister's statement in the legislative does not amount to a promise or representation by Government.[2] But where an Industrial Unit failed to obtain benefit of exemption owing to its own acts of omission and commission, no such benefit can be given.[3] It has been clarified that though the doctrine of promissory estoppel has been so called in judgments and text books and it has been described as "equitable estoppel" "*quasi* estoppel", or "new estoppel" it is not really based on the principle of estoppel, but it is a doctrine evolved by equity in order to prevent injustice where a promise was made by a person knowing that it would be acted upon by the person to whom it was made and in fact it was so acted upon and it is inequitable to allow the party making the promise to go back on it. There is no justification to say that this doctrine should not be allowed to found a cause of action if in order to satisfy the equity, it is necessary to do so. (*Ibid*)

48. SECTION 116.—No tenant of immovable property, or person claiming through such tenant, shall, during the continuance of the tenancy, be permitted to deny that the landlord of such tenant had, at the beginning of the tenancy, a title to such immovable property; and no licensee of the person in possession thereof, shall be permitted to deny that such person had title to such possession at the time when such license was given.

49. This is an instance of estoppel by agreement based on principle of approbate and reprobate.[4] The estoppel under this section is against denial of landlord's title "at the commencement of tenancy". It is open to tenant, even without surrendering possession, to show that after the date of tenancy, landlord's title came to an end or he was evicted by paramount title.[5]

The section applies even where the lease itself discloses defect in title.[6] There is no bar against the denial of derivative title of somebody who claims under the original lessor. There is no estoppel where tenant has restored possession by surrender. If there has been attornment to a derivative title-holder, this Section applies unless the attornment was by mistake, misrepresentation, fraud

---

1. *Motilal Padampat Sugar Mills Co. Ltd.* v. *State of Uttar Pradesh*, AIR 1979 SC 621: 1979 (2) SCJ 185: (1979) 2 SCR 641; *Gujarat State Financial Corporation* v. *Lotus Hotels Pvts. Ltd.*, AIR 1983 SC 848: (1983) 3 SCC 379: (1983) 2 SCWR 144; *State of Punjab* v. *Nestle India Ltd.*, AIR 2004 SC 4559: 2004 AIR SCW 3703: (2004) 6 SCC 465; *Mahabir Vegetable Oils (P) Ltd.* v. *State of Haryana*, (2006) 3 SCC 620: 2006 AIR SCW 1500; *Tandon Brothers* v. *State of West Bengal*, AIR 2001 SC 1866: 2001 AIR SCW 1521: (2001) 5 SCC 664.
2. *Union of India* v. *Ganesh Rice Mills*, (1998) 9 SCC 630: JT 1998 (9) SC 51; *State of Karnataka* v. *K.K. Mohandas*, AIR 2007 SC 2917: 2007 AIR SCW 5311: (2007) 6 SCC 484.
3. *A.P. Steel Re-Rolling Mill Ltd.* v. *State of Kerala*, AIR 2007 SC 797: 2007 AIR SCW 501: (2007) 2 SCC 725; *Motilal Padampat Sugar Mills Co. Ltd.* v. *State of Uttar Pradesh*, AIR 1979 SC 621: 1979 (2) SCJ 185: (1979) 2 SCR 641.
4. *Pal Singh* v. *Sunder Singh*, AIR 1989 SC 758: (1989) 1 SCC 444: JT 1989 (1) SC 67.
5. *Kumar Krishna Prasad Lal Singh Deo* v. *Baraboni Coal Concern Ltd.*, AIR 1937 PC 251: 63 IA 311: ILR 1938 IC 1; *Jitendra Nath Roy Chaudhury* v. *Narendra Kumar Karforma*, AIR 1988 Cal 392: (1988) 1 Cal HN 316: (1988) 92 Cal WN 956; *D. Satyanarayan* v. *P. Jagadish*, AIR 1987 SC 2192: (1987) 4 SCC 424: JT 1987 (3) SC 571; *Mangat Ram* v. *Sardar Meharban Singh*, AIR 1987 SC 1656: (1987) 4 SCC 319: JT 1987 (3) SC 571; *Seth Fida Hussain* v. *Fazal Hussain*, AIR 1963 MP 232: 1963 MPLJ 248: ILR 1964 MP 623; *Tej Bhan Madan* v. *II Additional District Judge*, AIR 1988 SC 1413: (1988) 3 SCC 137.
6. *Currimbhay and Co. Ltd.* v. *L.A. Creet*, AIR 1933 PC 29: 60 Ind App 297; *Kumar Krishna Prasad Lal Singh Deo* v. *Baraboni Coal Concern Ltd.*, AIR 1937 PC 251: 63 IA 311: ILR 1938 IC 1.

or *bona fide* ignorance.[1] Principle of the section is explained.[2] A tenant cannot acquire by prescription a permanent right of occupancy in derogation of the title of the landlord by mere assertion of such a right to the knowledge of the landlord.[3] Tenant cannot set up adverse possession until he has first surrendered possession. Where landlord accepted rent after notice to quit, he cannot contend that the lessee had no interest in the land.[4] Where a tenant paid rent to the landlord, he cannot deny the latter's right.[5] But payment by mistake does not lead to estoppel.

50. Immovable Property.—The section applies only to tenants and licensees of immovable property. Enjoyment of such property by permission is the basis of the bar. If the tenant has not been put in possession, the bar does not apply.[6]

The Section presupposes a tenancy. Tenant can plead mistake or fraud etc. As long as lease has not been proved, this section does not apply. Where the tenant purchases absolute interest in a part of the property, with reference to that share, he is entitled to enforce his rights against the lessor. If the lease is void, there is no estoppel.[7]

The section applies to representatives of tenant also.[8]

51. Mortgage.—The same principle applies between mortgagor and mortgagee, unless the mortgagee has acquired title by adverse possession or the mortgage is void.[9] Similarly, mortgagor is also estopped from derogating from the grant. Once a mortgage always a mortgage.

52. Continuance of Tenancy.—Estoppel is confined to the period during the continuance of tenancy, that is, if possession was received by or under the tenancy in question. Even if the landlord's title is defective, it continues till the restoration of possession.[10] This is so, except to the extent already noticed. Even symbolical possession delivered through court in execution of an *ex parte* decree obtained against the landlord terminates possession. If in that case the tenant attorns to the decree-holder, he is not precluded from denying his old landlord's title.[11]

1. *Jitendra Nath Roy Chaudhury* v. *Narendra Kumar Karforma*, AIR 1988 Cal 392: (1988) 1 Cal HN 316: (1988) 92 Cal WN 956.
2. *Subhash Chandra* v. *Mohammad Sharif*, AIR 1990 SC 636.
3. *Atyam Veerraju* v. *Pechetti Venkanna*, AIR 1966 SC 629: (1966) 1 SCR 831: 1967 (1) SCJ 17; *Sri Ram Pasricha* v. *Jagannath*, AIR 1976 SC 2335: (1976) 4 SCC 184: (1977) 1 SCR 395.
4. *Narendra Bahadur Tandon* v. *Shankar Lal*, AIR 1980 SC 575: (1980) 2 SCR 821: (1980) 2 SCC 253: 1967 All 405.
5. *Tej Bhan Madan* v. *II Additional District Judge*, AIR 1988 SC 1413: (1988) 3 SCC 137.
6. *Kumar Krishna Prasad Lal Singh Deo* v. *Baraboni Coal Concern Ltd.*, AIR 1937 PC 251: 63 IA 311: ILR 1938 IC 1 *see* Contra AIR 1917 Mad 789 (2) (FB).
7. *Shamsher Bahadur* v. *State of Uttar Pradesh*, AIR 1964 All 395.
8. *P.G. Venkataswamy* v. *Mir Zahid Hussain Saheb (Sha)*, AIR 1973 Mys 145.
9. *C. Krishnamurthy Setty* v. *Abdul Khadar*, AIR 1956 Mys 14: ILR 1955 Mys 562; *N. Nanjappa* v. *Siddiah*, AIR 1973 Mys 28; *Venkategowda* v. *Shivanegowda*, 1990 (1) Ker LJ 134.
10. *Sant Lal Jain* v. *Avtar Singh*, AIR 1985 SC 857: 1985 2 SCC 332: 1985 UJ (SC) 609; *Bhogadi Kannababu* v. *Vuggina Pydamma*, AIR 2006 SC 2403: 2006 AIR SCW 3052: (2006) 5 SCC 532; *Currimbhoy and Co. Ltd.* v. *L.A. Creet*, AIR 1933 PC 29: 60 Ind App 297; *Chandrika Prasada* v. *Bombay Baroda and Central India Rly. Co.*, AIR 1935 PC 59: 39 Cal WN 552: 154 Ind Cas 945 (PC); *State Bank of India* v. *M. Selvaraj Daniel*, AIR 1966 SC 1654: (1964) 1 Lab LJ 29: (1966) 3 SCR 280; *Vashu Deo* v. *Bal Kishan*, AIR 2002 SC 569: 2002 AIR SCW 152: (2002) 2 SCC 50; *J.J. Lal Pvt. Ltd.* v. *M.R. Murali*, AIR 2002 SC 1061: 2002 AIR SCW 794: (2002) 3 SCC 98.
11. *Adyanath Ghatak* v. *Krishna Prasad Singh*, AIR 1949 PC 124.

53. "At the Beginning of the Tenancy".—The estoppel relates to title at that point of time. Title can be derived at a time prior to such commencement or subsequent thereto.[1]

If a person in possession attorns to another, the section applies as between them.[2]

54. Licensee.—The principle applies to a case of a person coming into possession with permission as a licensee.[3]

55. Section 116 is not exhaustive and does not deal with all kinds of estoppel which might arise between a landlord and his tenant.[2]

56. SECTION 117.—No acceptor of a bill of exchange shall be permitted to deny that the drawer had authority to draw such bill or to endorse it; nor shall any bailee or licensee be permitted to deny that his bailor or licensor had, at the time when the bailment or license commenced, authority to make such bailment or grant such license.

Explanation (1).—The acceptor of a bill of exchange may deny that the bill was really drawn by the person by whom it purports to have been drawn.

Explanation (2).—If a bailor delivers the goods bailed to a person other than the bailor, he may prove that such a person had a right to them as against the bailor.

57. Bill of Exchange.—An acceptor of a bill of exchange cannot deny that the drawer had authority to draw such bill or to endorse it, though he may deny that the bill was really drawn by the person by whom it purports to have been drawn. Under section 41 of N.I. Act, an acceptor is bound by a forged endorsement even if he knew or had reason to believe the endorsement as forged. According to section 42 of N.I. Act, an acceptor is liable though the bill is drawn in a fictitious name. Section 120 of N.I. Act says that maker of a promissory note, a drawer of a bill of exchange or cheque and acceptor of a bill of exchange for the honour of the drawer are, in a suit by the holder in due course, estopped from denying the validity of the instrument as originally made or drawn. Section 121 of that Act says that a maker of a promissory note and an acceptor of a bill of exchange payable to, or to the order of, a specified person are, in a suit by the holder in due course estopped from denying the payees' capacity at the date of the note or bill to endorse the same. According to section 122, an endorsee of a negotiable instrument is, in a suit thereon by a subsequent holder, estopped from denying the signature or capacity to contract of any prior party to the instrument. Section 26 of the Paper Currency Act says that a hundi made payable to bearer on demand is invalid and an endorsor of such a hundi is not estopped as against the endorsee from setting up it's invalidity. In an action on a bill of exchange or a promissory note against a

1. *India Electric Works Ltd.* v. *B.S. Mantosh*, AIR 1956 Cal 148: ILR (1957) 2 Cal 613; *Udaypratap Singh Deo* v. *Krushna Padhano*, AIR 1952 Ori 95; *Guruswami Nadar* v. *Ranganathan*, (1953) 2 MLJ 511: AIR 1954 Mad 402: ILR 1954 Mad 341; *Bobbili Gowresu* v. *Kottu Subhadramma*, AIR 1957 AP 961: 1956 Andh WR 1090; *Kumar Krishna Prasad Lal Singh Deo* v. *Baraboni Coal Concern Ltd.*, AIR 1937 PC 251: 63 IA 311: ILR 1938 IC 1; *S.A.A. Annamalai Chettiar* v. *Molaiyan*, AIR 1970 Mad 396: (1970) 2 Mad LJ 562: 1969 Ren CR 1114.
2. *Kumar Krishna Prasad Lal Singh Deo* v. *Baraboni Coal Concern Ltd.*, AIR 1937 PC 251: 63 IA 311: ILR 1938 IC 1.
3. *Bansraj Laltaprasad Mishra* v. *Stanley Parker Jones*, (2006) 3 SCC 91: AIR 2006 SC 3569: 2006 AIR SCW 1073.

person whose name properly appears as a party to the instrument, it is not open either by way of claim or defence to say that the signatory was in reality acting for an undisclosed principal. There is nothing in sections 24 to 26 of the N.I. Act to support any contention to the contrary.[1]

58. Bailee or licensee.—The bailee and licensee are put in the same position as a tenant in Section 115. The bailee is protected by the bailor's title as long as any better title is not advanced. A bailee is estopped from claiming that the bailor had no title at the time of the bailment. But the bailee has no better title than the bailor. A bailee or licensee cannot deny the right of the bailor or licensor at the commencement of the bailment or license. But a bailee, if he delivers the goods to a third person, may prove that such a person had a right to them as against the bailor. (*Expln. (2)*).

---

1. *Sadasukh Janki Das* v. *Maharaja Sir Kishan Prasad*, 46 IC 33: 46 C 663: AIR 1918 PC 146: 50 IC 216.

CHAPTER 21

WITNESSES (SECTIONS 118 TO 134)

This Chapter deals mainly with competency and compellability of witnesses. Competency is the rule and in-competency the exception. This Act declares all to be competent except those wanting in intellectual capacity. Weight depends on a host of circumstances. Ordinarily witnesses are both competent and compellable, but the two are distinct and separate. In certain cases, persons though willing, are not permitted to give evidence (privilege, prohibition, etc.). Where there is exclusion, it is generally based on considerations of public policy or grounds of privilege. Rules of discovery in C.P.C. also have relevance. (Order XIV rule 1). No one can be indirectly compelled to disclose what he cannot be directly called upon to state. There is difference between privilege and in-competency. Incompetent persons cannot be examined at all. If examined, the evidence is not legal evidence. A person who is privileged may be examined and his testimony is not illegal if privilege is waived. Competency is to be judged in the light of Section 118; compellability arises under provisions such as sections 122, 124, 125 and 129.[1]

2. SECTION 118.—All persons shall be competent to testify unless the court considers that they are prevented from understanding the questions put to them, or from giving rational answers to those questions, by tender years, extreme old age, disease, whether of the body or mind, or any other cause of the same kind.

Explanation.—A lunatic is not incompetent to testify, unless he is prevented by his lunacy from understanding the questions put to him and giving rational answers to them.

3. There is always competency unless the court considers otherwise within the meaning of this section.[2] Understanding is the sole test of competency. Young, very old persons or sick can testify if they satisfy the requirements of the section.[3]

Section 4 of Oaths Act makes oath imperative. Yet under section 7 of that Act, omission to make oath or irregularity in the form does not invalidate

1. Phipson on Evidence, 13th Edition, pages 690, 693.
2. *Rameshwar* v. *State of Rajasthan*, AIR 1952 SC 54: 1952 SCJ 46: 1952 Cr LJ 547: (1952) 3 SCR 377; *Ratansing Dalsukhbhai Nayak* v. *State of Gujarat*, AIR 2004 SC 23: (2004) 1 SCC 64: 2004 Cr LJ 19: 2003 AIR SCW 5547.
3. Phipson on Evidence, 15th Edition, pages 152, 153, *Ratansinh Dalsukhbhai Nayak* v. *State of Gujarat*, (2004) 1 SCC 64: 2004 Cr LJ 19: 2003 AIR SCW 5547; *Yuvaraj A.M* v. *State of Maharashtra*, (2006) 12 SCC 512: (2006) 10 SCALE 369; *Acharaparambath Pradeepan* v. *State of Kerala*, (2006) 13 SCC 643: 2007 AIR SCW 2140.

proceeding or render the evidence inadmissible. This is so even if the omission is deliberate in view of the clear language of section 7 of Oaths Act.[1] Omission of an oath may affect credibility of the witness.[2]

4. The modern practice is to interrogate the witnesses before swearing him or to elicit facts upon chief examination. If then his incompetency appears, he is rejected. This preliminary examination is *"VOIRE DIRE"*. Competency under Oaths Act depends upon his comprehension of his duty to speak the truth and of the nature of oath or affirmation. If a child witness has capacity to understand questions and give rational answers, his evidence is admissible even if oath is not and cannot be administered. Abuse of oath does not render the evidence illegal.[3] The Judge must certify that the witness is competent and why it is so. If either side has any doubt about the competency of a witness, that should be brought to the notice of court so that a preliminary examination is conducted and a view taken. It is advisable to record questions and answers; but failure to do so is no ground to reject the evidence.[4] But it is necessary to do so to enable appellate court to review the decision.[5] Child's capacity can be adjudged even without putting preliminary questions. Preliminary enquiry is a rule of prudence and not legal requirement and omission is an irregularity which does not vitiate trial.[6] But it is the duty of court to record the finding.[7] But failure to do so does not vitiate the judgment.[8] The deposition itself will show if the child is competent.[9] The decision arrived at initially is tentative, subject to completion of his evidence.[10]

5. Child Witness.—That a witness is a child does not, *Ipso facto*, render him incompetent. It is in the discretion of court to decide competency. All discretion must be exercised judicially. No precise age is fixed by law within which there is total prohibition. Children of 8, 6, 5 and 4 years have been held to be competent.[11]

1. *Mohamed Sunal Esa Mamasn Rer Alalah* v. *King*, AIR 1946 PC 3: 1946 ALJ 100: 222 IC 304 (PC); *Rameshwar* v. *State of Rajasthan*, AIR 1952 SC 54: 1952 SCJ 46: 1952 Cr LJ 547: (1952) 3 SCR 377.
2. *Rameshwar* v. *State of Rajasthan*, AIR 1952 SC 54: 1952 SCJ 46: 1952 Cr LJ 547: (1952) 3 SCR 377.
3. *Sudhakaran Aniyan Kunju* v. *State of Kerala*, 1983 Ker LT 594; *Ponnumani* v. *State of Kerala*, 1987 II Ker LT 1042.
4. *Bipin Bihari Sahu* v. *State of Orissa*, 1986 Cr LJ 406: 1985 (60) Cut LT 375; *Srinivasa Murthy* v. *State of Karnataka*, 1977 II KLJ 341.
5. *Ratna Munda* v. *State*, 1986 Cr LJ 1363; *Sudhakaran Aniyan Kunju* v. *State of Kerala*, 1983 Ker LT 594; *Santosh Mandal* v. *State*, 1983 Cr LJ 773.
6. *State of Orissa* v. *Machindra Majhi*, AIR 1964 Ori 100: (1964) 1 Cr LJ 422; *Santosh Mandal* v. *State*, 1983 Cr LJ 773.
7. *Rameshwar* v. *State of Rajasthan*, AIR 1952 SC 54: 1952 SCJ 46: 1952 Cr LJ 547: (1952) 3 SCR 377.
8. *Jai Singh* v. *State*, 1973 Cr LJ 1466; *State* v. *Lobsang Sharap*, 1973 Cr LJ 85: (1972) 2 Sim LJ (HP) 216.
9. *Bipin Bihari Sahu* v. *State of Orissa*, 1986 Cr LJ 406: 1985 (60) Cut LT 375; *State of Rajasthan* v. *Vijairam*, 1968 Cr LJ 270: 1968 Raj LW 1; *Ram Hazoor Pandey* v. *State*, AIR 1959 All 409: 1959 All LJ 239: 1959 Cr LJ 796.
10. *Govind Natha* v. *State*, AIR 1961 Guj 11: (1961) 1 Cr LJ 57; *Municipal Committee, Malerkotla* v. *Mohd. Mushtaq*, 1960 Cr LJ 111: AIR 1960 Punj 18.
11. *Suresh* v. *State of Uttar Pradesh*, AIR 1981 SC 1122: 1981 Cr LJ 746: (1981) 2 SCC 569; *Rameshwar* v. *State of Rajasthan*, AIR 1952 SC 54: 1952 SCJ 46: 1952 Cr LJ 547: (1952) 3 SCR 377; *Jalwanti Lodhin* v. *State*, AIR 1953 Pat 246.

A boy of thirteen with mature understanding is competent.[1] Competency is not judged merely by age, but by the degree of understanding possessed by him.

The Section refers to a person of tender years, without prescribing any age limit, though the Oaths Act refers to the aspect of age. Similarly, the section does not lay down any precise rule regarding the degree of intelligence and knowledge which will render a child a competent witness. The common sense and discretion of the judge must govern a decision on this aspect.

A child represents innocence in all its dimensions and hence is likely to speak the truth and also likely to have good memory. At the same time, one must bear in mind that child witness is susceptible to tutoring.[2] Generally, court looks to corroboration of the evidence of child witness, as a matter of prudence.[3] The real rule of corroboration is that the necessity of corroboration as a matter of prudence, except when the circumstances make it safe to dispense with it, must be present in the mind of the court before a conviction without corroboration can be sustained.[4] Where the court finds a trace of tutoring, corroboration may be insisted upon.[5] What should be the nature and extent of corroboration will depend on the facts and circumstances of each case. That, since the occurrence, the child has been living with the accused (say, father or mother) has a bearing on credibility. If on close scrutiny of the evidence of a child witness it is found to bear the impress of truth, there is no obstacle in the way of accepting the evidence even without corroboration.[6] In the case of narration by a child witness to relations about the occurrence immediately after the occurence and such narration is spoken to by them in court, such evidence has corroborative value for the evidence of the child witness. The need for corroboration is more a rule of practical wisdom than of law.[7]

The testimony cannot be rejected merely on the ground that the witness is likely to be tutored. Evidence requires careful scrutiny.[8] Each case depends on its particular facts and circumstances. The test is how consistent the story is with itself, how it stands cross-examination, and how for it fits in with rest of the evidence and circumstances of the case.[9] The court has to see the surrounding circumstances and probabilities to assess the credibility of a child witness.[10] Where a child witness stands the test of rigorous cross-examination, minor contradictions in his evidence do not matter.[11] Evidence, should, however,

1. *Tehal Singh* v. *State of Punjab*, AIR 1979 SC 1347: 1979 Cr LJ 1031: 1980 Supp SCC 400: 1979 SCC (Cri) 722; *Dhanraj* v. *State of Maharashtra*, (2002) 7 SCC 425: AIR 2002 SC 3302: 2002 Cr LJ 4325.
2. *State of Bihar* v. *Kapil Singh*, AIR 1969 SC 53.
3. *Brij Bhushan Singh* v. *E.*, (1946) 47 Cr LJ 336: AIR 1946 PC 38: 223 IC 1: 73 IA 18: 50 Cal WN 348; *Ulla Mahapatra* v. *King*, AIR 1950 Ori 261: 16 Cut LT 102: ILR 1950 Cut 293; *Jalwanti Lodhin* v. *State*, AIR 1953 Pat 246.
4. *Rameshwar* v. *State of Rajasthan*, AIR 1952 SC 54: 1952 SCJ 46: 1952 Cr LJ 547: (1952) 3 SCR 377; *Mohd. Kadam* v. *State of Bihar*, (2008) 7 SCC 257.
5. *Arbind singh* v. *State of Bihar*, AIR 1994 SC 1068: 1994 AIR SCW 1041: 1994 Cr LJ 1227.
6. *Mohamed Sunal Esa Mamasn Rer Alalah* v. *King*, AIR 1946 PC 3: 1946 ALJ 100: 222 IC 304 (PC).
7. *Acharaparambath Pradeepan* v. *State of Kerala*, (2006) 13 SCC 643: 2007 AIR SCW 2140.
8. *Prakash* v. *State of Madhya Pradesh*, AIR 1993 SC 65: 1992 AIR SCW 2582: 1992 Cr LJ 3703.
9. *Bhojraj* v. *Sita Ram*, AIR 1936 PC 60: 1936 All LJ 755: 160 IC 45.
10. *Ramchandra Rambux* v. *Champabai*, AIR 1965 SC 354: (1964) 6 SCR 814: 1965 (2) SCJ 557.
11. *State of Karnataka* v. *Maruthi*, (1997) 11 SCC 473.

be accepted with caution and credibility carefully considered. Possibility of influence and tutoring must be considered.[1]

6. Disease of body or mind or extreme old age.—The mere existence of such a disease or extreme old age by itself does not render a witness incompetent. The condition must be such that the person concerned is, in the opinion of the court, prevented from understanding the questions put to him or from giving rational answers to these questions. The test is the degree of comprehension and capacity to formulate rational answers. Whenever a court entertains a doubt on this score or even when the opposite party raises an objection about the competency of the person proposed to be examined as a witness, the court may study his appearance and put some questions to him and apply its mind regarding the nature of the answers given before coming to a conclusion regarding his competency.

7. Any other causes of the same kind.—For example, habitual drunkenness which incapacitates the mind.

8. Accused as a witness.—Accused can testify for the defence (not prosecution) in view of section 315 of the Cr.P.C..[2] An accused who is discharged can be a witness.[3] No accused shall be compelled to be witness against himself.[4] This privilege can always be waived.[5] He is competent to give evidence.[6] Only a person against whom formal accusation relating to commission of an offence has been made which, in the normal course, may lead to prosecution is an accused.[7]

An accomplice who would have been jointly tried with the accused, but was not, is competent to be a witness.[8] In his case, generally, court looks to corroboration, direct or circumstantial, as a matter of prudence.[9] *See* illustration (b) to section 114 of Evidence Act.

9. Counsel.—Counsel representing a party is not incompetent to be a witness; but it is undesirable for him to be a witness.[10] After giving evidence, he can continue to act as counsel.

10. SECTION 119.—A witness who is unable to speak may give his evidence in any other manner in which he can make it intelligible, as by writing or by

---

1. *Sanghvi Jeevraj Ghewar Chand* v. *Secretary, Madras Chillies, Grains and Kirana Merchants Workers Union*, (1969) 1 SCR 366: AIR 1969 SC 530; *Chandran* v. *State of Tamil Nadu*, AIR 1978 SC 1574: 1978 Cr LJ 1693: 1978 Cr LR (SC) 455; *Tehal Singh* v. *State of Punjab*, AIR 1979 SC 1347: 1979 Cr LJ 1031: 1980 Supp SCC 400: 1979 SCC (Cri) 722; *Shivaji Genu Mohite* v. *State of Maharashtra*, AIR 1973 SC 55: 1973 Cr LJ 159: (1973) 3 SCC 219.
2. *Subedar* v. *State*, AIR 1957 All 396: 1957 All LJ 263: 1957 Cr LJ 698.
3. *A.J. Peiris* v. *State of Madras*, AIR 1954 SC 616: 1954 Cr LJ 1638.
4. *M.P. Sharma* v. *Satish Chandra*, AIR 1954 SC 300: 1954 SCR 1077: 1954 Cr LJ 865.
5. *Banwarilal* v. *State*, AIR 1956 All 341: 1956 Cr LJ 664.
6. *State of Maharashtra* v. *R.B. Chowdhari*, AIR 1968 SC 110: 1968 Cr LJ 95: (1968) 3 SCR 708.
7. *Ramesh Chander Mehta* v. *State of West Bengal*, AIR 1970 SC 940: 1970 Cr LJ 863: (1969) 2 SCR 461; *Balakishan A. Devi Dayal* v. *State of Maharashtra*, AIR 1981 SC 379: 1980 Cr LJ 1424: (1980) 4 SCC 600.
8. *Laxmipat Choraria* v. *State of Maharashtra*, AIR 1968 SC 938: (1968) 2 SCR 624: 1968 Cr LJ 1134: (1968) 2 SCJ 589.
9. *Devan* v. *State*, 1988 Cr LJ 1005: 1987 (2) IJR (SC) 111: 1987 (2) Ker LT 187; *Chandan* v. *State of Rajasthan*, AIR 1988 SC 599: 1988 Cr LJ 842: (1988) 1 SCC 696.
10. *Seth Biradhmal* v. *Sethani Prabhabhati Kunwar*, AIR 1939 PC 152: ILR (1939) Kar (PC) 258.

signs; but such writing must be written in and the signs made in open Court, evidence so written shall be deemed to be oral evidence, provided that if the witness is unable to communicate verbally, the court shall take the assistance of an interpreter or a special educator in recording the statement, and such statement shall be videographed.

The section has been amended to some extent by Criminal Law (Amendment) Act 13 of 2013. The amending Act also incorporated a new proviso to the section as indicated above.

There must be a record of signs and not record of interpretation of signs.[1] Evidence of a deaf-mute by signs must be translated by a skilled interpreter who should be sworn. A person who has taken vow of silence is regarded as a person unable to speak. A deaf and dumb witness should not be examined without the help of an expert. Court has no expertise in the matter.[2]

11. SECTION 120.—In all civil proceedings the parties to the suit and the spouse of any party to the suit, shall be competent witnesses. In criminal proceedings against any person, his spouse shall be a competent witness (*See* also sections 51, 52 of Indian Divorce Act).

12. SECTION 121.—No Judge or Magistrate shall, except upon the special order of some court to which it is subordinate, be compelled to answer any questions as to his own conduct in court as such judge or magistrate, or as to anything which came to his knowledge in court as such judge or magistrate; but he may be examined as to other matters which occurred in his presence while he was so acting. However, they do not cease to be competent witnesses. This section is based on convenience and public policy. The privilege is that of the judge, who is the witness. He may waive the privilege specifically or by not raising any objection. If so, it is not for any one else to raise objection. Arbitrator is not entitled to this privilege.[3]

13. SECTION 122.—No person who is or has been married shall be compelled to disclose any communication made to him during marriage by any person to whom he is or has been married; nor shall he be permitted to disclose any such communication, unless the person who made it, or his representative in interest, consents, except in suits between married persons, or proceedings in which one married person is prosecuted for any crime committed against the other. The principle is based on the premise that it would otherwise disturb families and destroy or weaken the mutual confidence upon which marital happiness depends.[4] The prohibition cannot be waived. Scope of the section is explained.[5] This section is a kind of limitation on section 120. Such communications cannot be disclosed by any spouse without the consent of the other who made the communication.[5]

---

1. *Kumbhar Musa Alib* v. *State of Gujarat*, AIR 1966 Guj 101: 1966 Cr LJ 542.
2. *Kadungoth Alavi* v. *State of Kerala*, 1982 Cr LJ 94 (Ker): 1982 Ker LT 287.
3. *Union of India* v. *Orient Engineering and Commercial Company Limited*, AIR 1977 SC 2445: (1978) 1 SCC 10: (1978) 1 SCR 632.
4. *S.J. Choudhary* v. *The State*, 1985 Cr LJ 622: 1985 (2) All Cri LR 144.
5. *M.C. Verghese* v. *T.J. Ponnan*, AIR 1970 SC 1876: (1969) 1 SCC 37: 1970 Cr LJ 1651: (1969) 2 SCR 692.

The section prevents disclosure of marital confidence.[1] This section does not bar evidence under other sections.[2] The bar is only regarding communications between spouses.[3] A third party cannot be permitted to intrude into their privacy.[4]

The section applies to communications and not acts and conduct.[3] Section does not apply in the matter of proving or disproving "access".[5]

Under this section, a married person shall not be:

(a) compelled to disclose any communication made to him during marriage by any person to whom he is married, and

(b) permitted to disclose any such communication, except

  (i) When the person who made it or his representative in interest consents, or

  (ii) In suits between married persons, or

  (iii) In proceedings in which one married person is prosecuted for any crime committed against the other.

The bar does not apply to communication made before marriage. The bar continues even after divorce or death. Relevant date of status is the date of communication and not date of examination as witness.[6] Communication after divorce is not privileged.[7] Equally so, a communication made after death of a spouse. A communication can be proved in any other manner without putting either of the spouses in the witness box.[6]

The bar applies only where a spouse is a witness and claims privilege. It does not apply to letter written by spouse to the other and produced by father of one spouse. (*Ibid*). A wife can testify to the acts of her husband of which she was an eyewitness.[8]

They must be legally and technically spouses. They are not so if the marriage is void (*ibid*). Section does not apply if the lady was only a mistress.[9]

This section relates to evidence given in the witness box. It does not prevent police or any other from listening to the statement of a spouse suspected of a crime or a spouse from exercising himself or explaining the circumstances even though thereby he may implicate the other spouse. Statement of a wife which was neither given in evidence nor disclosed as evidence against the other spouse

---

1. *T.J. Ponnen* v. *M.C. Varghese*, 1967 Cr LJ 1511: 1966 Ker LT 1010: 1967 Ker LJ 56; *A. Manibhushana Rao* v. *Alapati Suryakantam*, AIR 1981 AP 58: (1980) 2 Andh LT 412: (1981) 1 Andh WR 212.
2. *M.C. Verghese* v. *T.J. Ponnan*, AIR 1970 SC 1876: (1969) 1 SCC 37: 1970 Cr LJ 1651: (1969) 2 SCR 692; *Appu* alias *Ayyanar Padayachi* v. *State*, AIR 1971 Mad 194: (1971) 2 Mad LJ 53: 1971 Cr LJ 615.
3. *Ram Bharose* v. *State of Uttar Pradesh*, AIR 1954 SC 704: 1954 Cr LJ 1755.
4. *Baldev Singh* v. *Surinder Mohan Sharma*, (2003) 1 SCC 34: AIR 2003 SC 225: 2002 AIR SCW 4674.
5. *Chilukuri Venkateswarlu* v. *Chilukuri Venkatanarayanan*, AIR 1954 SC 176: 1954 SCR 424: 1954 SCJ 84.
6. *M.C. Verghese* v. *T.J. Ponnan*, AIR 1970 SC 1876: (1969) 1 SCC 37: 1970 Cr LJ 1651: (1969) 2 SCR 692.
7. *S.J. Choudhary* v. *The State*, 1985 Cr LJ 622: 1985 (2) All Cri LR 144.
8. *Ram Bharose* v. *State of Uttar Pradesh*, AIR 1954 SC 704: 1954 Cr LJ 1755.
9. *Shankar* alias *Gauri Shankar* v. *State of Tamil Nadu*, (1994) 4 SCC 478: 1994 Cr LJ 3071 (SC).

would be admissible for and against the statement maker.[1] A document, even though it contains a communication between spouses, in the hands of a third person, is admissible. In producing it, there is no compulsion or permission to either of the spouses to whom the communication was made to disclose any communication. The section protects the individuals and not the communication, if it can be proved without examining either of them. A letter by one to the other seized by police on house search and containing a confession is admissible against the writer.[2] Evidence of overhearer is admissible. Only the spouse cannot be compelled to disclose it. Absence of an objection does not matter.

The prohibition being absolute, unless the disclosure is consented to by the other spouse who made the communication, mere failure to raise objection at the time of recording evidence did not render the answer admissible. Consent cannot be implied.[3] The spouse can give evidence on aspects other than communications.[4]

The bar does not apply in relation to suits between spouses or in cases in which one spouse is prosecuted for any crime committed against the other.[5] The exception does not take in the case of a crime against a child.

14. SECTION 123.—The section applies to evidence derived from unpublished official records relating to any affairs of State. No one is permitted to give such evidence, except with the permission of the officer or the Head of the Government concerned; the latter shall give or withhold such permission as he thinks fit. The section is based on grounds of public policy, broad principles of state policy and public convenience. Thus, the ground for non-disclosure is not that document is "confidential".[6] Private interest must give way to public interest.[7] The section protects confidentiality of state documents. Court can direct production of confidential records for the Court or other side to see, on condition (implied) that they will not be used for any other purpose.[8] The principle is that the information cannot be disclosed without injury to public interest and not that documents are confidential.[9]

The understanding of the statutory provision does not remain static, in this dynamic world, particularly in a democratic country with egalitarian values, developmental perspective. Law does not operate in a vacuum. This is so particularly when right of information as part of rule of law is being increasingly accepted.[10] It is no longer restricted to a clash of public interest and private interest. Fair administration of justice, which is a matter of vital public interest,

1. *Daniel Youth* v. *King*, AIR 1945 PC 140: (1945) 2 Mad LJ 578: 1945 ALJ 269 (PC).
2. *Appu* alias *Ayyanar Padayachi* v. *State*, AIR 1971 Mad 194: (1971) 2 Mad LJ 53: 1971 Cr LJ 615.
3. *S.J. Choudhary* v. *The State*, 1985 Cr LJ 622: 1985 (2) All Cri LR 144.
4. *Jitendra Kumar Baidya* v. *Surendra Kumar Seal*, (1965) 1 Cr LJ 88: AIR 1964 Tri 71.
5. *Norendra Nath Mozumdar* v. *State*, AIR 1951 Cal 140: 87 CLJ 58: 52 Cr LJ 1241.
6. *Asiatic Petroleum Co. Ltd.* v. *Anglo-Persian Oil Co. Ltd.*, (1916) 1 KB 822: 85 LJKB 1075; *Hanry Greer Robinson* v. *State of South Australia*, AIR 1931 PC 254: 1931 AC 704: 35 Cal WN 1121 (PC).
7. *S.P. Gupta* v. *Union of India*, AIR 1982 SC 149: 1981 Supp SCC 87: (1982) 2 SCR 365; *State of Uttar Pradesh* v. *Raj Narain*, (1975) 4 SCC 428: AIR 1975 SC 865: (1975) 3 SCR 333.
8. *Doypack Systems Pvt. Ltd.* v. *Union of India*, AIR 1988 SC 782: JT 1988 (1) SC 304: (1988) 2 SCC 299.
9. *Henry Greer Robinson* v. *State of South Australia*, AIR 1931 PC 254: 135 IC 625.
10. *S.P. Gupta* v. *Union of India*, AIR 1982 SC 149: 1981 Supp SCC 87: (1982) 2 SCR 365.

may require disclosure and openness. Court should balance two kinds of public interest and come to a decision. Right to information is implicit in article 19(1)(a) {Right to free speech and expression}. Right to know leads to concept of open government. The correct approach is to restrict the area of secrecy as much as possible consistently with requirements of public interest, bearing in mind that disclosure also serves an important aspect of public interest. (*S.P. Gupta's* case). This decision disagreed with the view in an earlier case.[1] It is public interest in the fair administration of justice and what is necessary is balancing between the two. The foundation of the law underlying sections 153 and 162 of the Evidence Act is that the injury is to public interest or even national interest.[2] To give immunity from disclosure of unpublished state documents, the documents must relate to affairs of State and disclosure thereof would be against the interest of the state or public interest.[3]

There is heavy burden on the authority which makes the claim for class immunity, immunity based not on the contents of the document, but upon the membership of a class. A wide and liberal approach to the claim of immunity is destructive of concept of open government. Grant of immunity is the exception. Earlier in *State of Punjab* v. *Sodhi Sukhdev Singh*,[4] it was held that the court has no power to inspect the document. In *Amar Chand Butail* v. *Union of India*,[5] it was held that if no affidavit was filed in support of the claim of privilege, the claim is liable to be rejected. In *S.P. Gupta's* case[6] court did inspect the documents. Inspection may be necessary to decide on the claim of privilege. The statement of the head of the department is not final. The final decision rests with the Court. (*See* section 162). The affidavit claiming privilege should be sworn to by the Minister or Government Secretary. It should state that the department has carefully read and considered the document and the department has formed the opinion that the document should not be disclosed because of it's actual contents or because of the class to which it belongs. Court should consider the two kinds of public interests, the nature of the proceedings, issues arising in it and likely effect of the documents on the decision on the issues. (*Ibid*). The affidavit must show that each document has been carefully read and considered.[7] It should state reasons also.

15. There may be classes of documents which public interest requires should not be disclosed, irrespective of the nature of the individual documents in the class, for example, class of document which it is really necessary for the proper functioning of public service, such as cabinet minutes, minutes of discussion between heads of departments, high level inter-departmental communications, dispatches from abroad of Ambassadors etc.[2] Also papers

1. *State of Punjab* v. *Sodhi Sukhdev Singh*, AIR 1961 SC 493: (1961) 1 SCJ 691: (1961) 2 SCR 371: (1961) 2 MLJ 203.
2. *State of Uttar Pradesh* v. *Raj Narain*, AIR 1975 SC 865: (1975) 3 SCR 797: (1975) 4 SCC 428: 1975 Cr LJ 772.
3. *People's Union for Civil Liberties* v. *Union of India*, AIR 2004 SC 1442: (2004) 2 SCC 476.
4. (1961) 2 SCR 371: AIR 1961 SC 493: 1961 (2) SCJ 691.
5. AIR 1964 SC 1658: (1964) 67 Pun LR 90: 1965 (1) SCJ 243.
6. *S.P. Gupta* v. *Union of India*, AIR 1982 SC 149: 1981 Supp SCC 87: (1982) 2 SCR 365.
7. *State of Punjab* v. *Sodhi Sukhdev Singh*, AIR 1961 SC 493: (1961) 1 SCJ 691: (1961) 2 SCR 371: (1961) 2 MLJ 203; *Amar Chand Butail* v. *Union of India*, AIR 1964 SC 1658: (1964) 67 Pun LR 90: 1965 (1) SCJ 243.

for the purpose of preparing submission to cabinet, documents which relate to framing of government policy at a high level, notes and minutes of officers on relevant files, information expressed or reports made and gist of official decisions reached in the course of determination of questions of policy. This is to ensure complete freedom and candor at high level in stating facts, tendering advice, exchanging opinions and possibility of ultimate publication might affect frankness and candor in preparing them. There is no absolute immunity to any class of documents. (*S.P. Gupta's* case). That a privilege claimed against an accused has been upheld in a criminal case is no ground to acquit him on the ground of prejudice. It is generally accepted that documents relating to public security, defence and foreign relations are documents relating to affairs of state. Documents relating to trading, commercial or contractual activities of the state are not generally regarded as documents relating to affairs of State. Each case has to be considered on its own merits. Court's power to inspect is clearly accepted in *S.P. Gupta's* case. Claim of privilege cannot prevail over the constitutional mandate of disclosure under article 22(5) of the Constitution.[1]

It is not sufficient that documents are "State" documents or "official" documents or documents marked "confidential". That, if produced, they might involve Government in parliamentary discussion or public criticism, or might necessitate attendance of officials as witnesses, might expose inefficiency or tend to open government to compensation claim or might help the opposite party in the case, is no ground to claim privilege.[2] Privilege should not be allowed for each and every document.[3] The test is only injury to public interest. In doubtful cases, Court can direct production to see whether its production would be injurious or not.[4] The oath of secrecy under article 75(4) of the Constitution does not absolve the minister to state reasons in support of "public interest" to produce state documents or as to how the matter was dealt with or for their production when the discovery order was passed. The minister has to act in aid of the court.[3]

Power of court to order production of documents under section 91 of the Cr.P.C. is subject to sections 123, 124 of Evidence Act.[5] These two Sections and section 173(2) of the Cr.P.C. cater to two different situations.[6]

16. Records covered by this Section.—Confidential notes in official files, deliberations of Parliament, confidential papers, communications between public officials, political communications, documents that pass between two States, documents between Government and subject, documents that pass between

1. *Lawrence Joachim Joseph D'Souza* v. *State of Bombay*, AIR 1956 SC 531.
2. *Henry Greer Robinson* v. *State of South Australia*, AIR 1931 PC 254: 135 IC 625; *Amar Chand Butail* v. *Union of India*, AIR 1964 SC 1658: (1964) 67 Pun LR 90: 1965 (1) SCJ 243; *Sub-Divisional Officer (Compensation Officer) Mirzapur* v. *Raja Srinivasa Prasad Singh*, AIR 1966 SC 1164: (1966) 2 SCR 970: (1966) 1 SCA 556.
3. *Doypack Systems Pvt. Ltd.* v. *Union of India*, AIR 1988 SC 782: JT 1988 (1) SC 304: (1988) 2 SCC 299; *People's Union for Civil Liberties* v. *Union of India*, AIR 2004 SC 1442: (2004) 2 SCC 476.
4. *S.P. Gupta* v. *Union of India*, AIR 1982 SC 149: 1981 Supp SCC 87: (1982) 2 SCR 365.
5. *Chandubhai Jethabhai Desai* v. *State*, AIR 1962 Guj 290: 1962 (2) Cr LJ 610: (1962) 3 Guj LR 833.
6. *Subhash Chandra* v. *Union of India*, 1988 Cr LJ 1077: 1987 (3) Crimes 159: 1987 (1) Raj LR 269.

departmental heads or between ministers relating to affairs of State, orders relating to deployment of armed forces.[1]

Privilege can be claimed only in respect of "unpublished" documents, not if they have already been published.[2] "Unpublished" means not disclosed to any member of the public. If it is produced in Court by order, that amounts to publication, though not voluntary.

"Affairs of State" should receive narrow, restricted meaning.[3] If a broad meaning is given, it may affect constitutionality of the provision. The expression means matters of a public nature in which the state is concerned and whose disclosure will be prejudicial to public interest. Affairs of state generally has reference to matter which affects defence and relations with another country as also affect freedom and candour of expression in the determination and execution of further policies.[4]

17. The following documents have been held to be not privileged.—Diary of a P.C. shadowing a suspect, departmental enquiry papers, material which led to compulsory retirement, statements made in course of investigation, records kept in police station regarding activities of any person, accident register, report by one officer to another, accounts books.[5]

On the other hand, jail diary book, report of I.G. of Police under police manual, Character rolls of Government employees have been held to be privileged.[6] So also notings made by officers by way of comment or opinion on reports of public speeches made at election meetings.[7]

See section 137 of I.T. Act.[8]

Materials on which ministerial advice is based are not privileged.[9] Advice tendered by council of ministers to President or Governor is privileged under article 74(2) of Constitution[10] To decide this question, court will not permit any evidence about the contents.

---

1. *State of Orissa* v. *Jagannath Jona*, AIR 1977 SC 2201: (1977) 2 SCC 165; *Subhasini Jena* v. *Commandant of 6th Battalion, O.S.A.P., Cuttack*, 1988 Cr LJ 1570: 1988 (65) Cut LT 551: 1988 OCR 159; *Doypack Systems Pvt. Ltd.* v. *Union of India*, AIR 1988 SC 782: JT 1988 (1) SC 304: (1988) 2 SCC 299; *State of Bihar* v. *Kripalu Shankar*, AIR 1987 SC 1554: 1987 Cr LJ 1860: (1987) 3 SCC 34; *Bachhittar Singh* v. *State of Punjab*, AIR 1963 SC 395: 1962 All WR (HC) 746: 1962 Supp 3 SCR 713.
2. *Henry Greer Robinson* v. *State of South Australia*, AIR 1931 PC 254: 135 IC 625; *Union of India* v. *Sudhir Kumar Roy*, AIR 1963 Ori 111: 29 Cut LT 179: ILR 1963 Cut 213.
3. *S.P. Gupta* v. *Union of India*, AIR 1982 SC 149: 1981 Supp SCC 87: (1982) 2 SCR 365.
4. *State of Orissa* v. *Jagannath Jona*, AIR 1977 SC 2201: (1977) 2 SCC 165.
5. *North Eastern Railway* v. *Ram Lal Golcha*, AIR 1960 Pat 489: 1960 BLJR 669.
6. *State of Punjab* v. *Surjit Singh*, AIR 1975 Punj 11: (1975) 1 Serv LR 433: ILR (1976) 1 P&H 541; *D.P. Maheshwari* v. *Delhi Admn*, (1983) 4 SCC 293: (1983) 2 Serv LJ 542: AIR 1984 SC 153; *State of Uttar Pradesh* v. *Chandra Mohan Nigam*, AIR 1977 SC 2411: (1978) 1 SCR 621: 1977 SCC (Lab) 535.
7. *Kanwar Lal Gupta* v. *Amar Nath Chawla*, AIR 1975 SC 308: (1975) 2 SCR 259: (1975) 3 SCC 646.
8. *Dagi Ram Pindi Lall* v. *Trilok Chand Jain*, AIR 1992 SC 990: (1992) 2 SCC 13: (1992) 1 SCR 545.
9. *S.R. Bommai* v. *Union of India*, 1994 AIR SCW 2946: (1994) 3 SCC 1: (1994) 2 SCR 644.
10. *State of Rajasthan* v. *Union of India*, AIR 1977 SC 1361: (1978) 1 SCR 1: 1978 (1) SCJ 78; *R.K. Jain* v. *Union of India*, AIR 1993 SC 1769: 1993 AIR SCW 1899: (1993) 3 SCR 802; *Doypack Systems Pvt. Ltd.* v. *Union of India*, AIR 1988 SC 782: JT 1988 (1) SC 304: (1988) 2 SCC 299.

18. Head of the department.—The Government has to decide to claim privilege and authorize an officer to swear to an affidavit on its behalf. If the Government is not a party, it should be claimed by the department head.[1] He is, ordinarily, the officer who is in control of the department, namely, the Secretary to Government.[2] Department is the one in whose custody the documents are. An affidavit of the minister cannot be insisted on.[3] Minister or Government Secretary of Railway is the Head.[4]

Section 123 prevails over Order XI rule 9 C.P.C.[5] Sections 123 and 162 apply also where the State is a party.[6]

The officer called upon to produce the document must bring it to court. If the plea is overruled, the document must be admitted in evidence. Court can inspect the document before the decision, for the limited purpose of deciding on the objection as held in *S.P. Gupta's* case. The contrary view in *State of Punjab* v. *Sodhi Sukhdev Singh*,[6] has been over ruled.

The privilege under section 123 cannot be waived.[7]

Privilege has to be claimed in an affidavit of the Minister or Head of Department[6] or Secretary to Department.[7]

19. SECTION 124.—No Public officer shall be compelled to disclose communications made to him in official confidence, when he considers that the public interest would suffer by the disclosure. This section supplements section 123 to safeguard official communications made in official confidence; public interest may be prejudiced by disclosure as otherwise, it will be impossible to communicate freely.

It is for the officer to decide, not the Court.[8] What the officer is to consider is whether public interest would suffer by disclosure. It is for the Court to decide whether the document is a communication made to a public officer in official confidence.[9] The officer need not be head of department. The privilege extends only to a communication upon the subject to which privilege extends.[10] In *Dagi Ram Pindi Lall* v. *Trilok Chand Jain*,[11] the court held that under both sections 123 and 124, it is for the court to decide whether to grant privilege or not.[12] Once

1. *Miss Rajul Raoji Bhai Shah* v. *Provincial Government of C.P. and Berar*, AIR 1951 Nag 212: 1950 Nag 690.
2. *State* v. *Abdurahiman Baffakki*, AIR 1954 Mad 926: 1954 Mad WN 409: 67 Mad LW 533; *In re Hanumantha Rao*, AIR 1957 AP 456: 1956 Andh WR 360: 1957 Cr LJ 930; *State of Punjab* v. *Sodhi Sukhdev Singh*, AIR 1961 SC 493: (1961) 1 SCJ 691: (1961) 2 SCR 371: (1961) 2 MLJ 203.
3. *Lady Dinbai Dinshaw Petit* v. *Dominion of India*, AIR 1951 Bom 72: 53 Bom LR 229.
4. *Union of India* v. *Indradeo Kumar*, AIR 1963 Pat 129: 1963 BLJR 138; *Union of India* v. *Indra Deo Kumar*, AIR 1964 SC 1118: (1964) 1 SCWR 399: 1965 (2) SCJ 520.
5. *Lakhuram Hariram* v. *Union of India*, AIR 1960 Pat 192: 1959 BLJR 658: ILR 39 Pat 255.
6. AIR 1961 SC 493: (1961) 1 SCJ 691: (1961) 2 SCR 371: (1961) 2 MLJ 203.
7. *S.P. Gupta* v. *Union of India*, AIR 1982 SC 149: 1981 Supp SCC 87: (1982) 2 SCR 365.
8. *Nagaraja Pillai* v. *Secretary of State*, AIR 1915 Mad 1113: ILR 39 Mad 304.
9. *Pandiri Satyanandam* v. *Paramkusan Mangayya*, AIR 1935 Mad 342.
10. *V.R. Bhate* v. *State of Maharashtra*, AIR 1970 SC 1362: 1970 SCD 598: 1970 Cr LJ 1261; *Bishnu Ram Borah* v. *Parag Saikia*, AIR 1984 SC 898: 1984 Tax LR 570: (1984) 2 SCC 488.
11. AIR 1992 SC 990: (1992) 2 SCC 13: (1992) 1 SCR 545.
12. *Mohd. Hussain Umar* v. *K.S. Dalipsinghji*, 1970 Cr LJ 9: AIR 1970 SC 45: (1970) 1 SCR 130.

there was disclosure, privilege cannot be claimed. Court has the inherent power to look into the document and decide the question.[1]

Sections 123 and 124 are distinct and separate, though there may be cases where they overlap. Section 124 applies even where affairs of state are not involved. Neither section should be made a cloak to conceal truth.[2]

20. Official confidence.—It is not every communication which is covered by the section. It must be made in "official confidence". There must be express or implied promise of secrecy. The test is whether the disclosure would result in the betrayal of the person confiding, having regard to the nature thereof.[3] If the communication was made under the process of law, it cannot be said to have been made in official confidence. If not, or if the communication was for gathering information, official confidence is implied.[4] A communication made voluntarily is not made in official confidence.[5]

Statement made in I.T. returns is not made in official confidence. So also communication by I.T.O. to superiors regarding assessment and penalty. Statement made during Forest offence investigation and during police investigation are not covered by the section.[6] That is because the investigation was under due process of law.

A communication by a private individual to a public officer could attract the section.[7] Police officer cannot be compelled to disclose from whom he received information about an offence. Information supplied by a citizen leading to search and recovery of contraband is privileged.[7]

Privilege should be claimed at the earliest opportunity by filing an affidavit.[4] Where the probity of the conduct of a public officer is in issue, state cannot screen his conduct claiming privilege.[8] Cables sent to or received through telegram office are not communications sent in public confidence.[9]

21. SECTION 125.—Source of information of Magistrate or Police officer regarding commission of an offence or of Revenue Officer regarding an offence against public revenue are protected. They cannot be compelled to disclose the source of such information received by them. This rests on public policy, *e.g.*, identity of spy, informer cannot be disclosed for fear of consequences.[10]

---

1. *S.P. Gupta* v. *Union of India*, AIR 1982 SC 149: 1981 Supp SCC 87: (1982) 2 SCR 365; *Central Bureau of Investigation* v. *A.K. Agarwal*, (2007) 10 SCC 736.
2. *Excelsior Film Exchange* v. *Union of India*, AIR 1968 Bom 322: 69 Bom LR 878: 1968 Mah LJ 126; *L.K. Koolwal* v. *State of Rajasthan*, AIR 1988 Raj 2: (1987) 4 Reports 53: 1987 MCC 431; *Ganga Ram* v. *Union of India (UOI)*, AIR 1964 Pat 444: ILR 45 Pat 241.
3. *S.P. Gupta* v. *Union of India*, AIR 1982 SC 149: 1981 Supp SCC 87: (1982) 2 SCR 365.
4. *In re: Killi Suryanarayana Naidu*, AIR 1954 Mad 278: 66 Mad LW 927.
5. *B.R. Srinivasan* v. *Bramhatantra Parakalaswamy Mutt, Mysore*, AIR 1960 Mys 186: ILR 1960 Mys 332.
6. *Natha Apparao* v. *Narulasetti Suryaprakash Rao*, AIR 1951 Mad 864: 6 DLR Mad 282: 52 Cr LJ 984.
7. *Public Prosecutor Andhra Pradesh* v. *Pocku Syed Ismail*, 1973 Cr LJ 931: (1972) 2 Andh LT 202: (1973) 1 Andh WR 31.
8. *Niranian Dash Sehgal* v. *State of Punjab through Secy. to Govt. of, Punjab Dept. of Forests*, AIR 1968 P&H 255: 1968 Lab IC 804: 1968 Serv LR 183.
9. *Mohd. Hussain Umar* v. *K.S. Dalipsinghji*, 1970 Cr LJ 9: AIR 1970 SC 45: (1970) 1 SCR 130.
10. *Munna Singh Tomar* v. *State of Madhya Pradesh*, 1989 Cr LJ 580: 1989 MPLJ 414: 1988 (18) Reports 86.

But the officer may disclose the information.[1] The nature of the information is not protected. It does not apply to sworn information laid by an informer. FIR is not a privileged document.[2]

22. SECTION 126.—No barrister, attorney, pleader or lawyer and vakil shall at any time be permitted, unless with his client's express consent, to disclose any communication made to him in the course and for the purpose of his employment as such barrister, pleader, attorney or vakil, by or on behalf of his client, or to state the contents or condition of any document with which he has become acquainted in the course and for the purpose of his professional employment or to disclose any advice given by him to his client in the course and for the purpose of such employment:

Provided that nothing contained in this section shall protect from disclosure:—

(1) any such communication made in furtherance of any illegal purpose;

(2) any fact observed by any barrister, pleader, attorney or vakil, in the course of his employment as such, showing that any crime or fraud has been committed since the commencement of his employment.

It is immaterial whether the attention of such barrister, pleader, attorney or vakil was or was not directed to such fact by or on behalf of his client.

Explanation:—The obligation stated in this section continues after the employment has seized.

23. The privilege is that of the client and not of the lawyer and can be waived by the client. Intercourse between a client and his legal counsel is privileged, unless waived by the client.[3] Law officers are within the scope of this section.[4] So also an insurer.[5] A lawyer cannot withhold information regarding a crime.[6] Once privileged, always privileged.

Section 126 relates only to private and confidential communications.[7] Section 126 applies also to facts observed by the lawyer in the course of employment and for the purpose of the employment. Letter containing mere statement of facts is not privileged. Letter written by one accused to another and in the custody of the lawyer has no privilege. Statement by client to his lawyer in the hearing of the opposite party or another has no privilege.[8]

---

1. *D. Narmperumal* v. *State*, 1987 III Crimes 91.
2. *Munna Singh Tomar* v. *State of Madhya Pradesh*, 1989 Cr LJ 580: 1989 MPLJ 414: 1988 (18) Reports 86.
3. *Ayeasha Bi* v. *Peerkhan Sahib*, AIR 1954 Mad 741: 1954 Cr LJ 1239; *Superintendent and Remembrancer of Legal Affairs, West Bengal* v. *Satyen Bhowmick*, AIR 1981 SC 917: (1981) 2 SCC 109: (1981) 2 SCR 661.
4. *Municipal Corporation of Greater Bombay* v. *Vijay Metal Works, Bombay*, AIR 1982 Bom 6: 1982 Mah LJ 798: 1982 Hindu LR 93.
5. *M. Ramalingam* v. *P.R. Thakur*, AIR 1982 Del 486: (1982) 21 DLT 430: 1982 ACJ 440.
6. *People's Union for Civil Liberties* v. *Union of India*, AIR 2004 SC 456: 2003 AIR SCW 7233: (2004) 9 SCC 580.
7. *Ayeasha Bi* v. *Peerkhan Sahib*, AIR 1954 Mad 741: 1954 Cr LJ 1239; *Kallu* v. *Kallu Singh*, AIR 1918 All 38.
8. *Mahableshwar Devershetti* v. *Badku Venka Naij*, AIR 1925 Bom 1 (FB); *Pratti Rajamma* v. *Pratti Chintaiah*, 1973 Cr LJ 1489: (1972) 2 APLJ 62: (1972) 2 Andh WR 253.

The privilege under section 126 is qualified privilege.[1] The privilege is not intended for committing an offence.[2] Lawyer may be compelled to disclose collateral facts such as client's name and address, facts showing mental capacity of the client, the fact of engagement, handwriting etc.

"Disclosure" implies what is not known to others. If it is referred to in the notice or reply, there is already disclosure and section 126 does not apply.[3]

The privileges under section 126 extends to original documents coming into the lawyer's possession from his client.[4] He may prove that the particular document is in his possession, but not anything else with reference to it.

A Judge can ask the lawyer if he was making a particular allegation on instructions.[5]

24. SECTION 127.—Section 126 applies to interpreter, clerk or servants of legal counsel.

25. SECTION 128.—A party giving evidence in his case shall not be deemed to have thereby consented to disclosure as is mentioned in section 126. If a party calls his legal counsel as a witness, he shall be deemed to have consented to such disclosure only if he questions such counsel on matters, which, but for such question, he would not be at liberty to disclose. (*See* also II proviso to section 165).

26. SECTION 129.—Confidential communication between a person and his legal professional advisor cannot be compelled to be disclosed unless he offers himself as a witness, in which case he may be compelled to disclose any such communication as may appear to the Court necessary to be known in order to explain any evidence he has given, but no others. The Bar is against compulsion; a party may of his own accord disclose any such communication.

Sections 126, 127 and 128 apply when the legal counsel or his clerk etc., is examined as a witness. Section 129 applies when the client himself is examined as a witness. All the four Sections apply to communications between them. This privilege may be waived only by the client. The idea is that a person seeking assistance of a lawyer must be in a position to communicate to him freely, without fear of disclosure.

See also 9th *explanation* to section 499 I.P.C., the scope of which is explained by the Supreme Court.[6] That provision contemplates qualified privilege.[7] There is an initial presumption in favour of good faith of the lawyer.

If the communication has already being disclosed, section 129 will cease to apply.[8]

---

1. *Deepchand* v. *Sampathraj*, AIR 1970 Mys 34.
2. *S. Antony* v. *G.S. Naidu*, AIR 1967 Mad 395: (1966) 2 Mad LJ 443: 1967 Cr LJ 1527.
3. *Pratti Rajamma* v. *Pratti Chintaiah*, 1972 II Andh WR 253.
4. *Chandubhai Jethabhai Desai* v. *State*, AIR 1962 Guj 290: (1962) 2 Cr LJ 610: (1962) 3 Guj LR 833.
5. *Mohunt Gopal Das* v. *Maharaja Rameswar Singh*, AIR 1915 Cal 396.
6. *Chaman Lal* v. *State of Punjab*, AIR 1970 SC 1372: 1970 Cr LJ 1266: 1970 SC Cri R 452; *Harbhajan Singh* v. *State of Punjab*, AIR 1966 SC 97: 1966 (1) SCJ 753: (1965) 3 SCR 235; *Sukra Mahto* v. *Basdeo Kumar Mahto*, AIR 1971 SC 1567: 1971 Cr LJ 1168: 1971 (Supp) SCR 329.
7. *Bai Shanta* v. *Umrao Amir Malek*, AIR 1926 Bom.
8. *Rev. Fr. Bernad Thattil* v. *Ramachandran Pillai*, 1987 Cr LJ 739: 1987 (1) Crimes 27.

The client can waive the privilege.[1] An advocate of one party cannot be cited as a witness of the opposite party to give evidence on his side. Advocate cannot be compelled to show to the court notes made by him of his client's instructions. The relationship need not be with reference to a case; it can be in the context of arranging a conveyance or sending a notice.

A view has been taken that sections 126 and 127 do not override section 91(i) of the Cr.P.C. and power of court to order production of a document is limited by these Sections. But since the discretion is judicial, it should not ordinarily be exercised in such a way as to nullify the privilege conferred by sections 126 and 127.[2]

27. SECTION 130.—No witness who is not a party to a suit shall be compelled to produce his title deeds to any property, or any document in virtue of which he holds any property as pledgee or mortgage, or any document the production of which might tend to incriminate him, unless he has agreed in writing to produce them with the person seeking the production of such deeds or some person through whom he claims.

This section is based on the principle that great inconvenience and mischief would result to witnesses if they are compelled to disclose their title by the production of their title deeds. The underlying object is that title of such persons may not be disclosed and examined. It is open to that person to waive this privilege. Reference may be made to Order XI and Order XVI rule 6 C.P.C. and Section 162 of the Evidence Act. If a person refuses to produce his title deed, the party who wants its production may be allowed to give secondary evidence of the contents of the document.

28. SECTION 131.—No one shall be compelled to produce documents in his possession or electronic records under his control, which any other person would be entitled to refuse to produce if they were in his possession or control, unless such last mentioned person consents to their production. This section applies to documents in the possession of a person on behalf of others, say agents, attorneys, mortgagees, pledgees, trustees etc. This principle will protect such categories of persons from being compelled to speak to contents of such documents.[3] Refusal under this section cannot lead to an adverse inference regarding the contents, being drawn.

29. SECTION 132.—A witness shall not be excused from answering any question as to any matter relevant to the matter in issue in any suit or in any civil or criminal proceeding, upon the ground that an answer to such question will criminate such witness, or that it will expose, or tend directly or indirectly to expose such witness to a penalty or forfeiture of any kind.

Provided that no such answer, which a witness shall be compelled to give, shall subject him to any arrest or prosecution or proved against him in any criminal proceeding, except a prosecution for giving false evidence by such answer.

A witness cannot refuse to answer a question which may incriminate and expose him to penalty or forfeiture. But the answer shall not subject him to

1. *Rev. Fr. Bernad Thattil* v. *Ramachandran Pillai*, 1987 Cr LJ 739: 1987 (1) Crimes 27.
2. *Chandubhai Jethabhai Desai* v. *State*, AIR 1962 Guj 290: (1962) 2 Cr LJ 610: (1962) 3 Guj LR 833.
3. Field on Evidence, 11th Edn. Page 1433.

arrest or prosecution or proved against him in a criminal case, except for giving false evidence.[1]

The Section relates only to a person examined as a witness. It applies even where an accused in a criminal case is examined in other proceeding.[2]

The question must relate to any matter relevant to the matter in issue in the case.

The protection of the proviso is not available where he answers questions voluntarily, without raising an objection.[3]

Where a witness hesitates to answer a question and is asked by the court to answer it, the proviso applies. This is so even if he did not specifically raise an objection.[4] This controversy has been set at rest in AIR 1989 SC 598. Whether answer is given to question put by counsel on either side or court, it cannot be said to be a voluntary one and it is immaterial whether he objects or not. This may not be so in the case of a party-witness in a civil case or the case of accused giving evidence as a witness. Where witness is present on summons or otherwise, his answer cannot be said to be voluntary and without any compulsion.[5]

The compelled answer can be used in a later civil case. The incriminating answers cannot lead to his prosecution, unless it be for false evidence.[6] This includes case of evidence given by an accused as an approver. Where an accused enters the witness box and gives evidence, it does not amount to being compelled to be a witness against himself under article 20(3) of the Constitution.[7]

Liability for criminal defamation must be decided with reference to section 499 of Code. Liability for damages for defamation (by witness in earlier case) is not governed by statute and requires to be decided by principles of justice, equity and good conscience.[8] Section 94 of Representation of Peoples' Act is an exception to this Section and hence a voter cannot be compelled to divulge to whom he voted.[9]

Benefit of section 132 is not available to a witness interrogated under section 161 of Code.

---

1. *Tara Chand* v. *State of Rajasthan*, AIR 1980 SC 1361: (1980) 2 SCC 321: 1980 Cr LJ 1015; *Laxmipat Choraria* v. *State of Maharashtra*, AIR 1968 SC 938: (1968) 2 SCR 624: 1968 Cr LJ 1134: (1968) 2 SCJ 589; *State (Delhi Administration)* v. *Jagjit Singh*, AIR 1989 SC 598: (1988) 2 SCALE 1578: (1988) 3 SCR 1093: 1989 CAR 37: 1989 Cr LR 140: (1989) 1 Crimes 343B: 1989 Cr LJ 986: (1989) 2 SCC 770: JT 1988 (4) SC 715.
2. *Maniklal Soni* v. *Union of India*, 1984 Cr LJ 1359: 1984 ECR 584: 1984 (16) ELT 33; *Janardan Subrao Pai* v. *Chandra Kamalaksha Pai*, 2003 Cr LJ 2909: 2003 (4) All Cri LR 167: 2003 (4) Mah LJ 342.
3. *Bai Shanta* v. *Umrao Amir Malik*, AIR 1926 Bom 141: 28 Bom LR 1: 27 Cr LJ 423 (FB).
4. *Chotkan* v. *State*, AIR 1960 All 606: 1960 All LJ 668: 1960 Cr LJ 1285; *Bai Shanta* v. *Umrao Amir Malik*, AIR 1926 Bom 141: 28 Bom LR 1: 27 Cr LJ 423 (FB).
5. *Murali* alias *Muraleedharan* v. *State of Kerala*, 1989 II Kerala LT 448; *Tukaram G. Gaokar* v. *R.N. Shukla*, AIR 1968 SC 1050: 1968 Cr LJ 1234: 1968 (2) SCJ 727.
6. *State (Delhi Administration)* v. *Jagjit Singh*, AIR 1989 SC 598: (1988) 2 SCALE 1578: (1988) 3 SCR 1093: 1989 CAR 37: 1989 Cr LR 140: (1989) 1 Crimes 343B: 1989 Cr LJ 986: (1989) 2 SCC 770: JT 1988 (4) SC 715.
7. *Tukaram G. Gaokar* v. *R.N. Shukla*, AIR 1968 SC 1050: 1968 Cr LJ 1234: 1968 (2) SCJ 727.
8. *Rajindra Kishore Sahi* v. *Durga Sahi*, AIR 1967 All 476: 1967 All LJ 158: 1967 All WR (HC) 163.
9. *Raghubir Singh Gill* v. *Gurcharan Singh*, AIR 1980 SC 1362.

30. SECTION 133.—An accomplice shall be a competent witness against an accused. A conviction is not illegal merely because it proceeds upon the uncorroborated testimony of an accomplice. (*See* section 313 of Code, Illustration (b) to section 114). The combined effect of Section 133 and illustration (b) to Section 114 is that though conviction of an accused on the testimony of an accomplice is not illegal, the court, as a matter of practice, will not ordinarily accept his evidence without corroboration in material particulars.[1]

An accomplice is one who is concerned with another or others in the commission of a crime.[2] He is a *participis criminis* except in two cases; that is, receiver of stolen property is not always an accomplice and accomplice in previous similar offences committed by the accused on trial are deemed to be accomplices in the offences for which the accused is on trial, when evidence of the accused having committed crimes of identical types on other occasions be admissible to prove the system and the intent.[3] Accomplice who has received conditional pardon on the undertaking that he will tell all he knows, may at any time be relegated to the dock if he fails in his undertaking. Conviction can rest on his evidence if the Court is satisfied as regards his truthfulness. It is not necessary to seek corroboration in regard to every minor detail. It is not possible to formulate the kind of evidence which should be regarded as corroboration. Its nature and extent must be according to the particular circumstances of the offence charged. There need not be independent corroboration of every material circumstance in the sense that independent evidence by itself must be sufficient to sustain conviction. What is necessary is that there is some additional evidence rendering it probable that the story of the accomplice is true and it is reasonably safe to believe the particular crime was committed and the additional evidence reasonably connects or tends to connect the accused with the crime by confirming in some material particulars the testimony of the accomplice. The corroboration must come from independent source ordinarily, not another accomplice. Corroboration can be by direct or circumstantial evidence.[4] It

1. *Bhuboni Sahu* v. *King*, AIR 1949 PC 257: 50 Cr LJ 872: 51 BLR 955: 53 CWN 609: 1949 ALJ 283: 51 PLR 311: 76 Ind App 147; *Abdul Sattar* v. *Union Territory, Chandigarh*, 1985 SCC (Cri) 505: AIR 1986 SC 1438: 1986 Cr LJ 1072; *C. Chellappan* v. *State of Kerala*, (1979) 4 SCC 312: AIR 1979 SC 1761: 1979 Cr LJ 1335; *Dagdu* v. *State of Maharashtra*, AIR 1977 SC 1579: 1977 Cr LJ 1206: 1977 SCC (Cri) 421: (1977) 3 SCC 68; *Bhiva Doulu Patil* v. *State of Maharashtra*, AIR 1963 SC 599: 1963 Cr LJ 489: (1963) 3 SCR 830; *R.* v. *Baskerville*, (1916) KB 658; *Rameshwar* v. *State of Rajasthan*, AIR 1952 SC 54: 1952 SCJ 46: 1952 Cr LJ 547: (1952) 3 SCR 377; *Kashmira Singh* v. *State of Madhya Pradesh*, AIR 1952 SC 159: 1952 SCR 526: 1952 SCJ 201: 1952 Cr LJ 839.
2. *R.K. Dalmia* v. *Delhi Administration*, AIR 1962 SC 1821: (1962) 2 Cr LJ 805: (1963) 1 SCR 253.
3. *R.K. Dalmia* v. *Delhi Administration*, AIR 1962 SC 1821: (1962) 2 Cr LJ 805: (1963) 1 SCR 253; *Mohd. Hussain Umar* v. *K.S. Dalipsinghji*, 1970 Cr LJ 9: AIR 1970 SC 45: (1970) 1 SCR 130; *Kishan Chand* v. *State of Rajasthan*, AIR 1982 SC 1511: (1982) 3 SCC 466: 1983 SCC (Cri) 92.
4. *Vadivelu Thevar* v. *State of Madras*, AIR 1957 SC 614: 1957 Cr LJ 1000: 1957 SCJ 527; *Saravanabhavan and Govindaswamy* v. *State of Madras*, AIR 1966 SC 1273: 1966 Cr LJ 949: (1966) 1 SCWR 840; *State of Maharashtra* v. *Chandraprakash Jain*, AIR 1990 SC 658: (1990) 1 SCC 550: JT 1990 (1) SC 61: 1990 Cr LJ 889; *Abdul Sattar* v. *Union Territory, Chandigarh*, 1985 SCC (Cri) 505: AIR 1986 SC 1438: 1986 Cr LJ 1072; *Tribhuvan Nath* v. *State of Maharashtra*, AIR 1973 SC 450: 1972 Cr LJ 1277: (1972) 3 SCC 511; *Ram Narain* v. *State of Rajasthan*, AIR 1973 SC 1188: (1973) 3 SCC 805: 1973 Cr LJ 914; *G.S. Bakshi* v. *State (Delhi Administration)*, AIR 1979 SC 569: 1978 Cri LR (SC) 438: (1978) 4 SCC 482; *Mukhtiar Kaur* v. *State of Punjab*, AIR 1980 SC 1871; *Union of India* v. *Metal Corporation of India Limited*, AIR 1967 SC 637: (1967) 1 SCR 255: 1967 (1) SCJ 182; *Kanbi Karsan* v. *State of Gujarat*, 1962 Supp 2 SCR 726: 1966 Cr LJ 605: AIR 1966 SC 821; *Shankar alias Gauri Shankar* v. *State of Tamil Nadu*, (1994) 4 SCC 478: 1994 AIR

Contd. on next page

was held in *Kanta Goel* v. *B.P. Pathak,*[1] that the rule is that the necessity for corroboration must be present in the mind of the court and if the court finds sufficient justification to rely on the uncorroborated evidence of an accomplice, it can dispense with corroboration.

All accomplices cannot be treated alike. The nature of the offence, the circumstances under which the accomplice makes his statement must be always considered. Caution is always necessary.

31. A person who is willing to offer bribe in order to get his work done and having got the work done and complains to the police is an accomplice in respect of the crime committed.[2] Persons who are forced to give bribes are not accomplices. In every case the judge should first decide if the witness is or is not an accomplice. Victim of rape is not an accomplice.[3] Previous and subsequent abettors are accomplices.[4] A person who knowingly advances money to the bribe giver is an accomplice. An unblushing giver who gains an advantage and later gives evidence is an accomplice of the darkest colour. At the other extreme is the reluctant bribe giver who, without intention to give the bribe, makes a show of it so as to catch the dishonest bribe taker. He is a good citizen who deserves to be encouraged.[5] Between the two are many gradations. Ordinarily a trap witness is a partisan witness and cannot be taken at face value.[6] Traps are of two kinds. One is where bribe is going to be paid in the ordinary course and police on receiving information lay a trap. No legitimate objection can be taken to this trap. Another is a case in which it is not the intention of the giver to pay any

---

Contd. from previous page

SCW 2083; *Bhiva Doulu Patil* v. *State of Maharashtra,* AIR 1963 SC 599: 1963 Cr LJ 489: (1963) 3 SCR 830; *Sadashiv Mahadeo Yavaluje and Gajanan Shripatrao Salokhe* v. *State of Maharashtra,* AIR 1990 SC 287: 1990 Cr LJ 600; *Chandan* v. *State of Rajasthan,* AIR 1988 SC 599: 1988 Cr LJ 842: (1988) 1 SCC 696; *Ranjeet Singh* v. *State of Rajasthan,* AIR 1988 SC 672; *Ravinder Singh* v. *State of Haryana,* AIR 1975 SC 856: (1975) 3 SCC 742: (1975) 3 SCR 453; *Ram Narain* v. *State of Rajasthan,* AIR 1973 SC 1188: (1973) 3 SCC 805: 1973 Cr LJ 914; *Jnanendra Nath Ghose* v. *State of West Bengal,* AIR 1959 SC 1199: (1960) 1 SCR 126: 1959 Cr LJ 1492; *State of Bihar* v. *Basawan Singh,* AIR 1958 SC 500: 1958 Cr LJ 976: 1959 SCR 195; *S. Swamirathnam (in re:),* AIR 1957 SC 340: 1957 Cr LJ 422; *Harbans Singh Bhan Singh* v. *State of Punjab,* 1957 SCR 953: AIR 1957 SC 637: 1957 Cr LJ 1014: 1957 SCJ 699: 1957 SO 699; *Balwant Kaur* v. *U.T. of Chandigarh,* AIR 1988 SC 139: (1988) 1 SCC 1: 1988 Cr LJ 398; *Kashmira Singh* v. *State of Madhya Pradesh,* AIR 1952 SC 159: 1952 SCR 526: 1952 SCJ 201: 1952 Cr LJ 839; *Rao Shiv Bahadur Singh* v. *State of Vindhya Pradesh,* AIR 1954 SC 322: 1954 SCR 1098: 1954 Cr LJ 910; *Bhuboni Sahu* v. *King,* AIR 1949 PC 257: 50 Cr LJ 872: 51 BLR 955: 53 CWN 609: 1949 ALJ 283: 51 PLR 311: 76 Ind App 147; *Mahadeo* v. *E.,* AIR 1936 PC 242: 163 IC 681: 37 Cr LJ 914; *Kanta Goel* v. *B.P. Pathak,* (1977) 2 SCC 814: AIR 1977 SC 1599: (1977) 3 SCR 412.

1. (1977) 2 SCC 814: AIR 1977 SC 1599: (1977) 3 SCR 412.
2. *Rameshwar* v. *State of Rajasthan,* AIR 1952 SC 54: 1952 SCJ 46: 1952 Cr LJ 547: (1952) 3 SCR 377; *M.O. Shamsudhin* v. *State of Kerala,* (1995) 3 SCC 351: 1995 AIR SCW 2717.
3. *Sidheswar Ganguly* v. *West Bengal,* 1958 Cr LJ 273: AIR 1958 SC 143: 1958 SCR 749; *Narayan Saa* v. *State of Tripura,* AIR 2005 SC 1452: 2004 AIR SCW 7361: (2004) 7 SCC 775; *State of Himachal Pradesh* v. *Shree Kant Shekari,* AIR 2004 SC 4404: 2004 Cr LJ 4232: 2004 AIR SCW 5162; *Rameshwar* v. *State of Rajasthan,* AIR 1952 SC 54: 1952 SCJ 46: 1952 Cr LJ 547: (1952) 3 SCR 377.
4. *Mahadeo* v. *E.,* AIR 1936 PC 242: 163 IC 681: 37 Cr LJ 914; *Jeannette Robinson Belyea* v. *Samuel A. McBride,* AIR 1943 PC 4; *State of Bihar* v. *Srilal Kejriwal,* AIR 1960 Pat 459: 1960 BLJR 565: 1960 Cr LJ 1360.
5. *K.M. Narayanaswami* v. *State of Kerala,* AIR 1957 Ker 134: 1957 Ker LJ 476: 1957 Cr LJ 1127.
6. *Rao Shiv Bahadur Singh* v. *State of Vindhya Pradesh,* AIR 1954 SC 322: 1954 SCR 1098: 1954 Cr LJ 910; *In re: Venkatarama Iyer,* AIR 1957 AP 441: 1956 Andh LT 256: 1956 Andh WR 288.

bribe and it is only the police who want the bribe to be paid in order that an offence may be staged and detected. This kind of trap has been disapproved.[1] In *Hazari Lal* v. *State*,[2] Supreme Court held that there is no rule of prudence which has crystallized into a rule of law, nor indeed into any rule of prudence, which requires evidence of trap witness or officer should be treated on the same footing as that of an accomplice with insistence on corroboration. His uncorroborated testimony can be acted upon if justified by circumstances.[3] There can be no rigid formula laid down in the matter of assessment of value of evidence and degree of corroboration required.[4] Those who participated in the actual crime are accomplices. If not, they are interested witnesses.[5] Where circumstances justify it, court may or may not act on uncorroborated testimony of trap witness.[6] If he has no animus against the accused, he is ordinarily reliable.[7] In appropriate cases, court can insist on corroboration in material particulars. No hard and fast rule can be prescribed.[8] It is wrong to disbelieve trap officers merely because they are police officers. It is better to weigh the evidence in the light of probabilities.[9] In *Kamalabai Jethamal* v. *State of Maharashtra*,[10] practice of using a student as a trap witness (SITA Act) is condemned. A trap witness becomes an accomplice if he actually instigates the offence. Where an officer was deliberately goaded to accept bribe, the evidence was not accepted.[11]

Spies, informers are not accomplices.[12] A Food Inspector is not an accomplice.[13]

---

1. *Kamalabai Jethamal* v. *State of Maharashtra*, AIR 1962 SC 1189: (1962) 2 Cr LJ 273: 1963 (2) SCJ 82; *Major E.G. Barsay* v. *State of Bombay*, AIR 1961 SC 1762: 1962 (1) SCJ 231: (1962) 2 SCR 195; *Public Prosecutor* v. *A. Thomas*, AIR 1959 Mad 166: 1959 Cr LJ 484.
2. AIR 1980 SC 873: (1980) 2 SCC 390: 1980 SCC (Cri) 458: 1980 Cr LJ 564.
3. *Prakash Chand* v. *State (Delhi Administration)*, AIR 1979 SC 400: (1979) 3 SCC 90: 1979 Cr LJ 329: 1979 MLJ (Cri) 419; *Jadunath Khatua* v. *State*, 1982 Cr LJ 954; *Bharatkumar Jaymanishanker Mehta* v. *State of Gujarat*, 1982 Cr LJ 1314: 1982 Guj LH 249: 1982 (23) Guj LR 605.
4. *State of Bihar* v. *Basawan Singh*, AIR 1958 SC 500: 1958 Cr LJ 976: 1959 SCR 195; *Sabramania Goundan* v. *State of Madras*, AIR 1958 SC 66: 1958 SCR 428: 1958 Cr LJ 238: 1958 SCJ 321.
5. *In re Ambujam Ammal*, AIR 1954 Mad 326: (1953) 2 Mad LJ 50: 1954 Cr LJ 417; *Bhuboni Sahu* v. *King*, AIR 1949 PC 257: 50 Cr LJ 872: 51 BLR 955: 53 CWN 609: 1949 ALJ 283: 51 PLR 311: 76 Ind App 147; *George Frier Grahame* v. *Attorney-General, Fiji*, AIR 1936 PC 224.
6. *Prakash Chand* v. *State (Delhi Administration)*, AIR 1979 SC 400: (1979) 3 SCC 90: 1979 Cr LJ 329: 1979 MLJ (Cri) 419; *Ram Prakash Arora* v. *State of Punjab*, AIR 1973 SC 498: (1972) Cr LJ 1293: (1972) 3 SCC 652; *Cheriyan Joseph Poppallil* v. *Geevarghese Philip*, AIR 1974 SC 2183; *State of Bihar* v. *Basawan Singh*, AIR 1958 SC 500: 1958 Cr LJ 976: 1959 SCR 195; *Faquira* v. *State of Uttar Pradesh*, AIR 1976 SC 915: (1976) 1 SCC 662: 1976 Cr LJ 677; *Bhanu Prasad Hari Prasad* v. *State of Gujarat*, AIR 1968 SC 1323: (1969) 1 SCR 22: 1968 Cr LJ 1505.
7. *State of Maharashtra* v. *Narsingrao Gangaram Pimple*, AIR 1984 SC 63: (1984) 1 SCC 446: 1984 Cr LJ 4.
8. *Hazari Lal* v. *State*, AIR 1980 SC 873: (1980) 2 SCC 390: 1980 SCC (Cri) 458: 1980 Cr LJ 564; *State of Maharashtra* v. *Narsingrao Gangaram Pimple*, AIR 1984 SC 63: (1984) 1 SCC 446: 1984 Cr LJ 4.
9. *State of Uttar Pradesh* v. *Dr. G.K. Ghosh*, (1984) 1 SCC 254; *Hazari Lal* v. *State*, AIR 1980 SC 873: (1980) 2 SCC 390: 1980 SCC (Cri) 458: 1980 Cr LJ 564.
10. AIR 1962 SC 1189: (1962) 2 Cr LJ 273: 1963 (2) SCJ 82.
11. *Ramjanam Singh* v. *State of Bihar*, AIR 1956 SC 643: 1956 Cr LJ 1254 (SC).
12. *Mahabir Parshad* v. *State*, AIR 1951 Punj 424: 52 Cr LJ 944: 1951 AWR (Supp) 87; *T.A. Basheeruddin Ahmed* v. *Government of Mysore*, AIR 1952 Mys 42: ILR 1951 Mys 464: 1952 Cr LJ 919; *In re Ambujam Ammal*, AIR 1954 Mad 326: (1953) 2 Mad LJ 50: 1954 Cr LJ 417; *State Government of Madhya Pradesh* v. *Hiralal Tejulal*, AIR 1952 Nag 58: ILR 1951 Nag 930: 1952 Cr LJ 325; *State of Orissa* v. *Minaketan Patnaik*, AIR 1953 Ori 160: ILR 1952 Cuttack 678.
13. *Babulal Hargovindas* v. *State of Gujarat*, AIR 1971 SC 1277: 1971 Cr LJ 1075: 1971 UJ (SC) 500.

32. SECTION 114 Illustration (b).—This is a rule of guidance and practice. Court may or may not invoke it in a given case. This illustration and section 133 are really not, though apparently are, inconsistent. section 133 deals with legality; illustration (b) has effect on propriety. This is one of the few provisions in the Act which deals with weight of evidence. The correct method of appreciation is already dealt with by reference to decisions of Supreme Court.[1]

This is a rule of practice.[2] Neither provision is to be ignored. Reasons must be given for departing from section 114 Illustration (b). The rule is that, the necessity of corroboration as a matter of prudence except when it is safe to dispense with such corroboration, must be present in the mind of the court.[3]

33. SECTION 134.—No particular number of witnesses shall be required to prove any fact. Indian Law goes by weight of evidence and not number of witnesses. Evidence has to be weighed and not counted.[4] Conviction can rest on the evidence of a single witness.[5] It is the quality of the evidence which matters.[6] The maxim under the old English Law "*UNUS NULLUS*" (One equal to none) is not followed in this Section. Out of the witnesses cited in the charge-sheet, prosecution has to select witnesses for actual examination, that is, witnesses regarded as relevant and material for the purpose of unfolding the prosecution case. The prosecution is not bound to call a witness about whom there is reasonable ground for believing that he will not speak the truth.[7] What counts is the quality of the witnesses and not the number of witnesses.[8] Evidence of witnesses examined cannot be thrown out on the ground that other witnesses were not examined.[9] If the evidence of the witness examined appers to be

1. Woodroffe and Amir Ali on Law of Evidence, Vol. 4, page 3460; *Nantu Roy @ Kalyan Roy* v. *State of West Bengal*, 1994 Cr LJ 3271 (SC).
2. *Chandan* v. *State of Rajasthan*, AIR 1988 SC 599: 1988 Cr LJ 842: (1988) 1 SCC 696; *State of Maharashtra* v. *Chandraprakash Jain*, AIR 1990 SC 658: (1990) 1 SCC 550: JT 1990 (1) SC 61: 1990 Cr LJ 889.
3. *Ram Narain* v. *State of Rajasthan*, AIR 1973 SC 1188: (1973) 3 SCC 805: 1973 Cr LJ 914.
4. *Vadivelu Thevar* v. *State of Madras*, AIR 1957 SC 614: 1957 Cr LJ 1000: 1957 SCJ 527; *Pawan Kumar* v. *State of Haryana*, 1997 Cr LJ 3631: 1998 (1) APLJ (Cri) 73: 1997 (4) All Cri LR 495 (SC).
5. *Jose* v. *State of Kerala*, (1973) 3 SCC 472: 1973 SCC (Cri) 372: AIR 1973 SC 944: 1973 Cr LJ 687; *Shivaji Sahabrao Babade* v. *State of Maharashtra*, (1974) 1 SCR 489: (1973) 2 SCC 793: AIR 1973 SC 2622: 1973 Cr LJ 1783; *Maqsoodan* v. *State of Uttar Pradesh*, AIR 1983 SC 126: (1983) 1 SCC 218: 1983 Cr LJ 218: 1982 ALJ 1524; *Ramji Surjya* v. *State of Maharashtra*, AIR 1983 SC 810: (1983) 3 SCC 629: 1983 Cr LJ 1105; *State of Uttar Pradesh* v. *Satish Chandra*, AIR 1986 SC 313: 1985 Cr LJ 1921: (1985) 2 Crimes 861; *Marwadi Kishor Parmanand* v. *State of Gujarat*, (1994) 4 SCC 549: 1994 SCC (Cri) 1294; *Brij Bhushan Singh* v. *E.*, (1946) 47 Cr LJ 336: AIR 1946 PC 38: 223 IC 1: 73 IA 18: 50 Cal WN 348; *Badri* v. *State of Rajasthan*, AIR 1976 SC 560: (1976) 1 SCC 442: 1976 Cr LJ 496.
6. *Vadivelu Thevar* v. *State of Madras*, AIR 1957 SC 614: 1957 Cr LJ 1000: 1957 SCJ 527; *Ramratan* v. *State of Rajasthan*, AIR 1962 SC 424: 1962 (1) SCJ 371: (1962) 3 SCR 590; *Vahula Bhushan* v. *State of Tamil Nadu*, AIR 1989 SC 236: 1989 Cr LJ 799: JT 1988 (4) SC 298.
7. *Mohd. Khalid* v. *State of West Bengal*, (2002) 7 SCC 334: JT 2002 (6) SC 486 relying on *Habeeb Mohammad* v. *State of Hyderabad*, AIR 1954 SC 51: 1953 SCJ 678: 35 Cr LJ 338: 1954 SCR 475 and referring to an early decision in *Mohd. Sugal Esa* v. *King Emperor*, AIR 1940 SC 3.
8. *Krishna Mochi* v. *State of Bihar*, (2002) 6 SCC 81: 2002 Cr LJ 2645: AIR 2002 SC 1965: JT (2002) 4 SC 186; *Joseph* v. *State of Kerala*, AIR 2003 SC 507; *Syed Ibrahim* v. *State of Andhra Pradesh*, (2006) 10 SCC 601: 2006 Cr LJ 4087: AIR 2006 SC 2908 (SC).
9. *Ramjee Rai* v. *State of Bihar*, 2006 Cr LJ 4630: 2006 AIR SCW 4816: 2006 (4) Crimes 225 (SC): (2006) 8 SCALE 440 (SC).

truthful, conviction can rest on his evidence.[1] Plurality of witnesses cannot be insisted upon.[2] Evidence of the lone witness, the investigating officer, if found to be truthful, could be relied on to convict an accused.[3]

---

1. *Chacko* v. *State of Kerala*, AIR 2004 SC 2688: 2004 AIR SCW 1244: (2004) 12 SCC 269.
2. *Vithal Pundalik Zendge* v. *State of Maharashtra*, AIR 2009 SC 1110: 2009 AIR SCW 297: 2009 (1) All Cri LR 362; *Vadivelu Thevar* v. *State of Madras*, AIR 1957 SC 614: 1957 Cr LJ 1000: 1957 SCJ 527; *Chittar Lal* v. *State of Rajasthan*, AIR 2003 SC 3590: (2003) 6 SCC 397: 2003 Cr LJ 3548: 2003 AIR SCW 3466; *Ravi* v. *State*, AIR 2009 SC 214: 2008 AIR SCW 7166: 2009 (64) All Cri C 447; Ratanlal Dhirajlal on Law of Evidence, 23rd Edition, pages 1668 to 1681.
3. *Lopchand Naruji Jat* v. *State of Gujarat*, 2004 Cr LJ 4241: AIR 2004 SC 4645: 2004 AIR SCW 5267.

CHAPTER 22
OF THE EXAMINATION OF WITNESSES (SECTIONS 135 TO 167)

Procedural aspects of summoning and examination of witnesses is dealt with by sections 31, 32, 135, and Order XVI of C.P.C., and sections 34, 61 to 94, 217 and 311 of Cr.P.C.

The mandate of section 5 of the Evidence Act is that parties can adduce evidence to prove only facts in issue and relevant facts and of no others. Generally witnesses should be examined out of the hearing of each other.[1] Court may refuse to examine a person who was present during the evidence of another witness.[2]

2. SECTION 135

The order in which witnesses are produced and examined shall be regulated by the law and practice for the time being relating to civil and criminal procedure respectively, and in the absence of any such law, by the discretion of the court. Courts rarely exercise this discretion and yield to practicality. Order XVIII, rule 1 to 3A C.P.C. and Chapter XVIII to XXIII of Cr.P.C. contain some relevant provisions. Court will, however, be slow to interfere with the discretion of the counsel, though it has power to do so. Rule 3A of Order XVIII C.P.C. requires the party to be examined first. The practice of calling the opposite party as a witness has been condemned. The order of proving depends on the burden of proof. Court has the power to ask an unexamined witness to remain outside court when another witness is being examined.

3. SECTION 136

When either party proposes to give evidence in proof of any fact, the court may ask the party purporting to adduce such evidence in what manner the alleged fact, if proved, would be relevant; and the judge shall admit the evidence if he thinks that the fact, if proved, would be relevant and not otherwise.

If the fact proposed to be proved is one of which evidence is admissible only upon proof of some other fact, such last mentioned fact must be proved before evidence is given of the fact first mentioned, unless the party undertakes to give proof of such fact, and the court is satisfied with such undertaking.

If the relevancy of one alleged fact depends upon another alleged fact being first proved, the judge may, in his discretion, either permit evidence of the first fact to be given before the second fact is proved, or require evidence to be given of the second fact before evidence is given of the first fact.

---

1. *Achyutana Pitchaiah Sarma* v. *Gorantla Chinna Veerayya*, AIR 1961 AP 420: (1961) 1 Andh WR 396: 1961 Andh LT 384.
2. *Chacko Varghese* v. *Karthiyani*, 1987 Ker LJ 990.

The illustrations to the section are instructive. Before adducing evidence to prove an alleged "dying declaration" under section 32, the fact that the declarant is dead must be proved.

Proof must be confined to facts which are in issue or which are relevant. Question of admissibility is to be decided by the judge. He can ask in what manner the evidence tendered is relevant and then decide on its relevancy. Summons need be issued on such satisfaction and not in a mechanical manner. This scrutiny is to be made irrespective of any objection raised by any party. Failure to object does not result in estoppel if a mandatory provision of Evidence Act has been violated.[1]

The Section applies to oral and documentary evidence. Any party has a right to adduce direct evidence, oral or documentary, to prove facts in issue or relevant facts in civil cases or the charged offence or ingredients of charged offence and relevant facts in criminal cases. If a document is produced or witness is sought to be examined to prove any fact which is not a fact in issue or a relevant fact, such evidence cannot be received by court; it is inadmissible. Illustrations (a) and (b) explain para 2 of the section, while illustrations (c) and (d) explain para 3 of the section. What are relevant facts is seen from chapter 2 of the Evidence Act. Question of relevancy and admissibility of a document has to be decided when an objection is raised by the opposite party or when the court entertains a doubt about it. Objection to the mode of proof of a document can be waived. The fact that no objection was raised before a civil court to the relevancy or mode of proof of a document does not mean that the party not raising such an objection has admitted the contents of the document. It is the duty of the court to exclude all irrelevant or inadmissible evidence, though no objection was taken by the any of the parties.[2]

Second para has to be read with section 104.

4. SECTION 137

The examination of a witness by the party who calls him shall be called his examination-in-chief. The examination of a witness by the adverse party shall be called in cross-examination. The examination of a witness, subsequent to the cross-examination shall be called his re-examination. Witnesses shall be first examined in-chief, then (if the adverse party so desires) cross-examined, and then (if the party calling him so desires), re-examined.

5. SECTION 138

The examination and cross-examination must relate to relevant facts, but the cross-examination need not be confined to facts elicited in chief-examination. Re-examination shall be directed to explain matters referred to in cross-examination. If new matter is introduced by permission of the Court in re-examination, the adverse party may further cross-examine upon that matter.

Court has control over the manner and extent of examination of witnesses. Judge may protect a witness against irrelevant questions and omit a question which is being repeated. He may allow sufficient time to a witness to answer a question before allowing the next question. He must control objectionable leading questions. But undue interference is undesirable. Court will not cross-examine

1. *Miller* v. *Madhu Das*, (1890) 19 All 192 (PC).
2. *Miller* v. *Madhu Das*, (1890) 19 All 192 (PC); *Sri Rajah Prakasarayanim Garu* v. *Y.P. Venkata Rao*, ILR 38 Mad 160: AIR 1915 Mad 793.

a witness. Witnesses should ordinarily be left to be dealt with by the counsel. In the case of omission of important aspects or in case of ambiguity, court may put questions and allow cross-examination on those answers. Court must bear in mind that it has a duty towards all the parties and to ensure fair trial. Court witnesses may be allowed to be subject to cross-examination by both the parties. Volunteering answers should be frowned upon. Objections to questions must be raised when they are asked. Omission to object suggests waiver of the form of the question. But on the aspect of relevancy or admissibility, omission to object at the time does not result in any waiver. Once chief-examination is commenced, the witness cannot be given up. He can be given up before such commencement.[1]

Court is empowered to note in the deposition about demeanor. Order XVIII, rule 12 of C.P. Code may be seen.[2]

Witnesses may testify to the existence, identity and execution of documents and where secondary evidence is admissible, may testify to their contents. Leading questions will not be ordinarily permitted in chief-examination.

6. Cross-examination.—A witness may be asked questions to test his veracity, to discover who he is and what his position in life is and to shake his credit by injuring his character.

Cross-examination has an important purpose to achieve; that is to expose the truth. Full opportunity should be given for the same. It should not be curtailed on one pretext or the other. He should not be cross-examined as to any collateral independent fact, irrelevant to the fact in issue. Leading questions can be put in cross-examination but not in chief-examination or re-examination. If a party had no opportunity to cross-examine a witness, the evidence is not legally admissible, except with his consent.[3] If a statement of fact is not challenged in cross-examination, ordinarily it must be taken to be not objected to.[4] Leading questions, but not misleading questions, can be put in cross-examination.

Failure to cross-examine leads to acceptance of the evidence unless there are some inherent improbabilities in it.[5] The mere fact that no record was made in the deposition that there was no cross-examination, does not lead to the inference that request for cross-examination was denied.[6] The evidence of a witness not cross-examined at all, need not necessarily be true; it may not be accepted, if on the face of it, the evidence is unacceptable.[7] If in the cross-examination of

---

1. *Lalitha* v. *Sarangadharan*, 1988 II Ker LT 394.
2. *Sita Lakshmi Ammal* v. *Venkata Subrahmania*, AIR 1930 PC 170: 123 IC 557; *Valarshak Seth Apcar* v. *Standard Coal Co. Ltd.*, AIR 1943 PC 159: ILR (1944) Kar PC 109 (PC).
3. *Neminath Appayya Hanamannanavar* v. *Jamboorao Satappa Kocheri*, AIR 1966 Mys 154: (1965) 1 Mys LJ 442; *Chandan Lal Joura* v. *Amin Chand Mohan Lal, a partnership firm*, AIR 1960 Punj 500: 62 Pun LR 624: ILR (1960) 2 Pun 506; *Gopal Saran* v. *Satyanarayan*, (1989) 3 SCC 56: AIR 1989 SC 1141: 1989 MPRCJ 53.
4. *State of Himachal Pradesh* v. *Thakur Dass*, 1983 CrLJ 1694: 1983 (10) Cr LT 370: 1983 Shim LC 240; *Traders Syndicate* v. *Union of India*, AIR 1983 Cal 337; *State* v. *Bhola Singh*, AIR 1969 Raj 219: 1969 Cr LJ 1002: ILR (1969) 19 Raj 273.
5. *Jawar Singh* v. *State of Madhya Pradesh*, AIR 1981 SC 373: 1980 Supp SCC 417: 1980 Cr LJ 1418; *State of Uttar Pradesh* v. *Nahar Singh*, AIR 1998 SC 1328: 1998 Cr LJ 2006: (1998) 3 SCC 561; *Sarwan Singh* v. *State of Punjab*, AIR 2002 SC 3652: (2003) 1 SCC 240: 2003 Cr LJ 21.
6. *Union of India* v. *T.R. Verma*, AIR 1957 SC 882: 1958 SCR 499: 60 Punj LR 126: 1958 SCJ 142.
7. *Jawar Singh* v. *State of Madhya Pradesh*, AIR 1981 SC 373: 1980 Supp SCC 417: 1980 Cr LJ 1418.

a prosecution witness, no suggestion was put to the witness suggesting the defence version, the defence version argued by the defence counsel may be rejected as an afterthought.[1]

There is no lawful procedure for tendering a witness for cross-examination, without chief-examination.[2]

Rambling cross-examination can be stopped.[3] But undue interference must be avoided. Irrelevant question can be disallowed. Every such question need not be recorded. If it is an important question, the same may be recorded as also reason for disallowing it. Cross-examination is one of the most important processes for elucidation of the facts of a case.[4] Suggestive questions in cross-examination do not amount to admission.[5]

One co-accused has the right to cross-examine a witness called by the other co-accused.[6] A defendant supporting the plaintiff has no right to cross-examine the other defendant or his witness.

7. Re-examination.—The object of re-examination is to explain any part of the evidence elicited during cross-examination, which is capable of being construed unfavourably to the party who called the witness. It is to give opportunity to reconcile discrepancies, if any, between statements in chief-examination and cross-examination or to explain any statement inadvertently made in cross-examination or to remove any ambiguity in the answers. In the absence of these features, question should not be put in re-examination with the sole object of giving a chance to the witness to undo the effect of an admission.

A witness may be recalled for further chief-examination in case of inadvertent omissions in chief-examination. It is in the discretion of court to allow it.

Re-examination cannot introduce new matters.[7] If it is allowed right of further cross-examination arises. If in cross-examination, a former inconsistent statement had been admitted, in re-examination the motive or reason for making such statement can be elicited. If in cross-examination facts had been elicited which impeach his credibility or character, in re-examination questions can be put to explain that such facts are consistent with his credibility. Re-examination can be used to clarify ambiguites which arose in cross-examination and aslo to obtain explanation required for anything referred to in cross-examination.[8]

Permission to treat a witness hostile can be granted even after cross-examination is over. A clever witness faithfully conforms in chief-examination to

1. *K.N. Mehra* v. *State of Rajasthan*, AIR 1957 SC 369: 1957 Cr LJ 552: 1957 SCC 192; *Yusufalli Esmail Nagree* v. *State of Maharashtra*, AIR 1968 SC 147: 1968 Cr LJ 103: 1967 SCR 720: (1968) 1 SCJ 511: 70 Bom LR 76.
2. *Sukhwant Singh* v. *State of Punjab*, AIR 1995 SC 1601: (1995) 3 SCC 367: JT 1995 (3) SC 495; *State of Uttar Pradesh* v. *Jaggo*, AIR 1971 SC 1586: (1971) 2 SCC 42: 1971 Cr LJ 1173; *Sukhwant Singh* v. *State of Punjab*, AIR 1995 SC 1601: (1995) 3 SCC 367: JT 1995 (3) SC 495.
3. *Yeshpal Jashbhai Parikh* v. *Rasiklal Umedchand Parikh*, AIR 1955 Bom 318: 1955 Cr LJ 1159: ILR (1955) Bom 675; *Raj Kumar* v. *Ram Sundar*, AIR 1932 PC 69: 1932 All LJ 198.
4. *Vassiliades* v. *Vassiliades*, AIR 1945 PC 38: 1945 All LJ 34; *Babu* v. *Babu*, (2003) 7 SCC 37.
5. *Binapani Roja* v. *Rabindranath Sarkar*, AIR 1959 Cal 213.
6. *K.L. Tripathi* v. *State Bank of India*, AIR 1984 SC 273: (1984) 1 SCC 43: (1984) 1 Lab LJ 2; *Dr. Suhas H. Pophale* v. *Oriental Insurance Co. Ltd. & Its Estate Officer*, (2008) 3 SCC 279.
7. *Chanan Singh* v. *State of Haryana*, AIR 1971 SC 1554: 1971 Cri App R (SC) 318.
8. *Rammi* v. *State of Madhya Pradesh*, (1999) 8 SCC 649: AIR 1999 SC 3544: 1999 Cr LJ 4561: 1999 AIR SCW 3546.

what he stated earlier to the police, but in cross-examination introduces answers in a subtle way contradicting in effect what he stated in chief-examination. If his design is obvious, the court can, in the course of his re-examination, permit the person calling him as a witness to put questions to him which might be put in cross-examination by the adverse party. The adverse party can have an opportunity to further cross-examine him on the answers elicited by putting such questions, as the court has the discretion to permit the adverse party to do so.[1] A witness whose evidence is closed may be recalled for the purpose of a just decision. He may be recalled even for further chief–examination, if the interests of Justice so demand.

Court is not bound to accept the evidence of a witness, which on the face it is unacceptable, merely because there was no cross-examination.[2]

8. What a Judge should do.—It is advisable to be always watchful of the witnesses. Fairplay must be assured to both parties and the witnesses. Unfair questions are to be discouraged. Court has to ensure that counsel comes prepared to conduct cross-examination. An unprepared cross-examination is a waste of time. Court should try to be in control of the situation and understand the contentions of both sides before commencement of oral evidence and follow the evidence intelligently. Then only the judge will be able to decide quickly any dispute regarding relevancy. He should ensure that counsel knows the limits of cross-examination or re-examination. Abuse of right of cross-examination must be prevented, as also unwarranted protraction of evidence. Scandalous or vexations questions must be avoided. Rudeness by or to witnesses, may be avoided. Judge must ensure that all relevant evidence is brought in; depositions may be recorded clearly, legibly and fairly using the facility of paragraphs. Each witness may be examined out of the hearing of the other witnesses. Sections 273 to 282 of Cr.P.C. must be scrupulously observed. Deposition must be read over to the witnesses immediately after the completion of examination. If necessary, it has to be interpreted to him. All this must be done in the presence of accused. Clerical errors may be corrected.

Court can put questions to a witness to elicite truth.[3] Court has the discretion to decise how far cross-examination may go and how long it may continue. This has to be done in a fair and reasonable manner.[4] Abuse in the matter of cross-examination which enormously increases the cost of litigation without any corresponding benefit to the parties has to be checked.[5]

9. SECTION 139

A person summoned to produce a document does not become a witness merely because he produces it and cannot be cross-examined unless and until he is called as a witness.[6] This section merely provides machinery for production

1. *Dahyabhai* v. *State of Gujarat*, AIR 1964 SC 1563: (1964) 2 Cr LJ 472: (1964) 1 SCWR 831: (1964) 7 SCR 361.
2. *Jawar Singh* v. *State of Madhya Pradesh*, AIR 1981 SC 373: 1980 Supp SCC 417: 1980 Cr LJ 1418.
3. *State of Rajasthan* v. *Ani* alias *Hanif*, AIR 1997 SC 1023: 1977 Cr LJ 1529: (1997) 6 SCC 162; *Ram Chander* v. *State of Haryana*, AIR 1981 SC 1036: 1981 Cr LJ 609: (1981) 3 SCC 191.
4. *Vassiliades* v. *Vassiliades*, AIR 1945 PC 38: 1945 All LJ 34; *Babu* v. *Babu*, (2003) 7 SCC 37.
5. *Raj Kumar* v. *Ram Sundar*, AIR 1932 PC 69: 1932 All LJ 198.
6. *State of Bombay* v. *Kathi Kalu Oghad*, AIR 1961 SC 1808: (1962) 3 SCR 10: (1961) 2 Cr LJ 856: 64 Bom LR 240; *Parmeshwari Devi* v. *State*, (1977) 2 SCR 160: AIR 1977 SC 403: 1977 Cr LJ 245.

of summoned documents. It is sufficient if the summoned person causes the document to be produced. Order XVI, rule 6 Code of Civil Procedure may be seen. Production of a document under the section 139 is not proof of custody for the purpose of section 90.

10. SECTION 140

Witness to character may be cross-examined and re-examined. This specific provision has been made in the face of the contrary practice in England. The word "Character" is a wide expression. Sections 53, 54 and 146(3) may also be seen. Character lies in the man; it is the mark of what he is, unlike reputation while depends upon others and it is what they think of him. Character is an expression of wide import which takes in all the traits, special and particular qualities impressed by nature or habit which serve as an index to the essential nature of a person.[1]

11. SECTION 141

Any question suggesting the answer which the person putting the question wishes or expects to receive, is called a leading question.

12. SECTION 142

Leading questions must not be asked in chief-examination or re-examination if objected to by the adverse party, except with the permission of court. The Court shall permit leading questions as to matters which are introductory or undisputed, or which have, in its opinion, been already sufficiently proved.

13. SECTION 143

Leading questions may be asked in cross-examination.

It is improper for a counsel to put leading questions (except introductory or undisputed or proved already) to his own witness without treating him hostile. It is improper for court to allow it. A leading question is one which either suggests the answer desired, or assumes the existence of disputed facts as to which the witness is to testify.[2] A question is leading when it suggests the answer, not when it merely directs the attention of the witness to the subject respecting which he is questioned.[3] What is a leading question in one case or situation depends on the case and situation. A question depends on it's suggestion more in the tone of voice then in the form of words.[4] It is a question framed in such a manner as to suggest a hint directly or indirectly which the examiner desires to elicit from the witness. Such questions can be put in cross-examination. A party who calls a witness, may with permission of court, put leading question if the witness turned "hostile". The prohibition is not absolute. Court can allow such questions under Order XVIII, rule 11 C.P.C., though objected to as leading question. This power is discretionary, and depends upon on the circumstances, such as demeanour and attitude of the witness, the tenor of the preceeding questions etc.[5] The object of putting leading questions to a witness is to revive or refresh his memory by drawing his attention to a particular topic. Leading questions in criminal cases offend the right of the accused to fair trial, under

1. Ratanlal and Dhirajlal on Law of Evidence, 23rd Edition page 1710.
2. Stephen's Digest on Law of Evidence, 12th Edition, Article 140.
3. Best on Evidence, 8th Edition, page 592.
4. Field on Evidence 1967 Edition, Vol. 6, page 4820.
5. Howrah Trading Co. Ltd., Vol. 4. Ind. Tribunal, (1966) 2 Lab LJ 282.

article 21 of the Constitution.[1] The rule is not strictly applicable in domestic enquiry.[2]

Rule against leading question in chief-examination has three exceptions, namely (1) introductory etc., (2) under section 154, and (3) discretion of court. Sometimes it is allowed in the case of witnesses with defective memory or in regard to complicated matters. Misleading questions should not be put in the garb of leading questions in cross-examination. Wigmore observes that if an opponent's witness proves to be in fact biased in favour of the cross-examiner, leading questions may be forbidden.

14. SECTION 144

Any witness may be asked, while under examination, whether any contract, grant or disposition of property as to which he is giving evidence, was not contained in a document, and if he says that it was, or if he is about to make any statement as to the contents of any document, which, in the opinion of the Court, ought to be produced, the adverse party may object to such evidence being given until such document isproduced, or until facts have been proved which entitle the party who called the witness to give secondary evidence of it.

Explanation:—A witness may give oral evidence of statements made by other persons about the contents of documents if such statements are in themselves relevant facts.

This is a matter in which provisions of sections 91 and 92 may be enforced by the parties. Even if the opposite party does not object, it is the duty of the Court to prevent production of inadmissible evidence. Section 144 comes into play only when the witness is asked questions, while under cross-examination, with regard to any contract, grant or disposition of property.

15. SECTION 145

The Section is in two parts.—(1) A witness may be cross-examined as to previous statements made by him in writing or reduced to writing and relevant to the matters in question, without such writing being shown to him or being proved, (2) To contradict him by the writing, his attention must be called to relevant parts of it (contradictory) before proving the writing.[3] This section applies to a party as also a stranger witness.

This is one way of testing the memory and integrity of a witness. The other relevant sections are 138, 140, 146 and 154 for impeaching credit. According to section 155(3), one method of impeaching credit is by proof of an inconsistent previous statement. The mode of proof by tendering in evidence for contradiction is provided in section 145. Section 155(3) is controlled by section 145. The object of this section is to give an opportunity to the witness to explain or reconcile the conflict before the contradiction can be used as evidence. This section is to be resorted to only if a witness denies that he made a former statement.[4] A witness

1. *Varkey Joseph* v. *State of Kerala*, AIR 1993 SC 1892: 1993 Cr LJ 2010: 1993 AIR SCW 1729.
2. *Employers of Firestone Tyre and Rubber Co. (Private) Ltd.* v. *Workmen*, AIR 1968 SC 236: 1968 (2) SCJ 83: (1968) 1 SCR 307.
3. *Tahsildar Singh* v. *State of Uttar Pradesh*, AIR 1959 SC 1012: 1959 SCJ 1042: ILR (1960) 1 All 136: 1959 Cr LJ 1231; *Bhogilal Chunilal Pandya* v. *State of Bombay*, AIR 1959 SC 356: 1959 Supp (1) SCR 310: 1959 Cr LJ 389; *Pawan Kumar* v. *State of Haryana*, 1997 Cr LJ 3631: 1998 (1) APLJ (Cri) 73: 1997 (4) All Cri LR 495 (SC).
4. *Bhagwan Singh* v. *State of Punjab*, AIR 1952 SC 214: 1952 Cr LJ 1131: 1952 SCR 812: 1952 SCJ 284.

can be contradicted only when he denies his statement and not when he admits it.[1] The first part of the section deals with cross-examination other than by way of contradiction and the second part by way of contradiction only.[2]

This section does not apply to admission in previous statements made by the parties.[3] Admissions of parties are substantive evidence by themselves, irrespective of whether the maker comes to the witness box or not or whether, if he so appeared, he was confronted with it or not. Admission of a party is used as proof of fact in issue or relevant fact while contradiction of a witness with reference to previous statement is to impeach his credit.[4]

Only the portions to which attention of the witness is drawn can be considered for assessing his credibility.[5] Marking of whole section 161 statement to prove an omission is wrong. A contradiction in a previous statement must be one of substance.

16. The previous statement of a witness (unlike a party) can not to be used as substantive evidence of the facts mentioned therein, but can be used only to contradict the witness to impeach his credibility. The section does not say it is to be taken to be a true statement. A witness may be contradicted by the statements in a diary kept by him or a document to which he was a party.[6] The same applies to statements under section 164 of the Code.[7] Proof of the contradiction through the investigator does not make it substantive evidence.[8] Where section 157 is attracted, a previous statement (say an FIS) can be used for corroboration of the evidence of the witness who made the previous statement. If a previous statement of a party or his agent or representative, otherwise admissible, contains an admission (section 21) it can be used as substantive evidence. So also if FIS contains a dying declaration (section 32). So also a FIS given by an accused as evidence of his conduct. (Section 8).

A defence witness in a Criminal trial cannot be cross-examined with reference to his section 161 statement.[9]

1. *Dhanabal* v. *State of Tamil Nadu*, AIR 1980 SC 628: (1980) 2 SCC 84: 1980 Cr LJ 439; *State of Rajasthan* v. *Kartar Singh*, AIR 1970 SC 1305: (1970) 2 SCC 61: 1970 Cr LJ 1144.
2. *Kanu Ambu Vish* v. *State of Maharashtra*, AIR 1971 SC 2256: 1971 Civ Ap R (SC) 181: 1971 Cr LJ 1547.
3. *Trichinopoly Mills, Limited* v. *National Cotton Textile Mills Workers Union*, AIR 1960 SC 1003: (1960-61) 18 FJR 99: (1960) 2 Lab LJ 46.
4. *Bharat Singh* v. *Mst. Bhagirthi*, AIR 1966 SC 405: (1966) 1 SCR 606: 1966 (2) SCJ 53; *Bharatiya Samskrithi Vidhyapith, Banglore* v. *G. Parthasarathy*, AIR 1977 Kant 113: (1977) 1 Kant LJ 87: ILR (1977) 1 Kant 275; *Biswanath Prasad* v. *Dwarka Prasad*, AIR 1974 SC 117: (1974) 1 SCC 78: (1974) 2 SCR 124.
5. *Som Nath* v. *Union of India*, AIR 1971 SC 1910: 1971 Cr LJ 1429: 1971 (Supp) SCR 848.
6. *Bhogilal Chunilal Pandya* v. *State of Bombay*, AIR 1959 SC 356: 1959 Supp (1) SCR 310: 1959 Cr LJ 389.
7. *Brij Bhushan Singh* v. *E.*, (1946) 47 Cr LJ 336: AIR 1946 PC 38: 223 IC 1: 73 IA 18: 50 Cal WN 348.
8. *Bharat Singh* v. *Mst. Bhagirthi*, AIR 1966 SC 405: (1966) 1 SCR 606: 1966 (2) SCJ 53; *Kanu Ambu Vish* v. *State of Maharashtra*, AIR 1971 SC 2256: 1971 Civ Ap R (SC) 181: 1971 Cr LJ 1547; *Judah* v. *Isolyne Shrojbashini Bose*, AIR 1945 PC 174: ILR (1945) Kar PC 351: 1945 OWN 287; *State (Delhi Administration)* v. *Laxman Kumar*, AIR 1986 SC 250: 1985 CAR 304: 1985 Cr LR 501: (1985) 2 Crimes 758: (1985) 2 SCALE 701: (1985) 4 SCC 476: (1985) 2 SCR 898: 1986 Cr LJ 155; *Hazari Lal* v. *State*, AIR 1980 SC 873: (1980) 2 SCC 390: 1980 SCC (Cri) 458: 1980 Cr LJ 564; *Collector of Customs and Central Excise* v. *Lekhraj Jessumal and Sons*, AIR 1997 SC 145: (1996) 7 SCC 489: (1996) 2 SCR 245.
9. *Laxman Kalu Nikalje* v. *State of Maharashtra*, AIR 1968 SC 1390: 1968 Cr LJ 1647: (1968) 2 SCWR 557; *Shakila Khader* v. *Nausher Gama*, AIR 1975 SC 1324: (1975) 4 SCC 122: 1975 Cr LJ 1105.

An omission of importance in a previous statement could be regarded as a contradiction.[1] This principle applies also to FIS or section 161 statement.[2] Omission must refer to something, which if it existed, could not have been missed by the witness. His attention must be drawn to it after asking him if he had mentioned it to police. Effect of an omission depends on the circumstances of the case.[3] This section applies to a Panchanama signed by a witness.[4] This section must be complied with in substance and not merely in form.[5]

The correct procedure is to tentatively mark the relevant part of the statement containing the contradiction and prove that part subsequently, if it is denied. (When the investigator is examined).[6]

The section applies only to previous statements reduced to writing. Regarding its applicability to a taped statement may be seen.[7] A previous oral statement can be used for contradiction under section 155(3) which applies to oral statements also. The statement in writing need not be signed.[8]

Witness must have an opportunity to explain.[9] His attention must be called to the contradictory part.[10] Failure to observe the requirement of this section is a fatal defect.[11]

17. PREVIOUS STATEMENT

Section 145 deals with previous statements, not subsequent ones. Prior deposition, prior pleading, prior statements under sections 161 and 164 of Code, letters, complaints, section 313 statements in other cases, are previous statements.[12] So also deposition before committal Magistrate under the old

1. *State of Madhya Pradesh* v. *Revashankar*, AIR 1959 SC 102: 1959 SCJ 86: 1959 SCR 1367; *Dahyabhai* v. *State of Gujarat*, AIR 1964 SC 1563: (1964) 2 Cr LJ 472: (1964) 1 SCWR 831: (1964) 7 SCR 361; *Matadin* v. *State of Uttar Pradesh*, AIR 1979 SC 1234: 1979 Cr LJ 1027 1979 SCC Cri 627; *Laxman* v. *State of Maharashtra*, AIR 1974 SC 308: 1974 (2) SCJ 371: (1974) 2 SCR 505.
2. *Mehr Vajsi Deva* v. *State State of Gujarat*, AIR 1965 Guj 143: ILR 1964 Guj 799: (1965) 1 Cr LJ 696.
3. *Laxman* v. *State of Maharashtra*, AIR 1974 SC 308: 1974 (2) SCJ 371: (1974) 2 SCR 505.
4. *Kanu Ambu Vish* v. *State of Maharashtra*, AIR 1971 SC 2256: 1971 Civ Ap R (SC) 181: 1971 Cr LJ 1547.
5. *Bhagwan Singh* v. *State of Punjab*, AIR 1952 SC 214: 1952 Cr LJ 1131: 1952 SCR 812: 1952 SCJ 284.
6. *Ahmed R.V. Peermohamed* v. *Jogi S. Bhar*, 1990 Cr LJ 2195: 1990 (1) Mah LR 126; *Puthenthara Mohanan* v. *State of Kerala*, 1990 Cr LJ 1059; *Podda Narayana* v. *State of Uttar Pradesh*, AIR 1975 SC 1252: 1975 Cr 1062: (1975) 4 SCC 153.
7. *Babu Lal* v. *State of Uttar Pradesh*, AIR 1964 SC 725: (1964) 1 SCWR 180: (1964) 1 Cr LJ 555; *C.K. Narayana Chary* v. *Pothepalli Ashanna*, AIR 1986 SC 317: (1986) 1 SCC 9: (1986) 1 Supreme 232; *Shiv Kirpal Singh* v. *V.V. Giri*, AIR 1970 SC 2097; *N. Sri Ram Reddy* v. *V.V. Giri*, AIR 1971 SC 1162: (1971) 1 SCR 399: (1970) 2 SCC 340.
8. *Narayanan* v. *Krishnan*, 1981 Cr LJ 563.
9. *Bal Gangadhar Tilak* v. *Shriniwas Pandit*, AIR 1915 PC 7: 39 B 441: 42 IA 135: 29 IC 639; *Tara Singh* v. *State*, AIR 1951 SC 441: 1951 SCR 729: 1951 Cr LJ 1491.
10. *Tara Singh* v. *State*, AIR 1951 SC 441: 1951 SCR 729: 1951 Cr LJ 1491; *Bhagwan Singh* v. *State of Punjab*, AIR 1952 SC 214: 1952 Cr LJ 1131: 1952 SCR 812: 1952 SCJ 284.
11. *Tara Singh* v. *State*, AIR 1951 SC 441: 1951 SCR 729: 1951 Cr LJ 1491.
12. *Ponnuswami* v. *Kalyanasundara*, AIR 1930 Mad 770: 125 Ind Cas 231; *Badri* v. *State of Rajasthan*, AIR 1976 SC 560: (1976) 1 SCC 442: 1976 Cr LJ 496; *Judah* v. *Isolyne Shrojbashini Bose*, AIR 1945 PC 174: ILR (1945) Kar PC 351: 1945 OWN 287; *Karachi Oil Products Ltd.* v. *Kumar Shree Narendrasinghji*, AIR 1950 Bom 149: 51 Bom LR 1012: ILR 1950 Bom 192; *Dinamani Dass* v. *Bimbadhar Padhan*, AIR 1969 Ori 28.

Code.[1] (Section 288 old Code), FIS is a previous statement.[2] Inquest report can be used under this Section.[3] So also Panchanama.[4]

This Section is controlled by section 162 of the Code. What is prohibited by the latter cannot be brought in under this section.

18. SECTION 146

When a witness is cross-examined, he may, in addition to questions hereinbefore referred to, be asked any question which tend—

(1) to test his Veracity,

(2) to discover who is and what his position in life is, or

(3) to shake his credit, by injuring his character, although the answers to such questions might tend directly or indirectly to criminate him or might expose or tend directly or indirectly to expose him to a penalty or forfeiture.

Provided that in a prosecution for an offence under section 376, section 376A, section 376B, section 376C, section 376D or section 376E of the Indian Penal Code or for attempt to commit any such offence, where the question of consent is an issue, it shall not be permissible to adduce evidence or to put question in the cross-examination of the victim as to the general immoral character, or previous sexual experience of such victim as to the general character, or previous sexual experience, of such victim with any person for proving such consent or the quality of consent.

The above proviso substituted an earlier proviso introduced by amending Act 4 of 2003. The earlier proviso read as follows:

Provided that in a prosecution for rape or attempt to commit rape, it shall not be permissible to put questions in the cross-examination of the prosecutrix as to her general immoral character.

19. Thus section confers very wide powers on the cross-examiner in addition to those given by section 138 which confines cross-examination to relevant facts. Sections 145 and 155 also may be seen in this context. Credibility of a witness assumes great importance when the main or crucial evidence is his or her oral evidence. Under this section, questions may be put to test and shake the witness's credit and obtain details of his identity and position in life which may have relevance on the question of his credit. Under section 153 (exception (1)) and section 155, he may be contradicted when he denies any fact.[5] Cross-examination can be directed show the antipathy of the witness to the party and to throw proper light on the bias of the witness. Sections 147 to 150 protect a witness when his character is sought to be impeached. Sections 148 and 155

1. *Tara Singh* v. *State*, AIR 1951 SC 441: 1951 SCR 729: 1951 Cr LJ 1491; *Jit Singh* v. *State of Punjab*, AIR 1976 SC 1421: (1976) 2 SCC 836: 1976 Cr LJ 1162; *Bhagwan Singh* v. *State of Punjab*, AIR 1952 SC 214: 1952 Cr LJ 1131: 1952 SCR 812: 1952 SCJ 284.
2. *Aghnoo Nagesia* v. *State of Bihar*, AIR 1966 SC 119: 1966 Cr LJ 100: (1966) 1 SCJ 193: (1966) 1 SCR 134; *Nanhku Singh* v. *State of Bihar*, AIR 1973 SC 491: 1972 Cr LJ 1204: (1972) 3 SCC 590; *Sheikh Hasib* v. *State of Bihar*, AIR 1972 SC 283: (1972) 4 SCC 773: 1972 Cr LJ 233; AIR 1957 SC 312.
3. *Pandurang Tukia* v. *Hyderabad*, AIR 1955 SC 216: (1955) 1 SCR 1083: 1955 Cr LJ 572 (SC).
4. *Kanu Ambu Vish* v. *State of Maharashtra*, AIR 1971 SC 2256: 1971 Civ Ap R (SC) 181: 1971 Cr LJ 1547.
5. *N. Sri Ram Reddy* v. *V.V. Giri*, AIR 1971 SC 1162: (1971) 1 SCR 399: (1970) 2 SCC 340.

seem to indicate that credit is shaken only if it is shown that he is not a person of veracity. Questions to impeach credit also must be relevant to that aspect. Vexatious questions which do not really impeach credit or do not challenge the evidence given in chief examination are not allowed. Sections 132 and 146 to 151 must be read together. Evidence is admissible under section 145(1), section 153 exception 2, and section 155 (3).[1] Section 146 (1) relates to questions to test veracity etc., section 153 deals with contradicting him to show he is not reliable or impartial. (*Ibid*). In putting questions under section 146(3), the lawyer must have some reasonable grounds.[2] Questions to harass or embarrass a witness should not be allowed.[3] Section 146 extends the field of cross-examination provided in section 132.

20. SECTION 147

If any question put under section 146 relates to a matter relevant to the case, section 132 shall apply thereto. He shall not be excused from answering any question as to any relevant matter on the ground that the answer will criminate or tend to criminate him or that it will expose or tend to expose him to a penalty or forfeiture. Section 132 may also be referred to. A witness is compellable to answer every question which is relevant to the issue, unless protected by public policy or privilege or unless the case is one in which evidence is excluded by documentary evidence. All cross-examination must be relevant to the issue or to the witness's credit.[4]

21. SECTION 148

If any such question relates to a matter not relevant to the case, except to the extent of affecting credit by injuring his character, court shall decide whether or not the witness shall be compelled to answer it, and may, if it thinks fit, warn the witness that he is not obliged to answer it. In exercising its' discretion, the Court shall have regard to the following considerations:—

(1) Such questions are proper if they are of such a nature that the truth of the imputation conveyed by them would seriously affect the opinion of court as to the credibility of the witness on the matter to which he testifies;

(2) Such questions are improper if the imputation which they convey relates to matters so remote in time, or of such character that the truth of the imputation would not affect, or would affect only in a slight degree, the opinion of court as to the credibility of the witness on the matter to which he testifies;

(3) Such questions are improper if there is great disproportion between the importance of the imputation made against the witness's character and the importance of the evidence;

(4) Court, may, if it sees fit, draw, from the witness's refusal to answer, the inference that the answer, if given, would be unfavorable.

Sections 148 to 152 are intended to promote protection for witnesses. Sections 132 and 146 to 151 are part of a design. Refusal to answer a question

1. *N. Sri Ram Reddy* v. *V.V. Giri*, AIR 1971 SC 1162: (1971) 1 SCR 399: (1970) 2 SCC 340.
2. *Deepchand* v. *Sampathraj*, AIR 1970 Mys 34: (1969) 1 Mys LJ 606: 1970 Cr LJ 260.
3. *Dr. Baburao Patel* v. *Bal Thackeray*, 1977 Cr LJ 1637: (1977) 3 UCR (Bom) 371.
4. Phipson on Evidence, 15th Edition Para 249.

may lead to an inference being drawn that the answer would be unfavourable as suggested in illustration (h) to section 114. If the truth of the imputation sought to be conveyed through the question would seriously affect the credibility of the witness, the question could be allowed. Prior character at any time may have relevance to show present character, and hence, indirectly, to show the probability or improbability as to truthful speaking. The only limitation to be applied is that the character must not be so distant in time as to be devoid of real probative value in showing present character.[1] Stephen in his general view of the law in U.K. observed that if a woman prosecuted a man for picking her pocket, it would be monstrous to inquire whether she had an illegitimate child ten years ago.[2] In a case relating to pornographic materials, Supreme Court held that the judge could make some arrangement in the procedure so as to minimise embarrassment to all concerned.[3] A previous conviction has relevance either because the particular offence shows a certain amount of moral delinquency or because having been sent to jail he has spent some time with men presumably of bad character which might have contaminated him. Relevancy is of a high order in cases where all depends on the court's belief or disbelief in the witnesses evidence.

Clauses (1)(2): The facts must affect the credibility of the witness. Recent but not ancient conviction has relevance. Errors of a man's life, since repented of and forgiven by the community, should not be recalled to memory at the pleasure of a future litigant.

Clause (3): A witness called to speak to a minor or unimportant matter should not be subjected to severe impeachment of character.

Clause (4): See section 114, Illustration (h). If a witness refuses to answer a question, an adverse inference can be drawn against him.

22. SECTION 149

No question as is referred to in section 148 can be asked unless the questioner has reasonable grounds for thinking that the imputation which it conveys is well-founded. This section calls for certain standards of decency and decorum. Scandalous, vexatious, cantankerous questions put with a view to harass or which do not advance the cause of justice should not be allowed. Advocates appearing for a party have some responsibility on their own and they shall not abuse their privileges. They shall not put questions without verifying the truth of the imputation conveyed by such questions.[4] There is a presumption that an advocate puts questions on the instructions of the client.[5] The advocate who puts such questions on instructions of the client is protected under 9th exception to section 499 I.P.C. If such questions had no reasonable basis, the client will be liable under section 500 I.P.C.[6] Where a witness is put questions *per se* defamatory, he can seek protection of court, or set the criminal law in motion or file a suit for damages.[2]

---

1. Wigmore on Evidence Section 928.
2. *Ayeasha Bi* v. *Peerkhan Sahib*, AIR 1954 Mad 741: 1954 Cr LJ 1239.
3. *Fatima Riswana* v. *State*, AIR 2005 SC 712: 2005 Cr LJ 900: 2005 AIR SCW 372.
4. *M. Banarjee* v. *Emperor*, AIR 1927 Cal 823.
5. *Anwaruddin* v. *Fathim Bai*, AIR 1927 Mad 379.
6. *Deepchand* v. *Sampathraj*, AIR 1970 Mys 34: (1969) 1 Mys LJ 606: 1970 Cr LJ 260.

23. SECTION 150

If such a question was asked without reasonable grounds, court may, if asked by the opposite lawyer, report the circumstances of the case to the High Court and Bar Council. The system expects members of the Bar to conduct their business with due sense of responsibility. But they cannot be dealt with harshly merely because of something they said in the course of arguments.[1]

24. SECTION 151

Indecent, scandalous questions, though having some bearing on the questions before court, can be forbidden, unless they relate to facts in issue or to matters necessary to be known in order to determine whether or not the facts in issue existed. Such questions which do not advance the cause of justice are not to be allowed. The lawyer owes a duty not only to his client, but also to his opponent, court and above all, to the cause of justice, as also to the public and the community.[2] Where the fact in issue related to kidnapping and murder of a child and not the paternity of the child, Court should not allow indecent and scandalous imputations on the moral character of the witness, the mother of the victim.[3] But such a question can be permitted if they fall within the scope of section 152.[4] An advocate should not make a personal attack on a party or a witness on matters not borne by the record, nor use language which is abusive or obscene.[1] Scandalous questions can be asked if they are of such a nature that the truth of the imputation conveyed by them would seriously affect the opinion of court regarding the credibility of the witness on the matter to which the witness testifies.[5]

25. SECTION 152

Court shall forbid any question which appears to it to be intended to insult or annoy, or which, though proper in itself, appears to the Court needlessly offensive in form. This Section is mandatory in nature while section 151 is enabling or permissive. Under section 152, even a question which relate to the facts in issue are forbidden if the question is intended to insult or annoy or is needlessly offensive in form.

A witness is not to have his whole past dug up and exposed merely because he attends court in response to court summons.[6] Courts tend not to interfere for fear of falling foul of the Bar which is not the correct attitude. Court's endeavour should be to ensure that such questions are not asked.[7]

26. SECTION 153

When a witness has been asked and has answered any question which is relevant to the inquiry only in so far as it tends to shake his credit by injuring his character, no evidence shall be given to contradict him; but if he answers falsely, he may afterwards be charged with giving false evidence. According to

1. *Harbano Kaur* v. *P.C. Chaturvedi*, (1969) 3 SCC 712: 1969 Cri App R (SC) 394.
2. *In re Vasantha Pai*, AIR 1960 Mad 73: ILR 1959 Mad 958: (1960) 1 Mad LJ 21.
3. *State of Uttar Pradesh* v. *Raghubir Singh*, (1997) 3 SCC 775.
4. *K. Saraswathi* v. *P.S.S.S Chettiyar*, (1970) 2 MLJ 119.
5. *Prakash Rajaram* v. *State of Maharashtra*, 1975 Cr LJ 1297: 1974 Mah LJ 416.
6. *Ayeasha Bi* v. *Peerkhan Sahib*, AIR 1954 Mad 741: 1954 Cr LJ 1239.
7. *Ayeasha Bi* v. *Peerkhan Sahib*, AIR 1954 Mad 741: 1954 Cr LJ 1239; *Prakash Rajaram* v. *State of Maharashtra*, 1975 Cr LJ 1297: 1974 Mah LJ 416.

exception (1), if a witness is asked whether he has been previously convicted of any crime and denies it, evidence may be given of his previous conviction. According to exception (2), if a witness is asked any question tending to impeach his impartiality, and answers it by denying the facts suggested, he may be contradicted. Illustrations (a) to (d) may be seen. The object of the Section is to prevent trials being dragged to unreasonable length. The section limits the scope of trial to reasonable proportions. Evidence to contradict every answer given by a witness unnecessarily protracts trial.[1] Sections 153 and 155 must be strictly construed if courts are to be spared the task of prosecuting, on most imperfect material, issues which have no bearing upon the issues really in contest between the parties.[2] The intention underlying the section is to discourage collateral issues. If the question relates to relevant facts, answers may be contradicted by independent evidence.[3]

This section enacts a restriction on the right to give evidence in contradiction of an answer given by a witness to a question tending to shake his credit by injuring his character. But he can be charged for perjury. The intention is to reduce evidence on collateral matters. Thus what the witness states on this aspect is conclusive in that context and for that case. The section has to be strictly construed.

Evidence of a witness on matters affecting facts in issue or relevant facts can be contradicted by independent evidence but not so in the aspect dealt with by this Section. Defence can adduce evidence to show that a witness was at a particular place and time at the time of crime, which is far away from the scene of crime. But no such evidence is admissible to show the reasons given by him for being at the scene at the time of crime as the evidence is not on a matter relevant to the issue.[4]

Exception (1).—Evidence may be given of previous conviction of a witness, which has been denied by him. Section 299 of the Code prescribes the manner of proving it, that is, record of conviction. If the dispute relates to his previous criminal activity contradicting evidence is inadmissible as it merely impeaches his character.[5]

Exception (2).—In the face of denial of the facts suggested, contradicting evidence is admissible. For example (that he has been bribed, he has suborned other witnesses, he has hostility).[6] Impeaching impartiality is different from impeaching credit.[7]

27. SECTION 154

In it's discretion, court may permit a party to cross-examine his own witness. (Questions in the nature of cross-examination). For example, leading question, question impeaching credit and impartiality, regarding previous statement to test

1. *State of Karnataka* v. *Yarappa Reddy*, AIR 2000 SC 185: (1999) 8 SCC 715: 2000 Cr LJ 400.
2. *Bhogi Lal Bhika Chand* v. *Royal Insurance Co. Ltd.*, AIR 1928 PC 54: 6 R 142: 108 IC 1: 47 Cr LJ 550; *N. Sri Ram Reddy* v. *V.V. Giri*, AIR 1971 SC 1162: (1971) 1 SCR 399: (1970) 2 SCC 340.
3. Taylor, 8th Edition, Sections 1295, 1438.
4. *Ram Bali* v. *State*, AIR 1952 All 289: 1952 Cr LJ 600; *Ayeasha Bi* v. *Peerkhan Sahib*, AIR 1954 Mad 741: 1954 Cr LJ 1239.
5. *Kamal Kanto* v. *State*, 1959 Cr LJ 694: AIR 1959 Cal 342: ILR (1960) 1 Cal 292; see Illustration (a), (b)).
6. *N. Sri Ram Reddy* v. *V.V. Giri*, AIR 1971 SC 1162: (1971) 1 SCR 399: (1970) 2 SCC 340.
7. *Kamal Kanto* v. *State*, 1959 Cr LJ 694: AIR 1959 Cal 342: ILR (1960) 1 Cal 292.

veracity etc. This is where the witness unexpectedly turns hostile. The questions are those covered by sections 143, 145, 146, 148, 151. Such questions cannot be asked without the permission of court.

The purpose of the relaxation of the general rule is only to find if he is a witness of truth. This can be done at any stage.[1]

This section is to be liberally construed.[2] Where a Prosecution Witness resiles from his section 161 statement on a significant aspect, court will exercise this discretion in favour of the prosecution.[3] A witness is not "hostile" merely because his evidence doesnot support the case of the party calling him or is not in accord with evidence of other witnesses.[4] The party seeking permission must demonstrate that the witness was not speaking the truth. When a witness departs from what is tentatively believed to be true, this Section can be invoked.[5] Court can grant permission when the witness'es temper, attitude, demeanour, etc., shows a deliberately hostile feeling towards the party calling him, or while not exhibiting signs of hostility (concealing it) he makes statement contrary to what he was called or expected to prove.[6] Such permission can be given at any stage, even in re-examination.[7] An oral request is sufficient. No such permission can be granted without any question being put in chief-examination. Inference of hostility can be drawn from the answers given by him and to some extent from his demeanor.[8] Information must be elicited to show hostility.[9] Discretion must be exercised in the light of the particular circumstances of the case.[10] Inspite of invoking this section, it is open to court to believe a part of his evidence.[11] Formal "declaration" as hostile is not necessary. Leave must be asked for and may be granted. This must be recorded in the deposition. Court should avoid using words "hostile", "unfavourable" in the order.[12] Tacit permission is not sufficient. A witness whose evidence is over cannot be recalled for invoking this Section. Discretion is wide and unfettered, but is judicious. Permission cannot be granted as a matter of course. Discretion must be exercised not in a casual manner, but after weighing the circumstances.[6] Discretion is unfettered.

1. *Dahyabhai* v. *State of Gujarat*, AIR 1964 SC 1563: (1964) 2 Cr LJ 472: (1964) 1 SCWR 831: (1964) 7 SCR 361; *Rabindra Kumar Dey* v. *State of Orissa*, AIR 1977 SC 170: (1976) 4 SCC 233: 1977 Cr LJ 173.
2. *Sat Paul* v. *Delhi Administration*, AIR 1976 SC 294: (1976) 1 SCC 727: 1976 Cr LJ 295.
3. *G.S. Bakshi* v. *State (Delhi Administration)*, AIR 1979 SC 569: 1978 Cri LR (SC) 438: (1978) 4 SCC 482; *State* v. *Balchand*, AIR 1960 Raj 101: 1960 Cr LJ 520.
4. *Saraswathamma* v. *Bhadramma*, AIR 1970 Mys 157; *Tulsiram Shaw* v. *R.C. Pal Ltd.*, AIR 1953 Cal 160: (1952) 89 Cal LJ 127.
5. *Sivhamurthy Swamy* v. *Agodi Songanno*, AIR 1969 Mys 12: 1969 Cr LJ 118.
6. *Rabindra Kumar Dey* v. *State of Orissa*, AIR 1977 SC 170: (1976) 4 SCC 233: 1977 Cr LJ 173.
7. *B.N. Chobe* v. *Sami Ahmed*, (1969) 1 Andh LT 32; *Dahyabhai* v. *State of Gujarat*, AIR 1964 SC 1563: (1964) 2 Cr LJ 472: (1964) 1 SCWR 831: (1964) 7 SCR 361.
8. *Sivhamurthy Swamy* v. *Agodi Songanno*, AIR 1969 Mys 12: 1969 Cr LJ 118.
9. *Saraswathamma* v. *Bhadramma*, AIR 1970 Mys 157.
10. *Sat Paul* v. *Delhi Administration*, AIR 1976 SC 294: (1976) 1 SCC 727: 1976 Cr LJ 295; *State* v. *N. Somasekhar*, 1993 II KAR LJ 227; *Krutibas Sahu* v. *Madhab Das*, AIR 1961 Ori 48; *Shamsundar and Co.* v. *Sha Sunnilal Vesaji and Co.*, AIR 1962 Mys 12.
11. *In re, Saibanna Tippanna*, AIR 1966 Mys 248: 1966 Cr LJ 1155.
12. *Sat Paul* v. *Delhi Administration*, AIR 1976 SC 294: (1976) 1 SCC 727: 1976 Cr LJ 295; *Krutibas Sahu* v. *Madhab Das*, AIR 1961 Ori 48; *Sivhamurthy Swamy* v. *Agodi Songanno*, AIR 1969 Mys 12: 1969 Cr LJ 118.

The evidence is not washed off the record. It is part of the record. In each case, Court has to consider whether the witness stands thoroughly discredited or can still be believed in regard to a part of the testimony. If credit has not been completely shaken, court may, considering the evidence as a whole, with due care and caution, accept, in the light of the other evidence on record, that part of his testimony which is found trustworthy and act upon it. If the witness has been squarely and totally discredited, his evidence has to be discarded in full.[1] The maxim *"Falsus in uno, falsus in omnibus"* does not apply in India. It is open to court to look to corroboration even regarding a part of the evidence.[2]

28. SECTION 155

The credit of a witness may be impeached in the following ways by the adverse party, or, with the consent of the court by the party who calls him:—

(1) by the evidence of persons who testify that they, from their knowledge of the witness, believe him to be unworthy of credit;

(2) by proof that the witness has been bribed, or has accepted the offer of a bribe, or has received any other corrupt inducement to give his evidence;

(3) by proof of former statements in consistent with any part of his evidence which is liable to be contradicted.

Explanation.—A witness declaring another witness to be unworthy of credit may not, upon his examination-in-chief, give reasons for his belief, but he may be asked his reasons in cross-examination, and the answers which he gives cannot be contradicted, though, if they are false, he may afterwards be charged with giving false evidence.

The section is to be construed strictly. *See* also Sections 145, 146, 151 to 153.

Clause (1): Independent evidence can be given to show that a witness is unworthy of credit, that is, general reputation for untruthfulness, moral turpitude, not general bad character. He cannot speak of reasons for his belief in chief-examination. Reasons may be asked in cross-examination and his answers to such questions cannot be contradicted but he can, later, be charged for perjury. That he was disbelieved in another case is not relevant. The impeaching witness cannot be asked his opinion whether the witness is in fact speaking the truth about the issue before the Court.[3] That is for the Court to decide. Evidence of persons of shady character cannot be rejected without scrutiny.[4]

Clause (2): Credit can be impeached by proof that a witness has been bribed, or has accepted the offer of a bribe, or has received any other corrupt inducement to give his evidence.

1. *Sat Paul* v. *Delhi Administration*, AIR 1976 SC 294: (1976) 1 SCC 727: 1976 Cr LJ 295; *Syad Akbar* v. *State of Karnataka*, 1979 CAR 273: AIR 1979 SC 1848: (1979) 85 Cr LJ 327: (1979) 85 Cr LJ 1374: 1980 ACJ 38: (1980) 1 SCC 30: (1980) 1 SCR 95; *Alma* v. *State of Madhya Pradesh*, AIR 1991 SC 1519: 1991 Supp (2) SCC 409: 1991 Cr LJ 1791.
2. *Karuppanna Thevar* v. *State of Tamil Nadu*, AIR 1976 SC 980: (1976) 1 SCC 31: 1976 Cr LJ 708; *Bhagwan Singh* v. *State of Haryana*, AIR 1976 SC 202: 1976 Cr LJ 203: (1976) 1 SCC 389; *Sat Paul* v. *Delhi Administration*, AIR 1976 SC 294: (1976) 1 SCC 727: 1976 Cr LJ 295; *Rabindra Kumar Dey* v. *State of Orissa*, AIR 1977 SC 170: (1976) 4 SCC 233: 1977 Cr LJ 173.
3. Phipson on Evidence 15th Edition, Page 265.
4. *Ram Sarup Charan Singh* v. *State of Delhi*, AIR 1967 Del 26: 1967 Cr LJ 744.

If the offer of bribe was not accepted, the offer would not be a ground for impeachment.

Clause (3): By proof of former statements inconsistent with any part of the evidence liable to be contradicted. *See* Illustrations (a) and (b).[1] Former statement need not be in writing or signed.[2] Mere variations occuring in the narration of the incident by the witnesses is not sufficient to discredit their testimony.[3] Subsection (3) is not confined to facts in issue or relevant facts.[4]

29. Sections 145 and 155 show that a previous statement can be used for cross-examination and contradiction.[5] Section 155 is controlled partly by section 145.[6] The previous statement could be even in a letter.[7] A tape recorded conversation can be used to contradict.[8] Counter proof to reestablish credit can be given.[9]

30. SECTION 156

Where corroboration is felt necessary of evidence of a witness on a relevant fact, he may questioned as to any other circumstance which he observed at or near the time or place at which such relevant fact occurred, if court opines that such circumstances, if proved, would corroborate his evidence as to the relevant fact which he testifies.[10] This provision is helpful where the Court is not inclined to reject the evidence of a witness to be false but has some doubts, and may find it necessary to have corroboration from other circumstances.

The evidence is not for proving a directly relevant fact, but for testing the witness's truthfulness *i.e.* evidence of surrounding circumstances. If evidence on these aspects given by the witness is corroborated, that will support his credibility.

31. SECTION 157

In order to corroborate the testimony of a witness, any former statement made by such witness relating to the same fact, (a) at or about the time when the fact took place, or (b) before any authority legally competent to investigate the fact, may be proved. This is contrary to the normal rule that a witness cannot corroborate himself.[11]

---

1. *Binay Kumar Singh* v. *State of Bihar,* AIR 1997 SC 322: (1997) 1 SCC 283: 1997 Cr LJ 362: 1997 SCC (Cri) 333; *Bhagwan Singh* v. *State of Punjab,* AIR 1952 SC 214: 1952 Cr LJ 1131: 1952 SCR 812: 1952 SCJ 284; *N. Sri Ram Reddy* v. *V.V. Giri,* AIR 1971 SC 1162: (1971) 1 SCR 399: (1970) 2 SCC 340; *Herbertsons Ltd.* v. *Workmen of Herbertsons Ltd.,* AIR 1977 SC 322: 1977 ICR (SC) 343; *State of Rajasthan* v. *Teja Ram,* AIR 1999 SC 1776: (1999) 3 SCC 507: 1999 Cr LJ 2588: (1999) 3 SCC 507.
2. *Narayanan* v. *Krishnan,* 1981 Cr LJ 563.
3. *Rammi* v. *State of Madhya Pradesh,* (1999) 8 SCC 649: AIR 1999 SC 3544: 1999 Cr LJ 4561: 1999 AIR SCW 3546.
4. *N. Sri Ram Reddy* v. *V.V. Giri,* AIR 1971 SC 1162: (1971) 1 SCR 399: (1970) 2 SCC 340.
5. *Kehar Singh* v. *State (Delhi Administration),* (1988) 3 SCC 609: AIR 1988 SC 1883: JT 1988 (3) SC 191.
6. *Bal Gangadhar Tilak* v. *Shriniwas Pandit,* AIR 1915 PC 7: 39 B 441: 42 IA 135: 29 IC 639.
7. *Judah* v. *Isolyne Shrojbashini Bose,* AIR 1945 PC 174: ILR (1945) Kar PC 351: 1945 OWN 287.
8. *Pratab Singh* v. *State of Punjab,* AIR 1962 SC 72; *N. Sri Ram Reddy* v. *V.V. Giri,* AIR 1971 SC 1162: (1971) 1 SCR 399: (1970) 2 SCC 340.
9. *R.R. Chari* v. *State,* AIR 1959 All 149: 1959 Cr LJ 268.
10. *Yudhistar* v. *State of Madhya Pradesh,* AIR 1971 SCC (Cri) 684.
11. *Lim Yam Hong* v. *Lam Choon & Co.,* AIR 1928 PC 127: 107 IC 457.

Corroboration, as a general rule, should come from an independent source, but this section is an exception to the rule. Even a former statement of a witness can be used to corroborate his evidence in the two situations referred to in the section. The witness must give evidence with respect to some fact. He should have made earlier a statement with respect to the same fact in one of the two situations referred to in the section, namely at or about the time when the fact took place or before any authority competent to investigate the fact. A previous statement may be relevant under sections 6 to 9, 14 and 33 or as an admission.[1] The section speaks of corroboration by previous consistent statements.

Value of the statement depends on the particular circumstances of the case.[2] The value is that it shows consistency of his testimony and conduct.[3] That a person may persistently adhere to falsehood if there is a motive for it should not be lost sight of. It could have been made designedly also.

An example is, uttering of a version on seeing as event.

Witness should have given evidence regarding a fact, he should have made an earlier statement regarding the same fact at or about the time when the fact took place or earlier statement should have been made before any authority legally competent to investigate the fact. One of the two conditions must be satisfied. If neither of the two conditions is present, this section will not apply.[4]

It is not necessary that the witness to be corroborated, must, in his evidence, refer to his former statement. Suffice that a person who heard it gives evidence.[5] Prior statement, in any case, is not substantive evidence.[6] A mere prior narration, without reference to time or occasion is not resgestae and is irrelevant under section 6. The same when corroborated by other witnesses is admissible under section 157.[7] The former statement need not have been made on oath; it could be verbal or in writing.[8]

Section 164 (Cr.P.C.) statement is not substantive evidence, though it can be used under this Section.[9] Section 161(Cr.P.C.) statement cannot be used under this section.[10] Statement recorded under section 202, Cr.P.C. is a former statement.[11]

---

1. *Ambika Charan* v. *Kumed*, AIR 1985 SC 1268.
2. *Gauranga Charan Mohanty*, (1968) 1 SCWR 23; *Moti Singh* v. *State of Uttar Pradesh*, AIR 1964 SC 900: (1964) 1 SCR 688: 1963 (2) SCJ 714.
3. *Samauddi Sekh* v. *Abinas Chandra Sharma*, 1972 Cr LJ 172: Assam LR (1971) Assam 384.
4. *Dwarka Nath* v. *Lalchand*, AIR 1965 SC 1549: 1966 (2) SCJ 95: (1965) 3 SCR 27; *Ramratan* v. *State of Rajasthan*, AIR 1962 SC 424: 1962 (1) SCJ 371: (1962) 3 SCR 590.
5. *Ramratan* v. *State of Rajasthan*, AIR 1962 SC 424: 1962 (1) SCJ 371: (1962) 3 SCR 590.
6. *Moti Singh* v. *State of Uttar Pradesh*, AIR 1964 SC 900: (1964) 1 SCR 688: 1963 (2) SCJ 714.
7. *Chandra Kala* v. *Ram Krishna*, AIR 1985 SC 1268: 1985 Cr LJ 1490: (1985) 4 SCC 212.
8. *Awadh Behari Sharma* v. *State of Madhya Pradesh*, AIR 1956 SC 738: 1956 Cr LJ 1372: 1957 Nag LJ 1.
9. *Bhuboni Sahu* v. *King*, AIR 1949 PC 257: 50 Cr LJ 872: 51 BLR 955: 53 CWN 609: 1949 ALJ 283: 51 PLR 311: 76 Ind App 147; *Brij Bhushan Singh* v. *E.*, (1946) 47 Cr LJ 336: AIR 1946 PC 38: 223 IC 1: 73 IA 18: 50 Cal WN 348.
10. *Rajindra Singh* v. *State of Uttar Pradesh*, 2007 Cr LJ 4281: AIR 2007 SC 2786: 2007 AIR SCW 5034.
11. *Sashi Jena* v. *Khadal Swain*, 2004 Cr LJ 1394: AIR 2004 SC 1492: 2004 AIR SCW 819: (2004) 4 SCC 236; *Moti Singh* v. *State of Uttar Pradesh*, AIR 1964 SC 900: (1964) 1 SCR 688: 1963 (2) SCJ 714.

32. "Statement" means something stated. It remains a statement even if not communicated, such as account books. *See* section 21 illustration (b) and sections 32(2)(6) and 39. Communication is not a necessary element. "Notes" kept by a witness or his conversation with another witness attract this section.[1]

33. "Fact" has a wider meaning than "event". It can be a continuing event like "possession".[2]

34. "At or about the time".—The proximity of time between the taking place of the fact and making of the statement has to be established clearly.[3] There is no hard and fast rule regarding the interval of time.[4] It must have been made as early as possible in the circumstances of the case and before there was opportunity for tutoring or concoction.[5] It must have been made at once or at least shortly after a reasonable opportunity for making it presented itself. What is "reasonable time" is a question of fact in each case.[6] Sometimes mere intervention of a few hours or days may not matter.[7]

Even a "belated" statement attracts the section if made to a person in authority legally competent to investigate the fact.[8]

"Dying declaration" of a person who survived his injuries would attract this section, if the necessary condition precedent is satisfied.[9] Statement in FIS can be used under this section.[10] Contents of search memo attract this section when search witness is examined in Court. Statements at T.I.P. can be used for corroboration when the maker is examined.[11] So also Panchnama regarding thing

---

1. *Bhogilal Chunilal Pandya* v. *State of Bombay*, AIR 1959 SC 356: 1959 Supp (1) SCR 310: 1959 Cr LJ 389.
2. *Muthalagiri Reddy* v. *Pappi Naicken*, AIR 1915 Mad 249.
3. *Ramratan* v. *State of Rajasthan*, AIR 1962 SC 424: 1962 (1) SCJ 371: (1962) 3 SCR 590.
4. *State of Tamil Nadu* v. *Suresh*, (1998) 2 SCC 372: AIR 1998 SC 1044: 1998 Cr LJ 1416.
5. *Rameshwar* v. *State of Rajasthan*, AIR 1952 SC 54: 1952 SCJ 46: 1952 Cr LJ 547: (1952) 3 SCR 377; *Mahabir Singh* v. *State of Haryana*, AIR 2001 SC 2503: 2001 AIR SCW 2757: 2001 Cr LJ 3945.
6. *Bhuboni Sahu* v. *King*, AIR 1949 PC 257: 50 Cr LJ 872: 51 BLR 955: 53 CWN 609: 1949 ALJ 283: 51 PLR 311: 76 Ind App 147; *Sheikh Zakir* v. *State of Bihar*, AIR 1983 SC 911: (1983) 4 SCC 10: 1983 Cr LJ 1285.
7. *Perajmal Ballaji* v. *State of Tamil Nadu.*, (1998) 2 SCC 372: AIR 1998 SC 1044: 1998 Cr LJ 1416 (SC) (See also *Nathuni Yadav* v. *State of Bihar*, AIR 1997 SC 1808: 1997 AIR SCW 1158: (1998) 9 SCC 238, *State of Tamil Nadu* v. *Suresh*, (1998) 2 SCC 372: AIR 1998 SC 1044: 1998 Cr LJ 1416; *Sheikh Zakir* v. *State of Bihar*, AIR 1983 SC 911: (1983) 4 SCC 10: 1983 Cr LJ 1285; *Ramashraya Yadav* v. *State of Bihar*, 1999 AIR SCW 4296: AIR 2000 SC 201: (1999) 5 SCC 169.
8. *Bhagwan Singh* v. *State of Punjab*, AIR 1952 SC 214: 1952 Cr LJ 1131: 1952 SCR 812: 1952 SCJ 284.
9. *Maqsoodan* v. *State of Uttar Pradesh*, AIR 1983 SC 126: (1983) 1 SCC 218: 1983 Cr LJ 218: 1982 ALJ 1524.
10. *Nisar Ali* v. *State of Uttar Pradesh*, AIR 1957 SC 366: 1957 SCR 657: 1957 Cr LJ 550: 1957 All LJ 447; *E.* v. *Khwaja Nazir Ahmad*, AIR 1945 PC 18: 46 Cr LJ 413; *Wilayat Khan* v. *State of Uttar Pradesh*, AIR 1953 SC 122: 1953 Cr LJ 662: ILR (1953) 1 All 189 (SC); *Thakur Prasad* v. *State of Madhya Pradesh*, AIR 1954 SC 30: 1954 Cr LJ 261 (SC); *Karnail Singh* v. *State of Punjab*, AIR 1954 SC 204: 1954 SCJ 269: 1954 Cr LJ 580; *Pandurang Tukia* v. *Hyderabad*, AIR 1955 SC 216: (1955) 1 SCR 1083: 1955 Cr LJ 572 SC; *Ramjanam Singh* v. *State of Bihar*, AIR 1956 SC 643: 1956 Cr LJ 1254 (SC); *State of Bombay* v. *Rusy Mistry*, AIR 1960 SC 391: 1960 Cr LJ 532; *Damodar Prasad and Chandrika Prasad* v. *State of Maharashtra*, AIR 1972 SC 622: 1971 Ind law SC 492: 1972 SCD 186; *Sheikh Hasib* v. *State of Bihar*, AIR 1972 SC 283: (1972) 4 SCC 773: 1972 Cr LJ 233; *Shankar* v. *State of Uttar Pradesh*, AIR 1975 SC 757: 1975 Cr LJ 634: (1975) 3 SCC 851.
11. *Sarju* v. *State of West Bengal*, (1961) 2 Cr LJ 71.

noted.[1] So also direct facts noted in Inquest Report.Statements recorded during Inquest are covered by section 162 of Cr.P.C..[2] Previous deposition attracts this Section.[3] Previous statement of accomplice attracts this section.[4] Section attracts entries in Register of Births when the officer is examined. So also entry in School Register. Panchnama cannot be regarded as a statement made to panch witnesses.[5]

35 "Authority Legally Competent to investigate".—This is not restricted to Police Officers. "Investigation" is not to be understood in the technical sense. These words are to be taken in their general sense. It is not "investigate a case", but "investigate a fact". "Legally Competent" means under some law, statutory or otherwise."Investigate" only means ascertainment of facts, sifting of materials, search for relevant data.[6] Statements under section 161 of Cr.P.C. cannot attract this section in view of bar in section 162 therein. This section is controlled by section 162 of Cr.P.C.[7]

36. "To Corroborate" First, the evidence sought to be corroborated must be given. Then the corroborating former statement must be referred to.[8] Evidence, under this section, can be used only for corroboration.[9] Autopsy report can corroborate the evidence of the doctor.[10] Commissioner's report can corroborate the evidence of the author. Former statements must be properly proved through the person who received or heard it being given. The document must be produced.

37. SECTION 158

Whenever any statement relevant under section 32 or 33 is proved, all matters may be proved, to contradict or corroborate it, or in order to impeach or confirm the credit of the maker which might have been proved if that person had been called as a witness and denied in cross-examination the truth of the matter suggested. This is to expose the basic statement to scrutiny, just as testimony in court is subject to scrutiny.[11] Curiously a subsequent statement is admissible to contradict or corroborate an earlier statement under section 32.[12]

---

1. *Kadiya Kanbi Bhavan Manji* v. *Ismail Mamad*, AIR 1955 Saurashtra 32: 6 Sau LR 517: 1955 Cr LJ 274; *Naginlal Nandlal* v. *State of Gujarat*, (1962) 1 Cr LJ142: (1961) 2 Guj LR 664.
2. *Rajik Ram* v. *Jaswant Singh Chauhan*, AIR 1975 SC 667: (1975) 4 SCC 769; *Rameshwar Dayal* v. *State of Uttar Pradesh*, AIR 1978 SC 1558: 1978 2 SCC 518: 1978 All LJ 1011.
3. *Bhagwan Singh* v. *State of Punjab*, AIR 1952 SC 214: 1952 Cr LJ 1131: 1952 SCR 812: 1952 SCJ 284.
4. *Rameshwar* v. *State of Rajasthan*, AIR 1952 SC 54: 1952 SCJ 46: 1952 Cr LJ 547: (1952) 3 SCR 377; *Bhuboni Sahu* v. *King*, AIR 1949 PC 257: 50 Cr LJ 872: 51 BLR 955: 53 CWN 609: 1949 ALJ 283: 51 PLR 311: 76 Ind App 147.
5. *Ram Kishan* v. *State of Bombay*, 1955 Cr LJ 196 (208): AIR 1955 SC 104: 1955 SCR 903.
6. *State* v. *Pareswar Ghasi*, 1968 Cr LJ 201: AIR 1968 Ori 20: ILR 1967 Cut 980.
7. *Tahsildar Singh* v. *State of Uttar Pradesh*, AIR 1959 SC 1012: 1959 SCJ 1042: ILR (1960) 1 All 136: 1959 Cr LJ 1231; *Gurbachan Singh* v. *State of Punjab*, AIR 1957 SC 623: 1957 SCJ 539: (1957) Cr LJ 1009.
8. *Muthu Goundan* v. *Chinniah Goundan*, AIR 1937 Mad 861; *Public Prosecutor (Andhra Pradesh)* v. *Kuraba Sanjeevamma*, AIR 1959 AP 567: 1959 Cr LJ 1279: ILR 1959 AP 681.
9. *Hubert P. James* v. *Gulam Hussein Pakseema*, AIR 1949 PC 151.
10. *Hadi Kirsani* v. *State*, 1966 Cr LJ 45: AIR 1966 Ori 21: ILR (1965) Cut 403.
11. Stephen's Digest Article 135.
12. *Ramrati Kuer* v. *Dwarika Prasad Singh*, AIR 1967 SC 1134: (1967) 2 SCJ 789: (1967) 1 SCR 153.

38. SECTION 159

A witness may, while under examination, refresh his memory by referring to any writing made by himself at the time of the transaction concerning which he is questioned, or so soon afterwards that court considers it likely that the transaction was of time fresh in his memory. The witness may also refer to any such writing made by any other person, and read by the witness within the time aforesaid, if when he read it he knew it to be correct. Whenever a witness may refresh his memory by reference to any document, he may, with the permission of the Court, refer to a copy of such document: provided, court be satisfied that there is sufficient reason for the non-production of the original. The witness must have made the writing or verified it while the facts were fresh in his memory. If the witness is blind, the document may be read over to him.[1] The section permits a witness to refresh his faded memory by looking at any writing contemporaneously made by him.[2] Sections 159 and 160 should be read together. Shorthand or long hand notes of speeches made can be used under this Section.[3] A witness can use a horoscope in proving date of birth stated in it under this Section or Section 160.[4] Where a witness has to depose to a number of transactions, he can refer to relevant account books.[5] A doctor can look at his report. So also police, diaries, panchanamas could be looked into.

39. SECTION 160

A witness may testify to facts mentioned in such writing as is mentioned in section 159, though he has no specific recollection of the facts themselves, if he is sure that the facts were correctly recorded in the document. The evidence is not from memory, but from the document. The principle underlying section 159 is carried forward in section 160. A witness may refresh his memory with the help of a document, though he has no specific recollection of the facts themselves, yet, however, he must be certain that the facts themselves were correctly recorded in the document. A trader who sues his customer for recovery of price of goods supplied to the latter in small quantities over a period may not recollect the particular transactions though he recollects the customer; but he remembers that all the transactions are contained in a book maintained by him and if conditions of section 159 are satisfied, the witness may look at the entries in the book and state that the entries are correct and he may read them out of the book. It is not necessary that the witness has any independent recollection of the facts recorded in the book.[6] It is sufficient that he remembers that he has seen the book or paper before and that when he saw it, he knew the contents to be correct or that even without any recollection of the facts themselves he can still, because he recognizes his handwriting or signature therein, vouch for its accuracy or swear to the particular facts in question because of the contents of the writing.[7] It would be sufficient if it appears from his evidence that the conditions in

1. Phipson on Evidence, 15th Edn, page 267.
2. *Emperor* v. *J. Mahton*, ILR 1882 Cal 739.
3. *Ziyauddin Burhanuddin Bukhari* v. *Brijmohan Ramdass Mehra*, AIR 1975 SC 1788: 1975 SCR 281: (1976) 2 SCC 17.
4. *V.P.P. Nair* v. *Grasim Industries*, AIR 1977 Ker 356.
5. *State of Andhra Pradesh* v. *Cheemalapati Ganeswara Rao*, 1963 (2) Cr LJ 671: (1964) 3 SCR 297: AIR 1963 SC 1850: (1964) 2 SCA 38; *Jewan Lal Daga* v. *Nilmani Chaudhuri*, AIR 1928 PC 80: 55 Ind App 107; *State* v. *Haris Chandra Kar Mohapatra*, AIR 1966 Ori 189: ILR 1965 Cut 426: 1966 Cr LJ 1042.
6. Phipson on Evidence, 15th Edn., page 272.
7. Taylor on Evidence, 12th Edn.page 896, 897.

section 160 are satisfied.[1] The witness can be allowed to testify even to a large number of transactions by referring to the document.[2] Even where a witness does not refresh his memory with reference to a document under section 159, he can make use of it under section 160, if the other conditions are satisfied.[3] Section 159 clearly states that a witness may refresh his memory by looking into a copy of a document only with the permission of the court; but the implication is that this condition applies to section 160 also.

40. SECTION 161

Any writing referred to in sections 159 and 160 must be produced and shown to the adverse party if he requires it and the latter may cross-examine the witness thereupon. While a witness will be allowed to refresh his memory with reference to a writing made by himself contemporaneously, fairness requires that the adverse party must be able to see it and cross-examine him with reference to it.[4] The writing, by itself, need not be admissible in law. For example, an insufficiently stamped D.P. Note, Account book belatedly produced could be refused to be admitted.

41. SECTION 162

A witness summoned to produce a document shall, if it is in his power or possession, bring it to court even if there is any objection to it's production or admissibility. Court shall decide on the objection. Court, if it sees fit, may inspect the document unless it refers to matters of State or take evidence to enable it to so decide. If translation is to be had, the translator shall be directed to keep secret the contents, unless the document is to be given in evidence; if he disobeys he shall be held to have committed an offence under section 166 I.P.C. *See* Order XI, rule 4 C.P.C. and rule 19(2).

Witness shall come to court with the document. There could be claim of privilege under Chapter IX. Document referring to affairs of State cannot be inspected by Court. But see *S.P. Gupta's* case which says there is power in the court to inspect such a document also.[5]

Validity of objection has to be decided after production.[6] If he does not produce it, secondary evidence can be produced (Section 65(a)); such evidence is inadmissible if the original is privileged.[7] Court has power to take evidence to enable it to decide the objection. A copy which is not a true copy cannot be looked into.[8]

1. *Kanti Prasad Jayshanker Yagnik* v. *Purshottamdas Ranchhoddas Patel*, AIR 1969 SC 851: (1969) 1 SCC 455: 1969 3 SCR 400.
2. *State of Andhra Pradesh* v. *Cheemalapati Ganeswara Rao*, 1963 (2) Cr LJ 671: (1964) 3 SCR 297: AIR 1963 SC 1850: (1964) 2 SCA 38.
3. *Laxminarayan* v. *Returning Officer*, AIR 1974 SC 66: (1974) 3 SCC 425: (1974) 1 SCR 822; *Kanti Prasad Jayshanker Yagnik* v. *Purshottamdas Ranchhoddas Patel*, AIR 1969 SC 851: (1969) 1 SCC 455: 1969 3 SCR 400.
4. *Republic of India* v. *G.A.N. Rajan*, AIR 1967 Ori 115: ILR (1967) Cut 148: 1967 Cr LJ 1039.
5. *S.P. Gupta* v. *Union of India*, AIR 1982 SC 149: 1981 Supp SCC 87: (1982) 2 SCR 365.
6. *State of Punjab* v. *Sodhi Sukhdev Singh*, AIR 1961 SC 493: (1961) 1 SCJ 691: (1961) 2 SCR 371: (1961) 2 MLJ 203; *Amar Chand Butail* v. *Union of India*, AIR 1964 SC 1658: (1964) 67 Pun LR 90: 1965 (1) SCJ 243; *State of Uttar Pradesh* v. *Raj Narain*, AIR 1975 SC 865: (1975) 3 SCR 797: (1975) 4 SCC 428: 1975 Cr LJ 772; *S.P. Gupta* v. *Union of India*, AIR 1982 SC 149: 1981 Supp SCC 87: (1982) 2 SCR 365.
7. *Lady Dinbai Dinshaw Petit* v. *Dominion of India*, AIR 1951 Bom 72: 53 Bom LR 229.
8. *Janki Vashdeo Bhojwani* v. *Industrial Bank Ltd.*, AIR 2005 SC 439: 2004 AIR SCW 7064: (2005) 2 SCC 217.

Order XI, rule 19(2) C.P.C. must yield to this section as it is only a procedural provision and the Evidence Act confers the privilege.

Apart from this Section, court has residual power of inspection of document.[1]

42. SECTION 163

Where a document is produced in response to a call by a party and inspected, he is bound to give it in evidence if required to do so by the party producing it.[2] The document needs no further proof.[3] The document becomes evidence for what it is worth. The party calling for it is not debarred from exercising right of cross-examination on the document. The only effect of this Section is that the party having called for and inspected the document, is debarred from objecting to its production under Order VII, rule 2, Order XIII, rule 7, Order XI, rule 15 C.P.C. Notice is the one contemplated in Order XI C.P.C.

43. SECTION 164

A party refusing to produce document after notice to produce, cannot afterwards use the document as evidence without the consent of the other party or the order of Court. Order XI, rule 15 C.P.C. may be seen. This section, in one sense, is a penalty for unfair tactics. *See* also section 89 of the Evidence Act. Adverse inference can also be drawn on failure to produce.

44. SECTION 165

The judge may, in order to discover or to obtain proper proof of relevant facts, ask any question he pleases, in any form, at any time, of any witness, or of the parties, about any fact relevant or irrelevant; and may order the production of any document or thing; and neither the parties nor their agents shall be entitled to make any objection to any such question or order, nor without the leave of court, to cross-examine any witness upon any answer given in reply to any such question:

Provided that the judgment must be based upon facts declared by this Act to be relevant, and duly proved:

Provided also that this Section shall not authorize any judge to compel any witness to answer any question, or to refuse to answer or produce under sections 121 to 131, both inclusive, if the question were asked or the document were called for by the adverse party; not shall the judge ask any question which it would be improper for any other person to ask under section 148 or 149; nor shall he dispense with primary evidence of any document, except in the cases hereinbefore excepted.

45. Court has extensive power for the purpose of getting at truth. Court can ask any question in any form, at anytime, of any witness or of the parties about any fact, relevant or irrelevant. Court can order production of any document or thing. This power is to be exercised to discover or obtain proper proof of relevant facts. Parties cannot object to such questions or orders. Parties cannot also cross-examine any witness upon any answer in response to court question, without leave of court. However, judgment can be based

1. *S.P. Gupta* v. *Union of India*, AIR 1982 SC 149: 1981 Supp SCC 87: (1982) 2 SCR 365.
2. *Liladhar Ratanlal Vyas* v. *Holkarmal Sohanlal*, AIR 1959 Bom 528: 60 Bom LR 203: ILR 1959 Bom 29; *Shrinarain* v. *Chunnilal*, AIR 1957 Raj 159: 1957 Raj LW 214: ILR (1957) 7 Raj 531.
3. *Phoolchand Garg* v. *Gopaldas Agarwal*, AIR 1990 MP 135.

only on relevant facts duly proved. But witness cannot be compelled to answer any question or produce, any document in regard to matters covered by sections 121 to 131, if asked or called by opposite party. Questions which are improper under Sections 148 and 149 cannot be asked. Court cannot also dispense with primary evidence of any document except in cases hereinbefore excepted. In some cases, the whole truth may not come out through the evidence adduced by the parties. In such a situation, court can exercise these powers, within the limitations indicated in the section. This is particularly so in criminal cases. The judge must cease to be a spectator and a mere recording machine, and become a participant in the trial evincing intelligence, active interest and elicit all relevant materials necessary for reaching the correct conclusion, to find out the truth, and administer justice with fairness and impartiality both to the parties and the community it serves.[1] This power of the court cannot be regarded as taken away by the omission of Order XVIII, rule 2(4) C.P.C. in 1999.[2] Court must try to find the truth.[3] Court has also the power to call a witness not called by either side, if deemed necessary in the interest of justice. Court has also the power to recall or re-examine any witness at any stage before judgment, even after reserving judgment.[4] Section 165 of Evidence Act and section 311 of Cr.P.C. are relevant in this connection.[5]

But Court must act within the limits of the law and do justice and ensure that justice is done.[6] Court should not act with bias or give any such impression.[7] It irrelevant matters are so brought out, they must be eschewed from consideration in arriving at a decision.[8] Section 165 does not enable court to order production of a document for inspection of the other party.[9]

Section 165 and section 311 of Cr.P.C. complement each other and vest court with widest possible jurisdiction to take all steps to bring on record all necessary evidence.[5] The responsibility of court is greater when the accused is not defended.[10] This power is wide.[11] This section overrides limitations imposed by section 162 of Cr.P.C.[12] Judicial interruptions should not be too many. Court

1. *Zahira Habibulla H. Sheikh* v. *State of Gujarat*, (2004) 4 SCC 158: 2004 SCC (Cri) 999: AIR 2004 SC 3114: 2004 AIR SCW 2325: 2004 Cr LJ 2050; *Himanshu Singh Sabharwal* v. *State of Madhya Pradesh*, AIR 2008 SC 1943: 2008 AIR SCW 2206: (2008) 3 SCC 602.
2. *Salem Advocate Bar Association, Tamil Nadu* v. *Union of India*, AIR 2005 SC 3353: 2005 AIR SCW 3827: (2005) 6 SCC 344.
3. *Ram Chander* v. *State of Haryana*, AIR 1981 SC 1036: 1981 Cr LJ 609: (1981) 3 SCC 191.
4. *Chhotey Badri Prasad* v. *State of Uttar Pradesh*, 2006 Cr LJ 711: 2006 (1) ALJ 181: 2006 (54) All Cri C 168.
5. *Jamatraj Kewalji Govani* v. *State of Maharashtra*, AIR 1968 SC 178: 1968 Cr LJ 231: (1967) 3 SCR 415.
6. *Municipal Corporation of Greater Bombay* v. *Lala Pancham*, AIR 1965 SC 1008: 1966 (1) SCJ 49: (1965) 1 SCR 542.
7. *State of Mysore* v. *Lulli Hanmantha*, AIR 1966 Mys 231: (1966) 1 Mys LJ 433: 1966 Cr LJ 1024.
8. *Hasan Abdulla* v. *State of Gujarat*, 1962 Guj LR 107: AIR 1962 Guj 214: (1962) 2 Cr LJ 55; *Nathubhai* v. *Chhotubhai*, 1962 Guj LR 418: AIR 1962 Guj 68.
9. *Hari Ram* v. *Hira Singh*, AIR 1984 SC 396: (1984) 2 SCC 36: 1984 Rajdhani LR 53.
10. *Sessions Judge, Nellore Referring Officer* v. *Intha Ramana Reddy*, 1972 Cr LJ 1485: (1972) 1 Andh WR 340: ILR 1972 AP 683.
11. *State of Rajasthan* v. *Ani* alias *Hanif*, AIR 1997 SC 1023: 1977 Cr LJ 1529: (1997) 6 SCC 162.
12. *Raghunandan* v. *State of Uttar Pradesh*, AIR 1974 SC 463: 1974 Cr LJ 453: (1974) 4 SCC 186; *Emperor* v. *Lal Mian*, AIR 1943 Cal 521: 45 Cr LJ 99; *Raghunandan* v. *State of Uttar Pradesh*, AIR 1974 SC 463: 1974 Cr LJ 453: (1974) 4 SCC 186.

should also not badger and bully a witness into saying something beyond his preferred recollection. The only purpose of exercise of the power is to seek the truth. The judge must not take sides. He must not descend into the arena. His action may have an intimidating effect upon witnesses. Over-activism may disable him from taking a detached view.[1] It may not be possible for him to observe demeanor. His vision may be clouded by the dust of conflict. The discretion must be exercised with circumspection to further the ends of justice and not in an inquisitorial manner.

46. The object of allowing questions which may not be relevant is to obtain "indicative" evidence which may lead to discovery of relevant evidence.[2] This power is only to get at relevant facts ultimately. Court should take care not to prejudice either party.

47. Ordinarily court questions should be put at the end of examination, though it can intervene in the course of examination. But it cannot lead to usurpation of function of lawyer.[1] It is courts duty to put questions to clarify obscure matters.[3] This power is to be exercised in order to disover or obtain proper proof of relevant facts. If material evidence is being suppressed, court can direct production of documents, particularly if there is danger of tampering or destruction. Inspection depends on the right of inspection under other provisions.

48. Regarding further cross-examination, Court will ordinarily give permission if the answers to court questions were adverse to that party.[4] It is in the discretion of court to be exercised judicially.[5]

49. This case is different from that of a court witness. In the case of court witness, parties have right of cross-examination. *See* section 311 of Cr.P.C.

50. Proviso (1): However, judgment must be based on relevant facts (Section 6 to 55) and duly proved (Section 56 to 100). This rule is made in view of power of Court to put irrelevant questions.

Proviso (2): *See* section 121 to 131, 148 and 149. Judges cannot do what parties are barred by the above provisions from doing.

51. SECTION 166

This section has no relevance now.

52. SECTION 167

Improper admission or rejection of evidence, by itself, shall not be a ground for a new trial or reversal of any decision in a case, if it appears to the Appellate or Rivisional court that, independently of the evidence objected to and admitted, there was sufficient evidence to justify the decision or that, if the rejected evidence

1. *Sunil Chandra Roy* v. *State*, 1954 Cr LJ 805: AIR 1954 Cal 305: 57 CWN 962.
2. *In re: Kovummal Ammal*, AIR 1934 Mad 199: 148 Ind Cas 177; *Santhamani* v. *S.N. Somasundaram*, 1983 1 MLJ 73.
3. *Damisetti Subbanna* v. *State of Andhra Pradesh*, 1976 Cr LJ 1242: (1975) 2 Andh WR 255: ILR 1975 AP 589; *Sessions Judge, Nellore Referring Officer* v. *Intha Ramana Reddy*, 1972 Cr LJ 1485: (1972) 1 Andh WR 340: ILR 1972 AP 683.
4. *In re: Mukhesh Ramachandra Reddy*, AIR 1958 AP 165: 1958 Cr LJ 343: ILR 1957 AP 742.
5. *Dwarka Dass* v. *State*, 1979 Cr LJ 550: 1979 Chand LR (Cri) 12 (J&K).

had been admitted, it ought not to have varied the decision.[1] If by the large body of inadmissible evidence trial has taken a course substantially different from that contemplated by law, the section will not apply. If the evidence to be excluded is the main evidence, it is impossible to say what the decision would have been but for the inadmissible evidence, the decision has to be set aside.[2]

•••

1. *Mirza Akbar* v. *E.*, AIR 1940 PC 176: 43 Bom LR 20: 41 Cr LJ 871: 190 IC 233: 67 IA 336; *Bhagwan Bakhsh Singh* v. *Mahesh Baksh Singh*, AIR 1935 PC 199: 38 Bom LR 1: 159 Ind Cas 325; *Chaturbhuj Pande* v. *Collector, Raigarh*, AIR 1969 SC 255: (1969) 1 SCR 412.
2. *Channoo Mahto* v. *Jang Bahadur Singh*, AIR 1957 Pat 293: 1956 BLJR 197; *K.S. Ramachandran* v. *Ragistrar of Co-operative Societies, Madras*, AIR 1963 Mad 105: (1962) 2 Mad LJ 407: (1963) 33 Com Cas 807; *Bibhuti Bhushan Bank* v. *Sadhan Chandra Sheet*, AIR 1965 Cal 199: 68 Cal WN 1043; *Habibur Rahman* v. *Tetri*, AIR 1972 Pat 43: 1971 BLJR 474; *Narain* v. *State of Punjab*, AIR 1959 SC 484: 1959 Supp (1) SCR 724: 1959 Cr LJ 537; *Ram Kishan* v. *State of Bombay*, 1955 Cr LJ 196 (208): AIR 1955 SC 104: 1955 SCR 903; *Nagindra Bala Mitra* v. *Sunil Chandra Roy*, AIR 1960 SC 706: (1960) 3 SCR 1: 1960 Cr LJ 1020.